The Soviet Capital Stock, 1928–1962

Publications of
The Economic Growth Center

LLOYD G. REYNOLDS, *Director*

THE SOVIET
CAPITAL STOCK,
1928–1962

by

RICHARD MOORSTEEN
Economist
The RAND Corporation

and

RAYMOND P. POWELL
Professor of Economics
Yale University

A Publication of
The Economic Growth Center
Yale University

 1966

RICHARD D. IRWIN, INC.
Homewood, Illinois

330.947
M78s

66459

July, 1969

Series Foreword

This volume is one in a series of studies supported by the Economic Growth Center, an activity of the Yale Department of Economics since 1961. The Center's Research program is focused on the search for regularities in the process of growth and structural change by means of intercountry and intertemporal analyses. The emphasis is on measurable aspects of economic growth and on the development and testing of hypotheses about the growth process. To provide more reliable statistical tests of theoretical hypotheses, the Center is concerned with improving the techniques of economic measurement and with the refinement of national data systems. The Center provides a home for the International Association for Research in Income and Wealth, which moved its headquarters from Cambridge University, England in 1962. The Center library endeavors to achieve a complete intake of significant economic and statistical publications from about 80 of the larger countries of the world.

Book-length studies supported by the Center are printed and distributed by Richard D. Irwin, Inc. Reprints of journal articles are circulated as Center papers.

LLOYD G. REYNOLDS, *Director*
GUSTAV RANIS, *Associate Director*
HUGH T. PATRICK, *Assistant Director*
SHANE J. HUNT, *Assistant Director*
MARIAM K. CHAMBERLAIN, *Executive Secretary*

Preface

The present study was in process over a rather long period, in the course of which we incurred more and larger obligations than we can adequately acknowledge.

Our first and greatest debt is to Abram Bergson, who made available to us the results of his research before their publication, advised us on various problems, and commented in detail upon the completed text. A further debt to Bergson we share with others, for the standard of rigorous scholarship in research on the Soviet economy which he has set. If this is rarely attainable, it serves nevertheless as a target at which to aim.

Robert W. Campbell, Janet G. Chapman, Nicholas DeWitt, Jerzy F. Karcz, Norman M. Kaplan, and Nancy Nimitz also permitted us to draw on their research before its publication. Without the assistance which they graciously gave, we could not have brought our study to completion. Gustav Ranis read and gave us helpful comments on portions of the study. Charles B. Westover, Jr., served long, conscientiously, and with great intelligence, as our research assistant. His contribution was so large that it is probably an injustice on our part not to credit him with co-authorship.

Several organizations provided us with financial support or with facilities for research: The American Council of Learned Societies, The Ford Foundation, The RAND Corporation, the Russian Research Center of Harvard University, the Committee on Faculty Research in International Studies of Yale University, and the Economic Growth Center of Yale University, under the last of whose auspices also the study is published.

None of the organizations or persons listed bears responsibility for what is said here.

Preliminary versions of some of the statistical estimates in this volume were cited in essays by Abram Bergson, Simon Kuznets, and Raymond Powell in a publication edited by Bergson and Kuznets, *Economic Trends in the Soviet Union,* Cambridge, 1963. The final estimates do not differ materially from the preliminary ones, but we would hope that reference hereafter to our estimates would be to those presented in this study.

Santa Monica, California
New Haven, Connecticut
June, 1966

RICHARD MOORSTEEN
RAYMOND P. POWELL

Table of Contents

Charts

Text Tables

Tabular Section Tables

PAGE

Appendix Tables

Chapter 1

Introduction

The purpose of this study will be clearer if its place in the existing body of research on the Soviet economy is understood. Since about the end of World War II, an extensive effort has been under way in the United States, and to a lesser degree in other Western countries, to compile usably reliable statistical series on the Soviet economy. These have been independent estimates in the sense that they are not derived from official series for national income or industrial output but are built up from detailed data for physical quantities, prices, and the like. The results of this effort are now largely in hand,[1] and a substantial consensus has been reached as to the general dimensions of Soviet growth. Conclusions are alike, at any rate, where the thing to be measured is agreed upon: output inclusive or exclusive of military production, with early or late price weights, over longer or shorter periods past.

Although the objectives of this research were various, there was undoubtedly in the minds of contributors to it an expectation that we should ultimately be able not only to measure Soviet performance but to explain it. Soviet growth has been rapid; most countries are now concerned with their growth rates and many economists with the analytical problems of growth; the Soviet experience presents a case which is practically significant and intellectually challenging. The information required for the analysis of Soviet growth, however, is still incomplete, and one major gap is acceptable data on the capital stock. Our objective is to fill this gap. The primacy of our purely statistical purpose should, perhaps, be stressed, because we do undertake a tentative exploration of the question of Soviet growth. The results of this exploration are not among our basic findings and will, we hope, be shortly displaced by more perceptive analyses than we are able to make. Our objective is a contribution to that corpus of empirical knowledge from which anyone may draw in order to elucidate the process of growth either in the Soviet Union or in general.

The capital stock estimates which we have compiled have the following principal characteristics. They cover reproducible fixed capital, livestock, and inventories. They refer to present values of assets as of each given date,

---

[1] The most important of the findings referred to are those of Abram Bergson's *The Real National Income of Soviet Russia Since 1928* (Cambridge, 1961). (Source citations hereafter are in abbreviated form, on which see p. 17 below.) Other studies, many of which are cited here in one or another context, contribute to Bergson's, or supplement it, or provide useful checks on it.

1

net of depreciation (we also present alternative calculations for fixed capital corresponding to gross values in the usual sense). They are composed for capital in being, but they may be taken to approximate, with some additional error, capital in use. Valuations are in constant prices, alternatively those of 1937, 1928, and 1950. The estimates in 1937 prices are the most reliable, and they are basic to the others. Prices are those internal to the Soviet economy, with adjustments for indirect taxes and subsidies where these are thought to be necessary.

The details of the procedures by which the estimates are obtained are presented in the chapters following, but they may usefully be summarized here—in broad and somewhat inaccurate terms. The stock of fixed capital is estimated, essentially, by the perpetual inventory method, from annual gross investment. Investment in equipment is obtained by the deflation of investment in current prices with indexes of equipment prices, construction from an index representing the quantity of materials consumed in construction, and "installation," a third and minor investment component distinguished in the Soviet data, from the other two. Livestock is obtained by the direct valuation of herds measured in physical units. Inventories are estimated, for the most part, by the deflation of current-price values of the stock.

Conceptual problems specific to each of the component estimates are also discussed in subsequent chapters. There are, however, conceptual difficulties common to the measurement of capital of all kinds, which we may better consider here. It is our impression that these are not of a totally different magnitude from those encountered in the measurement of naional product or labor supply or other such aggregates. Also, doubtless, acceptance of any statistical approximation to analytical variables requires a certain tolerance for conceptual impurity. Nevertheless, it is clearly desirable that, so far as feasible, statistical estimates be shaped by a firm notion of *what* is to be measured.

Unfortunately for our purposes, the large number of words written about the concept of capital have not brought agreement. It presumably would be agreed, since the principle is recognized to hold elsewhere, that the proper measurement of capital depends upon the analytical purpose in view and upon the analytical framework within which the data are to be used. As we have indicated, our ultimate objective is the analysis of growth. The logical point of departure for the explanation of our estimates, therefore, is a specification of the analytical framework for which we intend the estimates to be appropriate.

1. THE MEASUREMENT OF OUTPUT AND INPUTS[2]

Having in mind, in part, what the evidence will permit us to explain, we take as an acceptable objective of an analysis of growth that it account for the increase over time of the "production potential" of the economy, i.e.,

---

2 The argument of this section is, in substance, that developed in Moorsteen–61, to which reference should be made for a more detailed statement. For completeness, certain elementary propositions are also repeated here which the informed reader is welcome to pass over.

the outward shift in its transformation function. In terms of Chart 1–1, what we would like to know is how the movement in the transformation function from P_1P_1 to P_2P_2 was effected. In general, the shift in the function will not be equiproportionate for alternative possible product mixes, and in some cases, as in Chart 1–1, it may be extremely disproportionate. The amount of the outward shift, therefore, is measurable—and, evidently, definable—only for specified product mixes.

Assuming that the economy operates in both years on its transformation function, its actual output coincides with its production potential. But in each year we are able to observe its potential only for a single product mix, that of the proportions of the actual output, points A and B. In general, the proportions at B will not be the same as those at A, and we cannot say on the basis of the output data alone how far production potential has changed, even for the observed product mixes.

Further information is available in the form of relative prices of products. If prices are efficient (such as M_1M_1 tangent to P_1P_1 at A), equaling marginal rates of transformation, they register the *slope* of the transforma-

CHART 1–1

Interpretation of Aggregate Output Indexes

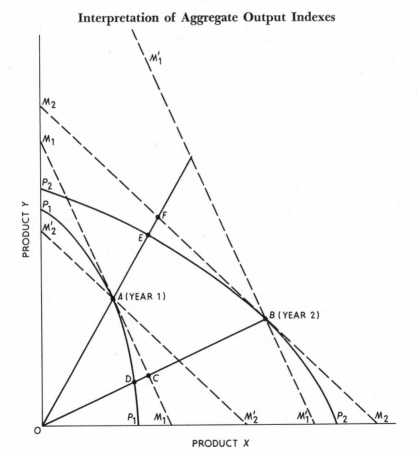

PRODUCT X

tion function at the point of actual operation. By extrapolating from that point along the price line (or market surface), we can estimate, approximately, the production potential of the economy in one year for the product mix of another: e.g., *OC* provides an approximation to the actual capacity, *OD*, of the economy in the early year to produce in the proportions of the late year. The capacity of the economy in the late year to produce its actual mix is observed directly, at *B*. By weighting both years' actual outputs with the prices of the *early* year, therefore, we obtain an approximate measure of the change in capacity to produce the *late*-year mix (*OB/OC*, the true change being *OB/OD*). Conversely, by weighting both with *late*-year prices, we measure approximately the change in capacity to produce the *early*-year mix (*OF/OA*, the true change being *OE/OA*). These are price-weighted output indexes of the usual sort, corresponding, respectively, to Laspeyres' and Paasche's indexes. For any pair of years, two indexes are possible, providing measures of the shift in the transformation function for two product mixes.

The position and shape of the transformation function in any year is determined by the quantities of productive inputs and the technology available. Changes in the function are therefore exhaustively explained by changes in these two factors. No data we shall be able to cite provide a direct measure of the change in technology. The change in productive inputs can be measured, approximately, by procedures analogous to those employed for output indexes.

Actual input quantities in early and late years are directly observable and, on the same assumptions as before, represent points on the production isoquants of the two years, as at *A* and *B* in Chart 1–2. In general, input proportions will differ, and the input quantities alone permit no unambiguous measure of their combined change. The relative prices of inputs, M_1M_1 and M_2M_2, reflecting the marginal rates of substitution in use (the relative marginal productivities) of inputs, give us the slopes of the isoquants at the actual points of operation. From these slopes we can approximate the quantity of inputs in one year, in the proportions of another, which would be "equivalent" to the actual inputs of the first year in the production of its actual output—equivalent in the sense that those inputs would just suffice for the production of the same output. Thus, in Chart 1–2, *D* is equivalent to *A* and *OC* is an approximation to *OD*. An index of inputs weighted with *early*-year prices provides an approximation to the change in inputs, equivalent to the actual change, in the proportions of the *late* year (*OB/OC* approximates *OB/OD*); one weighted with *late*-year prices gives an approximation to the equivalent change in *early*-year proportions (*OF/OA* approximates *OE/OA*).[3] Again, measures are possible only for the two input proportions corresponding to the observed points.

A further complication arises in the interpretation of input indexes. In general, marginal rates of substitution of inputs, and consequently their prices, are not independent of the product mix under which they are generated, and there is no presumption that they would remain the same for a

---

[3] To complete the analogy with output indexes, the input indexes could be regarded as measures of the shift in the production isoquants.

CHART 1–2

Interpretation of Aggregate Input Indexes

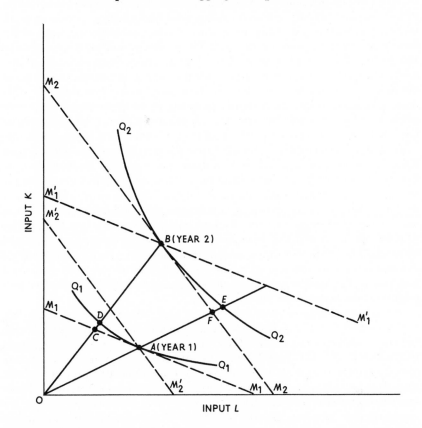

product mix different from the actual one. On this account, an input index in, e.g., early-year prices, is best interpreted as measuring the equivalent change in inputs with the output mix that of the same year, although the input mix is that of the late year. If the additional and probably unrealistic assumption is made, however, that relative input prices are independent of the product mix (depending, say, solely on factor proportions), an input index in early-year prices can be interpreted also as referring to both inputs and outputs of the late-year proportions. Converse propositions hold for indexes with late-year weights.

For any pair of years, then, four comparisons of aggregate inputs and outputs are possible. With inputs in early- and outputs in late-year prices, the reference is to the input mix of the late and the output mix of the early year. With inputs in late- and outputs in early-year prices, the reference is to the input mix of the early and the output mix of the late year. With both inputs and outputs in early-year prices, the comparison may be interpreted—but more hazardously—as for both input and output mixes of the late year; with both in late-year prices, to mixes of the early year.

To each of these pairs of input and output indexes, there corresponds a measure of technological change. The latter is defined, as in logic it must be, for specific mixes of inputs and outputs.

The kind of inferences that can be drawn from the comparison of an input and an output index, referring to specified proportions of both inputs and outputs, depends upon what can plausibly be assumed about economies (or diseconomies) of scale. The latter are not, of course, a third factor contributing to growth but a name for the disproportionality, relative to their initiating causes, of the effects produced by changes in inputs or in technology. Although in some cases economies of scale may be specific to increased inputs or to improved technology, this is unlikely to be true generally, and for all practical purposes they must be regarded as the effects of the two initiating causes acting in combination.

If returns to scale were constant, the increase in inputs could be read also as a measure of the increase in output specifically imputable to it, i.e., as the increase in output which would have resulted from the actual change in inputs if technology had remained constant. The change in the ratio of output to inputs could be read as a measure, albeit an indirect one, of the change in technology, i.e., the increase in output which would have resulted from the actual improvement in technology if inputs had remained constant. The change in inputs and in technology together account—in an explanatory sense—for the whole of the change in output, and their sizes relative to the change in output provide a meaningful measure of their relative contributions to it.[4]

We are unwilling to assume, however, especially for the case at hand, that returns to scale are constant. The index of aggregate inputs, consequently, cannot be taken to reflect accurately the contribution of inputs to growth, in that it disregards the role of increased inputs in the realization of returns to scale. If scale effects are positive, it must understate that contribution.[5] The ratio of output to inputs reflects not merely technological change but also the whole of scale effects, by whatever force engendered. For this reason, and for others which can be anticipated but which will be discussed subsequently (see Chapter 10, Section 1), we refer hereafter to the output/input ratio merely as a measure of "productivity."[6] It remains, however, on the assumptions made thus far, a measure of identifiable—if not simple—analytical content.

Two further explanations are required of the procedures for analyzing growth which motivate our choice of capital measures.

---

[4] In terms of percentage annual growth rates, if x is the rate of change of output, y that of inputs, and z that of technology, then $1 + x = (1 + y)(1 + z)$. In principle, y/x and z/x, the usual partial imputations, do not sum to 1 since the relation between changes in inputs and technology is multiplicative. They frequently do in actual calculations because of rounding.

[5] By estimating or guessing the size of returns to scale, it is still possible to answer the question, "How much would output have changed with the actual change in inputs, if technology had remained constant?" (in effect, this is done in, e.g., Powell-63). But the question is different from that of the contribution of the change in inputs to the actual change in output. The economies of scale that would have resulted from the change in inputs alone and from the change in technology alone may together more than exhaust the total economies produced by the two in combination.

[6] "Productivity" here is the same concept as "efficiency" in Moorsteen-61. The latter term is used here in the narrower, analytical sense.

impact of the choice between cost and productivity valuation falls largely, therefore, on the equipment component, and, in the Soviet stock as we have estimated it (net and in 1937 prices), equipment accounts for a quite small share of the total, rising from 6 percent in 1928 to 27 percent in 1962. Even for equipment, the problem of valuing new types of assets is considerably limited by the regime's practice of standardizing output and maintaining given models in production over long periods, although, for this single component, cost and productivity measures would doubtless diverge.[11]

Capital Services

In speaking thus far of capital values, we have not taken care to distinguish between the value of capital as an asset and the value of its services annually rendered, i.e., between the capitalized value, at a point in time, of its anticipated future earnings and the value of those earnings over a given period of time. In fact, the basic data from which our estimates commence are values for capital assets: of assets when new in the case of fixed capital, of values as of a given date for livestock and inventories. For this reason, chiefly, the explanation of the estimates proceeds through most of its length with reference to capital as an asset, which is to say to the "capital stock." The stock estimates are also of interest in themselves, and they are a familiar kind of capital measure—for which latter reason we also refer to the stock in the title of the study.

In the end, however, what the reasoning of the preceding section calls for is a measure of "capital services," i.e., a measure in which assets are weighted in proportion to the value of the marginal products imputable to them during the period of the weight year. It is this which determines their substitutability in use in the weight year, for one another and for other kinds of inputs. Assuming that all assets earn the same rate of interest on their capitalized values, the net services of capital, net of maintenance and depreciation, move with the net (depreciated) value of the stock, and the time series for the latter serves also as an index of net services, the absolute weight-year value of which can be set equal to total interest earnings in that year. As we have explained, however, we consider it more appropriate to our purposes that inputs and outputs be measured gross of depreciation, and gross capital services (interest plus depreciation) do not in general move with the value of the capital stock, either gross or net.

To illustrate, two assets yielding equal gross value products within a given period will, on the usual assumptions, command equal gross prices—rental charges—for their services. If the length (or shape) of their future service streams differ, they will at the same time command unequal prices as assets, since the discounted present values of their future earnings will be

---

[11] Even here, different conceptual premises may eventuate in similar statistical procedures. As noted earlier, we make use of given-year relative prices in estimating weight-year relative prices and, hence, weight-year relative productivities. In a recently published study of capital in the United States, in which the valuation principle is one of costs, given-year relative costs of equipment are used to estimate weight-year relative costs (cf. Jaszi–62, p. 10). If given-year costs and prices are equal, the two procedures yield identical results.

We have in Charts 1–1 and 1–2 drawn the transformation functions and isoquants as curvilinear and used straight price lines in estimating unobservable points on them. The implied errors in the estimates, as a result, are of particular sign. The curves are illustrative, and we do not mean at this juncture to offer a judgment of the probable shapes of the functions. Moreover, if the functions are curvilinear, it is possible that they may be better approximated by nonlinear than by linear aggregation, either being entirely feasible. In calculations made hereafter, partly for reasons of simplicity, outputs and capital inputs are each aggregated linearly. Total inputs, however, are obtained by adding the three major categories (capital, labor, and land) in the logs, allowance being made thereby for some convexity in the isoquants.

Secondly, it needs to be specified whether, in the foregoing argument, the annual values of outputs and inputs are to be taken net or gross of depreciation charges. We know of no absolutely compelling argument for choosing one rather than the other, but considerations of plausibility lead us to prefer gross measures. The transformation function derives from the concept of a production function; the production isoquants are single contours of such functions. That given inputs yield predictable outputs, as such functions imply, appears most plausible if inputs and outputs are conceived of in physical terms. Depreciation is a value construct having no evident physical analogue. Its deduction has no more apparent justification in the production function than would, say, the deduction of the "costs of maintaining intact" the labor force employed. We do, nevertheless, present alternative calculations using net measures—and also with total inputs aggregated arithmetically.[7]

2. THE CAPITAL CONCEPT

The capital estimates made here are intended to conform to two basic conceptual principles: (*i*) that assets are valued in proportion to their substitutabilities in use, i.e., their relative productivities, and (*ii*) that the substitutabilities in reference are those determined by the technology of the *weight* year—alternatively of 1937, 1928, or 1950, for the estimates in prices of each of those years.[8] That these are, for our purposes, appropriate criteria for the aggregation of different kinds of capital follows from the fact that they are the criteria we would apply in the aggregation of inputs of all kinds. Thus, in Chart 1–2, the input axes can equally well be regarded as referring to different kinds of capital (services). Their relative values per unit should approximate the slope of the weight-year isoquant,

---

[7] On the general analytical issue of gross vs. net measures, including the treatment of intersector purchases of current inputs in sectoral calculations, on which we shall touch subsequently, see Domar–61, pp. 714–17.

[8] We shall throughout use the expression, the "weight year," to mean the year from which price weights are drawn, for the aggregation of capital, of inputs in general, or for outputs. In any binary comparison with the weight year, we refer to the second year as the "given year." This usage proves somewhat awkward when we need to make reference to indexes involving comparisons of more than one weight year with a common "base year," i.e., indexes which are commonly described as "given-year weighted." We use the latter expression also, assuming that the meaning is clear from context.

in order that we may estimate the quantity of capital in given-year proportions that would be equivalent to the actual quantity in weight-year proportions (e.g., to estimate D from A). For such values, as in the valuation of inputs in general, we employ weight-year prices—for kinds of capital in existence (or produced) in the weight year. For kinds of capital not in existence in the weight year, prices are not observable and must somehow be synthesized. The derivation of such prices is the familiar problem of the treatment of "new products" or quality change, which is the central conceptual problem in the measurement of capital.

In principle, though by methods varying in detail and probable accuracy, we value "new" kinds of assets in accordance with the same criteria as old ones: their substitutability in use under the technology of the weight year. That is to say, one new asset is taken to equal the quantity of assets used in the weight year for which it could be substituted in the production processes of the weight year without altering either the output yielded or the quantity of other inputs required. The weight-year isoquant is, in effect, taken to register equivalent quantities of inputs for mixes inclusive of kinds of capital not actually employed in that year. Ours is, therefore, in the sense indicated, a "productivity" concept of capital.

In what degree does such a concept absorb into the quantitative measure of capital changes over time in its productivity? Productivity changes resulting from changes in the technology with which capital is *used* are not reflected in the measure. For example, the fact that a machine tool introduced in the given year is, with the technology of that year, more productive than a tool of weight-year type in the weight year is irrelevant for the valuation of the "new" tool. This is so whether the greater productivity of the new asset results from the "embodiment" of the changed technology in its physical characteristics or results solely from technological improvement of an organizational sort. If technological change in the *production* of capital, or changes in factor availabilities, result in a new type of asset which differs—as it need not—in productivity from the weight-year type, such differences are reflected in the measured quantity of capital: technology in the use of capital remaining unchanged, the new type could have been used as effectively in the weight year as in the given year. In all cases, the principle is the same: the productivities relevant for the measurement of capital are solely those observed or estimated with the technology of the weight year.

To repeat, the assumption is not made here that the weight-year productivities of new kinds of assets are equal to their given-year productivities.[9] Such a procedure would, indeed, absorb all changes in productivity associated with changes in the form of capital into the quantitative measure of capital. But, as capital is measured here, its productivity remains free to vary over time, subject to the condition that capital inputs of equal productivity *in the weight year* must be weighted equally in the capital aggregate.

---

[9] The reference is to absolute productivities. Relative given-year productivities do, in some instances, enter into our estimates as an approximation to relative weight-year productivities. See Chapter 2, pp. 40 ff.

The commonly proposed alternative to a productivity concept is a "cost" concept. If by cost is meant substitutability in producti weight year—the actual or hypothetical cost of producing an asset technology and factor prices of the weight year—the difference such a measure and ours would depend upon the importance o products" and upon the statistical procedures adopted for valuing for assets of kinds produced in both weight and given years, weig costs and prices (productivities) are, on the usual equilibrium assum equal. That capital estimates actually composed on the basis of costs differ grossly from those we obtain is in fact very doubtful.[10]

The principal reason for this is the practical difficulties encounter the valuation of structures, not only in the Soviet economy but i economies, and the large weight of this component in the total stock. heterogeneity of structures is such that virtually all given-year struc are "new." The compiler of statistics is, in consequence, brought al inevitably to reduce them to some homogeneous element or aspect—in present instance, in effect, to the materials of which they are compo Homogeneity of assets having by such a procedure been established follows that their weight-year costs and prices must be equal, and cap series weighted by either would behave in the same way. Of the remain of the total stock, inventories and livestock appear to consist largely constituents that can be treated as close to homogeneous over time. T

---

[10] How the two kinds of estimates might be expected, a priori, to behave relative one another is a complex matter which need not be explored here. Our suppositi would be that over periods in which technological change, both in the use and in th production of capital, is large, a cost measure would yield a *higher* growth rate f periods *following* the weight year. As assets from increasingly late years are valued, t case must be progressively approached of given-year assets which would be both unusab and unproducible in the weight year. Their weight-year productivity would approa zero and their weight-year cost infinity. Perhaps the same would be true of assets fro years increasingly antecedent to the weight year, their weight-year costs being relativ high and weight-year productivities relatively low, in which case the cost measure wou rise *less* rapidly than the productivity measure over periods *preceding* the weight ye But this seems less clear.

On occasion, what is intended by a "cost" measure of capital appears to be one which the valuation of assets produced in the given year is based on factor prices of weight year but the technology (in the production of capital assets) of the given ye i.e., on the weight-year cost of the inputs required for the production of assets in wh ever year they were produced. This comes to a measure of the change over time of t inputs utilized in the production of capital. We would suppose that, over the wh period covered by our estimates, such a measure would rise less rapidly than ours, this relation also is not simple. An approximation to such a measure is discussed Chapter 2, Section 3, where an alternative calculation for structures is made from input-price deflated series for construction.

The presumption that a cost measure in the sense of weight-year substitutabilitie production would not differ greatly from our estimates permits a statistical simplifica which is not justified in principle. As we have explained in the preceding section, inferences we would draw from output measures call for the valuation of outputs i cordance with costs—rates of transformation in the weight year. New types of ca goods should, therefore, enter the output measure with weights proportionate to estimated weight-year costs. The output measures we cite subsequently, however, capital goods as outputs the same as they are valued as inputs. Such error as this duces in the measured output of capital goods is greatly reduced in the output a gates of which they are a part.

unequal. Both may remain in production if the inequality in the capitalized values of their expected yields is matched by an inequality in their costs of production. The equal rental charges of the given period will consist of a relatively greater interest charge on the longer-lived and more valuable asset and a relatively greater depreciation charge on the shorter-lived and less valuable asset. If the share of the two in the total stock—the service-life distribution of assets—changes over time, the ratio of depreciation to interest charges will change, and gross capital services will not vary with the net capital stock. Under the same circumstances, the average depreciation rate on the gross value of the stock will change, and depreciation charges, like interest charges in any case, will not vary with the gross capital stock.

The service-life distribution of assets in the Soviet stock has changed, and we therefore compute, in Chapter 6, Section 4, an additional set of series representing gross capital services, obtained as the sum of interest and depreciation charges on the estimated stock. These are, despite their belated presentation, the capital input series which are the ultimate objective of our calculations. As it turns out, they do not behave over time much differently from the capital stock, although they rise somewhat more rapidly.

It should be understood that the depreciation component in the service calculations is not meant to represent merely a conventional charge (although it is derived by a conventional formula) but to correspond to the true decline in the capital value of assets in the course of a given period. That decline is itself estimated, for fixed capital, from the supposed length and shape of service streams and the rate of interest, so that, in logic, capital values beyond the date of an asset's acquisition are determined from the service streams and not vice versa. For livestock, although they are depreciable assets, our estimating procedures are such that they yield only net values of the stock, and depreciation on livestock is omitted from the service series. Inventories are assumed to be nondepreciating, and interest charges on them represent the whole of their services.

3. COVERAGE

We restrict the estimates to the three indicated categories of assets in part because this is the extent of the subject matter with which we are prepared to deal and in part on conceptual grounds: the similarity in the determinants and use of these categories of assets is probably greater than between them and any omitted kind. Financial claims, domestic or external, are excluded for the obvious reason that they are not physically productive assets. Consumer durables, for which data are in any case lacking, are acquired for motives remote from those operative with other assets (including, in the Soviet Union, the greater part of housing), and their inclusion in capital would create problems in the measurement of output which we would rather avoid. The nonreproducibility of land and natural resources sets them apart. "Capital" embodied in human beings is created and used with such a mixture of economic and noneconomic motives, even in the Soviet Union, that it is better treated separately. We do cite evidence hereafter on some of the omitted categories. There are also minor omissions, for lack of data, of assets which would fall within the categories covered, the most important of which is probably state stockpiles.

The capital stock estimates are annual, for the period from January 1, 1928, to January 1, 1962, omitting the years 1942 and 1943 (the service series end with 1961). The first date coincides approximately with the beginning of the era of five-year plans and the beginning of strenuous and deliberate efforts by the regime to attain rapid growth. It is also the earliest date covered by several previous studies upon which we have drawn. The year 1928 appears a reasonable starting point when the principal concern is the process of Soviet growth although, clearly, not for an over-all appraisal of the accomplishments of the regime since its accession to power. A very rough notion of the behavior of the capital stock in the years preceding 1928 can be obtained from Soviet sources.

According to official figures published in the late 1920's, total fixed capital, depreciated and valued in prices of 1925/26, increased by 1.5 percent in 1924/25 (October 1 to October 1), 3.6 percent in 1925/26, 4.8 percent in 1926/27.[12] Beyond serious doubt, the growth of fixed capital was slower before 1924/25 than after and, from 1917 to some date in the early 1920's, was probably negative. Inventories were reduced absolutely for a time, probably into the early 1920's, and were built up again at a rapid rate in the middle of the decade: in 1925/26 prices, they reportedly increased by 11.0 percent in 1925/26 and by 15.3 percent in 1926/27.[13] Judging from numbers and without adjustments for weight changes, livestock herds reached a trough in 1922 and recovered thereafter at a rate on the order of 6 percent per year.[14] The total stock presumably declined through a period following the Revolution, recovered from the early 1920's, and by the years immediately preceding 1928 may have been increasing at the quite rapid rate of 5 or 6 percent per year. The indicated rates are with valuations approximately the same as 1928 prices (and are, on various counts, not fully comparable with our estimates), and we are unsure how much they would differ with price weights from later years. Nor have we any clear notion of the size of the 1928 stock relative to that of 1913, although it can scarcely have been much larger.

Our estimates are carried to as recent a date as was feasible. Even to bring them as far forward as we did, required at several points rather crude extensions from earlier dates. We have been unable to make a thorough search of Soviet sources released after our estimates reached an advanced stage. We have made revisions when new data implied a substantial error in our calculations, but in a few instances we have merely noted the existence of errors which are relatively inconsequential or, al-

---

12 Cf. Gosplan–28, pp. 518–19, and Gosplan–29, pp. 426–29; we exclude the livestock included in "basic funds." Divergent figures are given in various sources for this period, but the general picture presented is the same.

13 Cf. Rozentul–29, pp. 310–11. We rely here generally on a discussion in the same source, pp. 301-2.

14 The reference is to a calculation employing numbers of livestock, as of the summer count (Volin–51, p. 153), weighted with 1928 average realized prices (Table 4–2 of the present study).

though of some consequence, could only be corrected by unjustifiably costly recomputations.

The estimates refer in all years to the actual territory of the Soviet Union. In particular, the figures for January 1, 1940, include assets acquired in new territories during 1939, and those for January 1, 1941, assets similarly acquired during 1940. These acquisitions in combination are thought to have amounted to approximately 10 percent of the stock in the pre-1939 territories.

The use of three alternative sets of price weights is intended to provide fairly widely spaced sample observations relating to capital substitutabilities in different periods of Soviet development. That not more than three are used is explained in part by the large cost of compiling (and reading) additional estimates, especially since our calculations rest upon earlier studies which employ the same weight years; the latter fact accounts also for our not undertaking calculations with weights later than 1950. For reasons we shall come to shortly, the limitation to these three years is due also to difficulties in interpreting observations on the Soviet economy for years intermediate to them.

The most serious deficiency in the coverage of the estimates, relevant to the analysis of growth, is that they contain little detail on the distribution of capital by sectors. We have separated capital in housing and in agriculture from the totals but have done so by procedures which, for fixed capital, are cruder than those used in obtaining the totals. Our estimates for agricultural capital are so unreliable that we do not present them; the errors to which they are subject are less significant for the nonagricultural remainder. Our inability to divide the totals for the nonagricultural nonresidential sectors among finer components is an unavoidable consequence of our estimating procedures (chiefly, those for fixed capital) and one which we cannot overcome without much more detailed data than are now available in Soviet sources.

4. RELIABILITY

Statistical estimates encounter two different kinds of problems of reliability. One is the familiar problem of the accuracy with which the data generated by an economy—prices, quantities—are observed, recorded, and processed. The second, which is implied by our earlier discussion, is a question of the accuracy with which the data so generated register the information required for analytical purposes. Reliability of the first sort, having to do with the quality of the statistician's own efforts, might be called purely statistical. Reliability of the second sort depends upon the characteristics of the economy observed and might, to distinguish it, be called conceptual. We commence with the second.

Conceptual Reliability

Analytical inferences from statistical series usually require that they relate to an economy which satisfies various equilibrium or efficiency or optimality conditions, the requirements depending upon the particular argument involved. For the argument we make in Section 1, the principal requirement of this kind is that the quantity data observed be for points *on* the transformation or production functions of the two years compared, i.e., that they represent efficient points of operation. The optimality of the observed points is not, as such, relevant.[15] Nor is it strictly necessary or even sufficient that prices, of inputs and outputs, be efficient—proportional to marginal rates of substitution and transformation respectively. Although we have not emphasized this in the Section 1 discussion, it can be seen from Charts 1–1 and 1–2 that, while efficient prices provide a rough approximation to the desired "slopes," a precise measure would require relative prices equal to rates of substitution or transformation over the *arcs* from the input or output proportions of the weight year to those of the given year. When the arcs are wide, the desired slopes may be more nearly approached by average than by marginal rates. Moreover, it is not necessary that the price structure in every detail satisfy the required conditions, but only that such distortions as exist are not *systematic* in their effects on the calculated indexes.

The particular inferences we want to draw, therefore, impose considerably less stringent requirements on the observed economy than would, say, an analysis resting upon optimality of resource allocation. Nevertheless, there is reason to doubt that the necessary conditions have typically been met in the Soviet economy. It is not an economy notable for its efficiency, and its prices have been subject to distortions, relative to efficient prices, which can scarcely have moved them in the direction of the desired substitution or transformation rates. These are difficulties which threaten all quantitative research on the Soviet economy, and no fully satisfactory solution to them is possible.

They are somewhat minimized by the choice of weight years in which the desired conditions may be most nearly approximated. Of the three weight years used here (as by Bergson), 1928 comes after the recovery from war and revolution and before the extreme dislocations of the early planning era. It antedates the introduction of large indirect taxes and subsidies. The year 1937 comes after the major price reform of 1936 and in the relatively orderly interlude between the early 1930's and World War II. The year 1950 also follows a major price reform and comes fairly late in the postwar recovery. Of the three years, however, 1937 undoubtedly provides the data most nearly reliable for our purposes, and this is the primary reason for treating calculations in prices of that year as basic.

We follow Bergson also, in principle, in adjusting prices for the incidence of turnover taxes and subsidies—from prevailing prices to "factor cost" valuations—which presumably corrects a major distortion in weight-year prices.[16] Bergson has discussed the reliability of factor cost valuations at length, and reference to his writings should be made on this point.[17] We take it as the broad import of his argument that Soviet prices, as

---

[15] We shall have occasion, however, to speak of preferences, meaning, we should note, those of the central authorities or "planners' preferences."

[16] The incidence of taxes and subsidies on the prices of assets produced in the three weight years appears to have been small for fixed capital, small—or perhaps more accurately, indeterminate—for livestock, but large for inventories. In fact, therefore, we make adjustments in the capital estimates only for the inventory estimates.

[17] See Bergson–61, chaps. 8 and 9, and earlier sources cited there.

adjusted and more certainly in 1937 than in the other two years, do in rough fashion reflect true economic scarcities; that the distortions to which they are subject are not necessarily systematic in their impact on aggregate measures; and, also, that they probably come closer to average than to marginal costing.

Despite such selectivity in the data used and adjustments in them, there remain discrepancies in both price and quantity data between what the economy permits us to measure and what our analytical system requires that we measure. For these, we make such allowance as we can in interpreting the implications of our findings for the analysis of Soviet growth in Chapter 10. In Section 1 of Chapter 10, we also examine more fully the several issues of conceptual reliability raised here.

Statistical Reliability

The reliability of our estimates viewed simply as recordings of the data provided by the economy depends in part upon the accuracy of the published statistics from which they are composed. The statistics utilized are in general detailed, and they have been collated, adjusted for differences in coverage, and checked for internal consistency as far as possible. That official data processed in this fashion merit considerable confidence is a conclusion to which the whole body of research on the Soviet economy has led. Of the data required for capital estimates, however, there are critical elements which are either totally lacking or for which the reliability is doubtful and untestable. These deficiencies we have had to handle by assumption or by procedures which are only the best of the alternatives available. We cannot conclude, therefore, on the basis of the quality of the data underlying them, that the estimates are reliable, even in a purely statistical sense.

In the face of this difficulty, we have adopted the procedural rule that we should, wherever feasible, test by alternative calculations the dependence of our results upon critical assumptions and estimating devices employed in their derivation.[18] In some cases, we can set limits to the possible values of relevant parameters and establish absolutely the range within which the true estimates must lie. In others, we can only try extreme assumptions and establish the likely range of the true estimate. The employment of alternative calculations accounts for the considerable complexity of the exposition which follows. It also, incidentally, allows the reader some choice among estimates, where he disagrees with our selection.

The outcome of the alternative calculations is, on the whole, reassuring. Our estimates prove quite insensitive—perhaps remarkably insensitive—to errors in those elements for which the reliability of the data is most questionable. To this generalization there is one important exception provided by the rate of interest. For this parameter, we have no usable information directly from the Soviet economy, and we must guess at a range of likely values.

The rate of interest enters into the calculations of the capital stock, capital services, and, in our discussion of growth, aggregate inputs. As it

---

18 One or two of the alternative calculations bear on "conceptual" rather than "statistical" reliability, but the bulk refer to the latter.

turns out, the stock estimates prove insensitive, for both absolute values and rates of change, to variations in the interest rate. The service estimates also prove insensitive for rates of change, but, understandably, highly sensitive for absolute values. Thus the weight of capital in aggregate inputs varies with the interest rate as, therefore, does the behavior of aggregate inputs and, in turn, the explanation of Soviet growth. With respect to this parameter, our alternative calculations are also our final estimates: a range of possible values for capital services and a range of possible explanations of Soviet growth.

Comparability

Related to the question of reliability is that of comparability—of our estimates with those made for other countries. Since it is our impression that procedures for estimating capital have not yet become standardized, we have followed our own judgment in choosing procedures, without regard for conformity with statistical practices elsewhere. Nor have we undertaken any systematic comparison of our results, either in the capital estimates or in our discussion of growth, with those obtained for other economies. International comparisons are illuminating. We would wish that they might have been made here, but they present statistical and conceptual difficulties too large to be dealt with in the limits of this single volume. At the risk of inconsistency, we have occasionally cited data for other countries, where they were helpful in judging the reliability of some element in our calculations, where the point of comparison was sufficiently broad that it could sustain some incomparability in the data, or where the comparison might provide a helpful point of reference. The comparisons we make, however, are casual. Any implications drawn from them are altogether tentative.

5. ORGANIZATION OF THE STUDY

The whole of the study consists of the textual chapters, a tabular section, and a number of appendixes. The appendixes contain the bulk of the detailed explanations of the origins of our data and the more mechanical aspects of their processing. Most of the material of this sort relevant to the fixed capital estimates was assembled by us, working separately, in earlier studies, and is not repeated here. Our livestock and inventory estimates originate with this volume, and the description of sources for the latter, in particular, occupy a sizable portion of the appendixes. The statistical series which constitute our basic findings are, because of their unwieldly size and for easy reference, grouped together in the tabular section. We show there also subsidiary series required for our discussion of growth. Absolute figures are given in old, pre-1961, rubles, and are uniformly rounded to the nearest tenth of a billion rubles. Throughout, components may not sum to totals because of rounding. Omitted figures, whether unavailable or inapplicable, are shown as a dash. Tables and appendixes are arranged approximately in the order of the discussion in the text.

The text itself is divided into two parts, one concerned with the capital estimates and the other with capital and growth. In the chapters of Part I, we explain the general rationale of our procedures, examine in detail the more critical data problems, and present our findings. Selected figures from the tabular section are repeated in the text, or series are shown graphically, in order that the findings may be made more accessible to the reader. The first part concludes with a comparison of our estimates with certain official series for the fixed capital stock. In Part II, we use the capital estimates in an analysis of Soviet growth, the exploratory character of which we would again emphasize.

The number of sources cited is large, and to make the citations manageable a system of abbreviated references is employed. Sources are indicated by the surname of the author or name of issuing organization and by the last two digits of the publication date. Where more than one publication in a year is cited for the same author, identifying letters are shown after the date of publication. A full list of sources is provided at the end of the volume.

PART I

The Capital Estimates

Chapter 2

Fixed Capital: The Stock in

1937 Prices

1. INTRODUCTION

With qualifications to be stated, the stock of fixed capital is estimated by the perpetual inventory method: that is, by cumulating and depreciating gross annual investment. For this purpose we rely largely on estimates of investment in fixed capital in constant prices made previously by us.[1] In addition, necessary extensions of these series and other data required to move from investment to stocks are estimated in the present study. The materials and methods employed in deriving the value of the fixed capital stock in 1937 prices are described in this chapter. Certain supplementary calculations relating to fixed capital—values in alternative prices, annual depreciation charges, distribution by economic sector, average age—are described in Chapter 3.

Our estimates of stock values are composed from the following elements: (*i*) Depreciation methods or, more concretely, the relationships by which the present value of a capital asset may be inferred from its value when new, its service life, the pattern of services which it delivers, expenditures on its maintenance, and the rate of interest. These are discussed in Section 2, which also summarizes the principal results of the calculations. (*ii*) Data on gross annual investment, which are described in Section 3. The annual investment data are compiled only for 1928–61, the same period covered by the capital stock estimates. If relied upon wholly, the perpetual inventory method requires investment data for a period prior to the first stock estimate equal in length to the service life of the longest-lived asset in the stock. In the absence of such data, we begin our calculations with an estimate otherwise obtained of (*iii*) the stock of fixed assets in place on January 1, 1928. For subsequent years, therefore, our estimates are the sum of two components: the cumulated and depreciated total of annual investment since January 1, 1928, plus the present (depreciated) value of those assets that were already in place on that date. The estimates of the January 1, 1928, stock—also referred to hereafter as the "initial

---

[1] On investment in equipment, see Moorsteen–62; on construction, see Powell–57 or the summary of that study in Powell–59a and, for later revisions, Powell–59.

stock"—are described in Section 4. (*iv*) Service lives of the various kinds of assets. These are considered in Section 5, in which are explained also, for different depreciation methods, the specifics of the derivation of present values for assets created by past investment or in the initial stock. (*v*) Extraordinary changes in the stock of assets, occurring through territorial change and war damage, which are discussed in Section 6.

Of those just listed, elements (*iii*), (*iv*), and (*v*) require the addition of substantial increments of information to the already existing investment series, and for these we have undertaken to estimate the necessary magnitudes. The quality of the data available for this work, however, leaves much to be desired, and the resulting estimates are subject to sizable errors. The consequences of such errors are explored by means of alternative calculations, based on varying assumptions concerning the elements in question. The objective is to establish some presumptions as to the size of the possible errors in the over-all calculations and to distinguish intervals for which the impact of such errors is relatively small. The method of alternative calculations is used also to determine the effects on the results of those items of data enumerated in element (*i*) for which no firm information is available: the time shape of the streams of capital services and the rate of interest.

Because there are many areas of ambiguity, the number of alternative calculations and the volume of accompanying exposition is, we fear, rather large. The reader who wishes to gain an impression of the magnitudes in question but is willing to forego the details will find our main conclusions summarized in the tables of the text, the titles of which indicate the problems under elaboration. Without at this point attempting a systematic summary of these materials, it may be in order to note that they point generally to more uncertainty about the absolute value of the stock of fixed capital than about its rate of growth over time.

2. PRESENT VALUES AND DEPRECIATION METHODS

The purpose of this section is to explain how the magnitude we seek to measure, the value of the fixed capital stock, is related to the statistical data at our disposal. To facilitate comparison of the alternative estimates made, this section also summarizes the main results. In this it anticipates subsequent sections of the chapter, which describe the data.

The Shape of Service Streams and the Rate of Interest

The present value of a capital asset is the discounted sum of future productive services, defined therefore by the following relationship:

$$V_j = \sum_{i=j}^{n} \frac{S_i}{(1+r)^{i-j}}, \qquad (1)$$

where V_j is the value of the asset at the beginning of its jth year, expressed here in 1937 prices; S_i is the productive service (marginal value product) in the same prices expected from the asset during its ith year, gross of depreciation but net of the costs of maintenance; r is the expected rate of interest; and n is the expected service life of the asset under conditions of appropriate maintenance. "Depreciation," the decline in present value, in the jth year, is $V_j - V_{j+1}$. The use of the formula entails certain simplifications, such as that the expected rate of interest is constant over the life of the asset, that scrap values are negligible, and that the discount applied to future services is compounded only annually. The value of the total capital stock at any point in time is the sum of the present values, as of that time, of all existing assets.

In our calculations, we use actual 1937 prices (or approximations to them) of new assets as estimators of the V_1's.[2] We are able to draw on Soviet data for actual and expected service lives to estimate the n's. We have virtually no evidence, however, from within the Soviet economy, either on r or on the pattern of change over time in the S_i's of assets. We therefore make alternative estimates for the V_j's ($j > 1$) intended to bound the values described by the following conditions: (i) that r, the interest rate, is non-negative; (ii) that the annual service (net of maintenance) rendered by an asset does not increase from year to year; and (iii) that if annual services decline, the average absolute rate of decline between the years 1 and i is no greater than S_1/n.

The first condition is surely unexceptionable. The second must hold for the great majority of assets. Although the empirical evidence even for Western economies is scant, it seems sufficient to indicate that, far from rising, net services typically decline.[3] Gross services tend downward through impaired operability, as assets lose reliability or precision, and through gradual obsolescence, the progressive degradation of function caused by the availability of new substitutes or changes in processes.[4] In addition, the difference between net and gross services tends to increase because maintenance costs rise with age.

The third condition, that net services decline no faster than the straight line which connects the initial service, S_1, with zero at the end of the asset's service life, is more conjectural. Indeed, without more empirical data it is impossible to judge accurately its probability, which, in any case, must differ as among assets. For most assets, however, and in particular for most structures, which make up the greater part of the fixed capital stock, services gross of repairs probably decline only gradually and are still substantially greater than zero up to the end of the asset's life. A warehouse, a road, or a bridge, to take extreme cases, will deliver approximately the same gross service throughout the service period. Repairs, which must be subtracted to arrive at the net services, are probably slight during the early years of service, increasing thereafter. This means that in the early part of the service life the net service stream, too, will not decline sharply. But even later there are factors making for a relatively flat net service stream. As the end of the service period approaches, it

---

2 These prices presumably reflect, in some degree, expectations as of 1937, which are those relevant for our purposes. In general, however, our information is much too limited to justify our attempting to maintain any systematic distinction between expectations and realizations.

3 See, for example, Terborgh–49, chap. ii, and pp. 69–72, 247–51, and Terborgh–54, chap. v.

4 Strictly, it is expected obsolescence that is relevant, not unexpected. Expectations of obsolescence may also, of course, affect the expected service lives of assets.

becomes economic to avoid fundamental repair work, employing instead less expensive short-run maintenance measures intended to keep each part of the asset functioning up to, but only up to, the anticipated date of retirement. The same result is likely to follow also from the fact that, other things equal, it is economic in the original design of new assets to provide parts of roughly equal durability. Thus the service stream must often end quite abruptly.

CHART 2–1

Alternative Service Streams of Fixed Capital Assets

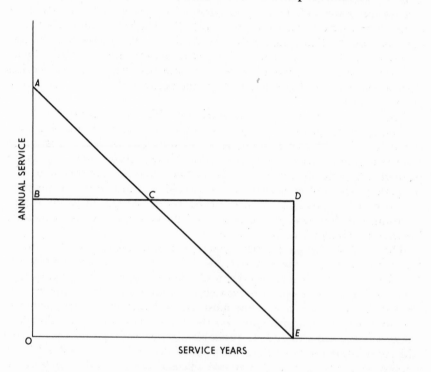

Taken all together, the foregoing considerations suggest to us that the tendency of the net service stream, although downward, is probably not, on average, as rapid as the straight line from S_1 to zero. The matter is illustrated graphically in Chart 2–1, which shows the alternative bounding service streams we consider, for an asset of known initial value and service life. If services are constant, the stream is the line BD; services have the value OB during the period OE and are zero thereafter. If services decline along a straight line from S_1 to zero, the service stream is AE. Because the initial value of the asset, i.e., the discounted sum of all services, is given, there must be some early services greater than in the constant service case, to offset the lesser services that will be rendered toward the end of the service life. Hence AE cuts BD from above. The area within our "bounds," thus, is that included in the two triangles ABC, in the first part of the service life, and CDE, in the latter part (where CDE is necessarily greater than ABC for any positive interest rate). The argument of the preceding paragraph is (*i*) that services decline slowly during the earliest and latest phases of the service life, and (*ii*) that they are substantially above zero during the latest phase. The end of the service stream, therefore, comes somewhere between *E* and *D*. As the stream cannot lie entirely above *AE* or entirely below *BD*, it is most plausible to assume that it commences somewhere between *A* and *B*. In other words, it declines, but not as rapidly as *AE*. We describe this as a "plausible" assumption to underscore that it is not a necessary one. It would not hold for assets with service streams that declined precipitously in the middle of the service life. Such a service stream could lie above *AE* during its early years and below during many of its later ones without contradicting any of the presumptions set forth above. Such a sharp, discrete, decline in services might occur, for example, as a result of a change in function due to partial obsolescence. For these reasons, our service-stream assumptions do not establish true bounds.

For the interest rate, our limiting assumptions clearly include rates that lie beyond the bounds of plausibility. The only explicit interest rates generated in the Soviet economy are on financial assets (government bonds, bank deposits, bank loans) and are purely nominal. They provide no guide to the rate of return on physical assets. Specific discount rates have been proposed in Soviet discussions of the problem of choosing among investment alternatives, but the method of their derivation is obscure and their meaning uncertain.[5] Various and serious obstacles block any effort to infer an interest rate from time series for inputs and outputs.[6]

In the absence of direct evidence, we attempt to bracket the *likely* value of the true rate of interest, in 1937, by taking quite extreme alternatives of 8 percent and 20 percent. The 8 percent rate is meant to correspond, roughly, to rates reached in developed, capitalist, economies.[7] It appears unlikely that the rate appropriate to the Soviet economy in 1937 should have been lower than this. The 20 percent rate is simply much higher than 8 percent, and also appears to be a plausible but undemonstrable limit.

We make, then, seven calculations, which show the values taken by the capital stock for zero, 8 percent, 20 percent, and infinite interest rates, with asset services assumed alternatively to hold constant over time or to decline along a straight line to zero. Only these parameters are varied. All of the calculations use the same values for assets when new—1937 prices—and the same service lives. The results are shown numerically in Tables T-1 to T-6 of the Tabular Section; they are shown here graphically, in Chart 2-2. In addition, the reader may find it helpful in the discussion following to refer to the graphs, given in Chart 3-2, p. 83, of the change over time in capital values under different depreciation methods.

---

5 E.g., Anonymous–60, p. 58, suggests "normative coefficients of relative effectiveness" of not less than 15 to 30 percent or, for transportation and power, 10 percent. The period in reference is much later than 1937. Kantorovich–59, p. 222, asserts that "normal effectiveness" in the U.S.S.R. has exceeded by "several times" normal profit rates in capitalist countries.

6 Besides the usual problem of multicollinearity, there is the difficulty, remarked on in Chapter 1, of the "disequilibrium" character of observations on the Soviet economy. Also, an identification problem arises in that capital is both a function of output, in the demand for annual investment, and a determinant of output (see pp. 221–22 below).

7 Various estimates suggest a figure of this approximate order of magnitude for the United States., e.g., Becker–60, p. 349; Kravis–59, p. 938, col. (8); and Bergson–63, p. 30, fn.

The first estimate, which, in conformity with ordinary usage, we refer to as the "gross value" of the capital stock, is a summation of present values for assets with constant services $(S_1 = S_i; i = 1 \ldots n)$ for r approaching infinity. As the interest rate becomes large, V_i approaches S_i, and therefore S_1 and V_1. The asset maintains throughout its life its initial value in 1937 prices. This method of valuation is also referred to in the literature of depreciation accounting as the "retirement" method.

Our second and third estimates retain the assumption of constant services but employ alternative interest rates of 8 and 20 percent to discount future services. The depreciation formula is that known in accounting as the "sinking fund" method.[8]

The fourth estimate, which for convenience we refer to henceforth simply as the "net value" estimate, is a summation of present values for straight-line depreciated assets. It may be interpreted as referring to assets with constant services when $r =$ zero. With that interest rate,

$$V_j = \sum_{i=j}^{n} S_i = (n + 1 - j)S_1, \text{ and} \tag{4}$$

$$V_j - V_{j+1} = S_1 = V_1/n, \tag{5}$$

which is the straight-line rate of depreciation. The first and fourth estimates together bound the values that a stock of constant service assets would assume for interest rates of zero or greater. The constant service

---

[8] Under the sinking fund method, the value of an asset is the difference between its acquisition cost and the amount of a sinking fund established by uniform annual payments from the time of acquisition. The payments are sufficient, given the interest rate, to provide a fund equal to the acquisition cost by the end of the asset's life.

If services are constant, then $S_1 = S_2 = \ldots S_n$, and expression (1) becomes

$$V_j = S_1 \sum_{i=j}^{n} \frac{1}{(1 + r)^{i-j}} \tag{2}$$

$$= [S_1/(1 + r)^n] \sum_{i=j}^{n} (1 + r)^n (1 + r)^{j-i}$$

$$= [S_1/(1 + r)^n] \sum_{i=j}^{n} (1 + r)^i, \text{ and}$$

$$V_1 - V_j = [S_1/(1 + r)^n] \left[\sum_{i=1}^{n} (1 + r)^i - \sum_{i=j}^{n} (1 + r)^i \right] \tag{3}$$

$$= [S_1/(1 + r)^n] \sum_{i=1}^{j-1} (1 + r)^i .$$

That is to say, at the beginning of the jth year, the end of the $(j - 1)$th year, the difference between the acquisition cost of the asset and its present value is the amount of expression (3). The latter, however, is the value at the end of $(j - 1)$ years of a sinking fund at interest r, built up through uniform annual contributions of the amount $[S_1/(1 + r)^n]$. By definition, $V_{n+1} = 0$. Hence from (3), we have

$$V_1 = V_1 - V_{n+1} = [S_1/(1 + r)^n] \sum_{i=1}^{n} (1 + r)^i .$$

Thus $[S_1/(1 + r)^n]$ is also the annual payment necessary to build a sinking fund equal to the acquisition cost of the asset over its life, n.

CHART 2–2

Total Fixed Capital Estimated with Alternative Depreciation Methods, in 1937 Prices, 1928–62
(January 1—Billion Rubles)

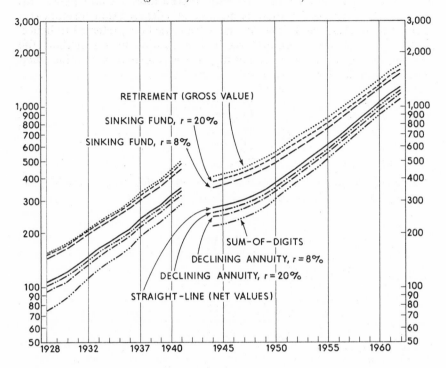

Sources: Tables T–1 to T–6, pp. 315–20.

assumption common to all of the first four estimates is equivalent to the assumption that assets are of the "one-hoss-shay" type, for which, as is evident, capital values vary with the interest rate at which services are discounted.

The straight-line depreciation estimate may also be interpreted as referring to assets with services declining along a straight line to zero (i.e., for which the average rate of decline in services between years 1 and i always equals S_1/n), as r approaches infinity. As the rate of interest increases, V_j approaches S_j or $S_1(n + 1 - j)/n$. The latter term approaches $V_1(n + 1 - j)/n$; and $V_j - V_{j+1}$ approaches V_1/n, the straight-line rate of depreciation. Thus the first and fourth estimates may also be interpreted as bounding the true value, as r approaches infinity, of a stock of assets with service streams lying somewhere between constancy, $S_1 = S_i$, and straight-line decline to zero, $S_i = S_n(n + 1 - i)$.

As the foregoing implies, the straight-line depreciated series may be interpreted in still a third way, as applying to assets with service streams lying somewhere between our two extreme cases, when the interest rate is positive but finite. Under this interpretation, services decline by a constant absolute amount each year, the rate of decline being determined by the interest rate.[9] In terms of Chart 2–1, the service stream is a straight line with terminal points between A and B at one end, between D and E at the other.

The fifth and sixth estimates are made on the assumption that services decline along a straight line to zero, with interest rates of 8 and 20 percent. So far as we can discover, there is no standard depreciation formula corresponding to these conditions. We have composed one, referred to henceforth as the "declining annuity" method. According to this method, the value of an asset at the beginning of its jth year is related to its value when new by the following expression:[10]

$$\frac{V_j}{V_1} = \frac{\sum\limits_{i=0}^{n-j} \sum\limits_{k=0}^{i} \dfrac{1}{(1+r)^k}}{\sum\limits_{i=0}^{n-1} \sum\limits_{k=0}^{i} \dfrac{1}{(1+r)^k}}. \tag{6}$$

Finally, the seventh estimate is made employing the "sum-of-digits" method—that is, where depreciation in the jth year is

$$[V_1]\left[\frac{(n+1-j)}{\sum\limits_{i=1}^{n} i}\right].$$

---

[9] From equation (1) above, we can obtain:

$$V_j = S_j + 1/(1+r) \sum\limits_{j+1}^{n} \frac{S_i}{(i+r)^{i-j-1}}$$

$$= S_j + [1/(1+r)]V_{j+1},$$

from which it follows that:

$$S_j - S_{j+1} = V_j - V_{j+1} - [1/(1+r)](V_{j+1} - V_{j+2}).$$

Under straight-line depreciation, since depreciation is the same absolute amount each year and the last year's depreciation is the last year's service, $V_j - V_{j+1} = V_{j+1} - V_{j+2} = S_n$. Therefore,

$$S_j - S_{j+1} = [r/(1+r)]S_n.$$

In other words, services decline each year by $[r/(1+r)]S_n$. Thus, so long as r is finite, services are not constant but decline; and, so long as r is greater than zero, the annual amount of the decline is less than S_n, the rate along the straight line which connects S_1 with zero at the end of the asset's service life.

[10] If services decline along a straight line to zero, then $S_i = S_n(n+1-i)$, and the value of an asset at the beginning of year j as given by expression (1) above is

$$V_j = S_n \sum\limits_{i=j}^{n} \frac{(n+1-i)}{(1+r)^{i-j}} = S_n \sum\limits_{i=0}^{n-j} \frac{(n+1-j-i)}{(1+r)^i}.$$

The last summation is

$$\left[\frac{(n+1-j)}{(1+r)^0} + \frac{(n-j)}{(1+r)^1} + \dots + \frac{2}{(1+r)^{n-j-1}} + \frac{1}{(1+r)^{n-j}}\right]$$

$$= \left[\frac{1}{(1+r)^0}\right] + \left[\frac{1}{(1+r)^0} + \frac{1}{(1+r)^1}\right] + \dots + \left[\frac{1}{(1+r)^0} + \dots + \frac{1}{(1+r)^{n-j}}\right]$$

$$= \sum\limits_{i=0}^{n-j} \sum\limits_{k=0}^{i} \frac{1}{(1+r)^k}.$$

This method may be interpreted as yielding capital values for assets with services declining along a straight line to zero when the interest rate is zero.[11]

Thus the fourth and seventh estimates together bound the values that a stock of such assets would assume for all interest rates of zero or more. They also bound the values, for a zero interest rate, of stocks with service streams between $S_i = S_1$ and $S_i = S_n(n + 1 - i)$. The first and seventh estimates, therefore, are bounds for any nonnegative interest rate and any service stream between $S_i = S_1$ and $S_i = S_n(n + 1 - i)$.

Table 2–1 repeats the results of the calculations for selected years in a form which may make comparison easier. As can be seen, the absolute values produced by the alternative methods of depreciation differ greatly. The lowest, those obtained by sum-of-digits, are some 35 to 50 percent below those gotten by the retirement method, the highest. Even a comparison of the next innermost set of estimates, which rest on less extreme assumptions, reveals substantial differences. The values produced by declining annuity with $r = 8\%$ are 27–39 percent below those obtained by the sinking fund method with $r = 20\%$. The size of this difference stems chiefly from our ignorance of the shape of service streams. If the assumption about changes in services is held constant, shifting the interest rate from 8 to 20 percent produces a much smaller difference in results—4–8 percent (compare rows 2 and 3 or rows 5 and 6 of Table 2–1). The straight-line depreciated values are intermediate but lie closer to the declining annuity than to the sinking fund estimates. Absolute values produced by the several calculations draw progressively closer together with time (except for a wartime reversal), which means, as we shall see, with the decline in the average age of the stock. This is to be expected, since the method of depreciation has greater impact on the present value of older assets.[12]

The estimated rate of growth proves to be less sensitive to the method of depreciation. Expressed in index form, all of the series move broadly together. Here too, varying the interest rate between 8 and 20 percent produces the smallest variation in results. Differences stemming from the service stream assumption are more consequential. The retirement and

----

11 Under these assumptions, $S_i = S_n(n + 1 - i)$, and

$$V_1 = \sum_{i=1}^{n} S_i = S_n \sum_{i=1}^{n} (n + 1 - i) = S_n \sum_{i=1}^{n} i .$$

Also, $V_j - V_{j+1} = S_n \left[\sum_{i=j}^{n} (n + 1 - i) - \sum_{i=j+1}^{n} (n + 1 - i) \right] = S_n(n + 1 - j) .$

Multiplying by V_1/V_1 and substituting, we get depreciation in the jth year as

$$V_j - V_{j+1} = [V_1] \left[\frac{(n + 1 - j)}{\sum_{i=1}^{n} i} \right],$$

which is the "sum-of-digits" formula.

12 Alternative depreciation methods also fall differently on assets of different service lives and, hence, affect the distribution of the total stock among its components. The effects here, however, are small, the share of structures in the total, e.g., varying from 87 to 88 percent in 1928 and 59 to 62 percent in 1962.

TABLE 2-1

TOTAL FIXED CAPITAL ESTIMATED WITH ALTERNATIVE DEPRECIATION
METHODS, IN 1937 PRICES, SELECTED YEARS
(January 1)

Depreciation Method	1928	1932	1937	1941	1945	1950	1955	1962
A. Billion Rubles								
1. Retirement (Gross Values)	157.4	215.4	335.3	503.5	420.6	558.5	859.3	1674.0
2. Sinking Fund, r = 20%	156.1	212.4	326.2	483.9	398.7	528.8	801.3	1569.2
3. Sinking Fund, r = 8%	148.8	201.3	307.2	453.4	368.4	486.4	745.5	1481.5
4. Straight-Line (Net Values)	107.6	151.0	240.5	359.6	281.3	376.6	603.9	1249.0
5. Declining Annuity, r = 20%	102.3	144.1	229.2	341.9	265.0	355.1	572.2	1187.8
6. Declining Annuity, r = 8%	95.0	135.3	217.5	325.3	249.7	335.8	545.9	1140.0
7. Sum-of-Digits	75.0	113.8	192.9	293.5	222.5	304.8	506.4	1070.7
B. Straight-Line Depreciated Values = 100								
1. Retirement (Gross Values)	146	143	139	140	150	148	142	134
2. Sinking Fund, r = 20%	145	141	136	135	142	140	133	126
3. Sinking Fund, r = 8%	138	133	128	126	131	129	123	119
4. Straight-Line (Net Values)	100	100	100	100	100	100	100	100
5. Declining Annuity, r = 20%	95.1	95.4	95.3	95.1	94.2	94.3	94.7	95.1
6. Declining Annuity, r = 8%	88.3	89.6	90.4	90.5	88.8	89.2	90.4	91.3
7. Sum-of-Digits	69.7	75.4	80.2	81.6	79.1	80.9	83.9	85.7
C. 1937 = 100								
1. Retirement (Gross Values)	46.9	64.2	100	150	125	167	256	499
2. Sinking Fund, r = 20%	47.9	65.1	100	148	122	162	246	481
3. Sinking Fund, r = 8%	48.4	65.5	100	148	120	158	243	482
4. Straight-Line (Net Values)	44.7	62.8	100	150	117	157	251	519
5. Declining Annuity, r = 20%	44.6	62.9	100	149	116	155	250	518
6. Declining Annuity, r = 8%	43.7	62.2	100	150	115	154	251	524
7. Sum-of-Digits	38.9	59.0	100	152	115	158	263	555

Sources: See text.

sum-of-digits calculations yield average growth rates over the period 1928–
62 of 7.2 and 8.1 percent respectively. Among the series for which the
assumptions are less extreme, the slowest rate is produced by the sinking
fund method with $r = 8\%$ and the most rapid by declining annuity with
$r = 8\%$, 7.0 and 7.6 percent respectively. The rate with straight-line depreciation, 7.5 percent, is roughly intermediate. Apparently, the calculations provide a more reliable guide to changes over time than to absolute
values.[13]

If it were easier than it in fact is to think in terms of broad ranges of
values—absolute values, since growth rates are similar—as against single-
valued estimates, we would be inclined to treat the whole of the foregoing

[13] The observed similarities in growth rates are in part a matter of coincidence, but
there is an element common to all the calculations—the shape of the gross investment
stream—which also provides an important part of the explanation. On this, see p. 241.

estimates as our findings on the fixed capital stock. Our knowledge of the shape of service streams and of appropriate interest rates is so slight that any substantial narrowing of the range of estimates must be highly speculative. Our best judgment, nevertheless, is that the net value series, computed with straight-line depreciation, is the most plausible of the alternatives.

It appears likely that service streams decline over time, but not so rapidly as in the most extreme case considered. It appears likely also that the rate of interest in the Soviet economy, if observable, would prove relatively high, although certainly not infinitely so. Both gross value and sum-of-digit estimates, therefore, can be ruled out as wholly implausible, on the basis of their implied assumptions on interest rates if not service streams. The sinking fund and declining annuity calculations are less certainly implausible, but their service-stream assumptions appear relatively extreme. Interpreted in the third of the three ways we have indicated, straight-line depreciation is consistent both with services declining at an intermediate rate and with high interest rates. These conditions are not sufficient to suggest whether present values decline over time at an accelerating or decelerating rate, but, in the face of that uncertainty, it may not be unreasonable to take a decline along a straight line as a best guess. On these grounds, we hereafter treat the calculations with straight-line depreciation as our preferred estimate, although we do make further reference to the alternatives.

While the acceptance of straight-line depreciation allows us to present our (net) stock estimates without identifying the interest rate assumed for their calculation, this is only a formal simplification and one which must be abandoned when we come to estimate the annual capital services associated with the stock. As indicated, we take the stock figures as appropriate for high but not infinite interest rates, and we shall subsequently take this to mean the 8 to 20 percent range considered heretofore. As the interest rate is varied within this range, it is implicitly assumed, of course, that the slope of the service stream rendered by assets over time varies accordingly, the 20 percent rate implying a more rapidly declining stream than does the 8 percent rate.

One final possibility should be considered. If, as suggested, services tend to decline more rapidly over time for equipment than structures, it might be appropriate to depreciate different kinds of assets by different methods. This is explored in Table 2–2, which presents the results of employing combined depreciation methods in comparison with those produced by the straight-line method.[14] Combination I shows values when structures are assumed to deliver constant services, equipment and installation (the last is a separate category in our estimates) services declining along a straight line to zero, with an interest rate of 20 percent.[15] In Combination II, structures are depreciated at straight line, which, as explained, can

---

14 Annual figures for the combined depreciation calculations of Table 2–2 are not shown in the Tabular Section, since they are of little interest or likely use other than as a check on our basic estimates. Other alternative calculations are treated similarly hereafter. The form of the tabular comparisons in the text is also varied hereafter, as suits the particular point under examination.

15 An interest rate of 8 percent would produce a nearly parallel series, some 4–8 percent lower in absolute level.

be interpreted as consistent with a finite interest rate; equipment and installation are again assumed to deliver services declining along a straight line to zero, and an interest rate of 8 percent is used.[16] The results of the calculation lead to much the same conclusions as those drawn from Table 2–1. Combination I develops much like the series computed by the sinking fund method ($r = 8\%$), and Combination II much like that derived by declining annuity ($r = 20\%$). The variation in growth among the series is about the same as among those computed by a uniform depreciation method (6.8 percent per year for Combination I, which is slightly slower than for any of the uniform series; 7.4 percent for Combination II), while the variation in absolute level is somewhat less than among the three innermost series of Table 2–1 (rows 3–5).

TABLE 2-2

TOTAL FIXED CAPITAL ESTIMATED WITH COMBINED AND STRAIGHT-LINE
DEPRECIATION METHODS, IN 1937 PRICES, SELECTED YEARS
(January 1)

Depreciation Method	1928	1932	1937	1941	1945	1950	1955	1962
A. Billion Rubles								
1. Combination I[a]...	149.6	203.1	308.5	454.0	370.9	487.4	732.5	1421.2
2. Straight-Line Depreciation ...	107.6	151.0	240.5	359.6	281.3	376.6	603.9	1249.0
3. Combination II[b]..	104.7	147.9	234.0	348.3	271.1	362.2	578.5	1190.6
B. Straight-Line Depreciated Values = 100								
1. Combination I[a]...	139	135	128	126	132	129	121	114
2. Straight-Line Depreciation ...	100	100	100	100	100	100	100	100
3. Combination II[b]..	97.3	97.9	97.3	96.9	96.4	96.2	95.8	95.3
C. 1937 = 100								
1. Combination I[a]...	48.5	65.8	100	147	120	158	237	461
2. Straight-Line Depreciation ...	44.7	62.8	100	150	117	157	251	519
3. Combination II[b]..	44.7	63.2	100	149	116	155	247	509

[a] Structures depreciated by sinking fund method ($r = 20\%$), equipment and installation by declining annuity method ($r = 20\%$).
[b] Structures depreciated by straight-line, equipment and installation by declining annuity method ($r = 8\%$).
Source: For rows 1 and 3, see text; for row 2, Table T–1.

The Capitalization of Major Repairs

The estimates considered thus far are based on certain, rather simple, parametric assumptions concerning the shape of capital service streams. Such regularities in the service streams are more likely in the case of assets which are "normally" maintained, i.e., when repairs are applied according to the schedule most economic under weight-year conditions. Thus, our basic calculations are most appropriately interpreted as referring to assets in a state of "normal" repair.

What happens when, in response to the exigencies of the time, repairs

---

16 A 20 percent interest rate would result in a nearly parallel series, some 1–2 percent higher in absolute level.

are postponed or augmented for assets generally? Clearly, for example, a stock of assets subjected to a parsimonious repair policy will soon accumulate a substantial backlog of repairs which must be performed sooner or later. Its ability to provide services will be impaired to some extent, and the mounting bill for future repairs will stand as a claim against services not yet rendered. On both counts, its present value will be smaller than that of a stock of like assets in normal condition. Our estimates of capital values would be improved, therefore, if we could capitalize repairs—allow for anticipated repairs in reckoning depreciation while adding to depreciated values the value of actual repairs as they are made.

Soviet investment data are unusual in that they include expenditures for major repairs, known in Soviet parlance as "capital repairs," as a separate item.[17] In calculating investment in 1937 prices, we have compiled a series inclusive of capital repairs, though it is less reliable than that for investment exclusive of such repairs.[18] In spite of the availability of these data and of the conceptual desirability of capitalizing repairs, we have derived our primary estimates from investment outlays for new assets only, taking our assumptions about service streams to refer to services net of capital repairs. To do otherwise it would be necessary *inter alia* to know how capital repairs are "normally" distributed over assets' service lives and the effect of postponing repairs on asset services and on the costs of future repairs, all of which we have been unable to determine satisfactorily. In what follows, therefore, some highly simplified assumptions concerning normal repairs are confronted with the data for repairs actually performed. The results, unfortunately, are indicative only very roughly of the implications for our estimates of not capitalizing repairs.[19]

The same considerations which lead us to choose 1937 as the weight year for our principal calculations[20] suggest the adoption of actual repair expenditures in 1937 as an approximation to normal repair expenditures for that year. On this basis and with the additional assumption that normal repair requirements vary with the gross stock of assets, we compute a time series for normal repairs for all years.[21] The difference between repairs

17 "Capital repairs are relatively large scale renovating activities in which defective parts of a fixed asset are replaced—e.g., the replacement of a heating system. The object of such activities is to restore the asset to full working power. If the object is to increase the working power of the asset, the activity is called not a capital repair but reconstruction (and is treated like other investments and not like repairs)." See Kaplan–51, p. 15.

18 The estimates of capital repairs to equipment, about 40 percent of the total, are based on a deflation of doubtful reliability; see Moorsteen–62, p. 456. In the case of construction, on the other hand, our basic investment series includes capital repairs and has been adjusted to exclude them for purposes of the present study; see Section 3, pp. 45–46. Errors in this adjustment, accordingly, would be partially compensated for by incorporating capital repairs as a separate item in the capital stock calculations.

19 Maintenance other than "capital repair" is known as "current repair." No systematic data on the volume of this item are available, but it is undoubtedly of considerable importance, possibly as great as that of capital repairs. See, e.g., Bunich–60, p. 187. Presumably, current repairs, like capital repairs, are subject to changes in relative amount, and for this reason the problems considered in this section would probably be intensified if account were taken of current as well as capital repairs.

20 See Chapter 1, p. 14.

21 In each year, normal repair requirements in the year i are computed as the product $R^{37}V^i$, where R^{37} is the ratio of actual repairs performed in 1937 to the gross value of assets in 1937 and V^i is the gross value of assets in the year i, all values in 1937 prices. Gross values are used, rather than net, because it is desired to measure the quantity of

actually performed in each year and normal repair requirements is plotted in billions of 1937 rubles in Chart 2–3.[22] Thus, a negative value in the chart indicates a repair deficit, an amount by which actual repairs were less than normal, and conversely.

CHART 2–3

Annual Deficits (−) and Surpluses (+) in Capital Repairs, in 1937 Prices, 1928–61
(Billion Rubles)

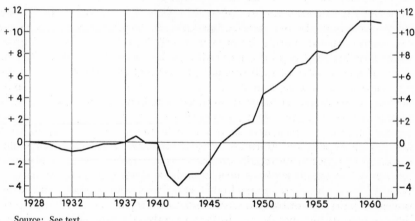

Source: See text.

Before the results of the calculation are considered, it may be well to comment further on the two main underlying assumptions. First, are actual 1937 repair expenditures a reasonable approximation to normal? This question cannot be resolved satisfactorily. An affirmative answer requires not only that the quantity of resources allocated to repairs in 1937 was appropriate under the circumstances of that year but also that the over-all condition of the fixed capital stock at the beginning of the year was roughly normal. In fact, Soviet sources frequently complain about inadequate maintenance in the prewar period, implying a persistent state of underrepair.[23] The difficulty with interpreting these discussions is that the standard against which judgments are made is not clear. It is not usually economic to maintain assets in mint condition, and it may be that under

assets physically extant. A flow of normal repairs is computed in this fashion for each of the three kinds of fixed assets distinguished in our calculations—structures, equipment, and installation. The series for total normal repairs is the sum of these three flows. The capital repair data for 1937 are obtained from Tables A–1 and A–2. The gross stock values are from Table T–1, except that figures for 1942 and 1943, which are not shown in that table, are calculated (by the same procedures as for other years) to obtain a continuous series here.

22 The actual repair data are from Table A–1.

23 See, e.g., Pavlov–57, p. 189, who cites a 1938 Council of People's Commissariats' decree: "The present neglect of repairs to industrial equipment and buildings inflicts large losses on the state and cannot be tolerated." The same source, p. 190, on the other hand, also reports that fixed assets were observed at this time to fulfill or even outlive their expected service lives.

1937 circumstances a relatively austere repair policy was justified, even though the assets, appraised by purely engineering criteria, would seem to be suffering neglect. According to the data in Chart 2–3, actual repair outlays throughout the prewar period stayed close to the relative 1937 level: none of the deficits or surpluses are as large as one billion rubles, during a period in which the estimated net stock increased from 108 to 360 billion rubles. This indicates that some potent factors consistent with this relative level of expenditures were at work. The persistence of the same relative level of expenditure prior to 1937 is also consistent with the assumption that the general state of repair at the beginning of 1937 was normal (and with normality in the state of repair at the beginning of 1928, on which none of our data bear directly). These data certainly suggest that normal repairs were unlikely to have been much *below* the actual level of 1937, because this would imply persistent repair surpluses throughout the prewar period. On the other hand, it is possible that the normal level was above anything actually attained prewar, in which case we have underestimated normal requirements and the whole curve in Chart 2–3 should be moved downward. The possibility that actual prewar repairs were below normal is consistent with the large postwar repair surpluses plotted in Chart 2–3, though the latter may reflect a rise in the normal level over time. For our purposes, of course, the normal should reflect only weight-year—1937—scarcities.

Secondly, we have estimated normal repair requirements on the assumption that they vary with the gross stock of assets. In fact, they no doubt also increase with asset age, over the greater part of the service life.[24] As will be shown later, the average age of Soviet fixed assets, over the long run, has tended downward. Thus, our method of calculation would tend, on this count, to overstate the growth of normal repairs, imparting a downward bias over time to the series in Chart 2–3.

Turning now to the substance of the matter, a relatively simple pattern emerges in Chart 2–3. The differences between actual and normal repairs were relatively small throughout the prewar period; substantial repair deficits occurred throughout the war, 1941–45; and growing repair surpluses occurred after 1946.

What does this flow of deficits and surpluses signify for the present value of the asset stock at any given point in time? The main obstacle to inference here is that neglected repairs of the past differ in their implications for present values. Some repairs, if not performed when normally indicated, must be performed eventually and at equal or increased cost. For example, delaying the replacement of a faulty roof may result in interior damage. The present value of an asset for which such a repair has been neglected would be less than that of one normally maintained by an amount equal to or greater than the unperformed repair. Other repairs, although reducing an asset's serviceability when not performed, may be obviated in the future at no cost by further normal maintenance. For example, a tractor which misses a scheduled overhaul may perform badly for a period but be restored to normal condition by the next regular overhaul. Thus, at any

---

[24] As is noted, pp. 23–24, repairs are likely to decline at the near approach of the retirement date.

point in time, the actual present value of the asset stock may differ from the normal by more or by less than the sum of past repair deficits and surpluses.

It is clear from the above that we can say nothing very precise about the effects on our calculations of not capitalizing repairs. The data in Chart 2–3 strongly suggest, however, at least the following general observations: (*i*) The prewar growth rates seem not to be significantly affected.[25] (*ii*) The state of repair was higher by the end of the postwar period than during the prewar. This implies that certain of our long-run growth rates would be increased if repairs were capitalized. (*iii*) The state of repair just after the war was lower, relative to normal, than before the war and lower still when compared with the later postwar years. This implies that growth rates within the postwar period would also be increased if repairs were capitalized—and by more than the long-run ones. (*iv*) If actual repairs in 1937 were in fact substantially below normal, the stock has probably been underrepaired throughout the period studied and all the normal values are overestimates. The implications of this for the measured growth rates, however, are not clear.

While it is not possible to quantify the foregoing with any accuracy, it may nevertheless be useful to arrange the data of Chart 2–3 in a somewhat different form. In Table 2–3, the repair deficits and surpluses are cumulated from 1928 and compared with the value of the net stock as previously estimated.[26] For reasons discussed above, the cumulated repair deficits and surpluses are not to be construed literally as estimators of the difference between actual and normal stock values, though they may serve very roughly to indicate the relative magnitudes involved. The cumulated deficit or surplus ranges in size to as much as 7 percent of the value of the stock with normal repairs. However, over the 17 years 1945–62, the algebraic difference changes by 12 percent of the normal value, from −5 percent to +7 percent. When it is noted that the estimated stock of fixed assets, normally repaired, increased by about 11 times between 1928 and 1962, it will be seen that variations of the size indicated in Table 2–3 for the later postwar years would not have a large effect on the long-run growth rates. However, for certain shorter intervals, especially those ending with immediate postwar years, the effect on the rate of change might be marked. Within the postwar period, the magnitudes of the changes from repair deficit to repair surplus amount to upwards of 1 percent per year of the estimated value of the net stock.

Problems akin to those presented by variations in repairs arise from variations in the intensity with which assets are used: from changes, for

---

25 This is strictly true only under the assumption that actual 1937 repairs approximated normal. But if, as is also possible, they were below normal, actual repairs would be below normal in almost all other prewar years. The stock of assets would be underrepaired throughout the period, but no change in the *growth rate* measured for the stock would necessarily be implied.

26 As will be explained subsequently, the latter series is adjusted for territorial gains and war damage. To provide comparability, therefore, the cumulated repair figures are similarly adjusted, using the allowance described in Section 6 of this chapter. No adjustment is made, however, for any divergence from normal in the 1928 stock or for the fact that part of the deficit or surplus accumulated by any given date may relate to assets retired before that date.

TABLE 2-3

CUMULATED CAPITAL REPAIR DEFICITS (-) AND SURPLUSES (+) RELATIVE
TO TOTAL NET FIXED CAPITAL, IN 1937 PRICES, SELECTED YEARS
(January 1)

	Net Fixed Capital, "Normally" Repaired (Billion Rubles)	Repair Deficits and Surpluses Cumulated from 1928 to Indicated Year	
		Billion Rubles	Percent of Net Fixed Capital, "Normally" Repaired
	(1)	(2)	(3)
1928 . . .	107.6	0	0
1932 . . .	151.0	-1	0*
1937 . . .	240.5	-3	-1
1941 . . .	359.6	-3	-1
1945 . . .	281.3	-14	-5
1950 . . .	376.6	-11	-3
1953 . . .	500.0	+4	+1
1955 . . .	603.9	+18	+3
1958 . . .	829.4	+43	+5
1962 . . .	1249.0	+86	+7

*Less than 0.5 percent.

Sources: For column 1, Table T-1. For columns 2 and 3, see text.

example, in the number of shifts worked or in operating rates. These not only produce "abnormalities" in the shapes of service streams, and consequently in the present values of assets, but they must also alter the volume of repairs required to bring an asset of given age back to its normal state. They may well alter also the actual service lives of assets.

We have no concrete evidence on the extent of such variations in the use of Soviet fixed capital. It is likely that an increase in shifts and operating rates occurred during the First Five-Year Plan, from 1928 to 1932, and the rate of use was probably exceptionally high during World War II. The latter reinforces the implication of the calculations for capital repairs that our estimates of the net stock, based on the assumption of normal (1937) repairs and rates of use, may significantly overstate the value of the stock in the immediate postwar years.

3. THE ANNUAL INVESTMENT DATA

The fixed capital calculations employ annual investment series for three classes of assets: structures, equipment, and installation. The series are described in detail in the previous studies from which they are largely drawn.[27] We need here only to summarize those descriptions and to draw attention to modifications of the original series made for use in the present study.[28]

The threefold classification of fixed capital investment follows Soviet practice and is dictated by the nature of the source materials. The "construction" series refers to outlays for the creation of structures, including, for example, housing, factory buildings, roads and railroads, dams, mine

---

[27] See p. 21, fn.

[28] Details of the extensions and revisions made are set forth in Appendix A, which also contains the annual series.

works, canals, sewers, power transmission lines, fences, blast furnaces, and the like. The "equipment" series refers to outlays for the acquisition of producer durables. Of these, the dominant component is machinery, such as trucks, tractors, locomotives, metal-cutting machines, steam boilers and turbines, ships, hoists and elevators, or laboratory equipment. But other durables, such as office furnishings or industrial containers, are also included. Investment in "installation" consists of outlays for the assembly and emplacement of machines that are attached to the structures in which they operate. A substantial share of these expenditures must go for labor, but there are also physical manifestations in the form of special foundations, framings, stairways, insulations, or electrical conduits, required for mounting the machines. At points, the distinction between the three kinds of outlays must be arbitrary. So far as possible, we are guided by Soviet accounting conventions in marking dividing lines, but, since the latter have not been entirely constant over time, some ambiguity and inconsistency in classification enters our data. For example, heating and plumbing devices have been treated as equipment in some periods but as building materials—and hence part of construction—in others. However, it is unlikely that these variations in scope have been large enough to have a significant impact on the capital stock calculations.

In addition to the three kinds of assets in our series, Soviet investment series include a category known as "other capital investments and outlays," a miscellany of expenditures, the scope of which has altered over time. It has included variously outlays for designing, geological, and prospecting work, associated with a specific construction project; outlays for land betterment; and "investments which do not increase the stock of fixed capital," i.e., outlays for designing, etc., which are *not* associated with a specific project, for training personnel of new enterprises, for the purchase of existing assets from collective farms and co-operative organizations, or for maintaining the administration of enterprises during the period of construction. Although, by Western concepts, some of these expenditures might appropriately be treated as outlays for the creation of new fixed assets, most of them, we judge, should not. We lack information on the distribution of outlays within the category and omit it entirely from our investment series—and, hence, from the capital stock values.[29]

Equipment

Our equipment series is based on one computed previously for investment in equipment excluding capital repairs, in 1937 prices. The original series covers the years 1928–30, 1934–40, 1944–46, 1949–56, and was obtained by deflation of investment in current prices.

The data on investment in current prices are for acquisitions of producer durables. Consumer durables and military procurements are excluded. In keeping with present Soviet practice, the data exclude, for all

---

[29] On the definitions of Soviet capital investment categories, see Kaplan–51, pp. 1–2; Moorsteen–62, pp. 423–25; TsSU–44, pp. 199–201; Anonymous–58, pp. 118 and 325; Petrov–61, pp. 184 ff. Some Soviet capital investment series also include outlays for acquisition of livestock. These are excluded from our series for investment in fixed capital. Capital and investment in livestock are considered in Chapter 4.

years, outlays for "small-valued and short-lived durables."[30] The outlays include the price paid the producer plus costs of distribution. For equipment requiring no special installation, the investment outlay is considered to occur when the durables are received at the investor's repository. In the case of equipment requiring installation, the investment outlay is considered to occur only when the machinery is issued from the repository near the project site for the purpose of installing it. Thus at any given moment, the sum of past fixed capital investment outlays includes some expenditures for durables not yet in operation. All equipment in transit and that requiring installation and still in the investor's warehouse are treated as inventories and excluded from fixed capital investment.[31] The prices paid producers are, in general, current wholesale prices. Peasant households and collective farms, however, have apparently paid higher prices than other purchasers, reflecting at least in part the higher costs of marketing to these units but possibly also some price discrimination against them.[32] Indirect taxes and subsidies are of little consequence in equipment prices, and no adjustment is made here for them.

The preceding paragraph describes the intended content of the current-price investment data which are deflated. It must be .emphasized, however, that systematic and consistent current-price investment series have not been published in Soviet sources since the mid-1930's, and that, even for early years, the share of total investment going to equipment is not always clearly indicated. The equipment series actually employed for our purposes is derived from data on total fixed capital investment in current prices, compiled by Norman Kaplan and generously made available to us in advance of publication, together with diverse information on the relative importance of equipment in the total. Under the circumstances, neither the estimates of totals nor the equipment shares can be counted free of error. For the series on current-price investment in equipment only, it is believed that the margin of error should not generally exceed about 10 percent, though of course it is impossible to determine this magnitude precisely.

The equipment deflator is essentially an index of Soviet producer prices for domestic machines. As is required for a deflation into constant prices of 1937, it is based on 1937 and computed with variable weights of the given year. For the years in which imports were of greatest importance—1928–30 and 1944—the index of domestic prices is adjusted from sample price data to take account of price differentials of imported machines as well. In all cases, the prices are exclusive of distribution and transportation charges.

---

[30] These are items having a service life of less than one year and/or a value less than normed. The latter magnitude has varied over time and, in any given period, is determined separately by different systems of investing organizations, but with an upper limit applicable to all systems. In the 1930's, the limit was 200 rubles; it was raised to 300 rubles in the 1940's and to 500 rubles in the 1950's. Assets of this sort were treated in official Soviet investment accounting as fixed capital until the latter half of 1936, as "working" capital thereafter. In our estimates, they are included throughout in inventories. On the official accounting, see Moorsteen–62, p. 424; Gozulov–53, p. 200; Ezhov–57, p. 167.

[31] See, for example, TsSU–44, p. 200; Petrov–61, p. 76.

[32] See Moorsteen–62, pp. 23–34.

In this respect, and because it includes only prices for machinery but not for other producer durables, the scope of the price index does not strictly coincide with the class of investment outlays to be deflated. The excluded outlays probably account for about 15 percent of total expenditures for equipment investment.

In form, the deflator is a value-weighted aggregation of price relatives. Taken from Soviet handbooks, the price quotations underlying the relatives are believed to provide a reasonably accurate reflection of the rates at which investors acquired machinery from Soviet producers. The weights refer to the value of output rather than of investors' acquisitions, but, given the intimate link between the two, the substitution of the one for the other should not in itself be a major source of error. Much more problematic is the effect on the index of the introduction of new types of machinery and the abandonment of old.[33]

Price relatives are constructed to span these changes in regimen by two methods. The first is to compare prices for machines which are not identical but are judged close substitutes from their technical characteristics. The presence of such substitutability must be read from the published descriptions of the machines and, where the descriptions are sparse, can be determined only roughly. Furthermore, differences in durability between otherwise substitutable assets are difficult to take into account. In a few important cases, prices for less closely substitutable machines are used to construct price relatives by adjusting for measurable differences in quality: for example, the difference in tractive power of tractors which in other respects are similar. The room for error here, too, is substantial.

The second approach to regimen change is the construction of price relatives by linkage. A relative for model "x" spanning 1928–34 is multiplied by one for model "y" spanning 1934–37 to produce a 1937-based relative for 1928. For these relatives the problem of comparing technical characteristics does not arise.[34]

In all, in computing the price relatives, about two thirds of the underlying comparisons are between prices for substantially identical machines. This was possible because, to attain serial production and avoid learning costs, the Soviets have standardized machinery output to an unusual degree, continuing over prolonged periods to produce the same models, and because new models often overlapped older ones, permitting linkage. In many cases where prices of nonidentical machines were compared, the differences were relatively small. Nevertheless, where nonidentical models are involved, many quality changes undoubtedly go unnoticed, with the result that, as quality improves, the deflator tends systematically to over-

---

33 The discussion following is based on that in Moorsteen–62, pp. 51 ff., to which reference may be made for a fuller treatment of the question.

34 In Moorsteen–62, pp. 58–59, it is argued that the use of linkage in itself produces a bias in the deflator. The argument is that the reason underlying regimen changes is often a change in relative cost—in the example in the text, that "x" ceased to be produced while "y" was introduced because "x" had grown relatively more, "y" relatively less, costly to produce. Thus the linked relative understates what it would have cost to produce "x" in 1937 (relative to 1928) and also understates what it would have cost to produce "y" in 1928 (relative to 1937). As should have been made clear, this consideration applies to a deflation intended to measure output, "production potential," but not to one measuring capital on the basis of substitutability in use.

state later price levels relative to earlier ones. This is no doubt a characteristic of machinery price indexes in all countries, but it is worth remarking that the difficulties in the Soviet case may be less than for economies in which producers are more flexible, which place less emphasis on "quantity" in the simplest sense, and in which, therefore, regimens tend to change more frequently.

Even if the price relatives were impeccable in having reference only to machines of closely similar quality, the question of representativeness would remain. This is the point at which the problem of new products becomes critical. The deflator contains price relatives for just under two hundred kinds of machines (though not all relatives are included for all years). The number of machinery models produced in the Soviet Union is many times this number. In constructing the deflator, each relative, although computed from prices for only one or a few machine models, is assumed to reflect price movements for all the models in a specified *group* of machines: for example, one relative for normal AC motors of 0–5 kilowatts, one for motors of 6–50 kilowatts, etc. Relatives common to a single category of machinery are aggregated to produce a category index, presumed to reflect price behavior for the category generally, even though the price relatives employed do not encompass all of the kinds of machinery in the category. Such indexes are composed for 19 categories, which, when aggregated, are taken to stand for all machinery price behavior, even though there are many other categories for which no individual index has been computed. Thus at three levels, the available data are taken to represent the unavailable.

The effect of this procedure on the deflated investment series may be described as follows. Within the indicated class of machines, *relative* given-year prices of individual items have been taken to stand for relative weight-year prices. For example, within the group of machines represented by a single price relative, prices for all individual items are assumed in effect to move together. Thus in deflating, say, current-price data for 1928 into 1937 prices, the price level for the group changes, but relative prices for items within the group retain their 1928 structure. Prices of items which are in one of the 19 included categories but which are not represented by individual price relatives are adjusted by the change in price level for the category as a whole but not for structural change within the category, and so forth. This reliance on representative price data introduces the assumption that, within the indicated classes, substitution rates, in use, are the same in the weight and given years. Obviously, the error in the assumption is the less, the narrower the indicated class. To characterize the error more concretely than this is difficult, however, because the relationships involved are not simple.

A large share of the machines omitted from the deflator are relatively standard items for which price sources, although known to have been published, are not now available. Another important group are new products, the introduction of which was occasioned by changes in relative costs in the machinery-producing industry. These are products of known design that were not produced earlier because it was not economic to do so. In the Soviet case, where so much that was "new" to the domestic economy was borrowed from abroad, shifts in cost structure may have been a major determinant of regimen change. But potential relative costs in the weight year of machines that were not produced are no guide to their rate of substitution in use for other machines under weight-year technological conditions. For both of these groups of omitted products, it would be difficult to establish a priori assumptions as to the dominant tendency of differences between relative weight-year and given-year *users'* substitution rates. The employment of given-year, rather than weight-year, relative values as weights in the deflated investment series no doubt yields errors, but it is not clear that these tend in a particular direction. The same is true where given-year relative values are used for new products introduced as a result of genuine innovation. Had the new machines been invented and produced in the weight year, their substitutability for existing machines would no doubt differ from that in the given year, but, again, the direction and magnitude of difference must vary among individual cases. Finally, there are products, known but not previously produced, which are introduced in response to changing relative costs in the machinery-using industries. In these cases, presumably, given-year relative values exceed those of the weight year, and use of the former as weights in the deflated investment series tends to overstate the volume of investment in the given year. It may be noted that this error, at least, is opposite in tendency to that stemming from unadjusted quality improvements in products judged closely substitutable in computing the price relatives.

The magnitude of the problem raised by omissions from the deflator is difficult to judge. As noted previously, errors are undoubtedly less within the relatively narrow groups of products represented by individual price relatives, greater for products represented only by category price indexes, and greater still for products represented only by the general deflator. In our deflator, the price relatives are believed to account for about 70–80 percent of all output within the 19 categories for which individual price indexes are computed, and the 19 categories, in turn, for about 55–70 percent of all Soviet investment in machinery. Of the omitted items, new products which differed radically from goods produced in the weight year no doubt accounted for a significant portion of the total, but it should be noted that by 1937 the Soviet Union was self-sufficient in machinery and produced some variants of virtually every type of machine required by the several branches of its economy. The introduction of machines embodying, say, an entirely new technological process, while by no means absent, was certainly less typical than the modification and improvement of designs already in production.

The preceding describes our equipment investment series, excluding capital repairs, in 1937 prices for the years 1928–30, 1934–40, 1944–46, and 1949–56 which are drawn from a previous study. For present purposes, the series has been extended to include all years from 1928 through 1961. Three methods of extension have been employed. For 1931–33, 1942, and 1943, data on current-price investment comparable to those described above are compiled and deflated, the deflator being obtained by interpolation from that previously existing. For 1941, 1947, and 1948, current-price investment data are not available, and investment in 1937 prices is interpolated directly between figures for contiguous years. For 1957–61, investment in 1937 prices is extrapolated from our 1956 figure by means of official Soviet data on investment in equipment "in prices of July 1, 1955." This use of an official series impairs materially the "independence" of our estimates. It is based on the finding, however, that for 1950–56 the Soviet equipment investment series moves closely with ours, together with the fact that, so far as we are able to ascertain, no significant change in Soviet machinery prices has occurred since 1956. The latter suggests that the danger of error in the Soviet deflation of investment is probably not great, though in the absence of an independent investigation this can hardly be assured.

Construction

The series for construction is derived from an index of annual investment in construction inclusive of capital repairs, in 1937 prices. Values of the index for 1928–40 and 1945–55 are taken from an earlier study. Values for 1956–61 are estimated here by the same procedures as those used previously. Values for 1941–44 are interpolated. Absolute values are obtained from the index by setting it equal in 1937 to total construction in current prices. Capital repairs are then deducted from the series in all years.

The construction estimates are meant to include investment in fixed works and structures of all kinds, the precise boundaries of the category being determined by Soviet usage.[35] They are inclusive of work in progress as well as work completed, though an insignificant fraction of work in progress is here, as in Soviet practice, attributed to inventories.[36] The estimates are meant to be comprehensive in all other respects: of both contract and force-account construction, socialized and private construction, and construction in kind as well as that requiring money outlays.[37] 1937 valuations are prices paid by investing organizations in that year. Adjustments for correspondence to factor cost valuations are not thought to be necessary.

The index of annual construction inclusive of capital repairs, 1941–44 aside, is a price-weighted index of quantities of materials consumed in construction (cement, bricks, lumber, etc.) rather than a direct measure of quantities of construction outputs produced (plants, houses, roadways). Extended arguments on the reliability of the index as a measure of materials inputs and as a measure of construction outputs are made elsewhere and will only be summarized here.[38]

The index is designed as a measure of materials actually consumed in construction rather than domestic output or total consumption of construction materials conventionally defined. Reported consumption data of the required kind, however, are fragmentary and relate entirely to prewar years. Consumption in most years is estimated from total materials available and from the construction share in the total in the years for which it is known. Materials available are estimated in turn as the sum of

---

[35] See the sources cited p. 21, fn.

[36] See Appendix E, p. 445, and Appendix H, p. 526.

[37] In Powell–59, p. 64, the current-price estimates of construction are exclusive of collective-farm investment in kind and of road-building in kind by the population. These exclusions were occasioned by lack of data and have no effect on the indexes of construction in constant prices.

[38] See Powell–57, Part I, pp. 11 ff., and Powell–59, pp. 4 ff.

domestic output and net imports, the statistics for both of which are subject to further errors. A number of materials which are of little weight individually but of substantial importance in total are omitted entirely. Systematic adjustments for changes in inventories of construction materials are not made. The quantity series are aggregated with 1937 wholesale prices at origin for state industries, though average delivered prices would be preferable in principle.

The net error likely to result from the foregoing deficiencies cannot be established. A broad consistency can be shown, however, between the estimates of materials inputs and estimates made of labor inputs, materials prices and wages, and the value of construction in current prices.[39] From this consistency check, we infer a rough reliability of the materials index as a measure of materials consumed in construction.

For 1941–44, data for materials inputs cannot be compiled, and values for the index in those years are interpolated: between contiguous years for 1941; on an input-price deflated index for 1942–44. Errors resulting from these procedures are likely to be large relative to the volume of annual construction. Since, however, wartime construction was undoubtedly small, the effect of such errors on the capital stock estimates, especially beyond the immediate postwar years, is probably small also.

The question of the reliability of a materials input index as a measure of construction outputs is essentially the same as the question of the proper treatment of new products or quality change in the measurement of construction. To an exceptional degree, construction is marked by an extreme heterogeneity of its products, both over time and within any given year. It is a custom industry in which single products are frequently unique. Even products which are otherwise alike may differ in costs and in services rendered because of differences in site. In the face of these difficulties, it has been usual in statistical practice to forgo entirely the direct measurement of outputs and to rely instead on indirect measures, typically measures derived from input data. From among these, we have chosen one.

By reducing the heterogeneous array of construction products to the homogeneous materials of which they are composed, we have in effect

---

[39] See Powell–59, pp. 5 ff. The consistency check referred to employs the series for construction in current prices exclusive of collective-farm and road-building investments in kind which is commented on in fn. 37, p. 43. Inasmuch as labor employed in such construction is thought to be omitted from the series for labor inputs and for wage rates, the force of the check is not greatly weakened by this exclusion; i.e., similar omissions occur for both inputs and outputs. On the other hand, the exclusion of labor involved in construction in kind may significantly affect the behavior of labor productivity in construction implied by the labor and materials indexes (cf. Powell–59, p. 89); in particular, it may cause a substantial overstatement in the rise of labor productivity between 1928 and 1937. Thus, Weitzman–61, p. 57, estimates that in 1937 collective farmers doing construction work and paid out of labor days numbered 823 thousand, which compares with figures for hired labor, presumably exclusive of such collective-farm employment, of 2,348 thousand "in construction" and 1,576 thousand in "construction-installation work." Since the hired labor totals are thought to be less than comprehensive, the relative importance of collective-farm labor is probably not so great as the figures suggest. However, an understatement of the rise in total numbers employed, over the time interval in which collective farms (and road-building by the population) became important, seems highly likely.

assumed away the problem of quality change. If, however, a measure of construction is conceived of in which the weight-year values of assets are somehow obtained directly and accurately, it is still possible to consider whether materials required per unit value of assets so measured, i.e., the productivity of materials, is likely to be constant over time, as the procedure requires. It can then readily be seen that materials productivity is liable to change from various sources, including substitution among inputs, changes in technology, and changes in the composition of output where materials required per unit value vary as among kinds of assets. On the whole, common observation suggests that substitutions of either labor or capital for materials in construction is likely to be limited, since the functions performed are totally different. Technological change of a relevant kind, i.e., design changes altering the services which assembled materials yield, appear also to be of limited significance. The effects of changes in the composition of output are those most likely to seriously distort the measure, although there is little apparent reason for expecting large and systematic biases from this source.

The statistically feasible alternatives to a materials input index are vulnerable without exception to variability in the productivity of labor in construction, productivity again being thought of in terms of an ideal measure of output. This is necessarily true of an index of labor inputs alone or of labor plus materials. It is true also of a measure obtained by deflating current values with an index of materials prices and wage rates— an input-price deflated index—which is the most commonly used indirect measure but which can be shown to correspond very nearly to an index of labor and materials inputs combined.[40] That the productivity of labor is likely to be much more variable than that of materials is suggested by the obvious possibilities of substituting equipment for labor, changes in the quality of labor employed, and changes in organizational and administrative efficiency. That the productivity of labor in Soviet construction was highly variable is virtually certain.[41]

The case for the relative superiority of a materials index is obviously better than for its absolute accuracy, and there is no way of establishing the actual degree of its accuracy.[42] It is our impression, however, that the materials input index, while hardly precise, is a serviceable approximation to a measure of construction output in which quality change has been properly allowed for. It probably traces more accurately the broad contours of change than year-to-year variations, but the former are more consequential for the capital stock estimates.

The procedures by which the materials index is derived make it most reasonable to interpret it as inclusive of capital repairs to structures. In order to separate repairs from the total, we assume that the share of repairs

---

40 See Powell–57, Part I, pp. 35–37.

41 A series for labor inputs, which can be compared with the materials input series used here, is given in Powell–59, p. 9. The labor series is faulty for a number of reasons, including its probable omission of labor employed in collective-farm and road-building construction in kind.

42 Some quite thin evidence that materials inputs may be a fairly reliable measure of U.S. construction is cited in Powell–57, Part I, pp. 37 ff.

in the total in 1937 prices equaled in each year the share of repairs in money investment in socialized construction and installation in current prices.[43] Errors may result from the restricted coverage of the latter data (repairs in private construction and construction in kind are not known). They may result also from the implicit assumptions that prices moved similarly in repairs and in new construction and that materials requirements in both were the same. Gross inaccuracies in the estimates exclusive of repairs are unlikely to result from these sources, but the precision of the estimates is doubtless still further impaired.

While we are reasonably confident of our grounds for preferring the materials input index, as a measure of *Soviet* construction, to one derived by deflation with input prices (wage rates and materials prices), we have, nevertheless, composed a deflated series for construction in 1937 prices and corresponding estimates of the (net) fixed capital stock. These alternative calculations are not intended to provide a test of the reliability of our basic estimates but to indicate how much our results would have differed had we used the more conventional estimating procedure. This is a question presumably of interest to those concerned with statistical methods for the estimation of construction. It is relevant also to international comparisons involving countries for which construction is estimated by deflation.

The Soviet series derived by deflation are compared for selected years with those based on materials inputs in Table 2–4.[44] The comparison is probably somewhat distorted by purely statistical errors in the deflated series for annual construction, which is obtained by cruder procedures than is the materials input series, but the general implications of the comparison are thought to be reliable. The stock estimates are derived from the deflated values of annual construction by the same procedures (some of which have yet to be described) as from materials inputs: the 1928 stock is valued in 1937 prices by means of the ratio of 1937 to 1928 input prices calculated for annual construction; annual construction is cumulated and depreciated (on a straight line); adjustments are made for territorial acquisitions and war losses. The equipment component in the total stock is unchanged from our previous calculations. Because of its small weight in the total, the installation component is also used without change.

As is evident from the table, the deflated series for annual construction in some periods differs greatly from the materials input series. In particular, the deflated series is relatively high in the early 1930's and again immediately after the war. Over the whole period, it rises at a substantially lower rate than does the materials inputs series. The likely explanation of these differences is that labor productivity in construction fell to a distinct low in the early 1930's and again in the postwar years but increased con-

---

[43] The share varies from a low of 4.5 percent to a high of 19.8 percent; see Table A–8.

[44] Annual figures for the deflated construction series are shown in Table A–13; the sources of the series are explained in detail in Appendix A. Annual figures for the corresponding stock estimates, gross and net, are shown in Table T–7 for the use of such readers as may prefer these to the materials input series. In Table 2–4, 1956 is used in preference to 1955, because deflated construction for the latter appears unrepresentative of contiguous years. Stock values as of years' end are cited so as to include the annual increment of the same year.

TABLE 2-4

ANNUAL CONSTRUCTION, ESTIMATED FROM MATERIALS INPUTS AND FROM INPUT-PRICE DEFLATION, AND CORRESPONDING NET FIXED CAPITAL VALUES, IN 1937 PRICES, SELECTED YEARS

	1928	1932	1937	1940	1945	1950	1956	1961
A. Billion Rubles								
Gross Annual Construction								
1. From Materials Inputs	7.2	13.6	20.3	19.8	8.3	28.8	52.0	80.1
2. From Input-Price Deflation	8.1	19.9	20.3	19.7	12.0	25.1	46.3	71.4
Net Value of Structures (end of year)								
3. From Materials Inputs	98.4	135.1	202.2	268.9	214.7	280.8	476.7	747.1
4. From Input-Price Deflation	110.9	159.5	233.0	299.3	243.3	300.5	462.7	696.5
Net Value of Fixed Capital (end of year)								
5. From Materials Inputs	113.7	166.4	263.6	359.5	290.6	415.0	746.5	1249.0
6. From Input-Price Deflation	126.2	190.9	294.4	389.9	319.2	434.7	732.5	1198.4
B. Series from Materials Inputs = 100								
Gross Annual Construction								
1. From Materials Inputs	100	100	100	100	100	100	100	100
2. From Input-Price Deflation	113	146	100	99.5	145	87.2	89.0	89.1
Net Value of Structures (end of year)								
3. From Materials Inputs	100	100	100	100	100	100	100	100
4. From Input-Price Deflation	113	118	115	111	113	107	97.1	93.2
Net Value of Fixed Capital (end of year)								
5. From Materials Inputs	100	100	100	100	100	100	100	100
6. From Input-Price Deflation	111	115	112	108	110	105	98.1	95.9
C. 1937 = 100								
Gross Annual Construction								
1. From Materials Inputs	35.5	67.0	100	97.5	40.9	142	256	395
2. From Input-Price Deflation	39.9	98.0	100	97.0	59.1	124	228	352
Net Value of Structures (end of year)								
3. From Materials Inputs	48.7	66.8	100	133	106	139	236	369
4. From Input-Price Deflation	47.6	68.5	100	128	104	129	199	299
Net Value of Fixed Capital (end of year)								
5. From Materials Inputs	43.1	63.1	100	136	110	157	283	474
6. From Input-Price Deflation	42.9	64.8	100	132	108	148	249	407

Sources: For row 1, Table A-2; row 2, Table A-13; rows 3 and 5, Table T-1. For rows 4 and 6, see text.

siderably over the long term. Surprisingly, perhaps, the large differences in annual construction produce relatively modest, though not insignificant, differences in the capital stock estimates. This is the consequence in part of differences in the valuation of the initial stock, in part of the fact that the discrepancies between the annual construction series fluctuate in size and sign. For our primary purpose of estimating the fixed capital stock, therefore, the choice between materials inputs and input price deflation turns out to be of rather limited importance.

Installation

The data at our disposal include estimates of annual investment in installation in current prices, but suitable deflators are lacking. In years in which prices and costs are believed to have roughly corresponded, installation has accounted for a small part of total investment in current prices, usually around 4 percent. Its composition is complex, and the construction of an appropriate deflator would be a substantial undertaking. In view of these factors, we have not attempted deflation but have instead assumed that, in constant prices, investment in installation changed at a rate intermediate to those displayed by investment in construction and equipment.

Throughout the period studied, the latter type of investment has grown more rapidly than the former. Installation must have increased more rapidly than construction because, first, it is required primarily in industrial projects, which have increased more rapidly than construction generally, and, secondly, because changes in productive processes must often require new installation in existing buildings. On the other hand, there must also be many times when it is possible to replace machines without replacing the installation in which they are embedded. Investment in installation, accordingly, probably grows less rapidly than investment in equipment. We estimate an index of the volume of investment in installation as the simple arithmetic average of the corresponding indexes for investment in construction and in equipment. Absolute values for investment in installation are obtained by applying the resulting index to the value in 1937 in 1937 prices.

This method of estimation can hardly yield accurate results. As will appear, we must also resort to very rough expedients in estimating the average service life and depreciation rate applicable to installation and its relative importance in the initial stock. The resulting annual stock estimates for installation are intended only to round out the totals for all fixed capital and should not be interpreted as more than the crudest indication of what happened to installation alone. In our estimates of the gross and net values of fixed capital in 1937 prices, as computed, the stock of installation grows considerably faster than that of structures but a bit more slowly than the stock of equipment. It increases from about 2 percent of the total in 1928 to about 4 percent by 1962. Clearly, the totals are not very sensitive to errors in this component. If the stock of installation in 1937 as estimated is held constant but it is assumed that the change over time was the same as for structures, the variation in the total stock, net or gross, is about 1 percent in 1928, 2 percent in 1962. If the stock of installation is assumed instead to move with that of equipment, the change in the totals is even smaller.

4. THE INITIAL STOCK

Our estimates of the fixed capital stock on January 1, 1928—the initial stock—are derived from official data for the capital stock. Soviet statistics of this sort do not otherwise enter our calculations for fixed capital (they do enter the inventory calculations), and their use for the initial stock introduces a particularly critical and troublesome element into the estimates. For this reason, we examine here in considerable detail the nature and reliability of the statistics used. A full description of our handling of them, however, is given in Appendix B.

Our estimates in 1937 prices of the stock of fixed capital in place on January 1, 1928, are shown in Table 2–5. The data are distributed by economic sector and, within sectors, among structures, equipment, and installation. Four sectors—education, health, administration, and housing—contain structures only, and for these no intrasectoral breakdown is shown. The "gross" values in the table are undepreciated values in 1937 prices. The "net" values differ from the gross, in principle at least, by the amount of straight-line depreciation. The values are intended to include all capital in place, both assets in operation and those still in the process of construction.

The Soviet data underlying Table 2–5 are from a document of Gosplan, the State Planning Commission,[45] which contains estimates of the capital stock on October 1, 1927, and October 1, 1928, in prices of 1926/27. Our estimates are obtained from these data by interpolation, to arrive at January 1 values, and by deflation, to obtain values in 1937 prices. The materials in the source are of diverse origins, as is explained later in this section. In anticipation, it may be noted here, however, that a partial survey of the relevant literature suggests, on the one hand, that the Soviet data are almost surely subject to significant errors, and, on the other, that further research on the problem is unlikely to provide a firm basis on which to adjust for these errors. The Soviet estimates in 1926/27 prices, which we take as equivalent to 1928 prices, appear to err in the direction of overstatement. The deflators with which we move from 1928 to 1937 prices most likely contain errors of opposite direction, though probably of smaller magnitude. The net error may still be substantial.

The consequences of error in the initial stock are explored but not necessarily delimited by means of alternative estimates, shown in Table 2–6, in which the quantitative variations in the outcome of our net value estimate are computed on the hypotheses of errors of plus or minus 20 percent in our estimates for the initial stock. The latter figure is based on various considerations presented below. These lead us to believe, at least provisionally, that 20 percent is probably large enough to encompass the actual error and, also, that there is a greater likelihood of overstatement than of understatement in our initial stock estimates. Both views, however, are based on a search of the literature which is less than exhaustive and might be subject to revision as a result of further research.

Table 2–6 largely speaks for itself. As might be expected from the rate

---

45 Gosplan–30, pp. 446–47, 462–65.

TABLE 2-5

TOTAL FIXED CAPITAL ON JANUARY 1, 1928, DETAILED DATA

	Value in 1937 Prices (Million Rubles)		Ratio of Net to Gross Value	Service Life When New (Years)	Remaining Service Life (Years)
	Gross	Net			
	(1)	(2)	(3)	(4)	(5)
1. Industry					
1a. Structures.........	9,857	6,800 ⎫		55	38
1b. Equipment.........	5,254	3,625 ⎬ 69		25	17
1c. Installation	2,424	1,673 ⎭		40	28
2. Electric Power					
2a. Structures.........	1,192	822 ⎫		55	38
2b. Equipment.........	342	237 ⎬ 69		25	17
2c. Installation	226	156 ⎭		40	28
3. Agriculture					
3a. Machines and Tools ..	3,246	1,947	60	8	5
3b. Tractors..........	36	25	70	12	8
3c. Productive Structures.	16,434	10,517	64	40	26
3d. Irrigation Works	1,446	1,012	70	40	28
4. Railroads					
4a. Structures.........	18,573	13,558	73	50	37
4b. Rolling Stock.......	6,591	4,812	73	45	33
5. Water Transport					
5a. Waterways	335	235	70	50	35
5b. Ports............	587	411	70	50	35
5c. River Craft........	521	365	70	45	32
5d. Sea Craft	216	152	70	45	32
6. Motor Transport					
6a. Roads............	1,841	1,288	70	40	28
6b. Vehicles..........	2	2	70	8	6
7. Communications					
7a. Structures.........	487	339 ⎫		40	28
7b. Equipment.........	86	60 ⎬ 70		25	17
7c. Installation	74	53 ⎭		40	28
8. Trade					
8a. Structures.........	1,325	928 ⎫ 70		65	46
8b. Equipment.........	232	162 ⎭		25	17
9. Municipal Facilities					
9a. Structures.........	5,078	3,554 ⎫ 70		50	35
9b. Equipment.........	888	622 ⎭		25	17
10. Education............	5,411	3,734	69	80	55
11. Health..............	2,869	1,951	68	80	54
12. Administration	1,497	1,137	76	80	61
13. Housing					
13a. Socialized Urban.	20,839	14,796	71	90	64
13b. Private Urban	14,706	10,295	70	70	49
13c. Rural	34,816	22,282	64	50	32
14. Total..............	157,431	107,550			
14a. Structures........	137,293	93,659			
14b. Equipment........	17,414	12,009			
14c. Installation	2,724	1,882			

Source: Table B-1, columns 4, 14–19, 26–31.

at which the fixed capital stock has grown, the impact of errors in our initial estimates falls mainly on the early years, 1928 to 1932. The average growth rates implied by our estimates are appreciably affected for intervals commencing with either of those years, except perhaps for relatively long intervals such as 1928–62 or 1932–62. The difference in growth rates is much narrower, less than a point, for intervals commencing with 1937. Even for the earliest period, the ambiguities in the initial stock figures are not so great as to blur the finding of a high growth rate. Apparently, however, the calculations are not fine enough to indicate whether acceleration occurred between 1928–32 and 1932–37 or whether the prewar growth rates differed significantly from those of 1950–62.

The remainder of this section is a discussion of the following aspects of the initial stock estimate: concepts of valuation underlying the Soviet net value estimates; sources of the Soviet estimates for four major cate-

TABLE 2-6

EFFECTS ON TOTAL NET FIXED CAPITAL OF ERRORS IN THE INITIAL
STOCK, IN 1937 PRICES, SELECTED YEARS
(January 1)

	True Initial Value 20% below Estimated	No Error (Billion Rubles)	True Initial Value 20% above Estimated	Columns 1 and 3 Differ from Column 2 by: (As Percent of Column 2)
	(1)	(2)	(3)	(4)
1928	85.9	107.6	129.1	±20.0
1932	132.2	151.0	169.8	±12.5
1937	224.8	240.5	256.2	± 6.5
1941	344.9	359.6	374.3	± 4.1
1945	272.2	281.3	290.4	± 3.2
1950	369.8	376.6	383.4	± 1.8
1955	599.2	603.9	608.6	± 0.8
1962	1,246.6	1,249.0	1,251.4	± 0.2

	Average Annual Growth Rate in Percent			In Percentage Points
1928-32	11.4	8.8	7.1	2.6 - 1.7
1928-37	11.3	9.3	7.9	1.9 - 1.5
1928-41	11.3	9.7	8.5	1.6 - 1.2
1928-62	8.2	7.5	6.9	0.7 - 0.6
1932-37	11.2	9.8	8.6	1.4 - 1.2
1932-41	11.2	10.2	9.2	1.0 - 1.0
1932-62	7.8	7.3	6.9	0.5 - 0.4
1937-41	11.3	10.6	9.9	0.7 - 0.7
1937-62	7.1	6.8	6.5	0.3 - 0.3
1950-62	10.7	10.5	10.4	0.2 - 0.1

Sources: See text.

gories of assets—industrial, housing, agricultural, and rail transport; and our deflation of the Soviet figures.

Valuation Concepts

In Soviet accounting, including the accounts from which the initial stock data in Table 2–5 are derived, major repairs are treated at least in principle as capital outlays, and depreciation charges are intended to recoup the decline in value suffered by the asset by the end of its service life and, also, to provide for major repairs needed during its term of service. Thus, the Soviet concept of net value corresponds to that referred to in the last part of Section 2 of this chapter rather than to the straight-line depreciated valuations used in our basic estimates. The ratios of net to gross values in the Soviet data (reproduced in column 3 of Table 2–5) show the assets to be youthful, relative to their total service lives. Since capital repairs occur in greater volume in the later years of the service life, net values reckoned according to the Soviet concept for assets of such age should tend to be less than those reckoned by straight-line depreciation.

In spite of this apparent difference in concept, we use the Soviet net valuations as estimators of the net value reckoned by straight-line depreciation. Under straight-line depreciation, the ratio of net to gross value is also the ratio of remaining to total service life. The remaining service lives in column 5 of Table 2–5 are computed on this basis. As may be seen, the average age of the assets in the initial stock thereby implied is quite low, given that the creation of new assets during the 8 years 1918–25 must have been modest. If the net values are interpreted according to the Soviet concept, however, the implied ages would be younger still, which seems implausible.

As will be explained below, most of the Soviet values for the initial stock in the different economic sectors were obtained as estimates of the value of capital in place in various years prior to 1928, with new investment added and depreciation subtracted to arrive at 1928 values. The high net values could have their origin in the estimates of capital in place, if the appraisers, as seems not unlikely, obtained their net values from estimated gross values and the ratio of estimated remaining life to total service life. This method, however, would yield straight-line depreciated values. In addition, the actual depreciation charges used in deriving the Soviet net investment series seem low, relative to the straight-line rates estimated by us.[46]

The foregoing does not offer much reassurance as to the reliability of the Soviet net values. It does seem to be implied, however, that the values are high, relative to the correct valuation by the Soviet concept. For this reason we take them instead as estimates of straight-line depreciated values.

The treatment of investment projects in progress in arriving at capital stock values is not made explicit by the source, but circumstantial evidence leads us to treat the values as inclusive of this item. With certain limitations to be explained in the next section, Soviet investment series include expenditures made on projects not yet put into operation. Since our source apparently estimates 1928 capital values largely by adding net annual investment to estimates of capital in place earlier, the portion of annual investment represented by outlays on projects not completed by 1928 would automatically be included. This leaves open the question of whether unfinished projects were included in the capital values from which our source began its calculation. The latter values, however, are drawn mainly from the mid-1920's. Gross investment at that time was limited in quantity and carried on to a considerable degree in the private sector of agriculture, where construction projects of long duration, and hence accumulations of unfinished construction, are unlikely to occur.[47] Thus, even if

---

[46] Compare the Soviet rates in Table B–1, column 3, with the corresponding straight-line rates in columns 32–34 of that table. Our estimates of service lives and straight-line rates are discussed in Section 5 of this chapter.

[47] For example, in 1924/25, total fixed capital investment reportedly amounted to 2.8 billion 1925/26 rubles, of which over half was in private agriculture. This may be compared with a total net value of the capital stock on October 1, 1927, of 53.1 billion 1925/26 rubles. The figures cited, from which we exclude livestock, are from Gosplan–28, pp. 518–21. The source is an antecedent of Gosplan–30, on which our 1928 estimates are based, and its data are not fully comparable with (or consistent with) those from the later source. We cite it here because its coverage extends to earlier years than that of Gosplan–30.

our source has been inconsistent in the treatment of this item, the amount of unfinished construction omitted on this score should be relatively small. On this basis, we interpret the initial stock data as inclusive of work still in progress. The inference seems the most plausible one to draw, but, as with other aspects of the initial stock values, it is not firm.[48]

Sources of the Soviet Estimates

About 85 percent of the initial stock of fixed capital (net value in 1928 prices) is accounted for by four sectors: industry, 14 percent; urban housing, 22 percent; agriculture, including rural housing, 31 percent; and railroading, 18 percent. In the following discussion, we consider the reliability of the Soviet estimates for these sectors.

(*i*) Industry. Our source distinguishes four kinds of industrial capital: private, co-operative, state industry planned by the Supreme Council for the National Economy (VSNKh), and "other" state industry. Of these, the third accounted for over 80 percent of all industrial capital in 1928, and, accordingly, the reliability of the Soviet figures for industry generally depends largely on the data for this group. The latter data, in turn, were based on an "inventory" of VSNKh industrial capital, which established both gross and net values in current prices, as of October 1, 1925. Our source used the net values, to which subsequent gross investment minus depreciation was added, the resulting totals being adjusted for changes in price.[49]

The inventory of 1925 was apparently a detailed and elaborate attempt to catalogue the industrial assets of the time, but, in spite of what must have been a large expenditure of effort, a comparison of the results with other available information indicates that they lacked reliability, tending to err in the direction of overstatement, probably by a substantial margin.[50] The evidence on the matter is various and includes the following. (*a*) Valuations in the inventory were based on the current costs of replacing the assets covered rather than on their productive capacities under current circumstances (cost valuations probably underlie the official data in general). For purposes of its own, the Commissariat of Finance (NKF) attempted a verification of the VSNKh inventory. Using construction cost estimates compiled for capacity per unit of output, estimates were made of the cost of constructing new industrial enterprises matching in capacity those under VSNKh. The results for gross values were compared with those of the inventory, revealing the latter on average to be about 40 percent

---

[48] For at least one economic sector, industry, there is also some independent confirmation. The January 1, 1928, values of fixed capital in census industry (including electric power), both inclusive and exclusive of unfinished construction, is given in Putilov–32, p. 105. Figures of approximately similar scope for October 1, 1927, are given in our source. While not coinciding precisely with Putilov's data, they seem mutually consistent (only) with his inclusive figure.

[49] A comparison of Gosplan–30, pp. 446–53, and Gosplan–28, pp. 518–19 and 525, indicates that the figures we have used are derived from October 1, 1925, figures from "*Svodnyi balans gosudarstvennoi promyshlennosti*," evidently a published source. For VSNKh industry, the latter uses the inventory described in the text. See Strumilin–58, pp. 582 ff.

[50] The discussion in this paragraph is based on the account given by Strumilin–58, pp. 582–93.

greater than the former. How reliable the NKF estimates are, however, is unknown. There was apparently a policy conflict between VSNKh and NKF at this time, the former favoring a larger flow of depreciation funds than the latter. Their respective estimates of the base against which these charges were to be reckoned may well have been affected accordingly. (*b*) For one branch of industry, textiles, the inventory figures seem to imply an implausibly large increase in the real net value of reproducible assets between 1913 and 1925, given the small amount of new investment occurring during the interval. (*c*) In the case of the textile industry, the inventory implies an increase in the relationship of net to gross value of assets between 1913 and 1925, whereas almost all the assets in the branch had aged by 12 years. For industry generally, the inventory indicates only a modest decline in the relationship of net to gross value, whereas, again, a substantial increase in the average age of the assets must have occurred.

The foregoing suggests, we believe, that the inventory's net value figures for October 1, 1925, were probably substantially overstated. The figures in Table 2–5 for 1928 also include assets created between October 1, 1925, and January 1, 1928, which account for about a third of the 1928 total. The post-1925 current investment data are not believed subject to the defects affecting the inventory. Even if this is the case, however, and even if the NKF estimates somewhat overstate the error in the 1925 inventory, the figures we have used for industrial capital as of January 1, 1928, may contain a sizable error of overstatement, perhaps on the order of 20 percent.

(*ii*) Urban housing. Our source does not indicate the origin of its figures for urban housing. It seems likely, though by no means certain, that they were based at least in part on the 1926 population census, which included questions designed to yield an inventory of urban housing in physical terms.[51] In any case, the census returns provide a point of reference for appraising the figures on urban housing we have used.

The stock of urban housing at the end of 1926 in physical terms as determined by the census is shown in Table 2–7, columns 2 and 3. Working from these data, two early Soviet writers made estimates of the net value of the stock.[52] Their method consisted of valuing the physical stock revealed by the census at average 1913 construction costs, taking account to the extent possible of differences in building materials and of the differences in average quality corresponding to different classes of ownership. The 1913 values were then converted to 1926/27 net values by price indexes of building costs, allowances being made for depreciation. The reason given for this somewhat indirect approach was that the average quality of the existing stock in 1926 was above the average quality of current construction. Hence, direct valuation at average 1926/27 construction costs would understate the true value of the existing stock. Average costs of 1913 were considered more representative. The method just described yields the value of dwellings proper. This figure was increased by the

---

[51] The census included a form to be completed for each urban dwelling, requiring information on: number of floors, materials of which the walls were constructed, ownership, number of rooms, utilities available, rent, and living space (*zhilaia ploshchad'*) in square meters. The age of the dwelling was not asked. See TsSU–27, pp. 3–11.

[52] See Gibshman–29, pp. 108 ff.

TABLE 2-7

THE URBAN HOUSING STOCK ON DECEMBER 17, 1926, DETAILED DATA

Ownership	Building Materials Used in Walls	Existing Stock (Million Square Meters of Living Space)	1926 Construction Costs (Rubles per Square Meter of Living Space)	Gross Value of Existing Stock in 1926 Prices (Billion Rubles)
(1)	(2)	(3)	(4)	(5)
State	Masonry	49.71	166.4	8.27
	Mixed	3.78	154.8	0.59
	Wood	15.93	143.3	2.28
	Other	1.71	137.0	0.23
	Total	71.12	--	11.37
Co-operative	Masonry	0.62	169.0	0.10
	Mixed	0.07	136.9	0.01
	Wood	0.42	104.9	0.04
	Other	0.06	120.2	0.01
	Total	1.17	--	0.16
Socialized (State and Co-operative)	Total	72.29	--	11.53
Private	Masonry	12.00	62.8	0.75
	Mixed	4.57	60.5	0.28
	Wood	49.97	58.2	2.91
	Other	15.11	46.1	0.70
	Total	81.65	--	4.64
All Owners	Total	153.94	--	16.17

Sources: For column 3, Gibshman–28, pp. 77, 79, Tables 2, 7. The figures for masonry are those given in the source as for *kamennyi*. For column 4, TsSU–29a, pp. 832–33. The data are from a nation-wide sample survey of construction costs, for 5,324 structures. The unit costs shown are computed from total cost and floor space. Those for masonry are for brick and stone; those for other materials are for clay and "other" materials as given in the source. Costs for mixed wall materials are simple averages of those for masonry and wood.

authors by 15 percent, to allow for auxiliary structures, such as fences and out-buildings, which are part of the housing stock but are not reflected in the average construction costs. They found the net value of socialized urban housing, state and co-operative, to be 9.6 billion 1926/27 rubles, the figure for private urban housing being 3.6 billion, yielding an urban total of 13.2 billion. The corresponding figures given in our source, as reproduced in Table B–1, column 6, are 7.23 billion 1926/27 rubles for socialized housing, 5.03 billion for private, with an urban total of 12.2 billion. In the latter set of figures, the value of socialized housing falls significantly short of that in the former set, the reverse relation holds for private housing, and the totals differ by somewhat less than 10 percent.

For purposes of comparison, we have made another, similar, computation in Table 2–7. Actual average 1926 construction costs for different kinds of dwellings are shown in column 4 of the table. Multiplying these unit costs by the existing stock, shown in column 3, we obtain a rough estimate of the *gross* value of the urban housing stock in 1926 prices, in column 5. The total is 16.17 billion rubles, about 7 percent *below* the value at the end of 1927 indicated by our source (Table B–1, column 5). According to the reasoning of the Soviet writers cited just above, however, the estimate in Table 2–7 is understated by the amount of auxiliary structures, etc., and also because the use of 1926 average unit costs fails to allow for the inferior quality of 1926 construction relative to the average of structures in the existing stock. Even a modest allowance for these two factors would bring our estimate, too, above the figure obtained from our source.

Finally, it is noted that the estimate in Table 2–7 for socialized housing, 11.53 billion rubles, is fairly close to the figure indicated by our source, 10.19 billion rubles, whereas the corresponding figures for private housing, 4.64 and 7.19 billion rubles respectively, differ substantially. If allowance is made for understatement in the estimates in Table 2–7, the result is to increase the difference for socialized housing while diminishing that for private. The Soviet calculations referred to earlier yield a similar result; relative to the figures in our source, they give a higher value for socialized housing and a lower value for private.

It is difficult to know what inference should be drawn from these findings. Both of the calculations imply some understatement in the totals in our source and an error in the distribution of the total between the socialized and private sectors. On the other hand, the data we have cited were without question familiar to the compilers of our source at the time their estimates were made. Given the coarseness of our calculations and the access of Gosplan to information we cannot review, the present discussion does not seem to provide a sufficient basis for revising the figures in the source. Perhaps, however, they can be taken as indicative of the margins of uncertainty surrounding those figures.

(*iii*) Agriculture. Our source states that its figures for agricultural capital, including rural housing, are derived from the peasant budget studies of 1925/26, 1926/27, and 1927/28. In these surveys, conducted by the Central Statistical Administration, questionnaires were completed by interviewers for several thousand peasant households.[53] The responses referred to various aspects of the household's economic activities and status, including its production, purchases, sales, and consumption of goods, and its ownership of land and reproducible assets. The individual responses, aggregated by means of demographic data, constituted the chief contemporary source of information about the decentralized peasant economy.

Because of their importance for economic and domestic political planning, the budget studies were a serious, continuing, and well-financed effort to obtain meaningful data. Unfortunately, the success attained remains in doubt. Three aspects are particularly troublesome. (*a*) Although the number of households surveyed was large, the method of selecting respondents, and therefore the representativeness of their responses, are unknown. Given the difficulties which plague this kind of survey, it would not be surprising to find the respondents above average in literacy and articulateness. In fact, the director of the survey considered the "level" of respondent to be atypically high.[54] An effort to adjust for this bias was made in aggregating the returns, but it was not believed entirely success-

---

[53] For example, the 1925/26 survey covered about 11,000 households. Not all households responded to all questions, however. See TsSU–29, pp. 22 ff., on which the discussion in the text is also based.

[54] *Ibid.*, p. 6.

ful.[55] (*b*) Despite the preceding consideration, respondents apparently tended to understate their incomes and holdings. The source from which we take the agricultural capital data specifies that the survey returns used were adjusted for understatement but does not explain the basis for, or extent of, the adjustment. (*c*) We have little information about the method used in the survey to value capital assets. Appropriate prices for items normally acquired through the market, such as machines and tools, were no doubt available, but we do not know the choices actually made. More troublesome is the treatment, also unknown, of assets created by the household itself. The latter might include a substantial share of agricultural structures and rural housing. It is easy to ascertain that the budget studies place a much lower valuation on rural than on urban private housing.[56] The difference is in the right direction, but the magnitude remains open to question.

The problems raised by the peasant budget data are such that no method of quantitative appraisal, however crude, suggests itself. They well may err, but the probable size and direction of the error are unknown.

(*iv*) Railroads. Our data on capital in railroading were derived by our source in three steps. (*a*) The net value in "prewar" prices of the stock of railroad capital as of October 1, 1923, the result of an official inventory, was taken as a starting point. These figures were revalued into prices of 1925/26 by the uniform application to all types of assets of a price index of 1.7 (prewar prices = 1.0).[57] (*b*) Annual depreciation was deducted from, and annual investment in 1925/26 prices was added to, the 1923 stock figures, to obtain the net value of the stock in subsequent years. (*c*) The values in 1925/26 prices were deflated into prices of 1926/27.

The problems raised by the last two steps are relatively small. The data at the disposal of the compilers of our source should have been more or less adequate to the task, and, in any case, substantial relative errors in either of these steps would have a limited impact on our 1928 figures: assets created between the end of 1924 and the beginning of 1928 accounted for less than 15 percent of the 1928 stock, and the change in the price of railroad capital goods between 1925/26 and 1926/27 amounted to only about 6–7 percent.[58]

More troublesome is the reliability of the 1923 inventory and the method of translating it into 1925/26 prices. The inventory was apparently carried out by estimating gross values at prewar prices, then allowing for differences between present and gross values on the basis of age, required repairs, etc.[59] The Soviet economist Strumilin attempted an independent estimate of the gross and net values at prewar prices of postrevolutionary railroads, working from estimates of the value of the prerevolutionary stock, adjusted for territorial changes, to which he added subsequent in-

---

[55] *Loc. cit.*

[56] See the discussion of housing costs in Section 6 of Chapter 3, especially in fn. 22, p. 89, and fn. 25, p. 91. The implied value of rural housing is about a quarter of that for socialized urban housing, about 40 percent of that for private urban.

[57] On this and the succeeding steps, see Gosplan–28, pp. 520–21, 526; NKPS–27, pp. 63–64; Gosplan–29, pp. 426–27, 433; Gosplan–30, pp. 451–52, 464.

[58] See the sources cited in the preceding footnote.

[59] Strumilin–58, p. 650.

vestment and subtracted subsequent depreciation.[60] He obtained estimates of both net and gross values in 1923 which differed from the results of the inventory by −9 percent and +5 percent respectively. He considered his own estimates as crude and probably erring on the side of understatement. Nonetheless, he believed, apparently on the basis of other information, that the inventory figures were somewhat overstated.[61]

The use of a single deflator to revalue all railroad assets from prewar to 1925/26 prices also raises problems. We are unable to appraise the reliability of the deflator as applied to all assets taken together. Furthermore, even if the over-all deflator was appropriate, it seems unlikely that the change in price would have been the same for structures as for rolling stock. Errors arising on the second count would be partially offsetting, but only partially, because our calculations apply different depreciation rates and, in revaluing from 1928 to 1937 prices, different deflators to the two components.

Table 2–8 presents a rough estimate, obtained from physical quantities and prices, of the gross value of the principal items of Soviet railroad rolling stock in 1927/28. The total value would probably be increased about 5 percent if account were taken of omitted items, such as locomotive tenders, switching engines, and narrow gauge cars and locomotives. In our capital stock calculations, the gross value of Soviet rolling stock on January 1, 1928, is put at 4.7 billion 1928 rubles (Table B–1, column 5), about 10 percent greater than the value suggested by the above calculation.

Deflation of Initial Stock Values

The data in our source are expressed in prices of 1926/27. These values are treated in our calculations, without great error, we believe, as identical with values in 1928 prices.[62] For our estimates, however, the 1928 values are deflated into prices of 1937. Any error in deflation, therefore, would be cumulative with errors in the 1928 Soviet estimates considered just above.

In the case of agricultural machines and tools and railroad rolling stock, which account collectively for about half of the initial stock of equipment, the nature of the physical assets underlying the value estimates is fairly clear, and a reasonable basis appears to exist for appraising the suitability of the deflators employed. Both of these categories of equipment were produced in substantial quantities in the Soviet Union of 1928, and the price data used in computing the deflators are believed to be relatively reliable and representative (for railroad rolling stock, the calculation presented in Table 2–8 may also be interpreted as a test of this proposition).

The equipment component of industrial capital, which accounts for most of the other equipment in the initial stock, on the other hand, is considerably more heterogeneous. The deflator employed is an aggregation of individual price indexes for 14 categories of machinery used in industry. It refers to changes in the level of domestic prices for Soviet produced

---

60 *Ibid.*, pp. 646–52.

61 *Ibid.*, p. 650.

62 Gosplan-30, pp. 452, 460, shows total capital investment in 1926/27 and 1927/28 prices for the fiscal year 1927/28. The implicit deflator for 1927/28 (1926/27 = 100) is 99.

TABLE 2-8

RAILROAD ROLLING STOCK (WIDE GAUGE) IN 1927/28

	Stock (Annual Average, Thousands)	Price (Rubles)	Gross Value of Stock in 1927/28 Prices (Billion Rubles)
Locomotives	17.6	95,000	1.67
Freight Cars (2-axle units)	467.8	3,700	1.73
Passenger Cars (2-axle units) . . .	25.8	23,000	0.59
Total			3.99

Sources: For column 1, TsSU–29a, p. 616; although the source does not so specify, the figures appear from context to be annual averages. For column 2, prices for locomotives and freight cars are from Moorsteen–62, Table A–1; that for passenger cars is computed from a 1937 price and a 1937-based price relative for 1927/28 given in *ibid.*, Tables C–1 and E–3. All three prices are domestic wholesale prices for Soviet produced equipment, f.o.b. the factory.

machinery. The chief problems in applying this deflator are, first, that some portion of the industrial equipment stock, probably about 10 percent but possibly more, consisted of imported equipment valued at import prices.[63] Since the latter were substantially lower than domestic prices for analogous machines,[64] the use of a domestic price index in the deflation produces a corresponding understatement in the values at 1937 and 1950 prices. The error, it may be noted, is opposite in direction to that produced by defects in the VSNKh inventory discussed above. Secondly, the behavior of the 14 component price indexes is quite diverse. For the deflation, they have been aggregated by means of Soviet 1927/28 output weights, the more appropriate 1928 capital stock weights being unavailable. In calculations presented elsewhere,[65] the variation in this deflator produced by using, alternatively, Soviet output weights of 1927/28, 1937, and 1955 is seen to be small. The possibility remains, however, that a larger difference would result if 1928 stock weights were used, in which case the deflation computed here would be in error. In any case, large variations in the behavior of components of the deflator reduce its presumptive reliability. The data from which it is computed are necessarily less than comprehensive, and the price behavior of the omitted items is no doubt also quite diverse.

For structures, we have component deflators neither for particular kinds of structures nor for structures in particular sectors. Lacking these, we employ a single index which relates to structures in the aggregate and, moreover, to annual investment rather than to the capital stock. The index used has (implicit) given-year weights and a 1937 base.

---

[63] The 1925 inventory of industrial capital was intended to value imported equipment at domestic prices of comparable Soviet produced machines. As noted earlier, however, about a third of the 1928 stock of industrial capital was the result of post-1925 investment. Imports, which were valued at cost computed according to the official exchange rate, accounted for 20–30 percent of post-1925 investment. On the valuation of imports, see Moorsteen–62, Appendix F. On the share of imports in investment, see Gosplan–30, p. 462.

[64] See Moorsteen, *loc. cit.*

[65] *Ibid.*, p. 75.

The application of a single deflator to structures in all sectors undoubtedly produces errors in the 1937-price estimates for individual sectors. While insufficient data are available to judge the probable size of these errors, they are likely to be large enough that the reliability of the sector estimates is much lower than that of their combined total. Whether the procedure also produces errors in the estimate of the total stock depends, in part, upon the extent to which the composition of the stock in existence at the beginning of 1928 differed from that of investment in the course of 1928.

In Table 2–9, we compare the percentage distribution by sectors of the initial stock with that of 1928 gross investment. The investment data are taken from the same source as the stock figures; like the latter, they are given in the source as in 1926/27 prices, which are here treated as the equivalent of 1928 prices. It is evident that the composition of the initial

TABLE 2-9

DISTRIBUTION OF STRUCTURES BY SECTOR IN 1928 STOCK AND
INVESTMENT, IN 1928 PRICES
(Percent of Total)

	Net Capital Stock, January 1, 1928	Gross Investment, 1928
	(1)	(2)
1. Industry..................	7.2	18.3
2. Electric Power.............	0.9	4.6
3c. Agriculture: Productive Structures	11.2 ⎫	13.7
3d. Agriculture: Irrigation Works....	1.1 ⎬	
4a. Railroads: Structures	14.4	9.5
5a. Waterways.................	0.3	0.3
5b. Ports ··················	0.4	0.5
6a. Motor Transport: Roads	1.4	2.0
7. Communications	0.4	1.0
8. Trade	1.0	4.6
9. Education..................	4.0	3.4
10. Health....................	2.1	2.0
11. Administration	1.2	1.4
12. Municipal Facilities...........	3.8	3.1
13a. Housing: Socialized Urban	15.8	10.3
13b. Housing: Private Urban........	11.0	4.4
13c. Housing: Rural.............	23.8	21.1
	100.0	100.0

Sources: Column 1 is computed from column 6 of Table B–1. Column 2 is computed from data given in Gosplan–30, pp. 446–53. Figures for 1928 are interpolated on a straight line from those given in the source for 1927/28 and 1928/29. The division of total investment in each sector between structures, equipment, and installation is, for simplicity, assumed the same as in the net stock: columns 6, 7, and 8 of Table B–1.

stock is not wholly unlike that of the 1928 flow, but substantial differences do appear. How far these differences would cause a deflator for the stock to differ from the deflator computed for investment would depend upon the dispersion of the component price indexes about the average. Although we have little information on the behavior of the subindexes, there is evidence to suggest that for at least one important component, housing, prices tended to rise more rapidly than for structures generally. By implication, of course, the average price level for nonresidential structures rose less rapidly than the average, and, insofar as the distribution of structures varies between investment and the capital stock in 1928, our use of the implicit investment deflator is a source of error.

Even the information on costs for housing is incomplete and of un-

determinable reliability. Taking 1928 as 100, we estimate the cost of socialized housing in 1937 to have been about 265.[66] Costs in the private sector
are unknown. In nominal terms, they may have risen even more than for
socialized housing, because private construction did not have access to
the same markets for building materials. But, if this is in fact what happened, the nominal price level would not be relevant to our purposes,
because it would differ for just this reason from the real rate of substitution
between the two kinds of housing. At any rate, it is not obvious that the
real costs of private housing should have risen relative to socialized. Let
us take the index for socialized housing, then, to stand for housing generally. By contrast, prices for all kinds of structures in 1937 were at 204.5
percent of 1928.[67] Thus the housing price level, by 1937, stood about 30
percent above that for structures generally.[68] Given the distribution of

---

[66] The derivation of this figure is as follows. Until 1935, Soviet statistical organs published annually the average cost per cubic meter of all socialized housing completed in
the given year (see *Nashe stroitel'stvo*, 1936:22, p. 36). Five individual series are available for buildings of different wall materials, but within these classifications no account
is taken of quality change—a defect of uncertain but possibly significant consequence.
Also, the average costs are affected by outlays made prior to the year of completion.
However, during two brief intervals, 1927–28 and 1934–35, construction costs generally
were relatively stable (see p. 58, fn. 62, for 1927–28, and Tables A–2 and A–5, which show
the value of construction in constant and current prices, for 1934–35). Thus, as between
these two years, the cost of houses *completed* may also be a reasonable reflection of the
relative level of costs *incurred*. For the five kinds of wall materials, the 1935 price level
(1928 = 100) ranged from 197, for clay, to 299, for the residual category "other," but the
three most important categories, brick-concrete, stone, and wood log, were closer
together, 238, 271, and 246 respectively (on the relative importance of wall materials, see,
for example, TsSU–29a, p. 832, or Table 2–7 above). The simple mean of these three
figures, 252, might be taken to stand for all housing without too great a risk that more
appropriate weighting would present sharply different results. According to our calculations, the price level for all construction rose between 1935 and 1937 by less than 5 percent (see Tables A–2 and A–5). Assuming a similar change for housing, the 1937 price
level (1928 = 100) would be about 265 (252 × 1.05 = 264.6).

Naum Jasny (Jasny–52, p. 165) estimates the 1937 level of state housing costs at 300
(1926/27 = 100). However, we have been unable to reconstruct this finding from the
underlying data cited by him. The latter seem to indicate an index number nearer to
450. His calculation, apparently, is based on a comparison of average costs of dwelling
space completed in 1926/27 (about 150 rubles per square meter) with a 1937 figure of
680 rubles per square meter derived as the quotient of total outlays planned for housing
construction in the Third Five-Year Plan, divided by the number of square meters of
housing space to be put into operation in the same period. The data are adjusted by the
author to allow for differences between actual 1937 and planned Third Five-Year Plan
costs (see *op. cit.*, p. 114, including fn. 61). In view of the data cited earlier in this footnote, the indicated 1937 index number of 450 seems implausibly high to us—as apparently it did also to Jasny. In particular, the figures for outlays and for housing space to
be put into operation must be incomparable in scope, the former, but not the latter,
including increments to the stock of housing projects in progress and, in all probability,
the cost of nonresidential space in buildings used only in part as dwellings (see the
discussion of the latter point in connection with the accounting of the Soviet capital
census of 1959, Chapter 7, below). Given the elliptic form in which the Third Five-Year
Plan data were published, it is possible that other incomparabilities have also escaped
notice.

[67] This is the 1928 investment weighted index number used to revalue all structures
in the initial stock, obtained from Tables A–2 and A–5.

[68] We cannot account for the relative rise in housing costs, although it would presumably be attributable to a relative increase in input prices and, as seems especially
likely, a relative decline in the productivity of labor in housing construction.

investment in structures in 1928, we can compute the implied average price level for nonresidential components, which is about 170 percent of 1928, or 17 percent below the general level.[69] If we recombine the housing and nonresidential price index numbers, using now the distribution of structures in the initial stock (Table 2–9, column 1), the over-all deflator for all structures in the stock would be 218, instead of the 204.5 we have used, a difference of 6–7 percent.

For the deflation alone, the higher index might provide a gain in accuracy. It will be recalled, however, that some nonresidential components of the initial stock appear to be overstated in 1928 prices. A nonresidential deflator which allowed for this, then, would move us back in the direction of the implicit investment deflator actually used. Two errors of opposite direction exist. Given this, the roughness of the data on housing costs, and the other ambiguities in the initial stock values, it has seemed as well to employ the implicit investment deflator without adjustment.[70]

5. SERVICE LIVES

A considerable amount of data on actual or expected service lives of fixed assets has been released in Soviet publications, and from these we have estimated lives for a number of categories of equipment and structures. The estimates by components, which are shown in Table 2–10, underlie in turn our estimates of the timing of retirements, in the computation of the gross value of the capital stock, and of the depreciation rates used to derive net values.[71] They refer to terms of service for assets receiving appropriate maintenance (by Soviet standards), including capital repairs.

The Soviet sources we have consulted often express uncertainty about the reliability of the figures they cite, and in some cases it seems likely that they have had reference to foreign data in compiling their estimates. In any case, a definitive determination of average service lives could be accomplished only by an extensive investigation in the field. At the time of writing, no such survey was available to us or to the authors of the sources we draw on. Accordingly, the estimates we have made, although not so far as we know subject to a systematic bias, must be viewed as approximate. For this reason, the sensitivity of our calculations to errors in the service lives is explored by means of alternative calculations, the results of which will be presented shortly.

As was explained earlier, 31 separate groups of assets are distinguished within the initial capital stock, 11 kinds of equipment, 17 kinds of struc-

---

[69] Table 2–9 indicates housing to have accounted for 35.8 percent of all structures built in 1928 (170 × 0.642 + 265 × 0.358 = 204).

[70] The procedure means that the distribution of structures in the initial stock in 1937 prices does not reflect changes since 1928 in relative prices among economic sectors. For our immediate purposes, this deficiency raises problems mainly in connection with the application of depreciation rates, which vary somewhat among structures in different economic sectors (see Table 2–10). In Section 5, we consider the consequences of errors in depreciation rates. On the other hand, in Chapter 3, Section 6, where stocks of residential and nonresidential fixed assets are distinguished, we take explicit account of differences in relative 1937 price levels for housing and other kinds of assets.

[71] Detailed sources are given in Appendix C.

TABLE 2-10

ESTIMATED SERVICE LIVES OF FIXED CAPITAL ASSETS, SOVIET AND U. S.
(Years)

	Soviet (1)	U. S.: Bulletin "F" (2)
Equipment		
Construction and Road-Building Equipment	10	6-10
Railroad Rolling Stock	45	25-28
Diesel Engines	30	20-25
Locomobiles	30	--
Oil Engines	30	20-25
Steam Turbines	30	20-25
Water Turbines	40	30-40
Electrical Equipment	25	17-20
Tractors	12	6-20
Motor Vehicles	8	3-10
Horse-Drawn Vehicles	11	8
Steam Boilers	30	20-25
Pumps and Compressors	11	15
Lifting and Handling Equipment	25	--
Woodworking and Handling Equipment	25	10-25
Textile and Sewing Machines	50	15-25
Metalworking Machines	25	17-20
Pneumatic Hand Tools	3	--
Agricultural Machines	8	15
Leather and Shoemaking Machines	25	15
Printing Machinery	25	15
Metallurgical Equipment	25	20-30
Coal Mining Machines	5	--
Petroleum Extraction and Refining Equipment	20	--
Structures		
By Kind of Structure		
Housing, Masonry (brick, stone, concrete)	100	
Housing, Mixed Masonry and Wood	80	
Housing, Wood Log (rublenye and bruskovye)	80	50-60*
Housing, Wood Frame (karkasnye)	30	
Housing, Other Materials	30	
Nonresidential Buildings	65	50-75
Other Structures (sooruzhenie)	37	--
Roads, Roadbeds, Squares	40	--
Canals, Wells, Reservoirs	50	--
Dredging	25	--
Power Transmission Lines	35	--
Mine Works	25	--
By Economic Sector		
Industry	55	--
Electric Power	55	--
Agriculture, Productive Structures	40	--
Agriculture, Irrigation Works	40	--
Railroad Structures	50	--
Waterways	50	--
Ports	50	--
Motor Roads	40	--
Communications	40	--
Trade	65	--
Education	80	--
Health	80	--
Administration	80	--
Municipal Facilities	50	--
Socialized Urban Housing	90	
Private Urban Housing	70	50-60*
Rural Housing	50	

*The U.S. housing lives are those for apartment buildings (50 years) and dwellings (60 years).

Sources: For column 1, see Appendix C. For column 2, U. S. Treasury Department-55, passim.

tures, and 3 items of installation. In computing the present gross value of the initial stock for years after 1928, service lives corresponding to each group of assets are obtained from Table 2–10. Thus, agricultural machines are assigned an average service life of 8 years, railroad rolling stock 45 years, installation 40 years, and so on. Structures take the service lives shown in the table by economic sector. The life remaining to assets in the initial stock is computed from the total service life and the ratio of net to gross value (see Table 2–5). Within each group, assets are assumed to have approximately the same remaining life. However, to avoid an unlikely lumpiness in the occurrence of retirements, present gross values are reduced uniformly over a seven-year period centered on the year of expiry of the average remaining life for the group as a whole.[72] In computing the present net, straight-line depreciated, value of the initial stock, the January 1, 1928, net value of each group of assets is reduced annually by the depreciation charge obtained as the product of the depreciation rate, that is, the reciprocal of the corresponding service life, and the gross value of the asset group, as shown in Table 2–5.[73]

Although the assets in the initial stock are broken down into a number of categories, there undoubtedly remains considerable heterogeneity within each category. In particular, the component assets must have been acquired at various dates and, hence, have varied remaining service lives. Even if the average service lives and the depreciation rates applied to each asset group are accurate as of January 1, 1928, an error will result from their flat application to the entire group. The straight-line depreciation charge calculated for 1928 is the same as the "true" charge—that is, the charge which would be made if assets were depreciated individually—only as long as all the assets in the group still exist. As the assets with short remaining lives are retired, the true charge falls below that of 1928 and the true present net value rises above that computed by applying the 1928 depreciation rates. Similarly, the true present gross value of the assets will be the same as that obtained by means of the average remaining life only until retirements of short-lived assets begin. Thereafter the former lies below the latter, rising above it as the *average* remaining life for the asset group expires. For at least some of the items in the initial stock, such as industrial equipment or rural housing, retirements must be distributed quite broadly about the average remaining life, much more broadly than the seven years our method assumes. However, the data do not permit a more refined treatment of these present values, and our estimates, consequently, contain errors of the sort just described. These errors are akin

---

[72] For example, the gross value in 1937 prices of communications structures in the initial stock was 487 million rubles at the beginning of 1928. These structures had an average service life of 25 years and a remaining life of 13 years (see Table 2–5). Their present gross value is taken as 487 million rubles for every subsequent year through the beginning of 1937. Thereafter, for each of seven consecutive years, it is reduced by one seventh.

[73] To obtain present values for the initial stock corresponding to the sinking fund, declining annuity, and sum-of-digits depreciation methods, assets within each group are treated as if they were all of the same age, the average for the group (column 4 minus column 5 of Table 2–5). For each group, a hypothetical acquisition date is determined (January 1, 1928, minus the average age), and the gross value of the group is depreciated by the appropriate method commencing with that date.

to others in our estimates of the parameters of the initial stock, and their consequences for our over-all calculations may also be thought of as illustrated by the alternative calculations of Table 2–6.

Of assets created after January 1, 1928, our data, the annual investment series, distinguish only the three broad categories of equipment, structures, and installation. We describe the computation of present values for each separately.

Data on the distribution of investment in equipment by kind are not available, but the general structure may be discerned from the composition of Soviet machinery output (measured in 1937 prices). Using the latter as a surrogate for the former, together with the service lives of Table 2–10, we compute in Table 2–11 the distribution of retirements of equipment for use in our gross value calculations.[74] Distributions applicable to investment in equipment in 1928, 1937, and 1955 are given in columns 1–3. These show, for example, that, according to the estimated service life data, machines which accounted for 0.3 percent of all machinery investment in 1937 would have been retired three years after their acquisition; that eight years after acquisition, machines accounting for 44.3 percent of the original total would have been retired; and so on. As may be seen, distributions for the three years are quite similar in spite of large differences in the composition of output. To simplify further computations, therefore, we combine them, somewhat freely, into a composite distribution (column 4), which is used in deriving present gross values of past annual investments in equipment for all of the years studied. The distributions, which show retirements ranging over 50 years, may be compared with the corresponding *average* terms of service. Computed from the service life data of Table 2–10 and machinery output weights, the average service lives of the machines acquired in 1928, 1937, and 1955, respectively, were 24 years, 20 years, and 19 years, implying a composite average life of about 21 years.

In columns 5–7 of Table 2–11, straight-line depreciation rates analogous

---

[74] In detail, the several series in Table 2–11 are derived as follows. Columns 1–3 are obtained from the expression:

$$R_i = \frac{\bar{V} - \sum_{j=1}^{i-1} V_j}{\bar{V}},$$

where R_i is the relative share of remaining assets in the ith year after acquisition; $\bar{V}$ is the total value of machinery production in the year of acquisition; and V_j is the value of production in the same year of machines having a service life of j. The value of output data are from Moorsteen-62, Table D–2. In computing the distribution for 1928, output data for 1927/28 are used. In column 4, the figures for the first 25 years after acquisition are simple averages of the corresponding entries in columns 1–3. Thereafter, the entries from column 1 alone are used, since assets remaining 26 years or more after acquisition affect the calculations only in the case of investment from the earliest years studied. The entries for columns 5–7 are obtained from the expression:

$$D_i = \frac{\sum_{j=i}^{50} [V_j/j]}{\bar{V}},$$

where D_i is the depreciation charge in the ith year after acquisition, expressed as a percentage of investment in the acquisition year; V_j is the value of output of machines having a service life of j years; and $\bar{V}$ is the total value of machinery output in the acquisition year. Column 8 is the simple average of columns 5–7.

TABLE 2-11

DISTRIBUTION OF RETIREMENTS AND AVERAGE DEPRECIATION CHARGES
FOR ANNUAL INVESTMENT IN EQUIPMENT
(Percent)

Years after Acquisition of Asset	Gross Value of Assets Remaining in Existence as a Share of Total Investment in:				Annual Depreciation Chargeable against Assets Remaining in Existence as a Share of Total Investment in:			
	1928	1937	1955	Composite	1928	1937	1955	Composite
	(1)	(2)	(3)	(4)	(5)	(6)	(7)	(8)
0-3	100.0	100.0	100.0	100	7.3	8.1	7.5	7.6
4-5	99.7	99.7	99.9	100	7.2	8.0	7.4	7.5
6-8	99.7	99.4	99.4	100	7.2	8.0	7.3	7.5
9-10	58.4	55.7	67.8	61	2.0	2.5	3.4	2.6
11	58.3	53.1	62.3	58	2.0	2.2	2.8	2.3
12	52.0	49.5	57.6	53	1.4	1.9	2.4	1.9
13-20	51.5	43.2	49.5	48	1.4	1.4	1.7	1.5
21-25	51.5	43.0	49.0	48	1.4	1.4	1.7	1.5
26-30	41.4	24.4	23.0	41	1.0	0.6	0.7	0.8
31-40	35.0	17.0	9.1	35	0.8	0.4	0.2	0.5
41-45	34.4	16.9	8.6	34	0.7	0.4	0.2	0.4
46-50	4.9	2.0	1.4	5	0.1	0.0*	0.0*	0.1
over 50	0.0	0.0	0.0	0	0.0	0.0	0.0	0.0

*Less than 0.05.

Source: See text.

to the retirement distributions are shown. For each period, the depreciation which would be charged against the assets still extant, as indicated by the service lives of Table 2–10, is shown as a percentage of the value of all the equipment acquired in the investment year. The arrays of charges are again similar for the three years considered, and, as with retirements, we construct a composite set of charges to be used for investment in all years.[75]

Clearly, the composite distributions of retirements and depreciation charges can fit the varying annual investment stream only loosely. However, the data do seem sufficient to indicate, if the service life estimates are correct, that retirements do not begin in substantial quantities until eight years or so after acquisition. Only two relatively minor categories of machinery have lives of less than eight years. The rapid increase in annual investment that characterizes most of the period suggests that only large errors in the distribution of retirements occurring more than eight years after acquisition would have a substantial impact on the computed capital stock values.

The distribution of retirements of structures raises less of a problem because structures are relatively long-lived. As the data in Table 2–10 indicate, the shortest service life for any of the categories of assets distinguished is 25 years. Over this interval, the present net and gross values

---

[75] For the sinking fund, declining annuity, and sum-of-digits computations, remaining value schedules for investment in equipment in all years are computed from the implicit composite service life distribution of Table 2–11, column 4.

of any past investment computed by using only the average depreciation rate or service life would coincide with values computed to take account of the time distribution of retirements. Because of the rapid growth of investment, the calculations are relatively insensitive to the treatment of assets more than 25 years old. Accordingly, we compute net and gross present values for annual investment in structures by employing a single average depreciation rate and service life for all such investment. The averages are computed from the service lives by kind of structure in Table 2–10, the distribution of investment in structures in 1934, for which year data are available, being used as weights.[76] The average depreciation rate is 2.0 percent; the average service life, 57 years.[77]

We have no independent information on service lives of installation. We use instead a simple arithmetic average of the estimates for structures and equipment, 40 years (the implied annual depreciation rate is 2.5 percent). It is no doubt true that the appropriate magnitude lies between those for structures and equipment. Installation can hardly outlive the structures in which it is enclosed, nor is it likely to be changed more frequently than the equipment to which it is ancillary. But the possible range is large, as may be, therefore, the error in the estimated service life and depreciation rate we apply to installation. The weight of installation in the total, however, is small.

For reasons indicated above, our various simplifications in obtaining depreciation rates and service lives for application to the annual investment series are unlikely to be a source of major error, provided that the underlying individual service life data are reasonably accurate. Unfortunately, there is no assurance that such is the case, and, in fact, neither the Soviet sources we have consulted nor our own reflections offer reassurance on the matter. To test the consequence of errors at this point, we have made alternative calculations of gross and net values, in which the service lives used in the basic calculations are varied plus or minus one third. The results are summarized in Table 2–12, which indicates, for example, that the substitution for all assets of service lives one third greater than those actually used would produce net values for the total stock which exceed those in our basic estimate by 5 percent in 1937, 12 percent in 1950, and 10 percent in 1962 (row 4). Although errors as great as one third for individual kinds of assets seem possible, unless the available evidence is quite misleading, it is unlikely that the average error for all assets taken together can be this large. An error of one third would imply an average life for structures of less than 39 years or more than 75 years, for equipment of less than 15 years or more than 27 years. None of the Soviet data we have assembled lend probability to a combination either of upper or lower extremes.

In Table 2–12, the alternative as well as basic calculations necessarily commence with the same values for the initial stock. Varying the service life for assets in the initial stock alters their present values only in years

---

[76] The distribution is shown in Table C–3. See also the discussion in Appendix C.

[77] In the sinking fund and declining annuity calculations, in order to produce results strictly comparable with the straight-line depreciation series, the service life for annual investment in structures is taken as the reciprocal of the average depreciation rate, 50 years.

TABLE 2-12

EFFECTS ON TOTAL GROSS AND NET FIXED CAPITAL OF VARYING
SERVICE LIVES ± 1/3, IN 1937 PRICES, SELECTED YEARS
(January 1--Difference as Percent of Corresponding Basic Calculation)

	1928	1932	1937	1941	1945	1950	1955	1962
			Service Lives Increased by 1/3					
Gross Values Increase by:								
1. Total.............	0	0	0	2	3	3	3	5
2. Structures	0	0	0	0	0	0	2	4
3. Equipment	0	3	2	7	14	11	6	8
Net Values Increase by:								
4. Total.............	0	3	5	7	11	12	11	10
5. Structures	0	2	5	6	9	11	11	10
6. Equipment	0	5	8	12	18	12	13	12
			Service Lives Decreased by 1/3					
Gross Values Decline by:								
7. Total.............	0	1	2	3	6	11	12	8
8. Structures	0	0	0	0	2	11	11	4
9. Equipment	0	3	10	15	19	12	17	15
Net Values Decline by:								
10. Total.............	0	4	9	11	15	15	13	12
11. Structures	0	4	7	9	13	14	11	10
12. Equipment	0	8	15	17	23	18	19	17

Source: See text.

after 1928. Thus the alternative calculations testify as to the consequences of errors in *our* estimates of service lives, but they do not show what the effects would be of similar errors on the part of the Soviet statisticians responsible for the net and gross values of the initial stock estimates. If both of us erred in the same direction, the result would be to reduce the variation over time in the errors shown in Table 2–12: the errors at the beginning of the period would be more nearly of the same magnitude as those toward the end. If we erred in opposite directions, the result would, of course, be to steepen the time trends. Secondly, the fact that the initial values are unvarying means that the series in Table 2–12 may also be read as showing the consequences of changes over time in service lives. For example, if service lives corresponded to the values actually used in the early period but, as seems not unlikely, declined in later years as capital became more abundant and Soviet recognition of obsolescence grew, the value of the stock at the end of the period would be less than we have estimated and errors of the sort tabulated in rows 7–12 would occur.

Of the alternative calculations in Table 2–12, the largest relative variations are produced for net values when service lives are decreased (rows 7–9). Taking this calculation to illustrate the effects on growth rates, we note that substitution of the shorter lives results in a reduction in the average annual growth rate during the prewar period of about one percentage point or a bit more and, for periods extending from the prewar to the postwar, of rather less than one point. Within the postwar period, the effect is negligible or increases the growth rate by about one half point or less.

The absence of suitable data prevents our taking account of one further problem. Even within narrowly defined classes, assets must differ stochastically in their terms of service. Hence the service lives used for classes of assets would be more realistic if they were stochastic distributions of retirements rather than single values. The tendency of this error is probably toward overstatement of the absolute value of the stock by a few percent, with relatively minor consequences for the observed rate of growth.[78]

Because of the uncertain reliability of the Soviet service life data, it may be helpful in this instance to cite similar data for the United States, although this is an aspect of U.S. capital which is scarcely known with precision. In Table 2–10, we reproduce the so-called Bulletin "F" lives (pre-1962) of the U.S. Treasury for categories which can be identified as corresponding more or less closely to those we use (comparisons are not possible for a number of classes of structures). The Bulletin "F" lives date largely from the 1930's, and their statistical foundations are not entirely clear.[79] On the whole, they appear similar in magnitude to the lives we obtain for Soviet assets, although ours tend to be somewhat longer.[80]

The average service lives (for annual investment) implied by our data, about 21 years for equipment and 57 years for structures, also resemble but are larger than those which have been calculated for the United States. Simon Kuznets, on the basis of data which were the antecedents of the Bulletin "F" lives, puts the service life for equipment at 13 years and that for structures at 50 years (Kuznets evidently takes straight-line depreciation rates, 8 percent and 2 percent, as the reciprocals of average service lives; our weighted averages of the reciprocals of component service lives are 7.6 percent and 2 percent).[81] George Terborgh, aggregating Bulletin "F" lives for individual kinds of assets, finds the average life for equipment to be 17.25 years, for structures 50 years.[82]

In 1962, the U.S. Treasury Department revised the Bulletin "F" lives, reducing those for equipment by 30–40 percent and those for buildings

---

[78] Terborgh–54, pp. 62–64, compares straight-line depreciation charges for the "amortization" method of accounting, which is essentially that employed by us, and the "correct" method, when service lives are distributed according to an empirically observed pattern. During the first half of the average service life, charges reckoned "correctly" exceed those generated by the "amortization" method by about 8 percent, declining below the latter shortly thereafter. Present values computed by the amortization method, then, would exceed those computed correctly during the first part of the service life, though by less than 4 percent until the half life, declining below the correct values in later years. As will be shown subsequently, the average age of assets throughout the period has been well below the expected half lives—hence our presumption of overstatement in absolute level. With respect to the growth rate, it seems unlikely that the introduction of stochastically distributed service lives would produce as much difference as that manifested among the different methods of depreciation displayed in Table 2–1, because the difference in absolute values is less.

[79] For a description of their origins, see Grant–49, p. 142.

[80] For housing, the difference is large, but it should be noted that, as against the Bulletin "F" lives of 50–60 years, Raymond Goldsmith (Goldsmith–51, p. 21) has argued that the useful lives of houses in the United States are nearer to 80–100 years.

[81] See Kuznets–46, p. 80. Kuznets cites as his source for service lives Solomon Fabricant's *Capital Consumption and Adjustment* (New York, 1938), pp. 176–83; Fabricant cites a U.S. Treasury publication, *Depreciation Studies—Preliminary Report of the Bureau of Internal Revenue*, 1931.

[82] Terborgh–54, pp. 83, 95, 177–78.

(not necessarily all structures) by about 25 percent.[83] The resulting service lives are clearly much shorter than those we estimate for the Soviet Union. The circumstances under which the reductions were made, however, and especially the declared intention to facilitate the rapid replacement of assets,[84] makes it uncertain to what extent the new lives can be taken to represent actual service lives.

It is difficult to judge how closely the lives of fixed assets in the Soviet economy should be expected to correspond to those of assets elsewhere. The Soviet use of capital appears to be more intensive than that of most other countries. On the other hand, Soviet practice has tended toward repairing ageing assets and resisting retirement because of obsolescence. On balance, the estimated Soviet lives do not appear grossly implausible in the light of U.S. data, although the revision of the Treasury's estimates puts this conclusion in more doubt than it would otherwise be.

6. ADJUSTMENTS FOR TERRITORIAL CHANGES AND WAR LOSSES

Our calculations are intended to cover the actual capital stock within contemporary borders, including therefore capital acquired or lost through territorial change and military action. The method of accumulating and depreciating (or withdrawing) gross investments does not of itself take account of such extraordinary acquisitions or losses.[85] This section describes two rough adjustments, designed to allow for fixed capital acquired through the territorial changes of 1939–40 and that lost as a result of enemy action during World War II.[86]

Table 2–13 summarizes the changes in Soviet population and area resulting directly from territorial changes during the period studied. In relative terms, the total territorial acquisition was small, as was the population acquisition of 1944–45. The areas acquired during 1939 and 1940, on the other hand, contained a population equal to about 13 percent of the Soviet pre-expansion total. According to Soviet estimates, the degree of urbanization in these territories was somewhat below that of the Soviet Union as a whole: city dwellers accounted for 21 percent of the total population in the newly acquired areas as opposed to 33 percent in the Soviet territory of January, 1939.[87] On this count, at least, it might be expected

---

[83] The reduction for equipment is stated in U.S. Treasury Department–62, p. 3; that for buildings is a simple average computed from data given in *ibid.*, p. 11, and in U.S. Treasury Department–55, p. 7.

[84] Cf. U.S. Treasury Department–62, p. 3.

[85] Our annual investment series, however, are intended to include investment utilizing reparations or war booty captured abroad.

[86] It is possible that extraordinary losses of significant size also occurred during the first two or three years of the 1930's in connection with the collectivization drive, but we make no adjustment in our figures for lack of suitable data. The affected assets would be those used for agricultural production and rural housing. By 1930, these two categories together probably accounted for about 60 billion rubles, in 1937 prices, out of total fixed assets of about 180 billion rubles. Thus rural losses of 10–20 percent could have affected the total stock by 3–7 percent over the collectivization period. (The value of rural fixed capital in 1930 is extrapolated from the 1928 figures in Table B–1, columns 17 and 18; the value of all fixed assets is from Table T–1.)

[87] TsSU–59, p. 9.

TABLE 2-13

TERRITORIAL CHANGES, 1939-45

Date (1)	Regions (2)	Absolute Increment		Relative Increment	
		Area (Thousand Square Kilometers) (3)	Population (Thousands) (4)	Area (5)	Population (As Percent of Total of January 17, 1939) (6)
November 1939	Polish Provinces (excluding Vilna District)	194.8	12,500	0.9	7.3
March 1940 – August 1940	Finnish Provinces, Rumanian Provinces (Bessarabia, N. Bukovina), Lithuania (including Vilna), Latvia, Estonia. . . .	258.6	10,118	1.2	5.9
September 1944 – September 1945	Petchenga Raion (Murmansk), Tuva Oblast, Memel, Kaliningrad Oblast, Transcarpathian area, Karafuto (S. Sakhalin), Kurile Islands, Bialistock-Suwalki area (ceded to Poland), Przemysl area (ceded to Poland)	216.9	1,000	1.2	0.5

Sources: For columns 1–4, Bergson-54, p.6; for columns 5–6, TsSU-59, p.7.

that the amount of fixed capital per inhabitant in the new territories would also be below the Soviet average. In addition, some destruction of capital probably occurred in connection with the Soviet occupation, for example, during military action in the Polish Provinces, and agriculture in the new areas was no doubt less mechanized than in the Soviet Union. Our method of computation without adjustment yields figures for January 1, 1940, and January 1, 1941, which equal (*i*) the total capital stock at the beginning of the preceding year plus (*ii*) gross investment during the preceding year in all territories covered by contemporary Soviet accounting minus (*iii*) depreciation or withdrawals during the preceding year, computed from our estimates of the existing capital stock within pre-expansion borders. We adjust for the territorial changes just described on the basis of the relative population increments indicated in Table 2–13, raising our unadjusted figures for January 1, 1940, by 5 percent and those for January 1, 1941, by 10 percent. In calculations for subsequent years, we compute the present value of assets created before World War II on the assumption that, as of the middle of 1941, they were 10 percent greater than indicated by our unadjusted figures. No adjustment is made in connection with the territorial changes of 1944–45.

On June 22, 1941, the Soviet Union was invaded by Germany and its allies, who soon occupied the western regions of the country. The invaders made their main advance during 1941, improved their positions further during most of 1942, were halted in the winter of that year, and were gradually pushed back during 1943 and 1944 until, by the beginning of 1945, they had been almost entirely removed from the country. At one time or another, according to a Soviet authority, they occupied territories which, prior to the war, contained 45 percent of the Soviet Union's total population, a third of its industrial output, 47 percent of its sown acreage, and 55 percent of its railway lines.[88] Those areas, accordingly, witnessed 3½ years of violent military activity, during which substantial losses of capital occurred. Our problem is to take such account of these losses as the evidence permits and also to estimate at least roughly the errors which may attend an adjustment of this sort.

Table 2–14, columns 3 and 4, lists Soviet statements about fixed capital losses sustained during the war. For purposes of comparison, prewar stocks of the items in reference are shown in columns 1 and 2, and the loss, expressed as a percentage of the prewar stock, is given in column 5.[89] For the first five items listed (Group I) the losses indicated in column 5 may tend slightly to understate the actual loss, because the decline in the stock of these assets would equal the loss minus concurrent acquisitions out of domestic production, lend-lease, and the like. If the language in the Soviet sources may be taken literally, the losses shown in rows 6–18 of the table (Group II) reflect gross reductions in the existing stocks of assets resulting directly from the war. Finally, the figures in column 5 for items 19–32 are overstatements of the actual losses, because they include partial damage.

---

[88] Voznesenskii–47, p. 157.

[89] The list of losses is not exhaustive, containing only those items for which prewar stocks could be ascertained. The items in rows 1–5 and 19 were included, however, because the Soviet description of the loss was expressed in terms of the prewar stock.

Items	Prewar Stock Date (1)	Prewar Stock Quantity (2)	Loss Caused by War Quantity (3)	Loss Caused by War Description of Loss (4)	Loss as Percent of Prewar Stock (5)
Group I					
1. Seagoing Ships	–	–	–	"Decline in Stock, 1940-42"	50
2. River Barges	–	–	–	" " " "	25
3. Locomotives	–	–	–	" " 1941-43	15
4. Railroad Freight Cars	–	–	–	" " " "	20
5. Self-Powered River Vessels	–	–	–	" " 1940-42	20
Group II					
6. Metal-Cutting Machines	Nov. 1940	710,000	175,000	"Destroyed, wrecked or looted"	25
7. Presses and Hammers	"	119,000	34,000	" " " "	28
8. Coal-Cutting Machines	End 1940	3,421*	2,700	" " " "	79
9. Pneumatic Hammers	"	19,997*	15,000	" " " "	75
10. Electric Generating Capacity (mill. kw.)	"1940"	11.2	5	" " " "	45
11. Blast Furnaces (cu. m.)	End 1940	58,340	42,875	" " " "	73
12. Open Hearth Furnaces	"	391	213	" " " "	54
13. Textile Looms	"	241,100	45,000	" " " "	19
14. Fiber Spinning Spindles	"	9,939,200	3,000,000	" " " "	30
15. Tractors	"	531,000	137,000	"Destroyed or carried off"	26
16. Combines	"	182,000	49,000	" " " "	27
17. Seed Drills, Tractor	"	312,000	46,000	" " " "	15
18. Railroad Track	–	–	–	" " torn up	29
Group III					
19. Collective Farms	End 1940	236,900	98,000	"Totally or partially wrecked or looted"	41
20. Machine-Tractor Stations	"	7,069	2,890	" "	41
21. State Farms	"	4,159	1,876	" "	45
22. Retail Stores and Restaurants	"	494,800	216,700	" "	44
23. Post Offices	"1940"	51,000	36,000	" "	71
24. Sanatoriums	"1939"	2,166	976	" "	45
25. Rest Homes	"	1,270	656	" "	52
26. Elementary and Secondary Schools	Fall 1940	191,500	82,000	" "	43
27. Technicums	"	3,773	1,520	" "	40
28. Institutions of Higher Learning	"	817	334	" "	41
29. Scientific and Research Institutes	End 1940	1,821	605	" "	33
30. Museums	"	991	427	" "	43
31. Public Libraries	"	277,000	43,000	" "	15
32. Theaters	"	908	167	" "	18

* U.S.S.R. Ministry of Coal Mining, only.

Sources: For columns 1 and 2, rows 9, 11-14, see TsSU-57a, pp. 120, 124, 149, 342; for the remaining items, TsSU-59, pp. 156, 206, 215, 349, 487, 490, 602, 699, 813, 830, 831, 842, 850, 863, 865, 895. For columns 3 and 4, row 11, see Clark-56, p. 50; for the remaining items, Voznesenskii-47, pp. 159, 160. Column 5 is column 3 divided by column 4, except for rows 1-5, which are from ibid., p. 100 (but see also ibid., p. 161), and row 19, which is computed from ibid., pp. 157, 160.

The extent of loss varies widely among the different classes of assets, ranging from 15 percent to 79 percent of the prewar stock. If the items listed in the table are representative, the average loss might be taken to fall somewhere between 20 and 40 percent of the prewar stock. But the Soviet writings from which the list is drawn are tendentious, and it may well be true that the choice of items or language is such as to exaggerate the actual damage.

Some global Soviet estimates of war losses are also available. According to the chief authority on the subject, "the direct losses inflicted on the state and the population as a result of the destruction and looting of state, co-operative, and private property during the war in the occupied areas of the U.S.S.R. amounts to 679 billion rubles at state prewar prices," which was "about two-thirds of the prewar national wealth contained in the occupied territories."[90] Judging from the share of the total population in the occupied area, the latter statement would imply a loss, relative to the national wealth of the Soviet Union as a whole, of around 30 percent. The total loss (in billion rubles) is broken down elsewhere, as follows:[91]

State enterprises and establishments	287
Collective farms	181
Individuals	192
Co-operatives, trade-unions, and other social organizations	19
Total	679

However, the estimation procedures underlying these figures are unknown and, for reasons just expressed, somewhat suspect.

With respect to fixed capital only, we are told that assets "of enterprises in the socialized sector declined by 215 billion 1945 rubles during the second half of 1941 in connection with the Hitlerite German occupation of Soviet territory, remaining at about this level in 1942."[92] This figure, which apparently includes all assets in the occupied areas, whether or not destroyed, amounts to about 30 percent of all fixed capital held by socialized enterprises in 1940.[93] The statement also implies that assets destroyed as the Germans advanced during 1942 were roughly offset by new assets created behind the lines. Since investment in 1942 amounted to only about 2 percent of the prewar stock of fixed assets and substantial quantities of assets must have been recovered in usable or restorable condition as the Germans retreated during 1943 and 1944, the permanent loss implied by the statement is something less than 30 percent. The relative magnitude of the loss is reasonably consistent with that indicated for all classes of property by the data cited in the preceding paragraph.[94]

90 *Ibid.*, pp. 161–62.
91 TsSU–58, p. 20.
92 Voznesenskii–47, pp. 65–66.
93 *Ibid.*, p. 12, which puts the value of such assets at 709 billion 1945 rubles. Unfortunately, the source does not indicate whether this figure is for the beginning or end of the year or the annual average. A difference of about 10 percent may be involved.
94 The absolute figures are difficult to compare. Property losses of all kinds by socialized enterprises *and establishments* are given as 487 billion prewar rubles, as compared with fixed capital losses by socialist enterprises of 215 billion 1945 rubles. The former figure is broader in coverage than the latter, including inventories, livestock, and all losses by establishments other than enterprises. The latter is expressed in 1945 prices, which should exceed "prewar" prices.

We adjust our various calculations to allow for war losses by reducing our estimates of fixed capital in place as of June 30, 1941, by 25 percent. Present values in subsequent years of assets created before the middle of 1941 are computed accordingly. No further adjustment is made with respect to assets created after mid-1941, on the assumption they must generally have been placed beyond the zone of military action.

The adjustment is intended to be consistent with the various Soviet statements on losses, allowance being made for some degree of exaggeration in the general picture they convey. We are also guided in part by data to be presented shortly on prewar and postwar stocks of specific kinds of assets. Without implying a spurious fineness in the interpretation of the various data in reference, we may properly note that they refer to capital taken in a gross sense, that is, undepreciated.[95] Thus, no allowance is made for the age distribution of the items lost, and the application of our adjustment to net values is tantamount to assuming that losses were distributed in like proportions over assets of all ages. This is, no doubt, a further source of error in our calculations.

The lacunae in data which prevent a more precise estimate of actual losses also make it impossible to establish narrow margins of error for the adjustment. The effects of an error of 10 percentage points, 40 percent of the adjustment, are illustrated in Table 2–15, in which the net value of

TABLE 2-15

EFFECTS ON TOTAL NET FIXED CAPITAL OF ALTERNATIVE ADJUSTMENTS
FOR WAR LOSSES, IN 1937 PRICES, SELECTED YEARS

	Value of the Stock Assuming War Losses Amounted to:			Columns 1 and 3 Differ from Column 2 by:
	15 Percent of Prewar Stock	25 Percent of Prewar Stock	35 Percent of Prewar Stock	
January 1	Billion Rubles			In Percent of Column 2
1941	359.6	359.6	359.6	--
1945	313.0	281.3	249.6	11
1950	402.3	376.6	350.9	7
1955	624.8	603.9	583.0	3
1962	1263.8	1249.0	1234.2	1
	Average Annual Growth Rate (in Percent)			In Percentage Points
1941-50	1.3	0.5	-0.3	0.8
1941-55	4.0	3.8	3.5	0.2 - 0.3
1941-62	6.2	6.1	6.0	0.1
1945-50	5.1	6.0	7.1	0.9 - 1.1
1945-62	8.6	9.2	9.9	0.6 - 0.7
1950-55	9.2	9.9	10.7	0.7 - 0.8
1950-62	10.0	10.5	11.1	0.5 - 0.6
1955-62	10.6	10.9	11.3	0.3 - 0.4

Source: See text.

95 This is clearly true of the data in Table 2–14. Although the source is not explicit on the matter, the figures cited for fixed capital of socialized enterprises are doubtless to be understood as referring also to gross values, since this is the usual Soviet valuation. There is no specific indication or precedent from which to judge the valuation of all property losses.

TABLE 2-16

REPORTED STOCKS OF FIXED CAPITAL, SELECTED PHYSICAL ASSETS, 1940 AND 1950
(End of Year)

Industrial Equipment	1940 (Thousands)	1950 (Thousands)	End 1950 as Percent of End 1940
1. Metal-Cutting Machine Tools	710.0[a]	1,507.0[b]	212
2. Presses and Hammers	119.0[a]	284.0[b]	239
3. Blast Furnaces (cu. m.)	58.3	58.8	101
4. Open Hearth Furnaces (cu. m.).	10.8	13.5	125
5. Bessemer Converters (capacity in tons).	0.4	0.3	75
6. Electric Steel Furnaces (capacity in tons)	1.0	1.4	140
7. Coal-Cutting Machines	3.4[c]	4.8[c]	141
8. Pneumatic Hammers	20.0[c]	36.9[c]	185
9. Electric Generating Capacity (kw.)	11,193.0	19,614.0	175
10. Textile Looms.	241.1	220.7	92
11. Fiber Spinning Spindles.	9,939.2	9,455.6	95
12. Grinding and Husking Mills for Cereals	105.5[d]	92.0	87
Simple Average			139

Agricultural Equipment

	1940	1950	End 1950 as Percent of End 1940
13. Tractors (physical units).	531	595	112
14. Tractors (15 hp. units)	684	933	136
15. Combines, Grain	182	211	116
16. Trucks.	228	283	124
17. Plows, Tractor	491	519	106
18. Cultivators, Tractor.	272	317	117
19. Seed Drills, Tractor.	312	352	113
20. Mowers, Horse	487	519	107
21. Rakers, Horse	484	513	106
22. Silage Cutters	189	172	91
Simple Average			113

Transportation and Communication Facilities

	1940	1950	End 1950 as Percent of End 1940
23. Length of Operating Line (km.)	106.1	116.9	110
24. Length of Internal Waterways (km.).	107.3	130.2	121
25. Length of Pipelines (km.)	4.1	5.4	132
26. Length of Automobile Roads (km.).	1,531.2	1,550.4	101
27. Postal-Telegraph Stations	51.4	51.0	99
Simple Average			113

Residences

	1940	1950	End 1950 as Percent of End 1940
28. Urban Dwellings (sq. m.)	421,000	513,000	122

Communal Facilities

	1940	1950	End 1950 as Percent of End 1940
29. Elementary Schools	191.5	201.6	105
30. Public Libraries	277	351	127
31. Hospital Beds	791	1,011	128
Simple Average			120

[a] November, 1940. [b] End of 1951. [c] U.S.S.R. Ministry of Coal Mining, only. [d] End of 1939.
Sources: For rows 1–2, TsSU–57e, p. 54; rows 3–12, TsSU–57a, pp. 120, 124, 125, 126, 149, 171, 342, 409; rows 13–32, TsSU–59, pp. 487, 490, 544, 564, 572, 573, 604, 641, 813, 850, 879.

the capital stock in selected years is shown for calculations made on the alternative assumptions that war losses accounted for 15, 25, and 35 percent of the mid-1941 stock. The second of these series repeats our basic calculations. The comparisons may also be used as a point of reference in judging the consequences of errors in the adjustments for territorial change and in the annual investment estimates for the war years.

The effect of the war loss adjustment falls most heavily, of course, on the years nearest to the German invasion. Table 2–15 shows a difference in absolute results for 1945 of 11 percent, which declines to 7 percent by 1950 and to 1 percent by 1962. These figures also express the relative difference that would occur for index numbers comparing prewar years and the indicated postwar years. For comparisons among postwar years, the difference would be less, because the figures for all years vary in the same direction. Growth rates measured for intervals commencing with 1941 or any earlier year and ending with 1950 or any later year would be affected by 0.8 percentage points or less. Growth rates for intervals commencing with 1945 or later would be affected by 1.1 percentage points or less.[96]

Some further data are presented in Table 2–16, which show Soviet stocks of specific items of fixed capital at the end of the years 1940 and 1950. Postwar stocks relative to prewar (column 3) vary widely. For each group of assets, the postwar relatives are summarized by a simple arithmetic mean, but, clearly, the significance of such averaging is quite limited. As with the Soviet data on war losses, the representativeness of information made readily available is questionable. The figures in the table refer to gross stocks and hence are most easily compared with our gross value estimates. According to the latter (Table T–1), the Soviet fixed capital stock at the end of 1950, in 1937 prices, was about 21 percent greater than it had been at the end of 1940. This is computed with war losses at 25 percent. Using 15 or 35 percent instead would yield stocks for the end of 1950 30 and 12 percent, respectively, above the level of the end of 1940. On the whole, the data in Table 2–16 seem most consistent with the 25 percent adjustment.

---

96 This finding is only illustrated in Table 2–15 but has been verified in calculations not reproduced here.

Chapter 3

Fixed Capital:

Additional Calculations

1. INTRODUCTION

In general, the purpose guiding our choice of the data and methods employed in the fixed capital estimates has been to maximize the reliability of the calculations described in the preceding chapter, i.e., the estimates of the value of fixed capital in 1937 prices. The latter estimates, however, taken together with certain collateral data, permit a number of further estimates to be made. While of lower presumptive reliability than the stock estimates in 1937 prices, the additional calculations are, nevertheless, either relevant to our basic purpose or of interest in other contexts. They include the stock of fixed capital valued in 1928, 1950, and acquisition prices; annual depreciation charges; the stock of nonagricultural fixed capital; the distribution of all fixed capital between residential and non-residential assets; the stock of fixed capital available for operation as opposed to capital in place; and the average age of the fixed capital stock. These are discussed in turn in the sections following.

2. VALUES IN 1928 AND 1950 PRICES

Gross and net values of the fixed capital stock in 1928 and 1950 prices are presented in Tables T–8 and T–9. The net value estimates are compared with those in 1937 prices in Chart 3–1. The calculations in 1928 and 1950 prices are derived by procedures analogous to those employed for the corresponding 1937- price estimates. The method is again a perpetual inventory, commencing from an initial stock. Service lives, straight-line depreciation rates, and adjustments for territorial change and war losses are the same.[1] Differences lie only in the prices used to value the initial stock and annual gross investment.

---

[1] Service lives and depreciation rates are the same in that, *inter alia*, the composite lives and rates for annual investment in equipment obtained in Table 2–11 are used also for the calculations in 1928 and 1950 prices, although the Table 2–11 distributions are calculated with 1937 price weights. From the marked invariance of those distributions to changes in the physical composition of investment, we assume that the distributions would be relatively insensitive to changes in price weights as well.

78

CHART 3–1

Total Net Fixed Capital in 1937, 1928, and 1950 Prices, 1928–62
(January 1—Billion Rubles)

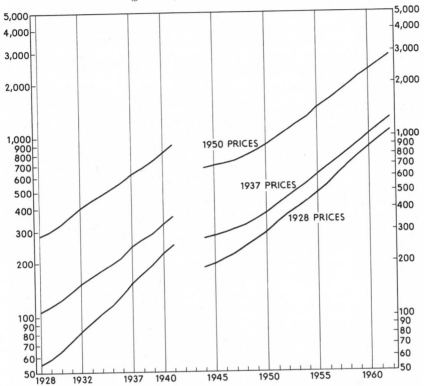

Sources: Tables T–1, T–8, and T–9.

The initial stock in 1937 prices is obtained, it will be recalled, from official data in 1928 prices, which are deflated to 1937 prices. For the initial stock in 1928 prices, the official data are used without deflation; for that in 1950 prices, the data are deflated to 1950 prices in the same way as to 1937 prices.[2] Annual gross investment in structures in 1928 and 1950 prices is again estimated from materials inputs in construction in physical units. In aggregation, the weights are, respectively, wholesale prices of 1928 and 1950[3]—instead of 1937. The absolute value of investment is obtained by applying the appropriate index numbers to the value in current prices of investment in structures in the calendar year 1928 or 1950. Annual investment in equipment in 1928 and 1950 prices is derived by deflation from the series in 1937 prices. The price index numbers used are of essentially the

---

2 The initial stock calculations are explained in detail in Appendix B. See in particular Table B–1, columns 6–11 and 20–25.

3 The 1950 price weights are for July–December of that year, but the resulting index is not thought to differ significantly from one weighted with average 1950 prices.

same character as the deflator used in compiling the 1937-price investment series. In particular, the resulting valuation of investment in equipment in 1928 prices is, like that of the initial stock, in domestic prices rather than actual acquisition prices, the two differing on account of the considerable volume of imported equipment in 1928 investment.[4] As in the 1937-price calculations, the change in the volume of investment in installation in 1928 and 1950 prices is estimated in index form as the simple average of the corresponding indexes for structures and equipment; absolute values are obtained by applying the appropriate index to the actual value of investment in installation in 1928 or 1950.[5]

The series in 1928 and 1950 prices are intended as alternative measures of the real change in fixed capital, reflecting rates of substitution in use in those two years as against rates of substitution in 1937. The relation of net to gross values is roughly similar in the prices of all three weight years. Net values in 1928 prices grow substantially and consistently more rapidly than in 1937 or 1950 prices, whereas the latter two sets of prices yield smaller differences in results. For the years 1928–37, the average annual growth rate is 11.7 percent when 1928 prices are used, as compared with 9.4 percent for 1937 prices and 9.0 percent for 1950 prices. Although we compute values in 1928 prices for the entire period, the estimates for later years are highly conjectural. Evidently, however, the difference in valuation produces smaller differences in growth rates for periods beyond 1937. Thus, for 1937–62, the average rate is 8.0 percent for 1928 prices, 6.8 percent for 1937 prices, and 6.3 percent for 1950 prices. The differences in growth rates may be described in terms of the following interactions: (*i*) 1928 prices produce a more rapid rate of increase in the equipment component of the capital stock than do 1937 or 1950 prices. For this component, differences between the latter two sets of prices are not very important. (*ii*) The equipment component grows more rapidly than the construction component in all sets of prices, and the relative weight accorded equipment is greatest when 1928 prices are used, least when 1950 prices are used. (*iii*) The construction component, which bulks large in the total, is not very sensitive to changes in the price weights. Thus factors (*i*) and (*ii*) operate to increase the growth displayed by the 1928 price weighted series, whereas only factor (*ii*) acts to distinguish the 1937 and 1950 price weighted series from each other.

3. VALUES IN ACQUISITION PRICES

As is implicit in the alternative calculations in constant prices, the price level of fixed capital investment goods has varied greatly over time. On the whole, but with the marked exception of some equipment prices in the early years covered, prices rose from 1928 to 1949, declined from 1949 to

---

[4] See Appendix A, p. 388. The disregarding of import prices increases the uncertainties which attach to 1928 prices as measures of rates of substitution in use. Since, however, foreign exchange was rationed in 1928, it is doubtful that import prices provide any guide to true substitutabilities.

[5] For details on the investment series, see Appendix A. The annual data are given in Tables A–3 and A–4.

1956, and were roughly constant thereafter. Consequently, the value of the stock in the prices at which it was acquired has diverged more or less pronouncedly from its value in current prices and has changed over time differently from its value in any set of constant prices.

Approximations to acquisition-price totals, gross and net, are calculated in Table T–10. For assets in the stock as of January 1, 1928, true acquisition-price valuations cannot be determined from our data, and 1928 values are used instead. For assets acquired after the beginning of 1928, annual gross investment in current—acquisition—prices for equipment, structures, and installation is derived from reported Soviet investment data[6] and is handled in the same way as in the constant-price estimates to obtain the stock totals: service lives, depreciation rates, and adjustments for extraordinary gains and losses are all the same. So calculated, the gross acquisition-price totals amount by 1937 to 67.8 percent of the value of the stock in (average) 1937 prices and by the end of 1950 to 52.7 percent of the value of the stock in (average) 1950 prices; the ratios for the net stock are 72.3 percent and 63.2 percent respectively.[7] In comparison, for example, with the net stock in 1937 prices, they rise more rapidly throughout the entire period from about the beginning of 1931, although the difference becomes slight from the mid-1950's on.

A point of interest in these estimates is that they correspond roughly to book values of fixed assets as typically carried in Soviet accounts. Although these are nominally in acquisition prices, they, like ours, are in fact somewhat mixed. The principal deviations from actual acquisition prices are stated to have been that assets acquired prior to 1925 were valued in 1925 prices and assets in occupied territory recovered after the German retreat were valued in 1941 prices. Since changes in capital goods prices were relatively small between 1925 and 1928, the valuation of assets in the 1928 stock should be similar in the two sets of accounts. However, the relative importance of assets recovered from occupied territory is unknown, as is, therefore, the difference in the two series introduced by varying treatment of this element. Other differences in valuation also exist: for example, assets socialized during collectivization are revalued in Soviet books but not in our accounts. Thus, our calculation illustrates, but does not reproduce, the effect on capital values of Soviet accounting methods.[8]

4. ANNUAL DEPRECIATION CHARGES

The depreciation charges implied by our calculations can be computed, for the most part, as the difference between gross and net investment in fixed capital, the latter being taken as the annual increment in the appropriate capital stock series.[9] For the years 1939–40, however, account must

---

6 See Table A–5.

7 Cf. Tables T–1, T–9, and T–10.

8 On the accounting methods referred to, see Petrov–61, p. 79, and Anonymous–58, p. 193. See also pp. 203–4 below.

9 The gross investment series are in Tables A–2, A–3, and A–4. The capital stock series are in the Tabular Section.

be taken, as in the stock estimates, of the effects of territorial acquisitions.[10] For straight-line depreciation charges, annual series in prices of 1937, 1928, and 1950 are presented in Table T–11. Results in 1937 prices for selected years are shown also in Table 3–1, which includes charges reckoned by other methods of depreciation. Depreciation under the retirement method is not shown, because the simplifications required in setting the retirement dates of assets in the initial stock distort the implicit depreciation series.[11]

TABLE 3-1

ANNUAL DEPRECIATION CHARGES ESTIMATED WITH ALTERNATIVE
DEPRECIATION METHODS, IN 1937 PRICES, SELECTED YEARS

	Depreciation Method	1928	1932	1937	1940	1945	1950	1955	1961
		A. Billion Rubles							
1.	Sinking Fund, $r = 20\%$	0.5	1.5	3.2	5.7	5.6	8.8	16.6	29.3
2.	Sinking Fund, $r = 8\%$	1.4	2.7	5.3	8.1	7.8	11.4	19.8	36.9
3.	Straight-Line	3.4	5.3	9.4	13.6	12.1	16.8	28.4	55.9
4.	Declining Annuity, $r = 20\%$	3.8	6.0	10.5	15.0	12.5	18.6	30.9	62.1
5.	Declining Annuity, $r = 8\%$	4.1	6.4	11.2	16.0	13.2	19.8	32.8	66.4
6.	Sum-of-Digits	4.5	7.0	12.1	17.3	13.8	21.0	35.3	72.6
		B. As Percent of Gross Value of Total Fixed Capital							
1.	Sinking Fund, $r = 20\%$	0.3	0.7	1.0	1.2	1.3	1.6	1.9	1.9
2.	Sinking Fund, $r = 8\%$	0.9	1.3	1.6	1.8	1.9	2.0	2.3	2.4
3.	Straight-Line	2.2	2.5	2.8	2.9	2.9	3.0	3.3	3.7
4.	Declining Annuity, $r = 20\%$	2.4	2.8	3.1	3.3	3.0	3.3	3.6	4.1
5.	Declining Annuity, $r = 8\%$	2.6	3.0	3.3	3.5	3.1	3.5	3.8	4.3
6.	Sum-of-Digits	2.9	3.2	3.6	3.8	3.3	3.8	4.1	4.8

Sources: See text.

Depreciation charges rise over time not only in response to the growth of the stock of fixed assets but also as the composition of the stock shifts toward assets with shorter lives. The shift is manifested primarily in the increased importance of equipment relative to structures but also within the equipment component. For example, in the initial stock, items such as railroad rolling stock and river and sea craft with 45-year service lives

---

10 For these years, depreciation is computed first from the capital stock figures unadjusted for acquired assets and from gross investment. The acquisitions of 1939 occurred near the end of the year (see Table 2–13), and the unadjusted depreciation figure is therefore used for 1939. The whole of the 1939 acquisitions were in the stock at the beginning of 1940, and the acquisitions made during 1940 occurred at roughly the middle of the year. The unadjusted depreciation for 1940 is therefore raised by 7.5 percent, the amount of the adjustment in the stock of January 1, 1940, plus approximately one half of the further adjustment in the stock for January 1, 1941.

11 In Table 3–1, depreciation as a percent of the gross value of the stock in 1940 is calculated from both stock and depreciation unadjusted for territorial acquisitions. The gross values of the stock in all other years are those of Table T–1.

account for over 40 percent of all equipment. The importance of long-lived equipment in annual investment since 1928, and hence in the post-1928 stock, is progressively less.[12] Because of changes in both the share and the composition of the equipment stock, depreciation charges relative to the gross value of assets rise over time (Table 3–1, Part B).

The change over time in the present values of assets under different depreciation methods and with different service lives is graphed in Chart 3–2. Changes in service lives do not affect at all the curves for present values

CHART 3–2

Capital Values with Alternative Depreciation Methods

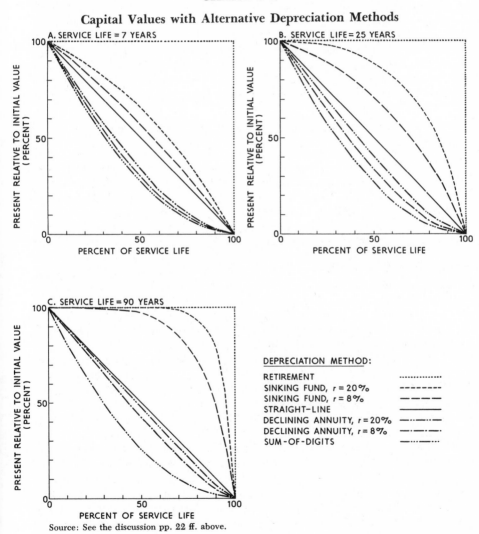

Source: See the discussion pp. 22 ff. above.

---

12 For the 1928 stock, see Table 2–5 of the present study; for investment, cf. Moorsteen–62, Table D–2.

computed with the retirement and straight-line methods and affect only slightly that computed with sum-of-digits. However, values computed by the sinking fund method resemble straight-line depreciated values for very short service lives but come increasingly to approach gross values (retirement method) as service lives lengthen. For the declining annuity method, a similar shift occurs, from the sum-of-digits curve toward the straight-line depreciation curve. Thus the shift over time toward assets with shorter lives is reflected in the relative rates of depreciation charges, the charges generated by the sinking fund method rising gradually relative to straight-line charges, those by the declining annuity method rising relative to sum-of-digits charges. As Chart 3–2 illustrates, the shift is much more marked for the sinking fund, as opposed to the declining annuity, method.

Relevant to the problem of acquisition-price accounting discussed in the preceding section, straight-line depreciation in acquisition prices can be calculated as 6.9 billion rubles in 1937 and 23.3 billion in 1950.[13] These figures amount to 73.4 percent in 1937 and 63.1 percent in 1950 of straight-line depreciation in the current prices of those two years.

5. NONAGRICULTURAL FIXED CAPITAL

Being global in scope, the investment data underlying our stock calculations do not readily lend themselves to estimates of the distribution of fixed assets by economic sector. We are able to make two basic estimates of this sort, one for the value of nonagricultural assets, which is described in this section, and one in which all fixed capital is distributed between the residential and nonresidential sectors, described in the next section. From these two, estimates for nonagricultural nonresidential assets are derived by simple arithmetic. Even for these series, the cost must be a perceptible diminution in reliability. The estimates are attempted, nonetheless, in part because circumstances of the calculation lead us to believe that for these sectors the risks of estimation are limited (and can be described), in part because the disaggregation seems of sufficient analytic interest to justify the additional hazard. Chart 3–3 presents graphically a portion of the results—for the net stock in 1937 prices.

The "nonagricultural" stock is defined to include all assets other than those used for agricultural production. It thus includes rural housing and assets which belong to agricultural enterprises but are used for nonagricultural purposes, such as cultural or industrial capital held by collective farms, excluding only productive structures and equipment employed for agricultural purposes.

The estimates are described in detail in Appendix D. The method consists essentially of estimating the real volume of annual investment for agricultural purposes in order to obtain, in the end, the stock of nonagricultural assets as a residual. In order to use the more reliable composite retirement and depreciation rates, however, we apply different procedures to structures and equipment. For the former, agricultural investment is subtracted from total investment in structures, and the residual investment

---

[13] The computation is made as for the constant-price series; net investment is derived from the stock figures in Table T–10.

CHART 3-3

Distribution of Net Fixed Capital by Sector, in 1937 Prices, 1928–62
(January 1—Billion Rubles)

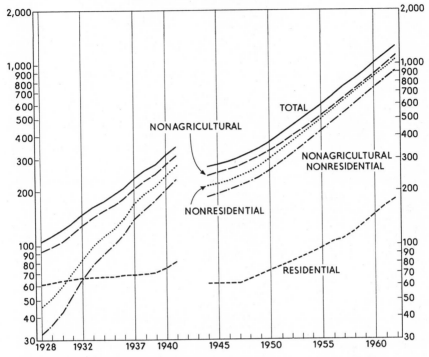

Sources: Tables T–1, T–12, T–15, T–16, and T–19.

series is cumulated together with the nonagricultural components of the initial stock to yield annual values for the stock of nonagricultural structures. For the latter, agricultural investment is cumulated, summed with present values of agricultural equipment in the initial stock, and the stock of nonagricultural equipment is determined as a residual by subtracting the agricultural stock from the total. Formally speaking, therefore, the calculations yield an estimate of agricultural capital as well, but the margin of error for this is difficult to delimit and may be large in relative terms, for which reason we do not report it among our findings. For the nonagricultural stock, on the other hand, the relative error is much reduced because of the smallness of agriculture's share in the total.

The crucial element in the calculation is the estimation of investment. For structures, we compile data from Soviet statistical sources on the distribution of annual construction between the agricultural and nonagricultural sectors. These distributions are applied to our estimates of total construction in 1937 prices to obtain a series for nonagricultural construction in those prices. The underlying distributions, however, are given in the sources in prices of years other than 1937. In the absence of information on changes over time in relative prices of structures, we make no adjustment for this disparity. Obviously, the procedure can yield correct results only to the extent that the implicit price indexes for investment in all and in nonagricultural structures have moved together. Given the preponderance of the latter in the former, the risks do not seem too great. According to our calculations, the agricultural share in the initial stock, in annual investment, and hence in the post-1928 stock of structures, has been generally between 10 and 15 percent.[14] Thus, unless relative prices of agricultural structures differed on average over time in one direction from the general price level of structures by something over 40 percent, which seems unlikely, the error produced in the nonagricultural stock of structures would not reach 5 percent.

For agricultural equipment, we compile data on investment in current prices for 1928–35 and effectively in current prices for 1956, obtaining values in 1937 prices by deflation. For intervening years, investment in 1937 prices is interpolated on an index of production (or, in the case of trucks, deliveries) in 1937 prices of machinery destined for agricultural use. For years beyond 1956, investment is extrapolated on an official series, as with total investment in equipment. Although imperfect in many respects, the resulting investment series should not be grossly in error. As agricultural equipment has typically accounted for about 15–25 percent of all investment in equipment,[15] the errors imparted to the nonagricultural residual are again correspondingly diminished.

Little of the equipment used in agriculture requires installation. Hence, the total stock of installation is ascribed to the nonagricultural sector.

The results of the computation in 1937 prices are given in detail, for both gross and net stocks, in Table T–12. The chief conclusion bearing on their reliability to which they point (see also Chart 3–3) is that the relative importance of nonagricultural fixed capital has remained virtually constant throughout the period studied at around 87–90 percent of the total. This means that nonagricultural growth rates are also about the same as for the total stock. At first glance, the outcome may seem at odds with the low priority generally accorded agriculture in Soviet economic policies. As will become evident subsequently, however, it appears differently when considered together with the behavior of other kinds of capital, notably livestock.[16]

The stock of nonagricultural fixed assets is also computed in prices of 1928 and 1950, by the same methods as those employed in the calculations just described (see Tables T–13 and T–14). The main ingredients are, again, initial stock and annual investment data for nonagricultural structures and for agricultural equipment, but valued now in the alternative prices. The calculation is also set forth in Appendix D. Briefly summarized, the initial stock data are those derived for our global calculations in 1928

---

[14] See Tables B–1 and D–8.

[15] See Table D–2.

[16] That agriculture's share in fixed capital investment remained relatively constant over time (at 16–19 percent) was noted much earlier by Norman Kaplan; see Kaplan-53, p. 53. On the stability of the share of agriculture in total fixed assets according to official Soviet statistics, see Chapter 7.

and 1950 prices, but with the appropriate exclusions, as indicated in Table B–1. For nonagricultural investment in structures, our global construction series in 1928 and 1950 prices are reduced by the same distributions used to derive nonagricultural investment in 1937 prices. For investment in agricultural equipment, the 1937-price series is deflated into 1928 and 1950 prices by appropriately weighted price index numbers for agricultural machines, tractors, trucks, and horse-drawn vehicles. Because we are unable to take account of differences in relative prices for agricultural and nonagricultural structures in the three weight years, and because our deflation of equipment is imperfect, the alternative price calculations reflect only part of the effects that complete reweighting would produce.

6. RESIDENTIAL AND NONRESIDENTIAL FIXED CAPITAL

Residential assets are defined as rural and urban housing, consisting therefore only of structures. Where a single building is used partially as a dwelling and partially for nondwelling purposes, only the former component is included in the residential stock. All other assets and the non-dwelling portion of mixed assets are counted nonresidential.

There are two main points of difference between the present calculation and that for nonagricultural assets described in the preceding section. The first is that the estimate for housing appears to be more reliable than that for agricultural capital, and, accordingly, we include the housing series among the findings of the study. The second is that the relative importance of housing in total fixed capital has at times been great, and its growth trends have often diverged markedly from those for nonresidential capital. Thus, errors in the housing estimate are more consequential for the nonresidential residual. For these reasons, the housing estimates and their subtraction from the totals are described here in some detail. Estimates gross and net, for residential and nonresidential assets, and in prices of all three weight years, are shown in Tables T–15 through T–18.

Gross and net values of the residential stock in 1937 prices are computed by the perpetual inventory method from the initial stock and estimates of annual gross investment, depreciation being calculated at straight line. The initial stock in 1928 prices[17] is deflated to 1937 prices by the separate index of housing costs obtained earlier: 265 in 1937 relative to 1928.[18] This, it should be noted, yields a 1937-price value of the initial housing stock different from the value at which housing enters into our total stock calculations; but, as has been explained, the apparent error in the latter is thought to be offset by other errors in the total stock estimates.[19] Housing in the initial stock is retired and depreciated as in the total. Annual investment also is depreciated (the period is not long enough for retirements to occur) in substantially the same way as in the total.[20] The same adjustment

---

17 Table B–1, columns 1 and 5.
18 See p. 61 above.
19 See p. 62.
20 Investment is depreciated at 1.52 percent per annum, which is the rate implied by the 1934 distribution of investment in housing by wall materials (Table C–3) and the corresponding service lives (Table 2–10).

for territorial changes and war losses are applied.[21] The new element required for the calculations is, then, the estimates of annual investment in housing.

Table 3–2 shows the derivation of the investment estimates. The data in physical units for housing constructed (or restored) and put into operation (columns 1–3) are taken directly from Soviet sources. The figures for urban housing refer to floor space used for dwelling purposes only, exclusive of those portions of buildings devoted to nonresidential uses. No similar distinction is possible with respect to rural houses, but, as will appear, the method of valuation employed is such as to imply that the nondwelling portion in rural houses built since 1928 is proportionately the same as in the stock of rural dwellings at the beginning of 1928.

TABLE 3-2

DERIVATION OF ANNUAL GROSS INVESTMENT IN RESIDENTIAL FIXED
CAPITAL IN 1937 PRICES, 1928-61

	Housing Constructed (or Restored) and Put into Operation				Annual Investment
	Socialized Urban	Private Urban	Private Rural	Total Value	(Billion Rubles; 1937 Prices)
	(Million Square Meters of Floor Space)		(Million Houses)	(Billion Rubles; 1937 Prices)	
	(1)	(2)	(3)	(4)	(5)
1928	--	--	--	--	2.5
1929-32.	32.6	6.1	0.6	2.5*	2.5
1933-37.	37.2	5.0	0.8	2.3*	2.3
1938-41 (1st Half) . . .	34.4	7.6	1.3	3.4*	3.4
1941 (2nd Half)-45 . .	41.3	8.5	1.8	3.3*	1.7
1946	12.6	4.8		4.8	2.4
1947	11.8	6.4		4.9	4.9
1948	14.7	6.4	0.54*	5.6	5.6
1949	15.5	6.4		5.8	5.8
1950	17.8	6.4		6.4	6.4
1951	20.3	7.3		7.0	7.0
1952	20.0	7.4		6.9	6.9
1953	23.2	7.6	0.46*	7.8	7.8
1954	24.4	8.1		8.1	8.1
1955	25.0	8.4		8.3	8.3
1956	29.5	11.5	0.5	10.0	10.0
1957	38.5	13.5	0.8	13.1	13.1
1958	46.7	24.5	0.7	16.7	16.7
1959	53.5	27.2	0.8	18.9	18.9
1960	55.8	27.0	0.6	19.1	19.1
1961	56.8	23.4	0.5	18.6	18.6

* Average annual value.

Sources: For columns 1–3, 1929–45, TsSU–61a, p. 191; 1946–55, *loc. cit.* and TsSU–57, p. 176; 1956–61, TsSU–62, p. 378. For columns 4 and 5, see text.

Total values in 1937 prices (column 4) of the indicated physical quantities are obtained by estimating for each of the three categories unit values in 1928 at 1928 prices, from stock data for January 1 of that year, and raising the unit values for each by the 1937/1928 housing cost index of

21 That is, the unadjusted stock is assumed to increase by 5 percent and 10 percent because of the territorial acquisitions of 1939 and 1940, respectively. War losses are put at 25 percent of the capital extant as of the middle of 1941. See Chapter 2, Section 6.

265.[22] Annual investment (column 5) is obtained with limited modifications from column 4: 1928 is assumed equal to the 1929–32 annual average; within the periods of several years duration, annual investment is assumed equal to the annual average (i.e., investment in each year from 1929 to 1932 is taken as 2.5 billion, in each year from 1933 to 1937 as 2.3 billion, etc.); investment from the second half of 1941 to 1946 is assumed equal to only half of the column 4 figures, to allow for the inclusion in the physical quantity data of the restoration of war-damaged houses as well as new construction.

Conceptually, the direct valuation of physical units is an appropriate way to measure investment, but the data and our procedures are both quite coarse. The data for physical quantities take no account of quality changes within the three categories, although a partial adjustment is effected by their separate weighting. The use of annual averages smooths the annual investment series in a manner which can hardly correspond to reality. For purposes of computing a stock, however, especially where, as in the present case, annual investment is small relative to the initial stock, the smoothing is of limited consequence. The size of the adjustment made for the inclusion of restored housing is arbitrary. According to the sources, moreover, such inclusions continued through 1950, although we suppose that new construction dominated the totals beyond 1946. Again, the results are not very sensitive to these procedures, because of the smallness of annual investment relative to the stock: the adjustment could be varied by half or the same adjustment could be extended to 1948 without affecting the stock by more than 5 percent. Because of the restriction of the quantity data to housing put into operation, annual investment excludes housing projects still in progress although the initial stock data may include them.[23]

For purposes of appraising the housing calculations, the main findings are these (see Table T–15 or Chart 3–3): (*i*) The rate of growth in the prewar period was limited, much below that for all fixed assets. From 1928 to 1939, the gross stock increases by 30 percent, an average annual rate of 2.4 percent. This means that by the beginning of 1939 over 75 percent of existing housing was still from the initial stock. Housing grows more rapidly from 1939 to 1941, but the increase reflects mainly territorial acqui-

---

[22] Gross values in 1928 prices of the stock of each kind of housing on January 1, 1928, are given in Table B–1, column 5. These values are believed to refer only to residential portions of the buildings in question. The questionnaire of the 1926 census, on which the urban housing figures are probably based, specifically excludes floor space used for nondwelling purposes (see TsSU–27, pp. 3–11). The peasant budget studies, from which the rural housing figures were probably drawn, divide the value of peasant structures by use (see TsSU–29, pp. 22 ff.). Stocks in physical units are, for urban floor space, from Table 3–3; the number of private rural houses is taken as 25.6 million or the same as the number of peasant households (see Bogoliubskii–29, p. 32). Values in 1928 prices divided by the number of physical units yield 1928 unit values. The latter raised to 1937 prices are 248 rubles per square meter of floor space for socialized urban housing, 157 rubles per square meter of floor space for private urban housing, and 1762 rubles per house for private rural housing. For 1946–55, only annual average physical data for rural construction are available, and the annual values are assumed equal to the averages.

[23] See p. 96 following.

sitions. Thus, throughout the prewar period, the dominant elements in the calculation are the initial stock and the adjustments for territorial change. (*ii*) The net stock grows more slowly in the prewar period than the gross, increasing only 15 percent from 1928 to 1939, an annual average rate of 1.3 percent. This is in contrast to the total stock, for which the ratio of net to gross is more or less constant, but is consistent with the fact that gross investment in housing grew more slowly than total gross investment. (*iii*) The acceleration in gross investment in housing in the postwar period is reflected in a marked increase in the growth of the housing stock, whether measured net or gross. The low ratio of net to gross which emerged at the end of the prewar period, together with the postwar acceleration in gross investment, results in a more rapid rate of growth for the net than the gross stock. Where relevant, further reference to these considerations will be made in the discussion following.

The various physical data used in the housing stock calculation may be judged with reference to the material in Table 3-3. Columns 1–3 show

TABLE 3-3

GROSS RESIDENTIAL FIXED CAPITAL ESTIMATED BY ALTERNATIVE
METHODS, IN 1937 PRICES, SELECTED YEARS
(January 1)

	Physical Stock (Million Square Meters of Floor Space)			Gross Value (Billion Rubles)	
	Socialized Urban	Private Urban	Private Rural	By Valuing Physical Data in Columns 1-3	By Perpetual Inventory
	(1)	(2)	(3)	(4)	(5)
1928	109	121	722	91.2	91.2
1929	114	124	731	93.4	93.7
1933	138	126	713	98.6	103.7
1936	187	120	680	107.7	110.6
1941	267	154	802	140.5	137.9
1951	340	173	449	139.5	137.4
1956	432	208	447	167.7	175.5
1960	541	355	430	216.8	212.9
1962	625	389	427	242.8	240.0

Sources: For columns 1 and 2, 1928 and 1929 are interpolated from October 1 data in Gosplan–30, p. 518; data for 1933 are from Gosplan–36, p. 554; for 1936 from Kobalevskii–40, p. 106; for 1941, 1951, and 1956, from TsSU–57, p. 177; for 1960 and 1962 from TsSU–62, p. 382. The sources cited for 1928, 1929, 1933, and 1936 give data for dwelling space. Following Nimitz–62, p. 169, we take 0.7 square meters of dwelling space to equal one square meter of floor space (floor space includes and dwelling space excludes so-called auxiliary areas such as corridors, stairways, kitchens, etc.). For column 3, floor space is estimated from the rural population and the assumption of 5.9 square meters per capita in the prewar period, 3.96 in the postwar. The population data are from Eason–59, p. 84, and TsSU–62, p. 29. The prewar per capita figure is from Tarasov–27, p. 336, and is indicated to refer to 1926. The postwar figure is from Strumilin–60, p. 141, which gives the rural housing stock "in 1959" as 430 million square meters. We take the figure to refer to the end of the year. For column 4, see text. For column 5, see Table T–15.

the stock of housing in physical units at various dates. The figures for socialized and private urban housing are taken more or less directly from Soviet sources. Those for 1928 and 1960 reflect the findings of urban housing censuses conducted at the end of 1926 and 1959, respectively. For the remaining years, the figures must be estimates, since no other housing census is known to have occurred.[24] The figure for rural housing in 1960 is also quoted directly from a Soviet source, while the figure for 1928 is obtained by applying a Soviet estimate of rural per capita floor space in 1926 to the 1928 rural population. For the remaining years, the figures are obtained from data on the rural population and the assumption that per capita floor space was at the 1926 level throughout the prewar period, at the 1960 level throughout the postwar period. The figures imply a decline in rural per capita floor space from 5.9 square meters prewar to about 4 square meters postwar and, also, a persisting decline in the total stock of rural housing interrupted only by the territorial acquisitions of 1939–40. In part, both tendencies may be associated with the reclassification from "rural" to "urban" of specific localities as population density increased and with unrecouped war losses. Nonetheless, the contrast between prewar and postwar seems unexpectedly sharp. None of the data result from direct enumeration and the possibility of error must be substantial.

In column 4 of Table 3–3, the physical stock data of columns 1–3 are valued in 1937 prices.[25] This series is conceptually equivalent to the gross values computed by the perpetual inventory method. For comparison, the latter are repeated in column 5. The two series are very close to each other, differing by as much as 5 percent only in 1933 and 1956. Similarity of this degree must in part be coincidental. Also, since both calculations use the same unit values, the observed similarity is significant only with respect to the two sets of underlying physical data. For these, however, the comparison indicates mutual consistency and suggests a greater degree of reliability than would be indicated by their derivations alone. In particular, it is noted that the physical stock data in Table 3–3 for 1928 and 1960 are independent both of each other and of the physical data and assumptions entering the perpetual inventory calculation. The latter, as will be recalled, depends on figures for new housing construction and also on highly simplified assumptions concerning the service lives of housing in the initial stock and the consequences of territorial expansion and war damage. The comparison made in Table 3–3 indicates that these do not produce results grossly in conflict with what is known of the physical stock, measured more directly.

The unit prices used for valuation in both calculations are derived from our initial stock estimates. As has already been explained, the relia-

---

24 One consequence of the 1959 census was that previously published estimates of urban housing for January 1, 1959, were revised from 524 to 500 million meters for socialized, from 257 to 332 million meters for private (compare TsSU–59, p. 641, and TsSU–61, p. 613). The figures shown in Table 3–3 for 1951 and 1956 are from precensus sources and quite possibly are subject to revision as well, though no revised figures for these years have yet appeared.

25 For socialized and private urban housing, the prices per square meter are the same as those used in the perpetual inventory calculation; see footnote 22, p. 89, above. For rural housing, the price is also the same as that used previously, but expressed now in terms of price per square meter rather than per house. Thus the gross value of rural housing in 1928 prices on January 1, 1928, 17,025 million rubles, is divided by the stock in square meters, 722 million, to yield the average unit value, 23.6 rubles. See Table B–1, column 5, and Table 3–3 for the underlying data. Multiplying by the 1937/1928 price index number for housing, 265, we obtain the 1937 reproduction cost, 62.5 rubles per square meter.

bility of the latter is open to question. Furthermore, even if essentially correct, they reflect the price *structure* of 1928 rather than 1937. How this structure might have changed between 1928 and 1937 is uncertain. The available data are scanty and ambiguous, and, even if they were not, they would be difficult to interpret, because different socioeconomic groups of builders purchased inputs in different markets, with the result that relative costs probably did not reflect producers' or users' substitution rates. The square meter values we have used for socialized urban, private urban, and private rural housing are in approximately the ratios 100/63/25. We can gain some notion of the sensitivity of the calculation to the weights by varying these ratios. For this purpose, we have revalued the physical stock data of Table 3–3, using, in addition to the above ratios, those of 100/80/40 and 100/40/15. These alternatives are arbitrarily chosen. They illustrate but need not bound the difference that might be produced by more appropriate weighting. For all intervals, the weights of 100/80/40 show the slowest rate of growth, those of 100/40/15 the most rapid, while the weights used in our calculation produce intermediate magnitudes. For the interval 1928–36, the three annual average rates are 1.4, 2.1, and 3.0 percent, respectively. The variation in relative terms is considerable, but the calculations agree that the prewar growth of housing before the territorial acquisitions was modest, much below the growth rates we have computed for fixed assets generally. For the latter, gross values increase by 8.4 percent annually over the same interval (Table T–1). After 1936, the variation in weights matters less. The increments in the housing stock for 1936–41 are 28, 30, and 33 percent, respectively; for 1941–51, −8, −1, and +6 percent, respectively. For 1951–62, the average annual growth rates are 4.8, 5.2, and 5.3 percent, in all cases markedly above the corresponding rates for 1928–36 and closer to the rates for all fixed capital, which, measured gross, increased over the same interval at 9.6 percent annually. For the entire period 1928–62, the three sets of weights yield annual growth rates of 2.4, 2.9, and 3.5 percent, respectively.

The considerations just presented, concerning the physical and unit value data underlying the housing calculation, insofar as they support the finding of low growth in gross residential investment before the war followed by marked acceleration after the war, tend also to confirm the changing ratios of net to gross in the value of the housing stock.[26]

The growth of the stock of fixed capital is sharply altered during the prewar period by the exclusion of housing (see Table T–16 or Chart 3–3). At the beginning of 1928, housing accounted for almost 60 percent of all fixed assets, but by 1941 this share had declined to around one quarter. As a result, the 1928–41 average annual growth rate for fixed capital is changed by the exclusion of housing from 9.7 to 14.8 percent, measured net, or from 9.4 to 14.0 percent, measured gross. This calculation i   .. very sensitive to the relative valuation of different kinds of housing. As was noted above, in the prewar period the housing stock calculation is dominated by the treatment of the initial stock and the adjustment for

---

[26] With respect further to the reliability of the housing estimates, reference should be made to the discussion of official data in Chapter 7.

territorial acquisitions. Thus, what is now subtracted varies in direct proportion to the values which represented housing in our original global calculation, that is, the present values computed for the housing items in the initial stock. Errors in the relative valuation of different kinds of housing in the initial stock are common to both the global and housing series and are eliminated, rather than compounded, when the latter is subtracted.

The subtraction, nonetheless, raises a problem of valuation, because the nonresidential residual is affected by the *absolute* value placed on housing. The latter, as will be recalled, is derived from 1928 values and an estimate of the change in housing costs between 1928 and 1937. Thus, errors in the cost index produce proportional errors in the absolute value of the housing stock, and, in consequence, affect both the absolute value and rate of growth of the stock of nonresidential assets. If the cost index, 265, were in error by as much as, say, 25 points in either direction, the variation in the absolute value of the net nonresidential residual would amount to about 13 percent in 1928, declining thereafter to about 4 percent by 1937, 3 percent by 1941, less than 2 percent by 1962. The growth rate of the nonresidential stock, then, is affected mainly in the years 1928–37 but little thereafter. For the interval 1928–37, the observed growth rate for the net nonresidential stock, 15.7 percent per annum, would vary by as much as 1.4 percentage points; that for 1937–62, on the other hand, by about 0.1 percentage points.

For the postwar period, the exclusion of housing produces relatively small changes in growth. From 1950 to 1962, total fixed assets increase annually by 10.5 percent, measured net, or 9.6 percent, measured gross, whereas, with housing excluded, the corresponding rates are 11.0 and 10.6 percent. The reasons are the dwindling relative importance of housing in the total and the acceleration in the rate at which the housing stock increased. For these reasons, too, the sensitivity of the nonresidential residual to errors in the housing calculation is quite limited.

To provide values in 1928 prices, the housing series in 1937 prices is deflated by the 1937/1928 index of 265. We assume that after 1937 housing costs moved with costs of construction generally. To obtain values in 1950 prices, therefore, values in 1937 prices are multiplied by the price index number implied by our estimates of 1950 construction in 1937 and 1950 prices, 250 with 1937 = 100.[27] Housing in 1928 and 1950 prices is then subtracted from the corresponding totals to obtain nonresidential fixed capital. Our procedures here, it may be noted, imply that changes over time in residential capital are the same in the prices of all three weight years. The behavior of the nonresidential residuals, in the three sets of prices, hence, varies with the value of housing relative to other assets in the weight years and with the behavior over time of the fixed capital totals.

The housing estimates also permit us to calculate the value of nonagricultural nonresidential assets, by subtracting residential from nonagricultural capital. Series of this scope are shown in Tables T–19 to T–21 (see also Chart 3–3). The problems of estimation are those in combination of the series employed for the calculation. Because the nonagricultural non-

---

[27] See Tables A–2 and A–5.

residential residual is smaller, however, it is more sensitive to errors in the housing estimates than is the nonresidential residual.

7. ASSETS IN PLACE VERSUS ASSETS AVAILABLE FOR OPERATION

Our method of estimating the fixed capital stock yields values for capital in place. The main difference between this and capital available for operation is the stock of investment projects begun but not yet completed, projects in progress. From an analytic point of view, assets of the latter sort are clearly inventories, since they are the goods in process of the construction industry. To treat them as such in deriving our fixed capital estimates, however, would be extremely complicating and would require much more detailed information than is available. It seems in order, nevertheless, to establish, as nearly as the data permit, the size of investment projects in progress and, hence, the quantitative implications of reclassifying them. The next paragraphs describe briefly the estimates we have made, the numerical results of which are shown in Tables T–25 to T–36.[28] Details of the calculations are explained in Appendix E.

For several years, 1933–35 and 1951–61, official statistics are available on "unfinished construction." This is a Soviet accounting category closely akin to investment projects in progress, and the data permit a reasonable estimate of the value of the latter category in acquisition prices.[29] The figures thus obtained for 1933–35 are extended backward to 1928 by means of official data on the volume of "unfinished construction" in industry, a sector accounting typically for something over half of the national total, and forward to 1938 by means of data comparing investments made with investments completed. The reliability of the estimates for 1928–32 and 1936–38 is substantially less than for 1933–35 or 1951–61, but they are at least derived from data which are independent of the annual investment (and hence capital stock) series and, accordingly, present a source of independent information on the difference between capital in place and capital available for operation.

For all years, the data just described are in acquisition prices. They are deflated into constant prices by implicit deflators derived from the annual investment series. For this purpose, it is assumed that the stock of projects in progress consists essentially of work begun during the preceding two years, though with the proportion of work carried over from the later year greater by 50 percent. These assumptions are quite conjectural. Some trial calculations (not reproduced here) using carry-overs in various proportions

---

[28] In these tables, total net fixed capital is distributed between capital available for operation and investment projects in progress, for all sectors and for the subsectors for which we make estimates, in prices of all three weight years.

[29] The scope of "unfinished construction" is explained in Appendix E. In broad terms, it coincides with projects in progress in including most construction, installation, and equipment outlays belonging to the latter category. "Unfinished construction" is broader, in that it includes some outlays for "other" investment, which, as is explained in Section 3 of Chapter 2, we exclude from fixed capital, and some projects actually, though not formally, in operation; narrower, in that it excludes some outlays for equipment not yet available for operation.

from three preceding years suggest that the stock of projects in progress in constant prices might vary by 10 percent or more if other equally plausible assumptions were employed.

For 1939–41, 1944–50, and 1962, we have no independent data on projects in progress. In order to provide annual capital stock series of consistent scope, estimates of projects in progress have been made for these years as well by extrapolating on the fixed investment series. The extrapolations may provide a rough but reasonable basis for distributing our totals between fixed capital and inventories, but they do not provide additional independent information on the difference between capital in place and capital available for operation.

The main findings with respect to projects in progress are summarized in Table 3–4, which shows capital available for operation as a share of capital in place in the years for which the estimates are not extrapolated

TABLE 3-4

TOTAL NET FIXED CAPITAL AVAILABLE FOR OPERATION AS A SHARE OF
CAPITAL IN PLACE, IN 1937 PRICES, 1928-38 AND 1951-61
(January 1--Percent)

Prewar		Postwar	
1928	97	1951	92
1929	96	1952	91
1930	95	1953	90
1931	93	1954	90
1932	92	1955	90
1933	92	1956	90
1934	93	1957	90
1935	93	1958	90
1936	94	1959	91
1937	95	1960	91
1938	95	1961	91

Source: Computed from Table T-25.

on investment. The data employed are in 1937 prices and refer to net values. If gross values were used, the differences between the two series would be less because projects in progress, which . ·e undepreciated in either case, are smaller relative to gross than to net values.[30] As may be ascertained from the series in Tables T–26 and T–27, the use of 1928 or 1950 prices would present largely the same picture as that drawn with 1937 prices.

The figures show capital available for operation to have ranged from 90 to 97 percent of capital in place. The average for the postwar period is somewhat below the prewar, but, if allowance is made for the roughness of the calculation, it is not clear that the difference is significant. The same must certainly apply to the trends indicated within the prewar and postwar periods. It is interesting to note, nevertheless, that these accord with what is known otherwise of accumulations of projects awaiting completion: the problem was considered most intense in the first part of the

---

[30] That is, the official data and hence our estimates of projects in progress are for undepreciated values. In the derivation of our stock estimates, annual investment is depreciated from the following January 1, whether or not it has by that date become available for operation.

1930's and again in the mid-1950's. For our purpose, the main significance of the calculation is the general magnitude of the level of capital available for operation and the indication that growth rates of fixed capital, whether for short or long intervals, would be little affected by substituting one concept for the other. It needs to be added, however, that capital available for operation is not the same as—and must by some margin exceed—capital actually in operation. We have no data for the latter.

The estimates of projects in progress are not distributed by kind of asset: data for 1958 indicate that structures and installation accounted for about 85 percent of the total in that year.[31] Distributions by sector are made, although they are unavoidably rough. In the prewar years for which data are available, 1933–35, agriculture accounted for about 6 percent of "unfinished construction" and hence, presumably, of projects in progress.[32] In postwar years, collective farms alone accounted for 3–5 percent of "unfinished construction."[33] Judging from relative volumes of capital investment, the figure for state agricultural enterprises and organizations would be of similar magnitude.[34] On the basis of these data, we assume that the nonagricultural sectors accounted for 94 percent of projects in progress in the prewar period, 92 percent in the postwar period. As previously explained, our estimates of the stock of housing are compiled from investment data for houses "put into operation." Our initial stock data for housing, on the other hand, may include projects in progress at the beginning of 1928. Thus, for the first year or two of the period studied, our housing series may correspond more to capital in place, but thereafter it must refer to capital available for operation. For this reason, we allot none of the estimated total of projects in progress to housing. Such projects in the nonagricultural nonresidential sectors, then, correspond to those in the nonagricultural sectors.

8. AVERAGE AGE

The age of a capital stock may be computed as an arithmetic mean, in which the age of each asset is weighted by its present value. There are, therefore, several possible measures, depending upon the prices and depreciation formula used to establish present values. One such calculation is made here, employing as weights gross values in 1937 prices.[35]

We define the average age simply as $\Sigma V_i a_i / \Sigma V_i$, where the V_i's are present gross values of individual assets and the a_i's are their ages. For assets created since January 1, 1928, the information required is readily available. The present values are those described previously, while the ages are the differences between the year in question and the year of acquisition, as indicated by the annual investment data. For the initial stock, the average age of each of the 31 classes of assets is obtained from the following identity:

---

[31] See Appendix E, p. 448.

[32] See TsUNKhU–36, p. 393.

[33] See Appendix E, p. 447.

[34] Cf. TsSU–61a, p. 155.

[35] An additional calculation, with net value weights but of incomplete coverage and for 1962 only, is described below.

$$A_k = n[1 - (T'_k/T_k)], \tag{11}$$

where A_k is the gross value weighted average age at the beginning of year k of a stock of assets with service life n (the stock being one in which none of the assets are older than k years), while T'_k and T_k respectively are the net (straight-line depreciated) and gross values of the stock at the beginning of year k.

That expression (11) holds for a single asset is no doubt obvious. It also holds for stocks of assets of different ages, provided all the assets have, when new, the same expected service life. Let V'_{rs} and V_{rs} respectively stand for the net and gross values at the beginning of the sth year since r of the assets that were new at the beginning of r. Then we may also write the following:

$$V'_{rs} = [V'_{r0}][1 - (s/n)], \tag{12}$$

from the straight-line depreciation formula,

$$V_{rs} = V_{r0} = V'_{r0}, \tag{13}$$

because gross values always equal initial values, and

$$T'_k = \sum_{i=0}^{k} V'_{i,k-i} = \sum_{i=0}^{k} [V_{i,0}]\{1 - [(k-i)/n]\} \tag{14}$$

$$= \sum_{i=0}^{k} V_{i,0} - (1/n)\{ \sum_{i=0}^{k} (V_{i,0})(k-i)\}$$

$$= T_k - (T_k/n)\{ [\sum_{i=0}^{k} (V_{i,0})(k-i)]/T_k\}.$$

But the last expression is a summation of the products of gross value times age, divided by total gross value—the average age, gross value weighted. Thus, from expression (14), we also have

$$T'_k = T_k[1 - (1/n)(A_k)], \tag{15}$$

and

$$A_k = n[1 - (T'_k/T_k)]. \tag{16}$$

Thus, the average age calculation proceeds from the same information and assumptions as the estimates of the gross value of the stock. The deficiencies of the latter calculation should be kept in mind, since they also find their reflection in the estimates of age.

In particular, if the initial stock estimates tend to overstate the ratio of net to gross value, the age computed for 1928 is too low. An error of the same direction would affect the calculations for later years as well, but to a continually lessening degree, and the observed rate of decline in average age would be understated. Secondly, the fact that we do not systematically distribute retirements over time for each kind of asset affects the calculation of average age. Although it is not possible to deduce the direction of error on purely a priori grounds, in a rapidly growing stock the tendency is probably toward overstatement of the average age. If assets are withdrawn gradually, our use of average service lives for broad classes of assets tends to overstate the value of assets of intermediate age, understating assets of greatest age. With rapidly growing investment, the former bulk much larger than the latter. Thirdly, errors in estimated service lives produce errors of like direction in the age estimates. It should be noted, too, that we make no allowance for the effects on average age of territorial acquisitions or war losses. This is tantamount to assuming that the capital acquired through expansion was of the same age as that in the old territory and that war losses fell equally on capital in all age groups. Judging from the relative growth rates of the Soviet Union and its pre-expansion neighbors and from the geographical distribution of prewar Soviet development, the former assumption probably tends to understate, the latter to overstate, average age in the affected years.

The results of the calculation are shown in Table T–22 and Chart 3–4. For capital in place at the beginning of 1928, the average age of structures was 18.5 years, of equipment 8.8 years, and of the entire stock 17.3 years, reflecting the preponderance of structures in the total.[36] It was argued in Section 4 of Chapter 2 that these ages probably are understated, though the matter is difficult to judge. The creation of new assets from the time of the Revolution until the mid-1920's was undoubtedly modest. On the

CHART 3–4

Average Age of Total Fixed Capital, Gross Value Weights, in 1937 Prices, 1928–62

(January 1—Years)

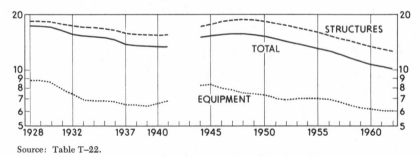

Source: Table T–22.

other hand, there was a considerable resumption of gross investment during 1925–27. Thus, the stock at the beginning of 1928 can almost be described in terms of the two groups of assets, one group created before 1918, all members of which, therefore, would be older than ten years, and a second group created during 1925–27 with an average age, therefore, of two years or less. In very rough terms, the latter group may have accounted for one sixth or so of the total stock of fixed capital at the beginning of 1928.[37] The average age of the fixed assets extant at the beginning of 1918

---

[36] For completeness, we include in Table T–22 the results calculated for installation, even though their significance is essentially limited to rounding out the picture conveyed by the totals. They are omitted from the chart.

[37] Capital values are taken gross. The proportion is impressionistic. From Gosplan–28, pp. 518–21, it appears that gross capital investment from the last quarter of 1924 until the beginning of 1928 amounted to about 12 billion 1925/26 rubles, while the net value

is, of course, unknown, but must have exceeded 15 years.[38] The attritions suffered between 1918 and 1928 must have been greatest for older assets. Even so, the average age of the assets remaining from 1918 must, by 1928, have been 25 years or more. This suggests a lower bound for the age of the entire 1928 stock of around 21 years,[39] as compared with our computation of 17.3 years. The implication for our calculations, then, is one of understatement. If the initial stock ages are understated, ages for subsequent years will also be affected in the same direction, though to a smaller extent as the importance of the initial relative to the total stock declines. The ages computed for, say, 1962 would scarcely be affected. The further implication is that our calculations also understate the rate at which the average age has declined.

The average age of each component of the stock declined continuously from 1928 until the last few years of the prewar period, with the average for the total declining (absolutely) more rapidly than either part as the relative importance of equipment, the more youthful component, increased.[40] The low rates of investment during and just after the war resulted in an increase in average age which continued only until 1945 for equipment, until 1948 for structures, and until 1947 for the stock as a whole. Although age declined continuously after these turning points, the minimum prewar levels were not regained until 1958, 1956, and 1955, respectively. By 1962, the average ages were below the prewar minimums by about 18 percent for structures, only 6 percent for equipment, but 25 percent for all fixed capital.

Average age could also be measured using present net values as weights, but the calculation would require information on the age distribution of assets within the 31 classes of the initial stock. In contrast to the measurement using gross value weights, the average age within these classes cannot be read from the relationship of net to gross value. We therefore make no separate calculation for the trend in the net value weighted average. However, the effect of shifting weights on the absolute magnitude of the average age may be illustrated from data for that portion of the total stock on January 1, 1962, which was generated by investment occurring from 1928 through 1961. For this portion, 1962 average ages with gross value weights were 9.0 years for structures, 5.9 for equipment, and 7.9 for all fixed capital, or considerably lower than ages computed inclusive of the relatively

---

of the stock of fixed capital at the beginning of 1928 was about 54 billion rubles in the same prices (on data from this source, cf. fn. 47, p. 52). If the ratio of net to gross was, say, 70 percent (cf. Table 2–5), the gross value would be about 77 billion rubles, of which something less than 16 percent had come from investment of the preceding 3¼ years.

38 At that time, Russian assets would have been mainly long-lived—structures and railroad rolling stock. The figure of 15 years is highly conjectural but is surely on the low side. By 1962, for example, after a considerable period of high and rapidly rising gross investment, the average age of the stock of structures was still about 13 years.

39 The weighted average of a stock of assets, one sixth having an age of two years, five sixths an age of 25 years.

40 The calculations show slight increases in the age of equipment after 1939 and in structures after 1940. Since the magnitudes involved are small and the calculations subject to error, these may not be true turning points, but whether they represent a reversal or merely a slackening in the rate of decline, they do reflect a significant phenomenon, the reduction in the rate of growth of gross investment in the late 1930's.

TABLE 3-5

DISTRIBUTION OF TOTAL FIXED CAPITAL AVAILABLE FOR OPERATION,
GROSS AND NET, BY PERIOD OF ACQUISITION, IN 1937 PRICES,
SELECTED YEARS
(January 1--Percent of Total)

	1928	1932	1937	1941	1945	1950	1953	1955	1958	1962
				A. Gross Values						
Assets Created before January 1, 1928. . .	100	77	48	35	30	23	17	14	9	4
Assets Created from January 1, 1928 to June 30, 1941	0	23	52	65	61	43	34	28	21	14
Assets Created from July 1, 1941 to January 1, 1962. . .	0	0	0	0	9	34	49	58	70	81
Total	100	100	100	100	100	100	100	100	100	100
Of Which, Assets 7 Years Old or Less	--	--	48	43	34	31	42	47	52	57
				B. Net Values						
Assets Created before January 1, 1928 . .	100	68	35	21	17	10	6	4	2	1
Assets Created from January 1, 1928 to June 30, 1941	0	32	65	79	71	45	32	25	16	9
Assets Created from July 1, 1941 to January 1, 1962. . .	0	0	0	0	13	45	62	71	82	90
Total	100	100	100	100	100	100	100	100	100	100

Source: See text.

minor (see Table 3–5) but quite aged assets surviving from the beginning of 1928. Average ages with net value weights, for the 1962 stock resulting from 1928–61 investment, were 7.5 years for structures, 4.1 for equipment, and 6.3 for the total stock, or 17 percent, 30 percent, and 20 percent less than the corresponding ages with gross weights.

The discussion thus far has been limited to capital in place, since it is only for this concept that our data are sufficient to indicate differences in the trend of average ages by kind of asset. For all assets taken together, however, we may also compute the average age, with gross weights, of capital available for operation.[41] The results are shown in the last column of Table T–22. As would be anticipated, they are slightly above, but move together with, the averages for capital in place. Periods in which there were especially large accumulations of unfinished investment projects, such as the early 1930's and mid-1950's, are marked by a widening of the difference.

Some further information on the age composition of fixed capital is

---

[41] The calculation is made on the assumption, stated on p. 94 above, that 40 percent of projects in progress consist of work done during the second year before a given January 1 (and, thus, having an average age of one year) and 60 percent of work done in the immediately preceding year (with an average age of zero). This permits us to subtract the projects in progress component from both the numerator and the denominator of the average age as defined on p. 96.

presented in Table 3–5, which shows the relative importance within all capital available for operation of assets created during three periods: the years before 1928, the period from the beginning of 1928 until the outbreak of the war (mid-1941), and the period after mid-1941. The choice of periods stems mainly from the organization of our calculations, though we believe it is not without intrinsic interest. The first grouping contains largely assets inherited from prerevolutionary Russia, as repaired and expanded in the years just prior to the Five-Year Plans. The second includes the period of the prewar Five-Year Plans, during which new assets, often crude but produced in the Soviet era, came to dominate the total. The third refers essentially to the postwar period and undoubtedly contains the more technologically sophisticated forms of capital. The tabulation also shows one other grouping which emerges readily from our data, the share of total capital aged seven years or less. The findings speak for themselves and need not be summarized here.

Chapter 4

Livestock

1. INTRODUCTION

The value of capital in livestock is calculated from stocks measured in physical units—in which respect the calculation is unique among our estimates—and from average realized prices in each of the three weight years, 1937, 1928, and 1950. The estimates take account of changes over time in the average weight of animals in the herds but not of other qualitative changes such as in age or breed. They include cows, other cattle, hogs, sheep, goats, and horses, but omit rabbits, fowl, bees, camels, mules, buffaloes, and the like. The results are given in Table T–23 and Chart 4–1.

The herd values we compute are to be interpreted as net values. Livestock are subject to depreciation in the sense that the true present value per liveweight pound of animal typically decreases with age. The average realized prices used here for herd valuations reflect prices paid per pound in marketings of animals of different ages, net in all cases, necessarily, of past depreciation. These prices are taken also to represent on average the present values of animals still on the hoof. Accordingly, the herd values derived are also net of depreciation. This means that for this component we proceed to net values without determining gross values or depreciation.

The various kinds of data entering the calculation are described in the remaining sections of this chapter. It may be well to make clear at the outset, however, that the results are of a provisional character. The data on livestock numbers are believed, on the whole, to be reliable. The adjustments for weight, while rough, are limited in magnitude and unlikely to form a major source of error, the immediate postwar years possibly excepted. The chief weakness of the calculation lies in the valuations. While we follow established convention in employing average realized prices, the institutional circumstances in which these prices are generated are not such as to permit a clear inference about the relationship between relative prices and users' substitution rates as among livestock and other forms of capital. As will be pointed out, there is reason to believe that the calculations give a reasonable picture of changes over time, but what remains in question is the appropriateness of the absolute values and, hence, the weight which should be accorded livestock in aggregation with other forms of capital.

As it happens, livestock herds have not moved at all closely with other

CHART 4-1

Livestock in 1937, 1928, and 1950 Prices, 1928–62
(January 1—Billion Rubles)

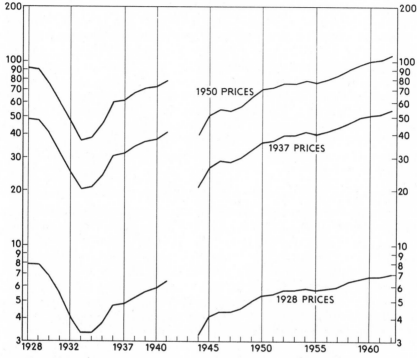

Source: Table T-23.

kinds of capital. The consequence is that the results of including livestock in the total stock of capital depend importantly on the weighting, and to this extent the provisional character of the livestock calculations is imparted not only to the total absolute values derived for all kinds of capital but also to their changes over time. The quantitative implications of this are explored further in Chapter 6. Meanwhile, it is noted that the independent movement of capital in the form of livestock, although an embarrassment from the viewpoint of computing a reliable series for total capital, also seems to provide a compelling reason for attempting, however tentatively, to include this item in the totals. As will be shown, even after allowance for a substantial degree of error in the livestock valuations, the behavior of the total capital stock inclusive of livestock is significantly different for some periods from that with livestock excluded. The role of capital in Soviet development is therefore the more obscure if no account is taken of this component. Of course, for many specific purposes it may be desirable to consider only capital other than livestock—or for that matter, other individual components of the total capital stock—and our presentation is intended to facilitate, insofar as our calculations permit, such discriminations among its parts.

2. NUMBERS

Table 4–1 shows livestock numbers by category. With a few exceptions, the information is reproduced directly from recent Soviet statistical sources. After a silence of many years, January 1 data for 1928–62 on the number of each kind of animal have been published. We have no independent basis for judging the reliability of the figures. The concept of the livestock count, however, is relatively unambiguous—as compared, for example, with that of an economic aggregate such as national income or of the resultant of an activity which is itself rather ill-defined, such as the harvest of a field crop. The dangers of misunderstanding the Soviet figures or of faulty methodology in their compilation seem correspondingly reduced. Generally, insofar as it has been possible to observe from a western vantage point, physical count data of this sort have been among the most reliable in Soviet sources. In the case of livestock, for the most part, the resources available to Soviet statistical organs should have been sufficient to permit the compilation of reasonably accurate data.

The main sources of information for the years before 1935 were sample surveys conducted in the spring and fall of the year. The scope of the surveys was broad, intended to include about 10 percent of all livestock-owning units, but the returns were used in levying taxes, and respondents apparently tended to understate their holdings. Offsetting corrections were applied by the collecting agencies, but the accuracy of their procedures has been questioned by later Soviet writers. Furthermore, the data obtained in the surveys must have required seasonal adjustments to produce figures for January 1, an additional source of error.

From 1935 to 1958, an annual census of livestock numbers was conducted, with physical verification by the census taker. For 1935–53 and 1957–58, censuses coincided with the date of the data used here, January 1. For 1954–56, however, the counts were taken only on October 1, and presumably again seasonal adjustments were required to yield January 1 figures. Since 1958, herds have been determined from the annual accounts of socialized agricultural enterprises and by sampling in the case of the private sector.[1]

The data in the sources are described as referring to the territory of the corresponding year. The implication is that the figures for January 1, 1940 and 1941, include livestock on the territories acquired during 1939 and 1940, respectively. For January 1, 1941, a detailed geographical breakdown is available which is consistent with this characterization in that it shows plausible numbers of livestock in the acquired territories. The same breakdown, however, strongly suggests that the January 1, 1940, figures refer only to the territory within the boundaries prevailing prior to the

---

1 The foregoing is from Gozulov–59, pp. 175–78. TsSU–57c, p. 3, which is the source of most of the data in Table 4–1, gives a similar, if rather terse, account, but states that the figures for 1930–34 are "based on calculations made by the financial and agricultural organs with the participation of the Central Statistical Administration." But presumably even these "calculations" had their origin in the survey data. Both sources note that no census was conducted in 1939 but do not indicate the alternative source of the data.

NUMBERS OF LIVESTOCK, BY KIND, 1928-62
(January 1--Million Head)

	Cows	Cattle Other than Cows	Hogs	Sheep and Goats	Horses
1928	29.3	30.8	22.0	107.0	32.1
1929	29.2	29.0	19.4	107.1	32.6
1930	28.5	22.1	14.2	93.3	31.0
1931	24.5	18.0	11.7	68.1	27.0
1932	22.3	16.0	10.9	47.6	21.7
1933	19.4	14.1	9.9	37.3	17.3
1934	19.0	14.5	11.5	36.5	15.4
1935	19.0	19.9	17.1	40.8	14.9
1936	20.0	26.0	25.9	49.9	15.5
1937	20.9	26.6	20.0	53.8	15.9
1938	22.7	28.2	25.7	66.6	16.2
1939	24.0	29.5	25.2	80.9	17.2
1940	25.5 (22.8)*	26.1 (25.0)*	25.1 (22.5)*	79.0 (76.7)*	19.4 (17.7)*
1941	27.8 (22.9)*	26.7 (24.6)*	27.5 (22.6)*	91.6 (86.2)*	21.0 (17.8)*
1944	16.5	17.4	5.6	63.3	7.7
1945	21.6	22.6	8.8	70.2	9.9
1946	22.9	24.7	10.6	70.0	10.7
1947	23.0	24.0	8.7	69.3	10.9
1948	23.8	26.3	9.7	76.8	11.0
1949	24.2	30.6	15.2	85.6	11.8
1950	24.6	33.5	22.2	93.6	12.7
1951	24.3	32.8	24.4	99.0	13.8
1952	24.9	33.9	27.1	107.6	14.7
1953	24.3	32.3	28.5	109.9	15.3
1954	25.2	30.6	33.3	115.5	15.3
1955	26.4	30.3	30.9	113.0	14.2
1956	27.7	31.1	34.0	116.2	13.0
1957	29.0	32.4	40.8	119.8	12.4
1958	31.4	35.4	44.3	130.1	11.9
1959	33.3	37.5	48.7	139.2	11.5
1960	33.9	40.3	53.4	144.0	11.0
1961	34.8	41.0	58.7	140.3	9.9
1962	36.3	45.6	66.4	144.1	9.2

* Figures in parentheses refer to livestock within pre-1939 boundaries.

Sources: For 1928–50, TsSU–57c, p. 6; for 1951–61, TsSU–61, p. 448; for 1962, *Pravda*, January 24, 1962 (data are preliminary), except that horses are extrapolated from 1961 and the 1958–61 trend. Data released after the completion of these calculations (TsSU–62a, p. 381) indicate that the 1962 figures for categories other than cows are slightly understated: the correct total in 1937 prices would be 43.0 billion as against the 42.8 billion shown in Table 4–3.

The 1940 figures outside parentheses are the sum of the figures in parentheses and the number of livestock on January 1, 1941, in the territories acquired during 1939: in the Belorussian Republic, the oblasts Brest, Grodno, Molodechno; in the Ukrainian Republic, the oblasts Lvov, Chernovitsy, Drogobych, Volyn', Rovno, Stanislav, Ternopol. The figures in parentheses for 1941 are the difference between the figures outside parentheses and the number of livestock on January 1, 1941, in the territories acquired during 1939 (as listed just above) and 1940: the Lithuanian, Estonian, Latvian, and Moldavian Republics; in the R.S.F.S.R., the Karelin A.S.S.R. The livestock herds in the indicated areas are from TsSU–57c. These areas coincide approximately, but not precisely, with the acquired territories (see Bergson–54, p. 6; Anonymous–56, front end-piece and p. 98).

Changes in numbers near the end of the war presumably reflect the acquisition of livestock in liberated territories and from defeated countries (cf. Jasny–49, p. 630).

1939 acquisitions, which is accordingly the interpretation we adopt.[2] The figures shown in Table 4–1 for the true boundaries of January 1, 1940, are estimated by adding to the reported totals for that date the January 1, 1941, number of livestock in the territories acquired during 1939. This procedure is adopted because of the form of the available data, but it is in error to the extent of changes in livestock numbers in the acquired territories during 1940. The figures for livestock in the old territory for January 1, 1941, are computed from the reported totals by subtracting the January 1, 1941, numbers in the areas acquired during 1939–40. In both cases, the data for the acquired territories are taken from distributions for administrative demarcations of the late 1950's. These correspond approximately, but only approximately, to the boundaries of the acquired areas.

The herds in the pre-1939 territories can be calculated to have had a total value in 1937 prices of 34.7 billion rubles on January 1, 1940, and 35.3 billion on January 1, 1941. The corresponding totals in 1928 prices are 5.3 and 5.4 billion; those in 1950 prices 66.5 and 67.5 billion. We shall at a later point use these figures in calculating annual investment in livestock.

3. AVERAGE REALIZED PRICES

The weight-year prices used to value livestock herds are shown in Table 4–2 (where we include also, for subsequent reference, 1955 and 1958 prices). These are intended to represent average realizations of Soviet livestock producers, private, collective, and state. In the years in which, for institutional reasons, more than one price for a single kind of livestock prevailed, the figures shown are averages of the several prices, weighted by the relative importance of each kind of marketing. No adjustment is attempted for the effects of turnover taxes or agricultural subsidies.

The suitability of any of the sets of prices for our purposes is problematic. Ideally, the prices should reflect rates at which kinds of livestock

---

[2] The evidence which seems most compelling is the following: The number of privately owned horses in the territory encompassed by the national totals reported in the source amounted to 1.1 million on January 1, 1940. The number of privately owned horses in the territories acquired during 1939 alone amounted to 1.6 million on January 1, 1941 (at which time the number of horses in the socialized sector of the same territories was less than 0.1 million). To conclude that the comprehensive January 1, 1940, figure includes the territory acquired during 1939, it would be necessary somehow to explain an increase during 1940 of well over 50 percent—that is, exceeding the biologically possible—in the number of privately owned horses in the newly acquired territories. (The implied number for the acquired territories for January 1, 1940, would be the national total, 1.1 million, minus the number in all other parts of the Soviet Union.) The socialized sector was surely too small to have supplied them, nor is it likely that they would have been sent in from other parts of the country. We infer instead, therefore, that the comprehensive figure for January 1, 1940, refers to the territory exclusive of acquisitions made during 1939. This is also consistent with the following data on the geographical distribution of privately owned horses on January 1, 1941: territory within pre-1939 acquisition boundary, 1.0 million; territories acquired during 1939, 1.6 million; territories acquired during 1940, 1.4 million. Presumably, the January 1, 1940, figures for livestock other than horses have the same geographical coverage.

The figure for privately owned horses on January 1, 1940, is from a forthcoming study by Nancy Nimitz and is the difference between all horses and the number held by collective farms and state agricultural organizations. The figures for January 1, 1941, are computed analogously from the sources cited in the notes to Table 4–1.

TABLE 4-2

AVERAGE REALIZED PRICES OF LIVESTOCK, 1937, 1928, 1950, 1955, AND 1958
(Rubles per Head)

	1937[b]	1928[a]	1950[a]	1955[a]	1958[a]
Cows	390	70	840	1200	2250
Cattle Other than Cows	195	34	600	800	1500
Hogs	140	11.5	400	560	700
Sheep and Goats	48	7.5	110	150	200
Horses	390	116	840	1200	2250

[a] Prices are for animals of the average weight of 1928.
[b] Prices are for animals of the average weight of 1932.
Source: Appendix F.

might be substituted for each other or for other types of capital while holding output constant. Agricultural production, including livestock breeding, and capital formation in agriculture were carried on in 1928 pre-
dominantly by the private sector. Transactions in livestock in the
countryside and in connection with meat sales to urban residents occurred
in a relatively free market. The state, the chief purchaser of other kinds of
capital, was also a purchaser of livestock from private agriculture, both on
capital and current account, and peasants in turn bought machinery from
the state. There was some administrative intervention in the establishment
of state purchase prices, but on average these were quite close to the prices
generated by the free market.[3] Peasant purchases of machinery were also
at levels corresponding more or less to costs of production and distribution.[4] There was, thus, a functional link between average realized livestock
prices and prices for other capital goods. On the other hand, as we shall
stress in Chapter 10, there is reason to doubt the equilibrium character of
the 1928 economy, and especially in the relation of agriculture to other
sectors.

By 1937, livestock marketings had grown more complex. Five major
channels of sale existed, each with its own prices: compulsory sales to the
state by collective farms and peasant households; "voluntary" sales to the
state by the same group; state farm sales to state procurement agencies;
sales of livestock on the hoof on the collective-farm market by collective
farms and peasant households; and sales of meat in cuts on the collective-
farm market by the same group. Of these five outlets, only the first four are
strictly for livestock on the hoof. Our average realized prices are therefore
computed from the first four kinds of prices only.[5]

The calculation yields average realized prices, and, for want of a better
alternative, we use the results to compute the 1937-price values of livestock
herds. The relationship of the livestock prices to prices for other capital

3 See Karcz–57, Section II, and pp. 340, 345.

4 See Moorsteen–62, pp. 9, 29.

5 We assume, however, that the opportunity foregone in selling livestock in the form
of meat cuts was sale on the hoof in the collective-farm market. The weight assigned
prices for the latter form of marketing, accordingly, includes both marketings of live
animals and of the liveweight equivalent of meat sold in cuts. Our treatment of this
matter was clarified in conversations with Abram Bergson.

goods, however, is quite obscure. Prices in the first three markets listed above were established by the state and probably bore little relationship to the alternatives foregone by the seller or the buyer. The fourth channel of sale opened into the consumer goods market, in which price levels were influenced by the levy of the turnover tax in other retail outlets. Since capital goods prices were, on the whole, not subject to the turnover tax, a difference arose here too between prices for livestock and for other capital goods, the effects of which may have been offset in part by agricultural subsidies.

This is not a very satisfactory outcome, though some limited reassurance may be derived from the following considerations. The livestock value series appear not to be sensitive in their movements over time to the structure of the prices used in valuation (cf. Chart 4–1). This suggests that our concern lies more with the price *level* than structure. With respect to the latter, state farm production costs in 1937 were below our estimated average price for cattle, above that for hogs. For cattle and hogs together, state farm production costs were at an average level close to that of realized prices.[6] As the state was also the primary producer and purchaser of other capital goods priced near costs in 1937, this might be taken as a willingness on the part of the state to trade between livestock and other capital goods at the rates indicated by their respective prices. On the other hand, the ultimate purposes, rationality, and accounting methodology of the state farm livestock breeding program in 1937 are all subject to question. Since state farms accounted for only a small percentage of all Soviet livestock holdings in 1937,[7] policies devised for them may not have been mainly influenced by the current—as opposed, say, to expected future—costs of obtaining output from them.

The average prices for 1950 (and for 1955 and 1958) share the defects of those for 1937 in that they are generated under circumstances largely isolated from those for other forms of capital. In addition, even the reassurance that may be derived from state farm production costs is dissipated by the fact that these costs tended after 1937 to rise more rapidly than average realized prices.[8]

4. ADJUSTMENTS FOR CHANGES IN WEIGHT

As is indicated in Table 4–2, the prices at which we value livestock herds refer variously to animals of the average weights in herds of 1928 or 1932. The livestock counts in Table 4–1 refer to the physical units and take no account of changes over time in weight. Table 4–3 shows the unadjusted

---

[6] Compare the average realized prices of Table 4–2 with the state farm production costs of 700 rubles per ton for cattle, 3,150 rubles per ton for hogs, cited in Karcz–57, p. 51. The value of 1937 marketings of cattle and hogs at average realized prices as computed in Table F–1 amounts to 3.53 billion rubles, whereas at state farm production costs it would be 3.57 billion.

[7] See Jasny–49, p. 774.

[8] See Karcz–57, p. 51, and Nimitz–59, p. 261, for costs, Table 4–2 for prices. Whereas prices in 1950 were at 2 to 3 times their 1937 levels, costs may have increased 5 to 10 times. After 1950, costs apparently remained constant or declined while prices continued to rise, but the former still exceeded the latter in 1955. By 1958, the two levels may again have come approximately together. See Nimitz–59, p. 261, for 1957 costs.

TABLE 4-3

LIVESTOCK, UNADJUSTED FOR CHANGES IN WEIGHT, IN 1937,
1928, AND 1950 PRICES, 1928-62
(January 1--Billion Rubles)

	1937 Prices[b]	1928 Prices[a]	1950 Prices[a]
1928	38.2	7.9	90.6
1929	37.6	7.8	88.9
1930	34.0	7.2	79.2
1931	28.5	6.1	66.2
1932	24.1	5.1	56.2
1933	20.2	4.2	47.4
1934	19.6	4.0	46.2
1935	21.5	4.2	51.7
1936	24.9	4.8	61.3
1937	24.9	4.8	60.8
1938	27.5	5.2	67.2
1939	29.2	5.6	71.3
1940	29.9 (27.5)[c]	5.8 (5.3)[c]	72.2 (66.5)[c]
1941	32.5 (28.0)[c]	6.3 (5.4)[c]	78.1 (67.5)[c]
1944	16.7	3.2	40.0
1945	21.3	4.1	51.3
1946	22.8	4.3	55.0
1947	22.4	4.3	54.0
1948	23.7	4.5	57.3
1949	26.2	4.9	64.1
1950	28.7	5.3	70.6
1951	29.4	5.4	72.3
1952	31.0	5.7	76.3
1953	31.0	5.7	76.1
1954	32.0	5.8	78.4
1955	31.5	5.7	77.1
1956	32.3	5.8	79.2
1957	33.9	5.9	83.7
1958	36.2	6.3	89.6
1959	38.3	6.5	94.9
1960	39.8	6.7	99.1
1961	40.4	6.7	101.1
1962	42.8	7.0	108.0

[a] Refers to animals of the average weight of 1928.
[b] Refers to animals of the average weight of 1932.
[c] Figures within parentheses refer to livestock within pre-1939 boundaries.
Source: See text.

products of price times herd number. These are the data which, after adjustment for changes in weight, constitute our series for the value of livestock as shown in Table T-23. The adjustments are made with the indexes derived in Table 4-4.

Since information on changes in the average weight of total livestock herds are lacking, we are guided instead by data on the weight of animals delivered for slaughter (Table 4-4, Part A). Even the latter data are not comprehensive in scope: some refer to obligatory deliveries from both private and socialized producers; some to all procurements, obligatory and "voluntary," but from collective farms only; some to all state procurements from all producers, but still exclusive of slaughterings for sale on the collective-farm market. Although the slaughter weights are an imperfect indicator of the magnitude we seek, there must be an important relationship between them and average herd weights. Moreover, the picture they convey is consistent with other information about Soviet animal hus-

TABLE 4-4

DERIVATION OF AVERAGE WEIGHT OF LIVESTOCK HERDS, 1928-62

A. Slaughter Weights

(Live Weight in Kilograms)

	Cattle Only	Cattle and Calves		Hogs		Sheep		
	a	a	b	a	c	a	b	c
1932	223	--	--	55	--	31	--	--
1933	228	--	--	54	--	29	--	--
1934	235	--	--	64	--	31	--	--
1935	242	--	--	76	--	33	--	--
1936	257	--	--	89	--	36	--	--
1937	258	225	--	92	--	37	36	--
1938	275	--	--	89	--	36	--	--
1940	--	--	238	--	85	--	--	36
1950	--	243	252	--	102	--	--	38
1953	--	--	240	--	96	--	--	38
1956	--	219	220	--	76	--	--	37
1957	--	235	234	--	85	--	37	38
1958	--	--	237	--	83	--	--	39
1959	--	--	248	--	82	--	--	40

[a]Obligatory deliveries.

[b]All procurements from collective farms.

[c]All procurements.

B. Index Numbers of Average Weight of Herds

	1928=100	1932=100
1928	100	126
1929	100	126
1930	93	118
1931	86	109
1932	79	100
1933	78	99
1934	83	105
1935	89	113
1936	98	124
1937	100	126
1938-62	100	126

Sources: For Part A, data for obligatory deliveries are from Narkomzem —36, p. 524, for 1932–34, and from Jasny—49, p. 798, for 1935–38. Jasny gives figures for 1934 which exceed those shown by one kilogram in each of the three categories. The 1932–34 figures for hogs exclude hogs raised for bacon. Data for all procurements from collective farms are from Nimitz —59a, p. 15; those for all procurements from TsSU–60a, p. 368. For Part B, see text.

bandry and suggests a development of which it seems desirable to take cognizance in the capital stock calculations: that the quality of the herds in 1932–33, at the end of the collectivization drive, was at a level substantially below that of, say, 1937, when adjustment to collectivization had largely been made. This appears to be a qualitative reflection of the reduced livestock numbers which occurred at the same time (Tables 4–1 and 4–3). For the period after 1937, the slaughter weights indicate no consistent trend. A decline very probably occurred to the immediate postwar years, but, in the absence of data and in view of the small weight of livestock in total capital by that period, we make no allowance for it. We lack data also on slaughter weights for 1928 but assume that the average at that time was at the peak post-1932 level.[9]

The indexes for average herd weights are computed for 1932–37 from the data for slaughter weights.[10] For 1937–62, the indexes are assumed to remain constant. As is noted above, average weights in 1928 also are taken to have been at the 1937 level. For the period 1929–31, we assume that changes in weight tended to occur roughly with changes in herd size, i.e., that no significant change occurred between 1928 and 1929, the change between 1929 and 1932 occurring in about equal amounts during each of the three years. The indexes, although calculated in part from annual data, are applied to the January 1 totals.[11]

Livestock herds are subject to considerable seasonal fluctuations, in which the January 1 herds must be near the low point. We shall have occasion subsequently to calculate annual average herds, which we shall take as equal to the average of herds at the beginning and end of each year. Data for a number of prewar years suggest that this procedure yields averages some 5–10 percent below those that would be obtained if July 1 totals, which are near the peak, were included in the averaging.[12]

---

[9] We are indebted to Lazar Volin for advice on this question, although responsibility for our procedures rests with us.

[10] A weighted average is computed from the following formula:

$$\frac{\Sigma\, N_1 W_1 P_{37}}{\Sigma\, N_1 W_{37} P_{37}},$$

where N refers to the number of animals in the herd (Table 4–1), W to the slaughter weight (Table 4–4), P to the price per ton (Table F–1), the subscript "1" to the given year and "37" to 1937. The index numbers are computed only for the animals for which slaughter weights are available, cattle other than cows, hogs, and sheep. Because of the form in which the herd data are available, however, slaughter weights for sheep are weighted by the number of sheep and goats combined.

[11] Except for the difference in their bases, the two indexes are meant to be identical. Because of rounding performed after the calculations were made, slight discrepancies appear.

[12] Herd counts as of July 1, 1928–38, are given in Jasny–49, p. 797; they are there indicated to refer to "June," but for 1928–34 they are identical with figures indicated to refer to July 1 in Narkomzem–36, p. 511. These data, together with the January 1 figures of Table 4–1, permit the calculation of annual averages on the assumption that herds increase at a constant (absolute) rate from January 1 to July 1 and decline similarly to the following January 1. The percentages cited in the text are based on calculations in 1937 prices. No allowance is made for changes in average weight within the course of the year.

Chapter 5

Inventories

1. INTRODUCTION

The estimates of inventories are intended to cover physical assets in the form of raw materials, goods in process, and finished products, held in all sectors engaged in the production and distribution of output. Essentially, function rather than service life provides the basis for the distinction between such assets and fixed capital, with the single exception of "small-valued and short-lived durables."[1] These are treated here, as in post-1936 Soviet accounting, as inventories. For brevity, they are referred to in this chapter simply as "small tools." Stocks of goods held by consumers are excluded. Stocks held by governmental agencies—administrative, educational, health, military—are largely or totally excluded. Data for the latter are lacking in any case, but their exclusion may be justified in principle on the ground that they are held for purposes of social consumption and, hence, are analogous to the consumption stocks of households.

Two omissions occur which are not justifiable on conceptual grounds: inventories in collective-farm market trade and state stockpiles. Data for the first are unavailable, but it is questionable whether it would be possible even conceptually to distinguish stocks held by peasants for sale on the collective-farm markets from their household consumption stocks. Considering the organization of these markets and the kinds of products traded in them, it is unlikely that the exclusion of such inventories has much effect on our estimates. However, the exclusion of state stockpiles, also occasioned by lack of data, may be of substantial consequence. Although stockpiles are not thought to be large relative to total inventories, changes in them in particular years may have been significant in comparison with the estimated changes in inventories.

Covered elsewhere in our estimates are two kinds of assets which might be treated as inventories: livestock and investment projects in progress.[2] Since the function of some part of livestock herds is similar to that of goods in process, this part could appropriately be included with inventories. The function of other livestock—draft animals, milk cows, breeding stock—more nearly resembles that of fixed capital. The mixed character of capital in livestock appears a sufficient justification for treating it as a separate category. Assets contained in investment projects in progress should, in

---

[1] See p. 39, fn. 30.
[2] See Chapter 3, Section 7, and Chapter 4.

principle, be included in inventories, but we have explained previously our reasons for including them in fixed capital.[3] We do not, of course, lose information by estimating livestock and investment projects in progress separately, and we examine at the end of this chapter the implications of combining one or both of them with inventories in the restricted sense in which we use the term here. It should be kept in mind, however, that our handling of these assets may differ from statistical practices elsewhere.

We follow the usual practice and that observed in Soviet accounting of treating inventories (for the most part) as nondepreciating assets. Although exceptions undoubtedly occur, inventories are typically held for a short enough period that significant deterioration in their physical qualities does not take place, and their values (in constant prices) when consumed or sold—their "scrap values," so to speak—are equal to their values when new. Gross and net values of the stock therefore correspond. An exception to the general procedure does arise in the case of small tools, which are depreciated in Soviet accounts[4] and, consequently, in our estimates. This category of assets, however, does not weigh heavily enough in the total to merit our distinguishing between gross and net stocks.

Inventories are valued in prices of the three weight years, 1937, 1928, and 1950, with adjustments in each case to a factor cost basis. The process of Soviet price formation as it bears on the valuation of inventories is in some areas (e.g., heavy industrial inventories) similar to that of fixed capital and in others (e.g., inventories of agricultural origin) more like that of livestock. Which is to say, inventory prices vary widely in their reliability as measures of substitutability in use—of goods used as capital assets. As will emerge, the component price indexes by which we reduce values in current to constant prices were designed essentially as output deflators. They do in considerable measure take into account quality changes, although the changes are probably not in all cases precisely those relevant to the substitutability of goods used as assets in production, as against, for example, their substitutability in final consumption.

Our estimates for total inventories and those in nonagricultural sectors, in prices (factor costs) of each of the three weight years, are presented in Table T–24; the total estimates are graphed as well in Chart 5–1. These series are derived from considerably more detailed estimates, some of which are of independent interest and will be cited subsequently. The discussion which follows is framed in terms of the more detailed calculations.

Total inventories are the sum of estimates obtained separately for eight sectors and two classes of assets. The sectors include producer goods industries, consumer goods industries, transportation and communications, procurement, domestic trade, contract construction, other nonagricultural sectors, and agriculture. The two asset classes are inventories on hand, within each given sector, and "goods shipped." The latter category is meant to approximate goods in transit between sectors, i.e., goods held physically in the transportation sector but title to which belongs to the

---

[3] See p. 94.
[4] Cf. *Vestnik statistiki*, 1957:2, p. 95, and the discussion of data from this source in Appendix G, p. 499.

CHART 5-1

Total Inventories in 1937, 1928, and 1950 Prices, 1928–62
(January 1—Billion Rubles)

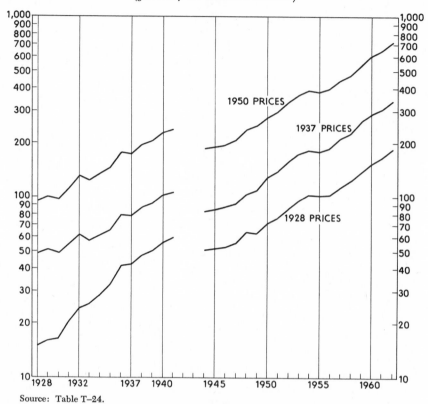

Source: Table T–24.

buyer or seller. Since we are not confident that the approximation is good, it appears preferable to retain the Soviet term for the category. In addition to the foregoing, a small amount of uninstalled equipment which is not otherwise accounted for in our estimates is included in inventories but not attributed to any sector.[5]

Broadly speaking, the estimates for sectors other than agriculture, contract construction in a number of years, and the uninstalled equipment category, are obtained by deflating values of inventories as of January 1 in current prices to constant prices of the weight years. The current-price data are obtained more or less directly from Soviet sources. It is worthy of note that this is the second point, the other being the initial stock of fixed capital, at which our estimates of the Soviet capital stock are derived from reported data for capital in value terms. The current values are first deflated by sectors to prevailing market prices of the three weight years and then adjusted to factor cost valuations. The three components which are

---

[5] On this component, see Appendix L, p. 581.

not derived by deflation are obtained essentially by extrapolation on output in constant prices.

The current-price estimates are shown in Table G–1, those in constant prevailing prices in Tables L–1, M–1, and M–2, and those in constant factor costs in Tables N–1, N–2, and N–3. Detailed explanations of the sources of the estimates are given in Appendixes G through N. We undertake to explain here the general rationale of our procedures and to summarize our methods. The discussion proceeds from the current-price estimates to those in constant prices and to a consideration of the reliability of the results.

2. THE OFFICIAL ACCOUNTS IN CURRENT PRICES

Accounting Procedures

The current-price estimates are pieced together from various reported aggregates and subcategories not only of assets but also of related liability and net worth accounts. To make clear the reasoning which underlies our use of the reported data requires a brief explanation of Soviet accounting terminology and procedures.[6] A useful point of departure for that explanation is provided by the accounts for January 1, 1960, which are shown in Table 5–1.[7] We consider subsequently variant terminologies and procedures.

The data in the table, which are derived from a single source, are unconsolidated accounts for all sectors covered in our constant-price estimates except for private and collective-farm agriculture and uninstalled equipment, n.e.c. They include state agriculture, which is included in our estimates in current prices but is not treated separately in the constant-price estimates. A few asset categories which are shown separately in the source are combined in the table because the distinctions involved are finer than need concern us. Some of the English captions used are rather free translations of their Russian counterparts. In a few instances, on the other hand, terms have been translated literally to avoid confusion with similar but not identical Western accounting terms. In two cases, the Russian terms have been retained without translation because no brief and appropriate rendering could be found.

The term translated in the table as "working capital," *oborotnye sredstva*, here comprehends the whole of current assets, both physical and financial. Total assets are divisible into two broad categories, normed and nonnormed, of which only the first is explicitly identified in the table. Nonnormed assets are those shown in items II through V.

The usual characteristics of normed assets are the following. They are assets for which minimal annual required stocks are prescribed for each

---

6 The bulk of what is stated here can be found in standard Soviet works on accounting and finance. We have drawn especially from Sobol'–37, *passim;* Shenger–40, *passim;* Sheremet–56, *passim;* Lavrov–56, pp. 65 ff.; Usoskin–56, pp. 21 ff.; and Barngol'ts–57, *passim.* We benefited at an early date from the reading of unpublished materials of Robert W. Campbell, part of which have since appeared in Campbell–63, chap. 9.

7 Data from the source from which Table 5–1 is obtained are considered at length in Appendix G, in the discussion of 1951 and related years.

TABLE 5-1

REPORTED WORKING CAPITAL ACCOUNTS, ALL SECTORS,* JANUARY 1, 1960
(Current Prices)

		Billion Rubles	Percent of Total
	Working Capital (Assets)		
I.	Normed assets (commodity-material values)	663.1	77.2
	A. Production supplies	257.3	30.0
	1. Raw materials and purchased semi-fabricates	151.2	17.6
	2. Fuel	8.0	0.9
	3. Packing materials	12.6	1.5
	4. Spare parts for repairs	13.3	1.5
	5. Small tools	42.4	4.9
	6. Seed and planting materials	4.0	0.5
	7. Feed and fodder	6.6	0.8
	8. Immature livestock	16.6	1.9
	9. Other production supplies	2.6	0.3
	B. Goods in process and internally produced semifabricates	61.7	7.2
	C. Supplies and goods in process of subsidiary agricultural organs	5.3	0.6
	D. Expenses of future periods	9.9	1.2
	E. Finished products	327.6	38.2
	F. Other normed assets	1.3	0.2
II.	Goods shipped and services rendered	83.2	9.7
III.	Monetary assets	54.0	6.3
IV.	Debitory	55.7	6.5
V.	Other assets	2.6	0.3
	Total Assets	858.6	100.0
	Sources of Finance of Working Capital (Liabilities and Net Worth)		
I.	Owned working capital and equivalents	326.3	38.0
II.	Bank loans	376.9	43.9
III.	Kreditory	135.7	15.8
IV.	Other liabilities	19.7	2.3
	Total Liabilities and Net Worth	858.6	100.0

* Private and collective-farm agriculture and uninstalled equipment, n.e.c., are omitted.
Sources: Absolute figures for total and normed assets and all percentage figures are from TsSU–61, pp. 92, 93, and 96. Other absolute figures are computed.

operating enterprise, on the basis of a "norm" or "normative."[8] Actual holdings do not ordinarily correspond to the norms, because of seasonal stocks and because of departures of nonseasonal holdings from the norms. The figures in the table are for actual holdings. Normed assets are physical assets, which fact is implied by the synonymous expression, "commodity-material values." They are inventories on hand rather than goods in transit. All physical assets on hand are included in normed assets.

Significant exceptions to the foregoing generalizations occur. (*i*) Norms for money balances are prescribed in retail trade and perhaps some minor other sectors,[9] though no monetary assets are included in the normed category in Table 5–1. (*ii*) Both production supplies and finished products include goods in transit which are carried on the books of the buyer

[8] Norms are discussed further, pp. 231 ff., below.
[9] See Atlas–37, pp. 126–27; Usoskin–56, p. 21.

(*material'nye tsennosti v puti*). These are purchased goods which the seller has dispatched and for which the buyer has received and accepted the bill but which have not yet been delivered. (*iii*) "Expenses of future periods" appear to be essentially financial assets, though Soviet accounting practice may suggest a contrary interpretation. They include certain development costs which are charged to expenses over an extended period and also items similar to "prepaid expenses" in Western usage.

"Immature livestock" represents that part of all livestock which is treated in Soviet accounts as working rather than fixed capital. The meaning of other detailed components of normed assets is clear from their titles.

Of nonnormed assets, "goods shipped and services rendered" are the financial claims of sellers against buyers for goods dispatched and services rendered for which payment has not been received. The category resembles "receivables," but, since receivables are also included elsewhere, it is preferable to retain the Soviet term. Monetary assets are principally currency and bank deposits but evidently include money orders and similar instruments. *Debitory* consist of financial claims other than those covered in goods shipped and monetary assets: claims against the Budget, credit institutions, and private persons (for example, for wage overpayments); advances made to industrial co-operatives and contract construction organizations; claims related to payments for equipment "on partial completion";[10] and sundry claims against other producing enterprises.[11]

The first category of sources of finance, "owned working capital and equivalents," combines two separable components. Owned working capital is that part of the total owned capital (net worth) of an enterprise which is not required, in the Soviet view of accounting, for the financing of fixed capital and other noncurrent assets. Its magnitude is determined as a residual: as total owned capital (plus any long-term or other liabilities allocable to noncurrent assets) *less* fixed and other noncurrent assets. The fact that it is a residual explains the equality, in Table 5–1, of total working capital assets and total sources of finance. Sources other than owned capital are "borrowed" or "attracted." Equivalents to owned working capital consist of portions of certain liabilities which are otherwise included in *kreditory:* accrued wages and related charges for social insurance, advances from buyers, claims owed for payments "on partial completion," and, in some cases, accrued tax liabilities. The portion of liabilities so designated is that regarded as "stable" or "minimal" and hence equivalent to owned capital as a source of finance. Owned working capital and equivalents are normed in combination, on the basis of the asset norms. As with assets, normed and actual magnitudes need not be equal.

Since Table 5–1 does not give separate data for owned working capital and for equivalents, the relation between these two categories—and between the working and fixed capital accounts—may be clarified by a numerical illustration taken from a Soviet source.[12] In a hypothetical enterprise, total owned capital is 4,300 (thousand rubles), equivalents to

---

10 The reference is to a procedure whereby the builders of equipment requiring long periods of construction are paid in installments, as the work progresses, by the purchasing enterprise.

11 For an extended list of the components of *debitory*, see Sobol'–37, p. 149.

12 Sheremet–56, p. 64.

owned working capital 270, or a total from these two sources of 4,570. Fixed capital and other noncurrent assets are 3,500, leaving 1,070 of owned working capital and equivalents. Owned working capital alone is 800, i.e., total owned capital *less* total noncurrent assets or, alternatively, total owned working capital and equivalents *less* equivalents.[13]

Bank loans in Table 5–1 are short-term loans, principally from the State Bank but also from the Construction Bank. Certain short- and intermediate-term loans are excluded, evidently on the grounds that they relate to fixed capital.[14] *Kreditory* include the remainder of those liabilities which are treated partly as equivalents to owned working capital: accrued wages and taxes, advances, etc. They also include, and presumably consist in larger part of, accounts payable for goods shipped and services rendered.

The several "other" categories in the table are of uncertain content, but their magnitudes are small.

The terminology employed in Table 5–1 approximates standard usage as nearly as does that of any single Soviet source. Unfortunately, the standard is not closely observed, and inconsistencies and ambiguities in the use of terms present a major difficulty in the reading of Soviet sources. Without attempting an exhaustive catalogue, we may usefully consider those variant meanings which are particularly troublesome and additional terms which are commonly encountered.

(*i*) The term, *oborotnye sredstva*, is about as loose in meaning as is the English expression "working capital." It does not necessarily denote assets rather than liabilities or total (current) assets rather than some component of the total. The term is frequently used in the sense of total sources of finance[15]—the terminology in Table 5–1 for this concept is not common. It is also frequently used to refer to the sum of owned working capital and bank loans, excluding *kreditory*.[16] Occasionally, it is given the meaning of normed rather than total assets.[17]

(*ii*) A second term of quite inclusive coverage and variable meaning also appears frequently in the literature: *oborotnye fondy* (literally "circulating funds"). In publications of the late 1920's and early 1930's, this consistently has the meaning which was subsequently attached to "normed assets" or "commodity-material values," i.e., essentially physical assets on hand.[18] In later publications, *oborotnye fondy* usually denotes assets "in production" in contrast to assets "in circulation" (*fondy obrashcheniia*), where the former are normed assets exclusive of finished products and the latter nonnormed assets plus finished products.[19] Although in some con-

---

[13] Actual figures similar to those in the illustration, for state industry in several prewar years, are given in Rubinshtein–58, p. 47. These do not, however, permit the separation of equivalents from owned working capital.

[14] See pp. 501 and 503.

[15] Cf., e.g., Popov–57, p. 66.

[16] Cf. Usatov–61, p. 26.

[17] Cf. Birman–56, p. 46.

[18] Cf. Gosplan–29, p. 432, and Putilov–32, p. 101.

[19] Cf. Khromov–37, pp. 70–71, and Atlas–47, p. 44. Assets in production or in circulation are often described as *sredstva* rather than *fondy*: cf. *Vestnik statistiki*, 1957:2, p. 95.

texts *fondy* refers to sources of finance,[20] *oborotnye fondy* appears consistently to mean current assets of some coverage.

(*iii*) Current assets are sometimes identified also as *oborotnye aktivy*.[21] The term is evidently not restricted to any particular array of assets, but it does unambiguously refer to assets.

(*iv*) The key source of our data for the mid-1930's, Usoskin–39, presents a number of terminological puzzles, the chief of which is an expression, "working capital invested in material assets" (*oborotnye sredstva pomeshchennye v material'nye fondy*). From various evidence, we infer that the reference is to normed assets in the Table 5–1 sense plus goods shipped. Usoskin also treats "normed assets" as inclusive of goods shipped.[22]

(*v*) Reported figures for normed assets are sometimes inclusive of the normed portion of monetary assets, the remaining money balances being attributed to nonnormed assets.[23]

(*vi*) Soviet sources often treat the assimilation of equivalents into owned working capital as understood without being specified. We follow the same practice in the appendixes and elsewhere.

(*vii*) Goods shipped and *debitory* are sometimes combined in a single category of "settlements" (*raschety*) or "resources in settlements."[24]

Because of the diversity and variability of terms, the meaning and coverage of reported data must often be judged from context. Where the context is unrevealing, it occasionally appears preferable to disregard data rather than risk a serious misinterpretation.

Additional problems arise from changes over time in Soviet accounting practices. The most consequential of these is the reclassification of small tools in 1936 from fixed to working capital.[25] The category of equivalents to owned working capital was introduced in 1938 and appears not to have been employed generally until 1939.[26] "Expenses of future periods" may not have been included with current assets before 1931, since they apparently are omitted from statistics for earlier years, but the evidence on this is inconclusive.[27]

Financial Procedures

The data presented in Table 5–1 reflect not merely accounting relationships but also administrative procedures which relate particular assets to particular sources of finance. These date from a government decree of July 23, 1931, which was a principal element in the Credit Reform of 1930–31.[28] In substance, the decree provided that minimal requirements of inventories on hand, i.e., the normed amounts of those assets which are

---

20 As in the expression, *ustavnye fondy*, or statutory capital. "Statutory capital in circulation" is sometimes used in place of "owned working capital": cf. Nusinov–37, p. 42.

21 Cf. Usoskin–39, p. 80.

22 See the discussion of this source in Appendix G, notes for 1933–39.

23 See the data from Atlas–37, p. 119, reproduced in Appendix G, notes for 1933-39.

24 Cf. *Vestnik statistiki*, 1957:2, p. 95.

25 See fn. 30, p. 39.

26 See Shenger–40, p. 40.

27 See Appendix G, notes for 1928–30.

28 See Shenger–34, pp. 80 ff.

subject to norming, should be financed by the owned working capital of an enterprise. Owned capital was to be obtained through budgetary grants and retained earnings. Seasonal inventories on hand, other inventories temporarily required, and goods shipped were to be financed by short-term bank loans. Loans, by the State Bank, were to be made only for such purposes.[29]

Modifications have been made in these principles over time, although only one was clearly of quantitative importance until the late 1950's. Beginning in 1933, the State Bank undertook to finance a substantial portion of nonseasonal inventories in domestic trade. The share of such inventories that was to be bank financed has differed as among the several components of the trade network and as between planned and above-plan inventories. It has also been altered on occasion by government decree or administrative action, most notably in 1954 when the Bank's share was sharply reduced, and in 1955 when it was again raised.[30] Similar arrangements for the Bank's financing a share of nonseasonal (normed) inventories in sales-supply organs and in heavy industry were introduced in 1939.[31] Data for the former are lacking, but the ratio of bank loans to all inventories in sales-supply appears to have been high before 1939 as well as after.[32] Loans on nonseasonal inventories in heavy industry were trivially small until 1957, after which they expanded to considerable volume.[33] The effect of these various changes has been to shift the relation between nonseasonal inventories and owned working capital, on the one hand, and that between seasonal inventories *cum* goods shipped and bank loans, on the other. Administrative procedures have been devised, however, which are intended to keep the relation of the combined sources and the combined uses unchanged.[34]

Other changes have altered somewhat the relation between total short-term loans and the assets to which they were initially tied. There has occurred a gradual extension of short- and intermediate-term loans to purposes ordinarily associated with fixed capital investment. The volume of these loans was insignificant until 1956 and modest thereafter.[35] In

---

[29] Financial procedures in effect before the Reform need not be described here because our inventory estimates for those years are derived entirely from asset data. They differed from post-Reform arrangements chiefly in that enterprises granted credit to one another on trade bills and other commercial paper, the Bank's lending was in large part against such paper, and the division of functions between owned capital and bank loans was not firmly fixed. Cf. Atlas–52, chap. ii.

[30] On the evolution of the financing of trade, see Atlas–47, pp. 224 and 328; Popov–57, pp. 78–79; Usoskin–56, p. 330; and Atlas–58, pp. 292–93.

[31] Sokolov–39a, p. 20.

[32] Cf. the figures for 1936 cited on page 474 with those for 1951 and later years given in Table G–6.

[33] See Table J–1.

[34] Enterprises in sales-supply and heavy industry, when shifted to the Bank for a part of the financing of their nonseasonal inventories, are required to make an equivalent payment to the Bank, thereby reducing their owned working capital by an equal amount (see Tiktin–40, p. 10; Batyrev–47, pp. 124 and 131). The increase in owned capital required by the 1954 reduction in the loan share to trade was provided by budgetary grants (Atlas–58, p. 292).

[35] See the data for loans "for the introduction of new techniques and mechanization and for increased production of consumer goods" in Table J–1.

Table 5–1, though perhaps not in all published data, these are excluded from sources of finance for current assets.[36] A second change has been the introduction of loans to guarantee the rendering of certain payments. These loans have reached substantial volume in the postwar period. They apparently are made largely to enterprises participating in clearing arrangements, the scale of which has increased since the war. We assume, perhaps mistakenly, that loans of this sort serve effectively as substitutes for loans on goods shipped.[37] Loans for extraordinary purposes were temporarily authorized during the war,[38] though these appear in part to have replaced various forms of peacetime lending and, outside of domestic trade, unlikely to have been large in volume.

Besides the changes over time in the arrangements introduced by the 1931 decree, there is a question whether variations may not have occurred in the closeness with which the procedures purportedly in force at any given time were observed. Controls bearing directly on owned working capital and bank loans and on their respective intended uses have been considerable. Superior administrative organs, both within particular sectors and at the national level (Council of Ministers, Budget, etc.), have had authority to transfer stocks between enterprises, to make grants which would increase owned working capital and withdrawals of funds which would reduce it.[39] The State Bank has had extensive authority to enforce the use of its loans for "legitimate" purposes.[40] Moreover, the predominance of owned capital and bank loans in total sources of finance and of normed assets and goods shipped in total assets must significantly limit the variations which can occur in the relation between these combined sources and uses.

On the other hand, the evidence is voluminous that nonseasonal inventories and owned working capital accounts have often diverged from their norms.[41] While administrative efforts are made to bring them into accord with their norms, these appear to be directed at a gradual rather than immediate adjustment.[42] There is evidence also that the Bank permits departures from its operating principles, primarily in the fact that it

---

36 See Appendix G, notes for 1951 and related years.

37 See Appendix J.

38 See Atlas–45, pp. 14 ff., and Golev–47, pp. 129 ff.

39 See Atlas–47, pp. 244 and 280; Lavrov–56, pp. 77–78; Shabanova–57, p. 51.

40 Bank controls are described in standard texts, e.g., Usoskin–56.

41 To cite a few examples: Nonseasonal inventories on hand in industry in excess of norms were reportedly 8–10 billion rubles or 6–8 percent of the norms in 1951–52, 3–4 billion or 2–3 percent of the norms in 1953–54 (Usatov–61, p. 28). Stocks of commodities in retail trade in excess of norms were 16 billion rubles or 10 percent of the norms on January 1, 1962 (Korovushkin–62, p. 8). In a source published in 1956 (*Den'gi i kredit*, 1956:9, p. 7), over half of the enterprises of union subordination in some branches of the economy were reported to have inadequate (below-norm) owned working capital; over 60 percent of enterprises of republican subordination were in the same state.

42 Lavrov–56, p. 77, states that excess owned working capital in an enterprise at the beginning of the planning year is allocated first to the planned increase in its normed assets; any remainder is transferred to the Budget. He states also that no provision is made in financial plans for covering inadequacies of owned capital, but other sources indicate these may be covered by administrative redistributions of funds within a sector or, on specific governmental authorization, by budgetary grants (cf. Shenger–40, p. 67; Sheremet–56, p. 17; budgetary grants evidently to cover such inadequacies are reported in Zverev–46, p. 51, and Kisman–56, p. 26).

regularly holds a significant volume of overdue loans.[43] In some degree, departures from the rules with respect to sources may produce or be accompanied by departures in the same direction with respect to uses, but no close correspondence appears necessary.[44]

A further ground for suspicion that the intended tie between particular sources and uses may not be firm is the fact that the official rationalization of financial procedures is incomplete and incoherent. Soviet sources are explicit that no deliberate provision is made for the financing of money balances.[45] Explanations offered as to how these are in fact financed—by economizing on physical assets, increasing sundry liabilities, etc.—vary considerably.[46] The desired relation between *debitory* and *kreditory*, and between these two and other accounts, also appears unsettled, although Soviet sources rarely comment upon the problem.[47] A tie of sorts between *kreditory* and bank loans can be inferred from the fact that the Bank does not make loans, which it otherwise would, against purchased materials which have not yet been paid for;[48] this also presumably weakens the tie between loans and inventories. Since *debitory* and *kreditory* for all enterprises together consist in part of offsetting claims, these two accounts are necessarily related to one another in some degree. But the absence of general principles for the determination of money balances, *debitory*, and *kreditory*, and the fact that these are not normed or planned for the individual enterprise, suggests that there is room for play in the connections between owned working capital and bank loans and their respective intended uses.

On balance, we would suppose that the administrative procedures employed do create a functional relation between the values of particular sources and uses. These relations have shifted over time and have probably been loose within any single period. Statistical evidence relevant to the issue is presented in the following section.[49]

Valuation

It is necessary for our calculations to establish also the principles of

---

[43] E.g., overdue loans averaged 9 billion rubles during 1957 (Mitel'man–58, p. 38). The asset against which any overdue loan was originally made may or may not be still in the possession of the borrowing enterprise.

[44] For example, a shortfall in profits may reduce an enterprise's owned capital and force it to reduce its normed inventories. It may react instead, however, by increasing its *kreditory* or, conceivably, by drawing down its money holdings.

[45] See, e.g., Nusinov–37, p. 46; Atlas–47, p. 255; Barngol'ts–50, p. 25. Normed money balances in trade are supposed to be covered from owned working capital (Shenger–40, p. 58).

[46] Soviet sources are in agreement that money balances are not meant to be financed from owned capital or bank loans.

[47] Cf. Nusinov–37, p. 44; Novikov–60, p. 33.

[48] Batyrev–47, pp. 131–32.

[49] In the reported statistics, it is generally true that the sum of normed assets and goods shipped exceeds the sum of owned capital and bank loans, though this is not always true of individual sectors (see Tables G–5 and G–6). We do not take this as evidence in itself of departures from the declared principles of finance. There are special arrangements additional to those we have described. There are undoubtedly lags between entries in the books of sellers and buyers and differences in the valuations they give to the same asset. And, the fact that the Bank does not lend against unpaid-for goods would work in the observed direction.

inventory valuation employed in Soviet accounting.[50] Although the procedures are obscure in some details, it is clear that the basic principle is valuation at cost. For inventories purchased by one enterprise from others, this amounts to valuation at official wholesale prices (plus transportation and handling charges). For inventories produced within an enterprise or value-added to purchased inventories, it evidently comes to valuation at internal cost. Turnover taxes payable upon sale of finished products are not included in their values while they are held by their producers. They are included in the price paid by purchasing enterprises and hence are reflected in their inventory valuations.

The speed with which changes in prices and costs are transmitted to inventories is clearest in the case of the general price reforms which have occurred periodically in the Soviet economy. Beginning with the changes associated with the abolition of rationing in 1935 and the reform of basic industrial prices in 1936, enterprises have been required to revalue inventories on hand immediately in accordance with the new official prices.[51] The revaluations have extended to goods in process and finished products as well as purchased materials. A simultaneous adjustment has been made also in the value of bank loans outstanding against the revalued inventories (with a corresponding adjustment in a special liability account of the Bank). The remaining capital gains or losses resulting from the price change have (in the main) been absorbed in owned working capital.

The rate of adjustment in inventory values to occasional changes in particular selling prices and to the continuous changes which occur in costs is less certain. A source published prior to the Credit Reform indicates that at that time inventories were revalued annually in accordance with existing prices.[52] The logic of the arrangements introduced in the Reform would appear to require a prompt adjustment of inventory values to changed prices and costs. Inspection of the statistical data on inventories leaves little doubt that cost changes occurring between major price reforms have been quite rapidly reflected in inventories. Although some lags in the adjustment are probable, it is our impression that inventories reported to be in current prices do very nearly reflect costs and prices as of the date of reference.

In contrast to inventories on hand, goods shipped are known to reflect price changes only with a significant lag. Goods are paid for at the price legally in force at the time they are dispatched.[53] Claims against such goods, therefore, remain unaltered in the face of a price revision occurring prior to receipt of payment. The reported values of goods shipped are not fully adjusted to the new prices until all claims outstanding at the time of the change have been paid. Correspondingly, no immediate change is made in bank loans against goods shipped, although these too come to reflect the new prices as old loans are paid off and new ones issued.

In one important instance, the reported data from which we work are thought to be for inventories valued at retail prices rather than at cost.

---

[50] The discussion following rests heavily on that in Bergson–61, pp. 406–7.

[51] See Arnold–37, p. 385 fn.; Pinus–35, pp. 7–11; Makarov–50, pp. 71 ff.; Shchenkov–52, pp. 207 ff.; and Shchenkov–55, pp. 308 ff.

[52] Rozentul–29, p. 303.

[53] Donde–53, p. 96.

These are data for inventories of finished products in retail and wholesale trade. They quite clearly reflect changes in prices as they occur.[54]

Sector Classifications

A final characteristic of the reported inventory data relates to Soviet statistical practices rather than accounting procedures. We have noted that our estimates are composed for separate sectors within the economy. In general, the sector classifications of the reported data and hence of our estimates are based on administrative divisions (ministries, for example) and not on product criteria. Since administrative arrangements have changed over time, the sector distributions of inventories are not constant in their coverage. On the other hand, the distributions do not necessarily reflect the organizational structure in existence as of each given date, because considerable stabilization of classifications is effected in the Soviet sources. Sharp discontinuities in the classifications almost certainly occur at about 1931 or 1932 and again between 1941 and the postwar years. Classifications within the period 1928–30 appear reasonably stable. Those within the period from the early 1930's to 1941 are likely to vary significantly. Those within the postwar period again appear relatively stable, and, moreover, may approach commodity classifications, since they are based, at least in part, on the operations of individual enterprises.

The intended coverage of the several sectors in our estimates is generally clear from their titles. Sales-supply organs and the antecedent syndicates are classed with industry. The category of "other nonagricultural sectors" in 1928–30 includes housing co-operatives and municipal enterprises. International trade organs in this period are evidently accounted for in the specified sectors. In subsequent years, the "other" category includes international trade, but its content is otherwise uncertain. It may again cover municipal enterprises; it quite probably covers economic organs administratively subordinate to noneconomic ministries; it may—but is not thought to—include some part of supplies and materials held in governmental organs.[55]

3. THE PRESENT ESTIMATES IN CURRENT PRICES

Estimates Based on Reported Asset Data

The initial step required for the derivation of inventory estimates from the published Soviet data is to determine which of the current assets shown in Table 5–1 are properly regarded as inventories. Clearly, all inventories on hand and all goods in transit are recorded in the table either under normed assets or under the account for goods shipped and services rendered. From the first, we exclude expenses of future periods, on the ground that they are not physical assets, and immature livestock, which are included in our separate estimates for livestock. From the second, we exclude "services rendered," which presumably do not relate to physical assets. From the source of the Table 5–1 data, it can be seen that services rendered refer only to transportation and communications and to contract construction. From the character of the operations of these sectors, we judge that

---

54 See Appendix K.

55 For more detailed discussions of the sector classifications of the data, see Appendixes G and I.

most of the category is likely to represent services rendered, and we therefore exclude it entirely from our estimates for these sectors.

The foregoing adjustments having been made, we take normed assets
as the equivalent of inventories on hand, goods shipped as the equivalent
of goods in transit. That this is a questionable procedure follows from the
facts, already noted, that normed assets include goods in transit entered
on the books of buyers and that goods shipped are literally goods dispatched for which payment has not been received. The kinds of errors
which may result from the procedure can be seen by considering the combinations of buyer and seller accounts relating to goods in transit which
may occur:[56]

(*i*) Goods actually in transit may appear in sellers' books as shipped and
not appear in buyers' books at all. This will be the case when the bill for
goods still in transit has not reached the buyer or has not been accepted
by him. Goods in transit are here properly recorded in goods shipped and
appear nowhere else in the accounts.

(*ii*) Goods actually in transit may appear in buyers' books as in transit
and not appear in sellers' books. This will be the case when payment has
been received by the seller before the goods reach the buyer. Goods shipped
here understate goods in transit; normed assets overstate inventories on
hand by an equivalent amount; total inventories are still accurately recorded.

(*iii*) Goods actually in transit may appear on sellers' books as shipped
and on buyers' books as in transit. This will occur when the buyer has
accepted the bill for goods still in transit but payment has not yet been
received by the seller. Goods shipped accurately record goods in transit.
Normed assets overstate inventories on hand, and total inventories are
overstated by an equal amount.

(*iv*) Goods already delivered to the buyer may be recorded in his books
as on hand but may appear on sellers' books as goods shipped. This will
occur when the buyer has accepted the bill for goods actually received but
payment has not yet reached the seller. Normed assets properly record
inventories on hand. Goods shipped overstate goods in transit, and total
inventories are overstated by an equal amount.

The circumstances of the first case described obviously give rise to no
error.

We have one fragment of information bearing on the size of the errors
arising in the second and third cases in combination. Goods in transit on
the books of buyers reportedly amounted on January 1, 1958, to 2.4 percent and on January 1, 1959, to 2.1 percent of the production supplies of
industrial enterprises subordinate to the *sovnarkhozy*.[57] If the 1959 ratio

---

[56] We disregard the fact that the book entries of enterprises may fall behind their
actual operations. For example, goods dispatched may be carried for a time as stocks on
hand, until documents are prepared, etc. (cf. Barngol'ts–57, p. 28). Presumably a similar
lag may occur at the receiving end. We also disregard the complications that arise from
differences between buyer's and seller's valuations of the same good.

[57] Novikov–60, p. 34. In an early source (*Economic Survey*, February 15, 1930, p. 2),
"materials and fuel not yet to hand" are shown as 169 million rubles out of a total of
about 3.7 billion rubles of current physical assets in VSNKh industries on October 1,
1929. We are unsure whether assets "not yet to hand" are necessarily in transit. The
payments arrangements of that period do not much resemble those in force after 1931.

had held in that year for production supplies in all sectors and for finished products in those sectors in which they are largely purchased rather than produced (domestic trade, procurement, sales-supply), goods in transit on the books of buyers would have amounted to about 9 billion rubles or 1.7 percent of inventories on hand and some 12 percent of goods shipped.[58] Normed assets would here overstate inventories on hand by the full 9 billion. Goods shipped would understate goods in transit by that portion of the 9 billion which represented goods already paid for.[59] Total inventories would be overstated by 9 billion less the understatement of goods in transit.

No quantitative evidence is available on the size of errors likely to result from the fourth case described. Soviet sources disagree somewhat on the matter, but they generally indicate that for nonlocal shipments, at least in the 1950's, the "payment period" was usually shorter than the period required for the movement of goods.[60] For local shipments, the relation may be different, although we would suppose that the local "float" of both goods and payments is relatively small.

It appears, then, that our use of normed assets (excluding expenses of future periods and immature livestock) to represent inventories on hand and of goods shipped to represent goods in transit is likely to produce relatively insignificant percentage errors in the estimates of total inventories, somewhat larger percentage errors in the estimates of inventories on hand, and possibly considerable percentage errors in the estimates of goods in transit. Moreover, changes which have occurred over time in the speed with which goods are moved and payments rendered may have altered the size and possibly the sign of the error in the estimate of goods in transit. It is because of the unreliability of these accounts that we retain the title, "goods shipped."

In one instance, we make a deliberate correction for a presumed distortion in the goods-shipped account. During 1936, the normal period permitted to buyers for the rendering of payments was markedly lengthened. Reported goods shipped (in major sectors only) increased in the course of that year by 91 percent, normed assets by 31 percent.[61] We are unable to trace the full consequences of this change in payment arrangements upon the inventory accounts.[62] As a rough adjustment, we link goods shipped for all years through 1936 to those for 1937 on the assumption that the ratio of goods shipped to inventories on hand (in each sector) was the same at the beginning of 1936 as at the beginning of 1937. We do not

---

58 The figures are calculated from detailed data for 1959 given in TsSU–61, pp. 92 ff., which is the source also of the Table 5–1 data for 1960.

59 This portion may be significant. Payments made under letter-of-credit arrangements ("accreditives" and "special accounts") follow promptly after shipment. While they account for a small share of total payments (see Popov–57, p. 247), the in-transit accounts under consideration are also small. Payments made under "special loan accounts" (essentially an open line of credit) appear also to be made immediately after shipment, and these are quite extensively used (cf. Chernyshova–57, pp. 28 ff.).

60 Cf. Mitel'man–54, p. 58; Frontas'eva–56, p. 59.

61 See Table G–4.

62 Compare on this Sobol'–37, pp. 146–47; *Den'gi i kredit,* 1939:9–10, p. 25; Atlas–58, p. 143.

make a compensating adjustment in the estimates for inventories on hand, although this might be a superior procedure.[63]

Our inventory estimates rest on reported statistics of normed assets and goods shipped to the extent that they are available. For many years, they are not available, and for these years the estimates are based on data from the liability side of the accounts. To convey in summary fashion the statistical origins of the estimates, we indicate in Table 5-2 the general

TABLE 5-2

TYPE OF REPORTED DATA UNDERLYING THE INVENTORY ESTIMATES
IN CURRENT PRICES, 1928-62
(January 1)

	Reported Data for Assets	Reported Data for Owned Working Capital and Bank Loans	Reported Data for Bank Loans
1928	X		
1929	X		
1930	X		
1931			
1932			X
1933	X		
1934	X		
1935	X		
1936	X		
1937	X		
1938	X		
1939	X		
1940		X	
1941		X	
1944			X
1945			X
1946	X		
1947			X
1948			X
1949			X
1950			X
1951	X		
1952			X
1953			X
1954			X
1955		X	
1956	X		
1957		X	
1958			X
1959	X		
1960	X		
1961		X	
1962		X	

Source: See Appendix G.

character of the reported data underlying the estimates for each year. The tabulation is unavoidably imprecise, as is the discussion immediately following. Reference should be made to the appendixes for complete explanations of sources and methods.

Reported data on assets underlie the estimates for 14 of the 33 years covered. In almost all of these years, the sources provide considerable

---

[63] On January 1, 1959, the previously existing arrangement by which the buyer was permitted to defer payment for a stated interval after acceptance of the bill was abolished (see Kazantsev–61, p. 15). We find no evidence of a sharp discontinuity in the statistical series at this date, presumably because the area of application of "deferred payments" had been progressively narrowed over the years preceding it (cf. Popov–57, p. 106). We therefore make no allowance for this change in composing our estimates.

detail by sectors. The data for the four postwar years, of which Table 5–1 contains a part, are the most detailed and comprehensive, although the division of total industrial inventories between producer and consumer goods is not given in our principal source and is obtained by quite round-about procedures. For the period from 1933 to 1939, the reported data are restricted for the most part to major sectors (state industry, state agriculture, procurement, and domestic trade); minor sectors are estimated from fragmentary data or by extrapolations on bank loans. The exclusion of small tools from inventories prior to their reclassification in 1936 is corrected for on the assumption that half of them were included in reported inventories by January 1, 1937, and all by January 1, 1938. Data on the value of small tools in this period are slight and inconsistent, and the adjustment is rough. Goods shipped are more or less crudely estimated in much of the 1930's; for all years before 1933, they are simply extrapolated (by sector) from 1933 on inventories on hand. The figures for inventories on hand of January 1, 1928, to 1930, are based on detailed reported data for the October 1 preceding.

The entries in Table 5–2 somewhat understate the amount of statistics for assets which are utilized in the estimates. In particular, inventories of finished products in domestic trade, valued in retail prices, are available for all the years covered from 1936 through 1961, although inventories in state wholesale trade organs are unreported in some periods. Inventories in industry are obtained from reported data in 1931 and 1932, and are therefore fairly solid—and considerable—components of the otherwise weak estimates for those years (we show no entry for 1931 in Table 5–2 because we make current-price estimates only for industry on that date; other sectors are interpolated in constant prices between 1930 and 1932).

Estimates Based on Reported Liability Data

The source of the asset data for 1951, 1956, 1959, and 1960 provides data as well for the liability accounts, by sectors; similar accounts can be estimated for 1939. These years provide benchmarks from which we interpolate or extrapolate inventories for seven additional years primarily on the basis of data for owned working capital and bank loans. With few exceptions, the figures reported for owned working capital in the interpolated years are given as totals only, without breakdowns by sectors (considerable detail is given for 1957 and some for 1962). We distribute the totals among sectors by interpolation (or extrapolation) on bank loans or, for domestic trade, on the finished product series. Inventories are then interpolated by sectors on the combined sums of owned capital and bank loans or in trade on the finished product series.[64]

The probable behavior of the relation between the combined sources of finance and total inventories can be judged from what has been said previously about the functional relation between them and from the statistical data presented in Table 5–3. Assets are shown there as they are reported in the sources, prior to the various adjustments for coverage made

---

[64] The data for inventories in trade of finished products valued at retail prices are compared for a few years with finished products at acquisition costs and total inventories at acquisition costs in Appendix K, p. 550.

TABLE 5-3

OWNED WORKING CAPITAL PLUS BANK LOANS RELATIVE TO NORMED
ASSETS PLUS GOODS SHIPPED, IN CURRENT PRICES, SELECTED YEARS*
(January 1)

	Owned Working Capital and Bank Loans (Billion Rubles)	Normed Assets and Goods Shipped (Billion Rubles)	Col. 1/Col. 2 (Percent)
	(1)	(2)	(3)
1935	32.3	36.5	88.5
1936	49.7	55.3	89.9
1937	70.1	75.8	92.5
1938	79.6	87.3	91.2
1939	90	99	91
1951	331.0	343.3	96.4
1956	433.9	450.0	96.4
1959	609.3	648.2	94.0
1960	703.2	746.3	94.2

* Figures for 1935–39 include state industry, state agriculture, procurement, and domestic trade; equivalents are excluded from owned working capital. Figures for 1951–60 include in addition industrial co-operatives, transportation and communications, contract construction, and other nonagricultural
sectors; equivalents are included in owned working capital.
  Sources: For 1935–38, Table G–5. For 1939, owned working capital is the
figure cited on p. 486 from Shenger–40, bank loans are calculated from Table
I–1. For 1951–60, Table G–6.

in our estimates. The data are for aggregates of sectors, but similar relations hold for individual sectors.[65] On the whole, the combined sources
appear to provide a good estimator of the combined uses. The lack of data
for owned working capital by sectors in the years being estimated reduces
the reliability of the procedure, but the known totals for owned capital
significantly limit the potential errors in the estimates. The estimates for
1940 and 1941 are adjusted for an apparent undercoverage in the reported
data on assets in the newly acquired territories.

For 11 of the years covered, the inventory estimates are largely interpolations or extrapolations on bank loans—and on the series for finished
products in trade. The loan data employed contain considerable detail by
sectors,[66] and we utilize the detailed data by industrial sectors in the interpolations: producer goods industries are estimated from separate loan
data for heavy and timber industries; consumer goods from loans to food,
light, and local industries, and to industrial co-operatives; sales-supply
organs are treated separately in the postwar years. Bank loans on goods
shipped are used as an estimator of total goods shipped;[67] the distribution
of the total among sectors is generally interpolated on total inventories in
each sector. No effort is made, as in principle it should be, to adjust the
sector loan data for differences in the share of loans on goods shipped in
total loans.

Other things equal, the higher the loan share in total sources of finance,
presumably the greater the likelihood of a close functional relation between bank loans and inventories in a particular sector. The distribution
of loan shares among sectors is, however, unfortunate for our purposes.
Loans are an important source of finance for domestic trade, but, for rea-

[65] See Tables G–5 and G–6.
[66] See Appendix I.
[67] On the relation of such loans to goods shipped, see Appendix J.

sons which have been explained, the ratio of loans to inventories is unlikely to have been stable. Because of this, we use the series for finished products when available instead of bank loans as an interpolator for trade. Loans are also important in procurement, but this sector holds a small part of total inventories. Producer goods industries (other than timber), which account in nearly all years for a larger share of inventories than any other sector for which we make current-price estimates, rely relatively little upon bank financing. Only consumer goods industries both rely substantially upon bank loans and account for a significant share of total inventories.

As a rough indication of the behavior of the relation of loans to inventories, we present in Table 5–4 data for all industry, domestic trade, and for a nearly comprehensive aggregate of sectors. The inventory figures are our final estimates and hence reflect various adjustments for coverage we have made (an exception in 1940 and 1941 is noted on the table). They include estimates derived from data for owned capital plus bank loans as well as those based directly on reported assets. The loan data include loans for nonseasonal inventories in heavy industry and loans related to fixed capital investment, for which we have made adjustments when employing the loan series as interpolators. Comparisons for more detailed sectors can be made with data provided in the appendixes. Such comparisons are likely, however, especially if carried over a long span of years, to be strongly affected by differences between the sector classifications of the loan and inventory data. These differences also affect the Table 5–4 comparisons.[68]

Clearly, loans do move broadly with inventories—and even in trade, though the anticipated variations in this sector are evident. The relation between loans and inventories is more stable from the mid-1930's on, which is also the period in which we rely most heavily on loans as interpolators. However, the inventory estimates for 1940–41 are not themselves highly reliable. The marked rise in the loan ratio to the mid-1930's, while partly the consequence of our adjustments of the asset data and partly attributable to known changes in lending procedures, gives little ground for confidence in our inventory estimates for 1932 (other than for industry, which are based on assets). It similarly gives reason to doubt the accuracy of various estimates for minor sectors in the 1930's which are extrapolated on loans.

The use of the loan data is particularly hazardous in estimating inventories in 1949, 1950, and 1952. In each of these years, general price reforms were made effective as of January 1. Bank loans on normed assets as of these dates presumably reflect the new prices, loans on goods shipped do not. To cope with this difficulty, we estimate from data for nearby years

---

[68] The calculations in the table provide a poorer measure of the consistency with which the State Bank has observed its declared lending principles than of the reliability of loans viewed simply as inventory interpolators. Besides the deficiencies mentioned in the text and the modifications of lending principles which have occurred over time, the Bank's rules are meant to apply to particular kinds of assets rather than to total inventories. As the composition of inventories within a sector changes, the ratio of loans to inventories may change, although the Bank's lending procedures remain constant. A similar result can occur also from shifts in the relative importance of the industries composing any observed sector.

TABLE 5-4

BANK LOANS RELATIVE TO INVENTORIES, IN CURRENT PRICES, SELECTED YEARS
(January 1)

	Short-Term Bank Loans (Billion Rubles)			Inventories on Hand and Goods Shipped (Billion Rubles)			Ratio of Loans to Inventories (Percent)		
	Industry	Domestic Trade	All Sectors[a]	Industry	Domestic Trade	All Sectors[b]	Industry	Domestic Trade	All Sectors
1932	3.60	--	--	14.3	--	--	25.2	--	--
1933	4.15	2.58	10.39	18.6	6.5	32.3	22.3	39.7	32.2
1934	5.80	4.39	14.11	22.0	7.6	38.0	26.4	57.8	37.1
1935	7.10	5.86	17.39	25.5	10.1	45.4	27.8	58.0	38.3
1936	13.08	7.46	26.56	38.6	14.6	66.7	33.9	51.1	39.8
1937	19.3	9.4	34.8	51.0	18.5	82.6	37.8	50.8	42.1
1938	21.47	11.52	40.22	55.6	21.2	90.8	38.6	54.3	44.3
1939	25.25	11.80	44.95	64.4	20.7	101.2	39.2	57.0	44.4
1940	29.27	10.94	47.95	75.2[c]	21.4[c]	113.5[c]	38.9	51.1	42.2
1941	32.1	13.5	55.0	83.7[c]	27.6[c]	129.6[c]	38.4	48.9	42.4
1946	35.3	15.2	60.6	87.4	22.2	127.3	40.4	68.5	47.6
1947	--	21.4	--	--	32.7	--	--	65.4	--
1948	--	30.1	--	--	46.0	--	--	65.4	--
1951	95.6	50.3	167.2	208.9	74.2	319.9	45.8	67.8	52.3
1953	--	72.7	--	--	107.3	--	--	67.8	--
1954	--	70.3	--	--	107.1	--	--	65.6	--
1955	117.2	51.0	190.5	266.6	99.1	401.1	44.0	51.5	47.5
1956	115.8	59.6	199.8	261.0	115.2	417.6	44.4	51.7	47.8
1957	127.6	83.5	244.2	287.0	133.5	475.5	44.5	62.5	51.4
1958	141.8	86.6	--	308.8	139.5	--	46.0	62.1	--
1959	172.1	104.7	320.8	354.8	173.3	601.9	48.5	60.4	53.3
1960	184.5	125.4	383.1	380.2	200.6	690.8	48.5	62.5	55.5
1961	198.2	131.0	412.7	414.7	209.0	748.3	47.8	62.7	55.2
1962	213.0	146.0	451.0	453	236	828	47.0	61.9	54.5

[a] Excluding contract construction.
[b] Excluding contract construction, private and collective-farm agriculture, and uninstalled equipment, n.e.c.
[c] Figures are unadjusted for undercoverage of assets in the acquired territories; see pp. 490–91.
Sources: Tables I–1, I–3, and G–1.

the division of loans between normed assets and goods shipped, in each sector, when both are valued in the same prices. Using indexes of the change in prices occurring on January 1, we revalue loans on goods shipped in the new prices. The interpolation then proceeds as for other years.[69]

Reported Data Not Utilized

Soviet sources contain a considerable amount of data of two sorts of which we make little or no use. One of these is figures on the ratio of bank loans to "working capital" in individual sectors. We have noted the ambiguity of the term, "working capital." The bank loan term in such ratios is also typically unidentifiable: it may refer to all loans or loans on normed assets; it may, in industry, be inclusive or exclusive of sales-supply organs; it may define the sector inconsistently with the available absolute loan figures. In the face of these uncertainties, it appears preferable to disregard such ratios. We do, however, make some use of them in dividing total industrial inventories between producer and consumer goods in the postwar period.[70]

The second sort of data which we disregard, altogether, is annual *planned* increases in owned working capital, which are reported for the postwar years. Besides the obvious drawback that these are planned rather than realized, their sector coverage is uncertain. It is unclear also to what extent inventory gains and losses resulting from price changes are reflected in them. Where asset data are unavailable, the realized loan figures appear a better basis of estimation than the planned changes of owned capital.[71]

4. THE ESTIMATES IN CONSTANT PRICES

The derivation of the constant price estimates can be explained quite briefly.[72] We begin with inventories in 1937 prevailing prices, which are basic to the whole of the constant-price estimates.

For all sectors for which we estimate inventories in current prices except domestic trade, we obtain inventories in 1937 prices by deflating the current-price estimates. For domestic trade, we deflate instead, in the years for which it is available, the series for finished products valued at retail prices, and adjust its absolute level for consistency with the 1937 value of all trade inventories at cost. For years before 1936, we deflate the estimates of total trade inventories valued at cost. Because of the unreliability of the division of total inventories between inventories on hand and goods shipped, we do not attempt to deflate the two categories differently.

The price indexes from which sector deflators are composed (retail prices, machinery prices, basic industrial prices, etc.) are drawn largely from Bergson–61 and from the several specialized studies which contribute to Bergson's. Since these indexes are more or less restricted to the years covered by Bergson, we undertake here to fill in the missing years: gen-

---

[69] For detailed explanations, see the discussion of these years in Appendix G.

[70] See Appendix G, notes for 1951 and related years.

[71] Considerable use is made of these data in Bergson–61 (see his Appendix G). However, almost all of the data employed in our postwar estimates were not available at the time of Bergson's writing.

[72] For details, see Appendixes L, M, and N.

erally those between 1928 and 1937, 1937 and 1940, 1944 and 1948, and those beyond 1955. Our interpolations for the intermediate years are rough, and the extensions beyond 1955, except for retail prices, come by various dates to the assumption that prices remained unchanged, despite some evidence that this was not strictly the case. For the most part, the component indexes are indexes of selling prices, though we construct a cost index for producer goods industries for use in those periods in which subsidization was large. Most of the component indexes either are given-year weighted or can be argued to approximate such indexes. The weights employed, however, relate to current flows of output or sales, not stocks of inventories.

Sector deflators are obtained by combining various price indexes with weights based usually on the composition of inventories by kind (raw materials, goods in process, finished products)[73] but, in the case of producer goods industries, on a distribution by sectors. An effort is made to approximate given-year weights in the aggregation of the component indexes, but it is limited. In the choice both of component indexes and weights, we are guided by the procedures devised by Bergson for the deflation of his estimates of annual investment in inventories, although we depart from them in some degree.[74]

The one consequential sector for which we cannot estimate inventories in current prices and hence do not obtain constant-price data by deflation is agriculture (the series for state agriculture in current prices is not utilized for the constant-price estimates). From the estimated value of all agricultural inventories (state, collective-farm, and private) on January 1, 1938, we extrapolate inventories in all years on gross agricultural production in 1937 prices. Inventories in contract construction, which are derived by deflation in some years, are interpolated or extrapolated to other years on the volume of contract construction in 1937 prices. The minor category of uninstalled equipment, n.e.c., is estimated as a constant fraction of fixed capital in investment projects in progress.

Inventories in 1928 and 1950 prevailing prices are obtained from those in 1937 prices. In its essentials, the procedure is to convert the values of the latter, for each sector, to 1928 prices in 1928 and 1937 and to 1950 prices in 1950 and 1937. The sector deflators required for the conversions are the given-year weighted indexes previously described and 1937 weighted indexes which are calculated for the purpose. Sector estimates are then interpolated on the 1937 price series between 1937 and the new weight year and extrapolated similarly beyond 1937 or the new weight year.

Inventories at factor cost valuations in all three weight years are derived from the corresponding series in prevailing prices. Adjustments from prevailing prices are made only for domestic trade and consumer goods industries, which are the sectors in which inventory values are thought to be significantly affected by turnover taxes. For trade, the percentage adjustments are those made by Bergson in his estimates of annual investment in trade inventories. For consumer goods industries, the adjustment required is assumed to equal one half that made for trade. The adjustments are

---

[73] See Appendix H.
[74] See Bergson–61, Appendix G.

uniform within each sector for all years in prices of any one of the weight years.

5. RELIABILITY OF THE ESTIMATES

In Current Prices

The reliability of the inventory estimates depends, to begin with, upon the quality of the current-price data which underlie them.

The original sources of data for inventories proper—normed assets and goods shipped—are generally not specified in the publications from which we obtain them. Occasional references are made to the "balance sheets" of industries or ministries,[75] and we suppose that the data for the most part originate in the books of individual enterprises or of the administrative bodies to which they are subordinate. Published data for the late 1920's are stated to include estimates for some sectors based on norms, sample surveys, extrapolations, and the like.[76] No similar statement appears in later sources.

We have no direct evidence on the accuracy of the accounts of enterprises or other administrative organs. Unintentional bookkeeping errors undoubtedly occur and are likely to have been common in the early years covered. The financial arrangements originating in the Credit Reform appear to require reasonable accuracy in accounts. The Ministry of Finance, the State Bank, and other agencies have broad powers to audit books and inspect inventory holdings. Motives to falsify inventory records deliberately are imaginable—for example, to exaggerate goods in process when they are counted as part of output[77]—but it is not obvious that these should operate in one direction or lead to large and cumulative errors.

We cannot know either with what accuracy the published sources have reproduced the data available in the accounts of operating sectors. Inventory data have not ordinarily been cited by Soviet spokesmen as a significant measure of the regime's accomplishments. Distortions deliberately contrived to mislead the reader appear highly unlikely.

On the other hand, much of the inventory data, especially for the 1930's, does not emanate from agencies such as the Central Statistical Administration or Gosplan, which might be presumed to have reviewed it for internal consistency and comprehensiveness. Indeed, the strongest ground for distrusting the data is that they are frequently inconsistent and ambiguous in coverage—by assets and by sectors. Much of Appendix G is taken up with an effort to identify and reconcile the reported data, but numerous unexplained discrepancies remain. To the inaccuracies arising from the reported data must be added those created by our adjustments, which are invariably crude, for small tools, expenses of future periods, the 1936 change in the payment period, etc.

The owned working capital totals employed in the interpolations come typically from the Ministry of Finance. The sector coverage of the figures

---

[75] Cf. Putilov–32, p. 102; Khromov–37, p. 72 fn.; Omel'chenko–39, p. 10; Rubinshtein–58, p. 47 fn.

[76] See Appendix G, notes for 1928–30.

[77] Cf. Sobol'–37, pp. 143–44.

is frequently uncertain. The origin of the figures raises the possibility that they are based in part on cumulated totals of past budgetary grants and retained earnings and, hence, do not adequately reflect gains and losses from price changes. The bank loan data come from publications of the State Bank or, in the postwar period, the Central Statistical Administration. The statistical accuracy of the figures is presumably high, except for years immediately following the Reform when the Bank's accounts may have been in considerable disorder.[78] Incongruities in the sector classifications of loans, however, are pervasive. Evidence on the reliability of the interpolations on owned capital and bank loans has been presented in the preceding section.[79]

In Constant Prices

While the potential errors in the current-price estimates are large, gross errors are more likely to result from the deflation procedures. The price indexes obtained from Bergson and used for deflation to prevailing 1937 prices are thought to be statistically reliable, but the fact that their internal weights are based on output or sales rather than on inventories may give them a significant bias for our purposes. The interpolations which we make in some of these price indexes, especially between 1928 and 1937, are probably the most vulnerable element in the whole of the 1937-price calculations: price data for the early 1930's are fragmentary and our interpolations are effectively freehand in large measure. The weights with which we compose sector deflators from the price indexes may be the source of additional errors.

No claim of reliability can be made for the constant-price estimates of agricultural inventories. Some evidence suggests that the extrapolation on output may not be wide of the mark in linking 1928 and 1937,[80] which is an important link. In general, however, the estimates for agriculture can be taken to serve only as a rough adjustment in the absolute level of total inventories. The other components extrapolated on output are unreliable but of slight significance in the total.

The adjustments from prevailing prices to factor cost valuations are crude, although the results appear plausible in comparison with the effects of similar adjustments for GNP. In Bergson's estimates, GNP in factor costs is lower than that in prevailing prices by 8 percent in 1928, 23 percent in 1937, and 24 percent in 1950.[81] In our estimates, inventories in factor costs are lower than those in prevailing prices by 7 percent, 15 percent, and 17 percent respectively.[82] Considering that turnover taxes are imposed at intermediate or advanced stages in the process of production and dis-

---

[78] There is also an unexplained discrepancy in reported loan totals for 1951. See p. 530.

[79] Data becoming available too late for incorporation in the estimates indicate that our current-price totals for 1961 and 1962 are some 2–3 percent too high (see Appendix G, pp. 515–16).

[80] See p. 584.

[81] See Bergson–61, pp. 130, 150, and 154.

[82] See Tables L–1, M–1, and M–2, and Tables N–1, N–2, and N–3. The percentages cited refer to averages of inventories as of the beginning and end of each year.

tribution, it is understandable that their effects on inventories should be less than on output. The effects will, of course, vary with the composition of both inventories and output.

The estimates in 1928 and 1950 prices suffer from deficiencies additional to those of the 1937-price calculations. The conversions from 1937 to 1928 prices in 1928 and 1937 and to 1950 prices in 1937 and 1950 alter growth rates in the inventory stock—raising the rate for the 1928–37 interval from 5.9 percent per annum in 1937 prices to 12.4 percent in 1928 prices and lowering that for 1937–50, from 3.7 percent in 1937 to 3.4 percent in 1950 prices[83]—in approximately the same proportions as similar weight shifts alter the growth rates of GNP.[84] Since inventories originate in a large share of the sectors which contribute to GNP, this similarity in sensitivity to price weights appears plausible. On the other hand, the component price indexes we use are largely GNP deflators, and the weights with which we combine them are rather arbitrarily chosen, so that we would not stress the price-weight sensitivity of the inventory measures as additional or independent evidence of such sensitivity in general.

The least defensible element in the 1928- and 1950-price estimates is the interpolations and extrapolations from the weight years on the series in 1937 prices. This is a kind of device to which we have not had to resort elsewhere in our estimates, and its employment here very greatly reduces the reliability of the inventory series in alternative prices, in years other than the indicated weight years, relative to that of the basic estimates in 1937 prices. The difference is somewhat minimized by the fact that the interpolations and extrapolations are done by detailed sectors, and 1950 prices are similar enough to those of 1937 that large errors may not result in the 1950-price series. The estimates in 1928 prices, however, other than for 1928 and 1937, are clearly usable only to complete estimates of the total capital stock in prices of that year.

Viewed as a whole, the inventory estimates are subject to significant error from a variety of sources. In their appraisal, however, it is relevant to note that they do not rest—especially those in 1937 prices and the agricultural component aside—on bold or critical assumptions. They are put together from a large quantity of detailed data, both for current values and for prices. Their potential errors are independent of one another, do not work predictably in one direction, and are likely to be mutually offsetting in some degree. For these reasons, we suppose that the estimates are usably reliable for purposes such as ours where considerable tolerance is permissible. Used with caution, they will, we believe, support analysis in broad terms, of a sort which we shall make hereafter, of the behavior of inventories as such, as well as that of the total capital stock into which they enter as a constituent.

---

[83] See Table T–24. The rates cited are calculated from annual averages, as in the preceding footnote.

[84] Bergson's GNP estimates (see Bergson–61, pp. 128, 149, and 153) imply 1928–37 growth rates of 5.5 percent in 1937 prices and 11.9 percent in 1928 prices, 1937–50 rates of 3.1 percent in 1937 prices and 2.9 percent in 1950 prices. We subsequently utilize a 1937-price GNP series which differs from Bergson's, but the difference, which is small in any case, is insignificant for the immediate purpose.

The Estimates Smoothed

In comparison with those for fixed capital and for livestock, the inventory estimates are probably relatively reliable for the order of magnitude of the absolute value of the stock. The implied growth rates for periods of several years' length appear also reasonably firm. The estimates are most questionable for the year-to-year changes which they imply and for some years are almost certainly wide of the mark. This is so because misreadings of the current-price data or faulty interpolations may produce small but erratic percentage errors in the annual stock estimates which amount to large percentage errors in the annual changes. Moreover, a slight misjudgment on our part of the timing of price changes may displace the resulting inventory gains or losses from the year in which they occurred to a contiguous year. Errors from either of these sources will not be cumulative over time. Even the agricultural estimates are likely to be more accurate for spans of several years than for periods of a single year's length.

Soviet sources occasionally contain commentaries on short-period changes in inventories, of which we have cited a few in Appendix N. These relate solely to industry but do lend credibility to some of the less plausible features of the estimates of industrial inventories: their absolute decline (in 1937 prices) in 1929, their large increase in 1931 and small increase in 1932, their relatively high level and slow rate of increase immediately after the war, and their absolute decline during 1955. The extremely large increase both in industrial and in total inventories during 1935 cannot be similarly substantiated. Some of the evidence on which it rests appears firm, and a limited corroboration from other evidence is possible.[85] But, on the whole, we are confident only that the increase during 1935 was large and not that it was as large as our estimates imply.[86]

To test the sensitivity of the estimates to short-period errors, we have calculated in Table 5–5 how far our results would be altered if we were to average the three years centered on each given year. The effects upon the stock figures are limited, not exceeding about 6 percent, and the general shape of changes over time is not significantly altered. For our basic purpose, the insensitivity of the estimates in this respect is relevant. The effects of the smoothing upon the annual increments, however, are radical. Since the increments (for 1939 and 1940, the increments excluding acquired assets) represent investment in inventories, it follows that our estimates are not a reliable guide to short-run changes in investment of this kind. When we come subsequently to consider the implications of our calculations for Soviet investment, we shall on this account refer again to the smoothed incremental series.

We do not suggest that the smoothed series, for either totals or incre-

---

[85] See Appendix N.

[86] Interestingly, the percentage increase in livestock herds in 1935, 27 percent in 1937 prices, was even higher than the 21 percent estimated increase in inventories proper. The livestock figure, however, is itself open to question because of the roughness of the adjustment for changes in weight.

ments, is the more accurate measure of the actual behavior of inventories, since all the evidence available to us supports the original estimates. It is noteworthy, moreover, that the increments vary about as erratically between 1951 and 1960, for which period the current price data are good

TABLE 5-5

EFFECTS ON TOTAL INVENTORIES OF SMOOTHING THE ANNUAL
ESTIMATES, IN 1937 PRICES

	Total Inventories (January 1)			Annual Increments	
	As Estimated (Billion Rubles)	Three-Year Moving Average (Billion Rubles)	Col. 2/Col. 1 (Percent)	As Estimated (Billion Rubles)	Three-Year Moving Average (Billion Rubles
	(1)	(2)	(3)	(4)	(5)
1928	48.8	--	--	1.5	--
1929	50.3	49.4	98.2	-1.2	1.9
1930	49.1	51.3	104	5.3	3.6
1931	54.4	54.9	101	6.8	2.7
1932	61.2	57.6	94.1	-3.9	2.2
1933	57.3	59.8	104	3.5	1.3
1934	60.8	61.1	100	4.4	7.3
1935	65.2	68.4	105	13.9	5.8
1936	79.1	74.2	93.8	-0.9	7.4
1937	78.2	81.6	104	9.2	4.3
1938	87.4	85.9	98.3	4.7	7.9 (6.3)*
1939	92.1	93.8	102	9.7 (4.9)*	5.8 (2.5)*
1940	101.8	99.6	97.8	3.0 (-2.0)*	--
1941	104.8	--	--	--	--
1944	82.5	--	--	1.9	--
1945	84.4	84.9	101	3.4	3.0
1946	87.8	87.9	100	3.8	6.6
1947	91.6	94.5	103	12.6	7.3
1948	104.2	101.8	97.7	5.4	12.2
1949	109.6	114.0	104	18.6	11.2
1950	128.2	125.2	97.7	9.5	14.9
1951	137.7	140.1	102	16.8	14.1
1952	154.5	154.2	99.8	15.8	14.0
1953	170.3	168.2	98.8	9.5	7.8
1954	179.8	176.0	97.9	-1.9	4.6
1955	177.9	180.6	102	6.2	9.3
1956	184.1	189.9	103	23.7	14.4
1957	207.8	204.3	98.3	13.2	23.6
1958	221.0	227.9	103	33.9	26.3
1959	254.9	254.2	99.7	31.7	28.9
1960	286.6	283.1	98.8	21.1	28.2
1961	307.7	311.3	101	31.9	--
1962	339.6	--	--	--	--

* Figures in parentheses exclude increments from territorial acquisitions.
   Sources: For column 1, Table T-24. All other figures outside parentheses are calculated from column 1. The column 4 figures in parentheses are calculated on the assumption that 5 percent of the stock of January 1, 1940, is attributable to the territorial acquisitions of 1939, and 5 percent of the stock of January 1, 1941, to the acquisitions of 1940. The column 5 figures in parentheses, for 1938 and 1939, are computed from the 1937 and 1938 actual increments and the 1939 and 1940 increments exclusive of acquisitions.

and the deflators pose few problems, as they do in earlier years, for which the data are less reliable. The smoothed series may, however, for reasons explained in Chapter 8, provide a measure of sorts of the level of inventories or annual investment intended by the Soviet authorities, in contrast to those actually realized.

6. DISTRIBUTION BY SECTOR

The inventory estimates of principal concern to us, those shown in Table T–24, cover either the whole economy or its nonagricultural sectors. Although some inventories attributable to the residential sector are included in the estimates for the earliest years and possibly those for later years, they are undoubtedly of inconsequential volume. We therefore take the total and nonagricultural series to represent also inventories in non-residential sectors and nonagricultural nonresidential sectors respectively. This gives us estimates corresponding in coverage to the sector categories which we have treated separately throughout the study. Of these, the series for sectors other than agriculture are obviously much the more reliable.

As noted, the aggregate series are composed from estimates for considerably more detailed sectors, and for inventories on hand and goods shipped taken separately. Of this detail, only two portions are sufficiently reliable to be of independent use: the estimates for all industry (producer and consumer goods in combination) and for domestic trade.[87] These also are of uneven reliability for various time periods, but they appear firm enough to permit us to explore, at least tentatively, hypotheses bearing on the determinants of inventory holdings.[88] Industry and trade together have accounted typically, in 1937 prices, for about two thirds to three quarters of nonagricultural inventories (the nonagricultural share in the total rising, according to our estimates, from 72 percent in 1928 to 92 percent in 1962). The remaining sector components are individually unreliable—and, in some cases, not necessarily plausible on their face. Their errors, however, are likely to be of minor effect for the aggregates and, in part at least, off-setting. The estimates for goods shipped, by sector or in total, are not usable in isolation. The relative reliability of the sector estimates inclusive or exclusive of goods shipped varies with the character of the underlying data, which differs from period to period.

So much of the sector detail as is of interest and use is presented graphically in Chart 5–2. Industry figures are omitted for 1944–45 because industrial inventories in these years are estimated as part of a combined total. The series for industry and trade are shown exclusive of goods shipped, as probably the analytically more relevant concept for these sectors; series inclusive of goods shipped can be obtained from Table N–1.

7. INVENTORIES HELD VERSUS INVENTORIES EMPLOYED

Like our other capital estimates, those for inventories are composed for assets in existence rather than for assets actually in use. No doubt, some part of fixed capital, for example, that held in standby reserves, could be regarded as not truly engaged in the production process, at least in the short run, and in that sense as inoperative or unemployed.[89] A more seri-

---

87 Some weight could be put on the two industrial components individually, but the risks of error in the distribution of the total between them are large.

88 See pp. 230 ff.

89 Fixed capital in investment projects in progress is inoperative as fixed capital, but it is not necessarily unemployed since it functions as inventories. As the latter, it poses the same problem as do inventories in the strict sense.

CHART 5-2

Distribution of Inventories by Sector, in 1937 Prices, 1928-62*

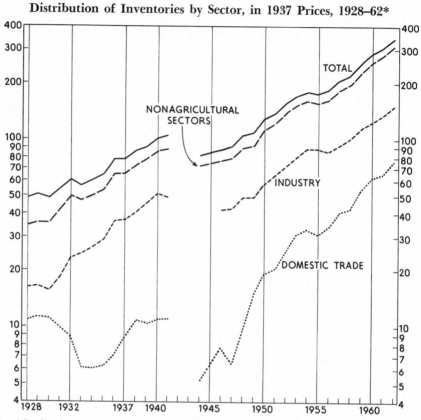

* Total and nonagricultural are shown inclusive, industry and trade exclusive, of goods shipped.
Source: Table N-1.

ous question on this score arises, however, with respect to inventories. The Soviet literature is heavily dominated by complaints of excessive inventories and inventory hoarding.

Like all Soviet "self-criticisms," these complaints are difficult to interpret. There are, first, assertions that on the contrary inventories are too small—which are no less convincing because they are rare.[90] Secondly, it is usually unclear whether the extreme unreliability of materials deliveries,

---

[90] Khromov-37, pp. 79–80, cites, critically, Professor (M. I.?) Bogolepov, in a lecture delivered November 8, 1936, as saying that until recently working capital of industry had been held at a rather low level, for lack of resources; that resources were now ample, and that forthcoming plans should provide for the "transition from somewhat stingy norms to full norms." Gerashchenko-57, p. 5, proposes an increase in the norms for raw materials and goods in process in industry, until such time as the system of materials supply is reorganized. L. V. Kantorovich, the mathematician and linear programmer, asserts the following (Kantorovich-59, p. 223): "While resources have often been allotted to long-term investments with small effectiveness, even of the order of 5–10 percent per year, the working capital of enterprises has been extremely curtailed, which has prevented the creation of normal stocks [*zadelov*], normal supplies of materials. . . . As a result there have here remained unrealized, for lack of the necessary resources, monetary

which appears endemic to the system, is taken as given.[91] That source of uncertainty being given, the rational manager and the rational norm-setter have good reason to insure against the disruption of operations by holding inventories which would be excessive under other circumstances, and such contingency reserves are properly regarded as employed. At the same time, the pressures to maximize output are likely to work against the holding of totally functionless inventories, especially of materials which can be converted into current inputs. Nor is there the incentive, which exists in other economies, to hold inventories which serve no productive purpose as a mode of speculating on price increases.

We do not exclude the possibility that on occasion inventories have been excessive in the aggregate and that, more often, they have been inefficiently distributed. Nor is it unlikely that some holdings represent insurance against highly unlikely contingencies; that some are held for lack of an adequate mechanism for transferring (as against consuming) them; and that some are held for such long periods that physical deterioration occurs. But we are unaware of evidence that the various inefficiencies bearing on inventories are of a totally different sort from those occurring with other kinds of capital or, for that matter, with other inputs in general, or that they are of a magnitude which produces a greatly disproportionate exaggeration of the quantity of inventories actually employed. We therefore do not attempt to estimate the quantity of inventories employed as distinct from the quantity held or in existence.

8. INVENTORIES INCLUSIVE OF PROJECTS IN PROGRESS AND LIVESTOCK

We remarked at the beginning of this chapter that our estimates of inventories were less comprehensive than could be justified on conceptual grounds and perhaps less comprehensive than inventory estimates for other economies. While our data for assets which we omit but might include, fixed capital investment projects in progress and livestock, are accessible, it may be well to emphasize how different a picture of Soviet inventories would be obtained with one or another more comprehensive concept of the category. For this purpose, we have shown in Chart 5–3 alternative series, in 1937 prices, combining inventories proper with projects in progress and livestock.

The chart largely speaks for itself. The most comprehensive concept would imply a total more than twice the size of inventories as estimated in 1928 and close to 50 percent greater in 1962. The pattern of change over time is most radically altered by the inclusion of livestock and over the first four or five years, during which livestock herds declined absolutely. The

---

or material, a large number of possible investments with effectiveness of 10–20 percent per *month*." (Italics are ours.) See also *ibid.*, pp. 192–93.

91 Sobol'–37, p. 140, however, is explicit to this degree: "With some directors of producing enterprises there is a striving to accumulate production supplies to an extent which would insure production not only against the fortuities of the work of transport and suppliers but also against the clumsiness and carelessness of their own supply apparatus."

CHART 5-3

Inventories, Investment Projects in Progress, and Livestock: Alternative Combinations, in 1937 Prices, 1928–62
(January 1—Billion Rubles)

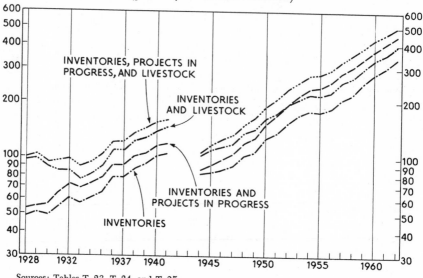

Sources: Tables T–23, T–24, and T–25.

inclusion of projects in progress significantly increases the rate of change to the early 1930's and again, within the postwar period, to the mid-1950's. Beyond about 1932, short-period fluctuations in any of the series are roughly similar to those in inventories proper.

Chapter 6

Summary of Findings

1. INTRODUCTION

The preceding chapters cover all the components of the Soviet capital stock for which we make estimates: fixed capital, livestock, and inventories. We are now in a position to consider the implications of the component estimates when they are taken together.

The level and behavior of the total stock, obtained simply as the arithmetic sum of the components, is described in Section 2 below. This discussion provides an opportunity also to review the possible errors in the component estimates and to examine their effects upon the total calculations. In Section 3, we consider the size and behavior of the asset components and, so far as our data permit, the distribution of the total stock by sector and by age. The following two sections of the chapter are devoted to additional information which can be obtained from our estimates. In Section 4, we present our calculations of the annual flow of capital services, which, as is explained in Chapter 1, we take to be the appropriate measure of capital regarded as a productive input. In Section 5, we compile the series for annual investment which underlie or can be obtained from our stock estimates. The final section provides a very limited comparison of the stock estimates made here with similar data for the United States.

2. THE TOTAL CAPITAL STOCK

The Findings

Series for the net value of the total stock in prices of 1937, 1928, and 1950 are graphed in Chart 6-1. The corresponding numerical series are given in Tables T-25, T-26, and T-27.[1] We confine our discussion initially to the series in 1937 prices.

Over the entire period of 34 years from 1928 to 1962, the total capital

---

[1] The total stock is shown in the tables cited as the sum of fixed capital available for operation, fixed capital investment projects in progress, livestock, and inventories. The distribution of the fixed capital component among structures, installation, and equipment, can be read from Tables T-1, T-8, and T-9. Capital stock totals are not shown in the tabular section with fixed capital measured by other than straight-line depreciation (net values). Gross values in prices of all three weight years can be obtained by using fixed capital series presented in Tables T-1, T-8, and T-9.

CHART 6–1

Total Net Capital Stock in 1937, 1928, and 1950 Prices, 1928–62
(January 1—Billion Rubles)

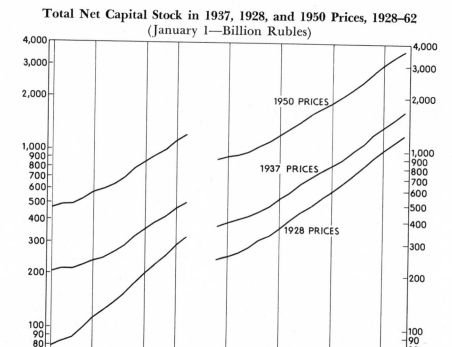

Sources: Tables T–25, T–26, and T–27.

stock in 1937 prices increased from 204 to 1,642 billion rubles, or at an average annual rate of 6.3 percent. This rate appears relatively high, even if the historical circumstances under which it was generated are disregarded. In the light of those circumstances, it appears quite remarkable. Livestock lost in the course of collectivization amounted to 58 percent of the value of herds at the beginning of 1928 and 14 percent of total capital at that date.[2] War losses of capital in all forms, together with continuing capital consumption and a low rate of gross investment, reduced the stock by the beginning of 1944 to 75 percent of its 1941 level. The prewar level was not regained until after the beginning of 1949, or after an interval of eight years. Against the adverse circumstances, however, should be set the extraordinary gain of assets, estimated at about 10 percent of the then-existing stock, through the territorial acquisitions of 1939–40.

Over the prewar years, 1928–41, the stock increased at an average rate of 7.2 percent or, excluding assets acquired in the new territories, about 6.4 percent, which is only slightly above the rate for the entire 34-year period. The average increase to the beginning of 1933, or approximately

---

[2] Losses are measured as the reduction in herds from January 1, 1928, to January 1, 1933. See Table T–23.

over the years of the First Five-Year Plan, was 3.6 percent,[3] which is the lowest of any period of similar length for which we make estimates excepting the war years. This is a significant finding with respect to the accomplishments of the First Plan, although it should be viewed in conjunction with changes in the distribution of the stock among assets and among sectors which occurred in the same period (and with the much more rapid rise of the stock when valued in 1928 prices). From 1933, the increase accelerated to a peak of over 10 percent in the mid-1930's (1935–37). The rate was maintained near this level through the remaining prewar years if the assets acquired in the new territories are included but declined rapidly if these assets are omitted.

The postwar period also begins with a modest rate of increase, which accelerates rapidly to a level of over 10 percent by 1949. Thereafter the rate shows some fluctuations, with a perceptible sag in 1953–55 and a decline following a peak in 1958. But over the whole period since 1949, the growth in the stock has remained in the neighborhood of 10 percent per annum. Indeed, the most nearly spectacular result of our enquiry is the implied rate of growth for the recent past: the total stock of capital doubled from 1955 to 1962 and tripled from 1950 to 1962. The growth rate from 1945 to 1962, 8.8 percent, is substantially above the prewar average; the rate of near 10 percent has been sustained much longer postwar than prewar. Retardation, therefore, can scarcely be identified in comparisons between these two periods. Nor is it apparent within the postwar period unless significance is attached to the decline from 1958 to 1961—which is from a rate of 12.0 percent to one of 9.9 percent.

Reliability

The foregoing summary is phrased as though the total stock estimates were entirely firm. That this is not the case has been explained in the preceding chapters, in which also we have tested the sensitivity of the estimates for the component asset categories to alterations in critical assumptions underlying them. It can readily be inferred that potential sources of error in a single component which have been shown to be insignificant for it will prove still less significant in the total; those which may seriously affect a component will necessarily have their effects attenuated in the total. Nevertheless, since the sensitivity of our results to such errors is crucial to an appraisal of their reliability, we recapitulate the relevent evidence in Tables 6–1 and 6–2.

The net value series (row 1), which is used as a basis of comparison in the tables, can be identified as that in which the fixed capital component is calculated with straight-line depreciation, war losses are assumed equal to 25 percent of the prewar stock, and annual construction is derived from materials inputs. This is the fixed capital series which we take as our preferred estimate. The livestock and inventory components of the row 1 totals have no special identifying characteristics but are also the best estimates which we can obtain from the information available to us.

---

[3] The rate is the same whether measured from January 1, 1928 or 1929, to January 1, 1933. The Plan commenced from the fourth quarter of 1928.

TABLE 6-1

EFFECTS ON TOTAL NET CAPITAL STOCK OF ALTERING ESTIMATING PROCEDURES, IN 1937 PRICES, SELECTED YEARS
(January 1)

A. Billion Rubles

	1928	1932	1937	1941	1945	1950	1955	1962
1. Total Net Value, as Estimated	204.4	236.3	350.1	505.3	392.5	541.0	821.5	1642.5
Fixed Capital:								
2. Sinking Fund Depreciation, r = 20%	253.0	297.7	435.8	629.6	509.9	693.2	1018.9	1962.7
3. Sinking Fund Depreciation, r = 8%	245.7	286.6	416.8	599.1	479.6	650.8	963.1	1875.0
4. Declining Annuity Depreciation, r = 20%	199.2	229.4	338.8	487.6	376.2	519.5	789.8	1581.3
5. Declining Annuity Depreciation, r = 8%	191.9	220.6	327.1	471.0	360.9	500.2	763.5	1533.5
6. Service Lives Increased by 1/3	204.4	240.7	362.9	531.8	423.2	584.5	890.1	1773.0
7. Service Lives Reduced by 1/3	204.4	229.6	329.4	466.2	351.0	484.0	741.7	1493.7
8. Initial Stock Increased by 20%	226.0	255.1	365.8	520.0	401.6	547.8	826.2	1644.9
9. Initial Stock Reduced by 20%	182.8	217.5	334.4	490.6	383.4	534.2	816.8	1640.1
10. War Losses 15% of Prewar Stock	204.4	236.3	350.1	505.3	424.2	566.7	842.4	1657.3
11. War Losses 35% of Prewar Stock	204.4	236.3	350.1	505.3	360.8	515.3	800.6	1627.7
12. Construction Deflated by Input Prices	216.3	255.0	381.7	535.6	418.1	565.3	821.7	1591.9
13. Livestock Increased by 1/3	220.4	244.3	360.6	518.9	401.4	553.1	834.7	1660.5
14. Livestock Reduced by 1/3	188.4	228.3	339.6	491.7	383.6	528.9	808.3	1624.5
15. Inventory Estimates Smoothed	--	232.7	353.5	--	393.0	538.0	824.2	--
16. Initial Fixed Capital Increased by 20% and Livestock Increased by 1/3	242.0	263.1	376.3	533.6	410.5	559.9	839.4	1662.9
17. Initial Fixed Capital Reduced by 20% and Livestock Reduced by 1/3	166.8	209.5	323.9	477.0	374.5	522.1	803.6	1622.1

B. Total as Estimated = 100

	1928	1932	1937	1941	1945	1950	1955	1962
1. Total Net Value, as Estimated	100.0	100.0	100.0	100.0	100.0	100.0	100.0	100.0
Fixed Capital:								
2. Sinking Fund Depreciation, r = 20%	123.8	126.0	124.5	124.6	129.9	128.1	124.0	119.5
3. Sinking Fund Depreciation, r = 8%	120.2	121.3	119.1	118.6	122.2	120.3	117.2	114.2
4. Declining Annuity Depreciation, r = 20%	97.5	97.1	96.8	96.5	95.8	96.0	96.1	96.3
5. Declining Annuity Depreciation, r = 8%	93.9	93.4	93.4	93.2	92.0	92.5	92.9	93.3
6. Service Lives Increased by 1/3	100.0	101.9	103.7	105.2	107.8	108.0	108.4	107.9
7. Service Lives Reduced by 1/3	100.0	97.2	94.1	92.3	89.4	89.5	90.3	90.9
8. Initial Stock Increased by 20%	110.6	108.0	104.5	102.9	102.3	101.3	100.6	100.1
9. Initial Stock Reduced by 20%	89.5	92.0	95.5	97.1	97.7	98.7	99.4	99.9
10. War Losses 15% of Prewar Stock	100.0	100.0	100.0	100.0	108.1	104.7	102.5	100.9
11. War Losses 35% of Prewar Stock	100.0	100.0	100.0	100.0	91.9	95.2	97.5	99.1
12. Construction Deflated by Input Prices	105.8	107.9	109.0	106.0	106.5	104.5	100.0	96.9

EFFECTS ON TOTAL NET CAPITAL STOCK OF ALTERING ESTIMATING PROCEDURES, IN 1937 PRICES, SELECTED YEARS
(January 1)

		1928	1932	1937	1941	1945	1950	1955	1962
13.	Livestock Increased by 1/3	107.8	103.4	103.0	102.7	102.3	102.2	101.6	101.1
14.	Livestock Reduced by 1/3	92.2	96.6	97.0	97.3	97.7	97.8	98.4	98.9
15.	Inventory Estimates Smoothed	--	98.5	101.0	--	100.1	99.4	100.3	--
16.	Initial Fixed Capital Increased by 20% and Livestock Increased by 1/3	118.4	111.3	107.5	105.6	104.6	103.5	102.2	101.2
17.	Initial Fixed Capital Reduced by 20% and Livestock Reduced by 1/3	81.6	88.7	92.5	94.4	95.4	96.5	97.8	98.8
				C. 1937 = 100					
1.	Total Net Value, as Estimated	58.4	67.5	100	144	112	155	235	469
	Fixed Capital:								
2.	Sinking Fund Depreciation, r = 20%	58.1	68.3	100	144	117	159	234	450
3.	Sinking Fund Depreciation, r = 8%	58.9	68.8	100	144	115	156	231	450
4.	Declining Annuity Depreciation, r = 20%	58.8	67.7	100	144	111	153	233	467
5.	Declining Annuity Depreciation, r = 8%	58.7	67.4	100	144	110	153	233	469
6.	Service Lives Increased by 1/3	56.3	66.3	100	147	117	161	245	489
7.	Service Lives Reduced by 1/3	62.1	69.7	100	142	107	147	225	453
8.	Initial Stock Increased by 20%	61.8	69.7	100	142	110	150	226	450
9.	Initial Stock Reduced by 20%	54.7	65.0	100	147	115	160	244	490
10.	War Losses 15% of Prewar Stock	58.4	67.5	100	144	121	162	241	473
11.	War Losses 35% of Prewar Stock	58.4	67.5	100	144	103	147	229	465
12.	Construction Deflated by Input Prices	56.7	66.8	100	140	110	148	215	417
13.	Livestock Increased by 1/3	61.1	67.7	100	144	111	153	231	460
14.	Livestock Reduced by 1/3	55.5	67.2	100	145	113	156	238	478
15.	Inventory Estimates Smoothed	--	65.8	100	--	111	152	233	--
16.	Initial Fixed Capital Increased by 20% and Livestock Increased by 1/3	64.3	69.9	100	142	109	149	223	442
17.	Initial Fixed Capital Reduced by 20% and Livestock Reduced by 1/3	51.5	64.7	100	147	116	161	248	501

Source: See text.

TABLE 6-2

EFFECTS ON ANNUAL GROWTH RATE OF TOTAL NET CAPITAL STOCK OF ALTERING ESTIMATING PROCEDURES, IN 1937 PRICES, SELECTED PERIODS
(January 1)

Average Annual Growth Rate
(Percent)

	1928-1932	1932-1937	1937-1941	1941-1945	1945-1950	1950-1955	1955-1962	1928-1941	1941-1950	1945-1962	1928-1962
1. Total Net Value, as Estimated	3.7	8.2	9.6	-6.5	6.6	8.7	10.4	7.2	0.8	8.8	6.3
Fixed Capital:											
2. Sinking Fund Depreciation, r = 20%	4.2	7.9	9.6	-5.4	6.3	8.0	9.8	7.3	1.1	8.3	6.2
3. Sinking Fund Depreciation, r = 8%	3.9	7.8	9.5	-5.7	6.3	8.2	10.0	7.1	0.9	8.3	6.2
4. Declining Annuity Depreciation, r = 20%	3.6	8.1	9.5	-6.7	6.7	8.7	10.4	7.1	0.7	8.8	6.3
5. Declining Annuity Depreciation, r = 8%	3.5	8.2	9.5	-6.9	6.7	8.8	10.5	7.1	0.7	8.9	6.3
6. Service Lives Increased by 1/3	4.2	8.6	10.0	-5.9	6.7	8.8	10.3	7.6	1.1	8.8	6.6
7. Service Lives Reduced by 1/3	2.9	7.5	9.1	-7.4	6.6	8.9	10.5	6.5	0.4	8.9	6.0
8. Initial Stock Increased by 20%	3.1	7.5	9.2	-6.7	6.4	8.6	10.3	6.6	0.6	8.6	6.0
9. Initial Stock Reduced by 20%	4.4	9.0	10.1	-6.4	6.9	8.9	10.5	7.9	1.0	8.9	6.7
10. War Losses 15% of Prewar Stock	3.7	8.2	9.6	-4.5	6.0	8.2	10.2	7.2	1.3	8.3	6.3
11. War Losses 35% of Prewar Stock	3.7	8.2	9.6	-8.8	7.4	9.2	10.7	7.2	0.2	9.3	6.3
12. Construction Deflated by Input Prices	4.2	8.4	8.8	-6.4	6.2	7.8	9.9	7.2	0.6	8.2	6.0
13. Livestock Increased by 1/3	2.6	8.1	9.5	-6.6	6.6	8.6	10.3	6.8	0.7	8.7	6.1
14. Livestock Reduced by 1/3	4.9	8.3	9.7	-6.4	6.6	8.9	10.5	7.7	0.8	8.9	6.5
15. Inventory Estimates Smoothed	--	8.7	--	--	6.5	8.9	--	--	--	--	--
16. Initial Fixed Capital Increased by 20% and Livestock Increased by 1/3	2.1	7.4	9.1	-6.8	6.4	8.4	10.3	6.3	0.5	8.6	5.8
17. Initial Fixed Capital Reduced by 20% and Livestock Reduced by 1/3	5.9	9.1	10.2	-6.2	6.9	9.0	10.6	8.4	1.0	9.0	6.9

TABLE 6-2 (continued)

EFFECTS ON ANNUAL GROWTH RATE OF TOTAL NET CAPITAL STOCK OF ALTERING ESTIMATING PROCEDURES, IN 1937 PRICES, SELECTED PERIODS
(January 1)

Given Row Differs from Row 1 by:
(Percentage Points)

	1928-1932	1932-1937	1937-1941	1941-1945	1945-1950	1950-1955	1955-1962	1928-1941	1941-1950	1945-1962	1928-1962
1. Total Net Value, as Estimated	0.0	0.0	0.0	0.0	0.0	0.0	0.0	0.0	0.0	0.0	0.0
Fixed Capital:											
2. Sinking Fund Depreciation, r = 20%	0.5	-0.3	0.0	1.1	-0.3	-0.7	-0.6	0.1	0.3	-0.5	-0.1
3. Sinking Fund Depreciation, r = 8%	0.2	-0.4	-0.1	0.8	-0.3	-0.5	-0.4	-0.1	0.1	-0.5	-0.1
4. Declining Annuity Depreciation, r = 20%	-0.1	-0.1	-0.1	-0.2	0.1	0.0	0.0	-0.1	-0.1	0.0	0.0
5. Declining Annuity Depreciation, r = 8%	-0.2	0.0	-0.1	-0.4	0.1	0.1	0.1	-0.1	-0.1	0.1	0.0
6. Service Lives Increased by 1/3	0.5	0.4	0.4	0.6	0.1	0.1	0.1	0.4	0.3	0.0	0.3
7. Service Lives Reduced by 1/3	-0.8	-0.7	-0.5	-0.9	0.0	0.2	-0.1	-0.7	-0.4	0.1	-0.3
8. Initial Stock Increased by 20%	-0.6	-0.7	-0.4	-0.2	-0.2	-0.1	-0.1	-0.6	-0.2	-0.2	-0.3
9. Initial Stock Reduced by 20%	0.7	0.8	0.5	0.1	0.3	0.2	0.1	0.7	0.2	0.1	0.4
10. War Losses 15% of Prewar Stock	0.0	0.0	0.0	2.0	-0.6	-0.5	-0.2	0.7	0.5	-0.5	0.0
11. War Losses 35% of Prewar Stock	0.0	0.0	0.0	-2.3	0.8	0.5	0.3	0.0	-0.6	0.5	0.0
12. Construction Deflated by Input Prices	0.5	0.2	-0.8	-0.1	-0.4	-0.9	-0.5	0.0	-0.2	-0.6	-0.3
13. Livestock Increased by 1/3	-1.1	-0.1	-0.1	-0.1	0.0	-0.1	-0.1	-0.4	-0.1	-0.1	-0.2
14. Livestock Reduced by 1/3	1.2	0.1	0.1	0.1	0.0	0.2	0.1	0.5	0.0	0.1	0.2
15. Inventory Estimates Smoothed	-	0.5	-	-	-0.1	0.2	-	-	-	-	-
16. Initial Fixed Capital Increased by 20% and Livestock Increased by 1/3	-1.6	-0.8	-0.5	-0.3	-0.2	-0.3	-0.1	-0.9	-0.3	-0.2	-0.5
17. Initial Fixed Capital Reduced by 20% and Livestock Reduced by 1/3	2.2	0.9	0.6	0.3	0.3	0.3	0.2	1.2	0.2	0.2	0.6

Source: See text.

Straight-line depreciation can be interpreted, *inter alia*, as the true decline in the capital values of assets whose service streams decline over time, though less rapidly than along a straight line to zero, under conditions of a finite rate of interest.[4] This is the interpretation which we put upon it in accepting the net value estimates. Large uncertainties, however, attach both to the shape of service streams of fixed assets and to the appropriate rate of interest. The first two alternative calculations in the tables (rows 2 and 3) indicate the effects upon the total stock estimates of depreciating fixed capital by the sinking fund method, i.e., on the assumption that service streams are constant over time, at interest rates of 8 and 20 percent. The implied understatement in the accepted estimates of the absolute values of the total stock remains large, although on the order of 15 to 30 percent as against 20 to 45 percent in fixed capital alone.[5] Implied rates of growth differ relatively little from those of the net value estimates. The alternatives show an 0.1 percentage point slower growth rate over the entire 34 years; differences in shorter periods vary in sign and are as large as 1 percentage point only in the interval from 1941 to 1945. The assumption of constant services is extreme, and the sinking fund calculations for this reason exaggerate the likely error. The two specified interest rates are meant to bound the plausible values for this parameter rather than set extreme limits. Rates higher than those specified, however, yield results which differ little from those calculated with a 20 percent rate; rates lower than 8 percent yield results closer to those obtained with straight-line depreciation.[6]

The alternative calculations with declining annuity depreciation (rows 4 and 5) indicate the effects of assuming that capital services decline along a straight line to zero, with 8 and 20 percent interest rates. Absolute values here are lower than the net value estimates, although by no more than 8 percent. Growth rates are unaltered for the entire period and are altered by as much as 0.4 percentage points only in 1941–45. Straight-line declining services are less clearly an extreme limit than are constant services, but a more rapid decline appears unlikely. Interest rates higher than 20 percent yield results closer to the net value estimates; rates lower than 8 percent yield results which fall further below the net value estimates.[7]

The service lives of fixed assets employed for our estimates rest on some evidence but are subject to considerable error.[8] Since we are unable to vary the service lives underlying the official data from which we obtain the 1928 value of fixed capital, that value remains unchanged in any test we can make of the effects of altering service lives. For this reason in part, the difference produced in the absolute values of the total stock by the indi-

---

[4] See Chapter 2, Section 2, for discussion of the various depreciation formulas that are referred to here.

[5] See Table 2–1.

[6] Constant services with interest rates approaching infinity correspond to retirement depreciation (gross values), calculations for which are shown for fixed capital in Tables 2–1 and T–1 but are not repeated here. Constant services with a zero interest rate are one of the possible interpretations that can be put on straight-line depreciation.

[7] Services declining along a straight line to zero with an interest rate of zero correspond to sum-of-digits depreciation: see Tables 2–1 and T–6. Such services with an interest rate approaching infinity are a third possible interpretation of straight-line depreciation.

[8] See Chapter 2, Section 5.

cated one-third alteration (rows 6 and 7) rises for a time after 1928 (to about 1945) and then is approximately stabilized—at about 8 percent above the net value estimates for longer lives and about 10 percent below for shorter. The 1928–62 growth rate is raised or lowered by 0.3 percentage points. The difference arises almost entirely in the periods before 1945 and in no case is as great as 1 percentage point. The one-third variation in lives is almost certainly extreme.

The single potential error in the fixed capital estimates of which the effects are most happily mitigated in the total is that associated with the initial stock (see rows 8 and 9), for which the estimate is based on data of questionable reliability.[9] In the net value total, fixed capital on January 1, 1928, accounts for only slightly more than 50 percent of the stock. A 20 percent error for that date in fixed capital, therefore, is almost halved in the total. The impact of the error necessarily declines in subsequent years, although less rapidly in the total than in fixed capital, because the share of the latter rises. The 1928–62 growth rate is altered by 0.3–0.4 percentage points. Short-period effects are registered chiefly in prewar years and then do not exceed 0.8 percentage points. The 20 percent error is thought to bound the probable error in the initial stock, but it is not an extreme limit.

The assumption that war losses amounted to 25 percent of the prewar stock of fixed capital is also based on some evidence but is of doubtful accuracy.[10] The effect of an error of 10 percentage points, or 40 percent, in this element of the calculations (see rows 10 and 11) is reduced in the total stock to about 8 percent in 1945 and declines thereafter, to less than 1 percent in 1962. The 34-year growth rate is virtually unaffected. Rates are altered from 1941 to 1945 by roughly 2 percentage points but within the postwar periods by less than 1 point. The assumed margin for error is wide but not limiting.

The calculation with construction deflated by input prices (row 12) is not a test of a possible error in our estimates but of the effects of using a procedure different from ours which is commonly employed elsewhere.[11] In the total stock, input-price deflation raises the total by as much as 9 percent in 1937 and reduces it by as much as 3 percent in 1962. Growth rates are increased to 1937 and over the war years and are reduced in the late 1930's and in the postwar period, although in no interval by as much as 1 percentage point. The rate of increase for the entire period is reduced by 0.3 percentage points.

One possible source of error in our fixed capital calculations, our failure to capitalize major repairs, is discussed in Chapter 2 (Section 2) but not tested by an alternative calculation and, hence, not included in Tables 6–1 and 6–2. In Table 2–3 (p. 34), however, we estimate that repair deficits and surpluses cumulated from 1928 were negative and equal to about 5 percent of net fixed capital by 1945, positive and about 7 percent of net fixed capital by 1962, these two years representing the extremes in the ratio. The same deficits and surpluses relative to the total capital stock

---

9 See Chapter 2, Section 4.
10 See Chapter 2, Section 6.
11 See pp. 43 ff.

amount roughly to a negative 4 percent in 1945 and a positive 5 percent in 1962. This suggests that in the total also our assumption of "normal" repairs produces a considerable understatement in the rate of growth of the stock during the postwar period, though a smaller understatement than that in fixed capital alone. The calculation is only illustrative and does not establish limits for the possible error from this source.

The chief uncertainty associated with the livestock estimates relates to their absolute values: the average realized prices at which we have valued livestock may not accurately reflect their substitutability for other kinds of capital.[12] A variation of one third in this component (rows 13 and 14) alters the total stock by about 8 percent in 1928, the difference declining thereafter to slightly over 1 percent by 1962. The 1928–62 growth rate is altered by 0.2 percentage points. The rate is altered by over 1 point in 1928–32 but by no more than 0.2 points in succeeding short periods. The variation allowed for appears large enough to encompass any probable error in the calculation, although it is not limiting.

The alternative inventory calculations (row 15) are meant to illustrate the effects of short-run and noncumulative errors in this component. They are obtained by averaging the accepted inventory estimates for the three years centered on each given year.[13] The procedure cannot be used for 1928, 1941, and 1962, and comparisons involving these years cannot be made. The years 1932 and 1937, however, are years in which the smoothing has close to its maximum effects upon the inventory estimates. The total stock figures are reduced by 1.5 percent in 1932 and raised by 1.0 percent in 1937. The rate of growth from 1932 to 1937 is raised by 0.5 percentage points.

Errors from two or more sources may, of course, be compounded in the estimates. The effects of such compoundings are not easily read from the tables, since the alternative assumptions for fixed capital, where they are not mutually exclusive, produce errors which are not simply additive. Addition is possible of errors from any single source in the fixed capital estimates and those in the livestock or inventory estimates. Without attempting to explore all possible combinations, we show in the tables (rows 16 and 17) the results which would follow if errors in the initial fixed capital stock and in the valuation of livestock were to occur together and in the same direction. The likelihood of error in either of these elements of the calculations is high, and the assumed margins are wide but not extreme. The combination, therefore, indicates the effects of a particularly adverse but not altogether unlikely compounding. The total stock estimate is here altered by over 18 percent in 1928; the difference declines thereafter and is slightly over 1 percent by 1962. The rate of growth for the entire 34 years is altered by 0.5–0.6 percentage points, that for 1928–32 by 1.6–2.2 points, but those for subsequent short periods by less than 1 point.

How, in their entirety, the results of the alternative calculations can properly be characterized depends upon the probabilities which the viewer attaches to the various errors allowed for—singly and in combination—and upon the precision required for whatever analytical purpose he an-

---

12 See pp. 106 ff.
13 See pp. 137–38.

ticipates. Our own reading of the calculations is that they provide grounds for considerable confidence in the broad reliability of the total stock estimates. In effect, they illustrate a feature of the estimates which is fortuitous but highly advantageous: the results do not depend crucially upon any single assumption required for their derivation. Errors of the magnitude allowed for are not likely; they are generally independent and as likely to be offsetting as reinforcing; there are interesting analytical questions which will permit inaccuracies of the probable size. The calculations indicate also, however, that no high degree of precision can be attributed to our findings. This same conclusion can be drawn from the quality of the basic statistical data common to all of the alternatives, which is not tested in the calculations.

The implication of the net value estimates which appears least vulnerable to error is the rate of growth for the whole span of years from 1928 to 1962. This rate is changed by no more than 0.4 percentage points by any single alteration in assumptions and by no more than 0.6 points by the combined alteration of the initial fixed capital and livestock assumptions. The higher figure amounts to 10 percent of the accepted estimate of 6.3 percent per annum, which difference is not trivial if cumulated over 34 years but which also eventuates from a particularly adverse compounding of independent errors. Within the total period, the estimates are clearly least reliable—both because of the impact of questionable assumptions and because of the poor quality of the underlying statistics—in the early years and immediately after the war. Short-term growth rates are least certain within these periods and in comparisons involving years falling within them. Short-term rates become relatively firm for the mid and late 1930's except that the allowance made for the assets acquired in 1939–40 is rough. They are relatively firm again in the later postwar years. The reliability of the absolute values of the total stock is open to significant question, in addition, because of uncertainty of the true shapes of the service streams of fixed capital, although the choice of interest rates with any given depreciation formula appears relatively inconsequential. On this last point, however, reference should be made to the discussion of capital services in Section 4 below.

The sense in which we feel justified in characterizing the total estimates as broadly reliable may be better conveyed by considering the following question: What portions of the description of our results, with which we began, remain valid if errors in the initial fixed capital stock and in the livestock valuations were combined as in rows 16 and 17 of the tables? As noted, absolute values are substantially altered in 1928 but little altered by 1962. The following propositions continue to hold with either alternative calculation:[14]

(*i*) The growth rate for the entire period appears remarkably high.

(*ii*) The growth rate for 1928 to 1941, if assets acquired in the new territories are excluded, is not markedly different from that for 1928–62.[15]

---

14 Reference is made here to calculations for some years for which figures are not shown in the tables.

15 The ratio of the 1928–41 growth rate to that for 1928–62 is 5.5/5.8 for row 16, 7.6/6.9 for row 17.

(*iii*) The rate for 1928–33 is the lowest of that for any period of similar length, excepting the war years.[16]

(*iv*) From 1933, the rate accelerates to a level of over 10 percent per year in 1935–37. It remains high through 1940 if acquired assets are included but declines rapidly if they are omitted.

(*v*) The stock declines by about 25 percent in the course of the war and regains its 1941 level only after the beginning of 1949. Its rate of increase accelerates in the immediate postwar years to over 10 percent in 1949 and remains in the neighborhood of 10 percent thereafter. The stock (approximately) doubles from 1955 to 1962 and triples from 1950 to 1962.[17]

(*vi*) The growth rate from 1945 to 1962 is higher than that from 1928 to 1941, even if acquired assets are included for 1941. Clearly significant retardation is not evident between the two periods or within the postwar period, although some decline appears after 1958.

Alternative Price Weights

A different kind of question is posed by the effects upon the total stock estimates of altering the price weights with which assets are aggregated. The answer in the broad can be observed directly in Chart 6–1 (p. 144). The value of the stock in 1950 prices is generally about 2.2–2.4 times the value in 1937 prices; it rises at virtually the same rate over the 34 years (6.2 as against 6.3 percent); and it closely parallels the 1937-price series in short periods. The series in 1928 prices is less than 40 percent of that in 1937 prices in 1928 but 75 percent of it by 1962. The growth rate for the entire period in 1928 prices (8.4 percent) is much higher than in 1937 prices. The difference in rates (10.8 as against 6.2 percent) is especially great from 1928 to 1937. Between these dates the year-to-year variations in the series also differ substantially. In sum, 1950 prices raise the absolute value of the stock but do not much change its behavior over time; 1928 prices alter both the absolute value of the stock and its behavior, the latter radically in the early years covered.

The effects of alternative prices upon the behavior of the total estimates are the combined result of differences in weights within the component asset categories and differences in the weights with which the components are aggregated. To permit comparison of the sensitivity to weight shifts of the total stock with that of the components, calculated growth rates for each are shown, in prices of the three weight years, in Table 6–3. In principle, the calculations are for intervals between the weight years. Figures for 1950–62 are included, although we have no calculation in 1962 prices. The changes are measured from the beginning of the weight year, whereas the weights are average annual prices. Installation is not shown separately because of its small size and questionable method of derivation.

As we have noted previously, growth rates of structures and livestock

---

[16] Rates are 2.1 percent for row 16, 5.6 percent for row 17, calculating from January 1 of each year.

[17] The statements in this paragraph reflect the fact that the impact of the two errors involved in the calculations is primarily on the estimates for the early years. The relative insensitivity of the postwar estimates is better illustrated by the calculations (rows 10 and 11) for alternative war losses: these too are substantially consistent with the statements of the paragraph except that the size of the wartime decline varies considerably.

TABLE 6-3

ANNUAL GROWTH RATES OF NET CAPITAL STOCK, TOTAL AND BY KIND OF ASSET, IN 1937, 1928, AND 1950 PRICES, SELECTED PERIODS
(January 1--Percent)

	1928 – 1937			1937 – 1950			1950 – 1962			1928 – 1962		
	1937 Prices	1928 Prices	1950 Prices	1937 Prices	1928 Prices	1950 Prices	1937 Prices	1928 Prices	1950 Prices	1937 Prices	1928 Prices	1950 Prices
Structures	8.0	8.1	8.0	2.6	2.6	2.4	9.2	9.4	9.0	6.3	6.4	6.2
Equipment	16.1	21.7	13.8	6.3	8.0	4.6	13.1	12.6	13.2	11.2	13.1	10.0
Livestock	-4.9	-5.7	-4.5	1.1	0.8	1.2	3.4	2.3	3.6	0.3	-0.4	0.5
Inventories	5.4	12.0	6.9	3.9	4.1	3.5	8.5	8.2	8.3	5.9	7.6	6.1
Total..........	6.2	10.8	6.8	3.4	4.9	2.9	9.7	10.6	9.5	6.3	8.4	6.2

Sources: Tables T-1, T-8, T-9, T-25, T-26, and T-27.

are relatively insensitive to price weights, those of equipment and inventories are extremely sensitive, especially in the interval from 1928 to 1937.[18] The effect of alternative weights on the growth rate of the total stock is much like that on equipment and inventories despite the relative invariability of its structure and livestock components. That this is so is due to divergent movements of prices and quantities of the component asset categories, in particular those of equipment and livestock: between 1928 and 1937, the stock of equipment increased greatly and its price declined greatly relative to those of all assets; livestock quantities declined and prices increased relative to those of all assets. The difference between growth rates in 1937 and 1950 prices, which is small, in the 1937–50 interval is accounted for primarily by changes internal to the equipment component.

To what extent does the characterization of our results in 1937 prices remain accurate for the estimates in prices of the other weight years? The stock in 1950 prices moves closely enough with that in 1937 prices that no significant alteration is required other than for the absolute values. The stock in 1928 prices obviously moves quite differently. The initial slow growth is restricted to the two years, 1928 and 1929, after which the rate of increase rises above 10 percent, where it remains until the war. A sag in 1932–33 remains visible, and the rate declines rapidly after 1937 if acquired assets in the new territories are excluded. The postwar behavior of the 1928-price series does not differ radically from that in 1937 prices. A modest retardation between the postwar and prewar periods can be read from the 1928-price series, and slightly more retardation from a comparison of the postwar series in 1937 or 1950 prices with those for the earlier period in 1928 prices. No clearly significant retardation within the postwar years is evident in any of the three series.

3. COMPOSITION OF THE TOTAL STOCK

Our data provide evidence on the composition of the capital stock, in varying detail, in three dimensions: by kind of asset, by sector of activity, and by age. We consider these in turn.

By Kind of Asset

Composition in this dimension can be judged from Chart 6–2, in which time series for component assets in 1937 prices are graphed. Corresponding numerical series, in prices of all three weight years, can be obtained from Tables T–1 and T–25, T–8 and T–26, and T–9 and T–27. Investment projects in progress, which are included in the structures and equipment categories, are also shown separately in the chart (estimates for 1939–41, 1944–50, and 1962, it will be recalled, are simple extrapolations). Installation, which is small and unreliably estimated, is not graphed separately although it is included in the total.

In 1937 prices, structures are much the largest single component of the total net stock. Their share was 46 percent in 1928, rose to 55 percent in 1933, remained near that level until immediately after the war, and then

---

18 With respect to inventories, however, see p. 136 above.

CHART 6–2

Distribution of Net Capital Stock by Kind of Asset, in 1937 Prices, 1928–62
(January 1—Billion Rubles)

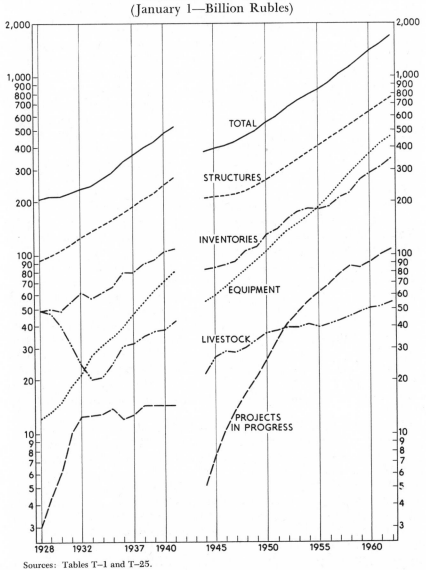

Sources: Tables T–1 and T–25.

declined, gradually and with some interruptions, to 45 percent in 1962. The rate of increase in structures over the 34-year period, 6.3 percent, is the same as that of the total stock. The growth rate is relatively steady except for marked upswings from the beginnings of the prewar and post-war periods and considerable fluctuations in the 1930's—peaks in 1931 and 1936, a trough in 1933, and a decline from 1936 to 1940 if acquired assets are excluded. No retardation in the growth rate is apparent.

The share of equipment in the total was 6 percent in 1928 and 27 percent in 1962, rising virtually without interruption between those dates except over the interval of the war years. Since, especially in methodological and theoretical discussions, equipment is sometimes treated as the epitome of capital, it is perhaps worth emphasizing that the equipment share in total Soviet capital (in 1937 prices) has been relatively small throughout the period covered here.[19] The rate of increase in the stock of equipment, on the other hand, has been remarkably high, amounting to 11.2 percent per year from 1928 to 1962, 15.5 percent from 1928 to 1941 (14.6 percent excluding assets acquired in the new territories), and 12.7 percent from 1945 to 1962. Within the prewar period, equipment shows fluctuations in its growth which resemble those in structures but are not precisely synchronous with them: a very high peak (over 20 percent per year) in 1930–32, a trough in 1934, a peak in 1936, and a marked decline after 1936 if acquired assets are excluded. In the postwar period, the rate of increase has lain generally within the range of 10–15 percent; a high rate is attained as early as 1945. There is an apparent sag in 1952–53 and a decline from 1958 to 1961 which are inevident, or less evident, in the structures series. Deceleration could conceivably be argued to exist in equipment, although it appears primarily in a more rapid growth in the early 1930's than is regained thereafter.

Total fixed capital, including installation, rose from 53 percent of the total in 1928 to 76 percent in 1962, with the greater part of the gain (to a 68 percent share) occurring by 1933. Its growth rate is 7.5 percent for the entire period, 9.7 percent for 1928–41 (8.9 percent excluding acquired assets), and 9.2 percent for 1945–62, all of which rates exceed those for the total stock although, again, the difference arises primarily between 1928 and 1933. Equipment weighs more heavily in fixed than in total capital, but its share (11 percent in 1928 and 36 percent in 1962) remains a minority one. Short-run variations in the growth rate of fixed capital are therefore closer to those in structures. Retardation is not apparent in total fixed capital.

The behavior of livestock is clearly unique in its enormous decline from 1928 to 1933 and its failure to regain the 1928 level until late in the 1950's. These movements reduce the share of livestock in total capital from 24 percent in 1928 to 8 percent in 1933 and to 3 percent in 1962. Beyond the 1933 trough, the short-run changes in livestock bear a perceptible resemblance to those in fixed capital—a burst of growth in the mid-1930's (1934 and 1935), a slower increase to 1941, an absolute decline over the war, and a postwar recovery—but the resemblance is not close. The wartime decline in livestock is larger than in other components. The postwar rise shows distinct interruptions, especially in 1946–47 and 1952–55.

The inventory component is notable on two scores: its relatively large weight in the total and its erratic growth over time. Inventories in 1928 accounted for 24 percent of total capital, and their share in all subsequent years remains within the range of 21 to 26 percent. Growth rates over long periods are similar to those in the total stock although somewhat lower

---

[19] See, however, the discussion of the "carrier" function of capital, pp. 306 ff., below.

from 1928 to 1962 (5.9 percent per year), materially lower from 1928 to 1941 (6.1 percent), and slightly lower from 1945 to 1962 (8.5 percent).

For reasons previously discussed, the apparent variability of the growth in inventories over short periods may be due partly to statistical errors, but these are unlikely to be the whole explanation.[20] In particular, it appears justifiable to infer that a sharp build-up of inventories occurred in the early 1930's (1930–31), which was followed by a roughly horizontal movement (1932–34), another upsurge (1935–37), and another near-plateau (1938 to 1941, acquired assets being excluded). These movements are similar to those in fixed capital but differ somewhat in timing. In the postwar period, the rise in inventories begins slowly but reaches very high rates in the late 1940's and early 1950's; it is sharply retarded in 1953–55 and then resumes at close to its earlier high rate to the end of the period.[21]

The weight of inventories in total capital is raised still higher if investment projects in progress are included with inventories.[22] These two categories in combination account, in the years for which we have reported data on projects in progress, for between 25 percent (in 1928) and 31 percent (in 1932 and again in 1953–54) of the total. They evidently fall as low as 23 percent in years near the war, although projects in progress are crudely estimated for these years. Projects in progress alone account in the early 1930's (1932–33) for as much as 5 percent of total capital and 8 percent of fixed capital in place, in the late 1950's (1957–58) for as much as 8 and 10 percent respectively. The inclusion of livestock with the other two categories would further increase the share of inventories in total capital (to 49 percent in 1928 and 30 percent in 1962). The inclusion of either projects in progress or livestock with inventories so-called materially alters the behavior of inventories over time.[23]

To summarize, the Soviet capital stock in 1937 prices has consisted of an equipment component which grows very rapidly but from a small to a modest share of the total; a structure component which is the largest single constituent and grows at about the rate of the total; an inventory component which is larger than equipment until 1955 and grows, erratically, somewhat less rapidly than the total; a livestock component which is reduced from substantial to minor significance in the first five years and shows little gain over the entire period; and, within fixed capital, a considerable volume of projects still in progress and unavailable for operation.

The effects upon the composition of the stock of measuring in 1928 or 1950 prices are indicated for selected years in Table 6–4; effects on growth rates can be read from Table 6–3 above; complete data are given in the

---

[20] Sources of error in the estimates are discussed pp. 134 ff. The interpretation of the apparent short-run changes in inventories is considered further in Chapter 8.

[21] The estimated rate of increase from (January 1) 1956 to 1962 (which is somewhat overstated; see p. 515) is 10.7 percent per year, that from 1947 to 1953 is 11.0 percent. The leveling-off of total inventories from 1953 to 1956, and even more pronouncedly from 1954 to 1956, appears also in most of the individual sectors from which the total estimate is composed (see Table N–1). There is no apparent element in the derivation of the sector estimates which would indicate that statistical error is a likely source of this pattern.

[22] See pp. 112–13.

[23] Cf. Chart 5–3.

TABLE 6-4

DISTRIBUTION OF NET CAPITAL STOCK BY KIND OF ASSET, IN 1937, 1928, AND 1950 PRICES, SELECTED YEARS

(January 1--Percent)

	1928			1937			1950			1962		
	1937 Prices	1928 Prices	1950 Prices	1937 Prices	1928 Prices	1950 Prices	1937 Prices	1928 Prices	1950 Prices	1937 Prices	1928 Prices	1950 Prices
Structures	45.8	58.0	52.1	53.4	46.6	57.5	48.0	35.3	53.9	45.5	31.0	51.1
Equipment	5.9	11.4	6.9	13.2	26.5	12.3	18.8	38.7	15.2	27.2	47.6	22.7
Installation	0.9	1.5	1.3	2.2	3.4	2.6	2.8	5.3	3.1	3.4	6.1	3.6
Livestock	23.5	10.0	19.3	9.0	2.4	7.1	6.7	1.4	5.7	3.3	0.6	2.9
Inventories	23.9	19.0	20.4	22.3	21.0	20.5	23.7	19.2	22.1	20.7	14.7	19.6
Total	100.0	100.0	100.0	100.0	100.0	100.0	100.0	100.0	100.0	100.0	100.0	100.0
Projects in Progress	1.5	2.0	1.7	3.6	4.9	3.6	4.7	6.4	4.6	6.5	8.0	6.3

Sources: Tables T-1, T-8, T-9, T-25, T-26, and T-27.

tabular section. The estimates in 1950 prices are much like those in 1937 prices except for differences in absolute values. In 1928 prices, the weight of equipment is much higher and that of livestock much lower than in 1937 prices; growth rates of equipment and inventories are much higher, especially in the early years covered.

By Sector

So much of a distribution of the total stock by sector of economic activity as we can obtain is shown, for valuations in 1937 prices, in Chart 6–3. Numerical series in prices of all three weight years are given in Tables

CHART 6–3

Distribution of Net Capital Stock by Sector, in 1937 Prices, 1928–62
(January 1—Billion Rubles)

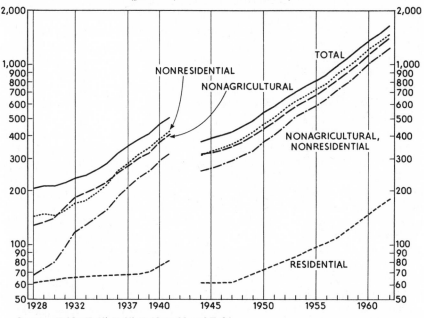

Sources: Tables T–15, T–25, T–28, T–31, and T–34.

T–15 and T–25 to T–36. Total residential capital is taken as identical with fixed capital in housing, and all other capital is attributed to non-residential sectors.[24] Agricultural capital, which is not shown, is taken as the sum of fixed capital and inventories in agriculture and all livestock; all other assets are attributed to nonagricultural sectors.

A feature of the sectoral breakdown which is immediately striking is the decline of the share of housing: from 30 percent of the total in 1928 to 11 percent in 1962. The decline is virtually uninterrupted until the last five years, 1957–62, over which housing grows at a rate equal to that of the

---

[24] Some inventories may properly be attributed to the residential sector, but they cannot be of significant volume.

total (10.5 percent per year).[25] The greater part of the change, however, occurs in the prewar years, reflecting the fact that housing in the unexpanded territory increased by less than 20 percent from 1928 to 1941. After a reduction to approximately the 1928 level in the immediate postwar years, it recovers at a quite rapid and evidently accelerating rate, although it regains its prewar level some two or three years later than does capital in other sectors.

Capital in the whole of nonresidential sectors behaves in the prewar years rather like the total stock minus a constant and in the postwar years, in which it predominates in the total, in much the same way as the total. Its growth rates (7.1 percent in 1928–62, 8.7 percent in 1928–41, and 9.1 percent in 1945–62) exceed those of the total in all long periods, but most markedly in the prewar period. Despite the greater relative increase in the prewar rate, the postwar rate still exceeds it and does not itself give evidence of diminishing significantly. The exclusion of housing necessarily reduces the share of structures in total nonresidential capital, and, in the prewar years, it raises the growth in nonresidential structures to a rate close to that in equipment (14.5 as against 15.5 percent). The latter conclusion is vulnerable to error on account of the 1937-price valuation of the 1928 housing stock.[26] On the other hand, error from this source has quite limited consequences for the estimate of total nonresidential capital because of the relatively small share of fixed capital in the total in the years in which housing bulks large.[27]

Capital in sectors other than agriculture rises from 63 percent of the total in 1928 to 80 percent by 1933; it remains close to 80 percent to the war, rises to 84 percent immediately after the war and to 86 percent by 1962. As these percentages imply, growth rates in the nonagricultural sectors diverge greatly from those in the total only in the first five years (8.5 percent as against 3.6 percent per year), but they are higher in all long periods (7.3 percent in 1928–62, 9.2 percent in 1928–41, and 8.9 percent in 1945–62). The slight excess of the prewar over the postwar growth rate is reversed if acquired assets are excluded from the 1941 total. The behavior of nonagricultural relative to total capital is dominated, although not fully explained, by the reduction in livestock in the first five years. Except for this component, the composition of nonagricultural capital broadly resembles that of the total stock. The exclusion of livestock does, because of the difficulty of valuing livestock,[28] significantly improve the reliability of the residual. The exclusion of agricultural inventories, which are extrapolated on output, works to the same effect. On both of these counts, the nonagricultural estimates are more reliable than those for all sectors and, on balance, they are probably the most reliable of the sector

---

[25] It should be kept in mind that the reference here is to net capital values. The gross value of housing increases at 5.9 percent per year from 1957 to 1962 (see Table T–15), that of total capital at 9.9 percent (see Tables T–1 and T–25).

[26] See p. 93.

[27] An error of 25 points in the housing cost index of 265 by which we convert the 1928 housing stock to 1937 prices alters total nonresidential capital by 4 percent in 1928 and 2 percent in 1937 and alters its growth rate between those years by no more than 0.3 percentage points in a growth rate of 7.8 percent. For the impact of the same error on nonresidential fixed capital, see *loc. cit.*

[28] See pp. 106 ff.

estimates we make. The indicated exclusions, however, also increase the leverage of potential errors elsewhere in the calculations—for example, in the initial stock of fixed capital—so the net effect on relative reliabilities is not certain.

While a series for total capital in agriculture can be derived from our estimates, it is not a usable finding of the study. The estimates of fixed capital in agriculture are subject to errors which are large for the agricultural stock although proportionately small for the nonagricultural residual.[29] Error in the weighting of livestock would have much larger consequences for agricultural capital than for capital in groups of sectors in which agriculture is a single component. The estimates for agricultural inventories can serve only to round out the estimates for larger groups and cannot be taken as a reliable measure for agriculture alone.

Capital in sectors other than housing and agriculture (i.e., essentially, industry, construction, transportation and communications, trade, and budget-financed activities) rose from 33 percent of total capital in 1928 to 75 percent in 1962 or at an average annual rate of 8.9 percent. Almost half of the relative gain, to a share of 53 percent, occurred by 1933. This is a change which significantly modifies the description of the period of the First Five-Year Plan given in Section 2 above. As noted there, the stock of capital in all sectors was enlarged at an exceptionally slow rate over the whole period of the Plan, the increase amounting to 19 percent over the five years from January 1, 1928, to January 1, 1933. The small increase in the total, however, was compounded of a large absolute decline in agricultural capital,[30] a slight increase in housing, and an increase of almost 90 percent in nonagricultural and nonresidential capital. What the regime accomplished, so to speak, in this period was not a notable increase in the total capital available to it but a radical transformation of the distribution of capital among sectors (and among kinds of assets). Further comment on this is made in Chapter 10 below.

The growth rate in nonagricultural and nonresidential capital is almost as high over the Second Five-Year Plan as the First (12.8 as against 13.6 percent per annum) but declines rapidly from 1938 to 1941 if acquired assets are excluded. The rate for the entire prewar period, 12.8 percent or 12.0 percent exclusive of acquired assets, is markedly above the 1945–62 rate of 9.4 percent. Within the postwar period, however, the rate appears generally to have accelerated, and the 1955–62 rate, 11.1 percent, is not far below the prewar average.

The composition of capital in this group of sectors is distinctive in that the share of inventories in the total in the early years covered is exceptionally high. In 1928, inventories accounted for 52 percent and fixed capital for 48 percent of the total. Throughout the 1930's the inventory share declines almost continuously and in the years immediately before the war falls to 25 or 30 percent, within which range it remains thereafter. The heavy weight of inventories accounts in part for the erratic movements in this series in the early years, although, in the main, short-run fluctua-

---

29 See p. 85.

30 This conclusion appears sustainable, despite the unreliability in general of the agricultural estimates, on the basis of the size of the reduction in livestock herds.

tions in the growth of capital in nonagricultural and nonresidential sectors parallel those in all sectors.

The effects of different price weights on the sectoral distributions, which are illustrated in Table 6–5, are similar to those on the distribution by kind of asset. The shares of component sectors in the total differ little in 1950 prices from those in 1937 prices. In 1928 prices, the shares of sectors other than housing, agriculture, or both, are higher than in later prices. In 1928 prices, growth rates, shown in Table 6–6, are higher in all sectors except housing, the behavior of which is taken to be invariant to price weights,[31] with the greater part of the excess arising in the 1928–37 period. The weighting effects in the estimates are produced in part by differences in the importance in the various sectors of major categories of assets (structures, equipment, livestock, inventories) and in part by differences in the deflators applied to assets of a given category within particular sectors.[32]

By Age

In Chapter 3, Section 8, we calculate time series for the average age of fixed capital, components and total, in 1937 prices, employing gross values as weights. The resulting series for total fixed capital (in place) is repeated in Chart 6–4. It implies that the average age of fixed capital was reduced by 23 percent from 1928 to 1941 (the age of assets in the 1928 stock being subject to considerable error), increased into the immediate postwar years, though to less than the 1928 level, and was reduced to 42 percent below the 1928 level by 1962. A considerably different picture emerges if the nonfixed components of the total stock are included in the calculation.

The average age of livestock on January 1, 1960, appears to have been on the order of four years. On that date, breeding and draft animals and other stock which are treated in Soviet practice as "basic funds" accounted, in current prices, for about half of total herds;[33] stock regarded as working capital accounted for the remainder. Published data suggest that the first of these categories may have had an average age of roughly six years, the second of roughly two.[34] We take the average of these figures and assume that it held in all years. For inventories, we have no reported data but assume an unvarying average age of one year. The ages for the total stock which these estimates, together with those for fixed capital, yield are shown in Chart 6–4 and Table T–37.

The casualness of the derivation of average ages for livestock and inventories appears justified by the insensitivity of the total series to the ages chosen. As calculated, the average age of the total stock is 11.6 years in 1928 and 8.4 in 1962. If the average age of inventories were ½ or 2 years, these figures would be 11.6 and 8.3 years or 11.8 and 8.6 years. If the aver-

---

[31] See p. 93.

[32] Differences of the latter sort occur in the deflating of residential and nonresidential structures (to 1937), agricultural and nonagricultural equipment, and agricultural and nonagricultural inventories.

[33] Total herds can be estimated (from Tables 4–1 and 4–2) as 228 billion rubles, the basic funds component as 122 billion (see p. 616), both in 1958 prices. Livestock prices are not thought to have changed significantly, however, from 1958 to 1960.

[34] See TsSU–60a, pp. 306–9.

TABLE 6-5

DISTRIBUTION OF NET CAPITAL STOCK BY SECTOR, IN 1937, 1928, AND 1950 PRICES, SELECTED YEARS
(January 1--Percent)

	1928			1937			1950			1962		
	1937 Prices	1928 Prices	1950 Prices	1937 Prices	1928 Prices	1950 Prices	1937 Prices	1928 Prices	1950 Prices	1937 Prices	1928 Prices	1950 Prices
Residential	30.0	29.4	32.7	19.6	13.0	20.1	13.3	7.4	14.6	11.0	5.5	12.4
Nonresidential	70.0	70.6	67.3	80.4	87.0	79.9	86.7	92.6	85.4	89.0	94.5	87.6
Nonagricultural ...	63.3	75.1	67.6	79.1	84.3	81.1	82.6	88.0	83.7	85.8	88.2	85.6
Nonagricultural Nonresidential	33.2	45.7	34.9	59.5	71.3	61.0	69.3	80.6	69.1	74.8	82.7	73.2
Total	100.0	100.0	100.0	100.0	100.0	100.0	100.0	100.0	100.0	100.0	100.0	100.0

Sources: Tables T-15 and T-25 to T-36.

TABLE 6-6

ANNUAL GROWTH RATES OF NET CAPITAL STOCK, TOTAL AND BY SECTOR, IN 1937, 1928, AND 1950 PRICES, SELECTED PERIODS
(January 1--Percent)

	1928 - 1937			1937 - 1950			1950 - 1962			1928 - 1962		
	1937 Prices	1928 Prices	1950 Prices	1937 Prices	1928 Prices	1950 Prices	1937 Prices	1928 Prices	1950 Prices	1937 Prices	1928 Prices	1950 Prices
Residential	1.2	1.2	1.2	0.4	0.4	0.4	8.0	8.0	8.0	3.2	3.2	3.2
Nonresidential	7.8	13.4	8.9	4.0	5.4	3.5	9.9	10.8	9.7	7.1	9.4	7.1
Nonagricultural	8.8	12.2	9.0	3.8	5.2	3.2	10.0	10.7	9.7	7.3	8.9	7.0
Nonagricultural Nonresidential	13.3	16.4	13.7	4.6	5.8	3.9	10.4	10.9	10.0	8.9	10.3	8.6
Total	6.2	10.8	6.8	3.4	4.9	2.9	9.7	10.6	9.5	6.3	8.4	6.2

Sources: Tables T-15 and T-25 to T-36.

CHART 6–4

Average Age of the Total Capital Stock, Gross Value Weights, in 1937 Prices, 1928–62
(January 1—Years)

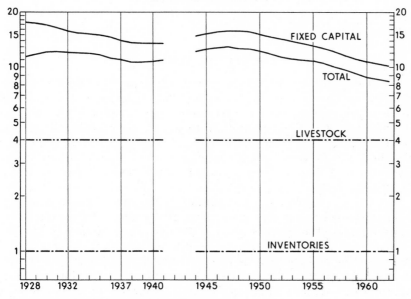

Sources: See Tables T–22 and T–37 and text.

age age of livestock were 2 or 6 years, the corresponding figures would be 11.3 and 8.4 or 12.0 and 8.5 years. The differences are inconsequential for our purposes. They also indicate that changes over time in the ages of inventories or livestock would have little effect on the calculations.

The average age of all capital is substantially shorter than that of fixed capital; in no year is it as long as 13 years. It remains virtually unchanged from 1928 to 1935, over which period the reduction in the age of fixed capital is offset, largely, by the fall in the share of livestock in the total. Thereafter the age of the total declines during three or four years but then rises slightly to 1941, in which year it is only 7 percent below the 1928 level. In the immediate postwar years (to 1947) it rises to a level above that of 1928 and then declines, at a rate which approximately parallels that in fixed capital. The 1928 level is not regained until about 1951 and the minimum prewar level until 1956, which is to say that throughout the first 28 years of the period covered the average age of all capital does not fall significantly (by as much as 10 percent) below its initial level. From 1956 to 1962 the average is reduced quite rapidly—more rapidly than in any previous period—and by 1962 is 27 percent below the 1928 level. The latter is a significant reduction but one materially smaller than that in fixed capital alone.

In Chapter 3 we compute also that for the portion of the fixed capital stock of January 1, 1962, which was created by investment occurring after January 1, 1928, the average age was 7.9 years with gross value weights and 6.3 years with net value weights. Since all livestock and inventories in existence in 1962 must have been created well beyond 1928, we can compute similar average ages for capital in all forms, of 6.7 years with gross value weights and 5.1 years with net value weights.[35] Clearly, that portion of the total stock dating from later than 1928, which by 1962 accounts for almost the whole, was by 1962 extremely youthful on the average.

4. CAPITAL SERVICES

From the capital stock estimates with which we have been concerned thus far, we obtain series for the annual flow of (gross) services rendered by the stock—which flow, we have argued (see Chapter 1, pp. 10–11), is the measure of capital appropriate to our primary analytical purpose. Service estimates, for total capital and for component sectors, in prices of the three weight years and for interest rates of 8 and 20 percent, are presented in Tables T–38 to T–43. The total series are also graphed in Chart 6–5.

Annual capital services are computed as the sum of depreciation and interest charges.[36] The first component is the same as the depreciation charge employed in the derivation of the net value estimates of the fixed capital stock, i.e., straight-line depreciation on the gross stock existing at the beginning of each calendar year.[37] Although depreciation on livestock should in principle be included also, our estimating procedures yield the net stock directly and do not permit calculation of a depreciation series. The omission cannot be consequential, especially beyond the earliest years covered. Inventories we regard as nondepreciating assets. The interest component of the service charge is computed by applying the 8 and 20 percent rates to average annual values of the net stock of assets of all kinds. Average annual stock values are assumed to equal the arithmetic average of January 1 values for the beginning and end of each calendar year.[38]

The use of annual averages to obtain interest charges is not entirely consistent with our procedures in deriving the January 1 values of the fixed capital stock, since in the latter the gross investment of each year is

---

[35] Strictly, the livestock weights are net values in both cases.

[36] A defect in the stock estimates which has been noted (see pp. 36–37), our failure to allow for variations in the intensity with which assets are used, may more significantly impair the service estimates. As with the stock estimates, we have no basis on which to adjust the estimates for such variations.

[37] The calculation of depreciation on total fixed capital, as the difference between gross and net investment, is described pp. 81–82. Analagous procedures are used to obtain depreciation in component sectors. The necessary sectoral data for net capital stocks are given in Tables T–12 to T–21. Annual gross investment in housing is given, for 1937 prices, in Table 6–5 and is converted to 1928 and 1950 prices with the indexes shown on p. 93. Annual gross investment in nonagricultural equipment in 1937 prices is given in Table D–2, that in agricultural equipment in 1928 and 1950 prices in Table D–6, and that in nonagricultural structures in Table D–8 (all installation is attributed to the nonresidential nonagricultural sectors). Other necessary series are computed as residuals. Adjustments in 1940 for assets acquired in the new territories are made for component sectors as in the total; see p. 82, fn. 10.

[38] For 1939, the average is computed from the figure for January 1, 1940, exclusive of acquired assets because the territorial expansion occurred near the end of 1939. In 1940, the figures used for January 1 of both 1940 and 1941 are those inclusive of acquired assets; the 1940 acquisitions occurred at about midyear (see Table 2–13).

CHART 6–5

Total Capital Services in 1937, 1928, and 1950 Prices, 1928–61
(Billion Rubles)

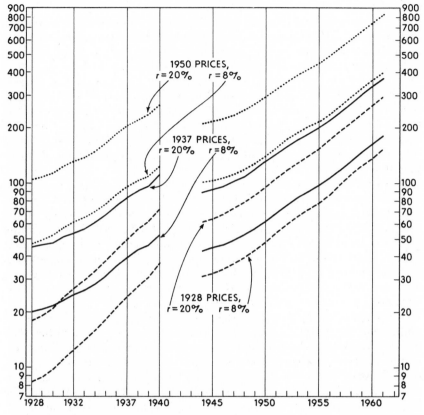

1950 PRICES,
r = 20%   r = 8%

1937 PRICES,
r = 20%   r = 8%

1928 PRICES,
r = 20%   r = 8%

Sources: Tables T–38 to T–43.

treated as though it were added to the stock at the end of the year.[39] The effect of this on the stock estimates is merely to defer briefly (presumably for about six months on the average) the charging of depreciation against assets, which error is small in any case and is offset in some degree by the depreciation at normal rates of investment projects in progress. That interest should in principle be charged against assets from the time of their creation appears unexceptionable. It is doubtless inaccurate also to assume that average annual stocks are equal to the average of the year-end values. In the case of livestock, we have cited evidence that average annual herds exceed the average of year-end herds.[40] Seasonal variations must occur also in inventories, at least in individual sectors, and probably in gross investment in fixed capital. But we have inadequate information to adjust com-

---

[39] For this reason also, there is a slight inconsistency between the service stream assumed in order to derive the present value of a fixed capital asset (see Chapter 2, Section 2) and the service stream computed for the same asset from the stock estimates. In principle, the two are identical.

[40] See p. 111.

ponents other than livestock, and we are unsure but what the understatement in the average for livestock may be offset by errors in the opposite direction in other components (for example, in inventories of livestock products). We therefore compute averages for all components from year-end values.

We have explained that the 8 and 20 percent interest rates are meant to correspond to rates observed in advanced, capitalist, economies and to a much higher rate, and to bound the likely values of the true interest rate in the Soviet economy—in 1937.[41] We here take the further step of assuming the same boundary rates for 1928 and 1950. The true rate of interest has undoubtedly changed over time, but it is not obvious in which direction. While the physical productivity of capital may have declined, the price of capital goods relative to the price of output in general has also declined, especially in the interval from 1928 to 1937.[42] For lack of better information, therefore, we assume the same range applicable in all three weight years.

Since we are here estimating for the aggregate of assets, in each given year, a flow whose shape for individual fixed capital assets, over time, is uncertain, it is appropriate to consider once again the sensitivity of the results to the choice of depreciation method. In Table 6–7, we compute capital services, in 1937 prices, for the total capital stock with fixed capital depreciated by straight-line, sinking fund, and declining annuity, methods, each for interest rates of 8 and 20 percent. Calculations with retirement and sum-of-digits depreciation are not repeated because of the extreme implausibility of the assumptions they reflect.[43]

With either of the two interest rates given, the absolute values of the alternative estimates of capital services differ less from one another than do their corresponding stocks. This results from the fact that differences in the interest components of the service series, which are proportional to differences in the stocks, are partially counterbalanced by differences in the opposite direction in depreciation charges. The narrowing of the dispersion is greater for the 8 percent rate than for 20 percent, but differences from the series with straight-line depreciation are no greater than 7 percent in any case except for sinking fund depreciation with a 20 percent interest rate. For the latter, the difference still reaches almost 20 percent.

With any given depreciation method, a great difference occurs in all cases between absolute values of services at 8 and at 20 percent interest rates. The difference approaches the 1 to 2.5 ratio of the interest rates, a result which is explained proximately by the dominance of interest charges in all of the capital service series. The ultimate explanation lies in the sizable share of assets in the total stock for which no depreciation is charged; the relative youth of fixed capital assets and, hence, high ratio of depreciated to undepreciated values; and the relatively high interest rates employed.

The foregoing implication of the service calculations is important and deserves emphasis. Whereas the absolute values of the capital stock show

---

41 See p. 25.
42 See Table 8–1.
43 See Chapter 2, Section 2.

TABLE 6-7

TOTAL CAPITAL SERVICES ESTIMATED WITH FIXED CAPITAL DEPRECIATED
BY ALTERNATIVE METHODS, IN 1937 PRICES, SELECTED YEARS

Depreciation Method	1928	1932	1937	1940	1945	1950	1955	1961
			A.	Billion Rubles				
r = 20%								
1. Sinking Fund . . .	52.1	62.2	94.5	126	110	153	229	404
2. Straight-Line . . .	45.0	53.3	83.0	110	92.1	130	200	370
3. Declining Annuity	44.3	52.6	81.7	108	89.1	127	196	364
r = 8%								
4. Sinking Fund . . .	21.4	26.0	40.2	53.9	46.9	65.6	100	180
5. Straight-Line . . .	20.0	24.5	38.8	52.3	44.1	62.0	97.0	181
6. Declining Annuity	19.7	24.3	38.7	52.1	42.6	61.6	96.6	184
			B.	Straight-Line Depreciated Values = 100				
r = 20%								
1. Sinking Fund . . .	116	117	114	115	119	118	114	109
2. Straight-Line . . .	100	100	100	100	100	100	100	100
3. Declining Annuity	98.4	98.7	98.4	98.2	96.7	97.7	98.0	98.4
r = 8%								
4. Sinking Fund . . .	107	106	104	103	106	106	103	99.4
5. Straight-Line . . .	100	100	100	100	100	100	100	100
6. Declining Annuity	98.5	99.2	99.7	99.6	96.6	99.4	99.6	102
			C.	1937 = 100				
r = 20%								
1. Sinking Fund . . .	55.1	65.8	100	133	116	162	242	428
2. Straight-Line . . .	54.2	64.2	100	133	111	157	241	446
3. Declining Annuity	54.2	64.4	100	132	109	155	240	446
r = 8%								
4. Sinking Fund . . .	53.2	64.7	100	134	117	163	249	448
5. Straight-Line . . .	51.5	63.1	100	135	114	160	250	466
6. Declining Annuity	50.9	62.8	100	135	110	159	250	475

Sources: See text.

considerable sensitivity to the shape of service streams and little to the interest rate at which the services are discounted, the absolute values of capital services vary almost in proportion to the interest rate and show substantial invariability to the service-stream assumptions. In the end, therefore, when capital is measured as a productive input, its value turns out to depend primarily, among the various elements entering into the calculation, upon the interest rate assumed appropriate for the Soviet economy. This is not a reassuring conclusion, since our ignorance of the appropriate interest rate is large, but it effectively pinpoints the single most critical source of uncertainty in our estimates.

The rate of growth of capital services shows little sensitivity to either service-stream or interest-rate assumptions. For the entire 33 years, rates range from 6.4 to 7.0 percent per annum, being somewhat higher (0.3 percentage points) for any given depreciation method at 8 percent interest than at 20 percent. The insensitivity follows from the similar behavior of capital stocks computed by the alternative methods and from the dominance of interest charges in capital services. The higher growth rates at the lower interest rate follow from the greater weight of depreciation charges in capital services at that rate and from the relative rise of depreciable assets in total capital and of short-lived assets (equipment) in depreciable assets.

The accepted service series—with straight-line depreciation—moves over time in much the same way as the net capital stock because, again, of the dominance of the interest component. Services rise somewhat more rapidly: from 1928 to 1961 in 1937 prices at 6.9 percent ($r = 8\%$) or 6.6 percent ($r = 20\%$) as against 6.3 percent in the corresponding annual averages of the stock. The relative gain is more or less continuous although somewhat more rapid in the early years: for example, from 1928 to 1933 services rise by 30 percent ($r = 8\%$) or 25 percent ($r = 20\%$) as against a 21 percent rise in the average stock. The averaging of the annual stock figures tends to smooth the service series, but it leaves the pattern of short-run changes recognizably like that in the stock: a slow initial growth to a peak in 1931 and a trough in 1933; several years of rapid growth in the mid-1930's (1935–38) followed by a decline if acquired assets are excluded; an acceleration from a slow start after the war to high growth rates from about 1950 but with a perceptible sag in 1953–55.

The conversion from stocks to annual services has sufficiently limited effects on the distribution of capital that no detailed description is required (reference may be made to Tables T–38 to T–43). The share of fixed capital in the total and the share of equipment in fixed capital are both raised. Sectoral distributions are practically unaltered. Growth rates of individual kinds of assets are altered little or not at all. Those of sector categories are generally raised, by amounts which are of the same order of magnitude as the increases in the total series.[44]

The relation of services to stocks in 1928 and 1950 prices is substantially the same as in 1937 prices.

In sum, the capital service calculations yield series which are conceptually more appropriate measures of capital inputs, for which absolute values differ from those of capital stocks by amounts heavily dependent upon the interest rate chosen, but which, except for a moderately more rapid rate of increase, change over time in conformity with the capital stock.

5. ANNUAL INVESTMENT

The Findings

Our capital stock estimates either are derived from annual investment data, in the case of fixed capital, or can be used to obtain investment as the increment in the stock, in the case of livestock and inventories. Annual depreciation emerges as a by-product of the computation of the net value of the fixed capital stock. Since interest attaches to investment as such, we assemble the various components to obtain total investment series.[45] These are shown, gross and net of depreciation (on fixed capital), in prices of each of the three weight years, in Tables T–44, T–45, and T–46. The gross

---

[44] Housing services rise less rapidly than the net stock because the initial stock of housing is depreciated at a higher average rate than are post-1928 additions.

[45] Gross investment in fixed capital is taken from Tables A–2, A–3, and A–4. Investment in livestock and inventories is computed from the stock estimates in Tables T–23 and T–24, except that adjustments are made for acquisitions through territorial expansion in 1939 and 1940. For livestock, investment is computed from the 1940 and 1941 herd totals in the pre-1939 territory; see pp. 104–6 above. For inventories, the territories added in 1939 are assumed to account for 5 percent of the stock on January 1, 1940, those added in 1940 for 5 percent of the stock on January 1, 1941. Annual depreciation is from Table T–11.

series are also graphed in Chart 6–6. The contributions of the component
asset categories to the whole, in 1937 prices, are indicated in Chart 6–7 (the
graph is drawn on an arithmetic scale because of the negative values in
some years of investment in livestock and inventories; investment in installation is included in the total but not shown separately).

CHART 6–6

Annual Gross Investment in 1937, 1928, and 1950 Prices, 1928–61
(Billion Rubles)

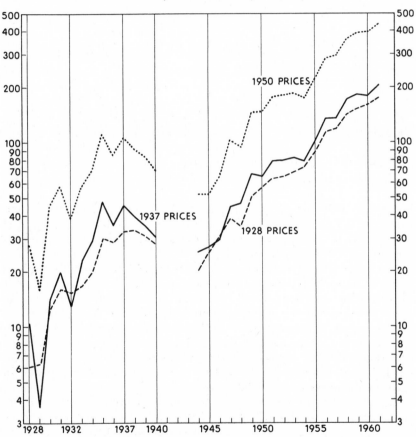

Sources: Tables T–44, T–45, and T–46.

In 1937 prices, gross investment increases at an average annual rate of
9.4 percent from 1928 to 1961, 9.5 percent from 1928 to 1940, and 13.6
percent from 1945 to 1961, all of which rates, measured between terminal
years, greatly exceed those of the stock over (roughly) comparable intervals.[46] Short-period variations in the volume of investment resemble those
in the growth rate of the stock. Troughs are evident in 1929, 1932, and
1940; peaks in 1931 and in 1935–37. The 1940 level of investment is almost

---

[46] See, however, the discussion of the functional relation between trend rates of
growth in investment and in the capital stock in Chapter 8, Section 5.

CHART 6–7

Annual Gross Investment, Total and by Kind of Asset, in 1937 Prices, 1928–61
(Billion Rubles)

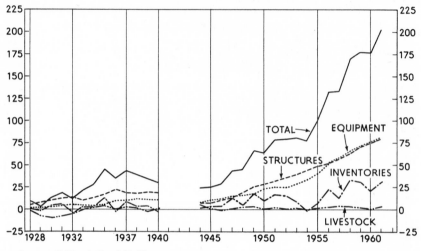

Sources: Tables A–2 and T–43.

regained by 1946 and the prewar peak by 1948. The rising postwar trend is broken by a pronounced leveling-off in 1952–54 and a possible retardation after 1958. Most remarkable, however, is the extreme variability of gross investment from year to year.

The latter characteristic of the series is explained largely by the variability of annual investment in inventories. How far this is true can be established by comparing total investment as estimated with a series obtained by smoothing the inventory component, which is done in Chart 6–8. The smoothed inventory series is that obtained in Chapter 5 (Table 5–5) by taking a three-year moving average.[47] Larger swings in annual investment remain visible, but the serrations in the total series are nearly eliminated. Again, we defer a final analysis of the apparent variability of investment in inventories to Chapter 8.

The annual investment series in alternative prices provide a striking if rather odd illustration of "index number relativity." Investment grows more rapidly in 1928 than in 1937 prices between 1928 and 1937 and (slightly) more rapidly in 1937 than in 1950 prices between 1937 and 1950, which are differences of the expected sort. But the relations among the series, and especially between the 1928-price series and those of the two later years, vary widely and unsystematically. The absolute value of investment in 1928 prices exceeds that in 1937 prices by as much as 68 percent—in 1929, which is clearly an especially odd year—and falls below it by as much as 42 percent. The sum of annual investments from 1928 through 1940 in 1928 prices equals 80 percent of that in 1937 prices (the

---

[47] The 1938 and 1939 figures for smoothed investment in inventories are those exclusive of assets acquired by territorial expansion.

ratio is 85 percent for 1944–61) although the 1928 stock in 1928 prices is less than 40 percent of that in 1937 prices. Periods can be selected over which investment in 1928 prices grows much more rapidly than that in 1937 prices and others in which it grows much more slowly. The 1928-price series exhibits less of the erratic year-to-year movements than do the series with later weights. Even between the 1950- and 1937-price series there are significant differences, e.g., in 1928–29–30 and in 1947–48.

CHART 6–8

**Annual Gross Investment as Estimated and with Inventories
Smoothed, in 1937 Prices, 1928–61**
(Billion Rubles)

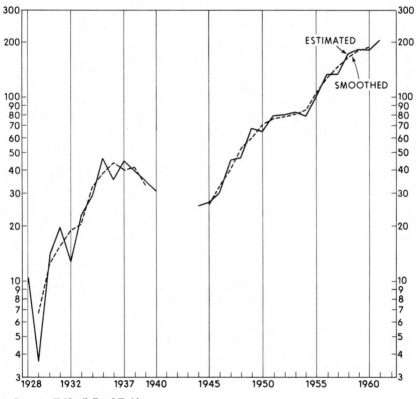

Sources: Tables 5–5 and T–44.

These various divergences can, of course, be explained by differences in the weights of component asset categories, notably of livestock and equipment, and by intracomponent weight differences, the effects of which we have explored with respect to the stock estimates.[48] They serve to empha-

---

[48] See pp. 154 ff. above. It should be recalled also that the valuations of inventories in 1928 prices, other than in 1928 and 1937, and in 1950 prices, other than in 1937 and 1950, are highly approximate.

size, nevertheless, how highly specific is any description of the course of investment in the Soviet economy to the price weights employed.

In view of the variability of gross investment, it is understandable that net investment moves still more erratically and the ratio of net to gross is also quite variable.[49] Absolute series for net investment are given in Tables T–44, T–45, and T–46; the ratio of net to gross investment is graphed in Chart 6–9. In 1937 prices, the net-to-gross ratio ranges from as low as 0 percent in 1929 to as high as 84 percent in 1935. In general, however, it has been high, averaging 66 percent in the prewar years and 71 percent in the postwar (1945–61). In both 1937 and 1950 prices, it shows no clear tendency to decline over the long run or within the postwar period. In 1928 prices, it fairly clearly does decline from a peak in the early 1930's although it shows an approximately horizontal trend in the last decade covered.

Comparison with Bergson's Estimates

Gross annual investment in constant prices is also estimated in Bergson–61 (Abram Bergson's *The Real National Income of Soviet Russia Since 1928*). Because of the authoritative character of this study, it is desirable that we establish with some precision the points at which, and reasons for which, our estimates differ from Bergson's. The two have common origins to a large degree so that consistency between them is not necessarily evidence of mutual corroboration. Differences between them, on the other hand, may not represent statistical errors in either but may reflect differences in the purposes for which they were made: as a component of Gross National Product in Bergson's case and as an element in the computation of the capital stock in ours. Bergson's finished estimates were available to us at the time our estimates were composed. In addition, we have been able to make use of official data released since the completion of his study.

The two estimates are compared in Table 6–8. Components are shown

CHART 6–9

Ratio of Net to Gross Annual Investment, in 1937, 1928, and 1950 Prices, 1928–61
(Percent)

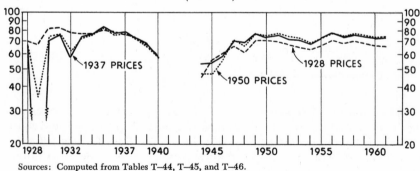

Sources: Computed from Tables T–44, T–45, and T–46.

---

[49] The functional relation between gross and net investment is discussed in Chapter 8, Section 5.

in as much detail as is feasible and revealing. The categories are matched as well as possible, but some inconsistencies in the coverage of nominally identical categories remain. The comparison is restricted to valuations in 1937 prices (1937 "factor costs" in Bergson's terminology), although both studies contain series in 1928 and 1950 prices as well. The years covered are all of those for which Bergson makes estimates. Bergson presents alternative estimates for 1954, one of which is shown in the table in parentheses.

If gross investment totals as they are presented in the two studies are compared directly (row 9), the differences between them are large and variable, ours falling short of Bergson's by 17 to 39 percent. Much of this difference, however, reflects the inclusion by Bergson of three categories of investment which we (largely) omit from our gross investment series: "other" fixed investment, miscellaneous investment, and capital repairs. "Other" fixed investment is essentially a Soviet statistical category, which we have described previously (p. 38). It includes outlays which, in the Soviet view, do not result in additions to the stock of fixed capital. Bergson questions whether these outlays ought to be considered investment but includes them for statistical reasons.[50] Miscellaneous investment is intended to encompass money investment in agricultural inventories insofar as these are omitted from Bergson's inventory estimates, increments in state stockpiles, "certain 'operational expenditures' of the investment type not elsewhere classified," and the net foreign balance on commercial account.[51] We include agricultural inventories in our inventory estimates and would include state stockpiles if adequate data were available for them. Bergson's inclusion of capital repairs is in accord with his general rule of following Soviet statistical methodology in the classification of expenditures as investment.[52] We omit capital repairs from our total investment series, although we have estimates for them, in order to maintain consistency with our capital stock estimates, which are derived from investment net of repairs.

If we correct these major inconsistencies in coverage by subtracting "other" fixed and miscellaneous investment from Bergson's series and adding capital repairs to ours (row 8), the orders of magnitude of the two estimates become similar. Ours, however, still ranges from as much as 21 percent below Bergson's (in 1928) to 11 percent above (in 1951). The principal sources of the remaining discrepancies can be explained here, but the reader desiring an exhaustive explanation must be referred to the detailed statements of sources and methods in the two studies.

Row 1: Construction in both estimates is obtained from the construction index, inclusive of capital repairs, provided in Powell–59. In setting a 1937 absolute value for the index, Bergson, following his general procedure of excluding imputed investment, omits investment in kind in collective farms and in road-building.[53] We include these items, which are of considerable weight, since they constitute gross additions to the capital stock. A 1944 value for the construction index is lacking in the original study and

---

[50] See Bergson–61, p. 379.
[51] *Ibid.*, p. 420.
[52] See *ibid.*, p. 379.
[53] *Ibid.*, pp. 379 and 384.

TABLE 6-8

BERGSON'S AND PRESENT ESTIMATES OF GROSS ANNUAL INVESTMENT, TOTAL AND COMPONENTS, IN 1937 PRICES, 1928-55
(Billion Rubles)

	1928	1937	1940	1944	1948	1949	1950	1951	1952	1953	1954	1955
A. Bergson's Estimates												
1. Construction and Installation, Including Capital Repairs	8.0	21.7	21.9	12.6	23.1	29.3	33.7	38.2	42.6	47.2	52.0	57.4
2. Equipment, Including Capital Repairs	2.6	12.5	13.4	9.9	18.3	21.6	29.2	31.1	31.7	35.4	41.6	49.8
3. Other Fixed Investment	0.5	1.3	4.4	1.9	3.3	5.2	4.3	5.2	5.3	5.7	6.4	6.2
4. Livestock	1.7	4.4	3.3	1.7	4.1	4.0	0.7	2.2	-0.3	0.9	2.0	1.9
5. Trade Inventories	2.4	2.1	0.0}	4.1	5.4	5.2	1.9	6.0	6.5	2.4	-2.2	4.4
6. Other Inventories	0.7	6.4	2.6}		5.1	9.1	7.7	6.2	6.2	8.5	0.0(5.7)	6.9
7. Miscellaneous	0.8	7.4	4.3	4.0	13.6	7.2	9.2	12.6	15.3	8.1	4.5	3.9
8. Total, Excluding Other Fixed and Miscellaneous	15.3	47.2	41.4	28.4	56.2	69.3	73.3	83.7	86.7	94.4	93.4(99.1)	120.6
9. Total as Estimated (Rows 1 to 7)	16.6	55.9	50.1	34.3	73.1	81.7	86.8	101.5	107.3	108.2	104.3(110.0)	130.7
B. Present Estimates												
1. Construction and Installation, Including Capital Repairs	8.8	24.2	24.5	10.4	26.0	32.9	38.0	43.1	47.8	53.0	58.5	64.8
2. Equipment, Including Capital Repairs	2.5	12.4	13.3	9.8	19.7	21.4	28.9	30.8	31.4	35.0	41.1	49.3
3. Other Fixed Investment	0.0	0.0	0.0	0.0	0.0	0.0	0.0	0.0	0.0	0.0	0.0	0.0
4. Livestock	-0.7	3.2	0.6	5.8	3.1	3.2	0.8	2.1	0.0	1.2	-0.6	1.0
5. Trade Inventories	0.4	1.9	-0.1	1.4	5.8	5.5	1.2	5.1	5.7	1.9	-2.2	2.9
6. Other Inventories	1.1	7.3	-1.9	0.5	-0.4	13.1	8.3	11.7	10.1	7.6	0.3	3.3
7. Miscellaneous	0.0	0.0	0.0	0.0	0.0	0.0	0.0	0.0	0.0	0.0	0.0	0.0
8. Total, Excluding Other Fixed and Miscellaneous	12.1	49.0	36.4	27.8	54.2	76.2	77.3	92.8	95.1	98.7	97.1	121.3
9. Total as Estimated (Row 8 Less Capital Repairs)	10.4	44.9	30.8	25.6	46.4	67.6	65.6	79.7	80.4	82.0	79.3	101.2

TABLE 6-8 (continued)

BERGSON'S AND PRESENT ESTIMATES OF GROSS ANNUAL INVESTMENT, TOTAL AND COMPONENTS, IN 1937 PRICES, 1928-55

(Billion Rubles)

	1928	1937	1940	1944	1948	1949	1950	1951	1952	1953	1954	1955
					C. Bergson's Estimates Minus Present Estimates							
1. Construction and Installation, Including Capital Repairs	-0.8	-2.5	-2.6	2.2	-2.9	-3.6	-4.3	-4.9	-5.2	-5.8	-6.5	-7.4
2. Equipment, Including Capital Repairs	0.1	0.1	0.1	0.1	-1.4	0.2	0.3	0.3	0.3	0.4	0.5	0.5
3. Other Fixed Investment	0.5	1.3	4.4	1.9	3.3	5.2	4.3	5.2	5.3	5.7	6.4	6.2
4. Livestock	2.4	1.2	2.7	-4.1	1.0	0.8	-0.1	0.1	-0.3	-0.3	2.6	0.9
5. Trade Inventories	2.0	0.2	0.1 ⎫	2.2	-0.4	-0.3	0.7	0.9	0.8	0.5	0.0	1.5
6. Other Inventories	-0.4	-0.9	4.5 ⎭		5.5	-4.0	-0.6	-5.5	-3.9	0.9	-0.3(5.4)	3.6
7. Miscellaneous	0.8	7.4	4.3	9.0	13.6	7.2	9.2	12.6	15.3	8.1	4.5	3.9
8. Total, Excluding Other Fixed and Miscellaneous	3.2	-1.8	5.0	0.6	2.0	-6.9	-4.0	-9.1	-8.4	-4.3	-3.7(2.0)	-0.7
9. Total as Estimated	6.2	11.0	19.3	8.7	26.7	14.1	21.2	21.8	26.9	26.2	25.0(30.7)	29.5

Sources: For Bergson's estimates, rows 1–7, series in 1937 prevailing prices are given in Bergson-61, pp. 388 and 392; data for adjustments to 1937 factor costs are given in *ibid.*, p. 130. The combined figure for inventories in 1944 is computed as the difference between 9.8 of "other" investment, *ibid.*, p. 128, and the figures for livestock and miscellaneous investment. Row 8 is row 9 minus rows 3 and 7. Row 9 is from Bergson-61, pp. 128 and 303. For present estimates, rows 1 and 2 are from Table A-1. Row 3 is not estimated. Row 4 is from Table T-44. Rows 5 and 6 are computed from Table N-1. Territorial acquisitions in 1939 are assumed to have accounted for 5 percent of inventories on January 1, 1940; acquisitions in 1940 for 5 percent of inventories on January 1, 1941. Row 7 is not estimated. Row 8 is row 9 plus capital repairs as shown in Table A-1. Row 9 is from Table-44.

is obtained differently by Bergson and by us.[54] Bergson assumes that installation moves with construction alone, we that it moves at a rate equal to the average of investment in construction and equipment.[55] Bergson makes a small upward adjustment, which we forgo, in all of the fixed capital components for the difference between prevailing prices and factor costs.

Row 2: Identical series, from Moorsteen–62, for investment in new machinery and capital repairs to machinery are used in both studies, except that 1948, which is lacking in the Moorsteen study, is obtained differently[56] and the slight adjustment is made by Bergson to a factor cost valuation.

Row 4: Bergson's livestock estimates for 1937 and 1948–52 are based on January 1 herd counts,[57] which are the basis of our estimates throughout. In these years, the two estimates differ little from one another, at least in relation to total investment. January 1 herd counts were not available to Bergson for other years. For 1928, he proceeds from a reported figure, of uncertain coverage, for gross investment in livestock in current prices. His resulting estimate appears implausibly high in the light of the herd data which have now been released.[58] For 1940 and 1944, Bergson describes his estimates as "arbitrarily" assumed. For 1953–55, he works with October 1 herd counts, with results which differ from ours by amounts which are modest in relation to total investment. Differences in the livestock estimates arise also from differences in valuation procedures—primarily from the fact that Bergson includes and we exclude prices of meat sold in cuts in the collective-farm markets in deriving average realized prices of livestock.[59]

Rows 5 and 6: The inventory estimates differ from one another chiefly because of differences in the current-price estimates since we follow Bergson's procedures rather closely in the deflation to constant prices.[60] For trade inventories from 1937 on, we proceed from the same current-price data as does Bergson and arrive at substantially similar estimates. For nontrade inventories from 1937 on, we have access to considerably more reported data than were available to Bergson, and we are not constrained, as he is, to reconcile the estimates of investment in nontrade inventories and miscellaneous investment with their combined total determined as a residual.[61] For both trade and nontrade inventories in 1928, we commence

---

[54] Bergson (p. 387) extrapolates 1944 from 1940 on an input-price deflated index, which procedure yields a 1944 value for the construction index which is much higher than that for 1945. We interpolate 1944 between 1940 and 1945, on the input-price deflated index (see Table A–6).

[55] For the defense of his procedure, see Bergson–61, p. 387; for the defense of ours, p. 48 of the present study.

[56] Bergson (p. 385) estimates 1948 equipment from construction in that year; we interpolate it between 1946 and 1949 (see Table A–1).

[57] Bergson's procedures are described in Bergson–61, pp. 393–95.

[58] See Table 4–1.

[59] See Chapter 4, Section 3, and Appendix F.

[60] On Bergson's procedures, see Bergson–61, Appendix G.

[61] It is at this point that the contrast between Bergson's concern with total GNP and ours with investment alone is registered most clearly. Bergson's total GNP in current prices is determined on the income side. When all other expenditures are accounted for,

from much the same data as Bergson; we obtain investments in current prices which are roughly the same as his; but, primarily because of differences in the way we read the sector distribution of inventories, we arrive at quite different figures in 1937 prices.[62]

Since our 1928 estimates of both inventories and livestock differ from Bergson's in the same direction and by large amounts, the difference between the total investment figures is very large. It follows that the rate of change in investment calculated for any period from 1928 appears materially different in our estimates than it does in Bergson's.

6. COMPARISONS WITH SOME U.S. DATA

Casual international comparisons are very likely to be misleading, and, for reasons we have explained, it is not possible to undertake systematic comparisons within this volume. However, especially for the reader who is unfamiliar with capital estimates for other countries, it may be helpful to have some points of reference in considering the results which we have described above. For this purpose, we cite here certain estimates for the United States which may be of particular interest. We restrict the comparisons to capital stock data, leaving aside services and investment flows, and, for the most part, to estimates made by Raymond W. Goldsmith.

While we are aware of "incomparabilities" between Goldsmith's estimates and ours, any careful discussion of these would carry us into the kind of systematic comparison which we are unprepared to make. In the absence of such a discussion, the reader will do well to keep in mind that capital estimates may differ significantly because of differences in capital concepts and, even where the conceptual objectives are the same, because of differences in statistical procedures. The behavior of the stock may be, as it demonstrably is in the Soviet case, heavily dependent upon the price weights chosen. Estimates in alternative prices are not available for the United States which extend into the early periods in which weight-sensitivity is likely to be large. Calculations made by Alexander Gerschenkron of U.S. machinery production, in prices of 1899, 1909, 1923, and 1939, suggest that the behavior at least of the equipment component of the

---

he is left with a residual which represents conceptually the sum of investment in nontrade inventories and miscellaneous investment, which residual he uses as a guide in estimating nontrade inventories (cf. *ibid.*, pp. 409–10). But this residual represents also any net error in his estimates. If, as is implied by his procedures, the error lies in the expenditure calculations, then his total GNP estimate in constant prices is in error only to the extent of differences in the deflators applicable to various expenditure components. Moreover, by his procedure he avoids making his annual GNP totals heavily dependent upon estimates of investment in inventories, which are unlikely in any case to be highly accurate (see our discussion in Chapter 5, Section 5). Our concern, on the other hand, is with annual investment as such, and for this it appears reasonable to make the best estimates we can without regard to any need to exhaust more aggregative totals.

[62] Bergson obtains his figure for 1928 investment in trade inventories from Rozentul–29, pp. 314–15. From related data given in Gosplan–29, p. 432, and from additional data in Rozentul, pp. 305 and 307, it can be inferred that Rozentul's figures for trade include industrial co-operatives (to a larger amount than the estimate made by Bergson, p. 396), agricultural co-operatives, and syndicates. We attribute inventories in industrial co-operatives and syndicates to industry and those in agricultural co-operatives to procurement. On our interpretation of these data, see Appendix G, notes for 1928–30.

U.S. capital stock might vary markedly with different price weights.[63] We leave it to the reader also to judge how far, in any comparative appraisal, account should be taken of differences in historical circumstances—the westward expansion of the United States in the 19th century or its depression of the 1930's, the initial backwardness of the Soviet economy or its losses in World War II.

Goldsmith's various estimates are straightforwardly comparable with ours—for the *net* stock—in that they are for depreciated values in constant prices, and they are given in sufficient detail that series can be obtained which have virtually the same coverage as ours: structures of all kinds, producer durables, livestock, and inventories other than those held in the public sector.[64] Goldsmith has presented estimates (in Goldsmith–52, Table I), in 1929 prices and for selected years, which extend backward—though presumably somewhat approximately—to as early a date as 1805. These imply annual growth rates, of the stock of the indicated coverage, of 5.1 percent in 1805–50, 5.4 percent in 1850–80, 6.3 percent in 1880–90, and 3.5 percent in 1890–1900. The estimates of his authoritative *A Study of Saving in the United States* (Goldsmith–56, Table W–3), also in 1929 prices but annual, commence from 1896 and imply average growth rates of 3.3 percent from 1896 to 1929 and 0.8 percent from 1929 to 1945. More recently (in Goldsmith–62, Tables A–6, A–39, and B–174), Goldsmith has made estimates, in 1947–49 prices, which indicate that the U.S. stock within the postwar period, from 1945 to 1958, has grown at about 3.3 percent per annum (from 1947 to 1957, at 3.6 percent).

Our estimates of the total Soviet stock, net, in 1937 prices, imply an average growth rate over the 34 years from 1928 to 1962 of 6.3 percent per annum. On its face, this appears a somewhat higher rate than that generally attained in the United States through the 19th century. It exceeds by a very large margin the rate of growth in the U.S. stock since the late 19th century, and, undoubtedly, by a still larger margin the U.S. rate for the interval 1928–62—by, one would judge, a factor of the order of 3 or 4. Within the recent postwar years, the Soviet rate of increase of roughly 10 percent per year must come close to triple that of the United States. If Soviet data in 1950 rather than 1937 prices are used in the comparison, the results are little altered. In 1928 prices, the growth rate of the Soviet stock, 8.4 percent for the 34 years, obviously greatly exceeds any of the U.S. rates cited.

With respect to the distribution of the total stock, by sector and by kind of asset, Goldsmith's estimates suggest a much greater stability over time than we find for the Soviet stock. Certain changes are in the same direction in both—a decline in agriculture, a rise in equipment—but sudden and radical changes of the sort which have occurred in the Soviet Union appear, doubtless understandably, not to have taken place in the United States. As in the Soviet case, the dominant component of the U.S. stock has been structures, and the share of equipment has been a minor one. Inven-

---

[63] See Gerschenkron–51, pp. 52–53.

[64] That is, the series cited here exclude land, consumer durables, inventories held in the public sector, monetary gold and silver, net foreign assets, and, for the period 1945–58, military assets other than structures (inside the United States) and equipment, which are included in Goldsmith's most comprehensive aggregates.

tories in the United States also have shown considerable variability. Their share in the total, however, appears typically to have been only about half as large as the 21 to 26 percent which we estimate, in 1937 prices, for the Soviet Union.[65]

A further comparison, although an even looser one, can be made between the capital stocks of the two economies. Estimates have been published, in Jaszi–62, p. 17, of the average age of *fixed business* capital in the United States, in 1954 prices. These include figures with assets weighted by gross values, as are our age estimates for the whole stock, but calculated alternatively with Bulletin "F" lives and with lives 20 percent shorter.[66] For this portion of the U.S. stock, at the end of 1961, average ages are estimated as 19.0 years for structures, 7.2 for equipment, and 13.6 for the total, with Bulletin "F" lives, or 13.8, 5.6, and 10.0 respectively, with the 20 percent shorter lives. In our estimates for fixed capital in all sectors, with gross value weights and in 1937 prices, average ages on January 1, 1962, are 12.8 years for structures, 6.0 for equipment, and 10.1 for the whole (see Table T–22). The U.S. ages with Bulletin "F" lives are materially greater than those we obtain but, with the shorter lives, not much different.[67] Fixed capital other than that held by business, however, weighs heavily in the total U.S. stock, consists largely of structures, and, for the most part, of long-lived (if not necessarily aged) structures.[68] From this, one would suppose that the average age of all fixed capital in the United States would prove considerably greater, even with the shorter lives assumed, than that of business capital alone and, hence, greater than that of the Soviet stock. Considering also the relatively small share of inventories and livestock in U.S. capital, the U.S. stock of all kinds of capital would doubtless prove markedly less youthful than that of the Soviet Union. Given the large difference in the growth rates of the two stocks, a contrary conclusion would be surprising although not impossible.

---

[65] At the end of 1958, the U.S. stock, of coverage comparable with our estimates and in 1947–49 prices (see Goldsmith–62, Tables A–6, A–39, and B–174) consisted 71 percent of structures, 17 percent equipment, 10 percent inventories, and 2 percent livestock. On January 1, 1962, in 1937 prices, the Soviet stock consisted 46 percent of structures, 27 percent equipment, 3 percent installation, 21 percent inventories, and 3 percent livestock. The latter shares in 1950 prices are about 5 points higher for structures and 5 points lower for equipment. See Table 6–4.

[66] The source also gives, *loc. cit.*, ages computed with net value weights, but we are unable to make a comprehensive calculation of this sort for the Soviet stock (see pp. 99–100 above).

[67] As we note elsewhere (p. 69), the Soviet lives used in our calculations are close to, but somewhat longer than, Bulletin "F" lives.

[68] For data on the composition of the stock, cf. Goldsmith–62, Tables A–57, A–58, A–62, and A–63.

Chapter 7

Comparison of Findings with Official Soviet Data

1. INTRODUCTION

Western estimates of Soviet economic magnitudes have in some cases, for example, those of industrial production or national income, represented the independent compilation of statistical series which were, at least in broad terms, the counterparts of official series published in Soviet sources. The same is true only in a very limited sense of the capital stock estimates made in this study. The regime has not since the late 1920's released time series in constant prices (or, for that matter, in current or acquisition prices) for any comprehensive measure of capital in the economy or for component series which could be combined into comprehensive measures. With one minor exception that we know of,[1] it has published no constant-price series for inventories, either in the whole economy or in subsectors, or global series inclusive of inventories. Nor has it published constant-price series covering all livestock (as against the part of livestock included in "basic funds"). As our calculations make clear, inventories and livestock have been important constituents of the total stock, and the absence of official data for these components restricts greatly the comparisons which can be made.

The history of official statistics for fixed capital (sometimes inclusive of livestock in "basic funds") is a fuller one, although we need not review it in detail here. Until the late 1950's, data released on the fixed capital stock were so restricted in coverage—to socialized or state capital or to particular sectors of production—as to make them incomparable with our estimates. Only with the increased flow of statistics following Stalin's death did data for fixed capital—time series in the form of index numbers—appear which could be taken as the official equivalents of the stock estimates we have compiled.

Even the official fixed capital indexes allow only isolated comparisons with our estimates. In their latest and revised version, they cover 7 of the 34 years from 1928 to 1962 and, within the 21-year interval between 1929 and 1951, they contain a single observation, for 1941. They are for gross

---

[1] The series for inventories in retail trade cited in Appendix L, p. 579.

184

values only, permitting no direct check of our time series for net values, and they provide no indication of the effects of alternative price weights. The stocks of structures and equipment are not shown separately, which forestalls comparisons with our component series. Within these limits, however, the official indexes provide a fairly direct check of our estimates in a few years and a few dimensions which, albeit loosely and inferentially, could be taken to extend to other years and dimensions as well.

While of lesser scope than our estimates in most respects, the official indexes differ from ours also in that they are given in considerably greater detail by productive sector. Comparison of the two sets of estimates, therefore, cuts both ways. To the extent that our estimates can be shown to confirm the official indexes at the points where comparison is possible, they can be inferred, again loosely, to lend credibility to those official sectoral indexes which have no counterparts in our estimates. To this extent, a way could be opened to remedy, at least in part, a major deficiency in the data which emerge from the present study.

Besides the fixed capital time series, official data have been released in the recent past for annual investment in fixed capital, nominally in constant prices, and the results have been published of an inventory of the fixed capital stock as of January 1, 1960. Although neither of these matches the stock estimates which are our primary concern, they obviously constitute an indirect check on them. They are relevant also to the interpretation and appraisal of the official stock indexes, and for this reason we discuss them first, in Sections 2 and 3 following. The official indexes are then considered in Section 4.[2]

With respect to all of the official data, it must be emphasized that Soviet descriptions of how they have been compiled and what they are supposed to represent are incomplete where not totally unavailable. Most Soviet comment is limited to how such statistics could or should be constructed, with no clear indication that the methods described are actually those employed by the Central Statistical Administration (TsSU).[3] On the contrary, the tentative nature of the exposition suggests that the methods are not public information and may even be unknown to Soviet writers on statistical methods. As will appear, the Soviet data contain certain anomalies, the origins of which are by no means obvious. Although in what follows some explanations and conjectures will be offered, we are unable to give an adequate account of the origins of the Soviet data and, hence, to comment satisfactorily on methodological differences between the official statistics and our own.[4] The comparisons, therefore, are largely formal, numbers compared with numbers, and the implications to be drawn correspondingly sparse.

---

2 Various preliminary operations with the official data have been performed in Appendix O.

3 A typical example is provided in Petrov–61, pp. 77–82. This text, published by the TsSU press, Gosstatizdat, illustrates the importance of measuring the capital stock by quoting the official index numbers but explains how such an index might be derived only with "a schematic [*uslovnyi*] and simplified example."

4 *Inter alia*, we do not attempt to explore systematically possible differences in the capital concept—use versus cost substitutabilities—between the Soviet data and ours. Comment on the matter is made where reasonably clear information is available.

Even this simple task is complicated by differences between the official data and ours in the prices used for valuation. As our calculations show, indicators of relative change in investment or stocks are affected by the price weights. Furthermore, comparisons of absolute values are impossible among data diversely valued. So far as feasible, therefore, we attempt to recast our series into prices at least roughly similar to those employed in the Soviet data, and to this extent we are forced out of complete agnosticism and into the adoption of provisional interpretations of the Soviet valuation standards.

2. FIXED CAPITAL INVESTMENT

The Official Data

Since 1956, TsSU has regularly published constant-price data on gross fixed capital investment made by the state and by co-operatives and collective farms. The first series of this sort, covering the period 1918–56, appeared in two statistical handbooks published respectively in early 1956 and early 1957.[5] The investment series are stated to be in "prices of July 1, 1955." Two subsequent handbooks published by TsSU in the latter parts of 1957 and 1958, respectively, contained revised series of the same scope, extending now to 1957, said to be in "prices of July 1, 1955, with account taken of new unit construction cost norms introduced in 1956."[6] Finally, the annual statistical handbooks published since 1959 contain series through 1961, of a scope broadened to include also private investment by individuals for home-building, said to be in "cost estimating prices of July 1, 1955, with account taken of new unit construction cost norms introduced in 1956; of the 1958 reduction in norms of overhead charges; and of the 1959 reduction in the schedule of charges for installation of equipment."[7] From the explanation appearing in one of the sources,[8] it may be taken that the "prices of July 1, 1955" and the "cost estimating prices of July 1, 1955" are the same, the difference in descriptions being one of ellipsis rather than substance. Aside from this, it is noted that the language employed in the sources—"with account taken of"—is ambiguous. It is not clear what concrete adjustments to the data are implied. If, for common years, we compare the various official series, the figures published in late 1957 are found to be identical with those published since 1959.[9] Thus, "taking account of" the 1958 and 1959 reductions in overhead and installation norms resulted in no revision of figures already published which did not take such account. What, if anything, the phrase means is unclear. Perhaps adjustments were made only in figures for years not previously covered (1958–60), values which reflect the 1958 and 1959 reductions being converted into values which do not. Or perhaps the figures for 1958 and thereafter are not in fact in the same prices as those used for earlier years; clearly, the series published in late 1957 could not

---

5 TsSU–56a, pp. 158–59, and TsSU–57, pp. 172–73. The former volume was set in type in April, 1956, the latter in February, 1957.

6 TsSU–57e, p. 207, and TsSU–58, p. 254.

7 E.g., TsSU–59, pp. 617–19, and TsSU–61, pp. 590–91, 891.

8 TsSU–57e, p. 207.

9 Compare the figures in TsSU–57e, p. 207, with those in TsSU–59, pp. 618–19.

have been adjusted for the 1958–59 reductions. On the other hand, for all common years, the series issued in late 1957 and subsequently are significantly greater than those published in 1956 and early 1957; "taking account of" the construction cost norms introduced in 1956 produced an upward revision of the previously published series in "prices of July 1, 1955." For present purposes, it is desirable to use the official series of greatest coverage, the third of those described above. But what, in principle at least, should we consider to be the prices in which it is expressed? Without more to go on, we take the basic valuation standard to be cost estimating prices *circa* 1956, i. e., prices of July 1, 1955, adjusted upward to reflect the cost norms introduced in 1956 but not further adjusted to reflect the various reductions of 1958 and 1959. This interpretation seems clearly the most appropriate for the figures in the series referring to years before 1958. As noted, the 1958–60 data may be differently valued, in which case, however, they should be viewed as reflecting a departure from "constancy" in the valuation standard.[10]

A systematic description of the "1956 estimating prices" would exceed the needs of this study. Essentially, cost estimating prices for individual capital investment projects indicate the value of normed input requirements and purchased equipment plus normed overhead charges, where wages are reckoned at prevailing rates of the indicated year, materials inputs and equipment at wholesale transfer prices of the indicated year (inclusive of normed distribution costs for items quoted f.o.b. the place of origin). Values at estimating prices differ, therefore, from actual investment outlays of the indicated year insofar as actual input consumption, overhead outlays, and distribution costs differ from the corresponding norms. For example, in 1956, according to official calculations, realized costs were below costs in 1956 estimating prices by 3.8 percent for construction and by 12.7 percent for installation work.[11]

There are difficult problems in the interpretation of global series expressed in estimating prices. For individual construction-installation projects, the value of work performed in estimating prices is used as a measure of physical volume ånd, hence, as a yardstick against which to measure plan fulfillment with respect to the quantity of work performed and the attainment of cost reduction goals. On both of these counts, therefore, there is an incentive for responsible administrators at the project level to reckon norms in such a way as to overstate values in estimating prices and for the degree of exaggeration to increase with time. Beyond this, we do not know how global accounts for the entire economy are reckoned in

---

10 Elsewhere we cite some of these same series as in prices of "July 1, 1955." At the cost of a minor inconsistency, it appears better to use here the somewhat more appropriate title of "1956 estimating prices."

11 TsSU–61a, p. 263. Although not specified in the source, the figures are believed to refer only to the state and co-operative sectors of the economy. Similar differences between values in actual and estimating prices may or may not exist for equipment. Acquisitions, f.o.b. the producer, are the same in both prices, but it is not clear if distribution costs are included in the estimating price accounts at normed or realized levels. Realized investment in equipment in 1956, according to our estimates, was 2.8 percent greater than the corresponding official figure in 1956 estimating prices (compare the figures in our Tables A–5 and A–11). The difference, however, may be due in part or wholly to errors in our estimate of realized investment in 1956.

estimating prices. During a period in which a given set of estimating prices is in use at operational levels, global figures might be compiled as a simple summation over all current projects. But, according to one Soviet source, there are technical difficulties which render this method impracticable.[12] Instead, it is stated, the physical volume of construction-installation work must be obtained by a rather complex method of deflation, in which, *inter alia*, the rate of current outlays for labor is independently adjusted for changes in labor productivity. The circularity of this approach, which is presented without further comment in the source, leaves the methodology essentially unexplained. Furthermore, this account, although purporting to describe methods actually employed by TsSU, appeared in 1955, before publication of the series under consideration here, and may not, therefore, actually have reference to those series. Thus, the nature of the valuation method remains obscure. The 1956 estimating prices, although no doubt closely related to actual prices of that year, are conventional and, until more is known, should be viewed with appropriate reservations.

Conversion of Present Estimates from 1950 Actual to 1956 Estimating Prices

Three sets of constant prices have been used in the investment series compiled in this study, those of 1937, 1928, and 1950, the last of which should presumably most nearly approach the 1956 prices of the Soviet investment series. In our calculations for construction, the growth rates measured differ only slightly over the three sets of price weights.[13] Thus, the substitution of 1956 for 1950 prices would probably also produce little difference in growth. For equipment, the substitution of 1937 or 1950 for 1928 prices yields a very marked reduction in the observed growth of investment.[14] As between 1937 and 1950 prices, the difference is much less. From calculations made elsewhere, we conclude that the substitution of 1956 for 1950 prices would produce an even smaller difference in growth.[15] Our treatment of installation, as has been explained, is unavoidably casual, and our calculations provide no basis for considering the true effects on this component of changes in price weights. Although its inclusion seems useful for rounding out totals, the individual significance of our figures for it are quite doubtful. For each of these components taken separately, therefore, the growth of investment measured in 1950 prices should be a reasonable approximation to that which we would measure in 1956 prices. In all of our investment series, however, the equipment component outpaces construction and installation. Thus the relative weight assigned the various elements affects the growth of the total. Furthermore, as among major components, there exists a significant difference between the 1950 and 1956 price structures.

---

12 Freimundt–55, pp. 182–88.

13 See Table A–6.

14 See Tables A–2, A–3, and A–4.

15 The calculations in reference are two production indexes for machinery, based on identical output data but employing alternatively price weights of 1950 and 1956. Taking 1937 as 100, the former takes value for 1927/28, 1940, and 1955, respectively, of 17, 84, and 333; for the latter, the corresponding figures are 18, 87, and 326. See Kaplan–60, Volume II, p. 235, and Moorsteen–62, p. 107.

In order to compare our series with the Soviet, therefore, we translate our figures in 1950 prices into 1956 estimating prices, reweighting among the three component series but not within them. We thus employ just three price index numbers, one for each component. Price indexes for this purpose are the implicit deflators indicated by the value of 1956 investment in 1950 prices and in 1956 estimating prices. The 1950 price data are those computed in this study; the 1956 estimating price data are from the official investment series. The computation is shown in Table 7–1.

Comparisons

The Soviet investment data are available annually for the state and co-operative sector of the economy, but, for coverage comparable with the series developed in this study (and with the official capital stock data), that is, inclusive also of collective-farm and private investment, the only series so far published refer to a scattering of individual years and to intervals of several years, grouped according to the periods conventionally recognized in Soviet economic historiography—First Five-Year Plan, Second Five-Year Plan, etc. The limitations are perhaps not too serious in assessing implications for a stock calculation. In any case, because of their greater comparability, the latter series are preferred for present purposes. They are reproduced in index form in Part A of Table 7–2 (odd-numbered columns). Entries for intervals (e.g., 1933–37) indicate the total value of investment during the stipulated period relative to investment in the base year, 1956. The series for construction-installation and equipment (columns 1 and 3) include all sectors of the economy except fishing collectives, a relatively insignificant omission,[16] and private investment for purposes other than home-building, an exclusion of significant proportions during the First Five-Year Plan but not thereafter.[17] The series for total investment (column 5) is more comprehensive than the two components, including investment by fishing co-operatives and, more importantly, a third component series, "other capital investments and outlays," not shown separately in the table.[18] The latter component is not included at all in the calculations made in this study and might better have been excluded also from the official series used here for purposes of comparison, had the form in which the data are available permitted. However, for years in which the official totals are available both inclusive and exclusive of "other" investment, the two series are found to differ by an almost uniform relative amount (about 6–8 percent)[19] with the result that a series expressed in index form, as in Table 7–2, is little affected by the difference

---

16 For example, in 1956, fishing collectives accounted for about 190 million 1956 rubles of investment as compared with 229 billion rubles for the rest of the economy. See TsSU–62a, pp. 538 and 546, and Table O–1 of this study.

17 Private investment in fixed assets other than housing has probably been negligible since the early 1930's. According to the calculations made for this study, however, it accounted for about 13 percent of all construction-installation work in 1928, declining to about 4 percent by 1930. In the case of equipment acquisitions, the corresponding figures are about 15 and 8 percent. These figures are in current prices. See Tables D–9 (row 2c) and A–7 (columns 5 and 8) for construction-installation; Moorsteen–62, p. 422, for equipment.

18 The scope of this category of outlays is explained p. 38 above.

19 Cf., in Table O–1, row 4a with the sum of rows 4b and 4c.

TABLE 7-1

DERIVATION OF IMPLICIT INDEXES OF "1956 ESTIMATING PRICES"
RELATIVE TO 1950 ACTUAL PRICES

| | 1956 Gross Investment (Billion Rubles) | | Implicit Index of 1956 Estimating Prices (1950 Actual Prices = 100) |
	In 1950 Actual Prices (1)	In 1956 Estimating Prices (2)	(3)
1. Construction	129.24	133.95	103.6
2. Installation	10.67	10.19	95.5
3. Equipment	97.43	68.45	70.3

Sources: For column 1, Table A–4. For column 2, the figure in row 1 (construction) is the sum of construction-installation work carried out by state and co-operative organizations, 113.20 billion rubles (TsSU–61a, p. 170), by collective farms, 15.75 billion rubles (*ibid.*, p. 170), and by private individuals for home construction, 15.19 billion rubles (*ibid.*, p. 188), minus the value of installation (row 2). The figure in row 2 (installation) is derived by simultaneous equations from the information in *ibid.*, pp. 44, 263, that construction and installation in the state and co-operative sector amounted to 113.20 billion rubles in 1956 estimating prices, actual cost was less by 4.6 percent for the total, by 3.8 percent for the construction component, and by 12.7 percent for the installation component. It is assumed that all installation occurred in the state and co-operative sector. The equipment figure in row 3 is from Table A–11. Column 3 is computed from columns 1 and 2.

in scope. The official series for nonagricultural and residential investment (columns 7 and 9) have the same scope as the totals. All of the series are specified in the sources from which they are drawn to be exclusive of outlays for capital repairs.

The columns adjacent to the official series in Part A of Table 7–2 contain the corresponding series developed in this study, calculated originally in 1950 prices and deflated to 1956 estimating prices by the price index numbers described above.[20] The ratios of our series to the official are shown in Part B of the table. As is explained elsewhere, our series for investment in equipment during 1956–61 is derived directly from the official series, on the basis of the close correspondence (also visible in Table 7–2) between our deflation and the official series for 1950–56. Hence the near-identity between the two equipment series for 1956–61 has no significance of its own.[21] For all other intervals and series, however, the official figures and ours coincide only to the extent that the two independent measurements of change in the physical volume of investment also coincide.

---

[20] Because we use only one price index number for each of our three component series, the indexes shown in Table 7–2 for equipment and housing are the same in 1950 or 1956 estimating prices. The construction-installation series is affected, but to a relatively minor extent because of the great relative importance of construction. The impact of the deflation, therefore, falls mainly on the aggregate series, "total" and "nonagricultural." For total investment, the effects of the deflation may be observed from the following comparisons: taking 1956 as 100, the index number for 1928 would be 10.8 in 1950 prices versus 11.6 in 1956 estimating prices; for 1940, the corresponding figures are 31.3 and 32.8; for 1950, 52.1 and 52.9; for 1961, 154 and 153. Thus the effect of changing prices is perceptible but not large. The index numbers in 1950 prices are computed from Table A–4; those in 1956 prices are from Table 7–2.

[21] The dependence of our equipment investment series on the official in this period should be kept in mind also in considering the comparisons of stock estimates which follow.

For the prewar period, 1928–40—or 1928 (4th quarter) to 1941 (1st half)—the official figures differ from ours by very large relative amounts, the latter uniformly exceeding the former. The differences are greatest for the earliest prewar years, least for the latest ones, with the corollary that the growth of the official series during the interval greatly outpaces that measured by us. For total investment, the official index in 1940 (relative to 1928) stands 2.3 times as high as ours. Much the same relationship is exhibited for the prewar period as a whole: taken relative to 1956, the total volume of investment measured by our indexes for 1928 (4th quarter) to 1941 (1st half) is some 90 percent greater than that indicated by the official series. The fact that our series do, whereas the official do not, include private, nonresidential, investment would alter the comparison for 1928 (4th quarter) to 1932—but not by much.[22] Comparisons for other intervals would be unaffected. Although there are many opportunities for error in our estimates for the prewar years, the latter constitute the period for which our underlying data are most abundant, and it is difficult to suggest plausible sources of error large enough to account for the differences between the two sets of investment data. We argue instead, therefore, that the official constant-price investment data for prewar years are essentially inconsistent with the raw data used in our investment calculations: physical consumption of building materials and wholesale price quotations and current-price investment data for machinery. These findings were foreshadowed in earlier studies, in which the official prewar investment series for the state and co-operative sector only (excluding collective farms and private individuals) were examined and found to be more nearly consistent with the change in investment in current than in constant prices.[23] As will appear subsequently, the official constant-price investment series for the prewar is also inconsistent with the official indexes of the change in the stock of fixed capital.

The disagreement between the official series and ours is also large for the wartime period, 1941 (2nd half) to 1945, for which our figure for construction-installation is 33 percent *below* the official, our figure for equipment, 33 percent *above* the official, and our total, 23 percent *below* the official. For most of this interval—that is, 1941–44—we not only estimate investment in equipment by means of deflation but also interpolate construction on a deflated index, data on building materials inputs being unavailable.[24] All of our calculations, therefore, are affected by errors in our indexes of materials and equipment prices, in our estimates of changes in construction wage rates, in the figures reported for total investment in current prices, and in our estimate of the division of this total between equipment and construction-installation. The fact that our investment figures for equipment exceed, while those for construction-installation fall

---

22 See footnote 17, p. 189, above. Our figure for total investment would probably decline by less than 5 percent, as would therefore the ratio in column 9.

23 For total investment and the construction component, see Powell–57, Part I, pp. 74–75, and Part II, pp. 513 ff.; and Powell–59, pp. 10–11. For equipment, see Moorsteen–62, pp. 98–100.

24 See Appendix A.

TABLE 7-2

GROSS INVESTMENT IN FIXED CAPITAL IN "1956 ESTIMATING PRICES," OFFICIAL AND PRESENT ESTIMATES, 1928-61

	Construction-Installation		Equipment		Total		Nonagricultural		Residential	
	Official	Present	Official	Present	Official	Present	Official	Present	Official	Present
	(1)	(2)	(3)	(4)	(5)	(6)	(7)	(8)	(9)	(10)
					A. Indexes (1956 = 100)					
1928	-	14.2	-	6.0	3.73	11.6	-	11.5	-	25.0
1940	30.0	38.4	-	21.1	24.2	32.8	26.0	34.5	21.5	34.0
1950	48.8	55.4	-	47.4	48.4	52.9	50.1	51.9	45.3	64.0
1955	89.2	94.0	-	79.0	87.0	89.2	85.4	88.1	85.0	83.0
1956	100	100	100	100	100	100	100	100	100	100
1957	114	109	110	111	113	110	115	109	139	131
1958	134	122	127	126	131	124	134	124	169	167
1959	155	136	137	136	148	136	153	139	186	189
1960	168	146	146	146	160	146	167	152	185	191
1961	171	152	157	156	167	153	172	160	176	186
1928 (4th Quarter)-32 . .	43.1	102	11.6	51.0	32.4	85.3	33.0	88.2	26.6	106
1933-37	93.0	174	34.2	87.3	73.4	146	77.8	148	49.2	115
1938-41 (1st Half). . .	95.9	135	38.7	78.2	76.8	117	82.5	122	69.0	119
1941 (2nd Half)-45 . . .	97.7	65.4	36.6	48.6	77.5	60.0	84.9	64.8	63.7	74.2
1946-50	197	194	156	167	183	185	194	187	186	251
1951-55	361	391	300	295	346	360	354	360	351	381
1956-61	841	766	778	778	820	769	841	785	955	964
1928 (4th Quarter)-41 (1st Half). . . .	232	410	84.5	217	183	348	193	358	145	340
1946-61	1400	1350	1230	1240	1350	1310	1390	1330	1490	1600
1928 (4th Quarter)-61	1730	1830	1360	1510	1610	1720	1670	1750	1700	2010

TABLE 7-2 (continued)

GROSS INVESTMENT IN FIXED CAPITAL IN "1956 ESTIMATING PRICES," OFFICIAL AND PRESENT ESTIMATES, 1928-61

B. Present as Percent of Official

	Construction-Installation	Equipment	Total	Nonagricultural	Residential
	(11)	(12)	(13)	(14)	(15)
1928	--	--	311	--	--
1940	128	--	136	133	158
1950	114	--	109	104	141
1955	105	--	103	103	98
1956	100	100	100	100	100
1957	96	101	97	95	94
1958	91	99	95	93	99
1959	88	99	92	91	102
1960	87	100	91	91	103
1961	89	99	92	93	106
1928 (4th Quarter)-32	237	440	263	267	398
1933-37 . . .	187	255	199	190	234
1938-41 (1st Half). . .	141	202	152	148	172
1941 (2nd Half)-45 . . .	67	133	77	76	117
1946-50	98	107	101	96	135
1951-55	108	98	104	102	109
1956-61	91	100	94	93	101
1928 (4th Quarter)-41 (1st Half).	177	257	190	185	234
1946-61	96	101	97	96	107
1928 (4th Quarter)-61	106	111	107	105	118

Sources: For the official investment series (columns 1, 3, 5, 7, 9), Table O-1. For our series in 1956 prices (columns 2, 4, 6, 8, 10), figures are computed from series in 1950 prices by applying the price index numbers of Table 7-1. The 1950 price series are from Table A-4 (for all construction, equipment, and installation); Tables A-4, D-6, and D-8 (for nonagricultural construction, equipment, and installation); Table 3-2 (for residential investment; the data in this table are in 1937 prices, but, as noted elsewhere, our calculations make no allowance for changes in price structure within this component). Columns 11-15 are computed from columns 1-10.

short of, the official does no doubt reflect a difference in the distribution of total investment among components. The data available for this purpose to the official compilers are no doubt superior to those we have used.[25] On the other hand, there are independent grounds for suspecting errors in the official distribution as well.[26] Our deflators are based on officially established prices, which may not in fact have been observed in transactions during this chaotic period, and on very rough estimates of money wage rates in construction. Economic accounting in general must have weakened during these years, and even the current-price investment data may contain serious errors. But these problems would also confront the compilers of the official series with obstacles difficult to surmount. Although they had better access to the needed data than we, it does not necessarily follow that they have used it well, as their prewar calculations testify. In brief, therefore, while we consider the reliability of our estimates for the war period as questionable indeed, we also have serious reservations regarding the official series.

For the postwar period, 1946–61, the official series and ours are much closer together. Only one of the comparisons in Table 7–2 (housing, 1946–50) shows a difference greater than 9 percent. Total investment during 1946–50 was at about the same level, relative to 1956, in both our and the official series. It is somewhat surprising to note, therefore, that our total for 1951–55 is in excess of the official, that for 1956–60 below the official. There is, thus, no consistent difference of trend between the two series for the postwar period as a whole, and, in fact, over the entire interval 1946–61, the total volume of investment measured by our index is just 3 percent less than that indicated by the official. From at least 1950, however, our total series tends to grow significantly more slowly than the official.

Both sets of indexes agree that the total volume of postwar investment greatly exceeds that made in the prewar period and during the war. Thus, for the entire period, 1928 (4th quarter) to 1961, the comparison is dominated by the postwar figures, and the total volume of investment (relative to 1956) measured by the two sets of indicators is similar, our series exceeding the official by 7 percent. For purposes of computing a stock in 1956 prices, the two sets of investment data might produce significantly different results for earlier years but considerable agreement for later ones.

Throughout the period under consideration, our indexes show a more rapid increase in investment in equipment than in construction-installation, the differential becoming quite small after 1956, however. The official series show the same inequality in growth rates until 1956 but indicate a significantly more rapid growth of construction-installation thereafter. There is nothing inherently impossible in this reversal of patterns, but it is unexpected and, perhaps, should be taken as adding to the reasons sug-

---

[25] See the discussions in Powell–57, Part II, pp. 424–26; Moorsteen–62, pp. 430–32. The possibility of an error of overstatement in our deflation of investment in equipment in 1944 has also been suggested elsewhere, on the basis of a comparison of investment data for 1944 and output data for 1945; see Moorsteen–62, p. 111.

[26] See Powell–57, Part II, pp. 513 ff., and Powell–59, pp. 10–11.

gested earlier for examining the origins of the official construction-installation series for indications of progressive exaggeration.

3. THE FIXED CAPITAL STOCK ON JANUARY 1, 1960

Soviet statistical handbooks published since 1960 contain data on the absolute value and various other aspects of the stock of "basic funds" as of January 1, 1960.[27] These figures were obtained mainly from an asset-by-asset inventory and revaluation conducted at the end of 1959 by all state and co-operative organizations that are required under Soviet economic regulations to set aside allowances for depreciation. This is a broad economic sector, accounting, according to reported totals, for about two thirds of all Soviet basic funds. The sectors not participating in the inventory include state organizations financed directly from the budget (schools, hospitals, administrative organs of government, etc.), collective farms, and private individuals. However, figures on basic funds in these sectors have also been published, according to which assets held by individuals, mainly livestock and houses, account for about 17 percent of the reported total, the remainder being held by budgetary organizations and collective farms.

The sources do not indicate the prices in which the global absolute values are expressed, but, from the instructions issued to organizations participating in the inventory, it is known that assets in this sector are valued essentially in estimating prices of July 1, 1955, adjusted for the new construction cost norms of 1956—that is, the same "1956 estimating prices" used in the official investment series described above. In the sources, the values used for this sector are described as being in "contemporary prices." The same appellation has also been authoritatively applied to the values published for other sectors,[28] from which it seems reasonable to infer that the value of fixed assets in these sectors is also expressed essentially in 1956 estimating prices.

For purposes of comparison, therefore, we also revalue our estimates of the gross value of the stock of fixed capital as of January 1, 1960, into 1956 estimating prices. This is done by means of the same set of price index numbers used above for revaluing our estimates of capital investment, commencing, as with investment, from our estimates in prices of

---

27 The following account is based on Kaplan–63 and Bunich–59, except where otherwise indicated. "Basic funds" are a Soviet economic category comprised mainly of fixed assets as defined in this study—structures, equipment, and installation—but including also certain kinds of livestock and a residual category, "other." For the conceptual and quantitative differences, see Appendix O of this study. For present purposes, we shall consider only the fixed asset portion of basic funds, and, except as noted, the ensuing discussions of the Soviet data and methods should be understood as referring only to the treatment of fixed assets.

28 In a private communication of November 14, 1962, to one of the present writers, Professor V. Starovskii, Chief of the Soviet Central Statistical Administration, stated that "the value of basic funds of collective farms, of budget organizations, and the value of basic funds of private individuals [*naselenie*], which were not subject to revaluation on January 1, 1960, have been computed in contemporary prices." For the indicated sectors, the revaluation was presumably done centrally, from global data. That this was probably the case was inferred earlier by Kaplan (*op. cit.*, pp. 112 ff.), by comparing the published figures with values for the same assets at acquisition costs.

1950.[29] This means, of course, we must again assume that revaluation from 1950 to 1956 estimating prices within the three main categories of assets—structures, equipment, and installation—is not importantly affected by the intracategory mix, and that the price index numbers derived for all structures and all equipment may also appropriately be applied to nonagricultural structures and equipment and, in the case of the index for structures, separately to residential and nonresidential assets. Thus the method of revaluation grows weaker with disaggregation. But this is also true, for similar reasons, of our underlying estimates in 1950 prices, for which reason it seems inappropriate to adopt a more complex procedure at this stage.

Comparison of Methods

Our estimates, thus revalued, will be compared with the official Soviet figures shortly. In anticipation, however, it may be helpful to summarize what is known of the methods of compilation underlying the Soviet data. Our knowledge, it should be emphasized, is limited to the procedures employed in the inventory and does not extend to the valuation of assets in other sectors of the economy. Within the inventoried sector, different methods were applied to structures, on the one hand, and equipment and installation, on the other.

For structures, 36 handbooks of replacement costs, differentiated for ten geographical regions, were used for more or less aggregative physical units of typical kinds of assets, for example, cost per cubic meter of building, per linear meter of pipeline, etc. In order to refine the matching of costs to specific structures, the data in the handbooks are classified according to the use of the structure (factory building, apartment house, etc.), according to the material of the walls (brick, stone, wood, etc.), and according to the number of stories. Within these breakdowns, costs are shown separately for the principal parts of the structure (basement, basic building, etc.). And, finally, the main technical characteristics of the elements (roof, walls, floor, etc.) from which the parts are constructed are specified and their relative importance in the total value indicated. For example, the "basic building" may be indicated to have brick walls which are 2.5 bricks thick and which account for 31 percent of total value. For purposes of the inventory, a building which coincided in all respects with the prototype in the handbook except in having walls 2 bricks thick would be given a value per cubic meter 6 percent less than that shown in the handbook (that is, the value would be reduced by $.31 \times .05/2.5$).[30] The geometry of

---

[29] That is, taking 1950 as 100, the price indexes used are: for structures, 103.6; for equipment, 70.3; for installation, 95.5 (see Table 7–1). Gross values of fixed assets in place in 1950 prices are from Table T–9. According to the communication cited in the preceding footnote, Soviet data refer to capital available for operation, i.e., exclusive of projects in progress. For the comparisons, therefore, we subtract the value of projects in progress from capital in place. The value of such projects in 1950 prices is given in Table E–1 and is converted to 1956 estimating prices by a price index number of 98.2 (1950 = 100). The latter is a weighted average of the indexes just listed for structures, equipment, and installation, using respectively weights of 80, 15, and 5 percent, roughly the relative importance of the three kinds of assets in projects in progress at the beginning of 1958, the only date for which such data are available (see Appendix E).

[30] The foregoing describes the basic method of valuing structures, but provision was also made for certain exceptions. Unique structures, resembling none of the prototypes

this method is not quite Euclidian, in that none of the elements on which the costing should, ultimately, be based—walls, floors, ceilings, etc.—need vary in direct proportion with the cubic volume of the structure. However, an adequate critique of the method would require an ambitious technical investigation, which we have not made, and it may well be that in practice the procedures employed yield good approximations to the desired magnitudes.

For purposes of the comparisons to be made here, it is important to note that the procedures of the inventory differ fundamentally from those employed in this study, the perpetual inventory computed from annual construction series, as estimated from building materials consumption. Our estimate of the *physical* stock of structures extant on January 1, 1960, may be thought of as essentially the sum of our estimates of building materials put in place in previous years, reduced for retirements and adjusted for territorial change and war loss. The Soviet inventory is essentially a physical measurement of the cubic volume of observable structures. In this respect, the two sets of data are independent. If the inventory was well conducted, it should, one would judge, yield the more reliable result. Even though, for reasons just mentioned, the findings of the inventory may not take account of all the physical particulars of the included structures, they do not suffer from the several vagaries besetting our estimates. To this it should be added, however, that many of the ambiguities in our estimates on the physical side are greatly attenuated for a year as late as 1960. As Tables 2–6, 2–12, and 2–15 indicate, sizable errors in our estimates for the initial stock, service lives, territorial change, and war losses would affect our stock estimates for 1960 by only a few percentage points. On the other hand, we have been able to compute no similar bound for the likely consequences of errors in our estimates of building materials consumed. Furthermore, the Soviet method of *valuation* takes explicit account for each kind of structure not only of the costs of materials inputs but of labor inputs, distribution charges, and overhead costs as well. Our method assumes that nonmaterial costs vary on average in proportion to the total value of materials inputs consumed, regardless of the kind of structure for which the materials are used.[31]

The valuation of equipment and installation in the inventory is somewhat simpler. Replacement values for individual items of equipment are

---

in the handbooks, were to be revalued by applying price indexes to values at original cost. Structures built according to obsolete specifications, for example, with walls of a thickness greater than required by current standards, were to be valued as though obsolete elements were replaced in accordance with current standards.

31 To state the matter precisely, our estimate of the stock may be expressed as the product Vk, where V is the value in weight-year prices of all building materials still in place and k is the ratio *in the weight year* between the value of materials consumed and the value of all construction outputs for that year. The Soviet estimate, if the inventory valuation procedures are accurate, is $\Sigma V_i k_i$ where V_i is the value in weight-year prices of materials still in place that were put there in the year i, and k_i is the ratio *in weight-year prices* between the value of materials and construction outputs still in place from the year i. The V_i's must sum to V. The implicit assumption of the materials inputs approach, therefore, is that k approximates the average of the k_i's weighted by the V_i's. The crux of the matter is the extent to which the k_i's vary, i.e., to which the ratio of materials cost to total costs varies with the product mix.

listed in 102 price handbooks. The values shown include the July 1, 1955, wholesale price of the asset, plus cost of distribution (when not already included in the wholesale price), of related installations, facings, linings, insulations, glazings, bases, and of related overhead charges, with adjustments for regional differentials in the costs of installation and transport. The handbooks show values for domestic machines in current production; they also show values for many imports and for domestic items no longer produced. How the latter values are obtained is not known. For items not included in the handbooks, prices of analogous items were to be used, adjusted for differences in economic characteristics. For example, a tractor developing 80 percent of the horsepower and consuming 120 percent (in value terms) of the fuel per horsepower-hour of its nearest analogue in the handbook would be valued at two thirds the value of the analogue (.80 × 1/1.20 = 2/3). A machine tool capable of milling half as many parts per hour as its nearest analogue is given half the value of the analogue. The method of adjustment implies a capital concept, like that of our estimates, based on user substitutabilities, but it seems quite rule of thumb. Under some circumstances, the value of a machine may vary more than in proportion to its capacity (for example, where operators' wages are a large share of costs); under others, by less (for example, where many diverse operations must be performed on small runs); and so forth. The bulk of durables in the inventory, presumably, is covered by the handbooks. But the question also arises whether handbook prices for items not currently in domestic production have been similarly derived.

The difference in method between the equipment inventory and our estimates may be summarized as follows: (*i*) The inventory provides enumeration of the equipment physically extant, whereas our estimates are subject to the limitations already noted in the case of structures. As with structures, our equipment estimates for 1960 are relatively insensitive to errors in the initial stock and in the treatment of territorial change and war loss. Because of the relative shortness of equipment service lives, however, errors in this aspect of the calculation are more consequential than for structures, ranging perhaps from 7 to 12 percent of the computed total, as Table 2–12 indicates. (*ii*) Because equipment prices were virtually constant from mid-1955 through the end of 1959, the method of valuing equipment acquired during this interval in the inventory and in our estimates are nearly the same: both accounts value assets at acquisition cost. In our calculations, such acquisitions account for just over half the gross value of the equipment stock extant on January 1, 1960.[32] (*iii*) Equipment acquired before mid-1955 but still currently produced and priced thereafter is valued item-by-item at actual 1956 estimating prices in the inventory but is valued by deflating global acquisition outlays in our calculations. The main obstacle to constructing an equipment deflator, the treatment of "new" products, does not arise here, but our deflator is based on prices for fewer than 200 items, whereas the inventory includes a complete matching of price to asset. According to our calculations, just over 20 percent of the 1960 equip-

---

[32] Compare equipment acquisitions in Table A–4 with the gross stock in Table T–9. Values are in 1950 prices.

ment stock was acquired during 1952–54 and in the first half of 1955.[33] Most of these acquisitions, as well as some from earlier years, would also have been produced and priced after mid-1955. (*iv*) Equipment not produced and priced after mid-1955 would be valued at synthetic prices in both accounts. In neither case are there strong grounds for expecting more than a rough correspondence with a theoretical ideal. Our calculations suggest, by elimination, that this group of acquisitions accounts for something less than a quarter of the stock of equipment at the beginning of 1960. (*v*) Our estimates of the stock of installation are extremely rough and, as is explained in Chapter 2 (Section 3), are intended only to round out the global totals. In the Soviet inventory, on the other hand, installation is reckoned as a surcharge on the replacement value of equipment actually in place. Although we have no independent means of appraising the precision of the Soviet method, it must strike much closer to reality than ours.

In brief, then, while we lack a basis for testifying to the accuracy of the results of the Soviet inventory as actually effected, the methods prescribed for it seem on superficial inspection to provide a significantly firmer basis of estimation than has been employed in this study. In this respect, it should be recalled that assets not included in the inventory, the value of which must have been estimated centrally by other methods, account for about one third of the reported total.[34] In addition, as with the compilation of many other Soviet aggregative statistics, there may have been economic pressures on participants in the inventory which produced distortions of which we are unaware.

Comparison of Findings

Our estimates of the stock of fixed capital at the beginning of 1960 are compared with the corresponding Soviet figures in Table 7–3. As is indicated, both sets of data refer to capital available for operation, exclusive, that is, of projects in progress. The table reproduces only those Soviet value data for which analogues have been computed in this study and hence does not show all the detail available in Soviet sources.[35]

For the total stock, the figures compared are extremely close, differing by only 2 percent (row 1). Roughly the same holds for nonagricultural assets. The Soviet figure exceeds ours by just 5 percent, the share of nonagricultural assets in the total being 89 percent in the Soviet figures, as opposed to 86 percent in ours (row 2). The division between residential and nonresidential assets, on the other hand, is quite different in the two sets of data. The residential sector accounts for 33 percent of the Soviet total but for only 20 percent of ours, the absolute value of residences in the Soviet figures exceeding that in ours by no less than 71 percent (rows 3 and 4). Similar but smaller disparities occur in the two distributions of assets by kind. The Soviet figure for all structures *exceeds* ours by only

---

[33] See Tables A–4 and T–9.

[34] Reservations concerning the results reported for private housing, a major item omitted from the inventory, are expressed below.

[35] We do not here or in the section following treat data for the nonagricultural nonresidential sectors separately. These can be obtained from the official data, but they provide no additional information.

7 percent (row 6), but, with residences excluded, the Soviet figure *falls short* of ours by 16 percent (row 7). The discrepancy in the case of equipment and installation is of like magnitude, the Soviet figure falling short of ours by 13 percent (row 8). Thus, in the distribution by kind, the Soviet data show a ratio of structures to equipment and installation of 77/23, as opposed to 73/27 in our estimates. If attention is limited to nonresidential assets only, the two ratios become 65/35 and 67/33, respectively, but with the total *absolute* value of the nonresidential stock in the Soviet figures falling 15 percent below that in ours.

TABLE 7-3

GROSS FIXED CAPITAL AVAILABLE FOR OPERATION, IN "1956 ESTIMATING PRICES," ON JANUARY 1, 1960, OFFICIAL AND PRESENT ESTIMATES

	Official	Present	Official as Percent of Present
	(Billion Rubles)		
	(1)	(2)	(3)
A. By Economic Sector			
1. Total	2840	2786	102
2. Nonagricultural	2525	2398	105
3. Residential	942	551	171
4. Nonresidential	1898	2235	85
B. By Kind of Asset			
5. Total	2840	2786	102
6. Structures	2185	2037	107
7. Nonresidential Structures	1243	1486	84
8. Equipment and Installation	655	749	87

Sources: For column 1 (official), the figures by economic sector (rows 1–4) are from Table O–2, as is the total figure (row 5) in the distribution by kind of asset. The figure for structures (row 6) is from TsSU–60, p. 69; that for nonresidential structures (row 7) is the difference between all structures (row 6) and total residential assets (row 3); that for equipment and installation (row 8) is the difference between all assets (row 5) and structures (row 6). For column 2 (present estimates), the data are computed from values for capital in place, less investment projects in progress. Values for capital in place in 1950 prices are from Tables T–9, T–14, and T–15. These are deflated to 1956 estimating prices by means of the price index numbers in Table 7–1. The value of projects in progress is computed at 194.4 billion rubles from the value in 1950 prices (Table E–1) and the price index number described on p. 196, fn. 29. Of this total, 92 percent is assumed to be nonagricultural, as explained in Chapter 3, Section 7. The figure in Table T–15 for residential assets refers to assets available for operation, and no deduction for projects in progress is made. The total of projects in progress is assumed to be distributed among structures, installation, and equipment in the proportions 80/5/15 (see Appendix E).

To clarify the import of Table 7–3, it may be helpful to elaborate on the comparisons for some individual items. We look first at structures and their distribution between the residential and nonresidential sectors, then at equipment and installation.

In our estimates, the stock of structures is computed from global data, embracing all sectors of the economy. Residential structures are estimated separately, the division of the total between residential and nonresidential assets occurring by subtraction. As is explained in Chapter 3 (Section 6), we feel that our estimates of the housing stock provide a reasonable basis for measuring relative change over time but that considerable uncertainty attaches to the absolute values. Only the latter, of course, enter into the present discussion. Thus, among our results, the estimate for all structures is the firmer figure, the distribution of this total between residences and other structures the more tentative. This presumptive appraisal is reinforced by the comparisons in Table 7–3, which show a relatively small disparity between our figure for all structures and the Soviet but very large differences for the residential component and the residential/nonresidential distribution.

If the Soviet figures are accurate, a large error in our valuation of housing is implied, and, in fact, the confrontation with the Soviet data leads us to emphasize the tenuousness of our housing valuations. At the same time, there is reason to believe that a more refined treatment of the data, if it were possible, would show smaller discrepancies than are presently indicated in Table 7–3. (*i*) Classification differences exist, as a result of which the portion of the Soviet residential stock covered by the inventory —essentially, the socialized urban part—includes certain assets considered nonresidential in our accounts: floor space used for stores, clubrooms, nurseries, restaurants, administrative offices, and other nonresidential purposes, in buildings devoted in "large part" to residential use; hotels, guesthouses, etc.[36] (*ii*) More conjecturally but perhaps also more importantly, the Soviet data, as noted earlier by Norman Kaplan, seem to imply an average unit value for private housing of upwards of 80 percent of that for socialized housing.[37] This is unexpectedly high, given the differences in construction, amenities, etc. Kaplan suggests the possibility that the Soviet accounts value private housing on the basis of the retail prices paid by individuals for building materials or that the Soviet "replacement" values are predicated on improved rather than identical housing.[38] Either procedure would be inappropriate in terms of the valuation standard adopted for this study, the real weight-year rate of substitutability among assets.

---

[36] For purposes of the Soviet inventory, the stock of residential structures (*zhilishchnoe khoziaistvo*) was defined as "all structures, permanent or temporary, in which all or a large part of the floor space is used as a habitation or dormitory . . . ; hotels and guest houses [*doma dlia priezzhaiushchikh*]" (see Bunich–59, p. 51). Our estimates are derived from residential floor space put into operation, the source indicating the figures to exclude "floor space designated for nonresidential use (stores, pharmacies, creches, kindergartens, libraries, service shops) and also . . . dormitories of sanatoria, rest houses and hotels" (see TsSU–61a, p. 191).

[37] Kaplan–63, pp. 111 and 113. The value of housing covered by the inventory is estimated by Kaplan at 450–470 billion rubles, private housing as the residual at 470–490 billion. Floor space in the two sectors on January 1, 1960, was 541 and 785 million square meters, respectively (see Table 3–3 above). If we reduce the inventory values by, say, 10 percent, to allow for nonresidential space, the implied average unit values are 750–780 rubles per square meter for the socialized sector, 600–625 rubles for the private, which is 77–83 percent of the corresponding socialized figures. By contrast, the data underlying our calculations in Table 3–3 suggest an average unit value for the stock of private housing on January 1, 1960, of 43 percent of that of socialized. In the latter calculation, our unit values refer to relative costs of 1928. As is noted in Chapter 3, usable data on changes in relative costs between the private and socialized sectors since 1928 are lacking, and this relationship may, accordingly, have little relevance to 1960. On the other hand, as is also argued earlier, it is by no means clear on a priori grounds that relative *real* costs should have tended against the private sector.

[38] *Op. cit.*, p. 113.

Both of these considerations suggest a better fit than is now shown between the two sets of figures in Table 7–3. But, while we can only conjecture on plausible magnitudes, it seems unlikely that we should alter the basic conclusions already drawn—that the Soviet figures are similar to ours with respect to total structures but considerably different with respect to the division between residences and other.[39] Unless there are further sources of overstatement in the Soviet figure of which we are unaware, the implication is that our valuation of housing in 1956 estimating prices is seriously understated. As is explained above and in Chapter 3, this figure is derived ultimately from values in 1928 prices, by means of price indexes for the intervals 1928–37, 1937–50, and 1950–56. How the error is distributed among these indexes is not clear. However, it will be recalled that for the first index, the 1928–37 link, use was made of data which, although incomplete, related specifically to changes in the cost of housing construction, whereas for the later links, 1937–50 and 1950–55, such data were unavailable and the cost of housing was assumed to move with the cost of construction generally. Presumably, therefore, it is the later links which are the more vulnerable.

There is less to be said about the comparisons for equipment and installation. The Soviet figure for this item is less than ours by 13 percent. Our figure, 749 billion rubles, includes 625 billion rubles of equipment, 124 billion of installation. Thus, installation, while constituting only 4 percent of the total stock, accounts for 17 percent of the equipment-installation total. On methodological grounds, we regard our estimates for this item as especially doubtful. The comparison in Table 7–3 suggests that a sizable error may indeed exist. Errors in the equipment component are most likely to originate in the equipment deflator or in the estimated service lives. As we noted earlier in this section, about three fourths of the stock of equipment available on January 1, 1960, as reckoned in our calculations, was acquired during 1952–59. For this period, our investment series for equipment in 1956 estimating prices corresponds closely with the official Soviet series, as Table 7–2 shows. Presumably, therefore, the values placed on these assets in the two *stock* accounts will also be alike. This would mean that the difference between the two stock values stems more from errors in our estimated service lives and from differences in the valuation of equipment acquired before 1952. For reasons already stated, it is possible that the Soviet accounts are also subject to error on the latter account.

To summarize, the Soviet figure for all structures is very close to ours, especially if allowance is made for some overstatement in the Soviet private housing component. In fact, the difference between the two figures is less,

---

[39] For example, if we reclassify as nonresidential 10 percent of the assets counted residential in the Soviet inventory and reduce the indicated value for private residences by 30 percent, the Soviet figures now shown in Table 7–3 would become: for all assets, 2,695 billion rubles; for all structures, 2,040 billion; for nonresidential structures, 1,290 billion; for residences, 750 billion. The figures for all assets and for all structures are again very similar to—within 3 percent of—our estimates. But the Soviet residential figure continues to exceed ours by 36 percent, the nonresidential to fall short of ours by 13 percent. (The calculation is based on values for socialized housing of 460 billion rubles, for private housing of 480 billion rubles; see fn. 37, p. 201.)

we should think, than the presumptive margin of error in either of the two figures considered singly, suggesting some degree of coincidence in the similarity. Nonetheless, the finding should no doubt be interpreted as tending to support the reliability of both figures. The respective figures for equipment and installation differ by a considerably greater relative amount, suggesting the presence of a significant error of overstatement in these components of our estimates. We conjecture that the relative error is likely to be greater for installation than for equipment. In any case, because of the dominance of structures in the total capital stock, the respective global figures for all fixed assets are also extremely close to each other —whether or not allowance is made for overstatement in the Soviet private housing figure. Our estimate of the nonagricultural stock of fixed assets is close to the corresponding Soviet figure, but our division of all assets or all structures between the residential and nonresidential sectors differs by a large margin from the Soviet, suggesting an error of understatement in our valuation of housing in 1956 estimating prices. This in turn points to an error of like direction in our valuation of housing in 1950 prices. The implications for our housing estimates in 1937 and 1928 prices, however, are not clear.

In addition to the figures for gross asset values, the Soviet data on basic funds included in the inventory contain information on the extent of wear and tear (*iznos*) and on the ratios of replacement to book values. These data are conceptually akin to calculations made in this study of the relations between gross and net asset values and between replacement (weight-year) and acquisition values. However, the restriction of the Soviet data to the economic sector participating in the inventory, and the inclusion of all basic funds rather than fixed assets only, make it difficult to construct clear-cut comparisons between the two sets of ratios.

According to the Soviet data, wear and tear on the assets included in the inventory amounted to 25 percent of their total replacement value in 1956 estimating prices.[40] The net value of all fixed assets available for operation in 1956 estimating prices according to our data would be 2,008 billion rubles, or 28 percent less than their gross value.[41] The sectors not participating in the inventory—budgetary organizations, collective farms, and private individuals—have tended to grow less rapidly than the included sector. Their assets, therefore, no doubt tend to be older. On the other hand, a larger part of their assets must consist of buildings, which have long service lives. These two factors affect the ratio of net to gross value in opposite directions. On balance, however, it seems likely that their ratio would be less than for the included sector and, hence, that total wear and tear for the national economy, if measured, would be greater than the 25 percent observed in the inventory.[42]

---

40 Kaplan–63, Table III–3.

41 The gross value is 2,786 billion rubles, as is shown in Table 7–3, above. The net value is computed from the net values of assets in place in 1950 prices in Table T–9, less the value of projects in progress, Table E–1. Conversion to 1956 estimating prices is made by means of the price index numbers given in footnote 29, p. 196, above.

42 For example, an inventory of collective farm assets taken as of January 1, 1962, put wear and tear at 29 percent of replacement value (see TsSU–62a, p. 425).

The replacement value of assets included in the inventory exceeds their book value by 12.4 percent.[43] For the most part, Soviet book values are undepreciated acquisition costs. However, at various times book values for certain groups of assets have been revised. Since the major revaluations have occurred after periods of price increase, total book values must tend to exceed acquisition cost.[44] According to our calculations, the gross value of all fixed assets in the national economy in 1956 estimating prices exceeds their value at acquisition cost by 23 percent.[45] Thus, the ratio of acquisition to replacement value is lower in our accounts than is the Soviet ratio of book to replacement value. The difference is due in part to the difference between book value and acquisition cost. In addition, the inclusion of assets not counted in the inventory would no doubt bring the Soviet figure closer to ours.[46] However, we are unable to estimate the probable size of the remaining difference.

4. FIXED CAPITAL STOCK INDEXES

To come to the Soviet indexes of the fixed capital stock, which are the official data most nearly duplicating the estimates which are our primary objective, we note first that two sets of such indexes have now been published. The first, which appeared in statistical handbooks issued during 1956–59, referred to basic funds exclusive of livestock. The series were stated to be in "comparable prices, gross of depreciation," but no indication was given of what prices were used. After the January 1, 1960, capital inventory, revised indexes were published. These, again, were described only as "in comparable prices, gross of depreciation." However, if the sectoral indexes are combined using the absolute data for January 1, 1960, as weights, the aggregative indexes (total, productive, nonproductive) can be closely reproduced.[47] In this sense, then, the indexes may be thought of as in the same prices as the absolute data, that is, in 1956 estimating prices. The revised indexes refer to basic funds inclusive of livestock. In order to obtain series comparable with ours, we attempt in Appendix O to reconstruct the nonlivestock components of the indexes. Although we are unable to do this with complete precision, there is reason to believe that the errors in our reconstruction are small in relative terms.[48] Even with livestock excluded, the coverage of the indexes extends beyond fixed capital to include a residual component, "other" assets, but the magnitude of the latter is quite small and it is believed that the adjusted indexes may be treated

---

[43] See *Vestnik statistiki*, 1960:10, p. 6.

[44] On Soviet book valuations of fixed assets, see Chapter 3, Section 3. In addition, the livestock component of basic funds was revalued after the increase in livestock prices of 1958 (see Kaplan–63, p. 97).

[45] The gross value is 2,786 billion rubles, as shown in Table 7–3, whereas the value at acquisition cost is 2,268 billion rubles. The latter figure is the value of assets in place at acquisition cost, 2,442 billion rubles (from Table T–10), less projects in progress at acquisition cost, 174 billion rubles (Table E–1).

[46] Thus, the inventory of collective-farm assets of January 1, 1962, showed a total replacement value 28 percent in excess of book value. For collective-farm buildings, the excess was 76 percent. See TsSU–62a, p. 424.

[47] See Appendix O.

[48] See *loc. cit.*

without significant error as referring to fixed capital only.[49] Values of the indexes are given in their original sources as for the end of each calendar year but are here ascribed to January 1 of the year immediately following.[50]

The revised and unrevised indexes are compared in Part A of Table 7–4, from which it may be seen that the effects of the revision were not great. The new and old indexes for the productive sectors of the economy (rows 2–7) are identical in several cases and in no instance differ by more than 6 percent of the smaller index number. Somewhat larger relative differences occur in the indexes for nonproductive sectors (rows 8–9). Differences between the two sets of indexes grow larger as the degree of aggregation increases, the largest differences occurring between the old and new global indexes (row 1). We have literally no information on the nature of the revision by which the new indexes were obtained from the old, other than the statement that the new series have been rendered "more precise than those published earlier, in connection with the revaluation" conducted at the end of 1959. How the information gleaned from the revaluation of assets extant on January 1, 1960, might have been used to revise indexes for earlier years is not clear. The fact that the aggregative indexes change by more than their respective components suggests that a principal element in the revision must have been reweighting. As Part B of the table shows, the distribution by sector was markedly altered by the revision. If reweighting also occurred *within* the finest sectoral categories shown in Table 7–4, it may even be that the sole revision was reweighting, indexes for finer categories of assets remaining unchanged. This, however, is conjectural. In any case, in what follows we limit consideration to the revised indexes. They represent the most recent conclusions of the responsible Soviet statisticians, and, since the differences in the two sets of indicators are small, the comparisons we shall make would be little affected by taking explicit account of both kinds of series.

Comparison of Findings

The revised Soviet indexes of fixed capital are shown in Table 7–5 with the corresponding series developed in this study, converted to index numbers. As noted, the Soviet data are for gross values in 1956 estimating prices. For this comparison, we show our series (gross) in 1950 prices, which involve no adjustment for fit to the official data, as well as series in which our data in 1950 prices are translated into 1956 estimating prices by means of the price index numbers used earlier (Table 7–1) for computing investment in these prices. As in the case of the investment series, only one price index number is used for each of the three kinds of assets distinguished in our calculations—structures, equipment, and installation. The rationale, and therefore the limitations, of the calculation are the same as for the investment data. Where stocks are computed by the perpetual inventory method, component investment series which are relatively insensitive to a change in price weights imply a like insensitivity in the component stock

---

[49] See Table O–2.

[50] Evidence that the revised indexes refer to the end of the year indicated in the sources is cited in Appendix O. There is no similar evidence on the dating of the unrevised indexes but, since some of these, for component sectors, are identical with their revised counterparts (see Table 7–4), we assume that their dating is the same.

TABLE 7-4

GROSS FIXED CAPITAL AVAILABLE FOR OPERATION, IN "1956 ESTIMATING PRICES," REVISED AND UNREVISED OFFICIAL SERIES, SELECTED YEARS

(January 1)

	A. Indexes (1941 = 100)				B. Distribution by Sector (Percent)			
	1929	1941	1951	1956	1929	1941	1951	1956
1. Total								
1a. Unrevised	32.0	100	123	189	100.0	100.0	100.0	100.0
1b. Revised	36.6	100	119	176	100.0	100.0	100.0	100.0
2. Productive Sectors								
2a. Unrevised	22.6	100	134	220	38.4	54.4	59.0	63.8
2b. Revised	24.0	100	131	215	30.1	45.9	50.6	56.3
3. Industry and Construction								
3a. Unrevised	12.2	100	158	--	9.8	25.7	32.8	--
3b. Revised	11.7	100	158	271	6.2	19.4	25.6	29.8
4. Industry								
4a. Unrevised	--	100	154	264	--	--	--	--
4b. Revised	--	100	--	263	--	--	--	--
5. Construction								
5a. Unrevised	--	100	242	431	--	--	--	--
5b. Revised	--	100	--	431	--	--	--	--
6. Agriculture								
6a. Unrevised	42.3	100	105	199	14.4	10.9	9.3	11.5
6b. Revised	44.1	100	104	197	12.4	10.3	9.0	11.5
7. Transportation and Communications								
7a. Unrevised	27.0	100	117	157	13.4	15.9	15.1	13.2
7b. Revised	27.0	100	117	157	11.0	15.0	14.7	13.4
8. Nonproductive Sectors								
8a. Unrevised	43.0	100	111	152	61.6	45.6	41.0	36.7
8b. Revised	47.4	100	109	142	69.9	54.1	49.4	43.7
9. Housing								
9a. Unrevised	49.3	100	108	--	54.8	35.5	30.9	--
9b. Revised	53.2	100	106	130	64.7	44.5	39.6	33.0

Sources: For the revised series, Table 0-1; for the unrevised series, TsSU-59, pp. 58-59, and TsSU-57e, pp. 15-16. The distribution by sectors for 1956 is computed from the distribution for 1941 and the 1941-based index number for 1956.

TABLE 7-5

GROSS FIXED CAPITAL AVAILABLE FOR OPERATION, IN 1950 OR "1956
ESTIMATING" PRICES, OFFICIAL AND PRESENT ESTIMATES, SELECTED YEARS
(January 1)

	Price Weights	1929	1941	1951	1956	1960	1961	1962
			A. Indexes (1929 = 100)					
1. Total								
Present	1950	100	286	323	480	696	763	833
Present	1956E	100	279	312	457	653	713	777
Official	1956E	100	273	326	480	685	754	825
2. Nonagricultural								
Present	1950	100	288	331	486	699	768	841
Present	1956E	100	281	319	463	655	717	782
Official	1956E	100	280	338	485	693	764	837
3. Residential								
Present	1950 }	100	147	147	187	227	242	256
Present	1956E }							
Official	1956E	100	188	200	245	348	374	398
4. Nonresidential								
Present	1950	100	452	534	832	1260	1389	1527
Present	1956E	100	452	529	813	1214	1335	1464
Official	1956E	100	430	557	911	1302	1449	1607
			B. Present Index as Percent of Official					
5. Total	1950	100	105	99	100	102	101	101
	1956E	100	102	96	95	95	95	94
6. Nonagricultural	1950	100	103	98	100	101	101	100
	1956E	100	100	94	95	95	94	93
7. Residential . . .	1950 }	100	78	73	76	65	65	64
	1956E }							
8. Nonresidential	1950	100	105	96	91	97	96	95
	1956E	100	105	95	89	93	92	91

Sources: For official indexes, Table O-3 (Part C). For present indexes, ruble
figures are obtained by the procedures described in the sources for Table 7-3
(column 2), and 1929 values are set equal to 100.

series, and the chief effects of reweighting are to be expected among, rather
than within, components. Since the Soviet data refer to capital available
for operation,[51] the series with which they are compared are computed net
of capital investment projects in progress. The table includes all the dates
for which revised official index numbers of scope comparable to ours are
available.[52]

We turn first to the indexes for all sectors of the economy (rows 1 and
5). For the prewar interval, 1929–41, both of our indexes grow slightly
more rapidly than the official, that using 1950 prices exceeding the official
by 5 percent by 1941, as opposed to 2 percent for our index using 1956
estimating prices. In both cases, our indexes fall by 6 percent relative to
the official between 1941 and 1951. Finally, both of our indexes move very
closely with the official throughout the postwar interval, 1951–62, that
using 1950 prices increasing relative to the official by 2 percent over the
interval, as opposed to a 2 percent decline relative to the official for our

[51] See footnote 29, p. 196.
[52] Some additional years are covered in the unrevised indexes, but only in the 1950's
for the global index (see TsSU–57, p. 38, and TsSU–59, pp. 58–59). The unrevised index
for capital in industry was released as an annual series, from 1938 but omitting the war
years (see TsSU–57a, p. 16).

index using 1956 estimating prices. Over-all, the degree of agreement between our and the official indexes is surprising.

Approximately the same relationships among the three indexes are observed for the nonagricultural sector (rows 2 and 6). As with our indexes, the official nonagricultural index moves closely with the official index for all sectors. This reflects the fact, as may also be observed directly in Table O-3, that nonagricultural assets according to the official data have remained over time a more or less uniform proportion of the total, a finding which also emerges from our calculations.[53]

In contrast to the foregoing, our index for the stock of housing diverges markedly from the official (rows 3 and 7).[54] Between 1929 and 1941, our index declines by 22 percent relative to the official. As with the indexes just discussed, the 1941–51 interval witnesses a 6 percent (5.index points) decline in our series relative to the official. In the postwar period, our index first rises slightly more rapidly than the official (1951–56), but during the next six years (1956–62) declines relative to the official by 16 percent (12 index points). Thus, from 1929 to 1962 our index declines relative to the official by over one third.

Our indexes for the nonresidential sector are again similar to the official, though not quite so close as the all-sector indexes (rows 4 and 8). In particular, during the postwar period, our indexes first decline (1951–56), then increase (1956–60), then decline again (1960–62) relative to the official, in contrast to the comparatively stable relationships among the all-sector indexes. The similarity otherwise of the nonresidential indexes is considerable, which is paradoxical in view of the marked divergences just noted between our and the official residential indexes. For example, having reference to our indexes using 1956 estimating prices, over the entire interval 1929–62, we note that our total index grows only 6 percent less than the official, our nonresidential index only 9 percent less, whereas our residential index lags behind the official by 36 percent (compare rows 5, 7, and 8). Both of our (jointly exhaustive) component indexes decline by more, relative to their official counterparts, than the global one. The explanation is that the official residential component outpaces ours but still grows more slowly than the official nonresidential index and has a greater weight in the official than in our total. Offsetting differences in the two sets of data exist. But this indicates that there is more, perhaps, than is immediately evident underlying the numerical similarities between the official indexes and ours.

As will be recalled: (*i*) the comparisons made previously, with reference to the 1960 inventory, between the Soviet and our absolute values for January 1, 1960, suggest an understatement in our valuation of the residential stock in 1956 estimating prices; (*ii*) our estimates are made independently for the total and for residential assets, nonresidential assets being computed as a residual; and (*iii*) our estimates for the residential stock show considerably less growth, especially in the prewar period, than

---

53 See p. 86.

54 Since the stock of residential assets includes only structures and, hence, is revalued in our calculations from 1950 to 1956 estimating prices by a single price index number, only one index of the change in the residential stock is shown in Table 7–5. The measured rate of change is the same in both sets of prices.

do our global estimates, with the result that the rate of growth of the nonresidential stock increases as the valuation placed on housing increases, again with greatest leverage in the prewar period. If the valuation placed on housing were increased to reconcile our estimate with the Soviet absolute figure for January 1, 1960, one consequence would be a marked increase in the growth rate of our prewar nonresidential *index*—which would increase the divergences between that index and its official counterpart.[55] The Soviet absolute data for January 1, 1960, show a value for housing on that date which is 71 percent in excess of ours. If that value is accepted and is used in conjunction with our global and residential indexes in 1956 estimating prices, the nonresidential residual for 1929 is actually negligible.[56] There is, therefore, a crucial inconsistency in the two sets of data. To retain the present degree of agreement between the Soviet and our indexes for all fixed assets and/or nonresidential assets while accepting the Soviet valuation of housing in 1960, it is necessary as well to accept the Soviet index of the growth of housing.

The Crucial Inconsistency

This is the major problem of interpretation which emerges from the comparison of our estimates with the official data. To recapitulate, our global estimates, which are our most reliable, agree closely with the corresponding Soviet figures. The same is true of our estimates for the non-agricultural sector, but the scope of the sector is so broad that this result is largely a repetition of the global finding. We are able to make only one other independent sectoral estimate, that for housing (with nonresidential complements emerging as a dependent residual). For this component, our findings are more tentative than for our global estimates and, in addition, are significantly at variance with the corresponding Soviet series. Should the agreement between the two sets of global data be interpreted as confirming the Soviet calculations, including the sectoral indexes? This would mean accepting the Soviet housing index where it disagrees with ours. It would have the important advantage of endorsing for use a number of sectoral indexes which our calculations do not provide. Or, should the discrepancy between the housing indexes be taken to create doubt that the apparent consistencies of the global data are in fact significant and, hence, that either set of estimates truly corroborates the other, in total or in detail? The problem is of sufficient weight to merit further examination.

---

55 To illustrate, in our series in 1956 estimating prices, a 15 percent increase in the value of housing—much less than the present difference between the Soviet value and ours—would produce a nonresidential index for 1941 (1929 = 100) of 526, which exceeds the corresponding Soviet index number by 22 percent. For the postwar years, our index thus recomputed would stand at 112 percent of the official for 1951; 106 percent for 1956; 112 percent for 1960. That is, from 1941, it would show about the same variations relative to the official as the indexes in Table 7–5.

56 Both the Soviet and our figures agree that the value of fixed assets in 1956 estimating prices was about 2,800 billion rubles at the beginning of 1960 (Table 7–3) and, therefore, around 420–425 billion rubles at the beginning of 1929 (applying the indexes of Table 7–5 to the absolute values of Table 7–3). If we accept the Soviet value for housing for 1960 (942 billion rubles) and our 1960 index number (1929 = 100) for housing of 227, the implied value of housing in 1929 is 415 billion rubles, almost as great as the total.

Let us consider first the indexes for the prewar period. The Soviet housing index for this interval seems to be seriously inconsistent not only with our index but also with the values placed on different kinds of housing in the Soviet absolute data for January 1, 1960, and what is known of the physical stock of housing. Table 7–6 (Part A) shows indexes of the physical stock of residential floor space. If these series are aggregated using *our* average unit values as weights, the index shown in row 4 results. As may be seen, for the interval 1929–41, this index exceeds the physical indicators for either private urban or private rural floor space (rows 2 and 3) and is itself exceeded only by the physical index for socialized urban floor space (row 1). Thus a lower index would be obtained by assigning a greater relative weight to either or both kinds of housing in the private sector, and vice versa. We noted earlier that the Soviet absolute data for January 1, 1960, imply an average unit value for private housing, relative to

TABLE 7-6

CHANGE IN RESIDENTIAL FIXED CAPITAL, SELECTED PERIODS
(January 1--Percent)

	1941/1929	1951/1941	1962/1951
A. Physical Stock of Residential Floor Space			
1. Socialized Urban	234	127	184
2. Private Urban	124	112	225
3. Private Rural	110	56	95
B. Gross Value of Housing Stock, All Sectors			
4. Aggregation of Physical Series Using Our Weights	150	99	174
5. Official Index	188	106	199

Sources: For rows 1-4, Table 3-3; for row 5, Table 7-5.

socialized, which is greater than that used in our calculations by about 85 percent.[57] The Soviet aggregative index should, on this account, be significantly lower than the one in row 4 of Table 7–6, whereas in fact it exceeds the latter by over 25 percent (compare rows 4 and 5). It is unlikely that the physical series could conceal an average improvement in quality that would reconcile these indicators. Given the construction standards of the early Five-Year Plans, the probabilities seem to lie in the opposite direction. For this interval, the Soviet index appears to overstate seriously the growth of the residential stock as measurable in the indicated prices. We are not inclined, therefore, to interpret the disagreement between it and our housing index as evidence of error in the latter. Rejecting the Soviet housing index (and retaining ours) tends to reinforce the indications noted earlier that the Soviet absolute values for housing are overstated. It also implies, insofar as *our* valuation of housing is *understated*, that the apparent degree of agreement between the Soviet and our nonresidential indexes for the prewar period is misleadingly high.

If the Soviet global index is constructed as an aggregate of components, this would mean that the similarity between it and ours is in large measure coincidental. Unfortunately, we do not know how the Soviet indexes are compiled. It is possible that the Soviet global index is computed inde-

---

[57] See footnote 37, p. 201.

pendently of the components, in which case the observed agreement between it and ours might still be taken as mutually corroborative, but only for the global calculations, not for the components.[58] Our principal conclusion is negative: whatever the significance otherwise of the agreement between the Soviet and our global indexes for the prewar period, it is difficult to read it as an endorsement of the Soviet component indexes for that interval. This conclusion suggests further that such similarity as exists between the official and our nonresidential indexes, allowance being made for possible error in our estimates, may be equally uninterpretable. It could conceivably result from the summation of official component indexes which are accurate, or from the summation of inaccurate components with weights having compensating errors, or from the computation of the total nonresidential index independently of its components.[59]

Over the interval 1941–51, all of our indexes decline relative to their Soviet counterparts by about the same amount, 6–10 percent. For this period, then, there is no greater agreement between the Soviet indexes and ours for global than for sectoral scope. An error of about the indicated magnitude could occur in our calculations through overstatements in our allowances for territorial acquisitions and war losses (cf. Table 2–15). Both kinds of error would understate the postwar stock relative to the prewar. We have just drawn attention to difficulties in accepting the Soviet 1941 index numbers relative to 1929 and would hesitate to endorse their standing relative to later years merely because of the possibility of error in our calculations. However, neither our results nor the data on the physical stock of housing[60] indicate patent implausibility in the Soviet indexes.

Finally, for the postwar period, 1951–62, the Soviet indexes and ours show similar trends. However, both the Soviet residential and nonresidential components tend to outpace our counterparts, the greater similarity between the respective global indexes again reflecting, perhaps coincidentally, the higher relative weight accorded housing in the Soviet aggregation. Roughly speaking, the differences in tempo seem to correspond to the differences noted earlier in growth rates of the Soviet and our postwar investment series. If the Soviet capital series are derived from

---

58 For example, if, as is quite possible, the Soviet global and component indexes were derived from data at original cost by means of a single set of deflators, if price movements were diverse among economic sectors, and if the deflators were global in reference, the result could be a set of indexes in which, although the components summed to the total, only the global index were accurate.

59 For one component index, industry and construction, the Soviet index for 1929–41 in Table 7–5 coincides approximately with certain official index numbers published earlier. The latter, given in sources cited in Kaplan–60, p. 272, indicate an index number for January 1, 1941 (average annual 1928 = 100), of 915. The Soviet index in Table 7–5 for January 1, 1941 (January 1, 1929 = 100), is 852, or about 7 percent lower, a difference in the proper direction and of a plausible magnitude to have resulted from the difference in bases. It is clear from the sources that the 1928–38 portion of the earlier index is in 1933 prices, though no prices are specified for the 1938–41 link. This suggests the possibility that older series, in prices other than those indicated, may be included in the currently published Soviet indexes.

60 See Table 7–6. The Soviet absolute value data cited earlier indicate the relative levels of socialized and private replacement costs but no relative levels within the private sector. Thus the Soviet housing index for 1951 (1941 = 100) of 106 could be consistent with the physical indexes shown.

the Soviet investment data, the considerations raised in connection with the latter would be applicable here as well—some error of overstatement in the rate of growth seems possible. We are puzzled to observe that, in spite of the stable relationship between the global indexes, the Soviet residential index falls (1951–56), then rises (1956–60) relative to ours, whereas the Soviet nonresidential index rises (1951–56), then falls (1956–60). We shall remark shortly on some anomalies in the Soviet indexes for 1956–60 that make these differences difficult to interpret.

For the entire period, the answer to the question with which we began this subsection may be summarized as follows. To consider that the agreement between our global index and the Soviet validates the Soviet component indexes as well, it is necessary to accept the Soviet housing index and the absolute values placed on housing in the Soviet 1960 stock data. Without this, the agreement at the global level must be taken either as coincidental or as the result of a Soviet global series which is independent of the sectoral calculations. We are inclined to believe, however, that both the Soviet absolute valuation of housing and the growth rate of the Soviet housing index are too high. This also removes the link with the global index needed to validate the various Soviet nonresidential sectoral indexes. The latter may receive some support from the similarity of the index for all nonresidential sectors to ours, but the reliability of our index is questionable, and we cannot exclude the possibility that numerical conformity here, as in the total, may be the coincidental result of offsetting errors in the official series. To the extent, of course, that our estimates fail to substantiate the official series, the latter fail to substantiate ours. The two may more firmly support one another in the postwar period than the prewar, but even this is not entirely clear.

Investment and Stock Data Compared

In the preceding paragraphs, it was suggested that part of the apparent agreement between our indexes and the Soviet may be coincidental. In addition, for the residential sector, there are significant visible divergences. But, even after allowance for these factors, a considerable measure of agreement seems to remain—especially in view of the large changes indicated by both sets of indexes. The similarities are the more surprising when it is recalled that our investment series differ sharply from their Soviet counterparts during the 1928–45 period.[61] We explore this paradox further in Table 7–7, in which comparisons are made of gross investment with increments in the gross fixed capital stock, as indicated in the Soviet statistics and in the estimates made in this study.

The main point to be examined in Table 7–7 is the relationship, for data of common origin, between gross investment and the increase generated by such investment in the gross stock. For the interval 1929–40, therefore, the capital increments are adjusted to exclude capital acquired through territorial expansion.[62] In the case of our data, the "adjustment"

---

[61] See Table 7–2.

[62] The increment is reckoned as the difference between the stock at the beginning and end of the indicated period. For all intervals other than 1929–40, increments refer to the stock on the enlarged territory.

TABLE 7-7

GROSS INVESTMENT IN FIXED CAPITAL AND INCREMENT IN GROSS STOCK,
IN "1956 ESTIMATING PRICES," OFFICIAL AND PRESENT ESTIMATES,
SELECTED PERIODS

A. Billion Rubles

	1929-1940[a]	1941-1950[b]	1951-1955	1956-1959	1960	1961
1. Total						
Official Investment	418	597	792	1127	367	383
Official Capital Increment	623	220	646	859	287	298
Present Investment.	739	521	765	998	310	326
Present Capital Increment	655	141	621	835	258	272
2. Nonagricultural						
Official Investment	365	526	669	947	315	325
Official Capital Increment	568	215	537	767	259	266
Present Investment.	632	445	635	835	269	282
Present Capital Increment	566	137	530	702	227	238
3. Residential						
Official Investment	65	112	157	265	83	79
Official Capital Increment	192	32	122	279	70	65
Present Investment.	88	84	99	152	49	48
Present Capital Increment	82	-1	99	97	36	34
4. Nonresidential						
Official Investment	353	485	635	862	284	304
Official Capital Increment	431	188	524	580	217	233
Present Investment.	651	437	666	846	261	278
Present Capital Increment	573	142	522	738	222	238

B. Capital Increment as Percent of Investment

	1929-1940[a]	1941-1950[b]	1951-1955	1956-1959	1960	1961
5. Total						
Official.	149	37	82	76	78	78
Present.	89	27	81	84	83	83
6. Nonagricultural						
Official.	156	41	80	81	82	82
Present.	90	31	83	84	84	84
7. Residential						
Official.	295	29	78	105	84	82
Present.	93	--[c]	100	64	73	71
8. Nonresidential						
Official.	122	39	83	67	76	77
Present.	88	32	78	87	85	86

[a] Investment is for 4th quarter 1928 to 1st half 1941.
[b] Investment is for 2nd half 1941 to 1950.
[c] Figure is negative.
Sources: For official data, Table O-1 (investment) and Table O-3, Part C (capital increment); see also the text discussion. For present estimates, data are the absolute ruble values corresponding to the indexes of Table 7-2 (investment) and Table 7-5 (capital increment).

consists only of undoing the allowance made previously to take account of such expansion. Whereas originally we had increased the stock accumulated on old territory by 10 percent as of the end of 1940, we now reverse the process, reducing the stock on new territory by 9 percent before reckoning the increments. An adjustment of the same magnitude is made in calculating the increments implied by the Soviet stock data. To the extent that our original allowance for territorial expansion was in error, our present adjustment to the Soviet data results in a misstatement of the increments out of capital investment those data imply. Another source of error derives from the fact that the intervals for which the Soviet investment data are available do not coincide exactly with those of the capital increments. To facilitate comparisons, our investment data are shown for the same intervals as the Soviet. Thus, in the first column of Table 7–7, the investment data refer not to 1929–40 but to 1928 (4th quarter) to 1941 (1st half), and, in the second column, not to 1941–50 but to 1941 (2nd half) to 1950. For later intervals, the investment and capital increment intervals coincide. Finally, the Soviet investment data are available only for capital put in place, rather than the more appropriate concept, capital available for operation. Again, for comparability, our investment data also refer to capital put in place. Although the presentation becomes untidy on these counts, it is unlikely that any of the inferences to be drawn are significantly affected.

Part A of Table 7–7 shows investment and capital in billions of rubles. In Part B, the increments are expressed as percentages of the corresponding investment figures. For all intervals, these percentages should be less than 100, reflecting the fact that stock increments are less than investment by the amount of assets withdrawn from use.

For the 1929–40 interval, however, the percentages computed from the Soviet data uniformly and significantly exceed 100. The magnitudes shown might be modified by a more exact adjustment for territorial change. However, the percentage presently shown would be *increased* if the investment data were limited to the interval 1929–40 and capital put into operation. It is, therefore, quite unlikely that refining the data could reverse the indicated inequalities,[63] and we conclude instead that there is a clear inconsistency between the Soviet investment and capital stock data.

We argued earlier that the Soviet investment data for the prewar period were understated relative to later years.[64] The present finding supports that contention. It also raises another, perhaps more disturbing, question. How did Soviet statisticians arrive at a capital stock index which is grossly inconsistent with their capital investment series? As indicated earlier, we do not know the answer. We have discovered no source which clearly describes the methods used in deriving the Soviet index. The reason the question is disturbing, nonetheless, is a Soviet account published in 1955,[65] according to which the TsSU computes its capital stock series by much the same procedures as those employed in this study: current investment is deflated into constant prices, and the stock is computed by cumulating

---

[63] To illustrate, the smallest ratio of capital increment to investment is that for the nonresidential sector, 1.22 (row 8). Total investment in this sector during 1928 (4th quarter) to 1941 (1st half), according to the Soviet data, was 353 billion rubles (row 4). To adjust this to exclude investment in the first half of 1941 and the increment over 1929–40 in projects in progress, it would be necessary to subtract about 24 and 33 billion rubles, respectively (see TsSU–62a, pp. 531, 535, 537). These figures refer to all investment by state, co-operative, and collective-farm organizations, and hence include some outlays for housing which ought not to be subtracted. No data are available which permit subtraction of investment during the last quarter of 1928. The foregoing adjustment would reduce the investment figure to 296 billion rubles. The stock of nonresidential assets at the beginning of 1929 was 148 billion rubles according to the official series (Table O–3). Thus, even if retirements during the 12 years 1929–40 were zero, the stock generated through investment at the end of 1940 would be 444 billion rubles (148 + 296 = 444), whereas the Soviet series put it at 636 billion (Table O–3). To reconcile these figures would require that territorial expansion increased the nonresidential stock of fixed assets by 43 percent (636/444 = 1.43), which is certainly implausible.

[64] See p. 193.

[65] Freimundt–55, pp. 182 ff.

new gross investment while subtracting retirements. If this is still the method employed, TsSU must use constant-price investment series that differ considerably from those currently shown in its statistical handbooks, a practice perilously close to double bookkeeping. Because the cited methodological discussion appeared before the publication of the capital stock indexes considered here, it may not be applicable to the latter. The matter is at best unclear. The implication, nevertheless, is surely that the Soviet stock and investment series may conceal more mysteries than strike the eye.[66]

Both sets of data show small ratios of capital increments to investment for 1941–50, reflecting the capital losses caused by the war. The Soviet ratios uniformly exceed ours, but, without knowledge of how the Soviet capital increments are computed, it is impossible to know what this signifies. Perhaps our calculations are predicated on greater relative allowances for war losses during 1941–44 or greater withdrawals of overaged assets during 1945–50. For example, we assume that assets were withdrawn at the end of their normal service lives throughout this period, although, in fact, lives may have been stretched to compensate for the capital loss produced by the war. We could easily err on either count, but, for reasons adduced previously, we are reluctant to use the Soviet series as a basis for adjustment until their origins are clearer.

From 1951 through 1961, our calculations tend to show a slightly larger ratio of capital increment to investment than do the Soviet data. This is consistent with the fact that our investment data include only investment in structures, equipment, and installation, whereas the Soviet data also include the residual category, "other." As noted previously, we suspect that a substantial part of "other" investment consists of expenditures classified in Soviet parlance as "not increasing the stock of basic funds."

Both sets of data for the residential sector for 1951–61 have their peculiarities. In our calculations, the ratio of capital increment to investment is 1.00 during 1951–55 but markedly lower during 1956–61. This reflects the oversimplification in our estimates of withdrawals from the initial stock of housing, as a result of which withdrawals are taken as virtually nil in the early postwar period and are bunched in the post-1955 years. A more refined procedure would undoubtedly spread the retirements, reducing the observed growth of the residential stock during 1950–55, increasing it thereafter. The Soviet data, on the other hand, show just the opposite pattern. The ratio of capital increment to investment is low during 1951–55 but rises to 1.05 during 1956–59. The latter ratio is, of course, anomalous, reflecting some inconsistency between the Soviet stock and investment data. It will be recalled from Table 7–5 that our residential index rises more rapidly than the Soviet during 1951–56, more slowly thereafter. The foregoing suggests that some redistribution of the observed growth of our index in the direction of the Soviet index would be in order—but that,

---

66 The methodological discussion just cited points, as a concrete example, to the derivation of the old Soviet index of industrial capital in 1933 prices during part of the prewar period. As noted in footnote 59, p. 211, the presently published index of industrial capital appears to be consistent—possibly even identical—with that 1933 price series. Though circumstantial, this evidence suggests that the methods described are in fact those still used in deriving the presently published indexes.

again, the ambiguities in the Soviet calculations make them a doubtful guide for adjustment.

For the nonresidential sector, our calculations show a lower ratio of capital increment to investment during 1951–55 than during 1956–61. This reflects the fact that the average age of the fixed capital stock increased during the war and early postwar period, when the flow of new investment was contracted, but declined in later postwar years as investment grew. Other things equal, withdrawals tend to vary with average age. If, as suggested, actual service lives were stretched during 1941–50, retirements during 1951–55 would probably have exceeded the norms used in our calculations, and a more accurate treatment would show a greater contrast between the 1951–55 and 1956–61 ratios. The Soviet ratios, however, show a pattern opposite to ours. They are higher during 1951–55 and lower during 1956–61. But the significance of this is doubtful because of the fact that the low Soviet ratio for 1956–59 is largely attributable to still another anomaly in the Soviet data—an implausibly low ratio for one year, 1959.[67] Again, therefore, the implications of the comparison are obscure.

Taken in their totality, the comparisons of our estimates with the official data do not much advance our knowledge of the Soviet stock of fixed capital. The official data can perhaps be taken to add a little to the credibility of certain of our estimates, for example, those for the total stock, and to increase the uncertainty which attaches to others, especially the division between residential and nonresidential assets. But the inconsistencies between our estimates and the official, and especially the inconsis-

---

[67] The data do not permit us to compute annual nonresidential ratios for 1956–59, but the annual variation in the ratio can be approximated within a reasonable error by comparing annual data, in 1956 estimating prices, on investment in productive basic funds in industry, agriculture, transportation, and communications with annual capital increments in all productive basic funds. The difference in scope between the two series consists of the exclusion of trade and "other" productive sectors from the investment data as opposed to their inclusion in the capital increment data. Because the omitted sectors are small, relative to all productive sectors—they accounted for less than 5 percent of all productive basic funds at the beginning of 1960, according to Table O–3—the incomparability should have only a limited effect on the year-to-year variation in the relative standing of the two series. As productive basic funds account for about 85 percent of all nonresidential basic funds (Table O–3), the two series also provide a reasonable picture of what happened in the nonresidential sector generally. The series are as follows:

Year	Investment in Productive Basic Funds by Industry, Agriculture, Transportation, and Communications (Billion Rubles)	Increment in the Stock of Productive Basic Funds, All Productive Sectors (Billion Rubles)	Stock Increment as Percent of Investment
1956	153	141	92
1957	161	129	80
1958	182	159	87
1959	208	92	44
1960	226	178	79
1961	240	178	74

We know of no historical or accounting reason for the exceptionally low capital increment of 1959 and suspect it reflects some distortion in the official stock series.

The investment data cited are from TsSU–62a, pp. 540–41. The capital increments are computed from the value of productive basic funds at the beginning of 1960, given in TsSU–60, p. 67, as 1,739.3 billion rubles, and the indexes of annual change in TsSU–60, p. 62, and TsSU–62a, p. 68.

tencies within the body of official data, make the import of the comparisons for the reliability of our estimates highly ambiguous. By the same token, it is impossible to read from the comparisons a confirmation of the reliability of those parts of the official data which, if confirmed, would significantly extend the information provided by our estimates. Until the regime chooses to release fuller explanations of the sources and methods underlying the statistics it has published, the true meaning of such comparisons as we can make will, necessarily, remain unclear.

PART II

Capital and Growth

Chapter 8

The Allocation of

Output to Capital

1. INTRODUCTION

While our intent in the preceding chapters has been to establish—not definitively but within tolerable margins of error—matters of statistical fact relating to capital in the Soviet economy, the issues to which we now address ourselves are of a kind which we can only treat tentatively and conditionally. As we have explained, our ultimate motivation in measuring capital is to make possible analysis of the sources of Soviet growth. The obstacles to such an analysis, however, scarcely inhere solely in capital statistics, and it would be presumptuous to suppose that all could be overcome within the limits of this study (and within the limitations of its authors). What we attempt, therefore, in this chapter and the two following, is at best a reconnaissance, which may be suggestive and which we hope may provide a point of departure for further research and less speculative inferences.

The first obstacle we encounter is deficiencies in the available data for variables other than capital. The body of data on the Soviet economy now assembled is large, and we have drawn heavily upon it, both in composing our capital estimates and for the supplementary series which we require. But important gaps remain. Some of these we fill, in the course of the following discussion, by procedures which, for the most part, are quite crude. The results of these efforts are not to be regarded as among the primary statistical findings of the study.

A second difficulty that arises is analytical, and it accounts for our inserting the present chapter before the discussion more specifically of the sources of growth in the last two chapters. As is immediately obvious, the functional relation between capital and output is not unidirectional. Capital is, on the one hand, a productive input and hence a determinant of the volume of output; this is the relation which is our primary concern. It is, on the other hand, dependent upon output. The gross addition to the stock in any period, external acquisitions aside, is determined by the volume of output in the period and by the complex of decisions which determines the share of output allocated to investment purposes. In effect, our capital estimates can be read both as observations on an independent variable in a production relation and as a reflection of the investment policy of the Soviet regime—and of such nonpolicy decisions as are operative. There are simultaneous relations between capital and output which, although we cannot undertake to handle them simultaneously, must both be considered. Of the two, we take up first the flow of output to capital, viewing capital, so to speak, as a dependent variable in its relation to output. This relation is also, of course, one of interest in itself.

For both kinds of relation, we require statistics of output, for which we employ series whose origins are described in the section immediately following.

2. OUTPUT DATA

For output, we have constructed annual estimates of Net and Gross National Product in 1937 prices for 1928–40 and 1945–61.[1] The basis of these estimates is primarily, but with some exceptions, physical quantities of output. These are aggregated for relatively detailed component sectors of origin with 1937 market-price weights. The output indexes for such components are, therefore, essentially measures of output inclusive of the value of intermediate purchases, although we assume they move with value added. The components are aggregated with net value-added weights to obtain Net National Product for the entire economy and for the major sectors or groups of sectors for which we make capital estimates, and for agriculture. Gross product in total and by major sectors is obtained by adding to the net product figures depreciation as estimated in the present study. Sectoral gross products, hence, are conceptually the sum of net value added and depreciation, not output gross of intermediate purchases. Numerical series for both net and gross products are shown in Table T–47. The gross product series are graphed in Chart 8–1, except that product in housing is not shown separately because of its small size. Agricultural product is shown, despite our lack of estimates for agricultural capital, because of the large significance of the sector.[2]

We stress as strongly as possible that our 1937-price GNP series is in no sense offered as an alternative to that estimated by Abram Bergson (Bergson's estimates are, in general but with some exceptions, obtained by deflating expenditures by final use categories with price indexes).[3] Part of the data used in our calculations is drawn from Bergson or is the same as his. More important, the grounds for supposing that our estimates are usably reliable are that, in years covered by both, ours conform quite closely to his.[4] The inadequacy of Bergson's estimates for our purposes is that they cover only a limited number of years: 1928, 1937, 1940, 1944,

---

[1] All national product estimates are explained in detail in Appendix P.

[2] Agricultural output is measured inclusive of changes in livestock herds, in which respect the present series differs from some others which have been published, e.g., in Johnson–59, p. 204. For years since 1957 at least, the series may be inflated due to falsification in reporting at the local level; see p. 625.

[3] See Bergson–61.

[4] With 1928 set equal to 100 in both, ours differs from Bergson's by no more than 3 percent in any year except 1937, in which ours is greater by 6 percent. On this, and on our reasons for not adjusting our estimates to complete conformity with Bergson's, see the introductory discussion of Appendix P.

and 1948–55. The point in composing a different series is solely to provide figures for the omitted years.[5] For these, however, our estimates are of questionable reliability, both because they lack the sanction of Bergson's estimates and because the underlying statistics are poor. Valuations are in factor costs in Bergson's sense of the term.

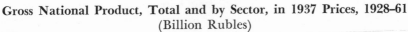

CHART 8-1

Gross National Product, Total and by Sector, in 1937 Prices, 1928–61
(Billion Rubles)

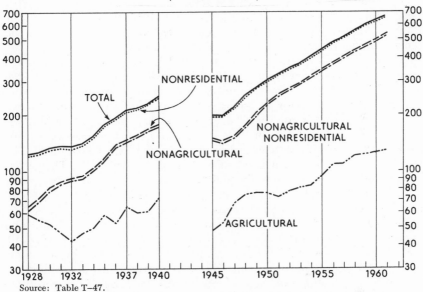

Source: Table T–47.

For GNP in 1928 and 1950 prices, we take Bergson's estimates directly and without alteration. His estimates in 1928 prices are for 1928 and 1937 only. Those in 1950 prices are for the same years as in 1937 prices, but, because of the similarity of the two, we use only selected years from the 1950-price series. From the GNP totals in both 1928 and 1950 prices, we derive NNP and product originating in major sectors. Data in these prices are presented in Tables T–48 and T–49.

Bergson has commented at length on the long-run behavior of Soviet GNP, and there is no need for us to do so here. In 1937 prices, GNP (in our estimates) grew at 5.2 percent per annum from 1928 to 1961, 6.1 percent from 1928 to 1940, and 7.8 percent from 1945 to 1961, all of which are relatively high rates. The most noteworthy information added by our estimates is that GNP rose very irregularly over the prewar years. After a modest rise from 1928 to 1931, output approximately leveled off in 1932–33, rose at a very rapid rate (over 10 percent per year) from 1934 through

---

[5] We are unable to obtain a 1944 figure by our procedures and are hesitant to link Bergson's into our series; see the discussion, p. 620. For 1944, Bergson's estimates are inclusive of Lend-Lease receipts and for 1948–53 of reparations receipts (see Bergson–61, pp. 98–100); the latter are small. Our output estimates are for product domestically produced although our investment estimates include materials obtained from external sources.

1937, and then slowed its growth markedly to 1940. As with capital, the gain during the First Five-Year Plan was exceptionally small, GNP increasing by less than 10 percent from 1928 to 1932. Output in 1945 was some 20 percent below the prewar level; it recovered rapidly in 1947–50, regaining the prewar level in 1948. Beyond 1950, the growth rate fluctuates considerably but perhaps can be characterized as decelerating. In particular, the rate for the last three years, 6.0 percent, is lower than that of any similar period since 1946 although about equal to the prewar average.

Net National Product declines over time relative to Gross National Product but only from a 97.3 percent ratio in 1928 to 91.6 percent in 1961. Long-term growth rates are, therefore, only slightly lower (5.0 percent for 1928–61, 5.8 percent for 1928–40, and 7.7 percent for 1945–61), and the general configuration of the series is much the same.

Among the component series, agricultural (gross) product is distinctive on several counts but particularly for its large absolute decline from 1928 to 1932. Thereafter, it recovers quite rapidly, with the erratic year-to-year fluctuations characteristic of Soviet agriculture, but to not much above the 1928 level except for the unusually good harvest of 1937 and, after the territorial enlargement, in 1940. In the latter year it is some 24 percent above 1928. By 1945, agricultural output is again well below 1928. The recovery to the 1940 level is rapid and is effected by 1948. Thereafter, output increases only gradually to 1954, spurts to 1958, and then slows greatly again to 1961. Over the entire period, the growth rate of agricultural output is 2.4 percent per annum, or less than half that of GNP.

Nonagricultural product exhibits more rapid growth rates in all long periods than does GNP (6.6 percent for 1928–61, 8.8 percent for 1928–40, and 8.3 percent for 1945–61), but the greater part of the gain occurs between 1928 and 1932, over which interval nonagricultural product increases by 43 percent while agricultural product falls by 27 percent. Nonagricultural product, like GNP, shows a retardation in 1932–33, a burst of growth for several years thereafter—but to 1936 rather than 1937—and a slower growth to 1940. As is evident from the chart, the inflection point which comes in 1936 in the nonagricultural sectors is delayed a year in total output by the good harvest of 1937. Nonagricultural output falls slightly less than the total from 1940 to 1945, starts its recovery somewhat more slowly, and then increases very rapidly through 1951. From 1952 to 1961 its growth rate is relatively steady, averaging 7.8 percent per year, but the last three years fall below the average, to 7.1 percent. The rate of the last decade is also below the prewar average, though probably not significantly if allowance could be made for the effects of the 1939–40 territorial acquisitions.

The product attributed to the housing sector is derived from the (gross) stock series and, like the latter, shows only a slow increase during the prewar period, a more rapid one during the postwar. Because of the small weight of housing, its effects on the totals in which it is included are barely perceptible: growth rates are raised slightly if residential product is deducted from GNP or from nonagricultural product. We comment further below on the valuation of the residential product.

Output in 1950 prices, total and by component sectors, behaves over time much like that in 1937 prices. In 1928 prices, however, GNP increases from 1928 to 1937 at 11.9 percent per annum (in Bergson's estimates) as against 6.2 percent in 1937 prices (in our estimates). Rates for neither the agricultural nor the housing components differ greatly in the two prices (the latter by assumption), but the weight of housing in the totals is small in both and the weight of agriculture less in 1928 than in 1937 prices. The nonagricultural nonresidential remainder is highly sensitive to the weight difference, increasing over the nine-year interval at 16.2 percent in 1928 prices as against 9.8 percent in 1937 prices.

For subsequent reference, it would be helpful if we could know to what extent the short-run fluctuations in the growth rate of output between 1928 and 1937, which are so marked in the 1937-price series, would appear also if output were valued in other prices. Although we cannot compose alternative series, various evidence strongly suggests that the pronounced sag in the rate of growth around the end of the First Five-Year Plan and the subsequent rapid acceleration into the mid-1930's would register clearly in computations employing any set of constant price weights.[6] What the effects would be of employing variable weights—given-year weights on a base, say, of 1928 or 1937—is less clear, but rapid change in the composition of output appears not to coincide with the 1932–33 trough,[7] and our impression is that such a trough would appear in a variably weighted output index as well.

3. THE INVESTMENT SHARE IN NATIONAL PRODUCT

The share of output devoted to investment in the Soviet economy appears differently depending upon whether it is measured in current or constant prices; if the latter, it depends upon the year from which the constant prices are taken. Our estimating procedures yield current-price

---

[6] In 1928 prices, we have from our estimates (see Table T–45) annual data for gross investment in fixed capital. Such investment rises very rapidly from 1928 to 1930, decelerates from 1930 to 1933 and declines absolutely in the last year, accelerates from 1933 to 1936, and declines from 1936 to 1937. This series must reflect roughly the behavior of the output of sectors producing commodities other than of agricultural origin. Agricultural output in 1928 prices can be approximated from data in 1926/27 prices given in Johnson–59, pp. 204 and 231–32, and our estimates of changes in livestock herds (see Appendix P, pp. 621 and 625) and can be taken as a rough measure of the output of all sectors producing and processing agricultural commodities: this, like its 1937-price counterpart, shows a continuous decline from 1928 to 1932 and a rapid upswing, interrupted in 1936, to 1937. Since the weight of investment goods is heavier and that of agricultural goods lighter in 1928 than in 1937 prices, the two in combination would probably show a more rapid rise from 1928 to 1930 in 1928 than in 1937 prices; beyond 1930, both conform to the general pattern of the 1937 price indexes. Both series err as measures of output in the intended sense because of large imports (of investment goods) and exports (of agricultural goods) in the earliest years referred to, but the errors are offsetting, at least in direction. The inclusion of munitions with investment goods would presumably heighten the acceleration to the mid-1930's and reduce the 1937 decline.

Other evidence points to the same conclusion. The official data for transportation of freight and passengers, in ton or passenger kilometers, show much the same pattern of change as does the gross investment series (see Table P–1, row 3, and the explanatory notes thereto). More debatably relevant, the official indexes of industrial production and national income, nominally in 1926/27 prices, accelerate and decelerate in the same phases as the investment and transportation series (see TsSU–62a, p. 169 and, for income, TsUNKhU–35, p. xx, and Baykov–48, p. 400). Those familiar with detailed physical output data published in Soviet sources will recognize the pattern described also as one common to a great variety of particular series.

[7] See the discussion of changes in the output mix, pp. 296 ff., below.

data only for the three weight years. In these, the share of gross investment in GNP is virtually the same: 20 percent in 1928, 21 percent in 1937, and 21 percent in 1950. Similar calculations with Bergson's more comprehensive definition of investment, which are available for a larger number of years, also indicate that the investment share in current prices has not risen greatly over the long run.[8]

Between 1928 and 1937, however, the price of products allocated to investment purposes fell enormously in relation to that of output in general. The size of the change differs as among the component kinds of investment and with the quantity weights of the price indexes, as can be seen from Table 8–1.[9] The most spectacular relative decline is in equipment prices. That in construction, and hence in all fixed investment, is also large. Investment prices in general fall by 60–65 percent relative to those of other GNP components. In consequence, the investment share, which in current prices is approximately unchanged between 1928 and 1937, rises in 1937 prices from 8 percent to 21 percent and in 1928 prices from 20 to 40 percent of GNP. Between 1937 and 1950, investment prices changed in about the same proportion as other prices, and investment shares are about the same in prices of either year: 21 and 22 percent in 1937 in prices of 1937 and 1950 respectively, 22 and 21 percent in 1950.

TABLE 8-1

PRICE INDEXES FOR GROSS INVESTMENT AND GROSS NATIONAL PRODUCT,
1928, 1937, AND 1950

	1937 (1928 = 100)		1950 (1937 = 100)	
	1928 Weights	1937 Weights	1937 Weights	1950 Weights
Gross Investment	173	136	232	223
Construction	205	199	260	250
Equipment.	143	71	197	191
Livestock	609*	655*	194*	195*
Inventories	325*	188*	233*	219*
Gross National Product	425	265	222	225
Noninvestment Components of GNP . .	489	353	219	225

* Weights are capital stocks, as of January 1, 1928, 1937, and 1950.
Sources: All figures are implicit deflators computed from expenditure (or stock) data for the two years involved in each comparison. The data for total investment are from Tables T–44 to T–46; for construction and equipment, Tables A–2 to A–4; for livestock, Table T–23; for inventories, Table T–24; and for GNP, Tables P–1 and P–4. For the last, our estimates in 1937 prices are set equal to Bergson's in 1937 (Bergson–61, p. 130), since we use his GNP figures in 1928 and 1950 prices. The indexes for the noninvestment components of GNP are computed from the GNP and gross investment data.

---

[8] Bergson's gross investment shares in 1928, 1937, and 1950 are 25, 26, and 28 percent, respectively (see Bergson–61, pp. 130, 150, and 154). For other years, see Bergson–60, p. 32, and Nimitz–62, p. 17. Neither Bergson's estimates nor ours provide evidence on the years between 1928 and 1937, and it is especially unsafe to infer the behavior of the current-price investment share within this period from its values in the terminal years.

[9] Livestock and inventories are shown with stock weights, because investment in them is small or negative in some of the years compared and their composition in a single year is unlikely to be representative. Both are included in gross investment with investment weights. The GNP and noninvestment deflators are affected, arbitrarily but in small degree, by differences in our estimates from Bergson's of the change in GNP in 1937 prices from 1928 to 1937 and from 1937 to 1950. For similar calculations covering more years, see Bergson–61, p. 238.

The behavior of the investment share in all years covered by our estimates, and in prices of all weight years, can be read from Table T–50 or,
in 1937 prices, from Chart 8–2. In 1937 prices, the gross share rises, very
irregularly, from the 8 percent level of 1928 to an average of 22 percent
in 1935–37, and then declines markedly with the approach of the war.
Presumably after a further fall during the war, it is back to the 1940 level
by 1945, regains the 1935–37 peak by the late 1940's, and rises to 31 percent
in 1961. The change from the beginning to the end of the entire period,
from 8 to 31 percent of GNP, is obviously very great. While the long-term
trend is difficult to describe in so variable a series, it seems clear enough
that the trend in the investment share in constant prices has been pronouncedly upward, the only large and sustained reversal being that associated with the war. Short-run fluctuations—troughs in 1929, 1932, 1940,
and peaks in 1931 and 1935–37; a postwar upswing broken by a decline in
1952–54 and a leveling-off in 1959–61—coincide with fluctuations in the
absolute volume of investment,[10] which is to say that the latter are not
matched by proportionate variations in GNP. The net investment share
moves generally with the gross, but fluctuates more widely. The significance
of the series with inventories smoothed (Chart 8–2) is discussed below.

CHART 8–2

Investment Share in National Product, in 1937 Prices, 1928–61
(Percent)

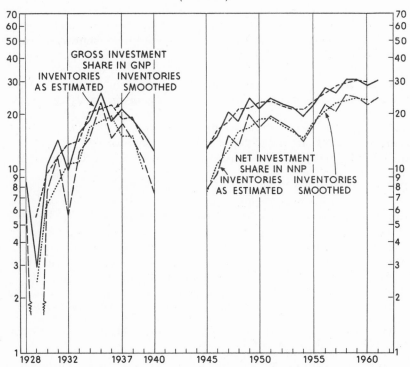

Sources: Tables T–44 and T–47, and for smoothed inventory series, Table 5–5, column 5.

---

[10] See pp. 173–74.

4. INVESTMENT POLICY

It appears reasonable to interpret the observed behavior of the investment share over fairly long intervals as the result of deliberate decisions
made by the central authorities, i.e., as an expression of the investment
policy pursued by the regime. Without attempting to survey such scant
direct evidence as there is on the reasoning processes of the authorities,[11]
we may justifiably infer from the declared aims of the regime and from
general knowledge of Soviet history that the rapid rise of the investment
share from 1928 to the mid-1930's was deliberate. The decline in the share
with the approach of war presumably reflects a decision to shift resources
to military uses, its rise after the war an intended shift back toward civilian
uses. That it remains high after 1953 and its trend continues to be upward
is explainable by the declared retention by his successors of Stalin's emphasis on investment and on the sectors producing investment goods. The
obverse of the long-term rise in the investment share is a fall in the share
of output available for current uses, and especially for household consumption. The resulting depression of living standards can be read as a measure
of the sacrifices the regime was willing to impose upon the public to
obtain the recorded rate of investment (and other allocations to noncon-
sumption uses).[12] Even in long periods, of course, the decision as to how
much of output to invest must have been conditioned by the realized size
of output and productivity of inputs, by anticipated reactions of enterprises and households, and by unexpected outcomes of decisions made at
earlier dates. But the Soviet economy is too tightly controlled from the
center to suppose that, over the long run, the investment share can be
viewed other than as a policy variable, set by the decisions of the authorities themselves.

In the short run, on the other hand, the apparent behavior of the investment share is difficult to interpret as solely or primarily the outcome
of decisions made by the central authorities. Circumstances are not readily
imaginable which would lead the authorities knowingly to determine that
3 percent of GNP should be devoted to investment in 1929 and 14 percent
in 1931, 26 percent in 1935, and 19 percent in 1936, etc. Rather, what appears to be operative here is a combination of centralized decisions, decisions made by subordinate agencies and individuals, surprise outcomes
contrary to all intentions, and—an explanation of a different order—statistical errors in our estimates.[13] Moreover, such deliberate decisions as are
reflected in the year-to-year movements of the series appear more likely to
have been focused on individual kinds of investment—in fixed capital,
livestock, or inventories—than on investment in the aggregate. This is
suggested by the behavior of the components relative to the total (see
Chart 6–7, p. 174). With exceptions in a few years, these do not behave
like parts of a predetermined aggregate, one component falling to offset

---

[11] For the early years covered here, Alexander Erlich's *The Soviet Industrialization
Debate, 1924–1928* (Erlich–60) is relevant.

[12] On real wages and per capita consumption, see Chapman–63.

[13] It is possible also that the variations would appear less extreme if the investment
share were measured in current prices.

a rise in another.[14] Each component appears, instead, to follow its independent course and the total to be determined as the sum of the parts.[15] Independence is especially marked in inventory investment. In addition, there are differences in the organizational and institutional arrangements under which investment in various forms is effected which support the supposition that in the short run each is differently and independently determined.

Fixed Capital

Investment in fixed capital occurs under circumstances which make tight central controls feasible, and it is, in fact, among the most tightly controlled activities in the economy. The products utilized in such investment, machinery and building materials, are typically the principal output of the industries in which they are produced, and the producing enterprises are themselves under close central direction. The conversion of machinery and building materials into investment in place occurs within a matrix of controls which leave neither investing enterprises nor contract construction organizations much autonomy in determining the volume of investment. The bulk of the machinery and materials involved are allocated by direct order. The flow of funds to finance fixed investment is channeled through a special bank (formerly several banks), which is responsible for the inspection and supervision of investment projects. Force-account construction is restricted in volume and segregated from the current operations of the enterprise. This is not to say that the central authorities have not sometimes been disappointed by the performance of the industries supplying investment goods and frustrated by the chronic inefficiencies of construction organizations. But even in short periods, the flow of output to fixed investment is likely to correspond at least roughly to the authorities' intentions. Unquestionably also, these intentions are conscious and highly specific, as is attested to by the prominence of fixed investment in published plans, plan-fulfillment reports, budget messages, statistical compendia, and the like.

---

14 The clearest instance of offsetting changes in the components is in 1936, when an exceptionally high rate of investment in fixed capital is coupled with an exceptionally low rate of investment in inventories. For the same reasons, however, that we are unsure of the accuracy of the very large investment in inventories estimated for 1935 (see p. 608), we are unsure of the accuracy of the 1936 estimate—and in the text have generally treated the 1935–37 period as a unit. On the other hand, there is a feature of our estimates of investment in construction which is likely to obscure somewhat offsetting variations in construction and in inventory investment: in general, the materials series from which construction is estimated do not allow for changes in inventories of building materials (see Powell–57, Part II, *passim*). Oddly, such an allowance is most nearly made in the construction estimates for the mid-1930's, for which considerable data on materials actually consumed by (or allocated to) construction are available. But we cannot show that this allowance helps to account for the inverse movements of construction and inventory investment in 1936 and contiguous years.

15 This is most evident for changes from one year to the next. Over periods of several years duration, the components do appear to be mutually related but more directly than inversely: all rise sharply from 1932 or 1933 to 1935–37, all decline to 1940, etc. (See Chart 6–7 and also the discussion of the capital stock by components, pp. 156 ff.). Some of these larger movements we have attributed to policy decisions, which could be expected to operate on all components. Others may reflect such decisions, about which we have no direct knowledge or strong presumption. Speculations to this effect appear below.

The intended absolute amount of fixed investment may be attained at the expense of production intended for current uses, or the latter may diverge from intentions for other reasons. In either case, the *share* of fixed investment in output is likely to prove less controllable than its absolute amount. In our estimates, nevertheless, the ratio of this investment to GNP changes relatively smoothly. From 8 percent in 1928, it rises to 19 percent in 1936, with a reversal only in 1933, but that a marked one. From 1936 to 1940 it declines (to 13 percent). From 1945 it rises continuously to 1961 (from 11 percent to 25 percent), with a single slight reversal in 1952. On the whole, this pattern appears interpretable as rather undistorted evidence of central policy decisions.[16]

Livestock

Investment in livestock is significant for the total volume of investment only in the early years, in which its large negative values work to offset the positive investment in other forms of capital. The drastic decline in livestock herds was, as is familiar, an indirect consequence of the decision of the regime to collectivize agriculture. But the immediate decision to liquidate livestock was made by individual peasants, and it is most improbable that the regime foresaw or intended this particular outcome. The long-run failure of livestock to recover to its 1928 level presumably also reflects the shape of agricultural policy in general more than a specific investment decision, although various measures bearing on livestock have been taken by the authorities. Central control over herds is unlikely to have been close at any time, because of the inherent difficulties in controlling the agricultural sector, the ease of converting livestock (like inventories) into a salable product, and the fact that a large part of total herds have been held privately, on the household plots of peasants and workers. Beyond the initial decline, investment in livestock exhibits year-to-year fluctuations which are as erratic as those in inventories, but its weight in the total is too small for these variations to register visibly in the investment share in GNP.[17]

Inventories

Investment in inventories has been, on the average, a substantial component of total investment. We have remarked in several earlier contexts on the extreme short-run variability of this component and on its dominance in short-run fluctuations in total investment. That it also accounts largely for year-to-year fluctuations in the investment share in GNP can be seen from the series with inventories smoothed in Chart 8–2.[18] For this reason, and because the forces determining the demand for inventories are

---

[16] The investment shares cited are for investment exclusive of capital repairs. Presumably, policy objectives are actually set in terms of totals inclusive of repairs, but the general pattern is not markedly different: the share is 9 percent in 1928, 21 percent in 1936, 15 percent in 1940, 13 percent in 1945, and 30 percent in 1961. For data on investment inclusive of capital repairs, see Table A–1.

[17] On the matter of this paragraph, see Jasny–49, *passim*, but especially pp. 343 ff. and chap. XXVI.

[18] The smoothed inventory series is obtained with a three-year moving average; see pp. 137–38.

peculiar in important respects, we devote considerable attention here to it. We should note, however, that the literature on what might be called "inventory management" in the Soviet Union is large, and we have sampled rather than exhausted it. The subject is one on which a separate monograph could usefully be written.

It is apparent, a priori, that inventories are a form of investment which is not easily controlled by the central authorities. The products used for inventory investment are produced by all the commodity producing sectors of the economy and handled by all parts of the transportation and distribution system. Raw materials purchased for additions to stocks are indistinguishable from those purchased for current consumption, and finished products sold from stocks are indistinguishable from sales of output currently produced. There is no observable material flow which represents additions to inventories or withdrawals from them, and no flow of expenditures or receipts which is identifiable as purchases or sales of inventories. The kinds of controls which serve for fixed investment, therefore, are not applicable and are not applied to investment in inventories.

The object of controls over inventories, rather, is the stock as such. As was noted in our discussion of the inventory estimates in Chapter 5, there has been in force in the economy since 1931 a system of prescribed inventory coefficients or "norms," which are intended to fix the relation between the inventory stock and some flow variable in the operations of the enterprise. For example, raw material stocks are related to raw material purchases, goods in process to gross output, finished products to sales or "commodity production."[19] The norms in force at any given time are, for the most part, constants, expressed as a fraction of the variable to which they relate or, equivalently, as so many days' requirements. In the short run, it would appear likely that the norms should tend to produce constancy in the ratio of inventories to output. This is obviously true of norms defined in terms of output or sales. It would be approximately true of norms of raw materials over periods short enough that the rate of raw materials consumption per unit of output (or the normed rate, since norms are set here also) remained roughly constant.

How nearly constant norms have remained over longer periods is less clear. Year after year, complaints have appeared in Soviet sources that the norms still in force were "basically" those set in 1931.[20] No general overhaul of the original norms was undertaken in the period covered by our estimates; the first such overhaul was called for by a decree of January, 1962, and preparation for it was to begin in early 1963.[21] On the other hand, piecemeal revisions have occurred.[22] Raw material norms relative to output may have changed because of changes in raw materials input

---

[19] Norming procedures are described in standard sources on inventories, finance, etc. See, e.g., Lavrov–56, pp. 66 ff.

[20] See, for example, Nusinov–37, pp. 36–37; Shenger–40, pp. 60–61; Kisman–56, pp. 92–93; Birman–63, p. 49. The last author, noting that the 1931 norms were intended to be temporary, adds wryly: "But it is well known that there is nothing longer-lasting than temporary norms."

[21] Birman–63, pp. 40 and 49. It is significant that the new norms were not to be revised more often than once every 5–7 years (*ibid.*, p. 50).

[22] Kisman–56, p. 92.

requirements. And the weighted average of norms may have changed with changes in the relative importance of various industries.

Chart 8–3 presents such evidence as we have on the behavior of inventory-output ratios over time. The detailed component sectors shown, industry and trade, are those for which our inventory estimates are reliable enough to justify analysis. The aggregate of sectors producing and distributing commodities, other than agriculture, includes inventories in all nonagricultural sectors for which we make estimates; output is that of industry, transportation and communications, construction, and trade. Agri-

CHART 8–3

Average Inventory-Output Ratio, Total and by Sector, in 1937 Prices, 1928–61

(Inventories/Net or Gross National Product)

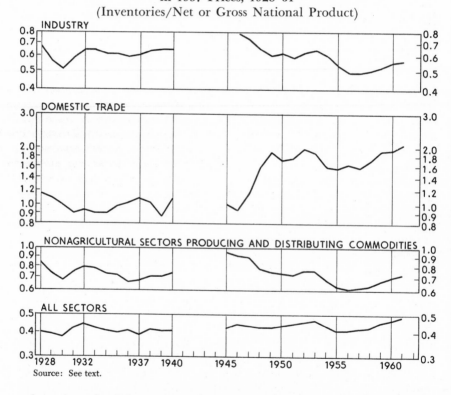

Source: See text.

culture is omitted because our inventory estimates are simply extrapolations on agricultural output. The calculation for "all sectors"—total inventories to GNP—is irrelevant to the question of norms, both because it includes the extrapolated agricultural inventories and because the non-commodity sectors (housing, finance, and services including government) do not hold significant inventories. The series is included for reference purposes. Inventories in industry and trade are those on hand only; goods shipped are attributed to transportation and are included for commodity sectors and all sectors. Inventories for each year are computed as the average of values at the beginning and end of each year to make them synchronous with the annual output flows (the averaging also somewhat smooths the inventory estimates). Output is net product originating for the component sectors, for which we do not have estimates gross of depreciation; the inclusion or exclusion of depreciation is of little consequence here.[23]

Over the nine prewar years following the introduction of inventory norms, 1932–40, inventory-output ratios evidence considerable stability. The extreme values of the ratio lie within 4 percent of their average for industry, in which sector norms are most likely to be firmly enforced, within 11 percent for domestic trade, and within 8 percent for all nonagricultural commodity sectors. Immediately after the war, the ratios for industry and the commodity sector aggregate are quite wide of the 1932–40 range; by 1949, all, with the marked exception of domestic trade, are back close to the prewar range and remain near it through 1953. The increase in the trade ratio over its prewar level is great, but the weight of trade in the aggregate is too small to much affect it.[24] From 1953, all ratios decline pronouncedly for two to four years and thereafter all rise, in varying

[23] Data used for the Chart 8–3 calculations are taken largely from Tables N–1 and P–1. These additional explanations are required: (*i*) Average inventories for 1939 are computed from estimated figures for January 1, 1940, reduced by the factor 1/1.05; the reduction is to exclude inventories acquired late in 1939 in the new territories. The 1940 averages are computed from the estimated figures for the beginning and end of the year, since the territorial acquisitions came in midyear. (*ii*) Net product in industry is the sum of that in civilian and munitions industries. (*iii*) Net product in domestic trade is computed from the index for state and co-operative trade (inclusive of private trade in 1928–30) given in Table P–3, extended to 1961 on the Table P–1 series for total trade. This index is used because the estimates for inventories in domestic trade exclude collective-farm market trade. The index is given a 1937 value of 9.1 billion rubles, or a fraction of total value added in trade equal to the share of state and co-operative in total trade (see p. 637). While the trade product series is for value added, the latter is estimated as a constant fraction of retail sales. Hence, the inventory-output series also constitutes an index of the inventory-sales ratio. (*iv*) Trade product is estimated in the same fashion for inclusion in the total product of commodity producing and distributing sectors. (*v*) Inventories in the latter include two components that are estimated partly or wholly from output: contract construction and uninstalled equipment, n.e.c. Their weights are too small to require their exclusion.

[24] Inventories on hand in domestic trade (both retail and wholesale trade are included) account for 12 percent of total nonagricultural inventories in 1940 and 17 percent in 1950. If the weight of trade inventories in the total were greater, it would be relevant to pursue the question of why their level relative to sales has been so much higher since the war than before, although we do not know a satisfactory answer. The data for both inventories and sales come largely from the same source, the Central Statistical Administration, which has itself published ratios similar to those calculated by us and with the same import (see TsSU–56, pp. 92–95; the data cited are for retail trade inventories only). The difference between the two periods appears not to result primarily from changes in the composition of trade, since similar differences appear in most individual commodity categories (see *loc. cit.*). Shifts in inventories between producing and distributing sectors appear not to be responsible, since the average ratio of inventories to output in industries producing consumer goods (output is computed from component data underlying row 2a of Table P–1) is about the same in 1949–61 as in 1932–40, .82 and .84 respectively. Differences in the relation of consumer demand to available supplies may be part of the answer: a recent Soviet source points to smaller excess demand in retail markets in the postwar period as a principal explanation (Afrutkin–62, pp. 72–73). We are inclined to suspect that a basic change has occurred also in the management of trade inventories, although we have no direct evidence of a change in norms. As noted elsewhere (p. 121, fn. 41), on January 1, 1962, inventories in retail trade exceeded their normed amounts by 10 percent. On the issue discussed here, see also Campbell–58, pp. 559–60.

degree. The ratio for all commodity sectors recovers by 1961 to approximately its level of the early 1950's and the prewar years.[25]

To the extent that inventory-output ratios approach constancy, they also approach, as will be recognized, the assumption underlying the "acceleration principle." It is a familiar implication of the latter that the demand for investment is a function not of the absolute level of output but of the change in output. If output changes erratically, erratic variations in investment demand will be induced. In Chart 8–4, we perform a simple test of the adequacy of an accelerator relation to account for the observed changes in inventories in the nonagricultural commodity sectors.[26] The acceleration coefficient for the series projected on output is assumed to be equal to the average value of the observed inventory-output ratio in all years for which we have data. The increments in inventories are for average annual stocks and therefore do not correspond strictly to annual investment. From 1928 through 1953, it appears that a constant inventory-output ratio would have produced increments in inventories which in general resemble the observed ones. Year-to-year fluctuations, while not identical in amplitude or timing with those observed, have a broadly similar shape and are at least as erratic. The similarity ends with 1953: actual increments are far below the projected ones in 1954–56 and well above them in 1959–61.

On this evidence, we would suppose that inventory investment, at least through 1953, has been determined in part by something like an accelerator relation. Output has changed erratically; the system of norms introduces an operating rule which makes it plausible that inventory demand should depend upon output; there is a considerable constancy in the ratio of inventories to output over long periods, although it is disrupted in the mid-1950's. The evidence is less convincing than it looks in that we have no direct knowledge of how nearly constant over time norms have been. It is possible also that a rough accelerator relation would hold in the absence of norms, as is suggested by the Chart 8–4 series for years prior to 1932.[27]

Beyond the uncomplicated operation of inventory norms posited thus far, there are other identifiable factors which modify the impact of the norms or work independently of them:

(*i*) Norms do not cover all inventories, and norms are not in all cases constant coefficients. Seasonal inventories and goods in transit are not normed. Collective-farm inventories were not normed, even nominally,

---

[25] The relatively greater stability of the inventory-output ratio for all sectors than for the nonagricultural commodity sectors is partly the result of the assumed constancy of the ratio for agriculture and partly is coincidental. In particular, the high immediate postwar ratio of inventories to output in the sectors holding inventories does not appear for all sectors because of the high share of services in GNP in that period. No causal connection appears likely.

[26] Data are the same as those employed in Chart 8–3. In Appendix G, p. 515, we note that our inventory estimates for nonagricultural sectors in current prices for January 1, 1961 and 1962, are some 2–3 percent too high. The impact of this error would be largest, among the uses we make of the inventory estimates, on the calculations of Chart 8–4. Assuming an error of 2.5 percent in 1937 prices, the increments shown in Chart 8–4 are reduced from 26.1 and 25.9 billion rubles in 1960 and 1961 to 22.7 and 22.2 billion, which differences are not great for the immediate purpose.

[27] Some norms were evidently in existence before 1931.

CHART 8-4

Increment in Average Annual Inventories in Nonagricultural Sectors Producing and Distributing Commodities, in 1937 Prices, 1929–61
(Billion Rubles)

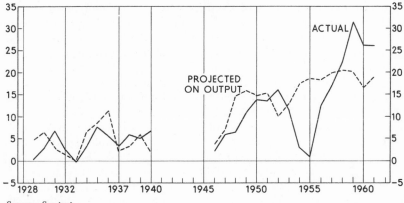

Source: See text.

up to 1952.[28] The absolute values of the normed amounts of spare parts and small tools are held constant except for large changes in output or product mix.[29]

(*ii*) The authorities, in exerting the physical and financial controls over inventories which they possess, appear to aim at a gradual rather than an immediate adjustment to the norms.[30] The latter, consequently, are targets, which actual inventories tend to reach only with a lag. Such a lag is evident in Chart 8–4: quite consistently, actual are below projected increments when projected increments are rising (i.e., when the increase in output is increasing) and above when projected increments are falling. If, moreover, actual inventories are for any reason pushed far out of line with their normed values, the path toward reattainment of the norms will be affected by the initial disequilibrium. Thus, the existence of large above-norm inventories in industry immediately after the war[31] undoubtedly explains in part the relatively small increments in inventories through 1949. The exceptionally small increments of 1954–56, whatever their explanation, probably account in part for the exceptionally high increments of 1959–61, the latter making good the deficits created in the earlier period.

(*iii*) Efforts to enforce established norms are not the whole of the measures taken by the central authorities. Campaigns to "accelerate the turnover of working capital" have been launched, most notably in 1949.[32]

---

28 Sorochinskii–56, p. 22.

29 Lavrov–56, p. 72.

30 See p. 121 above.

31 On the existence of such inventories, see the citation from Usoskin–46 on p. 607 below.

32 Turnover in the economy as a whole was to be accelerated during 1949 by 3 percent relative to the 1948 norms (Zverev–49, p. 47). Our estimates are not precise enough to judge the success of this campaign.

The sharp reduction in inventory-output ratios after 1953 almost certainly reflects a major policy decision, although the explanations for it which present themselves are *ad hoc* and inadequate.[33]

(*iv*) The controls which the central authorities have over inventories by no means fully constrain the managers of individual enterprises.[34] Managers, whose success depends heavily upon obtaining materials and ensuring against disruptions of supplies, have strong motivation to make their own decisions about inventories. That these are frequently contrary to the rules promulgated from the center is evidenced by continual reports in the literature of the "mismanagement" of inventories at the enterprise level.

(*v*) For reasons inherent in the way they are produced and acquired, inventories are particularly subject to unintended and unexpected outcomes. Delivery dates of raw materials and shipment dates of finished products are uncertain. The rate of flow of goods in process and in transit is not precisely controllable by anyone. Sales at retail are, at least over very short periods, unpredictable and uncontrollable. For these reasons, inventory totals as of any given date—such as the January 1 dates of our estimates—are likely to diverge significantly from those intended, both by the authorities and by individual managers. Surprises which are small relative to the inventory stock may be large relative to annual investment. In view of the disjointed character of economic processes in the Soviet Union, surprises may be large absolutely.

(*vi*) Surprise variations in inventory-output ratios may occur also, as in the total investment share in output, because of deviations of realized output from anticipations. This, together with the functioning of norms as targets, is a likely partial explanation of the fact that the fluctuations of several years length in the inventory-output ratios (1928 peak to 1930 trough to 1932 peak, etc.) parallel, in inverse, fluctuations in the productivity of inputs in general.[35] This is clearest for industry and for all non-agricultural commodity sectors, and for the period up to the early 1950's. If the fluctuations in productivity, and hence output, were unforeseen, unintended inverse fluctuations in the ratio of inventories to output would occur.

No doubt, the similarity of the behavior of the "productivity" of in-

---

[33] It is probably safe to assume that the timing of this change is significant. Insofar as it occurs in domestic trade and consumer goods industry, it can plausibly be interpreted as a part of the effort of Stalin's immediate successors to obtain a quick rise in consumption. But it is evidently at least as marked in producer goods industries (cf. Table N–1), which fact is not easily accounted for by this effort (note, however, that our division of industrial inventories between consumer and producer goods is subject to error). Above-norm inventories in industry were reportedly reduced in this period, but the reduction appears small relative to the calculated change in the inventory-output ratio (see the citations pp. 607–8). In 1953–55, various administrative changes were made which appear, on balance, to have broadened the discretionary authority with respect to inventories of enterprise managers, ministries, and the State Bank (for a handy summary, see Kisman–56, chap. 7). While these might have resulted in a more rational distribution and use of inventories, they are the sort of changes to which the inertia of Soviet bureaucracies rarely yields. Some were subsequently reversed.

[34] See pp. 121–22.

[35] Cf. Chart 8–3 with Chart 9–10.

ventories and of all inputs over such periods reflects, also, common factors affecting them as *determinants* of output. The circumstantial evidence appears strong, however, that the regime's attitude toward inventories is different from that toward other inputs. Here its decisions evidently proceed from expected output to inventory requirements rather than from expected availabilities and productivities to anticipated output. The result is, we suppose, that the observed ratio of inventories to output more nearly reflects the demand relation between the two variables than is the case with any other input. But it is a relation between the quantity of inventories demanded and *expected* output, and one which operates with lags, random disturbances, and occasional deliberate disturbances.

(*vii*) In some part, the apparent year-to-year fluctuations in inventory investment are spurious, the result of errors in our estimates.[36] We cannot specify where these errors lie or what share of the total fluctuations they account for, although the relative reliability of the estimates for individual years can be judged from the detailed statement of sources in the appendixes.

The likelihood of statistical error, the importance of unanticipated outcomes, and the considerable autonomy of managers in this area are the basis for our earlier assertion that the estimated series for inventory investment, and consequently for all investment, does not accurately reflect the short-run intentions of the Soviet authorities. The smoothing of annual investment in inventories, by averaging out discrepancies from these sources, may yield series which more nearly approximate the authorities' intentions (see Charts 6–8 and 8–2). The smoothing no doubt also eliminates, however, variations which are the consequence of inventory norms and, therefore, an expression of the inventory policy adopted by the regime.

It is obviously ironical, although not necessarily irrational, that the Soviet regime has as an act of policy introduced into its economy the prime source of short-run instability in the capitalist world. That this is likely to be of material consequence is suggested by the large size of the "accelerator coefficient," the average inventory-output ratio for the economy as a whole having remained in the neighborhood of 40–45 percent over the entire period covered (see Chart 8–3).[37] On the other hand, the instability of inventory investment in the Soviet economy, to our knowledge, affects only the distribution of output and not, or not in any direct way, its absolute amount.

5. FROM INVESTMENT FLOW TO CAPITAL STOCK

A decision to devote output to investment is necessarily equivalent to a decision regarding the capital stock, since investment flows, together

---

[36] See pp. 134 ff.

[37] The ratio of inventories to GNP in the United States in the 1950's, in current prices, was about 24 percent. U.S. inventories, of coverage comparable to our estimates, can be computed from Goldsmith–62; total inventories as shown in Table A–5, column (9), less government inventories as shown in Table A–39, columns (5) and (6). U.S. GNP is given in U.S. Department of Commerce–61, p. 2.

with pre-existing stocks and extraordinary gains and losses of assets, determine the level and behavior of the stock. It is unnecessary to ask, therefore, whether there has been in some sense a "capital policy" distinct from an investment policy. It is true that, within a given volume of total investment, a choice remains open as to how the total shall be distributed among various kinds of assets, which choice affects the size and growth rate of the stock as well as its composition. Presumably the Soviet authorities in making decisions about annual investment flows have had in mind some desired behavior of the stock, but, investment having been determined (deliberately or accidentally) in total and by components, the effects upon the stock follow mechanically. The workings of this mechanism, however, are not entirely self-evident, and it is these we mean to explore here.

For simplicity and because the more interesting questions lie there, we restrict the discussion to fixed capital investment and stock. Our livestock and inventory estimates are for depreciated or nondepreciable assets, so that (net) investment in either bears the usual mathematical relation to the stock in which it represents increments. Also, the discussion is framed in terms of trends, and the erratic behavior of these two investment components makes it more difficult to represent them by trend lines than is the case with fixed investment. Formally, however, investment in livestock and inventories could be incorporated into the analysis by treating these kinds of assets, for the immediate purpose, as assets of infinite service life.

We compare in Chart 8-5 our estimates of gross annual investment in fixed capital and the corresponding net stock series, i.e., the stock estimated with straight-line depreciation. We exclude from the latter, however, assets acquired through territorial expansion in 1939 and 1940, since these were not produced by the measured investment flow. For illustrative purposes, we fit trend lines (computed by least squares) to the investment data for 1928–40 and for 1950–61.[38] The trend for the earlier period is clearly a poor representation of the data to which it is fitted. That for 1950–61 fits observed investment quite closely for the period which it covers but not for the earlier postwar years. The extrapolation of the prewar trend line is also illustrative and is commented on hereafter.

During both periods, the growth rates of the investment trends are almost matched by those of the net stock. For 1928–40, the investment trend grows at 10.1 percent annually, the net stock at 9.2 percent. For 1950–61, the corresponding rates are 11.5 and 10.5 percent, respectively.[39]

A tendency toward such parallel development is inherent in the relationship of investment to stock, as may be shown symbolically. Consider a stock of assets of service life n, generated by an investment stream commencing with a value I_0 and growing each year by g percent. Let the present value of an asset i years old, relative to its original cost, be r_i. After at least n years have passed, the value S_t of the stock at the end of the year t, will be:

---

[38] The equation for the 1928–40 trend line is log $y = 1.057 + 0.0420x_1$, and that for 1950–61 log $y = 1.685 + 0.0474x_2$, where y = gross investment in billion rubles, x_1 = calendar year minus 1927, and x_2 = calendar year minus 1949.

[39] The stock growth rates refer to annual averages.

$$(17)$$

$$S_t = \sum_{0}^{n-1} I_0(1+g)^{t-i}\, r_i = I_0(1+g)^t \sum_{0}^{n-1} (1+g)^{-i}\, r_i = I_0(1+g)^t \sum_{0}^{n-1} \frac{r_i}{(1+g)^i}$$

By the same token, the value of the stock at the end of the year $t+1$ will be:

$$S_{t+1} = I_0(1+g)^{t+1} \sum_{0}^{n-1} \frac{r_i}{(1+g)^i} = (1+g)S_t. \qquad (18)$$

The stock, like the investment stream, grows at g percent per year.[40]

In the period before n years have passed, the stock may grow at a rate differing from g, depending on the initial value of the stock and its age structure (i.e., on the rate at which investment was growing prior to assuming the rate g). As n approaches, the stock and investment growth rates converge.

Equation (17) also defines an equilibrium relationship between the stock and investment. Thus gross investment I_t in the year t equals $I_0(1+g)^t$. According to equation (17), therefore,

$$S_t = I_t \sum_{0}^{n-1} \frac{r_i}{(1+g)^i}, \text{ and} \qquad (19)$$

$$\frac{S_t}{I_t} = \sum_{0}^{n-1} \frac{r_i}{(1+g)^i}. \qquad (20)$$

Equation (20) must be satisfied for the stock to grow at the same rate, g, as the investment stream. This relationship is relevant in considering the effects on the stock of major variations in the investment stream.

In the case, for example, where investment drops below the level indicated by equation (20), resuming growth at the rate g from a lower absolute level, the growth rate of the stock will be less than g, and the stock-gross investment ratio will decline. As it approaches the equilibrium level indicated by equation (20), the stock growth rate will accelerate. The stock will still not grow at the rate g with complete consistency until n years have passed, because the age structure of the stock will not be that indicated by equation (20) until the entire stock has been generated by an investment stream of consistent growth rate, g.[41] However, for high values

---

[40] Equations (17) and (18) hold only for assets of uniform durability, but the argument may be extended to assets with various service lives by summing stocks of like assets. What is necessary is that investment in each kind of asset grow at the same rate, g. The service-life distribution of investment must be constant over time. The latter condition is not met by the data in our calculations, the average durability of the investment stream having declined over time with the increased relative importance of equipment.

[41] The effect of an age structure inconsistent with equation (20) depends on the depreciation method used. For methods such as straight-line, where the percentage decline in the net value of the asset increases with its age, an average age for the stock greater than that indicated by equation (20) lessens the growth rate of the stock, and conversely. (It can be shown, from equation 11, p. 97, that depreciation, as a percent of the net stock, varies with the average age of the stock. Thus, $D/N = 1/(n-A)$, where D is depreciation, N is the net value of the stock, n the service life of the assets in the stock, and A their average age, measured with gross value weights).

CHART 8–5

Gross Investment and Net Stock of Fixed Capital, in 1937 Prices, 1928–62
(Billion Rubles)

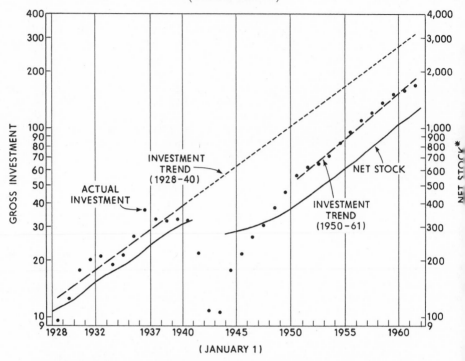

(JANUARY 1)

* 1940 and 1941 figures exclude assets in acquired territories.
Sources: Tables T–1 and A–2. Trend lines are computed (see text).

of g, the relative importance in the stock of older assets is small, and the growth of the stock may come very close to g as the stock-investment ratio approaches the value indicated by equation (20), even though the age structure of the older assets in the stock still does not strictly conform to that which is formally necessary. In other words, for high investment growth rates, the stock growth rate may approximate the investment growth rate well before n years are out.

A development similar to that just described may be seen in Chart 8–5 in the postwar period. Investment declined as a result of the war, growing rapidly again from a low level in 1943. At first, therefore, the growth of the stock is much slower than that of investment, accelerating, however, as the stock-investment ratio declines. By 1950, apparently, the stock-investment ratio approaches what would be an equilibrium level for the post-1950 investment trend, and henceforth the stock and investment grow at almost the same rate.[42] The last stages of a similar development which occurred at the beginning of the period studied are also visible in Chart

---

[42] That is, the stock grows almost 1 percent per year less rapidly than the investment trend, as noted earlier. The difference in rates may be explained in part by the age structure of the older assets in the stock. Another significant factor is no doubt the continuing shift toward assets with shorter service lives. As will be explained shortly, an

8–5. The growth of the net stock accelerates during 1928–30, as actual investment rises to and surpasses the level indicated by the 1928–40 trend line. Although we have made no estimates for the years before 1928, official data (in 1926/27 prices) indicate for those years lower levels of investment (relative to the trend) and slower rates of growth in the net stock than are shown for 1928–30 in Chart 8–5.[43] For the prewar years which are included in the chart, it can be seen that the growth of the net stock accelerates in periods during which actual investment exceeds the trend, decelerating in the contrary case.

A further aspect of equations (17)–(20), which is of particular relevance to the present study, is that they apply to stocks generated under any depreciation method in which the present value of an asset, relative to original cost, is strictly a function of the asset's age, i.e., they apply to all the depreciation methods employed in the alternative calculations of Chapter 2. Thus, when the growth of one such stock approaches the investment growth rate, all may be expected more or less to follow suit. Chart 8–5 shows that the growth of the net (straight-line depreciated) stock tended during 1928–40 and 1950–61 to parallel the growth of gross investment. If, as argued, this is explained largely by the high growth rate of the investment stream, a similar parallelism should appear in the growth of stocks computed under alternative depreciation methods. In fact, as noted in Chapter 2, the alternative stock calculations do show similar rates and patterns of growth. It is suggested, then, that this is not merely coincidental but is in large part a result of the high and relatively consistent investment growth trends.

From Chart 8–5, the stock-investment ratio appears on average to be lower during 1950–61 than in the 1928–40 period. The main reason for this, no doubt, is the larger proportion of relatively short-lived assets in the postwar stock. For example, the share of equipment in total fixed assets was 18 percent at the beginning of 1935 as opposed to 30 percent at the beginning of 1955 (see Table T–1). Shorter-lived assets result in higher depreciation charges, requiring therefore a larger flow of gross investment to generate a stock of given size. This means also that an investment stream of given growth rate, in which, however, there is a continuing rise in the proportion of shorter-lived assets, will generate a stock which grows less rapidly than investment.[44] Another factor which may explain the lower

---

increase over time in the relative importance of such assets causes the growth of the stock to be slower than the growth of investment. If the stocks and least squares investment trends for structures and equipment are compared separately for 1950–61, the annual net stock growth rates are 0.7 and 0.6 percent respectively below the corresponding investment trends. This difference must be mainly ascribable to asset age structure, most of the remaining 0.3–0.4 percent to the shift in relative importance of short-lived assets.

43 See Gosplan–30, pp. 452–53.

44 The same compositional shift, it should be recalled, will cause the rate of growth of (gross) capital services to exceed that of the capital stock. For depreciation methods such as straight-line, where the rate of depreciation is independent of the interest rate, the growth rate of services may exceed or fall short of the growth rate of investment, depending upon the rate of interest. With a rise in the proportion of shorter-lived assets, annual depreciation rises more rapidly than annual investment; depreciation is the whole of capital services at a zero interest rate. As the interest rate approaches infinity,

postwar ratio is the difference in investment growth rates. The rate appears to be somewhat higher in 1950–61 than in 1928–40. As may be seen from equation (20), the stock-investment ratio is a decreasing function of g, the rate of growth of investment.

Although both of these factors operate in the same direction on the investment-stock ratio, they are offsetting in their effect on the share of net investment in gross. The increased proportion of short-lived assets tends to increase depreciation—decrease net investment—relative to gross investment, but the acceleration in the investment growth rate tends to decrease the relative importance of depreciation—increasing that of net investment.[45] Thus in spite of the sizable increase in the share of shorter-lived assets in the stock between the prewar and postwar periods, the share of net in gross investment falls only slightly, from an average of 70 percent in 1928–40 to 69 percent in 1950–61.[46]

If the 1950–61 investment trend were to continue in the future, some slight acceleration in the growth of the stock would occur, as the age structure of existing assets conformed more closely to that of a stock generated by an investment stream of consistent growth rate. As long as the continuing increase in the relative importance of equipment persists, however, the stock must grow somewhat more slowly than investment.[47] This means, too, that a decline in future investment growth rates would in some small part be offset by the tendency of the stock's rate to rise, relative to investment's. A large decline in the investment growth rate would, nonetheless, produce a decline in the stock growth rate. The latter, however, changes more slowly than the former, so that, for example, even a sharp, discrete, decline in the investment growth rate would produce only a gradual decline in the growth of the stock. Any decline in the investment growth rate would decrease the share of net investment in gross, which tendency would be reinforced by a continuation of the trend toward investment in shorter-lived assets.

---

the growth rate of services approaches that of the capital stock, which is less than that of investment. Services from the fixed capital stocks shown in Chart 8–5, excluding assets from territorial expansion for the prewar period, increased at rates of 9.5 or 9.9 percent from 1928 to 1940, at interest rates of 20 percent and 8 percent respectively, and at 10.7 percent or 10.9 percent from 1950 to 1961 (the service figures are calculated as in Tables T–38 and T–39). Thus, both of these interest rates are high enough that services grow less rapidly than investment (measured from the trend line) though more rapidly than the stock.

[45] Other things the same, a decline in the stock-gross investment ratio will lead to a decline in the depreciation-gross investment ratio. This may also be put in terms of the symbols used in equations (17)–(20). If D_t, depreciation in the year t, is defined as gross investment less net investment, i.e., as $I_0(1 + g)^t - (S_t - S_{t-1})$, then from equation (17) it can be shown that:

$$\frac{D_t}{I_0(1 + g)^t} = 1 - \frac{g}{(1 + g)} \sum_{0}^{n-1} \frac{r_i}{(1 + g)^i}. \tag{21}$$

The right side of the equation is a decreasing function of g, the investment growth rate, as is, therefore, $D_t/I_0(1 + g)^t$, the ratio of depreciation to investment.

[46] See Table T–44.

[47] During 1956–60, in which housing construction was especially emphasized, investment in structures grew as rapidly as investment in equipment (see Table A–2). If, as however seems unlikely, these new proportions should be maintained, the consideration just expressed would not apply.

We remarked earlier that as the net (straight-line depreciated) stock approaches the investment growth rate, stocks computed under other depreciation methods should do the same. Thus, the ratio between the gross and net values of the stock becomes stabilized. From the relationships considered in Chapter 3 (Section 8), it can be seen that the average age of assets in the stock would also become constant. The relative closeness of the net stock and investment growth rates in the late postwar period, therefore, suggests that even if the 1950–61 investment trend is continued, the average age of each kind of asset in the stock will not decline very much further. The equilibrium average ages corresponding to the 1950–61 least squares investment trends taken separately for equipment and structures are, respectively, 5.8 and 9.8 years. As is shown in Table T–22, by the end of 1961, the actual average age of equipment had declined to 6.0 years. Hence, little further reduction is to be expected unless the rate of investment accelerates. For structures, the actual average age at the end of 1961 was 12.8 years. The service life for structures is 57 years, whereas the 1950–61 investment trend has prevailed for only 11 years. Even if investment continues indefinitely to grow at the trend rate, it would require 46 years for the average age of structures to decline by 3 more years, to the equilibrium level. Although no marked deceleration in the rate of decline in the age of structures has yet appeared, such is apparently to be expected —again, provided no acceleration in the growth of investment occurs. Conversely, of course, a significant decline in the investment growth rate could produce an upward tendency in the average ages of both equipment and structures.[48]

The projection in Chart 8–5 of the prewar investment trend into the postwar period is not meant to represent an estimate of what the course of investment would have been in the absence of war but to make clearer the nature of the loss in capital which the war, in all its consequences, entailed. The loss was not only that of direct destruction and of curtailed investment during the war but of a reduction in the economy's capacity to produce output, and hence to allocate output to investment, over some long—probably indefinitely long—period after the war. Thus, had it been possible to maintain the investment growth rate indicated by the prewar trend, the absolute volume of investment realized in each of the post-1950 years would have been attained 6–7 years earlier or, alternatively, it would have exceeded actual investment in each year by some 80 percent. From what has been said above, it follows that the same would have been true of the absolute value of the net capital stock. This too would have exceeded its actual values by something on the order of 80 percent, which difference amounts by 1962 to roughly 1,000 billion (1937) rubles. To put the point negatively, it is not the case that the value of the fixed capital stock, having by 1950 regained its prewar level, was thereafter unaffected by the impact of the war.

One final point emerges from the foregoing considerations. Discussions of the relation of investment to growth frequently run in terms of the

---

48 For the stock of all fixed assets, however, the average age might decline even though stability or increases in the age of each kind of assets occurred, because of a continued increase in the relative importance of equipment.

level of the investment share, of the ratio of investment to output. If the investment share remains constant over time, whether at a high or a low level, the rate of growth of investment necessarily equals the rate of growth of output. Since the growth rate of the capital stock tends toward equality with the growth rate of investment (disregarding changes in the service-life distribution of investment), the ratio of capital to output tends toward constancy.

As we have seen, it is not easy to characterize the level of the Soviet investment share (the reference now is to investment in all kinds of capital), but the trend of the share appears clearly upward. A rising investment share implies a growth rate of investment and, in due course, of the capital stock higher than that of output, and, hence, a rising capital-output ratio. Such a result appears in our estimates (see Chart 9–3 below), though the relations are complicated by the sizable fluctuations in output and in the investment share and by the extraordinary wartime losses from the stock.

The investment share cannot, of course, continue to rise (significantly) forever, and the relation between capital and output which appears characteristic of past Soviet growth cannot, therefore, be sustained into the indefinite future. Before investment absorbs the whole of output, the investment share must cease to rise and the capital-output ratio must do the same. Taken alone, however, this ultimate limitation appears not consequential for the shorter-run prospects of the Soviet economy (see p. 310 below).

Chapter 9

Aggregate Inputs and

Aggregate Productivity

We return now to the line of argument commenced in Chapter 1 (Section 1), in which we proposed to analyze the growth of Soviet output in terms of the increase in total inputs and changes in their productivity over time—a procedure which, in its broad features, is entirely conventional. The principal function of the present chapter is to bring together the necessary input data, combine them into indexes of aggregate inputs, and present the indexes of aggregate productivity which the input series imply when compared with measured output. We do, however, make one digression, to consider several partial relations between inputs and between particular inputs and output.

Beyond the statistical series assembled to this point, we require measures of inputs other than capital, to which we turn first. With respect to these, our earlier warning of the unreliability of our subsidiary estimates should be recalled.

1. INPUTS OTHER THAN CAPITAL

For labor inputs, we present in Table T–51 two alternative sets of series, for employment in the total economy and in the agricultural and non-agricultural subsectors.[1] Since housing is unlikely to absorb a significant amount of labor, we take these same series to represent labor inputs in the sectors exclusive of housing. The series measure average annual employment in man-years. In one set, which we refer to as unadjusted for changes in hours, civilian nonagricultural employment is measured in years of the length, in hours worked, prevailing in each given year in those sectors. Employment in agriculture, for which the original data are in man-days, is measured in years of the number of *days* prevailing in the nonagricultural sectors, but no allowance is made for differences in hours worked per day in the two sectoral categories. Numbers in the armed forces are included without adjustment for differences from the civilian nonagricultural sectors in either days per year or hours per day. The second set

---

[1] The derivation of the employment estimates is described in detail in Appendix Q.

of employment series, referred to somewhat inaccurately as adjusted for changes in hours, measures civilian nonagricultural employment in years of the number of hours per year worked in 1937, agricultural employment in years of the number of *days* worked per year in the nonagricultural sectors in 1937, and the armed forces again in numbers of men. The adjusted series, which we shall treat as our primary estimates hereafter, are also graphed in Chart 9–1.

The labor estimates derive largely from the research of Warren Eason, Nancy Nimitz, and Abram Bergson. It is in no way to the discredit of their work, but rather a commentary on the inadequacies of Soviet employment statistics, that the reliability of the estimates is open to serious question at a number of points.

CHART 9–1

**Employment, Total and by Sector, Adjusted for Changes
in Hours, 1928–61
(Million 1937 Man-Years)**

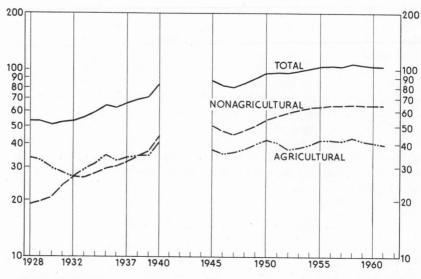

Source: Table T–51.

The labor series are thought to have some minor omissions, but in general they are quite comprehensive. They do, however, exclude penal labor. This exclusion is unavoidable because of the lack of data on the number of such laborers,[2] but it appears justified also by the fact that

---

[2] The nearest to a firm figure on the number of penal laborers is one of 3.5 million derived by Naum Jasny (Jasny–51a, p. 416) from the 1941 Plan. Jasny obtains the number, however, by assuming a productivity of penal relative to free labor. Since we are interested here in establishing the productivity of inputs, his estimate, which looks plausible on its face, is obviously inappropriate for our use. Bergson (Bergson–61, p. 443), proceeding from Jasny's 1941 Plan figure and from general historical knowledge, estimates totals of 3.0 million in 1937, 3.5 in 1950, and 2.0 in 1955, but the dependence of these figures on Jasny's makes them also inappropriate for our use. On the evidence on the number of penal laborers, see Bergson–61, p. 447, and Jasny–51a, *passim.*

our input series are intended to measure employed resources rather than
total resources available. It is our impression that the motivation for the
system of labor camps and related institutions, which grew to large significance under Stalin, was not primarily economic, and the product attributable to the labor involved was essentially incidental. The fragmentary data available (from the 1941 Plan) suggest that the product—the
measurable economic product—was small.[3] In any case, it is not a denial
of the importance of penal labor in Soviet history to treat it, as is done
here, as labor withdrawn from productive employment. It should be kept
in mind, however, that whatever output penal labor did yield is attributed
in subsequent calculations to other inputs. The productivity of the latter
is, therefore, somewhat overstated, presumably in larger proportion between the late 1930's and the mid-1950's than in other periods.[4]

Over the entire period from 1928 to 1961, employment adjusted for
hours increased at an average annual rate of 2.1 percent, as against a
growth rate of total population of about 1.1 percent.[5] Both employment
and population were affected by extraordinary losses, occasioned by the
famine of 1932–33 and by World War II, and by extraordinary gains from
the territorial acquisitions of 1939–40. The more rapid growth of employment than of population is attributable in part to the absorption of the
urban unemployed and rural underemployed which existed in 1928 and
to the increased participation of women in the labor force. Both the maintenance of something close to full employment, evidently from the early
1930's, and the extensive use of women in hired employments are distinctive features of Soviet labor policy. The statistical bias resulting from increased female participation, given the exclusion of housewives' services
from measured output, is familiar. The rate of increase in total employment was more rapid prewar (4.0 percent for 1928–40—but 2.8 percent
for 1928–39) than postwar (1.0 percent for 1945–61). Since the mid-1950's,
the total (adjusted for hours changes) has remained virtually constant.[6]

Employment in nonagricultural sectors has grown faster than in the
total in all long periods (3.8 percent per year in 1928–61, 7.2 percent in
1928–40, 1.5 percent in 1945–61). A large part of the relative gain occurred
from 1928 to 1932, reflecting again the structural changes of that period.
Labor in these sectors also has shown little change since the mid-1950's.
Labor in agriculture, which appears to have been more or less stabilized
since the mid-1930's, still accounted in 1961 for 38 percent of the total as
measured.

The principal change in hours which affects the series for nonagricultural labor is a sharp increase in the length of the normal working day
made in mid-1940 and remaining in force until 1956. Since 1956, hours
have been substantially reduced, with the consequence that nonagricul-

---

3 Jasny–51a, pp. 409 and 410, estimates that in the 1941 Plan the NKVD was to
account for 17 percent of construction and 1.2 percent of industrial production.

4 To judge from the estimates of penal labor cited in fn. 2, p. 246, the inclusion of
penal labor in productive inputs would not much alter our calculations. The numbers
of such laborers, relative to total employment as we estimate it (unadjusted for hours
changes) is 4.5 percent in 1937, 4.4 percent in 1940, 4.1 percent in 1950, and 2.1 percent
in 1955. These shares would be still smaller in aggregate inputs.

5 Population was 149.9 million on January 1, 1928 (Eason–63, p. 72), and 219.7 million
on January 1, 1962 (TsSU–62a, p. 8).

6 For a full discussion of factors affecting the labor force, see Eason–63.

tural employment adjusted for hours increases from 1955 to 1961 by only 2 percent over the entire period, whereas employment without the adjustment increases by 22 percent. The assumption that changes in hours represent an equivalent change in labor inputs is arguable. As will appear subsequently, the adjustment for hours affects significantly the apparent performance of the economy over the recent past.

Besides the changes in the quantity of man-years worked, it is unquestionably true that large changes in the quality of labor have occurred. In part, these are changes produced by formal education. Nicholas DeWitt has estimated that the educational "capital" associated with gainfully employed persons—the cumulated total of both direct outlays for education and incomes foregone—in 1937 prices rose from 24 billion rubles in 1926 to 113 in 1939 (expanded territory), 190 in 1950, and 327 in 1959.[7] This implies a much more rapid rise in educational capital than in man-years of labor, with the difference particularly great in the prewar years. It implies also a more rapid rise to 1950 in educational capital than in the material capital covered by our estimates, although a less rapid rise from 1950 to 1959. Educational capital apparently amounted to some 25 percent of material capital in 1950, 20 percent in 1959.[8] In addition, the quality of the labor force has undoubtedly been improved by the acquisition of skills and discipline through experience. We would not claim even an impressionistic notion of the magnitude of this gain, but it could have been large relative to that obtained through formal training.

We are unable to make adjustments for changes in the quality of labor within the agricultural and nonagricultural sectors taken separately. We do hereafter make an adjustment, in effect, for changes in the quality of labor in total by treating agricultural and nonagricultural labor as different inputs and weighting the two in proportion to their—highly unequal—earnings in the weight years. This procedure, with 1937 weights, increases the rate of growth of total labor inputs (adjusted for hours) over the entire period from 2.1 percent per year to 2.7 percent (the effect is virtually identical with 1928 or 1950 weights).

It is reasonably certain that agricultural (peasant) labor in the Soviet Union has generally been distinctly less skilled and well disciplined than labor in the nonagricultural sectors. Moreover, there is one respect in which the two categories are palpably different: in their location. By and large, although not entirely, agricultural employments are rural and nonagricultural urban. For this reason if no other, rural labor cannot be substituted for urban labor in the production of any given product and output be left unchanged. While this difference would be of no economic significance if one kind of labor could be converted into the other without cost, the costs of converting rural into urban labor had by 1937 probably become large. Training costs aside, the shortage of housing and other urban facilities was severe, and the costs of remedying it evidently more than the authorities were willing to incur.

---

[7] DeWitt–62, p. 144. We are indebted to the author for permission to cite these findings prior to publication.

[8] The percentages are calculated with our gross estimates since DeWitt's estimates are undepreciated.

Although the matter is difficult to judge, it is not obvious that in 1937 there was a gross misallocation of labor between agriculture and other sectors or, at least, that the misallocation was of a grossly different order of magnitude from those occurring elsewhere in the economy. According to Bergson's estimates, "real" earnings in agriculture in 1937 were about equal to those in other sectors, the difference in nominal earnings (including income in kind) being approximately matched by differences in living costs.[9] This was probably an unusually favorable year for agricultural earnings, but in years close to 1937 agricultural labor showed little inclination to move voluntarily into nonagricultural employments. From the point of view of the laborers themselves, then, their distribution between the two sectors was evidently near equilibrium. From the point of view of the authorities, the distribution may have been less nearly optimal, but their controls over the economy had been extensive for a number of years prior to 1937, and they did not undertake large transfers of labor out of agriculture thereafter. This suggests that the real costs of labor in the two sectors, as perceived by the planners, were also more or less proportionate to productivities. While there are identifiable factors distorting money earnings from real costs, these affect the valuation of labor in both sectors, and the direction of the net distortion is not certain.[10]

That proportionality between earnings and productivity held precisely is undoubtedly not the case. On balance, however, it appears more nearly accurate to interpret the 1937 wage differential as a difference in productivities of labor of unequal quality than as purely a distortion in the pricing of a homogeneous input. For 1928 and 1950, although we also weight the two labor categories with wages, the procedure is considerably less defensible. In 1928 in particular, a substantial misallocation between agriculture and other sectors is virtually certain (see below).

Inasmuch as part of the qualitative difference between agricultural and nonagricultural labor is due to differences in education, the separate weighting of the two categories amounts to a partial allowance for changes in the educational level of the labor force as a whole. In all probability, this is less than a full allowance for the effects of investment in education (or qualitative changes in general), because the education of labor within each of the two categories presumably has improved. However, we can-

9 See Bergson–61, pp. 118 ff., for the calculation referred to and for a general discussion of the issue here under consideration. The differential examined by Bergson, 1,600 rubles per man-year for collective farmers as against 2,800 rubles for industrial wage earners, is not identical with the difference implied by our labor and wage-share estimates.

10 To the extent that differences in money earnings are associated with differences attributable to location in the valuation of farm products consumed by rural and urban dwellers, the earnings differential corresponds to a difference in real costs. In part, however, the difference in product prices reflects low compulsory delivery prices in rural areas as opposed to high retail prices, inclusive of turnover taxes, in urban areas, on which account the relative real costs of rural labor are understated by the money wage. On the other hand, urban workers were the recipients of the bulk of the "social wage" (state expenditures for health, education, etc.) and of the state subsidy to socialized housing, on which account the relative real costs of urban labor are understated by the money wage. (Imputed rents of rural houses are not a wage but a return on the capital of the owner-occupant.)

not be sure that the error in the series for total labor inputs is an understatement of its growth, because the wage differential may overstate the difference in productivities of the two kinds of labor in the weight years.

Among inputs of natural resources, we compile data only for the sown area, in hectares, of agricultural land (see Table T–52 or Chart 9–2). Land inputs so measured rise at 1.8 percent per annum over the 1928–61 period or by over 80 percent between the terminal years, which is to say that the cultivated area was quite considerably extended. The bulk of the increase comes discontinuously: in 1928–31, in 1940 with the territorial acquisitions, and, after a postwar drop and recovery, in 1954–56 with the "new lands" campaign of Stalin's successors. The series omits other agricultural land (fallow, pasture, etc.)[11] and is unadjusted for changes in quality. Calculations made by D. Gale Johnson suggest, however, that, at least with respect to grain yields, the expansion of territory has not greatly altered the average quality of sown land.[12]

CHART 9–2

Sown Land, 1928–61
(Million Hectares)

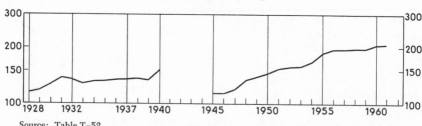

Source: Table T–52.

We are unable to estimate inputs of extractable natural resources, because suitable data for both physical quantities and weights are lacking: no charge is usually made for depletion in Soviet costing. The exploitation of such resources, principally minerals and timber, undoubtedly intensified over the period covered, and their omission may not be inconsequential.[13] We also omit site land, which is unlikely to be of great significance, and "weather," which is not easily treated as an economic input but in which variations from year to year are known to have large consequences for Soviet agriculture.

For component sectors, inputs include not only labor, capital, and land,

---

11 Cf. TsSU–60a, p. 126.

12 See Johnson–63, pp. 220–21.

13 The output of extractive industries included in our Table P–1 index of industrial production increases at an average annual rate of 7.8 percent between 1928 and 1961. The products included in the calculation are manganese ore, iron ore, coal, crude petroleum, peat, shale, firewood, and industrial timber; weights are 1950 wholesale prices. The high rate appears consistent with, but does not much strengthen, the supposition that inputs of extractable resources grew rapidly.

but purchases of the output of other sectors.[14] The principal such purchases between sectors which we distinguish are inputs of agricultural raw materials in the nonagricultural sectors and inputs in agriculture of industrial products, transportation services, etc. Of these two intersectoral flows, the first is evidently much the larger[15] and, given our lack of usable capital data for agriculture, the more relevant. If the assumption is made that inputs of agricultural raw materials in nonagricultural sectors vary as a constant proportion of the output of consumer goods industries, such inputs can be estimated to have risen by 4.5 percent per annum from 1928 to 1961, 5.1 percent from 1928 to 1940, and 11.7 percent from 1945 to 1961.[16] The long-term rate compares with a growth rate of agricultural production of 2.2 percent and of total industrial production of 7.5 percent. These differences reflect, on the one hand, the increasing share of output extracted by the regime from agriculture for use in the nonagricultural sectors and, on the other, the slow growth of industrial consumption of agricultural raw materials relative to total industrial output. The latter should be viewed in conjunction with the presumably rapid increase of mineral raw materials, the bulk of which went to industry.

2. SOME PARTIAL RELATIONS

A digression may be appropriate at this point. The separate input series described thus far permit comparisons of particular inputs with output and of one input with another. While the procedures employed here do not focus upon such partial relations, they may, nevertheless, be of significance or interest, and, in any case, their examination may make more comprehensible the statistical series with which we are dealing. With this in mind, we present in Charts 9–3, 9–4, 9–5, and 9–6 data in 1937 prices, for ratios of capital to output, capital to labor, and output to labor. The input and output measures used are intended to be appropriate to the analytical frameworks in which such ratios usually appear, but the reader may prefer other variants. If so, the necessary data are generally available in the tabular section, as are series in 1928 and 1950 prices. We do not attempt to explain here the behavior of the various ratios; some of the discussion hereafter may be relevant thereto.

---

14 On the general analytical issue of the inclusion of purchases from other sectors in aggregate sectoral inputs, see Domar–61, pp. 714–17. The matter is considered also in Powell–63, pp. 151–53.

15 For the 1941 Plan, the flow from agriculture is estimated at 27.0 and to agriculture at 7.5 billion rubles in current prices (Kaplan–52, p. 7); much of the 7.5 billion represents petroleum products, on which the turnover tax is high. In the official interindustry flow estimates for 1959 at "prices of final consumption," the flow from agriculture is 210 and to agriculture 85 billion rubles (TsSU–61, pp. 104 ff.).

16 For a defense of this estimating procedure, primarily on the grounds that the resulting series moves roughly with agricultural procurements, see Powell–63, pp. 166–68 and 198–200. Adjustments are not made here, as they are in Powell–63, for agricultural raw materials absorbed in increases in goods in process and for a possible understatement of consumer goods production in 1928. No allowance is made either for agricultural products going directly to nonagricultural sectors other than industry, principally to trade. The figures cited are derived from detailed data underlying Table P–1.

The average capital-output ratio, computed as the ratio of the net capital stock to GNP in 1937 prices (see Chart 9–3 or the corresponding numerical series in Table T–53) rises, irregularly, from 1.68 in 1928 to 2.35 in 1961 or by 40 percent over the entire period.[17] This appears a substantial but not spectacular increase. The capital-output ratio in nonagricultural sectors behaves broadly like that of the total, although the increase over the 33-year period is less, 22 percent. The exclusion of housing, on the other hand, makes a large difference: the increase is 75 percent for nonresidential sectors and 92 percent for nonagricultural and nonresidential sectors, with a large portion of the rise occurring in the prewar years. The extremely high ratio for housing reflects, in addition to the usual factors making for a high capital intensity in this sector, the low level of official rents in the Soviet Union. The variations in the ratio result largely from changes in the ratio of net to gross values of housing, where income originating in the sector is derived from gross values.

CHART 9–3

**Average Capital-Output Ratio, Total and by Sector,
in 1937 Prices, 1928–61**

(Net Capital Stock/Gross National Product)

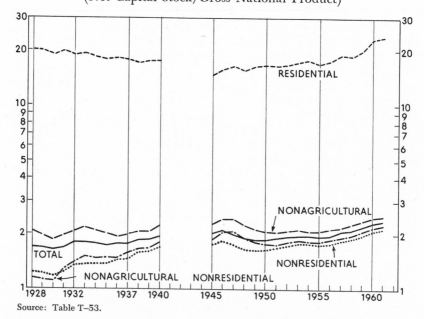

Source: Table T–53.

---

[17] The capital figures are averages of year-end values. For 1939, the figure for January 1, 1940, is taken exclusive of assets in the new territories.

As a possible point of reference, we note that in the United States, in 1958 and in current prices, the ratio of net capital stock, of coverage comparable to ours, to GNP was 2.59 (for the capital figure, see Goldsmith–62, Tables A–5, A–39, and B–175, and, in the present study, p. 182, fn. 64; for GNP, see U.S. Department of Commerce–61, p. 2). On the Soviet capital-output ratio in current prices, however, see p. 253 below. The Soviet ratio of *gross* capital stock to GNP, in 1937 prices, rises from 2.10 in 1928 to 2.97 in 1961 (see Tables T–1, T–25, and T–47).

As is implied by the variability of the average capital-output ratios, the incremental ratios are extremely erratic (for annual figures, see Table T–54). To make their pattern of change more visible, we show in Chart 9–4 incremental ratios for overlapping three-year intervals, with the calculated ratio attributed to the middle year. Despite the smoothing, the ratios vary widely over short periods, and any simple characterization of them is necessarily arbitrary. They might reasonably (having in mind discussions which follow) be interpreted, however, as indicating for the total economy a marked increase within the prewar period, from roughly 1.5 in the years centered on 1930 to about 3.0 by the late 1930's, and a retracing of rather the same path in the postwar period but to a higher terminal value, from close to 1.5 in the late 1940's to about 3.5 by 1958–60. The incremental ratios for each of the two periods as a whole are not greatly different, 2.2 for 1928–40 and 2.5 for 1945–61 (calculating from annual data). Changes in the component sectors are generally similar to those in the total.

The question has sometimes been argued whether in the early stages of development the incremental capital-output ratio is likely to be large or small in comparison with that of developed economies.[18] The answer suggested by Soviet experience depends in part on what segment, if any, of the period covered by our estimates can be regarded as corresponding to the early stages of development. If we take the interval 1928–37, over which the economy was transformed from a relatively unindustrialized to a substantially industrialized state, the incremental ratio in 1937 prices, 1.8, is fairly clearly small. If the same computation is made in 1928 prices, the ratio is 2.5, which by comparative standards probably is not notably small.[19] The effect of price weights can be illustrated similarly with the averages: the average capital-output ratio in current prices was much higher in 1928 (2.7) than in either 1937 (1.7) or 1950 (1.9). The apparent implication is that international comparisons of capital-output ratios, and a priori arguments about them, may be rather empty unless differences in price structures are taken into account.

Ratios of net capital stock, in 1937 prices, to employment, adjusted for hours but with no allowance for rural-urban quality differences, are shown in Table T–55 and Chart 9–5.[20] By 1961, the capital-labor ratio was 3.8 times its 1928 level in the economy as a whole, 3.0 in the nonagricultural sectors, 4.8 in the nonresidential sectors, and 4.9 in the nonagricultural nonresidential sectors. Manifestly, capital available per unit of labor has been raised enormously. The most remarkable increase occurs in the latest years covered, the capital-labor ratio doubling between 1953 and 1961 in the total economy and in the subsectors.[21] No similar increase occurs within

---

18 Cf., for example, Rosenstein-Rodan–54.

19 For fixed capital alone, the incremental ratio of net capital to GNP is 1.6 in 1937 prices, 2.0 in 1928 prices. With fixed capital taken gross, the ratios are 2.1 and 2.6 respectively, which may be compared with estimates for the Soviet Union made, from limited data, in Eckstein–56. With total capital taken gross, the ratios are 2.3 and 3.1 respectively; with net capital and NNP, the ratios are 1.9 and 2.8. For incremental capital-output ratios in other countries, see Kuznets–63, p. 354.

20 Capital figures are obtained as for the capital-output ratios.

21 With labor unadjusted for hours changes, the doubling occurs between 1950 or 1951 and 1961.

CHART 9–4

Incremental Capital-Output Ratio for Overlapping Three-Year Intervals, Total and by Sector, in 1937 Prices, 1930–60
(Net Capital Stock/Gross National Product)

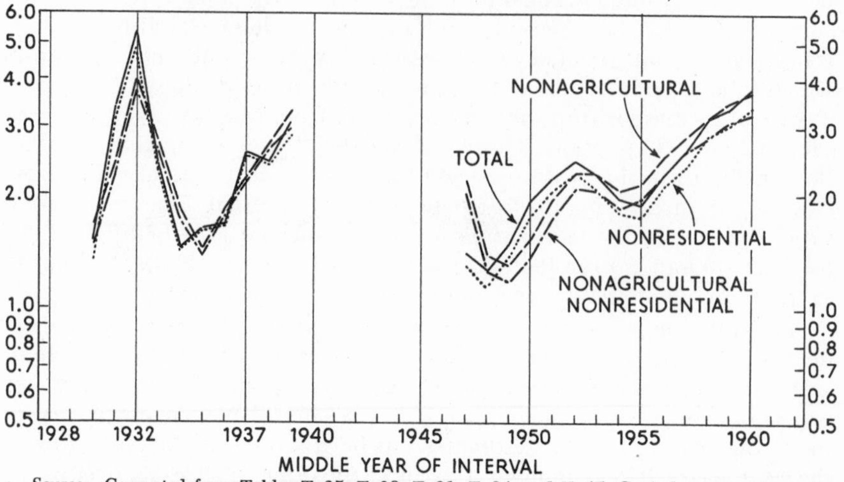

MIDDLE YEAR OF INTERVAL

Source: Computed from Tables T–25, T–28, T–31, T–34, and T–47. Capital increments are for average annual stocks, which are computed from January 1 data.

the prewar period, except for a near-doubling in the nonagricultural nonresidential sectors between 1928 and 1939.

For the nonagricultural sectors, the behavior of the capital-labor ratio in the early years covered resembles broadly that indicated by a model proposed by John Fei and Gustav Ranis.[22] In a developing economy, starting with redundant labor in agriculture, the capital-labor ratio in the nonagricultural sectors will tend to remain constant or to fall, so long as the labor redundancy in agriculture persists: strictly, the ratio will remain constant in the absence of innovation and economies of scale; it will fall unless innovations are very laborsaving. The model does not specify the prices in which capital is measured. The volume of surplus labor in Soviet agriculture in 1928 was, almost certainly, large (see below). Between 1928 and 1932, capital in the nonagricultural sectors increased by 42 percent in 1937 prices and by 62 percent in 1928 prices. Labor in the same sectors increased by 46 percent, presumably in large part because of transfers from agriculture.[23] The nonagricultural capital-labor ratio, hence, fell by 3 percent or rose by 11 percent depending upon the price weights used. It is not known that the redundancy of labor in agriculture was ended by 1932, although the rate of transfer evidently fell off sharply thereafter (cf. Chart 9–1), and the nonagricultural capital-labor ratio rose. The correspondence in detail of Soviet conditions to those posited by Fei and Ranis cannot be explored here.

Departing from capital altogether, we record in Chart 9–6 (and Table

---

[22] Fei–63.

[23] The figure is for labor without adjustments for changes in hours, as seems appropriate. Labor adjusted increased by 41 percent.

CHART 9–5

Capital-Labor Ratio, Total and by Sector, in 1937 Prices, 1928–61
(Thousand Rubles of Net Capital Stock per 1937 Man-Year)

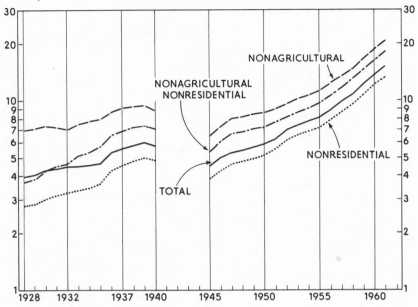

Source: Table T–55.

T–56) the series for labor productivity implied by our estimates of gross outputs, in 1937 prices, and of employment, adjusted for hours but not for rural-urban differences. Over the 33-year period, labor productivity in the economy as a whole increased to 2.7 times its initial level, in nonagricultural sectors to 2.4 times, and in agriculture—statistical errors aside— to 1.9 times.[24] The exclusion of housing from the output series raises the productivity increases slightly. The productivity gains are notably irregular in the prewar period, notably rapid in the last decade or so.

3. AGGREGATE INPUTS

Aggregation Procedures

Given the several component input series, we wish to establish how inputs in the aggregate have behaved over time, the components being weighted in proportion to their earnings in the weight years. Returns to labor we assume equal to those actually earned, including wage supplements and incomes in kind. For reasons explained previously (see pp. 248– 50), we treat labor in agriculture and in nonagricultural employments as separate inputs and allocate weights accordingly.[25] The system does not

24 With agricultural and nonagricultural labor weighted in proportion to their 1937 earnings, the productivity figure for the entire economy in 1962 is 2.2 times its 1928 level.

25 The absolute values for labor earnings in 1937 are 123.9 billion rubles for nonagri-

CHART 9–6

Labor Productivity, Total and by Sector, in 1937 Prices, 1928–61
(Thousand Rubles of Gross National Product per 1937 Man-Year)

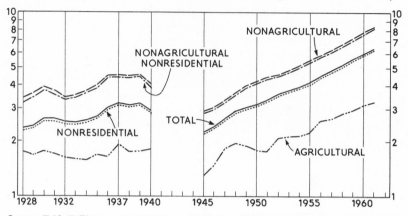

Source: Table T–56.

generate explicit (net) returns to material inputs, either capital, as we have previously considered, or land. For capital, we again take 8 percent and 20 percent as plausible bounding interest rates (see p. 170), in all three weight years. For the return on land, we follow Bergson in assuming, on the basis of U.S. data, that rent equaled 40 percent of labor earnings in agriculture[26]—in all three weight years. The extremely speculative character of these assumptions, and the essential arbitrariness of applying the same rates in all of the weight years, are self-evident.

The imputation of net returns to capital and land constitutes, unavoidably, a departure from the valuation principles which we have observed thus far, i.e., that the weight-year values of outputs are equal to "factor costs" in the sense of the sum of wage earnings, nominal profits, and depreciation. Consistency requires that nominal profits be deducted and interest and rent charges be added. But the matter is further complicated: capital is itself produced and its value determined in the same way as other outputs. The values of capital services, both interest charges and depreciation, are similarly determined. In order, therefore, to obtain consistent weight-year factor shares, we solve for that adjustment in the factor cost valuation of output which simultaneously satisfies the condition that output equal the sum of wages, rent, interest, and depreciation, and the condition that the gross rate of return on capital be unchanged by the revaluation. Since rent is estimated from an assumed relation to wages in agriculture, its value is taken to remain constant. Doubtless inaccurately, but for lack

---

cultural labor and 56.0 for agricultural; in 1928, 13.0 and 10.8 respectively; and in 1950, 422.5 and 138.4. Sources are Bergson–60, pp. 6 and 8, for 1937 and 1928; Hoeffding–59, pp. 4 and 6, for 1950. Total earnings are the sum of net income of households currently earned minus rental incomes plus social insurance payments. Agricultural earnings are those given as such.

[26] See Bergson–61, pp. 138–39, and Bergson–63, pp. 19–20. In an alternative calculation made below, we assume rent equal to 60 percent of labor earnings in agriculture.

of information, capital in all forms and in all sectors is assumed to be affected equiproportionately by the valuation change.[27]

This adjustment is not trivial. In 1937, it raises the value of output, and of capital and capital charges, by 16.6 percent at the 8 percent interest rate and 56.5 percent at 20 percent. The changes are similar for 1950, 11.3 and 54.5 percent respectively, but for 1928 they are extremely large, 31.8 and 142.2 percent, reflecting the high value of capital relative to output in the factor costs of that year.[28] The resulting capital shares in total inputs are 18.3 percent and 39.1 percent in 1937 at 8 and 20 percent interest rates respectively, 20.2 percent and 42.5 percent in 1950, and 28.0 percent and 60.8 percent in 1928. As is evident, the 20 percent interest rate implies capital shares in all years which are high—perhaps implausibly high—in comparison with those observed elsewhere.[29] Complete distributions of input shares are shown in Table T–57.

Given the weight-year values of the inputs, the choice remains of the manner in which the component input series are to be combined. As a rough allowance for the imperfect substitutability of inputs, we aggregate the three major components (labor, capital, and land) in the logs, i.e., on the assumption that the elasticities of substitution are unitary (as in a Cobb-Douglas). Within the major components, we aggregate the two categories of labor, like the several categories of capital, arithmetically. The assumptions in regard to substitutabilities are largely conventional, and, in the absence of information, more elaborate treatment of this element in the calculations is not justified. But, for reasons we shall explain below (see pp. 278–79), the resulting aggregative input indexes are highly defective for our analytical purpose.

To recapitulate, the estimates of aggregate inputs for the economy as a whole are the sum of agricultural labor in 1937 man-years, nonagricultural labor in 1937 man-years, capital services in weight-year prices, and hectares of sown land.[30] Weights are actual earnings of labor and assumed returns to capital and land, with the absolute value of capital returns

---

[27] Let:

$Y = $ GNP
$L = $ labor income
$R = $ land rent
$P = $ nominal profits and depreciation
$K = $ interest and depreciation charges

Symbols without primes represent valuations at factor cost, those with primes at recalculated valuations.

Then:

$$Y = L + P$$
$$Y' = L + R + K'$$
$$Y'/Y = K'/K, \text{ by assumption}$$
$$Y' = L + R + K\,(Y'/Y)$$
$$= (L + R)\frac{Y}{Y - K}.$$

[28] Our calculations of aggregate inputs differ significantly on this account from similar calculations made in Bergson–63, Johnson–63, and Powell–63. We consider below the effects of the revaluations on the GNP time series in 1937 prices.

[29] The capital shares cited are gross of depreciation. Shares of interest charges alone in Net National Product are approximately 3–4 percentage points lower.

[30] The several input series used are from Tables T–38 to T–43 for capital services, T–51 for employment, and T–52 for land.

adjusted for the effects of the assumed interest and rent charges on the value of output. Labor, capital, and land are summed logarithmically.

To obtain aggregate inputs by sector, we follow the same procedures as for the total economy, including aggregation in the logs. There is an obvious inconsistency between the assumption that inputs are substitutable in general along a logarithmic function, with coefficients equal to factor shares in the whole economy, and that they are substitutable within single sectors along the same kind of function, with coefficients equal to shares within those sectors. The procedure is, in fact, probably more defensible for the subsectors, within which the diversity of production processes is less than in the economy as a whole. The procedure is crude in any case and the effects of the inconsistency evidently small (see below).

The Findings

Indexes of aggregate inputs for the economy as a whole, with alternative prices and interest rates, are shown in Tables T–58 to T–63 and in Chart 9–7. In 1937 prices, inputs increase from 1928 to 1961 at an average annual rate of 3.4 percent with $r = 8\%$ and 4.2 percent with $r = 20\%$. The rates of increase from 1928 to 1940 (5.5 and 6.0 percent) are higher than those from 1945 to 1961 (2.9 and 4.4 percent), and retardation is apparent within the postwar period, although more clearly at the low interest rate than the high. Annual changes vary widely, especially in the prewar years. In 1950 prices, inputs parallel closely those in 1937 prices; in 1928 prices, they rise more rapidly, with a greater difference at the higher interest rate. The alternative weightings, it should be observed, are for quite broad categories of inputs except within the capital component. Weighting by more detailed categories, especially for labor, might produce significantly different results.

Series for aggregate inputs by sector, in alternative prices, are also shown in Tables T–58 to T–63. Those in 1937 prices are graphed in Chart 9–8. In 1937 prices, inputs in nonagricultural sectors increase over the 33-year period at 4.6–5.4 percent per annum, at $r = 8$ or 20%, as against the 3.4–4.2 percent for the economy as a whole. Inputs in nonresidential sectors increase at about the same rate as in the total, 3.4–4.3 percent, whereas inputs in housing (capital services only) increase at 3.1 percent with either interest rate; housing is considerably less laggardly when viewed against total inputs than against capital alone. The increase is most rapid in the nonagricultural nonresidential sectors, 4.8–5.8 percent, the relative gain being particularly large between 1928 and 1932.

The distribution of inputs among sectors cannot be read from the series aggregated in the logs and is shown instead, in 1937 prices, in Chart 9–9, with series obtained by arithmetic addition. Because of our procedure of weighting agricultural labor much less heavily than nonagricultural, the share of the nonagricultural sectors in total inputs is quite large in 1928, amounting to 52–54 percent at $r = 8\%$ or 20% respectively; by 1961, it is 76–80 percent. The imputation of interest to capital raises the share of housing (which is not shown separately but for which inputs correspond to capital services) disproportionately, but it remains only 4–10 percent of the total in 1928 and 4–6 percent of the total in 1961. The share of the

CHART 9–7

Aggregate Inputs in 1937, 1928, and 1950 Prices, 1928–61
(1937 = 100)

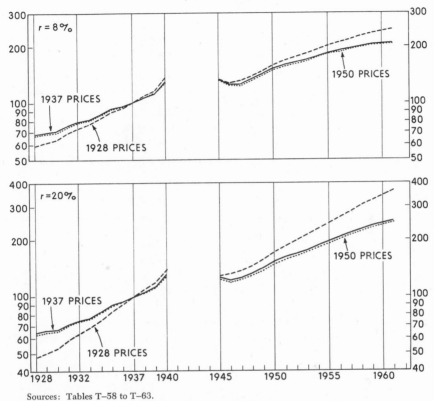

Sources: Tables T–58 to T–63.

nonagricultural nonresidential sectors increases from 48–45 percent to 73–73 percent over the 33-year period.

Alternative Calculations

The uncertainties which surround the aggregate input calculations are so numerous and so large that we cannot undertake to establish likely limits of error on all accounts. Certain elements, however, are sufficiently questionable on either statistical or analytical grounds, or differ sufficiently from procedures followed elsewhere, that it appears in order to examine the effects of altering some of the assumptions made. This is done, for selected years and in 1937 prices, in Table 9–1. The calculations are restricted to series for the total economy and for the nonagricultural nonresidential subsector, since series exclusive of housing parallel more or less closely those inclusive of housing.

Row 1 shows the series previously described.

Row 2: If labor is not adjusted for changes in hours, total inputs are considerably reduced from 1940 through to almost the end of the period.

TABLE 9-1

EFFECTS ON AGGREGATE INPUTS OF ALTERING ESTIMATING PROCEDURES, IN 1937 PRICES, SELECTED YEARS
(1937 = 100)

	1928	1932	1937	1940	1945	1947	1950	1953	1955	1958	1961
					All Sectors						
A. r = 8%											
1. Basic Estimates	68.5	79.4	100.0	130.0	131.4	125.6	151.4	168.5	182.7	198.3	207.0
2. Labor Unadjusted for Hours Changes	67.0	79.3	100.0	123.2	114.2	113.7	137.1	152.4	166.2	185.8	209.6
3. All Labor Assumed Homogeneous	74.1	78.7	100.0	127.3	125.0	120.6	144.8	156.7	171.0	185.5	191.8
4. Land Rent = 60% of Agricultural Wages	68.9	80.0	100.0	129.1	128.7	123.7	149.2	166.1	180.9	196.5	205.6
5. Inputs Aggregated Arithmetically	69.1	80.0	100.0	130.1	133.1	126.3	152.2	170.3	185.3	206.4	226.6
6. Inputs Aggregated by Sectors	68.0	78.9	100.0	130.2	132.7	126.1	152.0	169.1	182.8	198.2	206.9
7. Inputs Net of Depreciation	70.3	80.6	100.0	129.3	131.4	124.8	150.1	165.2	178.2	191.0	196.6
8. Inputs Excluding Labor in Service Sectors	70.6	80.7	100.0	127.4	116.7	120.9	145.6	160.8	176.2	196.0	206.4
B. r = 20%											
1. Basic Estimates	65.0	75.4	100.0	130.5	125.5	124.3	152.2	176.6	195.1	224.1	249.9
2. Labor Unadjusted for Hours Changes	63.9	75.3	100.0	125.4	113.0	115.5	141.4	163.9	181.7	213.6	252.2
3. All Labor Assumed Homogeneous	68.9	74.9	100.0	128.5	120.9	120.6	147.2	167.4	185.7	213.3	236.2
4. Land Rent = 60% of Agricultural Wages	65.3	75.8	100.0	129.8	123.5	122.9	150.6	174.8	193.7	222.7	248.9
5. Inputs Aggregated Arithmetically	65.7	76.1	100.0	130.6	127.1	124.9	152.8	178.6	198.2	235.4	279.3
6. Inputs Aggregated by Sectors	64.2	74.8	100.0	130.5	126.3	124.7	152.8	176.9	194.9	223.7	249.9
7. Inputs Net of Depreciation	66.5	76.4	100.0	129.9	125.2	123.6	151.1	173.7	190.9	217.1	239.6
8. Inputs Excluding Labor in Service Sectors	66.0	75.8	100.0	128.7	114.7	120.8	148.2	171.8	191.6	225.6	255.2

TABLE 9-1 (continued)

EFFECTS ON AGGREGATE INPUTS OF ALTERING ESTIMATING PROCEDURES, IN 1937 PRICES, SELECTED YEARS
(1937 = 100)

	1928	1932	1937	1940	1945	1947	1950	1953	1955	1958	1961
					Nonagricultural Nonresidential Sectors						
A. r = 8%											
1. Basic Estimates	52.3	76.7	100.0	138.2	153.3	143.1	173.2	200.3	213.2	231.1	244.2
2. Labor Unadjusted for Hours Changes . .	50.3	76.2	100.0	128.5	128.0	125.0	151.5	175.4	187.7	211.7	249.5
4. Land Rent = 60% of Agricultural Wages. .	52.0	76.4	100.0	138.3	153.0	143.2	173.4	200.7	213.9	232.4	246.3
5. Inputs Aggregated Arithmetically.	54.0	77.8	100.0	138.2	153.7	143.1	173.4	201.5	216.0	241.3	270.5
7. Inputs Net of Depreciation.	54.3	78.7	100.0	137.4	153.2	141.5	171.0	196.5	208.0	222.7	231.7
8. Inputs Excluding Labor in Service Sectors	51.5	78.0	100.0	135.8	131.4	139.4	168.8	195.8	211.0	238.2	257.1
9. Inputs Inclusive of Agricultural Raw Materials	54.1	74.3	100.0	131.3	116.1	121.2	156.9	190.4	207.9	231.5	248.6
B. r = 20%											
1. Basic Estimates	45.9	70.5	100.0	138.9	145.4	142.2	174.8	209.7	228.7	263.5	298.1
2. Labor Unadjusted for Hours Changes . .	44.6	70.2	100.0	131.6	127.1	128.5	158.1	189.9	208.0	246.7	302.9
4. Land Rent = 60% of Agricultural Wages. .	45.5	70.1	100.0	139.0	145.0	142.2	175.0	210.4	229.8	265.8	302.1
5. Inputs Aggregated Arithmetically.	48.2	72.1	100.0	138.9	146.3	142.2	174.9	211.3	232.6	278.4	337.9
7. Inputs Net of Depreciation.	47.5	72.1	100.0	138.1	145.1	140.6	172.6	206.2	223.8	255.3	285.2
8. Inputs Excluding Labor in Service Sectors	44.2	70.1	100.0	137.4	129.3	139.4	172.0	208.4	230.4	276.4	321.8
9. Inputs Inclusive of Agricultural Raw Materials	49.0	69.6	100.0	131.8	111.4	120.5	158.0	197.3	219.5	256.0	289.8

Source: See text.

CHART 9–8

Aggregate Inputs, Total and by Sector, in 1937 Prices, 1928–61
(1937 = 100)

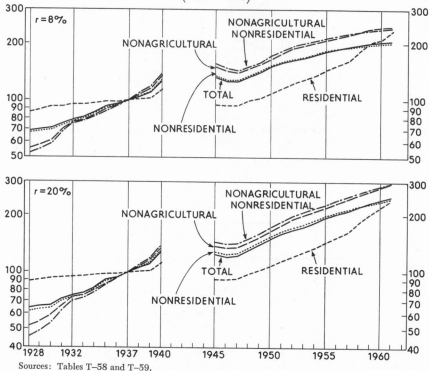

Sources: Tables T–58 and T–59.

The effect on the rate of increase between 1955 and 1961 is especially noteworthy: the rate for the entire economy is raised from 2.1–4.2 percent ($r = 8\%$ and 20%) to 3.9–5.6 percent; that for the subsector is similarly altered.

Row 3: If agricultural and nonagricultural labor are not weighted separately, the rate of increase in inputs in the total economy (the subsector is unaffected) over the 33-year period is considerably reduced: from 3.4–4.2 percent ($r = 8\%$ and 20%) to 2.9–3.8 percent. Much of the difference arises between 1928 and 1932.

Row 4: Since the assumption that land rent is equal to 40 percent of agricultural wages is questionable, we try the higher figure of 60 percent. The effects are slight for all of the series calculated.

Row 5: Arithmetic aggregation of the input series, which procedure has sometimes been used for similar calculations elsewhere, makes little difference in the series from 1928 until the early 1950's, but thereafter, essentially because of the disproportionately rapid increase of capital services relative to other inputs, it yields substantially higher growth rates for total inputs. For 1955–61, the rate in the total economy is increased from 2.1–4.2 percent to 3.4–5.9 percent; similar differences result for the subsector.

Row 6: With inputs aggregated logarithmically for both the total econ-

CHART 9–9

Distribution of Aggregate Inputs by Sector, in 1937 Prices, 1928–61
(1937 Total = 100)

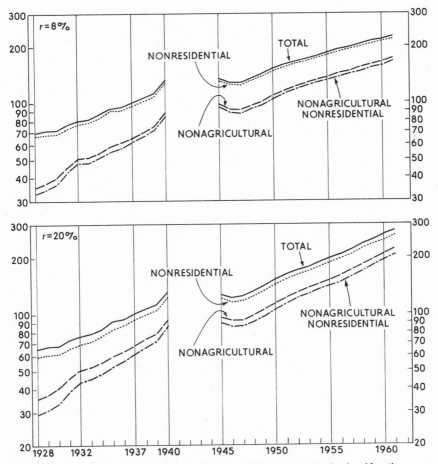

Sources: Data are the same as for Tables T–58 and T–59, but aggregation is arithmetic.

omy and the component sectors, the total does not equal the sum of the sectoral components. We can, however, obtain a total which equals the sum of the parts by adding arithmetically inputs in housing, agriculture (disregarding the unreliability of the capital estimates for agriculture), and the nonagricultural nonresidential sectors, with inputs in the first consisting solely of capital services and inputs within each of the latter two added logarithmically. The resulting series for the total economy differ little from the basic estimates.

Row 7: If, as is sometimes done, capital inputs are taken net of depreciation—i.e., capital inputs are assumed to vary over time with interest charges on the depreciated stock and the weight-year share is assumed equal to interest charges alone—the rates of increase of total inputs in the economy and in the subsector are reduced somewhat: by approximately 0.2 percentage points in all series over the entire period.

Row 8: Reference is made below to the productivity of aggregate inputs exclusive of labor in service sectors (including finance). The corresponding input series are those shown here. The procedure by which we deduct labor in these sectors is rough,[31] and, it should be noted, the resulting series are still inclusive of capital utilized in services.

Row 9: If in the nonagricultural nonresidential sectors we take inputs inclusive of agricultural raw materials and again aggregate the components in the logs, the rate of increase is considerably reduced in the prewar years, markedly increased in the postwar years, and reduced relatively little (more at $r = 20\%$ than $r = 8\%$) over the entire period.[32] While, over the long period, the growth of inputs of agricultural raw materials may have been low relative to that of total inputs in industry, it is not pronouncedly so relative to total inputs in the whole of the nonagricultural nonresidential sectors. The row 9 calculations, however, are not much more than illustrative. *Inter alia*, the assumption that agricultural raw materials are substitutable for other inputs along a logarithmic function in the subsector is not easily reconciled with the assumption that their quantity was a constant fraction of the output of consumer goods industries (see p. 251 above). On the other hand, the omission of mineral raw materials and timber from total inputs may produce a compensating error in the calculations.

4. THE PRODUCTIVITY OF AGGREGATE INPUTS

Imputed Returns and Measured Output

Our procedures for aggregating inputs, with assumed returns to capital and land, raise an immediate question of consistency with our estimates of the behavior of output over time. To what extent are the time series for output, composed with weights corresponding to "factor costs," likely to be altered if weights are adjusted to allow for imputed interest and rent charges? We are able to offer no more than an extremely tentative answer to this question, primarily because we lack a satisfactory weight-year distribution of fixed capital among sectors.

---

[31] Our indexes of output in services and finance are derived largely from employment in those sectors, unadjusted for changes in hours, and their 1937 weights are principally wages (see rows 6 and 7 of Table P–1 and accompanying notes). We therefore take total output in these sectors as a measure of total employment in them, adjust the series for hours changes, and deduct it from total nonagricultural employment with the 1937 value of the latter set equal to total nonagricultural wages. The reason for this procedure, which is not fully consistent with our treatment of employment elsewhere, is to take account of the employment imputed in row 7e of Table P–1 and in the absolute value assigned total services (row 7) in 1937.

[32] To obtain a 1937 value for agricultural raw materials, we begin with Bergson's estimate (Bergson–53, p. 105) that total agricultural marketings in 1937 amounted to 38.0 billion rubles at average realized prices gross of subsidies. This figure includes sales on the collective-farm market, which are excluded from the time series, but their share in physical quantities marketed was presumably limited. Since the value of agricultural output would, like capital, be affected by the imputation of interest and rent charges, we increase the 38.0 billion figure by the same factors as were estimated for total output and capital (see p. 257 above)—a procedure which is obviously very crude. The 1937 share of agricultural raw materials in total inputs in the subsector thus becomes about 23 percent. The valuation of these inputs differs from that followed in Powell–63, p. 200, both in the use of average realized, instead of procurement, prices and in the adjustment for the imputed charges.

If, in disregard of our previous assertions to the contrary, we accept as usable the fixed capital figure for agriculture implicit in our estimates, we can from our estimates distribute fixed capital, in 1937, among agriculture, housing, and all other sectors.[33] On the basis of published Soviet data, of which the valuation procedures and reliability in general are almost wholly unknown, we can distribute fixed capital in the nonagricultural and non-residential sectors among four components: industry and construction, transportation and communications, trade, and services including finance.[34] Given this six-sector distribution of fixed capital, corresponding distributions of other capital can be taken more or less directly from our estimates; interest charges at alternative rates can be obtained as in the calculations above of input shares. Wage distributions are provided in Bergson's studies.[35] Land rent, of alternative values, is assumed as before and charged entirely to agriculture. In this fashion, we reweight output series for the six sectors[36] with 1937 weights composed of wages, interest, and rent. Depreciation, also revalued for the effects of the assumed imputations, is added as in the factor cost calculation. The resulting estimates are compared in Table 9–2 with those at factor cost valuations in terms of growth rates for the 33-year period; the indicated differences arise fairly continuously over time.

The apparent effects of these revaluations are limited although not trivial. For sectors inclusive of agriculture, the growth rate is reduced, most markedly (by as much as 0.4 percentage points) with the lower interest rate in combination with the higher rent charge—which combination increases most the weight of agriculture. For all nonagricultural sectors, the growth rate is left unchanged at $r = 8\%$ and lowered (with a heavy weight for housing) by 0.2 points at $r = 20\%$. The rate in the nonagricultural non-residential sectors is raised, by 0.1 point at $r = 8\%$ and 0.2 points at $r = 20\%$. It is our impression, possibly mistaken, that the increase in the last sectors would be greater if more detailed component sectors, such as heavy and light industry, were distinguished. If so, the reduction for the total economy would be less.

On such evidence as we have, then, the output estimates at factor cost do not differ greatly from those that would be obtained with valuations adjusted for interest and rent charges. Because the evidence is poor, we cannot be sure that the apparent differences are close to the true ones, but, for the same reason, we can gain nothing in precision by substituting the alternative estimates for the factor cost calculations. We therefore use the latter, with the caveat that an accurate and detailed reweighting of outputs might disclose a significant error in the procedure.[37]

---

[33] The quality of the estimates described here is too low to merit their explanation in detail.

[34] The data referred to are taken from a processed appendix to Kaplan–53 and from Kobalevskii–40, p. 3.

[35] Wages in agricultural and nonagricultural sectors are those used in the input share computations. The distribution of nonagricultural wages is based on Bergson–53, p. 123.

[36] See Table P–1.

[37] Bergson makes a calculation (Bergson–61, pp. 138 ff.) of the effects on growth rates of assumed interest and rent charges with results similar to those described here. Although the two calculations differ in many particulars, they are alike in that they rely in some part upon official data for the distribution of fixed capital in 1937. Since this

TABLE 9-2

EFFECT ON ANNUAL GROWTH RATE OF GROSS NATIONAL PRODUCT OF
IMPUTING INTEREST AND RENT, IN 1937 PRICES, 1928-61
(Percent per Annum)

		Gross National Product		
Valuation	Total	Non-residential	Non-agricultural	Nonagricultural Nonresidential
Factor Cost	5.2	5.3	6.6	6.7
Interest Rate = 8%, Rent = 40% of Agri- cultural Wages	5.0	5.1	6.6	6.8
Interest Rate = 20%, Rent = 40% of Agri- cultural Wages	5.1	5.3	6.4	6.9
Interest Rate = 8%, Rent = 60% of Agri- cultural Wages	4.9	4.9	6.6	6.8
Interest Rate = 20%, Rent = 60% of Agri- cultural Wages	5.0	5.2	6.4	6.9

Source: See text.

We are unable to make similar calculations for gross products in 1928 or 1950 prices, and we have no grounds for assurance that these, and especially output in 1928 prices, would not be significantly affected by such reweightings.

The Findings

With output (gross product) taken at factor cost valuations and given the aggregate input series derived in the preceding section, the behavior over time of the ratio between the two—indexes of the productivity of aggregate inputs—are readily calculable.[38] Productivity indexes for the whole economy and for subsectors are shown in Tables T–64 to T–68. The calculations include ratios in which numerator and denominator are measured in prices of the same weight year: for 1928–40 and 1945–61 in 1937 prices, and for the selected years covered by the output estimates in 1928 and 1950 prices. Calculations are also made, comparing 1937 with each of the other weight years, in which outputs are weighted with prices from one year and inputs with prices from the other.[39] The annual series in 1937 prices are also graphed in Chart 9–10, along with the estimates in mixed 1937 and 1928 prices relating 1928 to 1937. The latter represent our extreme estimates for the 1928–37 interval.

Since we shall, in one way or another, be concerned with these calculations throughout the remainder of the study, little need be said here in characterization of them. Over the 33-year period from 1928 to 1961, the productivity of aggregate inputs in the whole economy, with both inputs

element is crucial to the calculations, the two cannot be regarded as independent or mutually corroborating.

[38] The necessary output data are given in Tables T–47 to T–49, the input data in Tables T–58 to T–63.

[39] On the logic of the several weight combinations, see Chapter 1, p. 5.

and output valued in 1937 prices, increases at 1.0–1.8 percent per annum ($r = 20\%$ or 8% in 1937). Over the period for which we can make estimates in 1950 prices, 1928–55, productivity in 1950 prices increases at 0.4–0.8 percent ($r = 20\%$ or 8% in 1950), as against 0.6–1.1 percent in 1937 prices, a difference which is not large in view of various peculiarities of the underlying statistics. Nor, for the interval from 1937 to 1950, does productivity with mixed 1937 and 1950 weights differ much from that measured in prices of either of the terminal years. For the 1928–37 interval, on the other hand, productivity with both inputs and output in 1928 prices rises at 3.1–5.6 percent ($r = 20\%$ or 8% in 1928),[40] as against 1.2–1.8 percent with both in 1937 prices. The use of mixed weights for this period, moreover, produces still more widely divergent results: 6.4–7.3 percent with output in 1928 and inputs in 1937 prices, and, with the weights reversed, a 2.2 percent per annum decline or 0.3 percent increase. Besides these features of the calculations, we shall hereafter regard as noteworthy also the short-run variability of productivity (as registered primarily in the 1937-price calculations) and the lack of any gain in productivity (in 1937 or 1950 prices) over the interval from 1936 or 1937 to the early 1950's.

Alternative Calculations (Total and Sectoral Productivities)

Alternative productivity estimates, calculated on assumptions corresponding to those made for aggregate inputs, are presented in Table 9–3. The greater part of these bear more or less directly on the relation of productivity in the economy as a whole to that in the component sectors for which we make estimates, and may usefully be examined at this point. The remainder, rows 2, 5, and 7, are discussed in the chapter following.

As may be seen from Chart 9–10, productivity (in 1937 prices) in the total economy has varied in a pattern quite similar to that in the non-agricultural sectors. This is explained partly by the large weight of the latter in the total. In addition, however, the productivity changes in agriculture implied by our estimates, while not statistically reliable, do nevertheless show considerable conformity in their broad fluctuations to those of the nonagricultural sectors.[41] The total series is not, so far as we can judge, an average of greatly disparate changes in agriculture and in all other sectors.

---

[40] It should be kept in mind here and in later discussions that the estimates in 1928 prices with an assumed interest rate in that year of 20 percent imply a capital share in total costs which may exceed the bounds of plausibility; see p. 257 above.

[41] The calculation, which is not shown because of its unreliability, implies a (much) lower level of agricultural productivity in 1932 than in 1928; a rise to a peak in 1937, which is not reattained in the subsequent three years; a very low level in 1945 followed by a rise to a maximum in 1961. The implied agricultural productivity differs from that in the nonagricultural sectors in that the decline is continuous from 1928 to 1932, the 1937 peak is much above the 1936 level, and the postwar upswing, which is irregular in general, is interrupted by a rough plateau from the late 1940's to the mid-1950's. The over-all growth in agricultural productivity is lower than that in other sectors. Something of the relation of productivity in agricultural and nonagricultural sectors can be judged also from the series for labor productivity alone (Chart 9–6 or Table T–56). The reference here, it should be repeated, is to the calculation in 1937 prices. With output valued in 1928 prices, the implied productivity in agriculture rises much less rapidly, from 1928 to 1937, than does productivity in other sectors. In 1928 prices, on the other hand, the weight of agriculture in the total is much less than in 1937 prices.

CHART 9–10

**Productivity of Aggregate Inputs, Total and by Sector,
Selected Series, 1928–61**

$(1937 = 100)$

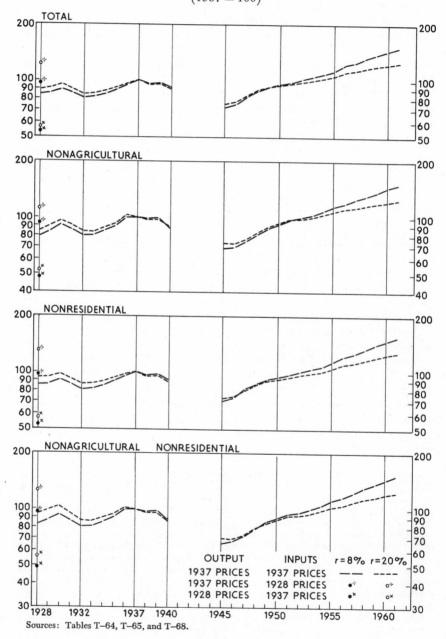

Sources: Tables T–64, T–65, and T–68.

TABLE 9-3

EFFECTS ON PRODUCTIVITY OF AGGREGATE INPUTS OF ALTERING ESTIMATING PROCEDURES, IN 1937 PRICES,
SELECTED YEARS
(1937 = 100)

	1928	1932	1937	1940	1945	1947	1950	1953	1955	1958	1961
					All Sectors						
A. r = 8%											
1. Basic Estimates	85.1	80.5	100.0	90.8	71.3	82.7	94.6	104.7	113.8	132.8	151.6
2. Labor Unadjusted for Hours Changes . . .	87.0	80.6	100.0	95.8	82.0	91.4	104.5	115.7	125.2	141.7	149.8
3. All Labor Assumed Homogeneous.	78.7	81.2	100.0	92.7	75.0	86.2	99.0	112.6	121.6	141.9	163.7
4. Land Rent = 60% of Agricultural Wages .	84.6	79.9	100.0	91.4	72.8	84.0	96.0	106.2	115.0	134.0	152.7
5. Inputs Aggregated Arithmetically.	84.4	79.9	100.0	90.7	70.4	82.3	94.2	103.6	112.3	127.6	138.5
6. Inputs Aggregated by Sectors.	85.7	81.0	100.0	90.6	70.6	82.4	94.3	104.3	113.8	132.8	151.7
7. Inputs and Output Net of Depreciation . .	84.4	79.8	100.0	90.3	70.1	81.8	94.4	104.7	114.3	133.8	153.1
8. Inputs Excluding Labor in Service Sectors and Output Excluding Services	84.4	77.6	100.0	90.5	67.9	81.9	96.8	109.7	120.9	142.1	161.7
B. r = 20%											
1. Basic Estimates	89.7	84.7	100.0	90.4	74.7	83.6	94.2	99.9	106.6	117.5	125.6
2. Labor Unadjusted for Hours Changes . . .	91.2	84.9	100.0	94.1	82.9	90.0	101.3	107.6	114.5	123.3	124.5
3. All Labor Assumed Homogeneous.	84.6	85.3	100.0	91.8	77.5	86.2	97.4	105.4	112.0	123.4	132.9
4. Land Rent = 60% of Agricultural Wages .	89.3	84.3	100.0	90.9	75.9	84.5	95.2	100.9	107.4	118.2	126.1
5. Inputs Aggregated Arithmetically.	88.7	84.0	100.0	90.4	73.7	83.2	93.8	98.8	104.9	111.9	112.4
6. Inputs Aggregated by Sectors.	90.8	85.4	100.0	90.4	74.2	83.3	93.8	99.7	106.7	117.7	125.6
7. Inputs and Output Net of Depreciation . .	89.2	84.2	100.0	89.9	73.6	82.6	93.8	99.6	106.7	117.7	125.6
8. Inputs Excluding Labor in Service Sectors and Output Excluding Services	90.3	82.6	100.0	89.6	69.0	82.0	95.1	102.7	111.2	123.4	130.8

TABLE 9-3 (continued)

EFFECTS ON PRODUCTIVITY OF AGGREGATE INPUTS OF ALTERING ESTIMATING PROCEDURES, IN 1937 PRICES,
SELECTED YEARS
(1937 = 100)

	1928	1932	1937	1940	1945	1947	1950	1953	1955	1958	1961
					Nonagricultural Nonresidential Sectors						
A. r = 8%											
1. Basic Estimates	82.2	80.8	100.0	87.5	66.5	72.7	90.2	100.2	111.9	130.1	151.4
2. Labor Unadjusted for Hours Changes	85.5	81.4	100.0	94.1	79.7	83.2	103.1	114.5	127.1	142.0	148.2
4. Land Rent = 60% of Agricultural Wages	82.7	81.2	100.0	87.4	66.7	72.6	90.1	100.0	111.5	129.4	150.1
5. Inputs Aggregated Arithmetically	79.6	79.7	100.0	87.5	66.4	72.7	90.1	99.7	110.4	124.6	136.7
7. Inputs and Output Net of Depreciation	80.8	79.8	100.0	86.9	65.2	71.4	89.7	100.2	112.3	131.2	152.7
8. Inputs Excluding Labor in Service Sectors and Output Excluding Services	78.1	76.0	100.0	86.5	61.5	68.9	92.7	106.5	121.5	141.8	163.4
9. Inputs and Outputs Inclusive of Agricultural Raw Materials	86.3	84.8	100.0	90.3	77.5	79.7	93.6	101.1	109.9	123.7	139.7
B. r = 20%											
1. Basic Estimates	93.7	87.9	100.0	87.0	70.2	73.1	89.4	95.8	104.3	114.1	124.0
2. Labor Unadjusted for Hours Changes	96.4	88.3	100.0	91.9	80.3	80.9	98.8	105.7	114.7	121.9	122.1
4. Land Rent = 60% of Agricultural Wages	94.5	88.4	100.0	87.0	70.3	73.1	89.3	95.4	103.8	113.1	122.4
5. Inputs Aggregated Arithmetically	89.2	86.0	100.0	87.0	69.7	73.1	89.3	95.0	102.5	108.0	109.4
7. Inputs and Output Net of Depreciation	92.4	87.1	100.0	86.5	68.8	71.8	88.9	95.4	104.4	114.4	124.1
8. Inputs Excluding Labor in Service Sectors and Output Excluding Services	91.0	84.6	100.0	85.4	62.5	68.9	91.0	100.0	111.3	122.2	130.5
9. Inputs and Outputs Inclusive of Agricultural Raw Materials	95.3	90.5	100.0	90.0	80.8	80.2	93.0	97.5	104.1	111.9	119.9

Source: See text.

The relation between these two sectoral categories and the total is also connected with our treatment of agricultural and nonagricultural labor as separate inputs. If, instead, all labor is assumed to be homogeneous and weighted equally (row 3 of Table 9–3), the 33-year growth rate of productivity in the total economy is raised from the 1.0–1.8 percent ($r = 20\%$ and 8%) implied by the basic calculations to 1.4–2.2 percent, which are higher rates than those of either the nonagricultural or agricultural components. This apparent parodox arises primarily, however, because of an inconsistency in the measurement of inputs and outputs. If labor is homogeneous, then the value-added weights used in the computation of the GNP time series are distorted by the difference in wage rates[42] and, doubtless, more consequentially than by the omission of interest and rent charges. By a rough calculation paralleling those in Table 9–2, the charging of equal wages for both kinds of labor (with interest and rent imputed) would reduce the growth rate of GNP from 5.2 percent at the factor cost valuation to 4.4 or 4.6 percent ($r = 8\%$ or 20%).[43] Productivity would be reduced to 0.8–1.4 percent, which are lower rates than those of the basic calculations but, like the latter, lie between the rates for agriculture (implicit in the calculations) and for nonagricultural sectors. As we have indicated, our judgment is that the 1937 wage differential is best interpreted as a reflection of differences in labor quality, on which interpretation no adjustment in output weights is called for. With respect further to the relation of agriculture to the total, productivity in the whole economy and in the nonagricultural sectors appears not to be particularly sensitive to the value of land rent assumed in aggregating the inputs, so long, at least, as rent is estimated from actual agricultural wages (Table 9–3, row 4).

The manner in which housing is incorporated in the calculations raises special problems here as in similar calculations for other economies. Because of the statistical practice of omitting activities occurring within residential structures ("housewives' services") from measured output, capital utilized in housing has the peculiar quality that it cannot affect the productivity of other inputs within the sector in which it is employed. Because of the statistical practice of estimating the output yielded by housing from some measure of the capital involved (the gross stock in the present instance), the productivity of capital within the sector is more or less fixed by assumption. While external effects from changes in the housing stock are not excluded by assumption and may be considerable, measures of aggregate productivity inclusive of housing are necessarily of dubious analytical significance. The inclusion or exclusion of housing does not, however, have much effect on the numerical values of the estimates.

The service sectors (including finance) pose problems similar to those with housing, except that here output is estimated by assumption from

---

42 On this point, see also pp. 276 ff., below.

43 The calculation, which shares all the defects of those in Table 9–2, is made by redistributing the 1937 total wage bill between agriculture and nonagriculture in proportion to man-years of employment (Table Q–4) and distributing the nonagricultural total among its components in the same proportions as previously. The calculation is made only for rent equal to 40 percent of agricultural wages—actual wages, since the underlying U.S. ratio refers to actual wages. The results could be read also as for a higher rent charge combined with some differential between rural and urban wages.

labor rather than capital. Again, changes in capital have no effect on labor productivity within the sector. If labor in services is excluded from inputs and service products excluded from output (Table 9–3, row 8), aggregate productivity rises somewhat more rapidly over the 33-year period (by 0.1– 0.2 percentage points in the total economy and by 0.2–0.4 points in the nonagricultural nonresidential sectors) and, understandably, varies somewhat more widely over shorter periods than in the basic calculations, but the general pattern is not greatly altered. Since the estimate of service labor is approximate and capital in services cannot be segregated from the totals, these results are merely indicative.[44]

Our method of aggregating inputs within component sectors is not, as we have noted, consistent with that for the entire economy. The two can be made logically consistent by assuming that each sector—agricultural, residential, and nonagricultural nonresidential—represents a productive activity totally independent of all others. Aggregate inputs for the whole economy can then be computed as the arithmetic sum of inputs within the component sectors, as in row 6 of Table 9–1, and compared with aggregate output to obtain what is in effect a weighted average of productivities within the components. The results of such a calculation, which are shown in row 6 of Table 9–3, differ insignificantly from those obtained in the basic calculations.

The economic rationale of the foregoing aggregation by sectors is questionable, since it assumes away the interdependence of sectors. The most that we can do to allow for such interdependence is to calculate productivity in the nonagricultural (and nonresidential) sector with both inputs and outputs taken gross of agricultural raw materials (Table 9–3, row 9).[45] The rate of change of productivity is by this alteration somewhat reduced (by 0.2–0.4 percentage points) for the 33-year period, although principally within the postwar portion, and its shorter-run fluctuations are damped— the trough of the immediate postwar years, in particular, is substantially reduced. Because of various crudities in their calculation, these results will not sustain much weight. They are suggestive of what one would suppose a priori to be true, that productivity within the nonagricultural sectors, however measured, is not uninfluenced by factors affecting the supply of agricultural raw materials, including changes in agricultural pro-

[44] Measured productivity is affected by assumptions made at two other points in our calculations: in trade and in construction. Value added in trade is assumed to move with the volume of retail sales (see Appendix P, p. 634). This has the consequence, among others, that changes in trade inventories relative to sales, which are likely to produce real changes in the services rendered to consumers, are not recorded in output. Our estimates may, on this account, understate postwar trade output relative to prewar, although the difference probably does not amount to much in the sectoral totals with which we are dealing. In construction, value added is assumed to move with materials consumed (Appendix P, p. 634). The productivities of capital, labor, and the two in combination, remain free to vary.

[45] The input series is that shown in Table 9–1, row 9. Output is obtained by adding to gross output as initially calculated the same series for agricultural raw materials as is included with inputs, its 1937 value being set equal to 38.0 billion rubles, the value of agricultural marketings at average realized prices. The latter figure, which is adjusted for imputed interest and rent in the input calculation, is not so adjusted for the output calculation since our output series are at 1937 factor costs. The merit of procedural consistency here is doubtful.

ductivity. Coincidentally, the effects of including agricultural raw materials are generally opposite to those of excluding services.

These qualifications of our basic estimates having been made, it needs to be emphasized that the estimates provide little evidence on the relation in general of productivity within sectors to that in the total. In particular, the nonagricultural nonresidential category, which accounts for a large part of the total and embraces diverse activities, cannot be disaggregated on the basis of our data beyond the illustrative exclusion of services.[46] As we shall argue shortly, productivity changes have undoubtedly differed greatly among sectors, especially in the early years covered, but the bulk of these are obscured in the nonagricultural nonresidential aggregate. Since, however, the broad patterns of productivity changes within the major sectors for which we make estimates are similar, we shall for the most part treat them as subject to common explanations.

---

[46] Productivity calculations for industry alone are made, by procedures roughly like those employed here, in Powell–63. These yield results which are broadly similar to those obtained here, for the nonagricultural nonresidential sectors. As is stressed in the source, however, the calculations are of highly questionable reliability, principally for lack of satisfactory data on fixed capital in industry. Nor is any evidence presented on the behavior of productivity within component industrial sectors.

Chapter 10

The Growth of Output

1. THE ANALYSIS AND THE DATA

The argument made in Chapter 1 (Section 1) is to the effect that, on the assumption that the economy satisfies certain conditions, particular analytical interpretations can be put on indexes of output, aggregate inputs, and aggregate productivity. Thus, an output index measures the shift in the economy's transformation function (for the given-year product mix). An input index measures the change in aggregate inputs in constant proportions equivalent to the actual change in varying proportions (for the input mix of the given year and the output mix of the weight year and, perhaps also, of the given year). An index of the ratio between the two, productivity, measures technological change and scale effects (for the output and input mixes of the two indexes from which it is computed).[1]

As is also explained in Chapter 1 (Section 4), we have, in the derivation of our statistical estimates, taken some account of the need for conformity of observed quantities and prices to the requirements of the analysis in our choice of weight years. We have made some adjustments in the data provided by the economy, by correcting for turnover taxes and subsidies and by imputing returns to capital and land in aggregating inputs. We have, although in a limited way, explored by means of alternative calculations the likely effects of distortions in the pricing of livestock and of the omission of rent and interest in the valuation of output. There remain, however, varied and serious discrepancies between analytical argument and statistical observation for which we can make no quantitative allowance and which bear significantly on the interpretation of the statistical results.

The Quantity Data

It has been remarked previously that there was substantial urban unemployment and rural underemployment in 1928, which evidently was absorbed by the early 1930's. The economy of 1928 and the immediately succeeding years was on this account operating within its transformation function. Output indexes involving these years, therefore, reflect not only the increase over time in productive capacity but the effects as well of

---

[1] It will be recalled that by the "weight year" we mean the year from which the price weights are drawn; by the "given year," any other year.

reduced unemployment. The productivity indexes relate to output per unit of employed resources, not to potential output per unit of available resources.

Secondly, in all years covered by our estimates, the economy undoubtedly has operated short of its transformation function because of inefficiency in the use of the resources actually employed. That is to say, realized output, in its actual proportions, has been smaller than was possible with the quantity of inputs utilized.[2] This is the result in part of a misallocation of resources among uses, for the actual product mix. It is due also to faulty organization and administration of resources in the uses to which they are assigned. Although we shall subsequently infer from our statistical results conclusions about the behavior of efficiency over time, we are not now anticipating those inferences but are proceeding from what is common knowledge among observers of the Soviet economy.[3]

If the degree of inefficiency—the percentage difference between actual output and that possible with the resources employed—were the same in all years, the interpretation of the output and productivity indexes would not need on this account to be altered. But there is no reason to assume that the degree of inefficiency was the same. Thus, the output indexes must be read instead as measures of the change in productive capacity together with such change in the relative shortfall from capacity as may have occurred. The productivity indexes must be read as reflecting technological change and scale effects plus changes in the efficiency with which employed resources are utilized. As is evident, these are major amendments to the meanings originally attached to the two kinds of indexes.

They are amendments which also, however, point to an awkward ambiguity in the concept of a transformation function and, hence, of the concept of inefficiency: to what extent are the specific physical characteristics of inputs taken as given in defining the efficiency frontier? That is, granted that the shape of the function will vary with the ratio of capital to labor in the aggregate, to what extent is it conceived of as varying with the ratio, for example, of machine tools to tractors? The more highly specific in form (the less "malleable") inputs are taken to be, the more will potential output for any given product mix depend upon the mutual *adaptation* of that mix and the inputs with which it is produced—and the more will dynamic factors complicate reasoning from the essentially static concept of a transformation function.

For expositional reasons, we mean to defer the discussion of problems of dynamics—of lags in adjustment and of the import of anticipations— to Section 3 below. It will suffice here to explain that we do not suppose that any of our observations on the Soviet economy are for an economy in which the form of inputs and the mix of products are fully adapted to one another. Indeed, we judge that the specific characteristics of inputs are

---

[2] When we speak hereafter of (static) efficiency and inefficiency, we shall generally mean efficiency in the use of employed resources, which is necessarily our meaning for individual subsectors.

[3] The reader unfamiliar with this aspect of the Soviet economy will find chaps. 6 and 7 of Nove–61 relevant.

of material consequence for the transformation function to which our observations relate. On the other hand, the weight years chosen, 1937, 1928, and 1950, are thought to be years of relatively full adaptation and years in which short-run immobilities and frictions are of relatively little consequence.

Clearly, inefficiency can be defined for a wide range of degrees of specificity in the form of inputs. For simplicity, however, we shall use the term, unless it is otherwise qualified, to mean shortfalls from the output possible with given inputs which are relatively well adapted to the uses for which they are employed—as well adapted, say, as in 1937. We shall, then, return in Section 3 to the question of variations over time in the degree of adaptation in the sense indicated.[4]

The Price Data

The conceptual appropriateness of prices is directly relevant to the argument only in the weight years, the prices of which pose two separable problems: (*i*) the accuracy with which they reflect rates of transformation or substitution at the actual point of operation, and (*ii*) the closeness with which extrapolations made with them approximate unobserved, hypothetical, points on the transformation function or production isoquant.

There can be little doubt that in all three weight years the structure of Soviet prices, even after such adjustments as we have made, differs in detail from true rates of transformation and substitution. In general, inefficiencies in the use of inputs must result in relative prices which diverge from those that would hold at capacity output (for the same product mix). In addition, prices in the economy are largely administered rather than market-determined, and various distortions are likely to result from deliberate or unwitting administrative actions. Nevertheless, so far as we can judge, factors working to distort relative prices were, in 1937 and perhaps in 1950,[5] quite pervasive and nonsystematic in their action and not clearly biasing for the statistical results.[6]

For 1928, on the contrary, there is an obvious potential source of a large and systematic distortion in the structure of relative prices, which is the "misallocation" of resources in that year between agriculture and other sectors. The precise nature of this misallocation is somewhat obscure.[7] In its bearing on prices, it evidently came in part to an excess of labor attached to agriculture relative to that available for urban employment, a more massive and longer-standing rural unemployment than ur-

---

4 There is a further question in the definition of inefficiency and of the transformation function of how much of existing institutions, allocational procedures, and quality of decision makers is to be taken as given. Loosely speaking, we mean to take as variable and not given those things which we conceive to have been within the power of the Soviet authorities to alter.

5 Evidence cited below on the level of efficiency in 1950 may cast considerable doubt on the quality of the prices of that year.

6 The effect on output indexes of the absence of interest and rent charges in 1937 prices appears to illustrate fairly well the kind of price distortions referred to here; see Table 9–2 and the accompanying discussion.

7 For discussion of the evidence, see Jasny-49, pp. 36 and 420–23.

ban.[8] In part, it consisted of an excessively high ratio of employed labor to other inputs in agriculture, i.e., of inefficiency in the use of employed resources. And in part, no doubt, it amounted to nonoptimality of the product mix, at a time when demand factors were of more consequence for price formation than they were subsequently (optimality is relevant to the argument as it affects the price structure although, it will be recalled, not otherwise). The production of agricultural relative to nonagricultural goods was, under the existing pattern of demand, too large to yield equal returns to labor of equal quality in the two sectors (land and capital receiving no net return). The movement of labor from one sector to the other was restricted by impediments of familiar sorts.

The effect of misallocation in all these respects was, we judge, a relative undervaluation of agricultural products and of agricultural labor in 1928. Since agricultural output and labor both grew relatively slowly after 1928, our indexes in 1928 prices of both output and inputs presumably overstate rates of growth from 1928 to subsequent years.[9]

It follows from the foregoing that the transfer of employed labor from agriculture to other sectors between 1928 and 1937, by which latter date we take the initial misallocation to have been largely corrected,[10] affects the estimated indexes of aggregate productivity for reasons of different analytical significance. Productivity is increased, on the one hand, by the improved efficiency which resulted from the sectoral redistribution. This increase would appear if output and inputs were valued in accord with true transformation and substitution rates, either of 1928 or 1937. With such valuations, the labor transfer also increases aggregate inputs, but not their productivity, through improvement of the average quality of labor.

On the other hand, with output valued in actual 1928 prices (factor costs), the shift of labor from the sector of low earnings to that of high raises measured productivity by more than the increase in efficiency, by increasing the weight in total output of the products which are overvalued in the 1928 price structure. The valuation of inputs in actual 1928 prices tends similarly to lower measured productivity. The two effects are off-setting (in direction) if productivity is calculated with both components in actual 1928 prices, but not if one or the other component is in 1937 prices. These effects, however, have no useful analytical meaning and, at least in principle, would better be eliminated by adjusting observed prices to conformity with transformation and substitution rates.[11] Where, as in the

---

8 While unemployment was general in 1928, it is unlikely that this reflected an abso-lute redundancy of labor, a zero marginal physical product, in the economy as a whole. The contrary is suggested by the behavior of the demand for labor in the years imme-diately following 1928 and by the existence of sectors, such as construction, which can be made labor intensive almost without limit and the product of which had an obvious utility for the central authorities.

9 This holds for sectoral categories inclusive of agriculture and also for the nonagri-cultural sectors if, at least, output and inputs are measured gross of purchases of agricul-tural raw materials.

10 See p. 249 above.

11 The calculation cited p. 271, in which agricultural and nonagricultural labor in 1937 are treated as homogeneous, illustrates roughly the sort of adjustment that would be required.

present instance, this is not possible, it appears preferable to describe the resulting calculations as biased than to ascribe to the bias some explanatory content in accounting for economic growth.

Given such price weights as we can obtain, the accuracy with which they permit the estimation of unobserved points on weight-year transformation functions and production isoquants depends on the shapes of the latter.

For the transformation function, we estimate unobserved points from the observed one by linear extrapolation on relative prices. The extrapolation is more accurate, therefore, the more nearly linear is the function itself. If, as we have surmised, the mutual adaptation of product mix and the specific form of inputs was relatively full at the observed points in the weight years, and if hypothetical points are conceived of as of similarly full adaptation, it may be inferred that in those years the functions are not extremely concave (downward). For the most part, moreover, Soviet prices are not so rapidly adjusted to changing conditions that they are likely to be strongly influenced by short-run immobilities and frictions. The extrapolators they provide may also, hence, be taken to reflect approximately the slope of a transformation function in which adaptation is relatively full.

The concavity of the function depends, further, upon the importance of scale effects. It appears likely that large potential economies of scale existed in 1928 in those sectors whose output was expanded most rapidly between 1928 and 1937.[12] In consequence, the departure from linearity of the 1928 function, between the 1928 and 1937 product mixes, may have been slight. The presumption which concavity would create, that output in 1928 prices understates the actual growth in production potential for the 1937 product mix (cf. Chart 1–1, p. 3), is, therefore, not strong. By 1937, the significance of economies of scale, for movements from the 1937 to the 1928 mix, was probably smaller than in 1928 because of the absolutely higher levels of output in the later year. Some concavity in the 1937 (and 1950) transformation functions is therefore not unlikely, and some *over*statement in the growth of production potential in 1928 proportions is possible (cf. Chart 1–1).

With respect to production isoquants, our aggregation in the logs of the major input categories allows for some convexity in the function. The direction of the allowance appears unexceptionable, but we cannot defend its size. If, moreover, as we judge to be the case, the weight-year transformation functions are in significant (although not extreme) degree affected by the specific characteristics of inputs, our arithmetic aggregation of various kinds of inputs within the major categories is in error: machine tools and tractors are not perfect substitutes for one another in the production of any given output mix, and the alternative input indexes reflect inadequately their dependence upon the product mix to which they could be inferred to relate. In addition and perhaps more consequentially, the relative prices employed in the aggregation of major input categories, since they rest largely on assumptions, can hardly be taken as reliable measures of the slopes of the isoquants. The assumption that the plausible range of

---

[12] See pp. 286–87 below.

interest rates is the same in all three weight years is particularly inde-
fensible.[13]

In the face of these defects in the aggregate input indexes, we propose
from this point forward to abandon the argument that the indexes we
actually obtain can be interpreted as referring to identifiable mixes of
inputs and outputs. We shall, instead, treat the indexes in different prices
as alternatives simply in a statistical sense, analogous to the estimates at
alternative interest rates. Since the output indexes can be interpreted with
some confidence as for particular product mixes (and, in 1928–37, differ
much more from one another than do the input indexes), we shall take it
as justifiable still to interpret the productivity indexes as for the product
mix of their output component, albeit for input mixes of uncertain proportions.

The Range of Observations

Given that our basic objective is to explain the outward shift in the
transformation function, to what extent do our output data permit us to
consider shifts, over long periods and short, for product mixes which are
unvarying over time?

Defects in the data aside, the mix for which we can most nearly approximate a long and continuous series is that of the year 1937. The change in
productive capacity (*cum* reduced unemployment and altered efficiency)
for the 1937 mix over the interval from 1928 to 1937 is given by output
measured in 1928 prices, the change over the interval from 1937 to 1950
by output measured in 1950 prices. For these three dates, we have observations which within the reasoning of the model are for a constant
mix. By somewhat looser inference, other dates can be added to the series.
For the 1937–50 interval, the change in output is virtually the same
whether valuation is in 1937 or 1950 prices, which result follows from the
similarity of both the product mix and the price structure of 1950 to that
of 1937.[14] For other years beyond 1937, with exceptions most likely in the
earliest postwar years, the similarity of either product mix or price structure, or the two in combination, to that of 1937 appears great enough
that the 1937-price estimates can be taken to provide an acceptable approximation to measures in given-year prices and, hence, measures for the 1937

---

[13] Inputs in 1928 prices with an assumed interest rate of 8 percent do not rise much
more rapidly, from 1928 to 1937, than inputs in 1937 prices with a 20 percent rate. With
a sufficiently low interest rate in 1928 or a sufficiently high one in 1937, the direction of
the difference would be reversed.

[14] Output series in prices of the two years are given in Tables T–47 and T–49. Assertions here and subsequently about the behavior over time of the composition of output
are based in part on general knowledge and in part on numerical calculations which are
described below, pp. 296–97 and 300. The latter, which are crude and which relate to
the distribution of product by sector of origin (in 1937 prices) rather than, as would be
appropriate, by kind of final product, indicate that 1950 product differed from that of
1937 by 9 percent for the entire economy and by 7 percent for the nonagricultural sectors, as against figures for 1928 relative to 1937 of 23 percent and 21 percent respectively.
Evidence on the similarity of 1950 and 1937 price structures is given in Table 8–1 above
and in Bergson–61, p. 238. Relevant to this also is the fact that output relatives computed
in the two sets of prices are similar for mixes as different as those of 1928 and 1955 (cf.
Tables T–47 and T–49).

mix.[15] For the years intermediate to 1928 and 1937, the same reasoning might be applied to some of the years immediately preceding 1937, but it is probably safer to regard the 1937-price series within this interval as for given-year mixes, which differ in varying degree from one another and from that of 1937.[16] For the 1937 mix, then, we have evidence, of the indicated kinds, for 1928 and, annually except for the war years, for 1937–61.

The year 1937 can reasonably be interpreted as within the "postindustrialization" phase of Soviet development, and its output mix can be viewed as more or less representative of the mixes with which the system has operated, in peacetime years, since industrialization was effected. This year is not representative in any precise sense, and it would no doubt be helpful if we could obtain a long and continuous series for mixes closer to those reached by the end of the period covered. But our best judgment is that this would not present a markedly different picture from that obtained for the mix of 1937. The same cannot be said for mixes in which the munitions component is, as in wartime, very large, and for which capacity may well have increased, at least after the mid-1930's, at a significantly more rapid rate than for the 1937 or other peacetime mixes.[17]

Clearly, 1937 is not representative of the "preindustrialization" output proportions with which the system commenced in 1928 and those which it traversed in the course of its movement to the 1937 mix. A question arises, nevertheless, whether the latter may not be for the earlier period also an appropriate mix on which to focus. The consideration which gives rise to the question is one, again, which is discussed more fully in Section 3 below.

As is there stressed, the movement from the 1928 to the 1937 mix reflects *intentions* held by the Soviet authorities throughout the entire period from 1928 to 1937. It is not simply the result of a difference in the preferences of the authorities in the two terminal years or of the combined action of a given preference map and coincidentally shifting production possibilities. Nor was the regime's decision to undertake rapid growth one to effect proportionate movement at all points on the function or rapid movement along those product rays on which the frontier chanced to yield easily. Rather, the consistent determination of the authorities was both that

---

[15] Extreme differences between the immediate postwar product mixes and those of 1937 are the principal reason for uncertainty about the estimates for those years. On this and on the post-1937 behavior of the product mix in general, cf. Chart 10–2. Actual prices in the interval from the beginning of the war to the 1949–50 price reforms bore little relation to true transformation rates, but we assume that changes in the latter were continuously in the direction indicated by the 1950/1937 comparison. Changes in price structure after 1950 can be judged roughly from the various indexes given in Appendix L.

[16] We shall argue below that the greater part of the change from the 1928 mix to that of 1937 (or 1936–37) was effected by 1932, which suggests that output relatives in 1937 prices may not, from that date, differ greatly from relatives in 1937 prices. It is not unlikely that the change in price structure (transformation rates) also occurred more rapidly between 1928 and 1932 than between 1932 and 1937, but we cannot establish that this was the case.

[17] According to Bergson's estimates (Bergson–61, p. 367), munitions prices rose much less than did other prices from 1937 to 1950, the difference presumably emerging in the course of the war. The weight of munitions in the 1937 and 1950 product mixes is not great enough for this difference to be significant in the aggregates of those years.

growth should be rapid and that it should, by some early date, maximize the economy's capacity to produce a more or less specific product mix—which mix was in the neighborhood of that actually attained by 1937.[18] In terms of the authorities' own objectives, therefore, Soviet growth up to 1937 is properly appraised by reference to the 1937 mix, which, for the interval from 1928 to 1937, is measured by output in 1928 prices.

The foregoing argument is put unqualifiedly in order to emphasize the substantial truth which we believe it contains: the character of Soviet intentions creates a valid case for focusing on growth in the 1937 proportions, over the 1928–37 interval. The qualifications called for, however, are weighty.

(*i*) Though the intended direction of movement was unquestionably toward the actual 1937 mix, the size of the change was probably not initially anticipated. Official declarations of intent, such as the First Five-Year Plan, suggest the existence of a target less distant from the 1928 mix than that actually reached. It is plausible to suppose, moreover, that errors and surprises encountered in the course of movement toward the 1937 horizon led to successive revisions of the initial intentions, to take advantage of resulting changes in opportunities foreseen for the future. The direction of these revisions was almost certainly toward the realized 1937 mix. The latter, consequently, gives an unduly favorable measure of the growth of production potential along the "intended" product ray.

(*ii*) Intentions held by the authorities at any point in time must have related to a continuum of future dates, both antecedent to 1937 and extending beyond it. For an appraisal of growth *throughout* the 1928–37 period, as against growth between its termini, intended mixes other than that of 1937 are relevant, and these must typically have been intermediate to those of 1928 and 1937. The 1937 target was not itself an ultimate objective of the regime but one instrumental to the attainment of remoter targets—say, for simplicity, rapidity of growth into the distant future. Its appropriateness as a basis for appraising the 1928–37 performance of the economy depends in part, therefore, upon its appropriateness to the longer-term objective it was meant to serve. In general, the existence of intentions relating to a multiplicity of future dates permits statements of the following sort to be true: such-and-such a measure was a failure in terms of 1932 objectives, a success in terms of 1937 objectives, and a failure, again, with respect to the attainment of long-term goals.[19] Intentions, that is to say, even in an economy where they are as deliberate and conscious as the Soviet, provide no simple guide to the choice of mixes on which to base appraisal.

(*iii*) There is no compelling reason that an economy's performance should be judged (or analyzed) solely by reference to objectives internal to it. The lessons of Soviet experience for other developing economies, espe-

---

18 It would probably be more accurate to say that the authorities, in choosing at pre-1937 dates among alternative transformation functions prospectively available for 1937, selected that function which maximized potential output for, approximately, the realized 1937 mix.

19 This particular statement could be argued to hold for the collectivization of agriculture. On this and other concrete aspects of Soviet development relevant to the present discussion, see pp. 299 ff.

cially those unwilling or unable to follow precisely the Soviet path, may lie along product rays different from those in fact selected. For international comparisons also, it may be relevant to consider shifts in potential for similar product mixes, whether or not these were actually chosen by the economies compared. In such cases, of course, it should be kept in mind that growth for an unrealized product mix is likely to be smaller than it would have been had that mix been the objective toward which the system was, with whatever deliberateness is characteristic of it, moving.

(*iv*) Finally, the evidence we have on the 1928–37 increase in potential for the 1937 mix—output valued in 1928 prices—almost certainly overstates the true change, principally because of the undervaluation of agricultural products. Besides the presumption of an upward bias in the 1928 price weighted index, there is a large uncertainty as to its reliability created, *inter alia*, by the difficulty of setting 1928 prices for products not produced in 1928.

In the upshot, then, we see grounds for attaching particular significance to growth in the 1937 proportions, over the 1928–37 interval, and grounds, both analytical and statistical, for not restricting our attention to growth in those proportions.

The considerations of statistical reliability which have occasioned our stress upon 1937 valuations throughout argue also, and strongly, for attaching significance to the 1937-price calculations for the 1928–37 interval as well as for later periods. These, we judge, measure growth over the early interval along the 1928 product ray without pronounced bias in either direction, though perhaps with more likelihood of overstatement than the contrary. While the 1928 mix lies at an extreme of the mixes actually produced thereafter, it differs from the 1937 mix in the same general direction as do other pre-1937 output proportions, and it provides an observation on a segment of the transformation function which is poorly represented by the 1937 mix. How capacity for the 1928 mix changed after 1937 we cannot say with confidence, though its increase was almost certainly less than that for the 1937 mix. Output in 1937 prices over the entire period, 1928–61, presumably overstates the long-term growth for the 1928 mix, understates that for the 1937 mix, and approximates most closely the change in capacity for the 1928 mix from 1928 to 1937 plus the change for the 1937 mix (or, more certainly, the 1961 mix) from 1937 to 1961.

The question remains of how far the data in 1937 prices, which are the only ones we have, permit us to reason about the changes which occurred within the period between 1928 and 1937. The variability of the product mix to which they relate necessarily creates a large ambiguity in their implications for the change in potential along any single product ray. We have previously suggested, however, that the wide fluctuations in the growth of output which are recorded for this period in 1937 prices would probably appear with any set of constant prices and also, though less certainly, for any constant product mix.[20] From the behavior of aggregate inputs in 1928 and 1937 prices, it appears unlikely that the comparatively steady change in aggregate inputs would be greatly disturbed by

[20] See p. 225.

an alteration of price weights.[21] We suppose, therefore, that the short-run fluctuations in productivity in 1937 prices would also appear with other weights. In any case, the timing of the fluctuations in output and productivity appears not to conform closely to that of changes in the product mix.[22] On these grounds, we shall hereafter treat the 1937-price series as indicative of the *pattern* of short-run change within the 1928–37 period, although the size and precise timing of fluctuations would doubtless appear differently with different weights.

In the discussion which follows, we explore the inferences about the process of Soviet growth which the data at hand, with their various limitations, appear to permit. For lack of comprehensive series in alternative prices and on the reasoning just explained, we shift rather freely from one to another portion of the data, as seems most appropriate to each point in turn. For simplicity, we cite on occasion extreme values of the calculations, it being understood that intermediate values are likely to lie closer to the truth. Where we mean only to illustrate a proposition, we refer generally to the estimates in 1937 prices, recognizing that details of an illustration may be dependent upon the particular valuation chosen.

2. THE GROWTH PROCESS: INITIAL HYPOTHESES

Short-Run Fluctuations

Inspection of the time series for the productivity of aggregate inputs (cf. Chart 9–10 and Tables T–64 to T–68) immediately suggests that the growth rate of Soviet output has varied in response to some potent factor additional to changes in inputs and technology. For example, productivity in 1937 prices, for the entire economy and at an 8 percent interest rate, rises by 6 percent from 1928 to 1930, falls by 10 percent from 1930 to 1932, rises by 24 percent from 1932 to 1937, falls by 9 percent from 1937 to 1940,[23] falls a further 21 percent to 1945, rises by 24 percent to 1948, and continues to rise, uninterruptedly but less rapidly, to 1961. Productivity in the non-agricultural nonresidential sectors at 8 percent interest fluctuates similarly, although the early changes are larger (a 13 percent gain from 1928 to 1930 and 13 percent loss from 1930 to 1932), the prewar peak is reached by 1936 rather than 1937, and the very rapid immediate postwar recovery extends through 1949. The pattern of short-run changes is much the same with the 20 percent interest rate as with 8 percent. It appears moreover, with minor variations in timing, in the productivities of labor and capital taken separately. Only from about 1950 and only markedly from about 1955 do the separate productivities move in opposite directions, the productivity of capital falling while that of labor is increasing.[24] The effects of changes in factor proportions upon the productivities of component inputs are evi-

---

21 Cf. Chart 9–7 or the corresponding tables.

22 Cf. pp. 296 ff.

23 The 1937–40 decline in 1937 prices can be compared also with the very rapid rise in productivity from 1928 to 1937 with output valued in 1928 prices. See Tables T–66 and T–68.

24 The behavior of the partial productivities can be read from Charts 9–3 (with the ratios inverted) and 9–6, although input series used in both are not precisely those relevant for the statement in the text.

dently obscured by the impact of forces affecting their combined productivity.

It is scarcely credible that such fluctuations should be accounted for by variations in technology. That their amplitude is in part the consequence of scale effects seems not improbable, but the single simple explanation which is most likely to be true is that these fluctuations reflect variations in efficiency, i.e., variations in the ratio of actual to potential output. As we have said, the existence of substantial inefficiency in the Soviet economy in all periods is beyond question, and there is no reason to think that its degree was unvarying over time. The pattern of the fluctuations, viewed as changes in efficiency, fits quite well, furthermore, that which would have been expected from historical knowledge, although the size of the fluctuations may be unexpected and the risks here of *ad hoc* explanations are obviously large.[25]

No strong historical evidence can be cited for the rise in productivity from 1928 to 1930, although is it probable that initiation of the drive toward industrialization did for a time stimulate managerial and administrative initiative, with favorable consequences which were not immediately offset by the ensuing disruptions. That efficiency fell to 1932 or 1933 is almost certainly the case, since the First Five-Year Plan ended with the economy in a state approaching chaos. This is most clearly illustrated by the crisis in rail transportation of that period, but disorder and disorganization pervaded planning and management, materials supply, and labor allocation and controls. The extremely rapid rise of productivity to 1936 or 1937 can be plausibly interpreted as a recovery from at least the worst inefficiencies of 1932–33. The leveling-off and decline of productivity in the late 1930's, which may be due in part to the correction in the mid-1930's of the most easily remedied inefficiencies, probably reflects also the impact of the Great Purges. The timing of the movements in the productivity series is revealing on this point: the nonagricultural series reach their peak by 1936, in which year the purges commenced; the peak for the total economy is delayed a year by the exceptionally good weather conditions in agriculture in 1937, which followed the poor harvest of 1936. The channels through which the purges affected efficiency are not easy to trace in detail, but there is little doubt that they were seriously demoralizing and disorganizing. The information available on the state of the economy immediately following the war is much less than for 1932–33, but such as there is is consistent with the occurrence of a similar low in efficiency in that period (efficiency levels during the war may have been well above that of 1945). The upswing of productivity from 1945–46 resembles that of the mid-1930's and presumably has a similar explanation. Here, however, the rise continues at a relatively rapid pace for a number of years, through 1961.

Were the short-run fluctuations in productivity less pronounced and less plausible historically than they are, we would less confidently exclude the possibility that they are the result solely of statistical error. In such

---

[25] The discussion immediately following resembles closely, in the time periods selected and in the characterizations made of them, that presented by Naum Jasny in Jasny–61 (see especially pp. 11 ff.).

calculations as those made here, "productivity" becomes a receptacle not only for all factors affecting growth other than measurable changes in inputs but also for any net error in the estimates of inputs and outputs. Small percentage errors in either may produce large percentage errors in the productivity estimate, and these are still further magnified in the percentage change of productivity from one year to the next. We have pointed previously to potential sources of error affecting the short-run behavior of the indexes,[26] and we would emphasize again the vulnerability of the estimates for the earliest years in both the prewar and postwar periods. There are, in addition, sources of error, associated with those historical events which give plausibility to the observed pattern of short-run change, which are likely to cause measured productivity to exaggerate the short-run fluctuations.

The sharp rise in productivity in the nonagricultural nonresidential subsector from 1928 to 1930 is probably due in part to an increase in the intensity (number of shifts worked, etc.) with which existing plant and equipment were utilized, which kind of change in capital inputs is not taken into account in our estimates. The depth of the 1932–33 trough is almost certainly the result in part of an overstatement in our estimates of labor inputs, in both the economy as a whole and in the subsector. Contrary to the assumption of our procedures, labor transferred from agricultural to nonagricultural employments does not immediately acquire the qualities, other than locational, of the labor previously in the nonagricultural sectors. Consequently, the large movement of labor out of agriculture between 1928 and 1932 reduced for a time the average quality of labor in the nonagricultural sectors and produced a smaller increase in the wage-weighted quantity of labor in the whole economy than is implied by our use of 1937 weights. Moreover, since 1932–33 was a period of severe famine, the capacities of labor in all sectors were probably reduced by low consumption levels. The effects of the purges were in part a deterioration of the quality of labor, through the removal of scarce administrative personnel and the demoralization of labor still employed. A low in the quality of labor must be part of the explanation, also, of the postwar trough in productivity, and a subsequent improvement part of the explanation of the postwar upswing.

As the foregoing remarks imply, the distinction between changes in inputs and in the efficiency with which they are used is a fuzzy one, and a good deal of what we have called short-run changes in efficiency could with considerable logic be described as changes in inputs. Inept managerial decisions, for example, even if not themselves evidence of low managerial quality, are likely to result in underutilization both of the capital available and of labor nominally employed. Poor allocation by planning organs of raw materials among plants or sectors may have the same effect. On the other hand, changes which we have ascribed to the quality of inputs, such as those caused by famine and by the purges, were themselves induced by decisions made by the regime and could probably, with a broader definition of the term, be included under the rubric of inefficiency. Indeed, our procedure in measuring inputs, verbal allowances for unmeasured quality

---

[26] Cf. especially rows 8 and 9 of Table 9–3 and the comment on them, pp. 271–73.

changes aside, has the peculiar consequence that the total removal of labor from employment (through undernourishment, imprisonment, or worse) by a given action of the regime appears as a decline in productive inputs, whereas the impairment by the same actions of the capabilities and incentives of labor still employed appears as a change in productivity. While, therefore, our estimates for 1932–33 or the late 1930's may understate the efficiency with which employed resources were used, they are likely to overstate the efficiency with which the total resources available to the regime were used.

On balance, and having in mind especially the similarity of the short-run fluctuations in the productivity of labor and capital taken singly, we suppose that the estimated fluctuations in aggregate productivity reflect a genuine and significant phenomenon in Soviet development. Growth has not been simply progress from one to the next, and higher, transformation function but has occurred in an erratic sequence of approaches to and retreats from the limit of production possibilities open to the economy. This conclusion has implications for interpreting the behavior of the economy over longer periods, as will be argued hereafter.

From 1928 to 1937, 1937 to 1953, and 1953 to 1961

Both inspection of the data and general historical knowledge suggest, next, a division of the whole 1928–61 period into three intervals of intermediate length.

Over the first of these, from 1928 to 1937, GNP increased at 11.9 percent per year if measured in 1928 prices and at 6.2 percent if measured in 1937 prices.[27] Allowing for some significant overstatement in the 1928-price measure because of distortions in the 1928 price structure, we suppose the difference between the two is explained chiefly by the character of the shift in the transformation function between 1928 and 1937: the capacity of the system to produce output in the 1937 product proportions grew much more rapidly than did its capacity to produce in the 1928 proportions. That over this interval the actual output of, for example, machinery increased more than the output of food is an observable fact. But the inference is only a little less secure that the economy's production potential for mixes with large machinery components increased more than its potential for those with large food components. The transformation function was shifted outward in a fashion much like that which was illustrated in Chart 1–1 (p. 3), at a highly disproportionate rate along different product rays.

In part, no doubt, though our input indexes do not permit us to establish that this is the case,[28] the disproportionate shift in the function is explained by disproportionate changes in productive inputs—not only in capital relative to labor or land, in the aggregate, but in capital assets of particular forms and labor of particular skills relative to others. For the rest, it is explained by differential changes in the productivity of inputs for different product mixes. For the 1937 mix, our productivity estimates with alternative prices of inputs and interest rates yield a wide range of figures, all of which, however, imply high rates of change: from 3.1 to 7.3

---

27 The 1928-price calculations, it will be recalled, are Bergson's; the 1937-price ours.
28 See pp. 278–79.

percent per year.[29] For the 1928 mix, productivity appears to have increased only moderately or perhaps to have declined absolutely, the estimated rates ranging from a positive 1.8 percent to a negative 2.2 percent.[30] The obvious explanation of the difference in productivity gains is that both technological change and scale effects were greater for the 1937 mix than for that of 1928. The regime's efforts to obtain a rapid improvement in technology appear to have been concentrated more on the production of "machinery" than on that of "food," and there is little question that its relative successes were similarly distributed. The production of machinery in 1928 was absolutely small, and in the ensuing nine years it was greatly expanded. If common observation is a reliable guide, machinery production—heavy industry in general—is subject to significant economies of scale, and these must have been realized in substantial measure by 1937. The change in product mix from 1928 to 1937 was large; it was towards those products for which much of the newly acquired inputs were well adapted and for which technological change and economies of scale were great.

There is a methodological moral in these conclusions which may be worth underlining. The "index number problem" in the measurement of early Soviet growth is serious, and the need to cope with it is a prime motivation for the analytical procedures used here. It is the import of the latter that the sensitivity of output measures to price weights over the 1928–37 interval is not merely a statistical nuisance but a meaningful reflection of the fact that the changes which occurred in the early phases of Soviet industrialization were extremely diverse. While more than one measure of output complicates the explanation of growth, reliance on a single measure makes for a spurious simplicity and may exclude relevant information. How far other economies over comparable (though, typically perhaps, longer) periods of their development have experienced changes of a diversity like that of the Soviet is a matter which, to our knowledge, has not been much investigated.[31]

Beyond the movement in the transformation function, the increase of measured output in both 1937 and 1928 prices is partly accounted for by the absorption of the unemployed labor existing in 1928. The increase in both is affected also by whatever change occurred in the level of efficiency. The 1928 level can scarcely have been high because, among other reasons, of the misallocation of resources between agriculture and the nonagricultural sectors. The 1930 peak in productivity (in 1937 prices) suggests that efficiency in 1928 may have been relatively low; the 1937 peak, which is the high point for the prewar period, suggests that efficiency in that year may have been relatively high.[32] On the other hand, inefficiencies peculiar

---

29 The lower figure is with inputs in 1928 prices at $r = 20\%$, the higher with inputs in 1937 prices at $r = 8\%$. Output is in 1928 prices.

30 The higher figure is with inputs in 1937 prices at $r = 8\%$, the lower with inputs in 1928 prices at $r = 20\%$. Output is in 1937 prices.

31 See, however, the citation to Gerschenkron–51, pp. 181–82 above.

32 For these reasons, comparisons solely between the two years, 1937 and 1928, may not be representative of the changes that occurred between the longer periods within which each falls. The year 1937 is clearly unrepresentative on account of its exceptional harvest, though there may have been adjustment problems created by the unforeseeably large output of one sector, and, as we have noted, efficiency in the nonagricultural sectors appears to have reached its peak in 1936.

to Soviet planning and allocative techniques are likely to have increased over the interval. Also, the fact that the 1928–37 increase in productivity for the 1928 mix may have been close to zero raises the possibility that efficiency within some sectors declined markedly relative to the 1928 level, and offsetting gains need not have occurred elsewhere.[33] What the net direction of change in the economy as a whole is likely to have been is not at all obvious.

The feature of the 1937–53 interval which is striking is still more so in comparison with that of 1953–61, and we take the two together. The dividing date, which might better be put as "the early 1950's," is the year of Stalin's death. Both intervals are discussed in terms of the 1937-price calculations.

By 1953, aggregate productivity in the economy as a whole was still approximately at the 1937 level, exceeding it by 5 percent at $r = 8\%$ and falling slightly below it at $r = 20\%$.[34] In the nonagricultural nonresidential subsector, 1953 productivity was slightly above ($r = 8\%$) or 4 percent below ($r = 20\%$) 1937 and as low or lower relative to 1936. Over an interval of some 16–17 years, then, or half of the entire period covered by our estimates, no significant gain in productivity was effected. Over the eight years from 1953 to 1961, in contrast, productivity rose at average annual rates of 2.9–4.7 percent ($r = 20\%$ or 8%) in the entire economy and 3.3–5.3 percent in the nonagricultural nonresidential subsector. The rise, moreover, was to levels well above any previous peak.

The conclusion appears to us inescapable that by 1953 efficiency was exceedingly low. If that is the case, it appears likely also that the rapidity of the subsequent rise in productivity was in large measure the result of improved efficiency. It is not conceivable that technology should have remained unchanged over so long a period preceding 1953. If it improved, even at a moderate annual rate, the shortfall of output from potential by 1953 must have been large. Nor are there evident grounds for expecting a spurt in technological improvement, at rates of the indicated order, in the post-1953 period.

However, differences in efficiency of the apparent magnitude cannot be said to conform to expectations. Inefficiencies in the Stalin period undoubtedly were large, and it is not surprising that they should have increased with the increasing rigidities and irrationalities of the regime in Stalin's later years. It is surprising that these should have so intensified as to counterbalance all gains from improved technology for a period of more than a decade and a half. The post-1953 rise in productivity is at least as difficult to account for in plausible historical terms. Most outside observers have not thought that the organizational and administrative changes made by

---

[33] If the productivity indexes were taken as weighted averages of sectoral productivities, which strictly they are not, the behavior of the average with alternative weights would almost necessarily imply a large fall in efficiency within some sectors. The large gains in productivity, in those sectors which experienced them and which are large in the 1937 mix, are presumably due primarily to technological change and economies of scale. The declines in productivity, which bring the average for the 1928 mix close to zero, can hardly be explained by negative changes in the same factors.

[34] With Bergson's GNP estimates, 1953 productivity would be approximately 5 percent higher relative to 1937 than the figures cited.

Stalin's successors are likely to have improved markedly the functioning of the system, although changes in agricultural policy and the greater rationality in general of the regime may have been beneficial. Also, the rise in productivity beyond 1953 is a continuation of a change previously under way—from the postwar trough—rather than a reversal of direction or a clearly significant acceleration of the rate of increase.[35]

Nevertheless, we see no credible alternative to the hypothesis that by 1953 efficiency was still at a very low level and that the rapid gains which followed represent in part the taking up of slack, as it were, left in the system at the time of Stalin's death. Given that efficiency quite clearly fluctuates over periods of a few years' length, there is no reason to exclude the possibility that large changes should occur over longer periods and no necessary reason that these should be foreseeable from a general knowledge of history. Here, therefore, we take the results of the statistical calculations as an addition to historical knowledge rather than as a quantitative verification of what was already known.

The 1937–53 interval does, of course, embrace the war years. Beyond any question, the war caused a severe setback in the growth of Soviet output, and the ground then lost was not recovered by 1953—or by 1961. The long-term character of the loss in capital has been argued previously.[36] Like capital, total population and labor force were reduced not only by the losses immediately due to the war but by a reduction for an indefinitely long period of the system's capacity to expand its labor force. On any reasonable assumptions, aggregate inputs were at all postwar dates lower than they would have been in the absence of war and, on this account, total output also was lower. Despite the war, however, aggregate inputs in the whole economy had by 1953 been raised approximately 75 percent above their 1937 level, and those in the nonagricultural nonresidential sectors had been doubled. These gains make still more remarkable the lack of growth over the same interval in productivity.[37]

The disturbing effects of war are no doubt multiform, pervasive, and often obscure in their workings. The low level of measured productivity in 1945 and for some years following was probably in part the unavoidable consequence of reconversion from military to civilian production.[38] On

---

[35] It is possible, perhaps without excessive straining, to see a fairly clear inflection at about 1953 in the series for productivity in the total economy; e.g., productivity rose at 2.2–3.4 percent per annum from 1948 to 1953 and 3.3–4.4 percent from 1953 to 1958. The rate of change in the nonagricultural nonresidential sectors, however, was about the same in both periods, and the difference in the total is almost wholly attributable to agriculture. While the implied difference in the behavior of agricultural productivity in the two periods is not implausible, it is not statistically reliable and it poses the usual problems in interpreting the short-run performance of Soviet agriculture. In any case, details of this fineness cannot safely be read from the estimates.

[36] See p. 243.

[37] Following the thought introduced pp. 280–81 above, it could be argued that Soviet intentions from 1937 to, say, 1944, were to maximize capacity for the 1944 mix and, from 1944 to 1953, to maximize capacity for the 1953 mix. Output over the early interval should then be measured in 1937 prices, which give a heavy weight to munitions, and over the later interval in 1953 (or 1950) prices, which give a light weight to munitions. The total growth in output, and probably in productivity, would be greater calculated in this manner than if calculated throughout in either 1937 or 1953 prices.

[38] See pp. 297–98 below.

the other hand, the effects of war on the determinants of productivity are favorable as well as unfavorable: it impedes technological development in some directions but stimulates it in others; it disrupts the functioning of existing administrative arrangements but provides an opportunity to break down existing bureaucratic rigidities and to displace entrenched bureaucrats. The extremely rapid rise of productivity to 1948 or 1949 looks like recovery from the worst effects of war and reconversion, and, if the recovery was not complete by 1953, the length of time required is perplexingly long and the portion of the recovery accomplished similarly small. The year 1953 stands as far removed from the end of World War II as 1928 from World War I, Civil War, and Intervention. Productivity in 1953, as we have stressed, was low, relative not merely to 1940, but relative to 1936–37 as well.

That there may be something in war which is long delayed in its action is suggested by the rapid rates of growth in output, and evidently in productivity, experienced in the 1950's by a number of countries which incurred severe damage.[39] Whatever the connection between war and their growth rates, however, other countries did not have all those features of the Soviet Union which would have made possible, one would think, a prompt overcoming of the disorder and disorganization resulting from war. Here, after all, was a firmly established political regime, unencumbered by domestic opposition, free of interference from an occupying power, committed to rapid growth as a fundamental objective of policy, and in possession of unusually extensive controls over its economy. Under these circumstances, it appears implausible that a 16–17-year hiatus in the growth of productivity could be accounted for as the inevitable consequence of war.

The absence of severe disturbances like the war—and like collectivization and the purges—in the post-Stalin years presumably did facilitate the rapid growth of productivity in that period. In considerable measure, however, the relative tranquility of the period is not fortuitous but is the consequence of the regime's own decisions and reflects credit upon it. On the other hand, the *ad hoc* quality of historical explanations is as dangerous here as for intervals where identifiable shocks are apparently recorded in statistical series. It is doubtful whether, should the statistical results have called for it, an explanation would have been hard to find for a marked decline in productivity immediately after Stalin's death or immediately following the industrial reorganization of 1957.

The larger difficulties in interpreting the post-1953 period are statistical. The productivity estimates in this period are highly sensitive to three elements in their calculation which in earlier years are of smaller consequence: the rate of interest, the method of aggregating inputs, and the adjustment of labor inputs for hours worked (see rows 1, 2, and 5, of Table 9–3). Primarily because of the wide divergence in the growth rates of capital and labor from the early 1950's (cf. Chart 9–5), aggregate inputs, and hence productivity, become heavily dependent upon the interest rate assumed, the rate of productivity change ranging, as noted, from 2.9 to 4.7 percent in the whole economy, for $r = 20\%$ or 8%, and from 3.3 to 5.3

---

39 Cf. data given in Kuznets–63, p. 355.

percent in the nonagricultural nonresidential subsector. The sensitivity of the results to the use of logarithmic as against arithmetic aggregation also reflects the rapid rise in the capital/labor ratio: with the latter, the productivity increase is reduced to 1.6–3.7 percent for the whole economy, $r = 20\%$ or 8%, and to 1.8–4.0 percent for the subsector. The superiority of logarithmic aggregation is clear in this instance, since it is under circumstances of large changes in input proportions that significant changes in relative marginal productivities are likely to occur. But the dependence of the calculations upon the form of the function assumed for aggregating inputs increases the uncertainities characteristic of the findings. It is also relevant if comparisons are attempted with other countries.

The single most problematic feature of the post-1953 evidence is the sensitivity of the calculations to the treatment of changes in hours in the estimation of labor inputs. This element has not inconsiderable consequences for earlier periods: without the hours adjustment, the decline in productivity between 1928 and 1932 is larger and that between 1937 and 1940 smaller; the 1945 trough is pronouncedly less deep; and productivity in 1953 is somewhat above the 1937 level (the 33-year increase in productivity is slightly lower). The omission of the hours adjustment alters the general shape of the findings most significantly, however, for the 1953–61 period. Not only is the rate of productivity gain for the entire eight years materially reduced, to 1.8–3.3 percent ($r = 20\%$ and 8%) for both the total economy and the subsector,[40] but a marked retardation in the rate of increase within the period is indicated. In the subsector, for example, in which productivity is less responsive to short-run variations in weather and for which the unadjusted labor series comes closer to numbers employed,[41] the rise in productivity at $r = 8\%$ declines from 5.4 percent per year in 1953–55 to 3.8 percent in 1955–58 and 1.4 percent in 1958–61, and, at $r = 20\%$, from 4.2 to 2.1 to less than 0.1 percent. The corresponding figures with labor adjusted for hours are 5.7, 5.2, 5.2 percent, and, at the higher interest rate, 4.3, 3.0, and 2.8 percent. Between the assumption that changes in hours represent a proportionate change in labor inputs and the assumption that they represent no change, the former appears to us the more reasonable. But we have little doubt that, because of the qualitative differences in the man-hours involved, the hours adjustment overstates the true changes in labor inputs, and that more accurate productivity indexes would depart from our basic calculations in the direction of the series unadjusted for changes in hours.[42]

Given this various evidence on the 1953–61 period, we conclude that the growth of productivity was rapid, and unquestionably so in comparison with the 1937–53 interval, although the precise value of the rate of increase is highly uncertain. To judge from calculations without the hours adjustment, the gain was less rapid than is indicated by our basic calculations and,

---

[40] As a contrary consideration, it should be noted that the number of penal laborers, which are not included in our employment series, is thought to have been greatly reduced within this period (see p. 247).

[41] It will be recalled that our basic employment data for agriculture are in man-days, which are converted to the equivalent of man-years in nonagricultural employments.

[42] There is here, however, an offsetting error of sorts in that leisure is omitted from calculated output.

within the eight-year interval, the rate decelerated significantly. If the gain over the whole period is explained by improvements in efficiency accomplished by Stalin's successors, the retardation in the growth rate can be plausibly accounted for by the progressive exhaustion of the opportunities for improvement as efficiency approached, not an imaginable maximum, but the maximum of which the system is capable so long as its more intractable sources of inefficiency remain operative.

The Long Run

Over the whole period covered by our estimates, 1928 to 1961, Gross National Product measured in 1928 prices to 1937 and in 1937 prices to 1961 increased at an average annual rate of 6.7 percent. This, as explained, can be interpreted as referring to growth in the 1937 product proportions. GNP measured in 1937 prices throughout, which is interpretable as for the 1928 product mix to 1937 and for the 1937 mix thereafter, increased at 5.2 percent. The output figures can be compared with extreme values of the growth rate of aggregate inputs of 3.4 and 5.1 percent.[43] The rate of increase of inputs thus amounts to 51–76 percent of that of output for the 1937 mix (3.4/6.7 and 5.1/6.7), to 65–98 percent for the linked 1928–37 mix. The ratios for the 1937 mix are understated because of the exaggeration of the growth rate of output measured in 1928 prices; the higher ratio for both mixes is overstated because of the exaggeration of the growth rate of inputs measured in 1928 prices. Similar ratios for the nonagricultural nonresidential subsector are 57–81 percent and 72–101 percent.[44]

For any broad appraisal of the Soviet experience, the high growth rate of inputs relative to output is the most important finding to come out of this study. Having in mind the direction of errors in the calculated ratios and considering that the ratios make no allowance for the contribution of increased inputs to the realization of economies of scale, it is clear that the dominant source of Soviet growth has been the increase in the quantity of productive resources employed. The relative importance of the latter differs, as is understandable, with the product mix in reference, but for either the 1937 mix or the linked 1928–37 mix, the "share" of increased inputs in total growth appears to have been significantly in excess of one half and may well have amounted to three quarters or better.

The increase in inputs reflects sources of growth which were, for the Soviet population, immensely costly: the rapid increase of the capital stock and consequent sacrifice of current consumption; the conversion of rural into urban labor, in substantial part by the violent measures of collectivization; the increased employment of women at the expense of their household functions; and, for previously non-Soviet peoples, the acquisition of resources by territorial expansion. These were not costs voluntarily incurred but costs imposed upon the population by the exertion of compulsion of the severest sort. In large degree, hence, the rapidity of Soviet

---

[43] The lower figure is calculated with 1937 prices and $r = 8\%$; the higher with 1928 prices for 1928–37, with 1937 prices for 1937–61, and with $r = 20\%$ in both 1928 and 1937.

[44] We attach no significance to the fact that the ratios are somewhat higher for the subsector than for the whole economy. All that is relevant here are general orders of magnitude.

growth is a testimonial to the efficacy of authoritarian political controls—
a demonstration of the potentialities of "growth by force."

Few of the measures referred to were without creditable consequences
for the population, and others—the absorption of unemployed labor and
the maintenance of full employment; the great improvement of educational levels (which may not be adequately accounted for in our estimates)
—represent positive gains quite apart from their effects on economic
growth. Moreover, by the single criterion of rapidity of growth, increasing
the quantity of inputs is as legitimate a device for achieving growth as is
raising the productivity of resources available. It may be an essentially
mechanical and uningenious method, but it is also, manifestly, one which
a sufficiently powerful and resolute regime can make work to the stated
end.[45]

Extreme values for the rate of change in productivity over the 33-year
period can be computed in the same manner as those for aggregate inputs.
In the economy as a whole, productivity growth rates range from 1.5 to
3.2 percent for the 1937 product mix, from 0.1 to 1.8 percent for the linked
1928–37 mix.[46] The higher figure for the 1937 mix is overstated; the lower
figures for both mixes are understated. Comparable rates for the nonagricultural nonresidential subsector are 1.5–3.4 percent and a negative 0.1 percent to a positive 1.9 percent.

The common expectation would have been, we suppose, that the growth
rate of productivity in the Soviet economy would prove exceptionally high,
primarily because of a rapid rate of technological improvement. Soviet
development began late relative to that of other industrialized economies.
The so-called "advantages of backwardness" are principally those of access
to advanced technology already developed elsewhere. The advantages of
this sort open to the Soviet Union were large, and the regime did deliberately import and utilize new techniques from the rest of the world. The
expectation would be reinforced by the likelihood that potential economies
of scale were relatively large also.

Whether or not the expectation is borne out is not answerable on the
evidence at hand. All the problems in international comparisons of output
or input growth rates are compounded in the comparison of productivity
rates.[47] If, moreover, numbers are simply compared with numbers, it is obvious that the calculated Soviet rates, ranging at their widest from 0.1
to 3.2 percent for the whole economy, are likely to bracket single rates
calculated for advanced economies. Long-term rates calculated for the
United States, for example, have generally lain within the range of 1.5 to
2.0 percent, which rates are roughly midway between the extremes esti-

---

[45] We consider subsequently, pp. 299 ff., the possibility that certain of the costs referred to were deliberately incurred for returns to be realized at a later date.

[46] In general, percentage rates of change in productivity are calculated from the
Tables T–64 to T–68 indexes rather than from the percentage rates of change in inputs
and outputs. Minor inconsistencies arise because of rounding errors.

[47] Comparisons of the growth rate of Soviet national product with that of the United
States are made in Bergson–63, pp. 6–7. Beyond question, the Soviet rate since 1928 has
been higher than that of the United States for the same period, but, depending upon the
Soviet price weights used, the Soviet rate since 1928 may not significantly exceed rates
attained in the United States in earlier periods. A limited comparison of growth rates in
Soviet and U.S. capital stocks is made above, pp. 181 ff.

mated here and far distant from both.[48] Until the spread of the Soviet rates can be narrowed by reducing the statistical uncertainties affecting them (especially of appropriate interest rates), and until U.S. rates for alternative product mixes become available, the most that can be said is that the Soviet rates, by such comparisons as can readily be made, are very high at one extreme and very low at the other.

It is perhaps surprising that the growth in Soviet productivity does not appear unambiguously high for whatever mix it is calculated. It should be considered, however, that the portion of the total economy in which technological change is thought to have been rapid (and scale effects large) is relatively small. Sectors of the economy in which changes in productivity are effectively excluded by assumption, housing and services, accounted in 1937, in 1937 prices, for 18 percent of total income originating (Net National Product).[49] In two other sectors, construction and trade, productivity is somewhat arbitrarily affected by the method of estimating output, and, in addition, these sectors are not thought to have been distinguished in other economies for the rapidity of their technical progress. These accounted in 1937 for 10 percent of output. In two sectors, agriculture and consumer goods industry, Soviet borrowings of advanced techniques appear in fact not to have been carried far, although the lags here presumably were large. These accounted for roughly 42 percent of output. The probable area of significant impact of borrowed techniques and of rapid productivity gains in general is, thus, reduced to the 30 percent of the 1937 economy (14 percent in 1928 and 46 percent in 1961, all in 1937 prices) represented by producer goods industries and transportation and communications. These sectors loom larger in the nonagricultural nonresidential category (27 percent in 1928, 45 percent in 1937, and 57 percent in 1961) than they do in the total economy, but even within them the rate of approach to Western technological levels is known to have been highly uneven. These sectors also loom larger when valuation is in 1928 prices, which accounts partially for the more rapid rise of productivity for the 1937 product mix than for the linked 1928–37 mix.

Secondly, the capacity of the Soviet economy to obtain and make use of new techniques has undoubtedly been limited at all times, though presumably increasing as experience accumulated and the stock of skilled personnel and sophisticated capital instruments grew.[50] Thus, the opportunities for rapid gains in productivity may have been smaller than they appear at first sight, and the period required for their exploitation may have been longer than the 33 years observed here.

We see no presumption, however, that the regime has exploited fully the opportunities for technological advance open to it. The leaders of

---

[48] E.g., Kendrick estimates rates for the United States for the period 1899–1957, on alternative assumptions, of 1.7 or 2.0 percent (see Kendrick–61, p. 65). Cf. also calculations made in Abramovitz–56 and Solow–57. The effects of several of the differences between our procedures and those used for one or another of the U.S. estimates (the netting out of depreciation, arithmetic aggregation, the treatment of all labor as homogeneous) can be seen by reference to Table 9–3.

[49] The percentage shares cited in this paragraph are based on the data in Table P–1, except that the division of civilian industry between producer and consumer goods is obtained from detailed, and not highly reliable, calculations underlying Table P–1.

[50] Cf. pp. 306–8 below.

the regime have not evidenced great wisdom in technical matters: this, it should be remembered, is the world of Lysenkoism, of official enthusiasm for perennial grass and then corn, for steel and then plastics. At the operational level, institutionalized impediments to the introduction of new techniques are large. In view of the inefficiencies which are elsewhere characteristic of the system, it seems unlikely that the difficult and complex problem of choosing among available techniques and applying them under the special circumstances of the borrowing economy should have been handled with notable efficiency and intelligence.[51]

To what extent do the calculated rates of productivity change from 1928 to 1961 reflect differences in allocative efficiency in the two terminal years? Even less than for the 1937/1928 comparison do we see grounds for a guess as to relative efficiency in these two years, and we make none. The difference could be large and it could lie in either direction. The significance of continuing inefficiency, throughout the 1928–61 period, however, is clear in its essentials.

On the one hand, inefficiency has not been so great as to prevent the attainment of a rapid rate of growth. Even in periods when actual output is thought to have fallen short of potential by a large margin, the regime has been able—as a less authoritarian regime might not have been—to devote enough output to additions to its stock of productive resources to maintain a high rate of growth in aggregate inputs. The growth of inputs, together with increased productivity, has been sufficient to produce a rapid growth in output. In effect, the economy has moved along a path more or less paralleling but lying substantially below that which it could have followed if in each year, with the given inputs, full efficiency had been attained. There is nothing necessarily inconsistent about a system which utilizes its resources inefficiently at all points in time and yet grows rapidly over time.

On the other hand, the costs of inefficiency have been large. If in each year potential output had been reached, annual additions to productive inputs equal to the actual ones could have been made and the output resulting from greater efficiency devoted to personal or social consumption. Alternatively, greater additions to productive resources could have been made and a third and higher path, reflecting the cumulative effects of sustained efficiency, followed. With the output level of 1928 taken as given, this path would also rise more rapidly over the 33-year period than that of maximum efficiency with the actual inputs. The consequences of inefficiency, therefore, have been some combination of growth at a lower absolute level, at a slower rate, and with greater sacrifice by the population, than was necessary.[52]

---

[51] Little systematic information is now available on the course and character of Soviet technical importations. Even a narrative history of this element in Soviet development would be extremely useful.

[52] Several of the arguments of the section immediately following bear on the possibility that inefficiency may have been the price of accelerated growth from other sources (on which, cf. Wiles–62, chap. 11). Also, the statements made here as to the consequences of inefficiency would, if the supply of labor were a negative function of the real wage (see p. 303 below), need to be altered to restrict the use of added output to increased investment, education, perhaps higher pensions, etc.

3. THE GROWTH PROCESS: FURTHER CONSIDERATIONS

The Rate of Change in Mix

In our previous discussion of short-run fluctuations in productivity, we assumed in effect an economy whose annual performance is unaffected by where it was in the past and where it is intended or expected to be in the future. We propose now to relax those assumptions.

In any single year, productivity must depend significantly upon how closely the product mix of that year resembles the mix of the year or years immediately past. This is so because inputs in existence at the beginning of the year are likely to have specific physical characteristics which are adapted to the uses in which the inputs are already employed and which can be changed only at a cost. Even without such specificity in the form of inputs, their reallocation from one use to another creates problems of adjustment which cannot be solved instantaneously. For these reasons, rapid changes in the composition of output are likely to depress productivity while they are occurring and to be followed by recoveries in productivity once they cease. Various complications in this relation could be allowed for. Changes which represent returns to earlier mixes are probably easier to make than are progressive departures from earlier positions. Changes which are accompanied by large additions to the stock of inputs are easier, on account of the greater malleability of new inputs, than are those made with inputs already formed and in use. Unequal changes in productivity among sectors will permit or cause changes in product mix which require no shifting of resources—short-run harvest fluctuations are an important case in point. But, where changes in the composition of output are as large and as rapidly effected as they are thought to have been in the Soviet Union, it appears reasonable to expect an inverse relation between productivity and the rate of change in product mix.

In Chart 10–1, we show a measure of sorts of this rate of change. The figures are calculated as the annual increase in the percentage share in total output of all sectors increasing their shares or, alternatively, the decline of all sectors whose share falls. Output is net product (value added) in 1937 prices. The total economy is divided into sixteen sectors and the nonagricultural portion into one less.[53] In principle, the measure ought to relate to the distribution of output among kinds of final product, not its distribution by sector of origin. The number of sectors distinguished is essentially arbitrary, although the classification appears fine enough to separate sectors of markedly unlike outputs. The several complications noted above are allowed for only in that the series exclusive of agriculture is shown because of the peculiarities of agricultural supply. The measure

---

[53] The sectors are agriculture; machinery industry; producer goods industries other than machinery; consumer goods industry; munitions industry; construction; transportation and communications; trade and restaurants; housing; finance; health; education; government and other administration; military services; repairs, domestic services, etc.; and other services. All data are given in Table P–1 or are detailed components of series in that table; "other services" are those not allocated among specified sectors (see p. 621). Data for net product are used because we do not allocate depreciation among such detailed sectors.

must lie between zero and 100—between constancy in the mix and the entire displacement of one group of products by another—but its absolute value is of no significance.

Over the prewar years, it is hard to see more than a trace of the expected relation between rate of change in the product mix and productivity. The change in mix of the First Five-Year Plan is most rapid in 1930, when productivity reaches a peak, and declines too quickly to account easily for the trough in productivity of the early 1930's. The 1936 peak in productivity in the nonagricultural sectors does coincide with a low in the rate of change—the series for the total economy in that year reflects a poor harvest—but no progressive slowing of change accompanies the productivity upswing to 1936–37. The leveling-off and decline of productivity

CHART 10–1

Annual Change in the Composition of Net National Product, by Sector of Origin, in 1937 Prices, 1929–61

(Percent of Total Product Gained or Lost by Component Sectors)

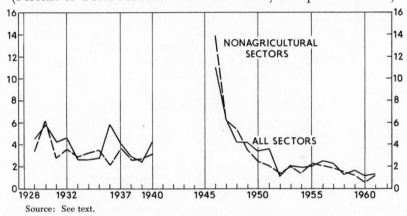

Source: See text.

after 1937 is associated with no pronounced rise in the change in mix. The latter is particularly significant because the conversion of industry from civilian to munitions production and the expansion of the armed forces might appear a likely explanation of the behavior of productivity in the late 1930's. These changes, evidently, were not large in the whole economy and in its nonagricultural portions relative to those which had occurred in earlier years, and it is not obvious that they should have been more difficult to effect.[54] With respect to 1940 in particular, however, we should note that the absorption of new territories may have posed short-run adjustment problems similar to those created by changes in product proportions.

The one instance in which the relation between rate of change in mix

---

[54] According to our estimates, which are not highly accurate on the point, munitions production accounted for 2.5 percent in 1937 and 5.9 percent in 1940 of value added in all sectors, for 3.6 percent and 8.4 percent in the nonagricultural sectors (cf. Table P–1). The armed forces accounted for 2.6 percent of total employment in 1937 and 4.2 percent in 1940 (cf. Table Q–4).

and productivity is as expected is in the immediate postwar years. The rate of change is very high in 1946 (and probably in 1945 also) and declines very rapidly for several years following; productivity is correspondingly low and rises rapidly. The change variable is here undoubtedly an important part of the explanation of the observed behavior of productivity, and, since the rapidity of change can properly be attributed to the war, war can here be charged with a specific and identifiable effect on productivity. Taken together with other factors on which we have commented earlier—the state of repair of the capital stock, the supply of agricultural raw materials to nonagricultural sectors, the hours adjustment in the estimates of labor inputs, unmeasured changes in the quality of labor, and the general disorganizing effects of war—the change in output proportions suggests that inefficiency, short-run immobilities being taken as given, was not so great in 1945–46 as our productivity estimates appear to indicate, nor, however, was its reduction in the years immediately following so rapid.

The rate of change in product mix does not help explain the low level of productivity in 1953 or the rapidity of its rise thereafter. By 1953, change was at a low rate by prewar standards and had been relatively low for some years previous. In the years following 1953, it remained low, which would account for a high level of productivity but not for a rapidly rising one. The change measure confirms the impression that the post-Stalin period was relatively tranquil, but it is not otherwise revealing. In these years, as in the prewar period, the rate of change in output proportions did in fact, we suppose, affect productivity in the manner posited, but its workings are largely obscured by those of other, more potent, factors.

Extending the period over which changes are measured to two or three years yields series—these are not shown—which conform not much better to the fluctuations in productivity, except that a peak rate of change is moved closer to the 1932–33 trough in productivity. A low in the rate of change does now occur in 1937, which sustains better than the series of Chart 10–1 our earlier assertion that 1937 was a year of relatively full adaptation of product mix and inputs. The rate of change in 1950, on the other hand, increases as the period is lengthened. The longer the period, of course, the less specific and immobile are resources and the less plausible that changes in product mix should depress productivity for the reasons postulated. Large and continuous changes in mix may, for another reason, reduce productivity, by disorienting and exhausting those responsible for decisions, which is to say that they may induce inefficiencies. Effects of this sort from changes in mix undoubtedly contributed to the inefficiencies of 1932–33.

A short-run adjustment problem analogous to that from changing output mixes arises from rapid changes in input proportions, but, again, the actual changes, at least for broad categories of inputs, are badly timed to explain the observed fluctuations in productivity. The most rapid increase in the ratio of capital to labor occurs from the early 1950's to 1961; within the prewar period, the ratio increases at a higher rate in 1932–37 than in either 1928–32 or 1937–40.[55] We judge that changes of this sort also tended

---

[55] The reference is to capital services and, for the whole economy, to the weighted labor series, but the general relations can be seen from Chart 9–5 or Table T–55.

to work in the expected direction but had their effects swamped by those of other forces—and by the reverse causation which makes changes in capital depend upon changes in output which are themselves the result of changes in productivity.

Although the fact is disregarded in the preceding discussion, the extent to which short-run changes in output or input mixes affect productivity depends also upon how far they are anticipated. The choice of output mix in one period is, foreseeably, a determinant of both the quantity and the kind of resources which will be available in subsequent periods and, hence, a determinant of both the position and shape of subsequent transformation functions. Such functions are not given but, over time, are themselves subject to decision. Thus, the depressive effects of a change in mix may be felt before the change actually occurs, as capacity more appropriate to the anticipated outputs than to the current ones is built up. Productivity may then recover as resources are put to the purposes for which they were designed. On the whole, however, allowing for a possible lead in the relation does not improve the fit of the change series to the observed fluctuations in productivity, with the possible exception that an anticipatory expansion of munitions capacity may have occurred in the late 1930's.

Growth Strategy

Whatever the relevance of anticipations to short-run fluctuations in productivity, it is unquestionably true that the Soviet authorities have made choices among product mixes in one period in anticipation of effects to be realized in later periods. Not only have they, as suggested earlier, held intentions expressed in terms of product mixes to be attained at future dates, but those intentions, including the goal of rapid growth,[56] have guided their choices among the alternatives open to them at antecedent dates. Objectives, as noted, have been revised with experience and with change in circumstance, but there is perceivable a sufficiently systematic sequence of choices, made with enough deliberation, to be properly called a "strategy" for growth.

By about 1928, the regime had determined on the broad features of the route to growth it intended to follow. These were, essentially, rapid industrialization and a rapid increase in investment, the two elements being mutually dependent. It was confronted initially, however, with a transformation function in which capacity was relatively large for the production and processing of agricultural goods but relatively small for the production of the kinds of investment goods required for industrial expansion. That is to say, it was confronted with a transformation function which was ill-suited to the generation of subsequent functions of the sort deemed necessary for rapid growth. In the course of the First Five-Year Plan, it effected an enormous reshaping of its transformation function. The reflection of this in the composition and distribution of the capital stock and labor inputs has been commented on previously. But the changes effected

---

[56] We assume in the discussion following, as we have implicitly heretofore, that the regime's objective was rapid growth in total output rather than in output per worker or per capita. The assumption appears the most nearly true of any simple one that can be made, but doubtless it is not wholly true.

were not solely in productive inputs or in technology. Institutional arrangements of every kind (administrative, planning, labor, credit, tax, agricultural) were reorganized into forms which persisted throughout the remainder of Stalin's life and, with limited modifications, thereafter. By 1932, the regime was substantially in possession of the kind of productive capacity and basic institutions which it judged appropriate to rapid growth, and for several years it moved along that rapid-growth path. Along the latter, further radical changes in the shape of transformation functions and in product mix were not required. In considerable measure, the system reproduced itself in its own image but on an increasing scale. Large outputs of machinery were selected from functions with large capacity for such outputs in order to create new functions with large capacity for machinery production, and so on. With the approach of war, the economy was forced off the path of rapid growth by the need to sacrifice investment to military preparations, and in the war itself it was driven far from that path. By 1945, it was again in a position similar to that of 1928, with a productive capacity much of which was adjusted to military uses and therefore ill-suited for rapid growth. In the course of a very few years, the system was moved back onto the path of the mid-1930's, along which it has proceeded since.

A still more schematized rendering of the same narrative is presented in Chart 10–2. We there employ again the—faulty—data, in 1937 prices, used for Chart 10–1, but we now calculate the difference between the product mix of each given year and that of 1936–37; the two-year base is intended primarily to average the good harvest of 1937 with the poor one of 1936.[57] Over the four years from 1928 to 1932, the system traversed roughly two thirds of the distance from the product mix of 1928 to that of 1936–37. Movement relative to 1936–37 was comparatively gradual from 1932 through 1938. By 1945, output proportions were far from those of the mid-1930's, but the latter were almost regained by 1948. Thereafter, the mix moved away from that of 1936–37 steadily but relatively slowly and smoothly.

As can be seen, there is a resemblance—though no more than a resemblance—between the curves of Chart 10–2 and the implications of the so-called "turnpike theorem."[58] The years 1928–32 and 1945–48 look like approaches to the turnpike, 1932–38 and 1948–61 like movements along it. The turnpike is not a straight line, with constant product proportions, but a broad curve, reflecting, among other things, a continuing shift from agriculture to industry and related activities and a continuing rise in the investment share in total output.[59]

---

[57] For convenience, Chart 10–2 is drawn with a vertical scale twice that of Chart 10–1. Although it cannot be read from the measure itself, changes in the shares of individual sectors are quite continuous over time.

[58] See Dorfman–58, chap. 12.

[59] The Chart 10–2 calculations record directly change in the share of fixed capital investment only, as income originating in machinery production and in construction, and not that of investment in inventories and livestock. For this reason, much of the erratic short-run fluctuations in the investment share (see Table T–50 or Chart 8–2), which could be taken as another measure of compositional change, are not recorded here. In the present context, however, differences in the physical characteristics of products appear more relevant than differences between commodities currently consumed and those added to stocks.

CHART 10-2

**Composition of Net National Product by Sector of Origin Relative to
1936–37 Average, in 1937 Prices, 1928–61**
(Positive or Negative Difference in Percent of Total Product Accounted
for by Component Sectors)

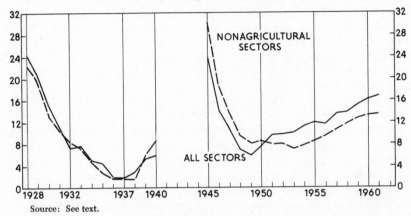

Source: See text.

The price paid in 1928–32 to get on the path of rapid growth was high.
We have noted the probable effects on output and productivity of the
rapidity with which product proportions were changed in this period.
Having in mind now the purpose for which they were changed, we should
add that the transition was effected in significant part by resort to international trade, of which little use was made again, at least before the late
1950's. In the face of a transformation function ill-suited to the production of machinery and steel, the regime for a time, especially in 1930–31,
produced and exported grain and timber products and petroleum in exchange for machinery and steel. The gains which the exchange yielded
were not only the immediate ones of comparative advantage but the rapid
expansion of domestic capacity to produce things of the sort which were
initially imported. Unfortunately for the regime and the population, the
terms of trade turned sharply against the Soviet Union in the course of
the exchange, and the large export of foodstuffs ultimately contributed to
the famine of 1932–33.[60]

Of all the changes effected in the First Five-Year Plan, the most costly
was collectivization. To this, chiefly, is attributable the loss of agricultural
capital which occurred between 1929 and 1933 and the loss of population
arising from the famine of 1932–33. That the system could sustain the
decline in agricultural output which occurred without a greater catas-
trophe is a reflection of its relatively high per capita output of food products
in 1928—high especially in comparison with countries which have attempted rapid development since. The absolute decline in agricultural

---

[60] On the material of this paragraph, cf. Holzman–63, *passim*. It should perhaps be
remarked that the transformation functions referred to here, throughout, are those for
domestic production, with no account taken of the possibilities of "producing" through
trade. A function for 1928 incorporating those possibilities presumably would have
differed less in shape from the functions of later years than did the 1928 function for
domestic possibilities only.

output, moreover, explains about as much as does the increase in nonagricultural production of the closeness of the 1932 product mix to that of subsequent peacetime years: the reshaping of the transformation function was effected by the "throwing away" of productive capacity of some kinds as well as by the creation of others. That collectivization was functionally related to the chosen path of rapid growth is a familiar proposition in Soviet history. By organizing the peasantry into large and controllable administrative units, the regime was able to extract from them, after the costs of transition were paid, the agricultural produce required to feed a growing urban labor force. This it was able to do by compulsion, without the necessity of diverting to the peasantry for their own consumption a large share of the growing industrial output.

From 1928 to 1932, GNP in 1937 prices increased by less than 10 percent. Almost certainly, the increase in 1937 prices, and probably in 1932 or even 1928 prices, would have been greater if institutions and product mix had been left as they were in 1928. The regime's accomplishment in the First Five-Year Plan was not primarily rapid growth but the laying of a basis for rapid growth. While the costs were unquestionably large, it may be that they tend to be magnified in retrospect because the realization of much of their prospective returns was prevented or deferred by the war. It is a defining characteristic of turnpikes that they are good routes for traveling long distances. The Soviet economy, having made its way on to a path of rapid growth, was quite shortly compelled to leave it and did not regain it for close to a decade.

What was the merit (the "efficiency") of the rapid-growth path chosen? Viewed broadly, it has an evident rationality. Industrialization and increased investment, and also improved education, full employment, the importation of advanced techniques, are all elements of a reasonable program for economic growth. The most that can be said about one or another such measure is that it was carried too far or not far enough, too fast or too slowly. There is also an obvious congruency between these measures and the institutional framework within which they operated: the collective farm permitted a large marketed share of agricultural output; authoritarian government made possible a rapid growth of investment. And, what is perhaps most convincing, a rapid rate of long-term growth was in fact attained, despite the losses of the early years and the war.

The regime's success has been most clearly notable, to repeat, in increasing aggregate inputs. There is in the process by which this was accomplished a possible logic which is worth comment. Except for the interruption of the war, the regime has persistently pushed upward the investment share in GNP (in constant prices).[61] This rise, however, has been accompanied by different patterns of change, in two distinguishable periods, in the level of real wages.[62] If some rather complex historical facts are simplified, the investment share may be said, in the Stalin era, to have increased while real wages were held at or below their 1928 level. In the post-Stalin years, the investment share has continued to rise, but wages have been allowed to rise also, and rapidly. How nearly either of these

---

[61] See Chart 8–2 or Table T–50.
[62] On real wages, see Chapman–63, p. 238 and *passim*.

policies maximized the total increase in inputs, capital and labor together, depends upon the shape of the supply function for labor.

If we suppose that the quantity of labor supplied, including all qualitative and motivational attributes, is independent of the return to labor for wage rates above subsistence requirements, the growth of aggregate inputs is maximized by holding wages at the subsistence level and devoting the remainder of output (beyond governmental expenditures) to investment. In the Stalin period, at least in its early phases, it may be that the supply of labor behaved in something like the manner posited. Promises of future rewards may be effective substitutes for present ones, and exhortations to sacrifice in the service of public goals may stimulate effort as well as does the expectation of immediate private gain. Where these inducements fail, the threat of punishment may work. All were tried in the Stalin years. Real wages were doubtless depressed too far even for the maintenance of the existing labor force in 1932–33, although this was probably accidental rather than deliberate. On the other hand, the depression of wages may help explain the willingness of housewives to enter the labor force, the labor supply function over a range being negatively sloped.

However, workers, like the authorities over them, learn from experience. Promises repeatedly unfulfilled lose their potency. Men long used to compulsion devise subtle forms of resistance to it. And, as the system advances to increasingly sophisticated production processes, it becomes increasingly dependent upon the volition of an educated and relatively informed labor force. Under these circumstances, the growth of aggregate inputs is likely to be maximized only with a continuous rise in the real wage. Workers must be rewarded here and now if the services of which they are capable are to be rendered. Conceivably, this was the kind of labor-supply function which confronted Stalin's successors, and they may have reacted to it in an intelligent way—not out of greater compassion than Stalin's but from a recognition that a critical function in the system, relevant to the same goal as Stalin's, had shifted.[63]

Nothing is more difficult to speculate about than the shape of the supply function for labor, account being taken not merely of the number of existing workers willing to offer their services but of the diligence with which they are willing to work and, what is still harder to discern, their willingness to reproduce themselves and expand their numbers. The Soviet authorities presumably know better than does an outside observer the likely shape of the function with which they deal. But, while granting that there may be logic in Soviet investment and wage policies in both the Stalin and post-Stalin periods and, hence, over the entire 33 years, we do not seriously propose that the regime has in fact maximized the growth of inputs. Investment policy under Stalin was so Spartan that in the long run it almost certainly depressed incentives and quite possibly slowed the growth of population and labor force. Both before 1953 and after, the

---

[63] The shift did not, of course, occur suddenly in 1953, though popular expectations of improved living standards may have been strengthened by Stalin's death. Nor did the rapid rise in real wages begin at that date. The preceding rise, however, was from what must have been a very deep trough at the end of the war, and it is indicative that as early as 1947 the investment share had been raised to 20 percent of GNP.

fetishism in the regime's devotion to heavy industry suggests that too many rather than too few resources went to investment. A more moderate rate of increase in the investment share might, because of its effects on the supply of labor, have yielded not only a more rapid increase in aggregate inputs but a more rapid increase in investment and hence in the capital stock.

For the rate of growth in productivity, the particular growth path chosen was clearly favorable in that it permitted the exploitation of economies of scale. The rapid increase in inputs presumably facilitated technological change, since new techniques could be introduced with new capital instruments adapted to them and with a more skilled and educated labor force, increasingly capable of using advanced techniques imported from abroad.[64] The opportunities for technological borrowings were undoubtedly large for the kind of product mixes that characterize the rapid-growth path. The product mix being taken as given, however, the extreme concentration of borrowings in a small portion of the economy gives reason, additional to those cited previously, to doubt that the opportunities were fully utilized. The best way to increase the output of heavy industry is not necessarily to maximize technological advance within heavy industry. Output in that sector can also be increased by devoting some part of the available capacity for acquiring new techniques to improvement within agriculture or light industry, releasing thereby resources for employment in heavy industry.

How nearly the institutions chosen were, even among those ideologically acceptable to the regime, the most appropriate for rapid growth is a question much too large to be dealt with here. Suspicion is obviously justified that, for example, the collective farm, while for a time perhaps advantageous, has proven in the long run a poor instrument for effective administration and for the provision of adequate labor incentives.

Given, in its broad features, the chosen path for rapid growth, there is a final question of the efficiency with which it was pursued. Efficiency here is largely a problem of maintaining a proper balance among interdependent sectors—coal and steel, fertilizer and agriculture—as they expand over time. This is in turn, in substantial measure though not wholly, a question of choosing appropriately among alternative forms and directions of capital investment.

Almost certainly, efficiency in the choice among kinds of new inputs has been even lower than efficiency in the allocation of existing inputs. The crisis in rail transportation of the early 1930's was not merely an error in allocation but a failure to anticipate and provide for the future demands of other sectors for transportation services.[65] In general, the system has proceeded from bottleneck to bottleneck, correcting its mistakes (sooner or later) once they become manifest but foreseeing its future needs and making present provision for them only very imperfectly. This has been the case despite the elaborate formalities of long-term planning.

There is, no doubt, an interesting implication in Soviet experience that a kind of shortsighted pragmatism, a sequential response to objective

---

[64] The "carrier" function of new capital is discussed more fully below, pp. 306 ff.
[65] Cf. Hunter-57, p. 50.

needs as each in turn becomes pressing, works better than one might have
thought. Such a procedure may in fact have a certain rationale in a system
short of skilled decision makers, without trustworthy sources of information on prospective requirements, and employing planned targets as much
to induce large efforts as to co-ordinate their results. It is hard to conceive,
nevertheless, that a more systematic and rational accommodation in this
year's decisions for next year's needs was not possible and would not have
yielded a higher rate of growth than that attained.

Failures to articulate the expansion paths of interdependent sectors
unquestionably contributed to the short-run fluctuations in productivity
which we attributed earlier to static inefficiencies. That attribution, therefore, should be amended to include "dynamic" inefficiencies. It is probable
also that the rapid rise in productivity since 1953 is due to more effective
foresight and long-run planning as well as to increased efficiency in the
use of existing resources.

The Contribution of Capital

In what we have said thus far, we have attached no special significance
to changes in capital, as against other inputs, as a determinant of growth.
Lacking firm knowledge of true interest rates, we are unavoidably forestalled from any pointed analysis of the specific contribution of capital.
It may be of interest, nevertheless, to make explicit the implications of
the change in capital which follow from our procedures.

Calculating extreme values as before, for the 33-year period and the
whole economy, aggregate inputs would have increased from the change
in capital alone, all other inputs remaining constant at their weight-year
magnitudes, at rates of 1.2 to 3.7 percent per annum.[66] These rates amount
to 35 and 73 percent respectively of the corresponding figures for the
actual increase in aggregate inputs (3.4 and 5.1 percent). They amount to
18 to 55 percent of the rate of change in output for the 1937 product mix
(6.7 percent), to 23 to 71 percent of that for the linked 1928–37 mix (5.2
percent). In the nonagricultural nonresidential subsector, aggregate inputs would have increased from the capital increase alone at 1.6 to 4.8
percent, which rates are about the same as in the whole economy relative
to actual rates of change in aggregate inputs (4.8 and 6.8 percent) and to
the change in output (8.4 and 6.7 percent). The increase of capital appears
thus, in this rather conventional sense, to account for roughly a fifth to a
half or more of the total growth in output. Allowance for the role of
capital in the realization of scale effects would increase its apparent importance. The range of possible estimates, however, is obviously extremely
wide.

The apparent importance of capital would be reduced somewhat if

---

66 The lower figure is computed from capital services in 1937 prices and with 1937
input shares, both at $r = 8\%$. Aggregation is logarithmic as before, the quantities of
labor and land being held constant at their 1937 values. The higher figure is computed,
for 1928–37, with 1928-price capital services, 1928 input shares, and labor and land at
their 1928 values; it is extended from 1937 to 1961 on the 1937-price data; for both intervals, $r = 20\%$. Because of interaction, the sum of the increase in aggregate inputs
resulting from the increase of each input taken separately is less than the total, but only
slightly so.

capital inputs and output were taken net of annual depreciation. In 1937 prices, for example, the long-term growth rates of net product are 5.0 percent for the whole economy and 6.5 percent for the subsector, or 0.2 percentage points less than the corresponding rates for gross product. Rates for aggregate inputs are reduced similarly, and productivity growth rates are therefore virtually unaffected (see Tables 9–1 and 9–3, row 7, where calculations are also shown for selected dates intermediate to 1928 and 1961). The rate of increase in aggregate inputs which would have resulted from the change in capital alone is reduced from 1.2–2.5 percent ($r = 8\%$ and 20%) to 0.9–2.3 percent for the total, and from 1.6–3.5 percent to 1.3–3.2 percent for the subsector. These rates are lower relative to those of aggregate inputs and of output than in the gross calculations, but by modest amounts. Our reasons for preferring measures gross of depreciation are stated in Chapter 1, p. 7.

The contribution of capital appears greater if the dependence of technological change upon capital is taken into account. Capital, it has been plausibly argued, serves as a carrier for new technology, or, more specifically, for that part of technology which is not organizational.[67] New techniques are embodied in new kinds of capital, and, given that technology progresses over time, the productivity of a unit of capital is higher the more modern it is, the more recent its vintage.[68] The productivity of a stock of capital depends upon the age distribution of its components, which may be approximated by an average.

While embodiment of new techniques in the use of capital requires changes in the quality of capital, not all qualitative changes represent the embodiment of new techniques, and those which do are not necessarily specific to the new techniques—which point we have discussed in Chapter 1 (Section 2). In our estimates, those qualitative changes which would have affected the productivity of capital in the weight year, under the technology of that year, are, in principle at least, allowed for in the measured quantity of capital. A further imputation to capital is required only for changes which affect productivity in the given year and not, or not proportionately, in the weight year.

The carrier function is unlikely to inhere equally in different kinds of capital. Although exceptions are imaginable, it is doubtful that either inventories or livestock embody in significant degree the technology of one period rather than another. Most structures appear not highly specific to particular technologies. Buildings, which are the larger part of structures, are generally adaptable, with or without remodeling, to the employment of new techniques within the space which they enclose. Other structures (blast furnaces, power transmission lines) may be closely shaped to the particular technology for which they were constructed but still others (roadways, bridges, dams) are not obviously so.[69] It is equipment,

---

[67] Cf. in particular, Solow–60.

[68] New techniques are doubtless embodied also, and perhaps as consequentially, in labor—in labor skilled or trained for their utilization. We restrict our attention, however, to capital.

[69] Some changes in technology, such as the introduction of the railroad, do require the creation of large quantities of structures which would have had a productivity close to zero in earlier periods. Such changes are not thought to have been characteristic of the Soviet economy in the period we are considering.

chiefly, which is visualized, when capital is described as the vehicle of technical change, and, even within this category, large differences in technological specificity must exist.[70] Equipment, as has been pointed out, accounted for 6 percent of the total Soviet capital stock, in 1937 prices, in 1928 and 27 percent in 1962; in 1928 prices, it accounted for 11 percent in 1928 and for 27 percent in 1937.

In the Soviet case, furthermore, there is no satisfactory way to date the technology embodied in assets created in any given year. For economies which have shared continuously in the technological progress of the world at large, it is reasonable to assume that the technology incorporated in an asset varies more or less continuously with the calendar date of its creation. But the Soviet Union drew from a pool of advanced techniques already in existence in 1928 and expanding thereafter. Moreover, it did not in each year following 1928 adopt what were then advanced techniques elsewhere in the world; its capacity to borrow was extended to increasingly sophisticated techniques over time; its practice of keeping equipment models in production over long periods caused the modernity of a given model to decline over time.[71] The vintage of Soviet capital, therefore, in an analytically relevant sense, cannot be read from the calendar date of an asset's creation.

For these reasons, we do not suppose that much can be inferred about the importance of capital as a carrier in Soviet growth from simple statistical measures. The behavior over time of the average age of the total capital stock (see Chart 6–4 or Table T–37), which does not in fact decline significantly before the mid-1950's, is dominated by inventories, livestock, and structures. We should note parenthetically that the decline by 22 percent in the average age of all capital from 1955 to 1962 probably is related to the increase of productivity in that period: given the considerable stability in the composition of output, the shortening of the average age suggests an improvement in the adaptation of the form and composition of capital to the particular uses to which it was put. But this is something different from the carrier hypothesis. The average age of equipment alone (see Chart 3–4 or Table T–22) is more nearly relevant to the latter and does conform in some instances to the observed changes in calculated productivity: equipment was relatively old in 1945; its age was materially reduced between 1955 and 1962. The sharpest reduction in equipment age, on the other hand, occurred between 1930 and 1933, when productivity was falling, and little further reduction was effected from 1933 to 1936–37, when productivity was rapidly rising. Because of the dating problem, how-

---

[70] Judging from official census data (see Table 7–3 of the present study; TsSU–60, p. 69; and TsSU–62a, p. 420), close to 40 percent of the stock of equipment existing on January 1, 1960, consisted of assets for the generation of electrical or mechanical power and of means of transportation. While not all of this is nonspecific in its use, a considerable part of the remaining equipment, such as tractors, cranes, pumps, etc., must be more or less equally usable under a wide range of technologies.

[71] For example, the "International tractor," introduced in the Soviet Union in 1930, was a copy of the 15/30 wheeled, general-purpose tractor, produced by the International Harvester Company from 1922 to 1928. The tractor "Universal," the locomotive "SO," and the 3-ton truck "Zis-5," which were introduced in 1933–34, were still in production in the 1950's. Models of some simpler machines, such as hand pumps, pneumatic hand tools, and small rectifiers, were produced without major modification from 1928 to at least 1958. See Moorsteen–62, pp. 51 and 266.

ever, neither the favorable nor unfavorable evidence is very compelling.

Nor is the reduction of the average age of equipment over the whole period, from 8.8 (which figure is not very reliable) to 6.0 years or by about one third, likely to be a satisfactory index of the extent of the modernization of the equipment stock. In terms of technological levels attained elsewhere, the stock of 1928 was older on the average than 8.8 years. Between 1928 and 1961, the gap between the technology embodied in new Soviet equipment and the new equipment of advanced economies was undoubtedly narrowed, although we cannot say by how many years or at what relative rates within particular subperiods. It is this reduction in the effective age of equipment, presumably by much more than one third, which is the principal ground for thinking that capital's contribution to growth was greater than is implied by the numerical calculations cited above and, also, for supposing that the role of equipment in particular was larger than would be inferred from its small share in total capital. The introduction of advanced techniques imported from the rest of the world was facilitated by a very rapid expansion of the stock of those kinds of assets in which a physical embodiment of the new techniques was required.

4. PROSPECTS

The future course of no economy is, in the present state of knowledge, predictable, and we shall not attempt predictions here. Even if substantial continuity in the behavior of functional relations is assumed, our analysis of the sources of past Soviet growth is scarcely firm enough to support reliable projections. Any one of innumerable shifts in policy or external events could produce large discontinuities in the evolution of the system which we cannot hope to foresee. It may be worth examining, nevertheless, a related but different question: whether there are characteristics of the development process of the past which put in doubt the sustainability of the same process into the fairly immediate future. To this purpose, we have performed the calculations shown in Table 10–1,[72] all of which relate to valuations in 1937 prices.

We take 1953–61 as the recently past period of the greatest interest. Over those eight years, the volume of capital inputs (capital services) more than doubled, which is a notable aspect of the growth of the period. We assume, for illustration, that capital inputs continue to grow at the 1953–61 rate, which means that they approximately double within each of the seven-year periods, 1961–68 and 1968–75. The estimates for labor and land inputs are meant to be realistic, but they are casual and imprecise. Labor inputs are assumed to grow at the rate estimated from demographic data for the population of "able-bodied" age.[73] The procedure appears reasonable in that it implies some allowance for recovery from the effects

---

[72] Abram Bergson has made calculations, unpublished, by procedures similar to those used in the table.

[73] The rates are calculated from estimates given in Brackett–62, p. 521; annual averages are computed from January 1 totals. From 1953 to 1961, population of able-bodied age increased at 1.1 percent per year, which is higher than the 0.7 percent estimated for labor inputs, but so large a reduction in hours as occurred between 1953 and 1961 is . probably not to be expected in the future.

TABLE 10-1

INPUTS, PRODUCTIVITY, AND OUTPUT, 1953-61 REALIZED, 1961-68 AND
1968-75 ILLUSTRATIVE PROJECTIONS, IN 1937 PRICES
(Percentage Annual Growth Rate)

		Productivity Growth Rate Equal to That of 1953-61		Productivity Growth Rate Equal to That of 1928-61	
	1953-61	1961-68	1968-75	1961-68	1968-75
			r = 8%		
Inputs					
Capital	10.3	10.3	10.3	10.3	10.3
Labor	0.7	1.2	1.7	1.2	1.7
Land	3.3	0.0	0.0	0.0	0.0
Aggregate	2.6	2.7	3.1	2.7	3.1
Aggregate Productivity . . .	4.7	4.7	4.7	1.8	1.8
Output					
Gross National Product. .	7.5	7.6	7.9	4.5	5.0
Gross Investment	12.0	10.3	10.3	10.3	10.3
Noninvestment Components of GNP. . .	5.9	6.3	6.4	1.2	-0.9
			r = 20%		
Inputs					
Capital	10.1	10.1	10.1	10.1	10.1
Labor	0.7	1.2	1.7	1.2	1.7
Land	3.3	0.0	0.0	0.0	0.0
Aggregate.	4.4	4.5	4.8	4.5	4.8
Aggregate Productivity . . .	2.9	2.9	2.9	1.0	1.0
Output					
Gross National Product. .	7.5	7.5	7.8	5.5	5.8
Gross Investment	12.0	10.3	10.3	10.3	10.3
Noninvestment Components of GNP. . .	5.9	6.1	6.2	2.9	1.7

Source: See text.

of low wartime birth rates on the flow of new entrants into the labor force, which were most severe in the late 1950's and early 1960's. No allowance for changes in hours, in participation rates, or in the distribution of labor between agriculture and other sectors (labor inputs have separate weights for the two categories) is attempted; the effects of these changes are likely to be in some degree offsetting.[74] In the absence of a major alteration in labor policy, the foreseeable growth of labor inputs is modest. The land estimates assume that no further expansion into "new lands" will occur; how far land in fallow, pasture, and the like may be reduced, we are unprepared to guess. Aggregate inputs are obtained by summation in the logs.

For aggregate productivity, we assume, alternatively, continuation of the high rates of the recent past and of the lower rates of the 33-year long term, both with valuations of output and inputs in 1937 prices. The higher rates are high also relative to the extreme long-term rates calculated

---

[74] If we assume that the calculated growth rates are for unweighted labor and, on the basis of its past stability, that the absolute quantity of labor in agriculture will remain constant, weighted labor inputs rise at 1.6 percent for 1961-68 and 2.1 percent for 1968-75. A further reduction in hours, however, is likely; the probable direction of change in participation rates is unclear.

for the 1937 product mix; the lower rates are high, at the lower limit, relative to those calculated for the linked 1928–37 mix. All of the assumed productivity rates are illustrative.

The output figures are inferred more or less directly from the posited inputs and productivities. The GNP growth rates are calculated from the rates for aggregate inputs and productivity. The investment figures, which are set equal to the higher of the capital input figures, are intended to approximate the investment which would be required to yield a capital stock which, in turn, would yield the capital services assumed. Between 1953 and 1961, gross investment in fixed capital increased slightly more rapidly than the corresponding net stock, of which the services increased at a rate still nearer the investment rate.[75] That is, the stock and flow relation for fixed capital was by this period near to equilibrium, and the change in the composition of fixed capital was small.[76] The considerable discrepancy between the 1953–61 growth rates of total investment and total capital services is explained chiefly by a large difference in the inventory and livestock components, reflecting the year-to-year variability of these forms of investment. On the assumption, which we make, that the future growth rate of total capital services is constant from year to year, at the 1953–61 rate, something like a constant growth rate of gross investment equal to that of total services will be required, the precise relation depending upon the extent and direction of further changes in the composition of the stock. The rate of increase in output devoted to noninvestment purposes is computed from the GNP and gross investment totals, which are derived from the actual 1961 values and the projected future changes. An error of 1 percentage point in the investment growth rate would produce an error of less than 1 percentage point in the noninvestment growth rate except for the 1968–75 period with the productivity rate assumed equal to that of 1928–61.

What the Table 10–1 calculations suggest is that the growth of the recent past is not unsustainable for another decade or more if the regime remains willing to maintain the growth rate of capital and if aggregate productivity continues to increase at the 1953–61 rate. This growth process requires in the future, as in the past, a continuing rise in the share (in constant prices) of gross investment in output, which rise, as was previously remarked (p. 244), cannot persist indefinitely. But, with no diminution in the rate of productivity gain, the increase in the investment share required to produce the assumed rate of increase in the capital stock (from 31 percent in 1961 to 42–43 percent in 1975) is small enough that noninvestment can continue to grow at close to the rapid rate of the last eight years. The disproportionately high growth rate of investment implies also an extremely large and rapid change in the capital-labor ratio—better than a tripling in the 14 years from 1961 to 1975—but this is no more rapid a change than that of 1953–61.

The critical assumption here, clearly, is that aggregate productivity should continue to rise at the 1953–61 rate. This rate, as we have pointed

---

[75] Investment grew at 11.4 percent per annum, the net stock (average annual figures) at 10.8 percent, and services at 10.9–11.1 percent.

[76] Cf. the discussion above, pp. 237 ff.

out, is probably explained in significant part by an exhaustible source of gain, improvements in efficiency. The apparent retardation of the growth in productivity within the 1953–61 period suggests that an effective if not ultimate limit to such gains may already have been approached. Productivity gains from borrowed technology are similarly exhaustible, although the remaining opportunities of this sort may be large. A further stimulus to increased productivity could come from increased expenditures for research purposes. And major institutional changes might increase the effective limit to efficiency. On balance, however, the maintenance of the 1953–61 rate of growth in productivity appears unlikely and a decline in it the most probable source of a decline in the rate of growth of output.

If the growth of productivity and hence output slows, the past rate of growth in capital can be sustained only by reducing the increase in output devoted to noninvestment uses. A reduction in the growth rate of personal consumption, especially if some positive gain in real wages can be maintained, is not necessarily one the regime would hesitate to make. A change in international relations (or of the Soviet view of them) could conceivably permit a reduction in the growth rate of military outlays. If, however, the productivity growth rate were to decline to the lower figures assumed and the investment growth rate were nevertheless maintained, the required deceleration in the growth of other uses of output would be very large. Understandably, the required deceleration would be less the more dependent the growth of output is upon the rapid increase of capital and the less it is dependent upon improved productivity, i.e., the nearer to reality are the calculations with $r = 20\%$ (in 1937, it will be recalled) as against those with $r = 8\%$. It is difficult to conceive, however, that the regime would think it feasible to hold the growth of investment at over 10 percent per year while the growth of other uses was reduced to any of the rates calculated at the lower figures for productivity change.

If, under these circumstances, the regime chose to reduce the rate of increase in investment, the growth of capital would be slowed also, albeit only gradually, as the stock adjusted to the lower trend value of the flow.[77] The effect of a given reduction in the investment growth rate upon the growth of output would be greater the nearer to reality is the assumption of $r = 20\%$ as against $r = 8\%$. Since the output figures calculated with the low productivity rate lie in the neighborhood of the 5.2 percent growth rate (in 1937 prices) attained over the entire 1928–61 period, the implication is that, under the assumed circumstances, the long-term growth rate also might prove unsustainable. This outcome, however, is heavily dependent upon the assumption that labor inputs in the future will increase at a materially slower rate than over the past 33 years: at 1.2 and 1.7 percent in comparison with 2.7 percent for 1928–61. Given the demographic changes in prospect, the reduced opportunity for shifts of labor from agriculture to other sectors, and the using up of the gains to be had from increased female participation, this assumption is not implausible, but its accuracy is highly uncertain.

Whether in fact the productivity growth rate will decline and by how

---

[77] We disregard here the dependence of technological change upon capital—and also the dependence of the labor supply upon the level of real wages.

much and with what response by the regime, we have, of course, no way of knowing. From 1958 to 1961, the growth of GNP declined relative to that of 1953–58, the share of investment in GNP leveled off, the growth rate of investment slowed markedly, and the growth rate of capital, moving gradually toward the investment rate, slowed somewhat. This may be the beginning of the retardation in Soviet growth which a decline in productivity gains is likely to engender. It may, on the other hand, be another of those short-run fluctuations in Soviet performance which have been characteristic of the past.[78]

We have made one other calculation relevant to the future. In order to facilitate extension of our capital stock estimates to years later than those covered, we show in Tables T–69 and T–70 projected future values, net and gross, of the fixed capital stock in existence on January 1, 1962. These are obtained by the same procedures as our estimates of remaining values for years to 1962. The calculations are restricted to valuations in 1937 and 1950 prices. They are carried as far into the future as 1975, although it is to be hoped that sufficient official data will become available to permit better estimates long before that date has been reached.

---

[78] As this is written, it appears that the growth rate of output declined further in 1962–63, though from what cause and with what significance we are not in a position to consider. For the whole of the retardation since 1958, an examination of the particular difficulties of the agricultural sector would be desirable, but that also we are unable to undertake.

Tabular Section

TABLE T-1

TOTAL FIXED CAPITAL, GROSS AND NET, IN 1937 PRICES, 1928-62
(January 1--Billion Rubles)

	Gross Values				Net Values			
	Structures	Equip-ment	Instal-lation	Total	Structures	Equip-ment	Instal-lation	Total
1928	137.3	17.4	2.7	157.4	93.7	12.0	1.9	107.6
1929	144.5	19.4	3.1	167.0	98.4	13.2	2.2	113.7
1930	153.5	21.7	3.5	178.7	104.8	14.9	2.5	122.2
1931	165.8	26.0	4.2	195.9	114.3	18.4	3.1	135.8
1932	179.4	31.1	4.9	215.4	124.8	22.5	3.7	151.0
1933	193.0	37.0	5.7	235.7	135.1	26.9	4.4	166.4
1934	204.9	42.4	6.4	253.7	143.4	30.7	5.0	179.1
1935	219.2	47.8	7.2	274.2	153.9	34.1	5.6	193.6
1936	236.9	54.9	8.2	300.0	167.5	38.8	6.4	212.6
1937	260.8	64.9	9.6	335.3	186.9	46.1	7.6	240.5
1938	281.1	74.9	10.8	366.8	202.2	52.8	8.6	263.6
1939	300.6	85.2	12.1	397.8	216.4	60.1	9.6	286.0
1940	336.8	99.0	14.0	449.8	242.3	69.3	11.1	322.7
1941	374.6	112.8	16.1	503.5	268.9	78.0	12.6	359.6
1944	305.9	87.9	13.8	407.6	209.9	55.1	10.2	275.2
1945	314.5	91.6	14.5	420.6	212.5	58.1	10.7	281.3
1946	322.8	98.7	15.5	436.9	214.7	64.7	11.2	290.6
1947	334.9	106.6	16.6	458.1	220.6	72.2	12.0	304.8
1948	349.4	116.3	17.8	483.5	228.6	81.1	12.8	322.5
1949	368.9	128.3	19.3	516.5	241.3	91.0	13.8	346.2
1950	394.3	143.0	21.1	558.5	259.7	101.8	15.1	376.6
1951	421.2	164.5	23.3	609.1	280.8	117.3	16.8	415.0
1952	452.2	187.6	25.8	665.6	305.5	132.6	18.7	456.8
1953	486.7	208.5	28.0	723.2	333.5	145.9	20.6	500.0
1954	524.5	231.2	30.5	786.3	364.2	160.8	22.8	547.8
1955	566.8	259.0	33.5	859.3	398.8	179.9	25.3	603.9
1956	613.3	293.2	36.9	943.5	436.6	204.8	28.2	669.6
1957	658.8	336.9	41.1	1036.8	476.7	238.1	31.7	746.5
1958	710.7	384.0	45.6	1140.4	520.3	273.6	35.6	829.4
1959	769.4	437.4	50.8	1257.7	569.4	314.8	40.0	924.2
1960	835.4	495.5	56.9	1387.7	624.8	357.7	44.7	1027.3
1961	906.5	557.9	63.4	1527.8	684.7	401.5	49.8	1136.0
1962	979.7	624.1	70.3	1674.0	747.1	446.7	55.1	1249.0

Source: See text of Chapter 2.

TABLE T-2

TOTAL FIXED CAPITAL, DEPRECIATED BY SINKING FUND METHOD
AT 20 PERCENT INTEREST RATE, IN 1937 PRICES, 1928-62
(January 1--Billion Rubles)

	Structures	Equipment	Installation	Total
1928	137.0	16.4	2.7	156.1
1929	144.1	18.0	3.0	165.2
1930	153.1	20.2	3.5	176.8
1931	165.3	24.2	4.1	193.6
1932	178.7	28.8	4.9	212.4
1933	192.2	33.8	5.6	231.7
1934	204.0	38.7	6.4	249.0
1935	218.1	43.2	7.1	268.5
1936	235.6	49.1	8.1	292.8
1937	259.2	57.6	9.5	326.2
1938	279.1	65.7	10.7	355.5
1939	298.2	74.3	11.9	384.5
1940	333.8	85.9	13.9	433.6
1941	370.9	97.2	15.9	483.9
1944	301.1	72.6	13.5	387.1
1945	308.7	75.9	14.2	398.7
1946	315.7	83.6	15.1	414.4
1947	326.4	92.5	16.1	435.0
1948	339.2	103.0	17.2	459.5
1949	356.7	115.2	18.6	490.5
1950	379.8	128.7	20.3	528.8
1951	405.7	147.3	22.3	575.2
1952	435.1	166.0	24.5	625.6
1953	467.7	182.9	26.9	677.5
1954	502.9	201.7	29.4	734.0
1955	544.2	224.8	32.3	801.3
1956	589.1	254.0	35.7	878.7
1957	636.8	292.2	40.0	969.1
1958	688.3	333.6	44.8	1066.7
1959	745.4	381.5	50.2	1177.2
1960	808.9	432.4	56.2	1297.4
1961	881.9	485.3	62.5	1429.7
1962	958.4	541.5	69.2	1569.2

Source: See text of Chapter 2.

TABLE T-3

TOTAL FIXED CAPITAL, DEPRECIATED BY SINKING FUND METHOD
AT 8 PERCENT INTEREST RATE, IN 1937 PRICES, 1928-62
(January 1--Billion Rubles)

	Structures	Equipment	Installation	Total
1928	131.2	15.1	2.5	148.8
1929	137.7	16.5	2.8	157.0
1930	146.0	18.4	3.2	167.7
1931	157.5	22.2	3.9	183.6
1932	170.1	26.6	4.6	201.3
1933	182.7	31.3	5.3	219.4
1934	193.5	35.7	6.0	235.2
1935	206.6	39.7	6.7	253.0
1936	222.9	45.0	7.6	275.5
1937	245.3	52.9	8.9	307.2
1938	263.9	60.4	10.1	334.4
1939	281.6	68.5	11.3	361.4
1940	314.8	79.0	13.1	406.9
1941	349.1	89.3	14.9	453.4
1944	280.3	65.6	12.5	358.4
1945	286.3	69.0	13.1	368.4
1946	291.8	76.2	13.9	381.9
1947	300.9	84.7	14.8	400.5
1948	312.1	94.5	15.9	422.5
1949	328.1	105.7	17.1	451.0
1950	349.7	118.0	18.7	486.4
1951	374.3	135.3	20.6	530.2
1952	402.6	152.5	22.7	577.8
1953	434.4	167.7	25.0	627.1
1954	469.1	184.9	27.4	681.5
1955	508.9	206.3	30.3	745.5
1956	552.4	233.7	33.6	819.7
1957	598.8	270.0	37.7	906.5
1958	649.1	309.1	42.2	1000.4
1959	705.6	354.3	47.3	1107.2
1960	768.9	402.2	52.9	1224.0
1961	839.2	451.6	58.8	1349.6
1962	913.0	503.4	65.1	1481.5

Source: See text of Chapter 2.

TABLE T-4

TOTAL FIXED CAPITAL, DEPRECIATED BY DECLINING ANNUITY METHOD
AT 20 PERCENT INTEREST RATE, IN 1937 PRICES, 1928-62
(January 1--Billion Rubles)

	Structures	Equipment	Installation	Total
1928	89.7	10.8	1.8	102.3
1929	94.2	11.9	2.1	108.1
1930	100.3	13.5	2.4	116.2
1931	109.5	16.9	3.0	129.4
1932	119.7	20.8	3.6	144.1
1933	129.6	25.0	4.2	158.9
1934	137.6	28.3	4.8	170.6
1935	147.7	31.1	5.4	184.2
1936	160.8	35.2	6.2	202.3
1937	179.9	42.0	7.3	229.2
1938	194.7	48.2	8.3	251.2
1939	208.3	54.9	9.3	272.5
1940	233.2	63.2	10.7	307.2
1941	258.7	70.9	12.2	341.9
1944	200.6	48.8	9.8	259.3
1945	202.8	52.0	10.2	265.0
1946	204.5	58.6	10.7	273.8
1947	209.8	65.9	11.4	287.1
1948	217.3	74.4	12.2	304.0
1949	229.6	83.6	13.2	326.4
1950	247.4	93.2	14.4	355.1
1951	268.1	107.5	16.1	391.7
1952	292.4	121.3	17.9	431.5
1953	319.9	133.1	19.7	472.8
1954	350.0	146.6	21.8	518.5
1955	383.9	164.0	24.3	572.2
1956	421.0	187.2	27.1	635.3
1957	460.3	218.6	30.5	709.4
1958	503.0	251.7	34.2	788.9
1959	551.3	289.9	38.5	879.7
1960	605.8	329.3	43.1	978.2
1961	664.1	369.0	48.0	1081.1
1962	725.0	409.7	53.1	1187.8

Source: See text of Chapter 2.

TABLE T-5

TOTAL FIXED CAPITAL, DEPRECIATED BY DECLINING ANNUITY METHOD
AT 8 PERCENT INTEREST RATE, IN 1937 PRICES, 1928-62
(January 1--Billion Rubles)

	Structures	Equipment	Installation	Total
1928	83.4	10.0	1.0	95.0
1929	87.6	11.0	1.9	100.5
1930	93.4	12.5	2.2	108.2
1931	102.3	15.9	2.8	121.0
1932	112.2	19.7	3.4	135.3
1933	121.8	23.8	4.0	149.7
1934	129.4	26.9	4.6	160.8
1935	139.1	29.5	5.2	173.8
1936	151.8	33.5	5.9	191.3
1937	170.4	40.1	7.0	217.5
1938	184.7	46.1	8.0	238.8
1939	197.8	52.6	8.9	259.3
1940	221.6	60.5	10.3	292.3
1941	245.9	67.7	11.7	325.3
1944	189.5	45.8	9.3	244.5
1945	191.1	49.0	9.6	249.7
1946	192.3	55.4	10.1	257.8
1947	197.2	62.6	10.8	270.5
1948	204.2	70.7	11.5	286.5
1949	216.0	79.5	12.5	308.0
1950	233.4	88.8	13.7	335.8
1951	253.5	102.5	15.2	371.2
1952	277.1	115.8	17.0	409.9
1953	303.9	126.9	18.8	449.6
1954	333.3	139.8	20.8	493.9
1955	366.2	156.6	23.1	545.9
1956	402.3	179.0	25.9	607.1
1957	440.3	209.4	29.1	678.9
1958	481.7	241.3	32.7	755.7
1959	528.5	278.2	36.8	843.6
1960	581.3	315.9	41.3	938.5
1961	637.8	353.8	46.0	1037.6
1962	696.5	392.6	50.9	1140.0

Source: See text of Chapter 2.

TABLE T-6

TOTAL FIXED CAPITAL, DEPRECIATED BY SUM-OF-DIGITS METHOD,
IN 1937 PRICES, 1928-62
(January 1--Billion Rubles)

	Structures	Equipment	Installation	Total
1928	65.1	8.5	1.3	75.0
1929	69.0	9.5	1.6	80.1
1930	74.5	11.0	1.9	87.5
1931	83.2	14.3	2.5	99.9
1932	92.7	18.0	3.1	113.8
1933	102.0	22.0	3.7	127.6
1934	109.2	24.9	4.2	138.2
1935	118.5	27.3	4.7	150.6
1936	130.8	31.1	5.4	167.4
1937	148.9	37.5	6.5	192.9
1938	162.7	43.2	7.3	213.3
1939	175.2	49.3	8.2	232.7
1940	197.2	56.6	9.5	263.3
1941	219.6	63.2	10.7	293.5
1944	168.1	41.6	8.3	218.1
1945	169.4	44.5	8.6	222.5
1946	170.2	50.8	9.0	230.0
1947	174.8	57.6	9.6	242.0
1948	181.6	65.3	10.2	257.1
1949	193.1	73.6	11.1	277.8
1950	210.1	82.4	12.2	304.8
1951	229.8	95.5	13.7	339.0
1952	252.9	107.9	15.3	376.1
1953	279.0	118.2	17.0	414.2
1954	307.5	130.2	18.8	456.5
1955	339.4	146.0	21.0	506.4
1956	374.2	167.3	23.5	565.1
1957	410.8	196.4	26.6	633.8
1958	450.5	226.6	29.9	707.0
1959	495.4	261.5	33.7	790.6
1960	546.1	297.0	37.8	880.9
1961	600.0	332.3	42.1	974.5
1962	656.0	368.1	46.6	1070.7

Source: See text of Chapter 2.

TABLE T-7

TOTAL FIXED CAPITAL, GROSS AND NET, WITH INVESTMENT IN STRUCTURES
DEFLATED BY INPUT PRICES, IN 1937 PRICES, 1928-62
(January 1--Billion Rubles)

	Gross Values		Net Values	
	Structures	Total	Structures	Total
1928	154.7	174.9	105.6	119.4
1929	162.8	185.3	110.9	126.2
1930	172.7	197.9	117.8	135.3
1931	185.8	215.9	127.7	149.3
1932	204.9	240.9	143.5	169.7
1933	224.8	267.5	159.5	190.9
1934	239.7	288.5	170.2	205.9
1935	258.0	313.0	184.0	223.8
1936	278.6	341.7	199.7	244.9
1937	302.6	377.1	218.5	272.1
1938	322.9	408.5	233.0	294.4
1939	342.3	439.5	246.3	315.9
1940	379.9	493.0	272.2	352.6
1941	419.7	548.6	299.3	389.9
1944	342.5	444.2	233.4	298.7
1945	353.8	460.0	238.2	306.9
1946	365.8	480.0	243.3	319.2
1947	380.9	504.1	251.3	335.5
1948	396.6	530.8	259.7	353.5
1949	417.0	564.7	272.3	377.1
1950	436.7	600.8	283.9	400.9
1951	459.6	647.5	300.5	434.7
1952	486.0	699.4	320.1	471.4
1953	517.3	753.8	344.6	511.1
1954	550.0	811.7	369.9	553.4
1955	587.0	879.4	399.0	604.1
1956	625.2	955.3	428.5	661.4
1957	664.2	1042.1	462.7	732.5
1958	709.4	1139.0	500.1	809.2
1959	760.6	1248.8	542.4	897.1
1960	818.2	1370.5	590.3	992.7
1961	880.5	1501.8	642.2	1093.5
1962	944.0	1638.3	696.5	1198.4

Source: See Chapter 2, p. 46.

TABLE T-8

TOTAL FIXED CAPITAL, GROSS AND NET, IN 1928 PRICES, 1928-62
(January 1--Billion Rubles)

	Gross Values				Net Values			
	Structures	Equip-ment	Instal-lation	Total	Structures	Equip-ment	Instal-lation	Total
1928	67.1	13.0	1.8	81.9	45.8	9.0	1.2	56.0
1929	70.6	14.4	2.0	87.0	48.1	9.9	1.4	59.4
1930	75.1	16.2	2.3	93.6	51.3	11.2	1.6	64.2
1931	81.4	19.7	2.8	103.9	56.2	14.1	2.1	72.4
1932	88.2	24.6	3.4	116.2	61.5	18.1	2.6	82.3
1933	95.1	31.1	4.2	130.4	66.8	23.7	3.3	93.8
1934	100.9	38.3	4.9	144.2	70.8	29.1	4.0	103.9
1935	108.0	45.8	5.8	159.5	76.0	34.4	4.7	115.1
1936	116.7	55.5	6.8	179.1	82.7	41.4	5.6	129.7
1937	128.7	69.9	8.4	207.0	92.5	52.6	7.0	152.1
1938	138.9	84.6	9.9	233.4	100.2	63.4	8.3	172.0
1939	148.6	101.3	11.7	261.7	107.3	75.9	9.9	193.1
1940	166.6	122.3	14.1	303.0	120.3	90.4	11.8	222.5
1941	185.3	141.8	16.4	343.4	133.3	102.8	13.7	249.9
1944	151.3	114.2	14.3	279.8	104.1	74.1	11.2	189.4
1945	155.6	121.0	15.4	292.1	105.5	79.6	12.1	197.1
1946	159.8	132.8	17.0	309.7	106.7	90.2	13.3	210.2
1947	166.0	144.3	18.7	329.1	109.7	101.0	14.5	225.3
1948	173.3	157.7	20.6	351.7	113.9	112.9	16.0	242.8
1949	183.3	174.6	22.8	380.8	120.5	126.8	17.6	265.0
1950	196.2	195.6	25.3	417.2	129.9	142.3	19.6	291.7
1951	209.9	225.7	28.5	464.1	140.6	164.2	22.1	327.0
1952	225.7	255.8	31.7	513.1	153.3	183.5	24.6	361.4
1953	243.3	283.0	34.7	561.1	167.6	200.7	27.1	395.4
1954	262.7	313.0	38.2	613.9	183.4	220.5	29.9	433.7
1955	284.4	350.8	42.4	677.5	201.2	246.7	33.3	481.1
1956	308.3	397.6	47.5	753.4	220.8	280.8	37.5	539.1
1957	332.0	456.2	53.7	841.9	241.6	325.4	42.8	609.8
1958	358.9	517.5	60.4	936.8	264.2	370.9	48.3	683.5
1959	389.4	585.7	68.0	1043.1	289.9	422.4	54.6	766.9
1960	423.6	660.6	76.5	1160.6	318.6	476.4	61.4	856.5
1961	460.8	740.9	85.5	1287.2	350.0	531.6	68.6	950.1
1962	499.1	825.9	95.1	1420.0	382.7	588.6	76.0	1047.3

Source: See Chapter 3, Section 2.

TABLE T-9

TOTAL FIXED CAPITAL, GROSS AND NET, IN 1950 PRICES, 1928-62
(January 1--Billion Rubles)

	Gross Values				Net Values			
	Structures	Equip-ment	Instal-lation	Total	Structures	Equip-ment	Instal-lation	Total
1928	358.8	47.7	8.5	414.9	244.8	32.6	5.9	283.2
1929	377.6	53.6	9.5	440.7	257.1	35.9	6.7	299.7
1930	401.7	59.5	10.9	472.1	274.4	40.5	7.8	322.7
1931	434.5	70.6	12.9	518.0	299.9	49.7	9.6	359.2
1932	470.3	82.4	15.1	567.9	327.7	58.7	11.4	397.8
1933	506.7	94.8	17.3	618.8	355.3	67.5	13.3	436.1
1934	538.0	105.5	19.2	662.8	377.2	74.8	14.8	466.8
1935	575.4	116.1	21.4	713.0	404.6	81.1	16.4	502.1
1936	621.1	130.4	24.1	775.7	439.4	90.2	18.6	548.2
1937	682.7	150.6	27.8	861.1	489.3	104.4	21.7	615.4
1938	735.4	169.3	31.0	935.7	529.1	116.5	24.3	669.8
1939	785.1	187.6	34.3	1007.0	564.7	129.1	26.8	720.6
1940	878.8	213.7	39.5	1132.0	631.7	145.8	30.6	808.1
1941	976.2	239.2	44.8	1260.3	699.7	161.1	34.5	895.3
1944	795.7	179.7	37.4	1012.7	544.5	109.5	27.0	681.0
1945	817.4	183.0	39.0	1039.5	551.0	112.3	27.7	691.0
1946	838.4	192.2	40.9	1071.5	556.2	121.0	28.7	705.8
1947	868.8	204.5	43.5	1116.8	570.4	133.4	30.2	733.9
1948	905.2	220.6	46.5	1172.2	589.9	148.8	32.1	770.9
1949	954.4	242.5	50.2	1247.1	621.7	167.2	34.6	823.4
1950	1018.2	270.6	54.6	1343.5	666.9	188.2	37.9	893.0
1951	1085.2	312.1	60.1	1457.4	719.2	218.7	41.9	979.8
1952	1162.7	356.6	66.1	1585.5	780.6	248.7	46.5	1075.7
1953	1249.4	396.9	71.5	1717.7	850.6	273.9	51.1	1175.6
1954	1343.9	440.4	77.4	1861.7	926.9	301.6	56.3	1284.7
1955	1449.4	492.0	84.3	2025.8	1012.8	336.1	62.2	1411.2
1956	1565.4	556.2	92.5	2214.2	1106.9	382.1	69.3	1558.4
1957	1677.7	638.2	102.2	2418.1	1205.8	444.3	77.7	1727.8
1958	1806.8	726.2	112.9	2645.9	1313.9	511.2	86.9	1912.0
1959	1952.9	824.3	125.2	2902.4	1436.1	587.2	97.4	2120.8
1960	2116.4	930.8	139.7	3186.9	1573.3	666.6	108.8	2348.8
1961	2292.1	1045.6	155.3	3493.0	1720.6	747.9	120.9	2589.3
1962	2470.3	1167.4	171.7	3809.5	1872.5	831.8	133.5	2837.7

Source: See Chapter 3, Section 2.

TABLE T-10

TOTAL FIXED CAPITAL, GROSS AND NET, IN ACQUISITION PRICES, 1928-62*
(January 1--Billion Rubles)

	Gross Values				Net Values			
	Structures	Equip-ment	Instal-lation	Total	Structures	Equip-ment	Instal-lation	Total
1928	67.1	13.0	1.8	81.9	45.8	9.0	1.2	56.0
1929	70.6	14.2	2.0	86.8	48.1	9.7	1.4	59.2
1930	75.0	15.7	2.3	93.0	51.2	10.7	1.7	63.6
1931	80.7	18.5	2.8	102.0	55.5	12.9	2.1	70.6
1932	90.0	22.2	3.8	115.9	63.3	15.9	3.0	82.2
1933	101.5	26.7	5.0	133.2	73.2	19.6	4.1	96.9
1934	110.9	31.5	6.4	148.8	80.7	23.0	5.4	109.0
1935	124.1	36.9	7.8	168.8	91.8	26.7	6.7	125.2
1936	141.0	43.5	9.1	193.6	106.3	31.3	7.7	145.4
1937	163.3	53.8	10.4	227.4	125.9	39.2	8.8	173.9
1938	183.5	64.1	11.6	259.2	143.0	46.7	9.8	199.5
1939	204.3	75.0	13.0	292.3	160.2	54.6	10.9	225.7
1940	239.2	89.1	15.4	343.7	188.8	64.1	12.8	265.7
1941	279.2	103.9	18.2	401.3	221.5	73.8	15.1	310.4
1944	253.8	84.4	19.2	357.5	197.4	54.4	15.7	267.5
1945	275.1	89.6	22.4	387.1	213.7	58.6	18.5	290.7
1946	298.2	99.2	25.6	423.0	231.4	67.4	21.1	319.9
1947	327.9	110.8	29.1	467.8	255.2	78.2	24.0	357.4
1948	361.1	127.5	32.6	521.2	281.9	93.3	26.8	402.1
1949	404.2	149.5	36.8	590.4	317.9	112.3	30.1	460.3
1950	470.1	195.9	42.5	708.5	375.9	153.2	34.9	564.1
1951	541.2	239.3	47.9	828.5	438.7	186.6	39.3	664.6
1952	621.4	284.0	54.1	959.5	509.1	218.0	44.2	771.3
1953	711.8	320.6	61.3	1093.7	588.3	240.0	50.3	878.6
1954	805.8	360.7	68.4	1234.9	669.3	264.6	56.1	990.0
1955	912.8	409.1	76.4	1398.3	761.6	295.8	62.6	1120.0
1956	1020.5	462.5	84.3	1567.3	852.3	331.2	68.8	1252.3
1957	1139.1	520.3	93.2	1752.6	953.9	370.2	75.7	1399.8
1958	1272.7	574.9	102.8	1950.4	1067.0	412.3	83.3	1562.6
1959	1424.4	642.5	114.2	2181.0	1195.5	463.3	92.2	1751.0
1960	1599.0	715.6	127.3	2441.9	1344.0	517.2	102.5	1963.8
1961	1792.5	796.1	142.1	2730.7	1508.2	573.2	114.2	2195.5
1962	1993.2	880.8	157.8	3031.7	1676.6	631.4	126.3	2434.3

*Assets in existence on January 1, 1928, are valued at 1928 prices.
Source: See Chapter 3, Section 3.

TABLE T-11

STRAIGHT-LINE DEPRECIATION CHARGES IN 1937, 1928,
AND 1950 PRICES, 1928-61
(Billion Rubles)

	1937 Prices	1928 Prices	1950 Prices
1928	3.4	1.8	9.3
1929	3.7	2.0	10.1
1930	4.1	2.3	11.2
1931	4.7	2.7	12.9
1932	5.3	3.2	14.4
1933	5.8	3.7	15.0
1934	6.5	4.4	16.6
1935	7.3	5.1	18.4
1936	8.2	6.1	20.6
1937	9.4	7.4	23.3
1938	10.6	8.7	25.6
1939	11.6	10.1	27.9
1940	13.6	12.3	32.2
1944	11.7	10.9	27.2
1945	12.1	11.2	27.4
1946	12.5	11.9	28.2
1947	13.3	12.7	29.5
1948	14.2	13.7	31.3
1949	15.3	14.9	33.7
1950	16.8	16.6	36.9
1951	19.0	19.1	41.5
1952	21.4	21.7	46.5
1953	23.5	23.9	50.9
1954	25.6	26.2	55.5
1955	28.4	29.2	61.2
1956	31.6	32.9	67.9
1957	35.7	37.5	76.3
1958	40.2	42.3	85.5
1959	45.2	47.7	95.6
1960	50.0	53.3	105.0
1961	55.9	59.7	116.9

Source: See Chapter 3, Section 4.

TABLE T-12

NONAGRICULTURAL FIXED CAPITAL, GROSS AND NET, IN 1937 PRICES, 1928-62
(January 1--Billion Rubles)

	Gross Values				Net Values			
	Structures	Equip- ment	Instal- lation	Total	Structures	Equip- ment	Instal- lation	Total
1928	119.4	14.1	2.7	136.3	82.1	10.0	1.9	94
1929	125.5	15.7	3.1	144.2	86.2	11.1	2.1	99.5
1930	133.3	17.8	3.5	154.6	91.8	12.7	2.5	107.1
1931	144.3	21.4	4.1	169.9	100.5	15.7	3.1	119.3
1932	156.2	25.7	4.9	186.9	109.9	19.1	3.7	132.8
1933	168.7	30.9	5.7	205.3	119.6	23.1	4.4	147.1
1934	178.8	35.2	6.4	220.4	126.7	25.8	5.0	157.5
1935	191.3	39.4	7.2	238.0	136.0	28.3	5.6	169.9
1936	207.0	44.9	8.2	260.1	148.2	31.8	6.4	186.4
1937	228.4	52.6	9.5	290.6	165.9	37.5	7.6	210.9
1938	246.0	60.5	10.8	317.3	179.2	43.2	8.6	231.0
1939	263.0	69.5	12.1	344.7	191.7	50.0	9.6	251.3
1940	294.8	81.7	14.0	390.5	214.7	58.6	11.1	284.5
1941	328.0	94.2	16.1	438.3	238.3	67.4	12.6	318.3
1944	267.8	77.0	13.8	358.7	186.2	50.7	10.2	247.2
1945	275.3	82.3	14.5	372.2	188.7	54.6	10.7	253.9
1946	282.6	90.5	15.5	388.6	190.7	61.4	11.2	263.3
1947	293.0	98.9	16.6	408.5	195.7	68.7	11.9	276.4
1948	305.4	108.4	17.8	431.7	202.6	76.6	12.8	292.0
1949	322.2	119.2	19.3	460.8	213.6	84.8	13.8	312.2
1950	344.1	130.6	21.1	495.9	229.3	92.1	15.1	336.5
1951	368.9	146.4	23.3	538.6	247.5	102.8	16.8	367.2
1952	397.0	163.6	25.8	586.4	268.5	114.0	18.7	401.2
1953	428.7	179.2	28.0	635.9	292.9	124.1	20.6	437.6
1954	463.7	196.7	30.5	690.9	319.9	136.4	22.7	479.1
1955	501.9	218.7	33.5	754.2	349.4	152.8	25.2	527.5
1956	542.4	246.5	36.9	825.8	380.3	174.5	28.2	583.0
1957	581.7	283.4	41.1	906.2	413.5	204.3	31.7	649.6
1958	624.6	324.7	45.6	994.9	449.4	236.6	35.5	721.5
1959	673.5	372.2	50.8	1096.5	490.3	273.6	40.0	803.8
1960	728.8	425.7	56.9	1211.3	537.0	314.2	44.7	895.9
1961	789.3	484.8	63.4	1337.5	588.3	357.4	49.8	995.5
1962	851.2	547.5	70.3	1469.0	641.9	401.7	55.1	1098.7

Source: See Chapter 3, Section 5.

TABLE T-13

NONAGRICULTURAL FIXED CAPITAL, GROSS AND NET, IN 1928 PRICES, 1928-62
(January 1--Billion Rubles)

	Gross Values				Net Values			
	Structures	Equip-ment	Instal-lation	Total	Structures	Equip-ment	Instal-lation	Total
1928	58.4	11.2	1.8	71.4	40.2	8.0	1.2	49.3
1929	61.4	12.4	2.0	75.7	42.1	8.7	1.4	52.3
1930	65.2	14.0	2.3	81.6	45.0	10.0	1.6	56.6
1931	70.8	17.1	2.8	90.7	49.4	12.5	2.1	64.0
1932	76.9	21.2	3.4	101.5	54.2	15.9	2.6	72.7
1933	83.2	27.2	4.2	114.6	59.2	20.8	3.3	83.3
1934	88.1	32.8	4.9	125.9	62.6	25.0	4.0	91.6
1935	94.2	38.5	5.8	138.5	67.2	28.9	4.7	100.7
1936	102.0	45.0	6.8	153.8	73.2	33.3	5.6	112.1
1937	112.8	55.0	8.4	176.2	82.1	41.3	7.0	130.4
1938	121.6	66.3	9.9	197.8	88.8	50.1	8.3	147.3
1939	130.1	79.8	11.7	221.7	95.1	61.1	9.9	166.1
1940	145.9	96.9	14.1	256.8	106.6	74.0	11.8	192.4
1941	162.2	113.4	16.4	292.1	118.2	86.1	13.7	218.0
1944	132.5	94.7	14.3	241.5	92.3	67.0	11.2	170.6
1945	136.3	103.1	15.4	254.8	93.6	73.7	12.1	179.4
1946	140.0	116.3	17.0	273.3	94.7	84.4	13.3	192.4
1947	145.2	128.0	18.7	292.0	97.3	94.3	14.5	206.2
1948	151.6	140.7	20.6	312.9	100.9	104.4	16.0	221.3
1949	160.2	156.1	22.8	339.1	106.6	115.4	17.6	239.7
1950	171.3	171.8	25.3	368.3	114.6	125.2	19.6	259.4
1951	183.8	194.0	28.5	406.2	123.9	139.8	22.1	285.9
1952	198.1	215.9	31.7	445.7	134.7	153.9	24.6	313.2
1953	214.3	235.3	34.7	484.3	147.2	167.0	27.1	341.3
1954	232.1	256.8	38.2	527.2	161.0	182.7	29.9	373.7
1955	251.7	284.0	42.4	578.1	176.2	203.1	33.3	412.6
1956	272.5	319.5	47.5	639.5	192.3	231.5	37.5	461.3
1957	292.9	366.0	53.7	712.7	209.5	270.2	42.8	522.5
1958	315.2	415.3	60.4	790.9	228.2	310.0	48.3	586.5
1959	340.6	471.6	68.0	880.2	249.5	354.5	54.6	658.6
1960	369.3	538.5	76.5	984.3	273.8	404.5	61.4	739.7
1961	400.9	612.3	85.5	1098.8	300.6	458.6	68.6	827.8
1962	433.4	689.9	95.1	1218.4	328.7	514.2	76.0	918.9

Source: See Chapter 3, Section 5.

TABLE T-14

NONAGRICULTURAL FIXED CAPITAL, GROSS AND NET, IN 1950 PRICES, 1928-62
(January 1--Billion Rubles)

	Gross Values				Net Values			
	Structures	Equip-ment	Instal-lation	Total	Structures	Equip-ment	Instal-lation	Total
1928	312.0	35.3	8.5	355.9	214.6	25.2	5.9	245.6
1929	327.9	39.4	9.5	376.9	225.2	28.2	6.7	260.2
1930	348.7	45.0	10.9	404.7	240.4	32.5	7.8	280.7
1931	378.1	54.3	12.9	445.3	263.7	40.1	9.6	313.4
1932	409.7	63.4	15.1	488.2	288.7	47.0	11.4	347.2
1933	442.8	73.8	17.3	533.9	314.6	54.7	13.3	382.6
1934	469.6	81.3	19.2	570.2	333.4	58.9	14.8	407.1
1935	502.2	88.9	21.4	612.6	357.6	62.8	16.4	436.8
1936	542.7	99.9	24.1	666.7	389.0	69.7	18.6	477.2
1937	597.9	113.3	27.8	739.0	434.2	80.7	21.7	536.6
1938	643.6	127.4	31.0	802.0	468.8	90.8	24.3	583.9
1939	687.1	142.4	34.3	863.8	500.5	103.1	26.8	630.3
1940	769.3	164.4	39.5	973.1	559.8	119.0	30.6	709.4
1941	854.6	187.7	44.8	1087.1	620.1	134.7	34.5	789.3
1944	696.7	148.8	37.4	882.8	483.3	98.9	27.0	609.1
1945	715.7	155.5	39.0	910.2	489.2	103.9	27.7	620.8
1946	734.1	168.2	40.9	943.2	494.1	113.6	28.7	636.3
1947	760.2	182.6	43.5	986.3	506.3	125.6	30.2	662.0
1948	791.5	199.0	46.5	1036.9	523.1	139.1	32.1	694.2
1949	833.8	218.6	50.2	1102.6	550.3	153.2	34.6	738.1
1950	888.6	239.5	54.6	1182.7	589.2	165.9	37.9	793.0
1951	950.5	269.4	60.1	1280.0	634.1	185.1	41.9	861.1
1952	1021.0	299.9	66.1	1387.1	686.4	204.8	46.5	937.6
1953	1101.0	326.8	71.5	1499.3	747.4	222.2	51.1	1020.8
1954	1188.6	357.3	77.4	1623.3	814.5	243.5	56.3	1114.3
1955	1284.1	394.0	84.3	1762.5	887.7	271.1	62.2	1221.0
1956	1385.3	441.8	92.5	1919.6	964.7	309.7	69.3	1343.7
1957	1482.6	505.8	102.2	2090.6	1046.5	363.8	77.7	1488.0
1958	1589.0	576.4	112.9	2278.3	1135.3	423.0	86.9	1645.2
1959	1710.6	657.3	125.2	2493.1	1236.9	489.5	97.4	1823.8
1960	1847.7	752.6	139.7	2740.0	1352.5	563.7	108.8	2025.1
1961	1997.0	859.7	155.3	3011.9	1478.9	643.6	120.9	2243.3
1962	2147.7	972.4	171.7	3291.9	1609.1	725.5	133.5	2468.0

Source: See Chapter 3, Section 5.

TABLE T-15

RESIDENTIAL FIXED CAPITAL, GROSS AND NET, IN 1937, 1928, AND
1950 PRICES, 1928-62
(January 1--Billion Rubles)

	Gross Values			Net Values		
	1937 Prices	1928 Prices	1950 Prices	1937 Prices	1928 Prices	1950 Prices
1928	91.2	34.4	228.0	61.4	23.2	153.5
1929	93.7	35.3	234.2	62.4	23.5	156.0
1930	96.2	36.3	240.5	63.4	23.9	158.5
1931	98.7	37.2	246.7	64.3	24.3	160.7
1932	101.2	38.2	253.0	65.3	24.6	163.3
1933	103.7	39.1	259.2	66.1	24.9	165.3
1934	106.0	40.0	265.0	66.8	25.2	167.0
1935	108.3	40.8	270.7	67.4	25.4	168.5
1936	110.6	41.7	276.5	67.9	25.6	169.7
1937	112.9	42.6	282.2	68.5	25.8	171.3
1938	115.2	43.4	288.0	69.0	26.0	172.5
1939	118.6	44.7	296.5	70.5	26.6	176.3
1940	128.1	48.3	320.2	75.6	28.5	189.0
1941	137.9	52.0	344.7	80.9	30.5	202.3
1944	109.0	41.1	272.5	61.1	23.1	152.7
1945	110.6	41.7	276.5	61.1	23.1	152.7
1946	112.3	42.3	280.7	60.9	23.0	152.3
1947	114.7	43.2	286.7	61.5	23.2	153.7
1948	119.6	45.1	299.0	64.7	24.4	161.7
1949	125.2	47.2	313.0	68.3	25.8	170.7
1950	131.0	49.4	327.5	72.1	27.2	180.3
1951	137.4	51.8	343.5	76.5	28.9	191.3
1952	144.4	54.4	361.0	81.3	30.7	203.3
1953	151.3	57.0	378.2	85.9	32.4	214.7
1954	159.1	60.0	397.7	91.4	34.5	228.5
1955	167.2	63.0	418.0	97.0	36.6	242.5
1956	175.5	66.2	438.7	102.7	38.8	256.7
1957	180.2	67.9	450.5	109.9	41.5	274.7
1958	188.0	70.9	470.0	120.2	45.4	300.5
1959	199.4	75.2	498.5	133.7	50.5	334.3
1960	212.9	80.3	532.2	149.3	56.3	373.3
1961	226.7	85.5	566.7	165.5	62.5	413.7
1962	240.0	90.5	600.0	180.9	68.3	452.3

Source: See Chapter 3, Section 6.

TABLE T-16

NONRESIDENTIAL FIXED CAPITAL, GROSS AND NET, IN 1937 PRICES, 1928-62
(January 1--Billion Rubles)

	Gross Values				Net Values			
	Structures	Equipment	Installation	Total	Structures	Equipment	Installation	Total
1928	46.1	17.4	2.7	66.2	32.3	12.0	1.9	46.2
1929	50.8	19.4	3.1	73.3	36.0	13.2	2.2	51.3
1930	57.3	21.7	3.5	82.5	41.4	14.9	2.5	58.8
1931	67.1	26.0	4.2	97.2	50.0	18.4	3.1	71.5
1932	78.2	31.1	4.9	114.2	59.5	22.5	3.7	85.7
1933	89.3	37.0	5.7	132.0	69.0	26.9	4.4	100.3
1934	98.9	42.4	6.4	147.7	76.6	30.7	5.0	112.3
1935	110.9	47.8	7.2	165.9	86.5	34.1	5.6	126.2
1936	126.3	54.9	8.2	189.4	99.6	38.8	6.4	144.7
1937	147.9	64.9	9.6	222.4	118.4	46.1	7.6	172.0
1938	165.9	74.9	10.8	251.6	133.2	52.8	8.6	194.6
1939	182.0	85.2	12.1	297.2	145.9	60.1	9.6	215.5
1940	208.7	99.0	14.0	321.7	166.7	69.3	11.1	247.1
1941	236.7	112.8	16.1	365.6	188.0	78.0	12.6	278.7
1944	196.9	87.9	13.8	298.6	148.8	55.1	10.2	214.1
1945	203.9	91.6	14.5	310.0	151.4	58.1	10.7	220.2
1946	210.5	98.7	15.5	324.6	153.8	64.7	11.2	229.7
1947	220.2	106.6	16.6	343.4	159.1	72.2	12.0	243.3
1948	229.8	116.3	17.8	363.9	163.9	81.1	12.8	257.8
1949	243.7	128.3	19.3	391.3	173.0	91.0	13.8	277.9
1950	263.3	143.0	21.1	427.5	187.6	101.8	15.1	304.5
1951	283.8	164.5	23.3	471.7	204.3	117.3	16.8	338.5
1952	307.8	187.6	25.8	521.2	224.2	132.6	18.7	375.5
1953	335.4	208.5	28.0	571.9	247.6	145.9	20.6	414.1
1954	365.4	231.2	30.5	627.2	272.8	160.8	22.8	456.4
1955	399.6	259.0	33.5	692.1	301.8	179.9	25.3	506.9
1956	437.8	293.2	36.9	768.0	333.9	204.8	28.2	566.9
1957	478.6	336.9	41.1	856.6	366.8	238.1	31.7	636.6
1958	522.7	384.0	45.6	952.4	400.1	273.6	35.6	709.2
1959	570.0	437.4	50.8	1058.3	435.7	314.8	40.0	790.5
1960	622.5	495.5	56.9	1174.8	475.5	357.7	44.7	878.0
1961	679.8	557.9	63.4	1301.1	519.2	401.5	49.8	970.5
1962	739.7	624.1	70.3	1434.0	566.2	446.7	55.1	1068.1

Source: See Chapter 3, Section 6.

TABLE T-17

NONRESIDENTIAL FIXED CAPITAL, GROSS AND NET, IN 1928 PRICES, 1928-62
(January 1--Billion Rubles)

	Gross Values				Net Values			
	Structures	Equip-ment	Instal-lation	Total	Structures	Equip-ment	Instal-lation	Total
1928	32.7	13.0	1.8	47.5	22.6	9.0	1.2	32.8
1929	35.3	14.4	2.0	51.7	24.6	9.9	1.4	35.9
1930	38.8	16.2	2.3	57.3	27.4	11.2	1.6	40.3
1931	44.2	19.7	2.8	66.7	31.9	14.1	2.1	48.1
1932	50.0	24.6	3.4	78.0	36.9	18.1	2.6	57.7
1933	56.0	31.1	4.2	91.3	41.9	23.7	3.3	68.9
1934	60.9	38.3	4.9	104.2	45.6	29.1	4.0	78.7
1935	67.2	45.8	5.8	118.7	50.6	34.4	4.7	89.7
1936	75.0	55.5	6.8	137.4	57.1	41.4	5.6	104.1
1937	86.1	69.9	8.4	164.4	66.7	52.6	7.0	126.3
1938	95.5	84.6	9.9	190.0	74.2	63.4	8.3	146.0
1939	103.9	101.3	11.7	217.0	80.7	75.9	9.9	166.5
1940	118.3	122.3	14.1	254.7	91.8	90.4	11.8	194.0
1941	133.3	141.8	16.4	291.4	102.8	102.8	13.7	219.4
1944	110.2	114.2	14.3	238.7	81.0	74.1	11.2	166.3
1945	113.9	121.0	15.4	250.4	82.4	79.6	12.1	174.0
1946	117.5	132.8	17.0	267.4	83.7	90.2	13.3	187.2
1947	122.8	144.3	18.7	285.9	86.5	101.0	14.5	202.1
1948	128.2	157.7	20.6	306.6	89.5	112.9	16.0	218.4
1949	136.1	174.6	22.8	333.6	94.7	126.8	17.6	239.2
1950	146.8	195.6	25.3	367.8	102.7	142.3	19.6	264.5
1951	158.1	225.7	28.5	412.3	111.7	164.2	22.1	298.1
1952	171.3	255.8	31.7	458.7	122.6	183.5	24.6	330.7
1953	186.3	283.0	34.7	504.1	135.2	200.7	27.1	363.0
1954	202.7	313.0	38.2	553.9	148.9	220.5	29.9	399.2
1955	221.4	350.8	42.4	614.5	164.6	246.7	33.3	444.5
1956	242.1	397.6	47.5	687.2	182.0	280.8	37.5	500.3
1957	264.1	456.2	53.7	774.0	200.1	325.4	42.8	568.3
1958	288.0	517.5	60.4	865.9	218.8	370.9	48.3	638.1
1959	314.2	585.7	68.0	967.9	239.4	422.4	54.6	716.4
1960	343.3	660.6	76.5	1080.3	262.3	476.4	61.4	800.2
1961	375.3	740.9	85.5	1201.7	287.5	531.6	68.6	887.6
1962	408.6	825.9	95.1	1329.5	314.4	588.6	76.0	979.0

Source: See Chapter 3, Section 6.

TABLE T-18

NONRESIDENTIAL FIXED CAPITAL, GROSS AND NET, IN 1950 PRICES, 1928-62
(January 1--Billion Rubles)

	Gross Values				Net Values			
	Structures	Equip-ment	Instal-lation	Total	Structures	Equip-ment	Instal-lation	Total
1928	130.8	47.7	8.5	186.9	91.3	32.6	5.9	129.7
1929	143.4	53.6	9.5	206.5	101.1	35.9	6.7	143.7
1930	161.2	59.5	10.9	231.6	115.9	40.5	7.8	164.2
1931	187.8	70.6	12.9	271.3	139.2	49.7	9.6	198.5
1932	217.3	82.4	15.1	314.8	164.4	58.7	11.4	234.5
1933	247.5	94.8	17.3	359.6	190.0	67.5	13.3	270.8
1934	273.0	105.5	19.2	397.8	210.2	74.8	14.8	299.8
1935	304.7	116.1	21.4	442.3	236.1	81.1	16.4	333.6
1936	344.6	130.4	24.1	499.2	269.7	90.2	18.6	378.5
1937	400.5	150.6	27.8	578.9	318.0	104.4	21.7	444.1
1938	447.4	169.3	31.0	647.7	356.6	116.5	24.3	497.3
1939	488.6	187.6	34.3	710.5	388.4	129.1	26.8	544.3
1940	558.6	213.7	39.5	811.8	442.7	145.8	30.6	619.1
1941	631.5	239.2	44.8	915.6	497.4	161.1	34.5	693.0
1944	523.2	179.7	37.4	740.2	391.8	109.5	27.0	528.3
1945	540.9	183.0	39.0	763.0	398.3	112.3	27.7	538.3
1946	557.7	192.2	40.9	790.8	403.9	121.0	28.7	553.5
1947	582.1	204.5	43.5	830.1	416.7	133.4	30.2	580.2
1948	606.2	220.6	46.5	873.2	428.2	148.8	32.1	609.2
1949	641.4	242.5	50.2	934.1	451.0	167.2	34.6	652.7
1950	690.7	270.6	54.6	1016.0	486.6	188.2	37.9	712.7
1951	741.7	312.1	60.1	1113.9	527.9	218.7	41.9	788.5
1952	801.7	356.6	66.1	1224.5	577.3	248.7	46.5	872.4
1953	871.2	396.9	71.5	1339.5	635.9	273.9	51.1	960.9
1954	946.2	440.4	77.4	1464.0	698.4	301.6	56.3	1056.2
1955	1031.4	492.0	84.3	1607.8	770.3	336.1	62.2	1168.7
1956	1126.7	556.2	92.5	1775.5	850.2	382.1	69.3	1301.7
1957	1227.2	638.2	102.2	1967.6	931.1	444.3	77.7	1453.1
1958	1336.8	726.2	112.9	2175.9	1013.4	511.2	86.9	1611.5
1959	1454.4	824.3	125.3	2403.9	1101.8	587.2	97.4	1786.5
1960	1584.2	930.8	139.7	2654.7	1200.0	666.6	108.8	1975.5
1961	1725.4	1045.6	155.3	2926.3	1306.9	747.9	120.9	2175.6
1962	1870.3	1167.4	171.7	3209.5	1420.2	831.8	133.5	2385.4

Source: See Chapter 3, Section 6.

TABLE T-19

NONAGRICULTURAL NONRESIDENTIAL FIXED CAPITAL, GROSS AND NET,
IN 1937 PRICES, 1928-62
(January 1--Billion Rubles)

	Gross Values				Net Values			
	Structures	Equip-ment	Instal-lation	Total	Structures	Equip-ment	Instal-lation	Total
1928	28.2	14.1	2.7	45.0	20.7	10.0	1.9	32.6
1929	31.8	15.7	3.1	50.6	23.8	11.1	2.1	37.0
1930	37.1	17.8	3.5	58.4	28.4	12.7	2.5	43.6
1931	45.6	21.4	4.1	71.1	36.2	15.7	3.1	55.0
1932	55.0	25.7	4.9	85.6	44.6	19.1	3.7	67.4
1933	65.0	30.9	5.7	101.6	53.5	23.1	4.4	81.0
1934	72.8	35.2	6.4	114.4	59.9	25.8	5.0	90.7
1935	83.0	39.4	7.2	129.6	68.6	28.3	5.6	102.5
1936	96.4	44.9	8.2	149.5	80.3	31.8	6.4	118.5
1937	115.5	52.6	9.5	177.6	97.4	37.5	7.6	142.5
1938	130.8	60.5	10.8	202.1	110.2	43.2	8.6	162.0
1939	144.4	69.5	12.1	226.0	121.2	50.0	9.6	180.8
1940	166.7	81.7	14.0	262.4	139.1	58.6	11.1	208.8
1941	190.1	94.2	16.1	300.4	157.4	67.4	12.6	237.4
1944	158.8	77.0	13.8	249.6	125.1	50.7	10.2	186.0
1945	164.7	82.3	14.5	261.5	127.6	54.6	10.7	192.9
1946	170.3	90.5	15.5	276.3	129.8	61.4	11.2	202.4
1947	178.3	98.9	16.6	293.8	134.2	68.7	11.9	214.8
1948	185.8	108.4	17.8	312.0	137.9	76.6	12.8	227.3
1949	197.0	119.2	19.3	335.5	145.3	84.8	13.8	243.9
1950	213.1	130.6	21.1	364.8	157.2	92.1	15.1	264.4
1951	231.5	146.4	23.3	401.2	171.0	102.8	16.8	290.6
1952	252.6	163.6	25.8	442.0	187.2	114.0	18.7	319.9
1953	277.4	179.2	28.0	484.6	207.0	124.1	20.6	351.7
1954	304.6	196.7	30.5	531.8	228.5	136.4	22.7	387.6
1955	334.7	218.7	33.5	586.9	252.4	152.8	25.2	430.4
1956	366.9	246.5	36.9	650.3	277.6	174.5	28.2	480.3
1957	401.5	283.4	41.1	726.0	303.6	204.3	31.7	539.6
1958	436.6	324.7	45.6	806.9	329.2	236.6	35.5	601.3
1959	474.1	372.2	50.8	897.1	356.6	273.6	40.0	670.2
1960	515.9	425.7	56.9	998.5	387.7	314.2	44.7	746.6
1961	562.6	484.8	63.4	1110.8	422.8	357.4	49.8	830.0
1962	611.2	547.5	70.3	1229.0	461.0	401.7	55.1	917.8

Sources: Calculated from Tables T-12 and T-15.

TABLE T-20

NONAGRICULTURAL NONRESIDENTIAL FIXED CAPITAL, GROSS AND NET,
IN 1928 PRICES, 1928-62
(January 1--Billion Rubles)

	Gross Values				Net Values			
	Structures	Equip- ment	Instal- lation	Total	Structures	Equip- ment	Instal- lation	Total
1928	24.0	11.2	1.8	37.0	17.0	8.0	1.2	26.1
1929	26.1	12.4	2.0	40.4	18.6	8.7	1.4	28.8
1930	28.9	14.0	2.3	45.3	21.1	10.0	1.6	32.7
1931	33.6	17.1	2.8	53.5	25.1	12.5	2.1	39.7
1932	38.7	21.2	3.4	63.3	29.6	15.9	2.6	48.1
1933	44.1	27.2	4.2	75.5	34.3	20.8	3.3	58.4
1934	48.1	32.8	4.9	85.9	37.4	25.0	4.0	66.4
1935	53.4	38.5	5.8	97.7	41.8	28.9	4.7	75.3
1936	60.3	45.0	6.8	112.1	47.6	33.3	5.6	86.5
1937	70.2	55.0	8.4	133.6	56.3	41.3	7.0	104.6
1938	78.2	66.3	9.9	154.4	62.8	50.1	8.3	121.3
1939	85.4	79.8	11.7	177.0	68.5	61.1	9.9	139.5
1940	97.6	96.9	14.1	208.5	78.1	74.0	11.8	163.9
1941	110.2	113.4	16.4	240.1	87.7	86.1	13.7	187.5
1944	91.4	94.7	14.3	200.4	69.2	67.0	11.2	147.5
1945	94.6	103.1	15.4	213.1	70.5	73.7	12.1	156.3
1946	97.7	116.3	17.0	231.0	71.7	84.4	13.3	169.4
1947	102.0	128.0	18.7	248.8	74.1	94.3	14.5	183.0
1948	106.5	140.7	20.6	267.8	76.5	104.4	16.0	196.9
1949	113.0	156.1	22.8	291.9	80.8	115.4	17.6	213.9
1950	121.9	171.8	25.3	318.9	87.4	125.2	19.6	232.2
1951	132.0	194.0	28.5	354.4	95.0	139.8	22.1	257.0
1952	143.7	215.9	31.7	391.3	104.0	153.9	24.6	282.5
1953	157.3	235.3	34.7	427.3	114.8	167.0	27.1	308.9
1954	172.1	256.8	38.2	467.2	126.5	182.7	29.9	339.2
1955	188.7	284.0	42.4	515.1	139.6	203.1	33.3	376.0
1956	206.3	319.5	47.5	573.3	153.5	231.5	37.5	422.5
1957	225.0	366.0	53.7	644.8	168.0	270.2	42.8	481.0
1958	244.3	415.3	60.4	720.0	182.8	310.0	48.3	541.1
1959	265.4	471.6	68.0	805.0	199.0	354.5	54.6	608.1
1960	289.0	538.5	76.5	904.0	217.5	404.5	61.4	683.4
1961	315.4	612.3	85.5	1013.3	238.1	458.6	68.6	765.3
1962	342.9	689.9	95.1	1127.9	260.4	514.2	76.0	850.6

Sources: Calculated from Tables T-13 and T-15.

TABLE T-21

NONAGRICULTURAL NONRESIDENTIAL FIXED CAPITAL, GROSS AND NET,
IN 1950 PRICES, 1928-62
(January 1--Billion Rubles)

	Gross Values				Net Values			
	Structures	Equip-ment	Instal-lation	Total	Structures	Equip-ment	Instal-lation	Total
1928	84.0	35.3	8.5	127.9	61.1	25.2	5.9	92.1
1929	93.7	39.4	9.5	142.7	69.2	28.2	6.7	104.2
1930	108.2	45.0	10.9	164.2	81.9	32.5	7.8	122.2
1931	131.4	54.3	12.9	198.6	103.0	40.1	9.6	152.7
1932	156.7	63.4	15.1	235.2	125.4	47.0	11.4	183.9
1933	183.6	73.8	17.3	274.7	149.3	54.7	13.3	217.3
1934	204.6	81.3	19.2	305.2	166.4	58.9	14.8	240.1
1935	231.5	88.9	21.4	341.9	189.1	62.8	16.4	268.3
1936	266.2	99.9	24.1	390.2	219.3	69.7	18.6	307.5
1937	315.7	113.3	27.8	456.8	262.9	80.7	21.7	365.3
1938	355.6	127.4	31.0	514.0	296.3	90.8	24.3	411.4
1939	390.6	142.4	34.3	567.3	324.2	103.1	26.8	454.0
1940	449.1	164.4	39.5	652.9	370.8	119.0	30.6	520.4
1941	509.9	187.7	44.8	742.4	417.8	134.7	34.5	587.0
1944	424.2	148.8	37.4	610.3	330.6	98.9	27.0	456.4
1945	439.2	155.5	39.0	633.7	336.5	103.9	27.7	468.1
1946	453.4	168.2	40.9	662.5	341.8	113.6	28.7	484.0
1947	473.5	182.6	43.5	699.6	352.6	125.6	30.2	508.3
1948	492.5	199.0	46.5	737.9	361.4	139.1	32.1	532.5
1949	520.8	218.6	50.2	789.6	379.6	153.2	34.6	567.4
1950	561.1	239.5	54.6	855.2	408.9	165.9	37.9	612.7
1951	607.0	269.4	60.1	936.5	442.8	185.1	41.9	669.8
1952	660.0	299.9	66.1	1026.1	483.1	204.8	46.5	734.3
1953	722.8	326.8	71.5	1121.1	532.7	222.2	51.1	806.1
1954	790.9	357.3	77.4	1225.6	586.0	243.5	56.3	885.8
1955	866.1	394.0	84.3	1344.5	645.2	271.1	62.2	978.5
1956	946.6	441.8	92.5	1480.9	708.0	309.7	69.3	1087.0
1957	1032.1	505.8	102.2	1640.1	771.8	363.8	77.7	1213.3
1958	1119.0	576.4	112.9	1808.3	834.8	423.0	86.9	1344.7
1959	1212.1	657.3	125.2	1994.6	902.6	489.5	97.4	1489.5
1960	1315.5	752.6	139.7	2207.8	979.2	563.7	108.8	1651.8
1961	1430.3	859.7	155.3	2445.2	1065.2	643.6	120.9	1829.6
1962	1547.7	972.4	171.7	2691.9	1156.8	725.5	133.5	2015.7

Sources: Calculated from Tables T-14 and T-15.

TABLE T-22

AVERAGE AGE OF TOTAL FIXED CAPITAL, GROSS VALUE WEIGHTS,
IN 1937 PRICES, 1928-62
(January 1--Years)

| | Capital in Place | | | | Capital Available for Operation |
	Structures	Equipment	Installation	Total	Total
1928	18.5	8.8	12.0	17.3	17.6
1929	18.5	8.8	11.6	17.2	17.7
1930	18.4	8.6	11.0	17.0	17.6
1931	17.9	7.9	10.1	16.4	17.3
1932	17.5	7.4	9.4	15.8	16.8
1933	17.2	6.9	9.0	15.4	16.2
1934	17.1	6.8	8.9	15.2	16.0
1935	16.9	6.8	8.8	15.0	15.7
1936	16.6	6.7	8.6	14.6	15.2
1937	16.0	6.5	8.2	13.9	14.5
1938	15.8	6.5	8.2	13.6	14.2
1939	15.7	6.4	8.2	13.5	14.0
1940	15.6	6.6	8.3	13.4	13.8
1941	15.7	6.8	8.5	13.4	13.8
1944	17.2	8.2	10.2	15.0	15.2
1945	17.7	8.3	10.6	15.4	15.7
1946	18.3	8.0	10.9	15.7	16.1
1947	18.6	7.8	11.1	15.8	16.3
1948	18.8	7.5	11.3	15.8	16.3
1949	18.7	7.4	11.3	15.6	16.3
1950	18.4	7.3	11.3	15.3	16.0
1951	18.0	7.0	11.1	14.8	15.6
1952	17.6	6.9	11.0	14.3	15.2
1953	17.1	7.0	10.6	13.9	14.9
1954	16.6	7.0	10.2	13.5	14.5
1955	16.1	7.0	9.9	13.1	14.1
1956	15.6	6.9	9.5	12.7	13.7
1957	15.0	6.6	9.1	12.1	13.1
1958	14.6	6.4	8.8	11.6	12.5
1959	14.1	6.2	8.5	11.1	11.9
1960	13.6	6.1	8.5	10.7	11.5
1961	13.2	6.0	8.6	10.4	11.1
1962	12.8	6.0	8.6	10.1	10.8

Source: See Chapter 3, Section 8.

TABLE T-23

LIVESTOCK IN 1937, 1928, AND 1950 PRICES, 1928-62
(January 1--Billion Rubles)

	1937 Prices	1928 Prices	1950 Prices
1928	48.1	7.9	90.6
1929	47.4	7.8	88.9
1930	40.1	6.7	73.7
1931	31.1	5.2	56.9
1932	24.1	4.0	44.4
1933	20.0	3.3	37.0
1934	20.6	3.3	38.3
1935	24.3	3.7	46.0
1936	30.9	4.7	60.1
1937	31.4	4.8	60.8
1938	34.6	5.2	67.2
1939	36.8	5.6	71.3
1940	37.7	5.8	72.2
1941	40.9	6.3	78.1
1944	21.0	3.2	40.0
1945	26.8	4.1	51.3
1946	28.7	4.3	55.0
1947	28.2	4.3	54.0
1948	29.9	4.5	57.3
1949	33.0	4.9	64.1
1950	36.2	5.3	70.6
1951	37.0	5.4	72.3
1952	39.1	5.7	76.3
1953	39.1	5.7	76.1
1954	40.3	5.8	78.4
1955	39.7	5.7	77.1
1956	40.7	5.8	79.2
1957	42.7	5.9	83.7
1958	45.6	6.3	89.6
1959	48.3	6.5	94.9
1960	50.1	6.7	99.1
1961	50.9	6.7	101.1
1962	53.9	7.0	108.0

Source: See Chapter 4.

TABLE T-24

TOTAL AND NONAGRICULTURAL INVENTORIES IN 1937,
1928, AND 1950 PRICES, 1928-62
(January 1--Billion Rubles)

	Total			Nonagricultural		
	1937 Prices	1928 Prices	1950 Prices	1937 Prices	1928 Prices	1950 Prices
1928	48.8	15.0	95.9	35.3	10.0	71.9
1929	50.3	16.0	99.2	36.5	10.9	74.6
1930	49.1	16.5	97.1	36.2	11.7	74.1
1931	54.4	20.1	111.6	42.2	15.5	89.9
1932	61.2	24.5	130.2	50.1	20.4	110.4
1933	57.3	25.7	123.8	47.3	22.0	108.0
1934	60.8	28.5	134.4	49.8	24.4	115.0
1935	65.2	32.3	145.2	53.6	28.0	124.7
1936	79.1	41.4	177.8	65.4	36.3	153.4
1937	78.2	41.7	174.6	65.9	37.1	153.6
1938	87.4	47.0	194.8	72.4	41.4	168.1
1939	92.1	49.9	206.3	78.3	44.8	181.7
1940	101.8	54.9	227.8	87.2	49.5	201.8
1941	104.8	59.1	235.5	88.2	52.8	206.0
1944	82.5	50.2	184.9	72.7	46.5	167.5
1945	84.4	50.9	188.3	74.6	47.2	170.9
1946	87.8	52.0	194.2	76.6	47.8	174.3
1947	91.6	55.7	204.5	79.3	51.1	182.6
1948	104.2	63.8	235.7	88.5	57.9	207.8
1949	109.6	62.4	239.1	92.3	55.9	208.3
1950	128.2	70.7	274.0	110.5	64.1	242.5
1951	137.7	76.2	294.7	120.2	69.7	263.5
1952	154.5	85.8	331.2	138.0	79.6	301.8
1953	170.3	95.3	366.0	152.6	88.7	334.5
1954	179.8	102.2	389.3	161.5	95.4	356.7
1955	177.9	101.7	386.1	159.1	94.7	352.6
1956	184.1	102.3	394.8	163.1	94.5	357.4
1957	207.8	112.1	440.0	183.6	103.1	396.9
1958	221.0	120.1	470.2	196.8	111.1	427.1
1959	254.9	135.5	537.0	228.1	125.5	489.3
1960	286.6	150.7	600.5	259.5	140.6	552.3
1961	307.7	163.9	649.2	280.3	153.7	600.4
1962	339.6	181.9	715.9	311.4	171.4	665.7

Sources:　Tables N-1, N-2, and N-3.

TABLE T-25

TOTAL NET CAPITAL STOCK IN 1937 PRICES, 1928-62
(January 1--Billion Rubles)

| | Net Fixed Capital | | | | |
	Available for Operation	Investment Projects in Progress	Inventories	Livestock	Total
1928	104.5	3.0	48.8	48.1	204.4
1929	109.4	4.3	50.3	47.4	211.4
1930	116.3	5.9	49.1	40.1	211.4
1931	125.8	10.0	54.4	31.1	221.3
1932	138.5	12.5	61.2	24.1	236.3
1933	153.8	12.6	57.3	20.0	243.7
1934	166.4	12.7	60.8	20.6	260.5
1935	180.1	13.5	65.2	24.3	283.1
1936	200.5	12.1	79.1	30.9	322.6
1937	227.9	12.6	78.2	31.4	350.1
1938	249.5	14.1	87.4	34.6	385.6
1939	271.9	14.1	92.1	36.8	414.9
1940	308.6	14.1	101.8	37.7	462.2
1941	345.5	14.1	104.8	40.9	505.3
1944	270.1	5.1	82.5	21.0	378.7
1945	273.8	7.5	84.4	26.8	392.5
1946	280.3	10.3	87.8	28.7	407.1
1947	291.6	13.2	91.6	28.2	424.6
1948	306.1	16.4	104.2	29.9	456.6
1949	325.8	20.4	109.6	33.0	488.8
1950	351.0	25.6	128.2	36.2	541.0
1951	382.7	32.3	137.7	37.0	589.7
1952	415.7	41.1	154.5	39.1	650.4
1953	452.0	48.0	170.3	39.1	709.4
1954	492.7	55.1	179.8	40.3	767.9
1955	543.0	60.9	177.9	39.7	821.5
1956	600.6	69.0	184.1	40.7	894.4
1957	668.2	78.3	207.8	42.7	997.0
1958	743.3	86.1	221.0	45.6	1096.0
1959	839.3	84.9	254.9	48.3	1227.4
1960	936.5	90.8	286.6	50.1	1364.0
1961	1036.0	100.0	307.7	50.9	1494.6
1962	1141.9	107.1	339.6	53.9	1642.5

Sources: Tables T-1, T-23, T-24, and E-1. Net fixed capital available for operation is total net fixed capital minus investment projects in progress. The total stock is the sum of components.

TABLE T-26

TOTAL NET CAPITAL STOCK IN 1928 PRICES, 1928-62
(January 1--Billion Rubles)

| | Net Fixed Capital | | | | |
	Available for Operation	Investment Projects in Progress	Inventories	Livestock	Total
1928	54.4	1.6	15.0	7.9	78.9
1929	57.1	2.3	16.0	7.8	83.2
1930	60.9	3.3	16.5	6.7	87.4
1931	66.6	5.8	20.1	5.2	97.7
1932	74.6	7.7	24.5	4.0	110.8
1933	85.2	8.6	25.7	3.3	122.8
1934	94.6	9.3	28.5	3.3	135.7
1935	105.1	10.0	32.3	3.7	151.1
1936	120.6	9.1	41.4	4.7	175.8
1937	142.3	9.8	41.7	4.8	198.6
1938	160.5	11.5	47.0	5.2	224.2
1939	181.6	11.5	49.9	5.6	248.6
1940	211.0	11.5	54.9	5.8	283.2
1941	238.4	11.5	59.1	6.3	315.3
1944	185.0	4.4	50.2	3.2	242.6
1945	189.8	7.3	50.9	4.1	252.1
1946	198.8	11.4	52.0	4.3	266.5
1947	211.3	14.0	55.7	4.3	285.3
1948	226.6	16.2	63.8	4.5	311.1
1949	245.5	19.5	62.4	4.9	332.3
1950	268.1	23.6	70.7	5.3	367.7
1951	297.0	30.0	76.2	5.4	408.6
1952	324.3	37.1	85.8	5.7	452.9
1953	353.7	41.7	95.3	5.7	496.4
1954	385.8	47.9	102.2	5.8	541.7
1955	426.9	54.2	101.7	5.7	588.5
1956	475.9	63.2	102.3	5.8	647.2
1957	535.9	73.9	112.1	5.9	727.8
1958	602.3	81.2	120.1	6.3	809.9
1959	687.6	79.3	135.5	6.5	908.9
1960	772.2	84.3	150.7	6.7	1013.9
1961	857.5	92.6	163.9	6.7	1120.7
1962	947.9	99.4	181.9	7.0	1236.2

Sources: Tables T-8, T-23, T-24, and E-1. Net fixed capital available for operation is total net fixed capital minus investment projects in progress. The total stock is the sum of components.

TABLE T-27

TOTAL NET CAPITAL STOCK IN 1950 PRICES, 1928-62
(January 1--Billion Rubles)

| | Net Fixed Capital | | | | |
	Available for Operation	Investment Projects in Progress	Inventories	Livestock	Total
1928	275.0	8.2	95.9	90.6	469.7
1929	288.2	11.5	99.2	88.9	487.8
1930	306.7	16.0	97.1	73.7	493.5
1931	332.3	26.9	111.6	56.9	527.7
1932	364.9	32.9	130.2	44.4	572.4
1933	403.8	32.3	123.8	37.0	596.9
1934	435.0	31.8	134.4	38.3	639.5
1935	468.8	33.3	145.3	46.0	693.4
1936	518.4	29.8	177.8	60.1	786.1
1937	584.6	30.8	174.6	60.8	850.8
1938	635.9	33.9	194.8	67.2	931.8
1939	686.7	33.9	206.3	71.3	998.2
1940	774.2	33.9	227.8	72.2	1108.1
1941	861.4	33.9	235.5	78.1	1208.9
1944	669.6	11.4	184.9	40.0	905.9
1945	675.2	15.8	188.3	51.3	930.6
1946	684.9	20.9	194.2	55.0	955.0
1947	706.5	27.4	204.5	54.0	992.4
1948	736.0	34.9	235.7	57.3	1063.9
1949	778.8	44.6	239.1	64.1	1126.6
1950	835.7	57.3	274.0	70.6	1237.6
1951	907.2	72.6	294.7	72.3	1346.8
1952	983.2	92.5	331.2	76.3	1483.2
1953	1066.6	109.0	366.0	76.1	1617.7
1954	1160.7	124.0	389.3	78.4	1752.4
1955	1275.2	136.0	386.1	77.1	1874.4
1956	1405.4	153.0	394.8	79.2	2032.4
1957	1555.8	172.0	440.0	83.7	2251.5
1958	1723.0	189.0	470.2	89.6	2471.8
1959	1934.8	186.0	537.0	94.9	2752.7
1960	2150.8	198.0	600.5	99.1	3048.4
1961	2371.3	218.0	649.2	101.1	3339.6
1962	2605.4	232.3	715.9	108.0	3661.6

Sources: Tables T-9, T-23, T-24, and E-1. Net fixed capital available for operation is total net fixed capital minus investment projects in progress. The total stock is the sum of components.

TABLE T-28

NONAGRICULTURAL NET CAPITAL STOCK IN 1937 PRICES, 1928-62
(January 1--Billion Rubles)

| | Net Fixed Capital | | | |
	Available for Operation	Investment Projects in Progress	Inventories	Total
1928	91.2	2.8	35.3	129.3
1929	95.5	4.0	36.5	136.0
1930	101.6	5.5	36.2	143.3
1931	109.9	9.4	42.2	161.5
1932	121.0	11.8	50.1	182.9
1933	135.3	11.8	47.3	194.4
1934	145.6	11.9	49.8	207.3
1935	157.2	12.7	53.6	223.5
1936	175.0	11.4	65.4	251.8
1937	199.1	11.8	65.9	276.8
1938	217.7	13.3	72.4	303.4
1939	238.0	13.3	78.3	329.6
1940	271.2	13.3	87.2	371.7
1941	305.0	13.3	88.2	406.5
1944	242.5	4.7	72.7	319.9
1945	247.0	6.9	74.6	328.5
1946	253.8	9.5	76.6	339.9
1947	264.3	12.1	79.3	355.7
1948	276.9	15.1	88.5	380.5
1949	293.4	18.8	92.3	404.5
1950	312.9	23.6	110.5	447.0
1951	337.5	29.7	120.2	487.4
1952	363.4	37.8	138.0	539.2
1953	393.4	44.2	152.6	590.2
1954	428.4	50.7	161.5	640.6
1955	471.5	56.0	159.1	686.6
1956	519.5	63.5	163.1	746.1
1957	577.6	72.0	183.6	833.2
1958	642.3	79.2	196.8	918.3
1959	725.7	78.1	228.1	1031.9
1960	812.4	83.5	259.5	1155.4
1961	903.5	92.0	280.3	1275.8
1962	1000.2	98.5	311.4	1410.1

Sources: Tables T-12 and T-24; for the division of fixed capital between its components, see p. 96.

TABLE T-29

NONAGRICULTURAL NET CAPITAL STOCK IN 1928 PRICES, 1928-62
(January 1--Billion Rubles)

| | Net Fixed Capital | | | |
	Available for Operation	Investment Projects in Progress	Inventories	Total
1928	47.8	1.5	10.0	59.3
1929	50.1	2.2	10.9	63.2
1930	53.5	3.1	11.7	68.3
1931	58.5	5.5	15.5	79.5
1932	65.5	7.2	20.4	93.1
1933	75.2	8.1	22.0	105.3
1934	82.9	8.7	24.4	116.0
1935	91.3	9.4	28.0	128.7
1936	103.5	8.6	36.3	148.4
1937	121.2	9.2	37.1	167.5
1938	136.5	10.8	41.4	188.7
1939	155.3	10.8	44.8	210.9
1940	181.6	10.8	49.5	241.9
1941	207.2	10.8	52.8	270.8
1944	166.6	4.0	46.5	217.1
1945	172.7	6.7	47.2	226.6
1946	181.9	10.5	47.8	240.2
1947	193.3	12.9	51.1	257.3
1948	206.4	14.9	57.9	279.2
1949	221.8	17.9	55.9	295.6
1950	237.7	21.7	64.1	323.5
1951	258.3	27.6	69.7	355.6
1952	279.1	34.1	79.6	392.8
1953	302.9	38.4	88.7	430.0
1954	329.6	44.1	95.4	469.1
1955	362.7	49.9	94.7	507.3
1956	403.2	58.1	94.5	555.8
1957	454.5	68.0	103.1	625.6
1958	511.8	74.7	111.1	697.6
1959	585.6	73.0	125.5	784.1
1960	662.1	77.6	140.6	880.3
1961	742.6	85.2	153.7	981.5
1962	827.5	91.4	171.4	1090.3

Sources: Tables T-13 and T-24; for the division of fixed capital between its components, see p. 96.

TABLE T-30

NONAGRICULTURAL NET CAPITAL STOCK IN 1950 PRICES, 1928-62
(January 1--Billion Rubles)

| | Net Fixed Capital | | | |
	Available for Operation	Investment Projects in Progress	Inventories	Total
1928	237.9	7.7	71.9	317.5
1929	249.4	10.8	74.6	334.8
1930	265.7	15.0	74.1	354.8
1931	288.1	25.3	89.9	403.3
1932	316.3	30.9	110.4	457.6
1933	352.2	30.4	108.0	490.6
1934	377.2	29.9	115.0	522.1
1935	405.5	31.3	124.7	561.5
1936	449.2	28.0	153.4	630.6
1937	507.6	29.0	153.6	690.2
1938	552.0	31.9	168.1	752.0
1939	598.4	31.9	181.7	812.0
1940	677.5	31.9	201.8	911.2
1941	757.4	31.9	206.0	995.3
1944	598.6	10.5	167.5	776.6
1945	606.3	14.5	170.9	791.7
1946	617.1	19.2	174.3	810.6
1947	636.8	25.2	182.6	844.6
1948	662.1	32.1	207.8	902.0
1949	697.1	41.0	208.3	946.4
1950	740.3	52.7	242.5	1035.5
1951	794.3	66.8	263.5	1124.6
1952	852.5	85.1	301.8	1239.4
1953	920.5	100.3	334.5	1355.3
1954	1000.2	114.1	356.7	1471.0
1955	1095.9	125.1	352.6	1573.6
1956	1202.9	140.8	357.4	1701.1
1957	1329.8	158.2	396.9	1884.9
1958	1471.3	173.9	427.1	2072.3
1959	1652.7	171.1	489.3	2313.1
1960	1842.9	182.2	552.3	2577.4
1961	2042.7	200.6	600.4	2843.7
1962	2254.3	213.7	665.7	3133.7

Sources: Tables T-14 and T-24; for the division of fixed capital between its components, see p. 96.

TABLE T-31

NONRESIDENTIAL NET CAPITAL STOCK IN 1937 PRICES, 1928-62
(January 1--Billion Rubles)

| | Net Fixed Capital | | | | |
	Available for Operation	Investment Projects in Progress	Inventories	Livestock	Total
1928	43.2	3.0	48.8	48.1	143.1
1929	47.0	4.3	50.3	47.4	149.0
1930	52.9	5.9	49.1	40.1	148.0
1931	61.5	10.0	54.4	31.1	157.0
1932	73.2	12.5	61.2	24.1	171.0
1933	87.7	12.6	57.3	20.0	177.6
1934	99.6	12.7	60.8	20.6	193.7
1935	112.7	13.5	65.2	24.3	215.7
1936	132.6	12.1	79.1	30.9	254.7
1937	159.4	12.6	78.2	31.4	281.6
1938	180.5	14.1	87.4	34.6	316.6
1939	201.4	14.1	92.1	36.8	344.4
1940	233.0	14.1	101.8	37.7	386.6
1941	264.6	14.1	104.8	40.9	424.4
1944	209.0	5.1	82.5	21.0	317.6
1945	212.7	7.5	84.4	26.8	331.4
1946	219.4	10.3	87.8	28.7	346.2
1947	230.1	13.2	91.6	28.2	363.1
1948	241.4	16.4	104.2	29.9	391.9
1949	257.5	20.4	109.6	33.0	420.5
1950	278.9	25.6	128.2	36.2	468.9
1951	306.2	32.3	137.7	37.0	513.2
1952	334.4	41.1	154.5	39.1	569.1
1953	366.1	48.0	170.3	39.1	623.5
1954	401.3	55.1	179.8	40.3	676.5
1955	446.0	60.9	177.9	39.7	724.5
1956	497.9	69.0	184.1	40.7	791.7
1957	558.3	78.3	207.8	42.7	887.1
1958	623.1	86.1	221.0	45.6	975.8
1959	705.6	84.9	254.9	48.3	1093.7
1960	787.2	90.8	286.6	50.1	1214.7
1961	870.5	100.0	307.7	50.9	1329.1
1962	961.0	107.1	339.6	53.9	1461.6

Sources: Tables T-16, T-23, and T-24; for the division of fixed capital between its components, see p. 96.

TABLE T-32

NONRESIDENTIAL NET CAPITAL STOCK IN 1928 PRICES, 1928-62
(January 1--Billion Rubles)

| | Net Fixed Capital | | | | |
	Available for Operation	Investment Projects in Progress	Inventories	Livestock	Total
1928	31.2	1.6	15.0	7.9	55.7
1929	33.6	2.3	16.0	7.8	59.7
1930	37.0	3.3	16.5	6.7	63.5
1931	42.3	5.8	20.1	5.2	73.4
1932	50.0	7.7	24.5	4.0	86.2
1933	60.3	8.6	25.7	3.3	97.9
1934	69.4	9.3	28.5	3.3	110.5
1935	79.7	10.0	32.3	3.7	125.7
1936	95.0	9.1	41.4	4.7	150.2
1937	116.5	9.8	41.7	4.8	172.8
1938	134.5	11.5	47.0	5.2	198.2
1939	155.0	11.5	49.9	5.6	222.0
1940	182.5	11.5	54.9	5.8	254.7
1941	207.9	11.5	59.1	6.3	284.8
1944	161.9	4.4	50.2	3.2	219.7
1945	166.7	7.3	50.9	4.1	229.0
1946	175.8	11.4	52.0	4.3	243.5
1947	188.1	14.0	55.7	4.3	262.1
1948	202.2	16.2	63.8	4.5	286.7
1949	219.7	19.5	62.4	4.9	306.5
1950	240.9	23.6	70.7	5.3	340.5
1951	268.1	30.0	76.2	5.4	379.7
1952	293.6	37.1	85.8	5.7	422.2
1953	321.3	41.7	95.3	5.7	464.0
1954	351.3	47.9	102.2	5.8	507.2
1955	390.3	54.2	101.7	5.7	551.9
1956	437.1	63.2	102.3	5.8	608.4
1957	494.4	73.9	112.1	5.9	686.3
1958	556.9	81.2	120.1	6.3	764.5
1959	637.1	79.3	135.5	6.5	858.4
1960	715.9	84.3	150.7	6.7	957.6
1961	795.0	92.6	163.9	6.7	1058.2
1962	879.6	99.4	181.9	7.0	1167.9

Sources: Tables T-17, T-23, and T-24; for the division of fixed capital between its components, see p. 96.

TABLE T-33

NONRESIDENTIAL NET CAPITAL STOCK IN 1950 PRICES, 1928-62
(January 1--Billion Rubles)

| | Net Fixed Capital | | | | |
	Available for Operation	Investment Projects in Progress	Inventories	Livestock	Total
1928	121.5	8.2	95.9	90.6	316.2
1929	132.2	11.5	99.2	88.9	331.8
1930	148.2	16.0	97.1	73.7	335.0
1931	171.6	26.9	111.6	56.9	367.0
1932	201.6	32.9	130.2	44.4	409.1
1933	238.5	32.3	123.8	37.0	431.6
1934	268.0	31.8	134.4	38.3	472.5
1935	300.3	33.3	145.3	46.0	524.9
1936	348.7	29.8	177.8	60.1	616.4
1937	413.3	30.8	174.6	60.8	679.5
1938	463.4	33.9	194.8	67.2	759.3
1939	510.4	33.9	206.3	71.3	821.9
1940	585.2	33.9	227.8	72.2	919.1
1941	659.1	33.9	235.5	78.1	1006.6
1944	516.9	11.4	184.9	40.0	753.2
1945	522.5	15.8	188.3	51.3	777.9
1946	532.6	20.9	194.2	55.0	802.7
1947	552.8	27.4	204.5	54.0	838.7
1948	574.3	34.9	235.7	57.3	902.2
1949	608.1	44.6	239.1	64.1	955.9
1950	655.4	57.3	274.0	70.6	1057.3
1951	715.9	72.6	294.7	72.3	1155.5
1952	779.9	92.5	331.2	76.3	1279.9
1953	851.9	109.0	366.0	76.1	1403.0
1954	932.2	124.0	389.3	78.4	1523.9
1955	1032.7	136.0	386.1	77.1	1631.9
1956	1148.7	153.0	394.8	79.2	1775.7
1957	1281.1	172.0	440.0	83.7	1976.8
1958	1422.5	189.0	470.2	89.6	2171.3
1959	1600.5	186.0	537.0	94.9	2418.4
1960	1777.5	198.0	600.5	99.1	2675.1
1961	1957.6	218.0	649.2	101.1	2925.9
1962	2153.1	232.3	715.9	108.0	3209.3

Sources: Tables T-18, T-23, and T-24; for the division of fixed capital between its components, see p. 96.

TABLE T-34

NONAGRICULTURAL NONRESIDENTIAL NET CAPITAL STOCK
IN 1937 PRICES, 1928-62
(January 1--Billion Rubles)

| | Net Fixed Capital | | | |
	Available for Operation	Investment Projects in Progress	Inventories	Total
1928	29.8	2.8	35.3	67.9
1929	33.0	4.0	36.5	73.5
1930	38.1	5.5	36.2	79.8
1931	45.6	9.4	42.2	97.2
1932	55.6	11.8	50.1	117.5
1933	69.2	11.8	47.3	128.3
1934	78.8	11.9	49.8	140.5
1935	89.8	12.7	53.6	156.1
1936	107.1	11.4	65.4	183.9
1937	130.7	11.8	65.9	208.4
1938	148.7	13.3	72.4	234.4
1939	167.5	13.3	78.3	259.1
1940	195.5	13.3	87.2	296.0
1941	224.1	13.3	88.2	325.6
1944	181.3	4.7	72.7	258.7
1945	186.0	6.9	74.6	267.5
1946	192.9	9.5	76.6	279.0
1947	202.7	12.1	79.3	294.1
1948	212.2	15.1	88.5	315.8
1949	225.1	18.8	92.3	336.2
1950	240.8	23.6	110.5	374.9
1951	260.9	29.7	120.2	410.8
1952	282.1	37.8	138.0	457.9
1953	307.5	44.2	152.6	504.3
1954	336.9	50.7	161.5	549.1
1955	374.4	56.0	159.1	589.5
1956	416.8	63.5	163.1	643.4
1957	467.6	72.0	183.6	723.2
1958	522.1	79.2	196.8	798.1
1959	592.1	78.1	228.1	898.3
1960	663.1	83.5	259.5	1006.1
1961	738.0	92.0	280.3	1110.3
1962	819.3	98.5	311.4	1229.2

Sources: Tables T-19 and T-24; for the division of fixed capital between its components, see p. 96.

TABLE T-35

NONAGRICULTURAL NONRESIDENTIAL NET CAPITAL STOCK
IN 1928 PRICES, 1928-62
(January 1--Billion Rubles)

	Net Fixed Capital			
	Available for Operation	Investment Projects in Progress	Inventories	Total
1928	24.6	1.5	10.0	36.1
1929	26.6	2.2	10.9	39.7
1930	29.6	3.1	11.7	44.4
1931	34.2	5.5	15.5	55.2
1932	40.9	7.2	20.4	68.5
1933	50.3	8.1	22.0	80.4
1934	57.7	8.7	24.4	90.8
1935	65.9	9.4	28.0	103.3
1936	77.9	8.6	36.3	122.8
1937	95.4	9.2	37.1	141.7
1938	110.5	10.8	41.4	162.7
1939	128.7	10.8	44.8	184.3
1940	153.1	10.8	49.5	213.4
1941	176.7	10.8	52.8	240.3
1944	143.5	4.0	46.5	194.0
1945	149.6	6.7	47.2	203.5
1946	158.9	10.5	47.8	217.2
1947	170.1	12.9	51.1	234.1
1948	182.0	14.9	57.9	254.8
1949	196.0	17.9	55.9	269.8
1950	210.5	21.7	64.1	296.3
1951	229.4	27.6	69.7	326.7
1952	248.4	34.1	79.6	362.1
1953	270.5	38.4	88.7	397.6
1954	295.1	44.1	95.4	434.6
1955	326.1	49.9	94.7	470.7
1956	364.4	58.1	94.5	517.0
1957	413.0	68.0	103.1	584.1
1958	466.4	74.7	111.1	652.2
1959	535.1	73.0	125.5	733.6
1960	605.8	77.6	140.6	824.0
1961	680.1	85.2	153.7	919.0
1962	759.2	91.4	171.4	1022.0

Sources: Tables T-20 and T-24; for the division of fixed capital between its components, see p. 96.

TABLE T-36

NONAGRICULTURAL NONRESIDENTIAL NET CAPITAL STOCK
IN 1950 PRICES, 1928-62
(January 1--Billion Rubles)

| | Net Fixed Capital | | | |
	Available for Operation	Investment Projects in Progress	Inventories	Total
1928	84.4	7.7	71.9	164.0
1929	93.4	10.8	74.6	178.8
1930	107.2	15.0	74.1	196.3
1931	127.4	25.3	89.9	242.6
1932	153.0	30.9	110.4	294.3
1933	186.9	30.4	108.0	325.3
1934	210.2	29.9	115.0	355.1
1935	237.0	31.3	124.7	393.0
1936	279.5	28.0	153.4	460.9
1937	336.3	29.0	153.6	518.9
1938	379.5	31.9	168.1	579.5
1939	422.1	31.9	181.7	635.7
1940	488.5	31.9	201.8	722.2
1941	555.1	31.9	206.0	793.0
1944	445.9	10.5	167.5	623.9
1945	453.6	14.5	170.9	639.0
1946	464.8	19.2	174.3	658.3
1947	483.1	25.2	182.6	690.9
1948	500.4	32.1	207.8	740.3
1949	526.4	41.0	208.3	775.7
1950	560.0	52.7	242.5	855.2
1951	603.0	66.8	263.5	933.3
1952	649.2	85.1	301.8	1036.1
1953	705.8	100.3	334.5	1140.6
1954	771.7	114.1	356.7	1242.5
1955	853.4	125.1	352.6	1331.1
1956	946.2	140.8	357.4	1444.4
1957	1055.1	158.2	396.9	1610.2
1958	1170.8	173.9	427.1	1771.8
1959	1318.4	171.1	489.3	1978.8
1960	1469.6	182.2	552.3	2204.1
1961	1629.0	200.6	600.4	2430.0
1962	1802.0	213.7	665.7	2681.4

Sources: Tables T-21 and T-24; for the division of fixed capital between its components, see p. 96.

TABLE T-37

AVERAGE AGE OF THE TOTAL CAPITAL STOCK, GROSS VALUE
WEIGHTS, IN 1937 PRICES, 1928-62
(January 1--Years)

1928	11.6
1929	11.8
1930	12.1
1931	12.1
1932	11.9
1933	12.0
1934	11.9
1935	11.7
1936	11.2
1937	11.0
1938	10.7
1939	10.6
1940	10.7
1941	10.8
1944	12.3
1945	12.6
1946	12.8
1947	12.9
1948	12.7
1949	12.6
1950	12.2
1951	11.8
1952	11.4
1953	11.1
1954	10.9
1955	10.8
1956	10.5
1957	10.0
1958	9.7
1959	9.3
1960	8.9
1961	8.7
1962	8.4

Source: See Chapter 6, pp. 164ff.

TABLE T-38

CAPITAL SERVICES, TOTAL AND BY SECTOR, AT 8 PERCENT
INTEREST RATE, IN 1937 PRICES, 1928-61
(Billion Rubles)

	Total	Non-agricultural	Residential	Non-residential	Nonagricultural Nonresidential
1928	20.0	13.1	6.5	13.7	6.8
1929	20.6	13.9	6.5	14.1	7.3
1930	21.4	15.3	6.7	14.7	8.5
1931	23.0	17.3	6.7	16.3	10.7
1932	24.5	19.2	7.0	17.6	12.1
1933	26.0	20.8	6.9	19.1	13.9
1934	28.2	22.4	7.1	21.2	15.4
1935	31.5	24.7	7.2	24.3	17.5
1936	35.1	27.4	7.2	28.0	20.3
1937	38.8	30.5	7.3	31.5	23.2
1938	42.6	33.4	7.5	35.1	26.0
1939	45.8	36.4	7.6	38.3	28.7
1940	52.3	41.7	8.3	43.9	33.5
1944	42.5	35.7	6.5	36.2	28.9
1945	44.1	36.8	6.7	37.2	30.3
1946	45.8	38.6	6.7	39.1	31.9
1947	48.5	40.9	6.7	41.8	34.2
1948	52.0	43.8	7.3	44.7	36.4
1949	56.5	47.4	7.6	49.0	39.8
1950	62.0	51.7	7.9	54.1	43.8
1951	68.6	57.0	8.5	60.1	48.2
1952	75.8	62.6	9.0	66.8	53.7
1953	82.6	68.1	9.4	73.2	58.7
1954	89.2	73.6	10.0	79.2	63.5
1955	97.0	79.8	10.6	86.3	69.2
1956	107.3	88.1	11.3	96.0	76.8
1957	119.4	98.1	12.0	107.5	86.1
1958	133.1	109.7	13.4	119.7	96.3
1959	148.9	123.4	14.6	134.2	108.9
1960	164.3	137.2	15.5	148.9	121.8
1961	181.4	152.7	17.1	164.2	135.7

Source: See Chapter 6, Section 4.

TABLE T-39

CAPITAL SERVICES, TOTAL AND BY SECTOR, AT 20 PERCENT
INTEREST RATE, IN 1937 PRICES, 1928-61
(Billion Rubles)

	Total	Non-agricultural	Residential	Non-residential	Nonagricultural Nonresidential
1928	45.0	29.0	13.9	31.2	15.2
1929	46.0	30.6	14.1	31.9	16.5
1930	47.4	33.6	14.4	33.0	19.1
1931	50.5	37.9	14.5	36.0	23.6
1932	53.3	41.8	14.8	38.6	26.9
1933	56.2	44.9	14.9	41.3	30.0
1934	60.9	48.3	15.1	45.7	33.2
1935	67.9	53.2	15.3	52.5	37.9
1936	75.5	59.2	15.3	60.1	43.8
1937	83.0	65.3	15.5	67.4	49.8
1938	90.6	71.4	15.8	74.8	55.6
1939	97.1	77.4	16.1	81.1	61.2
1940	110.3	88.4	17.6	92.6	70.8
1944	88.8	74.6	13.8	75.1	60.5
1945	92.1	76.9	14.0	77.9	63.0
1946	95.7	80.4	14.0	81.6	66.3
1947	101.4	85.1	14.3	87.1	70.8
1948	108.7	90.9	15.3	93.4	75.5
1949	118.3	98.4	16.0	102.3	82.5
1950	129.9	107.7	16.9	113.0	91.0
1951	143.0	118.6	18.0	125.0	100.4
1952	157.4	130.3	19.0	138.4	111.4
1953	171.2	142.0	20.0	151.2	121.9
1954	184.5	153.2	21.3	163.3	131.9
1955	200.0	165.8	22.6	177.3	143.2
1956	220.7	182.8	24.1	196.7	158.8
1957	245.0	203.2	25.8	219.3	177.3
1958	272.5	226.7	28.6	243.8	198.0
1959	304.3	254.6	31.6	272.7	223.1
1960	335.9	283.1	34.4	301.5	248.7
1961	369.6	313.9	37.8	331.7	276.0

Source: See Chapter 6, Section 4.

TABLE T-40

CAPITAL SERVICES, TOTAL AND BY SECTOR, AT 8 PERCENT
INTEREST RATE, IN 1928 PRICES, 1928-61
(Billion Rubles)

	Total	Non-agricultural	Residential	Non-residential	Nonagricultural Nonresidential
1928	8.3	6.3	2.5	5.7	3.7
1929	8.8	6.8	2.5	6.4	4.4
1930	9.7	7.6	2.5	7.3	5.2
1931	11.0	9.0	2.5	8.5	6.4
1932	12.5	10.4	2.6	10.0	7.8
1933	14.0	11.9	2.6	11.4	9.2
1934	15.9	13.3	2.7	13.1	10.6
1935	18.2	15.1	2.7	15.5	12.3
1936	21.1	17.1	2.7	18.3	14.5
1937	24.3	19.6	2.8	21.4	16.8
1938	27.6	22.3	2.8	24.8	19.5
1939	30.8	25.0	2.9	28.0	22.1
1940	36.2	29.4	3.1	33.1	26.2
1944	30.7	26.2	2.5	28.2	23.7
1945	31.9	27.8	2.5	29.3	25.2
1946	34.0	29.9	2.5	31.4	27.4
1947	36.6	32.3	2.5	34.2	29.8
1948	39.4	34.7	2.8	36.6	31.9
1949	42.9	37.4	2.9	40.1	34.4
1950	47.7	40.8	3.0	44.7	37.8
1951	53.6	44.9	3.2	50.5	41.8
1952	59.7	49.5	3.4	56.2	46.1
1953	65.4	53.9	3.5	61.9	50.4
1954	71.4	58.4	3.8	67.6	54.6
1955	78.6	63.6	4.0	74.7	59.7
1956	87.9	70.8	4.3	83.6	66.4
1957	99.0	79.7	4.5	94.4	75.3
1958	111.1	89.8	5.1	106.1	84.8
1959	124.6	101.3	5.5	118.9	95.6
1960	138.7	113.8	5.8	133.0	108.0
1961	154.0	127.7	6.5	147.4	121.2

Source: See Chapter 6, Section 4.

TABLE T-41

CAPITAL SERVICES, TOTAL AND BY SECTOR, AT 20 PERCENT
INTEREST RATE, IN 1928 PRICES, 1928-61
(Billion Rubles)

	Total	Non-agricultural	Residential	Non-residential	Nonagricultural Nonresidential
1928	18.0	13.6	5.2	12.6	8.3
1929	19.1	14.6	5.3	13.8	9.4
1930	20.8	16.5	5.4	15.5	11.2
1931	23.5	19.4	5.5	18.1	13.9
1932	26.6	22.3	5.6	21.0	16.7
1933	29.5	25.1	5.6	23.9	19.5
1934	33.1	28.0	5.7	27.3	22.2
1935	37.8	31.7	5.8	32.1	25.9
1936	43.5	36.1	5.8	37.7	30.3
1937	49.7	41.0	5.8	43.7	35.0
1938	56.0	46.3	6.0	50.0	40.3
1939	61.9	51.5	6.1	55.9	45.3
1940	72.1	60.2	6.6	65.4	53.5
1944	60.4	52.9	5.2	55.2	47.5
1945	63.1	55.8	5.3	57.6	50.5
1946	67.1	59.7	5.3	61.8	54.4
1947	72.3	64.4	5.4	67.1	59.1
1948	78.0	69.2	5.8	72.2	63.4
1949	84.9	74.5	6.0	78.9	68.4
1950	94.2	81.5	6.4	87.9	75.2
1951	105.2	89.8	6.8	98.6	83.1
1952	116.6	98.9	7.2	109.4	91.7
1953	127.7	107.8	7.5	120.2	100.3
1954	139.2	116.9	8.0	131.1	108.9
1955	152.8	127.4	8.5	144.3	119.0
1956	170.4	141.6	9.1	161.3	132.5
1957	191.3	159.1	9.7	181.5	149.4
1958	214.2	178.7	10.8	203.5	168.0
1959	240.0	201.1	11.9	227.9	189.1
1960	266.8	225.5	13.0	254.0	212.6
1961	295.4	252.0	14.3	281.0	237.7

Source: See Chapter 6, Section 4.

TABLE T-42

CAPITAL SERVICES, TOTAL AND BY SECTOR, AT 8 PERCENT
INTEREST RATE, IN 1950 PRICES, 1928-61
(Billion Rubles)

	Total	Non-agricultural	Residential	Non-residential	Nonagricultural Nonresidential
1928	47.6	32.7	16.2	31.4	16.5
1929	49.4	34.8	16.2	33.2	18.5
1930	52.0	38.3	16.7	35.3	21.5
1931	56.9	43.5	16.7	40.4	27.1
1932	61.2	48.2	17.5	43.8	30.9
1933	64.5	52.3	17.2	47.1	34.9
1934	69.9	55.9	17.7	52.3	38.2
1935	77.6	61.4	18.0	59.5	43.4
1936	86.1	68.1	18.0	68.1	50.2
1937	94.6	74.9	18.2	76.2	56.6
1938	102.8	81.6	18.7	84.1	62.9
1939	110.0	88.1	19.0	91.0	68.9
1940	124.9	100.7	20.7	104.2	80.1
1944	100.7	84.8	16.2	84.3	68.4
1945	102.8	86.8	16.7	86.2	70.1
1946	106.1	90.0	16.7	89.3	73.2
1947	111.8	95.1	16.7	94.8	78.2
1948	118.9	100.8	18.2	100.7	82.5
1949	128.3	108.1	19.0	109.3	89.1
1950	140.3	117.4	19.7	120.4	97.5
1951	154.7	128.4	21.2	133.3	107.1
1952	170.5	140.7	22.5	148.0	118.1
1953	185.7	153.0	23.5	162.4	129.5
1954	200.6	165.1	25.0	175.4	140.0
1955	217.5	178.0	26.5	190.9	151.5
1956	239.3	195.0	28.2	211.0	166.8
1957	265.2	216.1	30.0	235.1	186.2
1958	294.5	240.4	33.5	261.1	207.0
1959	327.6	268.7	36.5	291.1	232.1
1960	360.5	297.7	38.7	321.7	259.0
1961	397.0	330.4	42.7	354.3	287.9

Source: See Chapter 6, Section 4.

TABLE T-43

CAPITAL SERVICES, TOTAL AND BY SECTOR, AT 20 PERCENT
INTEREST RATE, IN 1950 PRICES, 1928-61
(Billion Rubles)

	Total	Non-agricultural	Residential	Non-residential	Nonagricultural Nonresidential
1928	105.0	71.8	34.7	70.3	37.1
1929	108.2	76.2	35.2	73.2	41.0
1930	113.3	83.8	36.0	77.4	47.8
1931	122.9	95.2	36.2	87.0	59.3
1932	131.3	105.1	37.0	94.3	68.1
1933	138.6	113.1	37.2	101.3	75.7
1934	149.9	121.0	37.7	112.1	83.1
1935	166.3	132.9	38.2	127.9	94.6
1936	184.3	147.4	38.2	145.9	109.0
1937	201.6	161.4	38.7	162.5	122.5
1938	218.6	175.4	39.5	179.0	135.8
1939	233.2	188.9	40.2	192.8	148.3
1940	263.9	215.0	44.0	219.8	171.0
1944	210.8	178.9	34.5	176.2	144.2
1945	216.0	182.9	35.0	181.1	147.9
1946	222.9	189.3	35.0	187.7	154.1
1947	235.1	199.9	35.7	199.3	164.1
1948	250.3	211.7	38.2	212.2	173.5
1949	270.1	227.0	40.0	230.1	187.0
1950	295.3	247.0	42.2	253.2	204.8
1951	324.5	270.2	45.0	279.4	225.2
1952	356.6	296.4	47.5	309.0	248.7
1953	387.9	322.5	50.0	338.0	272.5
1954	418.2	347.8	53.2	364.8	294.5
1955	451.9	374.5	56.5	395.4	318.0
1956	496.3	410.2	60.2	436.1	350.1
1957	548.6	453.5	64.5	484.0	389.1
1958	607.9	503.5	71.5	536.5	432.1
1959	675.7	562.1	79.0	596.7	483.1
1960	743.8	623.0	86.0	657.8	537.0
1961	817.1	689.0	94.5	722.4	594.5

Source: See Chapter 6, Section 4.

TABLE T-44

ANNUAL INVESTMENT IN 1937 PRICES, 1928-61
(Billion Rubles)

	Fixed Capital				Total	
	Gross	Net	Inventories	Livestock	Gross	Net
1928	9.6	6.2	1.5	-0.7	10.4	7.0
1929	12.2	8.5	-1.2	-7.3	3.7	0.0
1930	17.7	13.6	5.3	-9.0	14.0	9.9
1931	19.9	15.2	6.8	-7.0	19.7	15.0
1932	20.8	15.4	-3.9	-4.1	12.8	7.4
1933	18.5	12.7	3.5	0.6	22.6	16.8
1934	21.0	14.5	4.4	3.7	29.1	22.6
1935	26.3	19.0	13.9	6.6	46.8	39.5
1936	36.1	27.9	-0.9	0.5	35.7	27.5
1937	32.5	23.1	9.2	3.2	44.9	35.5
1938	33.0	22.4	4.7	2.2	39.9	29.3
1939	32.9	21.3	4.9	-2.1	35.7	24.1
1940	32.2	19.5	-2.0	0.6	30.8	18.1
1944	17.9	6.1	1.9	5.8	25.6	13.8
1945	21.3	9.3	3.4	1.9	26.6	14.6
1946	26.7	14.2	3.8	-0.5	30.0	17.5
1947	31.0	17.7	12.6	1.7	45.3	32.0
1948	37.9	23.7	5.4	3.1	46.4	32.2
1949	45.8	30.4	18.6	3.2	67.6	52.2
1950	55.3	38.4	9.5	0.8	65.6	48.7
1951	60.8	41.8	16.8	2.1	79.7	60.7
1952	64.6	43.2	15.8	0.0	80.4	59.0
1953	71.3	47.8	9.5	1.2	82.0	58.5
1954	81.8	56.2	-1.9	-0.6	79.3	53.7
1955	94.0	65.7	6.2	1.0	101.2	72.9
1956	108.5	76.9	23.7	2.0	134.2	102.6
1957	118.7	83.0	13.2	2.9	134.8	99.1
1958	134.9	94.7	33.9	2.7	171.5	131.3
1959	148.3	103.1	31.7	1.8	181.8	136.6
1960	158.7	108.7	21.1	0.8	180.6	130.6
1961	168.8	113.0	31.9	3.0	203.7	147.9

Source: See Chapter 6, Section 5.

TABLE T-45

ANNUAL INVESTMENT IN 1928 PRICES, 1928-61
(Billion Rubles)

	Fixed Capital				Total	
	Gross	Net	Inventories	Livestock	Gross	Net
1928	5.1	3.3	1.0	-0.1	6.0	4.2
1929	6.8	4.8	0.5	-1.1	6.2	4.2
1930	10.5	8.2	3.6	-1.5	12.6	10.3
1931	12.6	9.9	4.4	-1.2	15.8	13.1
1932	14.7	11.5	1.2	-0.7	15.2	12.0
1933	13.8	10.1	2.8	0.0	16.6	12.9
1934	15.6	11.2	3.8	0.4	19.8	15.4
1935	19.8	14.6	9.1	1.0	29.9	24.7
1936	28.5	22.4	0.3	0.1	28.9	22.8
1937	27.2	19.8	5.3	0.4	32.9	25.5
1938	29.8	21.1	2.9	0.4	33.1	24.4
1939	29.0	18.8	2.4	-0.3	31.1	20.9
1940	26.7	15.3	1.4	0.1	28.2	16.8
1944	18.6	7.7	0.7	0.9	20.2	9.3
1945	24.2	13.0	1.1	0.2	25.5	14.3
1946	27.0	15.1	3.7	0.0	30.7	18.8
1947	30.3	17.5	8.1	0.2	38.6	25.8
1948	35.8	22.2	-1.4	0.4	34.8	21.2
1949	41.7	26.7	8.3	0.4	50.4	35.4
1950	51.9	35.2	5.5	0.1	57.5	40.8
1951	53.6	34.4	9.6	0.3	63.5	44.3
1952	55.7	34.0	9.5	0.0	65.2	43.5
1953	62.2	38.3	6.9	0.1	69.2	45.3
1954	73.6	47.4	-0.5	-0.1	73.0	46.8
1955	87.2	58.0	0.6	0.1	87.9	58.7
1956	103.6	70.7	9.8	0.1	113.5	80.6
1957	111.1	73.6	8.0	0.4	119.5	82.0
1958	125.8	83.5	15.4	0.2	141.4	99.1
1959	137.2	89.5	15.2	0.2	152.6	104.9
1960	147.0	93.7	13.2	0.0	160.2	106.9
1961	156.8	97.1	18.0	0.3	175.1	115.4

Source: See Chapter 6, Section 5.

TABLE T-46

ANNUAL INVESTMENT IN 1950 PRICES, 1928-61
(Billion Rubles)

| | Fixed Capital | | | | Total | |
	Gross	Net	Inventories	Livestock	Gross	Net
1928	25.7	16.5	3.3	-1.7	27.3	18.1
1929	33.2	23.0	-2.1	-15.2	15.9	5.7
1930	47.7	36.5	14.5	-16.8	45.4	34.2
1931	51.6	38.6	18.6	-12.5	57.7	44.7
1932	52.7	38.3	-6.4	-7.4	38.9	24.5
1933	45.7	30.7	10.6	1.3	57.6	42.6
1934	52.0	35.3	10.9	7.7	70.6	53.9
1935	64.5	46.1	32.5	14.1	111.1	92.7
1936	87.7	67.2	-3.2	0.7	85.2	64.7
1937	77.6	54.4	20.2	6.4	104.2	81.0
1938	76.4	50.8	11.5	4.1	92.0	66.4
1939	76.9	49.0	10.6	-4.8	82.7	54.8
1940	74.2	44.3	-3.5	1.0	71.7	41.8
1944	37.2	9.9	3.4	11.3	51.9	24.6
1945	42.3	14.9	5.9	3.7	51.9	24.5
1946	56.3	28.1	10.3	-1.0	65.6	37.4
1947	66.4	36.9	31.2	3.3	100.9	71.4
1948	83.9	52.6	3.4	6.8	94.1	62.8
1949	103.2	69.6	34.9	6.5	144.6	111.0
1950	123.7	86.8	20.7	1.7	146.1	109.2
1951	137.3	95.9	36.5	4.0	177.8	136.4
1952	146.4	99.9	34.8	-0.2	181.0	134.5
1953	160.1	109.1	23.3	2.3	185.7	134.7
1954	181.9	126.4	-3.2	-1.3	177.4	121.9
1955	208.4	147.2	8.7	2.1	219.2	158.0
1956	237.3	169.5	45.2	4.5	287.0	219.2
1957	260.4	184.2	30.2	5.9	296.5	220.3
1958	294.3	208.8	66.8	5.3	366.4	280.9
1959	323.6	228.0	63.5	4.2	391.3	295.7
1960	345.6	240.6	48.7	2.0	396.3	291.3
1961	365.2	248.3	66.7	6.9	438.8	321.9

Source: See Chapter 6, Section 5.

TABLE T-47

GROSS AND NET NATIONAL PRODUCT, TOTAL AND BY SECTOR, IN 1937 PRICES, 1928-61

(Billion Rubles)

	Total		Agricultural		Nonagricultural		Residential		Nonresidential		Nonagricultural Nonresidential	
	Gross	Net	Gross	Net	Gross	Net	Gross	Net	Gross	Net	Gross	Net
1928	123.7	120.3	59.0	58.1	64.7	62.2	3.1	1.7	120.6	118.6	61.6	60.5
1929	127.0	123.3	55.2	54.2	71.8	69.1	3.2	1.7	123.8	121.6	68.6	67.4
1930	134.5	130.4	52.3	51.3	82.2	79.1	3.4	1.8	131.1	128.6	78.7	77.3
1931	137.2	132.5	48.0	46.8	89.2	85.7	3.3	1.8	133.9	130.7	86.0	83.9
1932	135.7	130.4	43.1	41.9	92.6	88.5	3.5	1.9	132.2	128.5	88.9	86.6
1933	141.3	135.5	47.0	45.9	94.3	89.6	3.5	1.9	137.8	133.6	90.8	87.7
1934	155.2	148.7	50.1	48.8	105.1	99.9	3.7	2.0	151.5	146.7	101.4	97.9
1935	178.6	171.3	58.9	57.3	119.7	114.0	3.8	2.0	174.8	169.3	115.9	112.0
1936	192.8	184.6	53.4	51.5	139.4	133.1	3.8	2.1	189.0	182.5	135.6	131.0
1937	212.3	202.9	65.1	63.0	147.2	139.9	3.9	2.1	208.4	200.8	143.3	137.8
1938	216.1	205.5	60.5	58.0	155.6	147.5	4.1	2.2	212.0	203.3	151.6	145.3
1939	229.5	217.9	61.2	58.5	168.4	159.4	4.1	2.2	225.4	215.7	164.2	157.2
1940	250.5	236.9	72.9	69.9	177.6	167.0	4.5	2.4	246.0	234.5	173.2	164.6
1945	199.0	186.9	49.1	47.1	149.9	139.8	4.1	2.1	194.9	184.8	146.1	137.7
1946	198.4	185.9	53.4	51.7	145.0	134.2	3.9	2.1	194.5	183.8	141.1	132.1
1947	220.5	207.2	67.6	65.8	152.9	141.4	3.9	2.2	216.6	205.0	149.0	139.2
1948	250.7	236.5	74.5	72.7	176.2	163.8	4.3	2.3	246.4	234.2	171.8	161.5
1949	277.7	262.4	76.3	74.3	201.4	188.1	4.3	2.4	273.4	260.0	197.1	185.7
1950	304.3	287.5	76.1	73.6	228.2	213.9	4.5	2.5	299.8	285.0	223.8	211.4

TABLE T-47 (continued)

GROSS AND NET NATIONAL PRODUCT, TOTAL AND BY SECTOR, IN 1937 PRICES, 1928-61
(Billion Rubles)

	Total		Agricultural		Nonagricultural		Residential		Nonresidential		Nonagricultural Nonresidential	
	Gross	Net	Gross	Net	Gross	Net	Gross	Net	Gross	Net	Gross	Net
1951 · · · · · ·	327.1	308.1	72.6	69.5	254.5	238.6	4.8	2.6	322.3	305.5	249.5	236.0
1952 · · · · · ·	351.8	330.4	78.3	74.3	273.5	256.1	5.0	2.7	346.8	327.7	268.6	253.4
1953 · · · · · ·	374.6	351.1	81.6	77.0	293.0	274.1	5.2	2.9	369.4	348.2	287.8	271.2
1954 · · · · · ·	404.1	378.5	84.0	78.9	320.1	299.6	5.4	3.0	398.7	375.5	314.6	296.6
1955 · · · · · ·	441.6	413.2	94.0	88.1	347.6	325.1	5.9	3.2	435.7	410.0	341.8	321.9
1956 · · · · · ·	483.4	451.8	108.3	101.6	375.1	350.2	6.1	3.3	477.3	448.5	369.0	346.9
1957 · · · · · ·	514.0	478.3	109.4	101.7	404.6	376.6	6.1	3.4	507.9	474.9	398.4	373.2
1958 · · · · · ·	558.9	518.7	121.1	112.6	437.8	406.1	6.9	3.6	552.0	515.1	430.9	402.5
1959 · · · · · ·	594.3	549.1	123.0	113.7	471.3	435.4	7.1	3.8	587.2	545.3	464.3	431.6
1960 · · · · · ·	627.0	577.0	125.2	115.2	501.8	461.8	6.9	4.0	620.1	573.0	494.8	457.7
1961 · · · · · ·	666.4	610.6	129.2	118.6	537.3	492.0	7.5	4.3	658.9	606.3	529.8	487.7

Source: See Appendix P.

TABLE T-48

GROSS AND NET NATIONAL PRODUCT, TOTAL AND BY SECTOR, IN 1928 PRICES, 1928 and 1937
(Billion Rubles)

	Total		Agricultural		Nonagricultural		Residential		Nonresidential		Nonagricultural Nonresidential	
	Gross	Net	Gross	Net	Gross	Net	Gross	Net	Gross	Net	Gross	Net
1928......	29.6	27.8	11.6	11.2	18.0	16.6	1.3	0.6	28.2	27.1	16.7	16.0
1937......	81.3	73.9	15.1	13.1	66.2	60.8	1.6	0.8	79.7	73.1	64.6	60.0

Source: See Appendix P.

TABLE T-49

GROSS AND NET NATIONAL PRODUCT, TOTAL AND BY SECTOR, IN 1950 PRICES, SELECTED YEARS
(Billion Rubles)

	Total		Agricultural		Nonagricultural		Residential		Nonresidential		Nonagricultural Nonresidential	
	Gross	Net	Gross	Net	Gross	Net	Gross	Net	Gross	Net	Gross	Net
1928......	298.6	289.3	126.2	123.5	172.4	165.8	7.1	3.3	291.5	286.0	165.3	162.5
1937......	478.4	455.1	145.9	139.8	332.5	315.3	8.6	3.9	469.8	451.2	324.1	311.4
1940......	561.7	529.5	159.2	151.4	402.5	378.1	9.8	4.8	551.9	524.7	392.8	373.3
1950......	694.1	657.2	161.6	155.7	532.5	501.5	10.4	5.4	683.7	651.8	522.1	496.1
1955......	1000.3	939.1	208.7	194.5	791.6	744.6	12.9	6.3	987.4	932.8	778.8	738.3

Source: See Appendix P.

TABLE T-50

INVESTMENT SHARE IN NATIONAL PRODUCT IN
1937, 1928, AND 1950 PRICES, 1928-61
(Percent)

	Gross Investment in GNP			Net Investment in NNP		
	1937 Prices	1928 Prices	1950 Prices	1937 Prices	1928 Prices	1950 Prices
1928	8.4	20.3	9.1	5.8	15.1	6.3
1929	2.9	--	--	0.0	--	--
1930	10.4	--	--	7.6	--	--
1931	14.4	--	--	11.3	--	--
1932	9.4	--	--	5.7	--	--
1933	16.0	--	--	12.4	--	--
1934	18.8	--	--	15.2	--	--
1935	26.2	--	--	23.1	--	--
1936	18.5	--	--	14.9	--	--
1937	21.1	40.5	21.8	17.5	34.5	17.8
1938	18.5	--	--	14.3	--	--
1939	15.6	--	--	11.1	--	--
1940	12.3	--	12.8	7.6	--	7.9
1945	13.4	--	--	7.8	--	--
1946	15.1	--	--	9.4	--	--
1947	20.5	--	--	15.4	--	--
1948	18.5	--	--	13.6	--	--
1949	24.3	--	--	19.9	--	--
1950	21.6	--	21.0	16.9	--	16.6
1951	24.4	--	--	19.7	--	--
1952	22.9	--	--	17.9	--	--
1953	21.9	--	--	16.7	--	--
1954	19.6	--	--	14.2	--	--
1955	22.9	--	21.9	17.6	--	16.8
1956	27.8	--	--	22.7	--	--
1957	26.2	--	--	20.7	--	--
1958	30.7	--	--	25.3	--	--
1959	30.6	--	--	24.9	--	--
1960	28.8	--	--	22.6	--	--
1961	30.6	--	--	24.2	--	--

Source: Computed from Tables T-44 to T-49.

TABLE T-51

EMPLOYMENT, TOTAL AND BY SECTOR, 1928-61
(Million Man-Years)

	Unadjusted for Changes in Hours (Prevailing Man-Years)			Adjusted for Changes in Hours (1937 Man-Years)		
	Agricultural	Non-agricultural	Total	Agricultural	Non-agricultural	Total
1928	33.5	18.1	51.6	33.8	19.0	52.8
1929	32.4	18.7	51.1	32.9	19.8	52.7
1930	30.8	20.7	51.5	29.9	20.9	50.8
1931	28.9	23.9	52.8	28.2	24.0	52.2
1932	26.9	26.5	53.4	26.6	26.7	53.3
1933	28.7	25.5	54.2	29.3	26.5	55.8
1934	30.9	26.8	57.7	31.7	27.8	59.5
1935	34.1	28.7	62.8	35.1	29.8	64.9
1936	32.1	30.2	62.3	32.6	30.5	63.1
1937	34.0	32.0	66.0	34.0	32.0	66.0
1938	34.8	34.3	69.1	34.8	34.3	69.1
1939	34.9	36.7	71.6	34.9	36.8	71.7
1940	39.0	40.1	79.1	40.4	43.8	84.2
1945	33.8	40.8	74.6	37.9	50.8	88.7
1946	32.6	39.2	71.8	35.6	47.2	82.8
1947	34.3	38.6	72.9	36.4	45.5	81.9
1948	35.7	40.6	76.3	37.9	47.9	85.8
1949	38.0	42.7	80.7	40.4	50.4	90.8
1950	39.8	46.2	86.0	42.2	54.4	96.6
1951	38.5	48.6	87.1	40.7	57.1	97.8
1952	35.7	50.8	86.5	37.7	59.6	97.3
1953	36.5	51.8	88.3	38.5	60.9	99.4
1954	37.7	53.8	91.5	39.7	62.8	102.5
1955	40.0	54.3	94.3	42.0	63.4	105.4
1956	40.2	55.3	95.5	42.0	64.3	106.3
1957	40.5	56.3	96.8	41.6	64.6	106.2
1958	41.9	58.5	100.4	43.1	65.1	108.2
1959	40.8	60.6	101.4	41.7	64.9	106.6
1960	39.5	63.2	102.7	40.2	64.4	104.6
1961	38.9	66.3	105.2	39.6	64.6	104.2

Sources: Table Q-1, columns 3-6, and Table Q-4. Nonagricultural employment is the sum of civilian nonagricultural employment and numbers in the armed forces.

TABLE T-52

SOWN LAND, 1928-61
(Million Hectares)

1928	113.0
1929	118.0
1930	127.2
1931	136.3
1932	134.4
1933	129.7
1934	131.5
1935	132.8
1936	133.8
1937	135.3
1938	136.9
1939	133.7
1940	150.4
1945	113.8
1946	114.0
1947	119.9
1948	133.7
1949	139.7
1950	146.3
1951	153.0
1952	155.7
1953	157.2
1954	166.1
1955	185.8
1956	194.7
1957	193.7
1958	195.6
1959	196.3
1960	203.0
1961	204.6

Sources: For 1928-32,
TsUNKhU-36a, p. 257; for 1933-
40 and 1945-59, TsSU-60a, p. 127;
for 1960-61, TsSU-62a, p. 311.

TABLE T-53

AVERAGE CAPITAL-OUTPUT RATIO,
TOTAL AND BY SECTOR, IN 1937 PRICES, 1928-61
(Net Capital Stock/Gross National Product)

	Total	Nonagricultural	Residential	Nonresidential	Nonagricultural Nonresidential
1928 ..	1.68	2.05	19.97	1.21	1.15
1929 ..	1.66	1.94	19.66	1.20	1.12
1930 ..	1.61	1.85	18.76	1.16	1.12
1931 ..	1.67	1.93	19.64	1.22	1.25
1932 ..	1.77	2.04	18.77	1.32	1.38
1933 ..	1.78	2.13	18.97	1.35	1.48
1934 ..	1.75	2.05	18.14	1.35	1.46
1935 ..	1.70	1.98	17.79	1.35	1.47
1936 ..	1.74	1.90	17.95	1.42	1.45
1937 ..	1.73	1.97	17.62	1.44	1.55
1938 ..	1.85	2.03	17.00	1.56	1.63
1939 ..	1.86	2.03	17.38	1.58	1.65
1940 ..	1.93	2.19	17.38	1.65	1.79
1945 ..	2.01	2.23	14.88	1.74	1.87
1946 ..	2.10	2.40	15.69	1.82	2.03
1947 ..	2.00	2.41	16.18	1.74	2.05
1948 ..	1.89	2.23	15.47	1.65	1.90
1949 ..	1.85	2.11	16.33	1.63	1.80
1950 ..	1.86	2.05	16.51	1.64	1.76
1951 ..	1.90	2.02	16.44	1.68	1.74
1952 ..	1.93	2.06	16.72	1.72	1.79
1953 ..	1.97	2.10	17.04	1.76	1.83
1954 ..	1.97	2.07	17.44	1.76	1.81
1955 ..	1.94	2.06	16.92	1.74	1.80
1956 ..	1.96	2.11	17.43	1.76	1.85
1957 ..	2.04	2.16	18.85	1.83	1.91
1958 ..	2.08	2.23	18.39	1.87	1.97
1959 ..	2.18	2.32	19.93	1.97	2.05
1960 ..	2.28	2.42	22.81	2.05	2.14
1961 ..	2.35	2.50	23.09	2.12	2.21

Sources: Computed from Tables T-15, T-25, T-28, T-31, T-34, and T-47.
Average annual stocks are computed from January 1 data.

TABLE T-54

INCREMENTAL CAPITAL-OUTPUT RATIO, ANNUAL,
TOTAL AND BY SECTOR, IN 1937 PRICES, 1929-61
(Net Capital Stock/Gross National Product)

	Total	Nonagricultural	Nonresidential	Nonagricultural Nonresidential
1929	1.06	0.99	0.78	0.84
1930	0.65	1.23	0.55	1.18
1931	4.63	2.83	4.11	2.58
1932	-7.47	4.82	-6.06	5.38
1933	2.16	7.18	2.02	6.05
1934	1.42	1.35	1.39	1.31
1935	1.32	1.52	1.31	1.50
1936	2.36	1.36	2.32	1.32
1937	1.62	3.31	1.60	3.29
1938	8.53	3.14	8.72	3.05
1939	1.99	1.98	1.88	1.89
1940	2.70	5.14	2.42	4.48
1946	-26.67	-2.78	-39.50	-26.60
1947	1.12	2.57	1.04	2.33
1948	1.06	1.05	0.96	0.93
1949	1.56	1.32	1.43	1.17
1950	1.89	1.55	1.75	1.40
1951	2.40	1.75	2.23	1.61
1952	2.43	2.71	2.25	2.45
1953	2.57	2.60	2.38	2.38
1954	1.90	1.78	1.72	1.59
1955	1.69	1.92	1.56	1.73
1956	2.10	2.67	1.95	2.46
1957	3.29	2.92	3.01	2.63
1958	2.57	2.99	2.34	2.70
1959	3.79	3.54	3.39	3.11
1960	4.07	4.00	3.58	3.48
1961	3.53	3.59	3.18	3.19

Sources are the same as for Table T-53.

TABLE T-55

CAPITAL-LABOR RATIO, TOTAL AND BY SECTOR,
IN 1937 PRICES, 1928-61
(Thousand Rubles of Net Capital
Stock per 1937 Man-Year)

	Total	Nonagricultural	Nonresidential	Nonagricultural Nonresidential
1928	3.94	6.98	2.77	3.72
1929	4.01	7.05	2.82	3.87
1930	4.26	7.29	3.00	4.24
1931	4.38	7.18	3.14	4.47
1932	4.50	7.06	3.27	4.60
1933	4.52	7.58	3.33	5.07
1934	4.57	7.75	3.44	5.33
1935	4.67	7.97	3.62	5.70
1936	5.33	8.67	4.25	6.43
1937	5.57	9.07	4.53	6.92
1938	5.79	9.23	4.78	7.19
1939	5.95	9.29	4.96	7.35
1940	5.74	8.88	4.82	7.10
1945	4.51	6.58	3.82	5.38
1946	5.02	7.37	4.28	6.07
1947	5.38	8.09	4.61	6.70
1948	5.51	8.19	4.73	6.81
1949	5.67	8.45	4.90	7.05
1950	5.85	8.59	5.08	7.22
1951	6.34	8.99	5.53	7.61
1952	6.99	9.47	6.13	8.07
1953	7.43	10.11	6.54	8.65
1954	7.75	10.57	6.83	9.07
1955	8.14	11.30	7.19	9.72
1956	8.90	12.28	7.90	10.63
1957	9.85	13.56	8.77	11.77
1958	10.74	14.98	9.56	13.03
1959	12.15	16.85	10.83	14.67
1960	13.66	18.88	12.16	16.43
1961	15.05	20.79	13.39	18.11

Sources: Computed from Tables T-25, T-28, T-31, T-34, and T-51. Average annual stocks are computed from January 1 data.

TABLE T-56

LABOR PRODUCTIVITY, TOTAL AND BY
SECTOR, IN 1937 PRICES, 1928-61
(Thousand Rubles of Gross National Product
per 1937 Man-Year)

	Total	Agricultural	Nonagricultural	Nonresidential	Nonagricultural Nonresidential
1928	2.34	1.75	3.41	2.28	3.24
1929	2.41	1.68	3.63	2.35	3.46
1930	2.65	1.75	3.93	2.58	3.77
1931	2.63	1.70	3.72	2.57	3.58
1932	2.55	1.62	3.47	2.48	3.33
1933	2.53	1.60	3.56	2.47	3.43
1934	2.61	1.58	3.78	2.55	3.65
1935	2.75	1.68	4.02	2.69	3.89
1936	3.06	1.64	4.57	3.00	4.45
1937	3.22	1.91	4.60	3.16	4.48
1938	3.13	1.74	4.54	3.07	4.42
1939	3.20	1.75	4.58	3.14	4.46
1940	2.98	1.80	4.05	2.92	3.95
1945	2.24	1.30	2.95	2.20	2.88
1946	2.40	1.50	3.07	2.35	2.99
1947	2.69	1.86	3.36	2.64	3.27
1948	2.92	1.97	3.68	2.87	3.59
1949	3.06	1.89	4.00	3.01	3.91
1950	3.15	1.80	4.19	3.10	4.11
1951	3.34	1.78	4.46	3.30	4.37
1952	3.62	2.08	4.59	3.56	4.51
1953	3.77	2.12	4.81	3.72	4.73
1954	3.94	2.12	5.10	3.89	5.01
1955	4.19	2.24	5.48	4.13	5.39
1956	4.55	2.58	5.83	4.49	5.74
1957	4.84	2.63	6.26	4.78	6.17
1958	5.17	2.81	6.73	5.10	6.62
1959	5.58	2.95	7.26	5.51	7.15
1960	6.00	3.11	7.79	5.93	7.69
1961	6.40	3.26	8.32	6.32	8.20

Sources: Computed from Tables T-47 and T-51.

TABLE T-57

SHARES OF INPUTS IN TOTAL COSTS, 1937, 1928, AND 1950

	Total (Billion Rubles)	Components (Percent of Total)			
		Agricultural Labor	Nonagricultural Labor	Capital	Land
1937					
r = 8%					
All sectors	247.5	22.6	50.1	18.3	9.0
Nonagricultural	159.5	--	77.7	22.3	--
Nonresidential	239.0	23.4	51.9	15.3	9.4
Nonagricultural Nonresidential	151.0	--	82.1	17.9	--
r = 20%					
All sectors	332.2	16.9	37.3	39.1	6.7
Nonagricultural	226.1	--	54.8	45.2	--
Nonresidential	307.8	18.2	40.2	34.3	7.3
Nonagricultural Nonresidential	201.8	--	61.4	38.6	--
1928					
r = 8%					
All sectors	39.0	27.7	33.3	28.0	11.0
Nonagricultural	21.3	--	61.0	39.0	--
Nonresidential	35.6	27.7	33.3	21.1	12.1
Nonagricultural Nonresidential	17.9	--	72.6	27.4	--
r = 20%					
All sectors	71.7	15.1	18.1	60.8	6.0
Nonagricultural	45.9	--	28.3	71.7	--
Nonresidential	58.6	18.4	22.2	52.1	7.3
Nonagricultural Nonresidential	33.1	--	39.3	60.7	--
1950					
r = 8%					
All sectors	772.5	17.9	54.7	20.2	7.2
Nonagricultural	553.2	--	76.4	23.6	--
Nonresidential	750.3	18.5	56.2	17.9	7.4
Nonagricultural Nonresidential	531.0	--	79.6	20.4	--
r = 20%					
All sectors	1072.5	12.9	39.4	42.5	5.2
Nonagricultural	804.1	--	52.5	47.5	--
Nonresidential	1007.5	13.8	41.9	38.8	5.5
Nonagricultural Nonresidential	738.9	--	57.2	42.8	--

Source: See Chapter 9, Section 3.

TABLE T-58

AGGREGATE INPUTS, TOTAL AND BY SECTOR, AT 8 PERCENT
INTEREST RATE, IN 1937 PRICES, 1928-61
(1937 = 100)

	Total	Nonagricultural	Residential	Nonresidential	Nonagricultural Nonresidential
1928	68.5	55.3	89.0	67.5	52.3
1929	69.8	57.8	89.0	68.7	54.8
1930	70.5	61.6	91.8	69.4	58.9
1931	75.6	70.5	91.8	74.7	68.7
1932	79.4	78.3	95.9	78.6	76.7
1933	81.5	79.3	94.5	80.8	78.1
1934	86.4	83.7	97.3	85.9	82.8
1935	93.5	90.3	98.6	93.2	89.7
1936	94.9	94.7	98.6	94.8	94.6
1937	100.0	100.0	100.0	100.0	100.0
1938	106.0	107.7	102.7	106.1	108.1
1939	111.2	116.0	104.1	111.5	116.5
1940	130.0	136.9	113.7	130.5	138.2
1945	131.4	149.3	91.8	132.8	153.3
1946	125.7	142.6	91.8	126.9	145.7
1947	125.6	140.4	91.8	126.7	143.1
1948	133.1	148.3	100.0	134.2	151.0
1949	141.1	157.0	104.1	142.3	159.9
1950	151.4	169.9	108.2	152.7	173.2
1951	158.1	180.3	116.4	159.2	183.3
1952	163.2	190.3	123.3	164.1	193.6
1953	168.5	197.2	128.8	169.2	200.3
1954	175.6	205.5	137.0	176.2	208.2
1955	182.7	210.8	145.2	183.1	213.2
1956	188.4	217.8	154.8	188.5	219.7
1957	192.2	224.0	164.4	191.9	225.1
1958	198.3	231.0	183.6	197.4	231.1
1959	201.1	236.6	200.0	199.5	235.7
1960	203.2	240.7	212.3	201.1	238.9
1961	207.0	247.2	234.3	204.2	244.2

Source: See Chapter 9, Section 3.

TABLE T-59

AGGREGATE INPUTS, TOTAL AND BY SECTOR, AT 20 PERCENT INTEREST
RATE, IN 1937 PRICES, 1928-61
(1937 = 100)

	Total	Nonagricultural	Residential	Nonresidential	Nonagricultural Nonresidential
1928	65.0	52.1	89.7	62.5	45.9
1929	66.2	54.6	91.0	63.6	48.6
1930	67.1	58.7	92.9	64.5	53.2
1931	71.8	66.8	93.5	69.5	62.8
1932	75.4	74.0	95.5	73.4	70.5
1933	77.8	76.1	96.1	76.1	73.2
1934	83.0	80.8	97.4	81.5	78.5
1935	90.5	87.7	98.7	89.7	86.1
1936	93.9	93.7	98.7	93.5	92.9
1937	100.0	100.0	100.0	100.0	100.0
1938	106.7	108.1	101.9	107.1	108.9
1939	112.5	116.6	103.9	113.3	118.0
1940	130.5	136.2	113.5	131.8	138.9
1945	125.5	138.7	90.3	128.4	145.4
1946	122.6	135.9	90.3	125.2	141.8
1947	124.3	136.7	92.3	126.9	142.2
1948	132.1	144.9	98.7	134.8	150.4
1949	141.1	154.4	103.2	144.0	160.6
1950	152.2	167.7	109.0	155.5	174.8
1951	161.0	179.8	116.1	164.2	187.0
1952	168.9	192.1	122.6	171.9	199.9
1953	176.6	202.1	129.0	179.5	209.7
1954	185.6	212.7	137.4	188.4	220.3
1955	195.1	221.6	145.8	197.7	228.7
1956	204.5	233.4	155.5	206.8	240.1
1957	213.2	245.5	166.5	214.8	251.3
1958	224.1	259.0	184.5	224.8	263.5
1959	232.8	272.5	203.9	232.3	275.4
1960	240.7	284.6	221.9	239.1	285.8
1961	249.9	298.8	243.9	247.1	298.1

Source: See Chapter 9, Section 3.

TABLE T-60

AGGREGATE INPUTS, TOTAL AND BY SECTOR, AT 8 PERCENT INTEREST
RATE, IN 1928 PRICES, 1928-61
(1937 = 100)

	Total	Nonagricultural	Residential	Nonresidential	Nonagricultural Nonresidential
1928	59.7	46.8	89.3	59.8	45.2
1929	61.4	49.4	89.3	62.0	48.9
1930	63.3	53.3	89.3	64.0	53.2
1931	68.7	61.9	89.3	69.6	62.3
1932	73.3	69.9	92.9	74.4	71.0
1933	76.6	73.4	92.9	77.5	73.9
1934	82.4	78.9	96.4	83.1	79.6
1935	90.0	86.5	96.4	91.0	87.1
1936	93.3	92.1	96.4	93.7	92.8
1937	100.0	100.0	100.0	100.0	100.0
1938	107.2	109.7	100.0	107.1	109.5
1939	113.7	119.8	103.6	113.3	119.3
1940	133.3	141.9	110.7	132.9	141.9
1945	131.7	152.0	89.3	132.9	156.3
1946	128.4	149.5	89.3	128.6	151.6
1947	130.1	150.7	89.3	129.9	151.1
1948	138.5	159.8	100.0	138.0	159.8
1949	147.4	169.8	103.6	146.7	169.3
1950	159.0	184.0	107.1	157.9	183.6
1951	167.8	196.7	114.3	165.8	195.4
1952	174.8	209.8	121.4	171.5	207.1
1953	181.8	219.7	125.0	177.8	215.6
1954	191.0	231.0	135.7	186.1	225.3
1955	201.2	240.3	142.9	195.3	232.5
1956	210.0	252.6	153.6	202.6	241.9
1957	217.2	265.4	160.7	208.0	251.2
1958	226.5	279.3	182.1	215.4	261.0
1959	232.6	292.2	196.4	219.3	269.1
1960	238.4	304.3	207.1	223.3	276.7
1961	245.6	318.9	232.1	228.3	286.2

Source: See Chapter 9, Section 3.

TABLE T-61

AGGREGATE INPUTS, TOTAL AND BY SECTOR, AT 20 PERCENT INTEREST
RATE, IN 1928 PRICES, 1928-61
(1937 = 100)

	Total	Nonagricultural	Residential	Nonresidential	Nonagricultural Nonresidential
1928	48.0	39.1	89.6	45.4	34.0
1929	50.0	41.7	91.4	47.9	37.3
1930	52.8	46.1	93.1	51.0	42.3
1931	58.3	53.9	94.8	57.1	51.0
1932	63.9	61.4	96.5	62.9	59.4
1933	68.5	66.7	96.5	67.8	65.1
1934	75.0	73.1	98.3	74.5	71.8
1935	83.6	81.5	100.0	83.8	81.0
1936	90.8	90.0	100.0	90.8	89.9
1937	100.0	100.0	100.0	100.0	100.0
1938	109.5	111.3	103.4	109.7	111.9
1939	118.2	122.5	105.2	118.5	123.6
1940	138.0	143.9	113.8	138.7	146.4
1945	128.9	142.2	91.4	131.9	149.8
1946	130.7	146.1	91.4	133.0	152.2
1947	136.2	152.7	93.1	138.1	157.8
1948	145.9	163.1	100.0	147.5	168.1
1949	156.9	174.5	103.4	158.5	179.6
1950	171.4	190.1	110.3	172.9	196.0
1951	185.4	206.6	117.2	186.1	212.2
1952	198.5	224.2	124.1	197.9	229.1
1953	211.4	239.9	129.3	209.8	244.0
1954	225.8	256.5	137.9	223.2	259.6
1955	242.2	273.6	146.5	238.5	275.0
1956	260.5	296.2	156.9	254.7	295.1
1957	279.5	322.5	167.2	270.9	318.0
1958	301.0	351.3	186.2	289.4	342.6
1959	321.5	382.0	205.2	305.8	367.6
1960	342.0	413.8	224.1	322.5	393.5
1961	363.9	448.5	246.5	340.0	421.6

Source: See Chapter 9, Section 3.

TABLE T-62

AGGREGATE INPUTS, TOTAL AND BY SECTOR, AT 8 PERCENT INTEREST
RATE, IN 1950 PRICES, 1928-61
(1937 = 100)

	Total	Nonagricultural	Residential	Nonresidential	Nonagricultural Nonresidential
1928	67.6	55.3	89.0	65.8	51.4
1929	68.9	57.9	89.0	67.3	54.4
1930	69.7	61.8	91.8	68.1	58.5
1931	74.9	70.6	91.8	73.7	68.4
1932	79.1	78.6	96.2	77.8	76.6
1933	81.1	79.6	94.5	80.1	78.0
1934	86.0	84.0	97.3	85.4	82.6
1935	93.2	90.5	98.9	92.9	89.6
1936	94.8	94.3	98.9	94.5	94.0
1937	100.0	100.0	100.0	100.0	100.0
1938	106.0	107.8	102.7	106.2	108.2
1939	111.3	115.7	104.4	111.7	116.4
1940	129.9	136.4	113.7	130.7	137.9
1945	130.9	147.6	91.8	132.5	151.0
1946	125.1	140.7	91.8	126.6	143.9
1947	124.9	138.6	91.8	126.3	141.5
1948	132.0	146.2	100.0	133.4	149.1
1949	139.9	154.4	104.4	141.5	157.7
1950	150.2	166.9	108.2	152.0	170.7
1951	156.9	177.0	116.5	158.7	180.9
1952	162.0	186.8	123.6	163.8	191.0
1953	167.7	193.7	129.1	169.5	197.8
1954	174.8	201.8	137.4	176.4	206.0
1955	181.7	207.0	145.6	183.3	210.8
1956	187.2	213.9	154.9	188.8	217.6
1957	191.5	219.9	164.8	192.7	223.4
1958	197.6	226.9	184.1	198.5	229.5
1959	200.6	232.2	200.5	201.1	234.5
1960	202.9	236.6	212.6	203.0	238.2
1961	206.9	243.1	234.6	206.5	244.0

Source: See Chapter 9, Section 3.

TABLE T-63

AGGREGATE INPUTS, TOTAL AND BY SECTOR, AT 20 PERCENT INTEREST
RATE, IN 1950 PRICES, 1928-61
(1937 = 100)

	Total	Nonagricultural	Residential	Nonresidential	Nonagricultural Nonresidential
1928	63.1	51.8	89.7	59.5	44.6
1929	64.4	54.4	91.0	61.1	47.6
1930	65.8	58.6	93.0	62.3	52.4
1931	70.8	67.0	93.5	68.1	62.2
1932	75.0	74.3	95.6	72.4	70.3
1933	77.5	76.5	96.1	75.3	73.1
1934	82.7	81.1	97.4	80.9	78.2
1935	90.2	87.9	98.7	89.2	86.0
1936	93.9	93.5	98.7	93.4	92.6
1937	100.0	100.0	100.0	100.0	100.0
1938	106.5	107.9	102.1	107.2	109.0
1939	112.4	116.0	103.9	113.3	117.6
1940	129.9	135.1	113.7	131.6	138.2
1945	123.5	135.3	90.4	126.6	141.4
1946	120.5	132.4	90.4	123.4	138.0
1947	122.3	133.2	92.2	125.2	138.7
1948	129.5	140.8	98.7	132.5	146.3
1949	137.9	149.4	103.4	141.2	155.4
1950	148.8	161.8	109.0	152.7	168.9
1951	157.6	173.3	116.3	161.5	180.9
1952	165.6	185.1	122.7	169.8	193.4
1953	173.7	194.8	129.2	178.0	203.5
1954	182.7	205.2	137.5	187.0	214.2
1955	192.0	213.6	146.0	196.3	222.5
1956	201.3	224.8	155.6	205.6	233.8
1957	210.3	236.4	166.7	214.2	245.3
1958	221.3	249.3	184.8	224.9	257.8
1959	230.4	262.3	204.1	233.1	269.8
1960	238.5	274.4	222.2	240.6	281.1
1961	248.4	288.3	244.2	249.6	294.1

Source: See Chapter 9, Section 3.

TABLE T-64

PRODUCTIVITY OF AGGREGATE INPUTS, TOTAL AND BY SECTOR,
AT 8 PERCENT INTEREST RATE, IN 1937 PRICES, 1928-61
(1937 = 100)

	Total	Nonagricultural	Nonresidential	Nonagricultural Nonresidential
1928	85.1	79.6	85.8	82.2
1929	85.7	84.4	86.5	87.4
1930	89.9	90.6	90.6	93.2
1931	85.4	86.0	86.1	87.3
1932	80.5	80.3	80.7	80.8
1933	81.7	80.8	81.8	81.2
1934	84.6	85.3	84.6	85.5
1935	89.9	90.0	90.0	90.2
1936	95.7	100.0	95.7	100.0
1937	100.0	100.0	100.0	100.0
1938	96.0	98.1	95.9	97.9
1939	97.2	98.6	97.0	98.4
1940	90.8	88.2	90.4	87.5
1945	71.3	68.2	70.4	66.5
1946	74.4	69.1	73.5	67.6
1947	82.7	74.0	82.0	72.7
1948	88.7	80.7	88.1	79.4
1949	92.7	87.1	92.2	86.0
1950	94.6	91.2	94.2	90.2
1951	97.5	95.9	97.2	95.0
1952	101.5	97.6	101.4	96.8
1953	104.7	100.9	104.8	100.2
1954	108.4	105.8	108.6	105.4
1955	113.8	112.0	114.2	111.9
1956	120.9	117.0	121.5	117.2
1957	126.0	122.7	127.0	123.5
1958	132.8	128.7	134.2	130.1
1959	139.2	135.3	141.3	137.5
1960	145.3	141.6	148.0	144.5
1961	151.6	147.7	154.8	151.4

Source: See Chapter 9, Section 4.

TABLE T-65

PRODUCTIVITY OF AGGREGATE INPUTS, TOTAL AND BY SECTOR,
AT 20 PERCENT INTEREST RATE, IN 1937 PRICES, 1928-61
(1937 = 100)

	Total	Nonagricultural	Nonresidential	Nonagricultural Nonresidential
1928	89.7	84.5	92.6	93.7
1929	90.3	89.4	93.4	98.6
1930	94.5	95.1	97.5	103.2
1931	90.0	90.7	92.5	95.5
1932	84.7	85.0	86.4	87.9
1933	85.6	84.2	86.9	86.6
1934	88.1	88.4	89.2	90.2
1935	92.9	92.7	93.5	94.0
1936	96.7	101.1	97.0	101.8
1937	100.0	100.0	100.0	100.0
1938	95.4	97.8	95.0	97.2
1939	96.1	98.1	95.5	97.1
1940	90.4	88.6	89.5	87.0
1945	74.7	73.4	72.8	70.2
1946	76.3	72.5	74.5	69.5
1947	83.6	76.0	81.9	73.1
1948	89.4	82.6	87.7	79.7
1949	92.7	88.6	91.1	85.6
1950	94.2	92.4	92.5	89.4
1951	95.7	96.2	94.2	93.1
1952	98.1	96.7	96.8	93.7
1953	99.9	98.5	98.8	95.8
1954	102.5	102.3	101.5	99.6
1955	106.6	106.5	105.8	104.3
1956	111.3	109.2	110.7	107.2
1957	113.6	112.0	113.5	110.6
1958	117.5	114.8	117.8	114.1
1959	120.2	117.5	121.3	117.6
1960	122.7	119.8	124.5	120.8
1961	125.6	122.2	128.0	124.0

Source: See Chapter 9, Section 4.

TABLE T-66

PRODUCTIVITY OF AGGREGATE INPUTS, TOTAL AND BY SECTOR,
IN 1928 PRICES, 1928 AND 1937
(1937 = 100)

	Total	Nonagricultural	Nonresidential	Nonagricultural Nonresidential
At 8 Percent Interest Rate				
1928	61.0	58.1	59.2	57.3
1937	100.0	·100.0	100.0	100.0
At 20 Percent Interest Rate				
1928	75.8	69.6	78.0	76.2
1937	100.0	100.0	100.0	100.0

Source: See Chapter 9, Section 4.

TABLE T-67

PRODUCTIVITY OF AGGREGATE INPUTS, TOTAL AND BY SECTOR,
IN 1950 PRICES, SELECTED YEARS
(1937 = 100)

	Total	Nonagricultural	Nonresidential	Nonagricultural Nonresidential
At 8 Percent Interest Rate				
1928	92.3	93.7	94.2	99.2
1937	100.0	100.0	100.0	100.0
1940	90.4	88.8	89.9	87.9
1950	96.6	95.9	95.7	94.4
1955	115.1	115.0	114.7	114.0
At 20 Percent Interest Rate				
1928	98.9	100.0	104.2	114.3
1937	100.0	100.0	100.0	100.0
1940	90.4	89.6	89.3	87.7
1950	97.5	98.9	95.3	95.4
1955	108.9	111.5	107.1	108.0

Source: See Chapter 9, Section 4.

TABLE T-68

PRODUCTIVITY OF AGGREGATE INPUTS, TOTAL AND BY SECTOR,
IN MIXED PRICES, 1928, 1937, AND 1950
(1937 = 100)

	Total	Nonagricultural	Nonresidential	Nonagricultural Nonresidential
Output in 1928 Prices; Inputs in 1937 Prices				
At 8 Percent Interest Rate				
1928	53.1	49.2	52.4	49.5
1937	100.0	100.0	100.0	100.0
At 20 Percent Interest Rate				
1928	56.0	52.2	56.6	56.4
1937	100.0	100.0	100.0	100.0
Output in 1937 Prices; Inputs in 1928 Prices				
At 8 Percent Interest Rate				
1928	97.7	94.0	96.8	95.1
1937	100.0	100.0	100.0	100.0
At 20 Percent Interest Rate				
1928	121.5	112.5	127.5	126.5
1937	100.0	100.0	100.0	100.0
Output in 1950 Prices; Inputs in 1937 Prices				
At 8 Percent Interest Rate				
1937	100.0	100.0	100.0	100.0
1950	95.8	94.2	95.3	93.0
At 20 Percent Interest Rate				
1937	100.0	100.0	100.0	100.0
1950	95.3	95.5	93.6	92.2
Output in 1937 Prices; Inputs in 1950 Prices				
At 8 Percent Interest Rate				
1937	100.0	100.0	100.0	100.0
1950	95.4	92.9	94.7	91.5
At 20 Percent Interest Rate				
1937	100.0	100.0	100.0	100.C
1950	96.3	95.8	94.2	92.5

Source: See Chapter 9, Section 4.

TABLE T-69

PROJECTED FUTURE VALUE OF TOTAL FIXED CAPITAL IN EXISTENCE
ON JANUARY 1, 1962, IN 1937 PRICES, 1963-75
(January 1--Billion Rubles)

	Gross Values				Net Values			
	Structures	Equip-ment	Instal-lation	Total	Structures	Equip-ment	Instal-lation	Total
1963 ..	971.4	605.8	70.3	1647.5	727.8	405.7	53.4	1186.9
1964 ..	967.2	584.5	70.3	1622.0	708.6	366.8	51.6	1127.0
1965 ..	963.0	559.6	70.3	1592.8	689.6	330.3	49.9	1069.7
1966 ..	958.8	531.9	70.3	1560.9	670.7	296.8	48.1	1015.6
1967 ..	955.3	499.8	70.3	1525.3	652.0	266.7	46.3	965.0
1968 ..	951.8	464.7	70.3	1486.8	633.2	240.3	44.6	918.1
1969 ..	950.5	426.6	70.0	1447.1	614.5	218.0	42.8	875.3
1970 ..	950.5	417.1	69.6	1437.3	595.8	200.1	41.1	837.0
1971 ..	950.3	374.6	69.1	1394.1	577.1	187.0	39.3	803.4
1972 ..	950.2	365.9	68.5	1384.5	558.4	174.8	37.6	770.8
1973 ..	950.0	358.2	67.8	1376.1	539.6	163.6	35.9	739.2
1974 ..	948.1	352.3	67.2	1367.6	520.9	153.2	34.2	708.3
1975 ..	946.2	345.6	66.6	1358.5	502.2	143.2	32.5	677.9

Source: See Chapter 10, p. 312.

TABLE T-70

PROJECTED FUTURE VALUE OF TOTAL FIXED CAPITAL IN EXISTENCE
ON JANUARY 1, 1962, IN 1950 PRICES, 1963-75
(January 1--Billion Rubles)

	Gross Values				Net Values			
	Structures	Equip-ment	Instal-lation	Total	Structures	Equip-ment	Instal-lation	Total
1963 ..	2448.6	1132.7	171.7	3753.1	1823.8	755.4	129.2	2708.4
1964 ..	2437.7	1092.2	171.7	3701.6	1775.5	682.8	124.9	2583.2
1965 ..	2426.7	1045.5	171.7	3643.9	1727.5	614.9	120.6	2463.0
1966 ..	2415.7	993.4	171.7	3580.9	1680.0	552.6	116.3	2348.9
1967 ..	2406.6	933.7	171.7	3512.0	1632.9	496.4	112.0	2241.3
1968 ..	2397.5	868.4	171.7	3437.6	1585.7	447.3	107.7	2140.7
1969 ..	2394.1	797.5	170.9	3362.5	1538.6	405.8	103.4	2047.8
1970 ..	2394.1	779.9	169.7	3343.7	1491.5	372.5	99.1	1963.1
1971 ..	2393.7	701.0	168.1	3262.8	1444.3	348.2	94.9	1887.4
1972 ..	2393.3	684.9	166.3	3244.4	1397.2	325.5	90.7	1813.4
1973 ..	2392.9	670.8	164.5	3228.2	1350.1	304.6	86.5	1741.2
1974 ..	2387.9	659.2	162.9	3210.0	1303.0	285.0	82.4	1670.4
1975 ..	2383.0	646.4	161.1	3190.5	1255.9	266.4	78.3	1600.6

Source: See Chapter 10, p. 312.

Appendixes

Appendix A

Annual Investment in

Fixed Capital

This appendix consists of three parts: (*i*) tables containing the basic statistical series employed in our calculations, together with statements of their immediate sources; (*ii*) discussion of the principal extensions and modifications made here of investment series obtained by us in previous studies, together with more detailed explanations of sources where these are called for; and (*iii*) a description of an input-price deflated construction series which is employed in an alternative calculation in the text.

THE ANNUAL INVESTMENT SERIES

Tables A–1 through A–5 contain our basic estimates of annual investment in fixed capital: in 1937 prices inclusive and exclusive of capital repairs; in 1928, 1950, and current prices, exclusive of capital repairs. Sources for the several tables are as follows.

Sources to Table A–1

Column 1: Investment in each year is computed by multiplying the figure for construction in 1937 in 1937 prices, including capital repairs, as shown in Table A–7, column 8, by the 1937 price weighted index of materials inputs to construction, Table A–6, column 1.

Column 2: For 1928–30, 1934–40, 1944–46, and 1949–56, see Moorsteen–62, Table G–21. For 1931–33, see Table A–9, rows 13 and 15. For the first half of 1941, half of the 1940 figure is used. For the second half of 1941, half of the 1942 figure is used. For 1942–43, see Table A–10, rows 5 and 8. For 1947–48, the figures are interpolations between 1946 and 1949. The 1957–61 figures are extrapolated from the 1956 figure by means of the index of equipment investment, excluding capital repairs, in July 1, 1955, prices, shown in Table A–11, column 8.

Column 3: The 1937 figure is that for socialized installation given in Table A–7, column 5; installation in private investment is unlikely to have been significant. For all other years, the figures are estimated as follows: (*i*) The construction and equipment series, columns 1 and 2 of this table, are expressed individually as indexes, 1937 = 100. (*ii*) These two

TABLE A-1

GROSS INVESTMENT IN FIXED CAPITAL, INCLUDING CAPITAL REPAIRS,
IN 1937 PRICES, 1928-61
(Billion Rubles)

	Construc-tion	Equip-ment	Instal-lation	Total	Capital Repairs Only
	(1)	(2)	(3)	(4)	(5)
1928	8.37	2.53	0.40	11.30	1.74
1929	10.26	3.26	0.50	14.02	1.83
1930	13.43	5.29	0.71	19.43	1.75
1931	14.52	6.25	0.80	21.57	1.66
1932	14.50	7.08	0.84	22.42	1.65
1933	13.04	6.63	0.78	20.45	1.99
1934	15.75	6.90	0.87	23.52	2.48
1935	19.45	8.80	1.10	29.35	3.09
1936	26.22	12.20	1.49	39.91	3.83
1937	22.80	12.40	1.40	36.60	4.09
1938	22.53	14.10	1.49	38.12	5.15
1939	23.03	13.40	1.46	37.89	4.94
1940	23.03	13.30	1.45	37.78	5.59
1941, 1st Half	11.51	6.65	0.75	18.91	2.78
1941, 2nd Half	3.49	2.23	0.28	6.00	0.56
1942	7.00	4.46	0.47	11.93	1.09
1943	7.30	4.88	0.51	12.69	2.11
1944	9.51	9.80	0.85	20.16	2.24
1945	9.78	14.00	1.09	24.87	3.58
1946	14.64	16.10	1.36	32.10	5.38
1947	18.10	17.90	1.56	37.56	6.60
1948	24.17	19.70	1.85	45.72	7.83
1949	30.78	21.40	2.15	54.33	8.57
1950	35.34	28.90	2.71	66.95	11.70
1951	40.13	30.80	2.97	73.90	13.06
1952	44.69	31.40	3.14	79.23	14.67
1953	49.48	35.00	3.49	87.97	16.71
1954	54.49	41.10	4.00	99.59	17.83
1955	60.19	49.30	4.63	114.12	20.09
1956	63.16	61.00	5.38	129.54	21.04
1957	68.63	67.10	5.90	141.63	22.97
1958	76.84	77.41	6.73	160.98	26.09
1959	85.96	83.69	7.36	177.01	28.73
1960	92.34	89.30	7.88	189.52	30.77
1961	97.36	95.77	8.40	201.53	32.69

indexes are combined in a simple arithmetic average. (*iii*) The resulting 1937-based index is taken as an index of the real volume of installation investment and applied to the 1937 figure, to obtain installation in billions of 1937 rubles in other years.

Column 4: The sum of columns 1, 2, and 3.

Column 5: Column 4 of this table minus column 4 of Table A–2.

Sources to Table A–2

Columns 1 and 3: The figures for each year are computed from the corresponding figures, inclusive of capital repairs, in Table A–1 (rows 1 and 3), on the assumption that capital repairs in 1937 prices in each series were the same share of the total as for investment in construction and installation taken together, in current prices, as shown in Table A–8.

Column 2: For 1928–30, 1934–40, 1944–46 and 1949–56, see Moorsteen–62, Table G–20. For 1931–33, see Table A–9, row 13. For the first half of 1941, half of the 1940 figure is used. For the second half of 1941,

TABLE A-2

GROSS INVESTMENT IN FIXED CAPITAL, EXCLUDING CAPITAL REPAIRS,
IN 1937 PRICES, 1928-61
(Billion Rubles)

	Construction (1)	Equipment (2)	Installation (3)	Total (4)
1928	7.20	2.02	0.34	9.56
1929	9.02	2.73	0.44	12.19
1930	12.30	4.73	0.65	17.68
1931	13.56	5.60	0.75	19.91
1932	13.62	6.36	0.79	20.77
1933	11.90	5.85	0.71	18.46
1934	14.35	5.90	0.79	21.04
1935	17.66	7.60	1.00	26.26
1936	23.92	10.80	1.36	36.08
1937	20.27	11.00	1.24	32.51
1938	19.48	12.20	1.29	32.97
1939	20.17	11.50	1.28	32.95
1940	19.84	11.10	1.25	32.19
1941, 1st Half	9.93	5.55	0.65	16.13
1941, 2nd Half	3.32	1.85	0.27	5.44
1942	6.69	3.70	0.45	10.84
1943	6.75	3.36	0.47	10.58
1944	8.55	8.60	0.77	17.92
1945	8.27	12.10	0.92	21.29
1946	12.10	13.50	1.12	26.72
1947	14.51	15.20	1.25	30.96
1948	19.50	16.90	1.49	37.89
1949	25.48	18.50	1.78	45.76
1950	28.84	24.20	2.21	55.25
1951	32.90	25.50	2.44	60.84
1952	36.87	25.10	2.59	64.56
1953	40.22	28.20	2.84	71.26
1954	44.68	33.80	3.28	81.76
1955	48.87	41.40	3.76	94.03
1956	51.97	52.10	4.43	108.50
1957	56.49	57.31	4.86	118.66
1958	63.24	66.11	5.54	134.89
1959	70.74	71.48	6.06	148.28
1960	75.99	76.27	6.49	158.75
1961	80.13	81.80	6.91	168.84

half of the 1942 figure is used. For 1942–43, see Table A–10, row 5. For 1947–48, the figures are interpolations between 1946 and 1949. The 1957–61 figures are extrapolated from the 1956 figure by means of the index of equipment investment in July 1, 1955, prices shown in Table A–11, column 8.

Column 4: The sum of columns 1, 2, and 3.

Sources to Table A–3

Column 1: Investment in each year is computed thusly: (*i*) A series for construction in 1928 prices, inclusive of capital repairs, is computed by applying the 1928 price weighted index of materials inputs, Table A–6, column 2, to the figure for 1928 construction, including capital repairs, in Table A–7, column 8. (*ii*) An analogous series, excluding capital repairs, is computed from the foregoing, on the assumption that capital repairs in 1928 prices were the same share of the construction total as for investment in construction and installation taken together, in current prices, as shown in Table A–8.

Column 2: Investment in each year is computed from the correspond-

TABLE A-3

GROSS INVESTMENT IN FIXED CAPITAL, EXCLUDING CAPITAL REPAIRS,
IN 1928 PRICES, 1928-61
(Billion Rubles)

	Construction (1)	Equipment (2)	Installation (3)	Total (4)
1928	3.52	1.41	0.22	5.15
1929	4.50	2.02	0.30	6.82
1930	6.21	3.78	0.50	10.49
1931	6.87	5.10	0.62	12.59
1932	6.91	7.00	0.77	14.68
1933	5.79	7.25	0.76	13.80
1934	7.03	7.73	0.84	15.60
1935	8.74	9.96	1.07	19.77
1936	12.02	14.90	1.56	28.48
1937	10.19	15.51	1.55	27.25
1938	9.73	18.30	1.76	29.79
1939	10.04	17.25	1.69	28.98
1940	9.74	15.43	1.53	26.70
1941, 1st Half	4.87	7.38	0.74	12.99
1941, 2nd Half	1.65	2.81	0.28	4.74
1942	3.32	5.62	0.55	9.49
1943	3.37	5.11	0.51	8.99
1944	4.32	13.07	1.17	18.56
1945	4.21	18.39	1.59	24.19
1946	6.14	19.17	1.72	27.03
1947	7.38	20.98	1.90	30.26
1948	9.99	23.66	2.19	35.84
1949	12.91	26.27	2.49	41.67
1950	14.59	34.12	3.17	51.88
1951	16.73	33.66	3.20	53.59
1952	18.82	33.63	3.26	55.71
1953	20.51	38.07	3.67	62.25
1954	22.85	46.31	4.40	73.56
1955	25.14	56.72	5.30	87.16
1956	26.80	70.34	6.43	103.57
1957	29.16	75.08	6.88	111.12
1958	32.74	85.28	7.80	125.82
1959	36.52	92.21	8.47	137.20
1960	39.54	98.39	9.06	146.99
1961	41.77	105.52	9.54	156.83

ing figure in 1937 prices (Table A–2, column 2), by applying the price index number for 1928 (1937 = 100) using weights of the year in question, as shown in Table A–12, column 2. This procedure yields investment in 1928 valued in domestic prices of that year, whereas the 1928 figure shown in Table A–5 is at actual acquisition prices and reflects the difference between domestic and import prices. This procedure also differs somewhat from that employed earlier, in Moorsteen–62, pp. 458–59, to derive investment in equipment in domestic 1928 prices in 1928. The figure in the latter source, which is greater than that shown here by about 10 percent, was derived from data of a sort which are not available for years other than 1928. In order to obtain a time series derived consistently for all years, the present, somewhat rougher, methods are employed.

Column 3: The 1928 figure is from Table A–5, column 3. For all other years, the figures are estimated in these steps: (*i*) The construction and equipment series, columns 1 and 2 of this table, are expressed individually as indexes, 1928 = 100. (*ii*) These two indexes are combined in a simple arithmetic average. (*iii*) The resulting 1928-based index is taken as an index of the real volume of installation investment and applied to the

1928 figure, to obtain installation in billions of 1928 rubles for other years.

Column 4: The sum of columns 1, 2, and 3.

Sources to Table A–4

Column 1: Investment in each year is computed as follows: (*i*) A series for construction in 1950 prices, inclusive of capital repairs, is computed by applying the 1950 price weighted index of materials inputs, Table A–6, column 3, to the figure for 1950 construction, including capital repairs, in Table A–7, column 8. (*ii*) An analogous series, excluding capital repairs, is computed from the foregoing, on the assumption that capital repairs in 1950 prices were the same share of the construction total as for investment in construction and installation taken together, in current prices, as shown in Table A–8.

Column 2: Investment in each year is computed from the corresponding figure in 1937 prices (Table A–2, column 2) by applying the price index number for 1950 (1937 = 100) using weights of the year in question, as shown in Table A–12, column 3.

TABLE A-4

GROSS INVESTMENT IN FIXED CAPITAL, EXCLUDING CAPITAL REPAIRS,
IN 1950 PRICES, 1928-61
(Billion Rubles)

	Construction (1)	Equipment (2)	Installation (3)	Total (4)
1928	18.81	5.88	1.06	25.75
1929	24.12	7.70	1.37	33.19
1930	32.84	12.82	2.01	47.67
1931	35.81	13.61	2.17	51.59
1932	36.34	14.12	2.22	52.68
1933	31.35	12.46	1.93	45.74
1934	37.41	12.39	2.16	51.96
1935	45.68	16.11	2.69	64.48
1936	61.61	22.46	3.67	87.74
1937	52.68	21.67	3.28	77.63
1938	49.65	23.55	3.28	76.39
1939	51.91	21.74	3.25	76.90
1940	50.52	20.54	3.13	74.19
1941, 1st Half	25.28	10.43	1.58	37.29
1941, 2nd Half	8.49	2.96	0.50	11.95
1942	16.98	5.92	1.00	23.90
1943	17.16	5.38	0.97	23.51
1944	21.76	13.76	1.64	37.16
1945	20.98	19.36	1.94	42.28
1946	30.40	23.36	2.54	56.30
1947	36.35	27.06	2.98	66.39
1948	49.26	30.93	3.70	83.89
1949	63.79	34.97	4.49	103.25
1950	72.05	46.22	5.47	123.74
1951	82.61	48.71	6.02	137.34
1952	92.89	47.19	6.32	146.40
1953	100.69	52.45	6.93	160.07
1954	111.77	62.19	7.93	181.89
1955	122.22	77.00	9.20	208.42
1956	129.24	97.43	10.67	237.34
1957	140.95	107.74	11.73	260.42
1958	158.02	122.96	13.28	294.26
1959	176.06	132.95	14.55	323.56
1960	188.25	141.86	15.54	345.65
1961	196.55	152.15	16.46	365.16

Column 3: The 1950 figure is from Table A–5, column 3. For all other years: (*i*) The construction and equipment series, columns 1 and 2 of this table, are expressed individually as indexes, 1950 = 100. (*ii*) These two indexes are combined in a simple arithmetic average. (*iii*) The resulting 1950-based index is taken as an index of the real volume of installation investment and applied to the 1950 figure, to obtain installation in billions of 1950 rubles for other years.

Column 4: The sum of columns 1, 2, and 3.

Sources to Table A–5

Column 1: The series is computed from the construction series, inclusive of capital repairs, in Table A–7, column 8, on the assumption that capital repairs were the same share of the total as for construction and installation together, as shown in Table A–8.

Column 2: For 1928–30, 1934–40, 1944–46, and 1949–56, see Moorsteen–62, Table G–20. For 1931–33, see Table A–9, row 11, below. For the first half of 1941, the figure for investment in 1937 prices (Table A–2) is inflated to the 1941 price level by the given-year weighted price index number from Moorsteen–62, Table E–2. For the second half of 1941, half of the 1942 figure is used. For 1942–43, see Table A–10, row 3, below. For 1947–48, equipment investment in current prices relative to 1946 is assumed to have moved with the official series for such investment in "comparable" prices, as given in TsSU–59, pp. 619–20. For 1957–61, equipment investment in current prices relative to 1956 is assumed to have moved with the official series for such investment in July 1, 1955, prices; see Table A–11, column 8, below.

Column 3: For 1928–61, the series is computed from the series, inclusive of capital repairs, in Table A–7, column 5, on the assumption that capital repairs were the same share of the total as for construction and installation together, as shown in Table A–8.

Column 4: The sum of columns 1, 2, and 3.

PRINCIPAL EXTENSIONS AND MODIFICATIONS OF PREVIOUS ESTIMATES

As is explained in the text, the series for investment in fixed capital are obtained for the most part from earlier studies (see references in footnote 1, p. 21). However, for use in the present context, the previous investment series have been modified and expanded in certain respects. It is intended here to describe the principal changes made and to draw attention to the points at which significant consequences for the capital stock estimates may arise. A list of the topics to be discussed follows, in the order of the subsequent exposition. The list also serves to indicate briefly the differences between the investment data shown in Tables A–1 through A–5 and those contained in the original studies.

(*i*) Interpolations in the construction series are made for the years 1941–44, which were not previously covered; estimates for 1956–58 are revised; and the estimates are extended through 1959–61. (*ii*) The value in current prices of certain forms of construction activity in kind is estimated and added to money investments in construction, as compiled previously. (*iii*) The original construction series, gross of capital repairs to

TABLE A-5

GROSS INVESTMENT IN FIXED CAPITAL, EXCLUDING CAPITAL REPAIRS,
IN CURRENT PRICES, 1928-61
(Billion Rubles)

	Construction (1)	Equipment (2)	Installation (3)	Total (4)
1928	3.52	1.21	0.22	4.95
1929	4.33	1.75	0.32	6.40
1930	5.74	2.98	0.54	9.26
1931	9.25	3.98	0.93	14.16
1932	11.55	5.02	1.22	17.79
1933	9.39	4.83	1.37	15.59
1934	13.21	5.60	1.46	20.27
1935	16.89	6.90	1.27	25.06
1936	22.25	10.70	1.28	34.23
1937	20.27	11.00	1.24	32.51
1938	20.76	12.20	1.38	34.34
1939	23.48	11.50	1.66	36.64
1940	26.03	11.80	1.90	39.73
1941, 1st Half	14.74	6.33	1.12	22.19
1941, 2nd Half	5.44	2.11	0.76	8.31
1942	12.32	4.22	1.72	18.26
1943	14.52	3.83	2.13	20.48
1944	21.24	9.80	3.24	34.28
1945	23.15	14.50	3.13	40.78
1946	29.65	17.00	3.55	50.20
1947	33.20	22.10	3.53	58.83
1948	43.09	27.00	4.12	74.21
1949	65.99	50.50	5.71	122.20
1950	72.05	46.30	5.47	123.82
1951	81.10	47.40	6.15	134.65
1952	91.58	41.40	7.43	140.41
1953	95.12	46.50	7.32	148.94
1954	108.24	55.80	8.20	172.24
1955	108.81	63.30	8.12	180.23
1956	121.80	70.40	9.05	201.25
1957	135.80	77.44	9.88	223.12
1958	153.90	89.34	11.52	254.76
1959	176.95	96.59	13.17	286.71
1960	195.87	103.07	14.81	313.75
1961	204.10	110.53	15.64	330.27

structures, are adjusted to exclude capital repairs. (*iv*) Interpolations and extrapolations in the equipment series in current and 1937 prices are made for years not previously covered: 1931–33, 1941–43, 1947–48, and 1957–61. (*v*) The equipment series, previously computed only in current prices, in 1937 prices, and in 1928 prices for benchmark years, are computed for all years in 1928 and 1950 prices. (*vi*) Investment in installation in constant prices is estimated.

Construction Indexes in Constant Prices

The original estimates of the volume of construction from which we work are indexes of materials inputs in construction, including capital repairs, valued in average prices of 1937, 1928, and, for 1950, average prices of the latter half of the year. Data for materials inputs are lacking for the years 1941 through 1944. An index can be composed, however, for the missing years other than 1941, by deflating current values of construction by prices of labor and materials inputs. The years 1942–44 are here estimated by straight-line interpolations between 1940 and 1945 on the deflated index. The first half of 1941 is assumed equal to one half of 1940, the second half to one half of 1942. Materials data of the required kind are available for 1959–61 and, with greater detail and accuracy than previously, for 1956–58. By the same procedures as those used previously, the estimates for 1956–58 are revised and the series extended through 1961. The complete construction indexes are shown in Table A–6, of which the sources in detail are the following.

TABLE A-6

INDEXES OF CONSTRUCTION INCLUDING CAPITAL REPAIRS, IN 1937, 1928,
AND 1950 PRICES, 1928-61
(1937 = 100)

	1937 Prices (1)	1928 Prices (2)	1950 Prices (3)
1928	36.7	35.7	36.9
1929	45.0	44.6	46.3
1930	58.9	59.1	60.5
1931	63.7	64.2	64.7
1932	63.6	64.2	65.3
1933	57.2	55.4	58.0
1934	69.1	67.3	69.3
1935	85.3	84.0	84.9
1936	115.0	115.0	114.0
1937	100.0	100.0	100.0
1938	98.8	98.2	96.7
1939	101.0	100.0	100.0
1940	101.0	98.6	98.9
1941, 1st Half	50.5	49.3	49.5
1941, 2nd Half	15.3	15.1	15.0
1942	30.7	30.3	30.0
1943	32.0	31.8	31.3
1944	41.7	41.9	40.8
1945	42.9	43.4	41.9
1946	64.2	64.8	62.1
1947	79.4	80.3	76.5
1948	106.0	108.0	103.0
1949	135.0	136.0	130.0
1950	155.0	156.0	149.0
1951	176.0	178.0	170.0
1952	196.0	199.0	190.0
1953	217.0	220.0	209.0
1954	239.0	243.0	230.0
1955	264.0	270.0	254.0
1956	277.0	284.0	265.0
1957	301.0	309.0	289.0
1958	337.0	347.0	324.0
1959	377.0	387.0	361.0
1960	405.0	419.0	386.0
1961	427.0	443.0	403.0

1928–40: All figures are from Powell–59, p. 3.

1941: First and second halves of the year are assumed equal to half of 1940 and 1942 respectively.

1942–44: Figures in all three series are interpolations based on an index composed by deflating total construction in current prices (Table A–7, column 8) by an index of prices of construction inputs weighted with 1937 quantities (Powell–59, p. 85).

1945–55: All figures are from Powell–59, p. 3.

1956–60: The three series are extended from 1955 on the basis of indexes composed from quantity series for 28 categories of construction materials. The share of construction in the total of each category is assumed the same in all years as in 1955. Where separate categories shown for 1955 in Powell–59 have been combined into a single category, the composition of the whole is assumed to remain the same as in 1955. The output statistics employed are taken from TsSU–60, pp. 166, 204, and 244, and from TsSU–61, pp. 241, 244, 281, 297, 301, 307, 309, 313, 315, and 319. The materials included are listed below, together with explanations of any peculiarities in their derivation.

(1) Steel rails.
(2) Steel beams and channels.
(3) Other rolled steel products (bars and sections, wire rod, flat products, roofing iron). This category is estimated from the total output of finished rolled steel minus rails and beams and channels.
(4) Steel pipe. Gas and oil pipe together are extrapolated on total pipe production.
(5) Sawnwood. Corrections for net exports are made only for this category, since a check of the trade statistics indicates that net exports of construction materials other than wood products has remained small. Net exports of sawnwood of 1.6 million cubic meters in 1955, 1.6 in 1956, and 2.9 in 1957 are calculated in Powell–59, p. 29. Net exports of 3.1 in 1958, 3.9 in 1959, and 4.5 in 1960 are calculated from data in Ministerstvo vneshnei torgovli–60, pp. 22 and 34, and from Ministerstvo vneshnei torgovli–61, pp. 22 and 23.
(6) Structural timbers, poles, piles, etc. From its behavior in the early 1950's and from the behavior of industrial roundwood shipped, the category is assumed to have remained at its 1955 level. Because of the method of estimation, no adjustment for net exports is appropriate.
(7) Railroad ties. Ties are extrapolated from 1955 on industrial roundwood shipped.
(8) Red clay bricks.
(9) Sand-lime bricks.
(10) Portland cement. Cement consumed in the production of asbestos-cement shingles is deducted. See Powell–57, Part II, p. 325, and Powell–59, p. 42.
(11) Trass and puzzolan cement.
(12) Portland-slag cement.
(13) Other cement.
(14) Building lime. Lime consumed in the production of sand-lime brick is deducted. See Powell–57, Part II, pp. 330–31.
(15) Gypsum.
(16) Window glass.
(17) Tar paper.
(18) Ruberoid.
(19) Pergamin.
(20) Roofing tiles. Numbers of tiles are extrapolated from 1955 on series given in square meters.
(21) Asbestos-cement shingles.
(22) Zinc white pigments.
(23) Drying oils.
(24) Radiators.
(25) Corrugated tubing.
(26) Heating boilers.
(27) Enameled cast-iron bathtubs.
(28) Cast-iron sewer pipe.

1961: 1961 is extrapolated from 1960 on indexes composed as for 1956–60 except that materials categories 14, 15, 20, and 22 through 28 are omitted. Production data used are those given in the annual plan fulfillment report, *Vestnik statistiki,* 1962:2, pp. 4 and 5. Deficiencies in the data require these further adjustments: Component categories of rolled steel (1–3), bricks (8–9), cement (10–13), and soft roofing (17–19), are extrapolated on reported total outputs. Industrial roundwood and total brick output are extrapolated from increases reported for output exclusive of collective farms. Sawnwood production is not reported; the amount consumed in construction is assumed equal to that in 1960, on the basis of the behavior of sawnwood relative to roundwood in the preceding years and an absolute decline in roundwood from 1960 to 1961.

Subsequent to the completion of the present calculations, fuller output data for 1961 were released in TsSU–62a. A recalculation of the series in 1937 prices on the basis of these data yields a 1961 figure which differs insignificantly from that shown in Table A–6.

Construction in Current Prices

Total investment in structures in current prices, including capital repairs, is estimated in Table A–7 as the sum of money investment in the socialized sectors (state, co-operative, and collective-farm), two forms of socialized investment in kind (by collective-farm members in collective-farm investment and by the "population" in road-building), and private investment. The estimates require the following comments.

(*i*) The series for socialized money investment in column 2 is conceptually the same as that given in Powell–59, p. 64, but the earlier series has been somewhat revised and extended here.

(*ii*) The figures (column 3) for collective-farm investment in kind for 1928–34 are official. For subsequent years, the annual figures in the table have been estimated from Soviet data on annual collective-farm money investment and the average relationship of such money investment to investment in kind over the intervals 1933–37, 1946–50, and 1951–53. In a purely nominal sense, this should provide a reasonable, if approximate, method of estimation. What remains unclear is the Soviet method of valuing investment in kind and, hence, the comparability of these figures with our money investment series.

(*iii*) Road-building investment in kind (column 4) is taken from a Soviet source for the years 1928–34 and is estimated for 1935–37 from official figures on annual money investment and the average relationship of road-building in kind to money investment for 1933–37. For all subsequent years, the estimates are derived on the assumption that the real volume of such investment remained at the 1937 level (or, for the war years, at half the 1937 level), the value in current prices varying with the level of money wages in construction. All of these data, accordingly, suffer from the ambiguity in valuation procedures adhering to collective-farm investment in kind; the post-1937 figures are intended only to round out the total and have no independent interest.

(*iv*) The private investment data (column 7) for the earliest years covered, 1928–32, are thought to be inclusive of both residential and nonresidential private construction and of investment in kind as well as money

TABLE A-7

CONSTRUCTION AND INSTALLATION INCLUDING CAPITAL REPAIRS,
IN CURRENT PRICES, 1928-61
(Billion Rubles)

	Socialized Construction and Installation				Social-ized Instal-lation	Social-ized Construc-tion	Private Con-struc-tion	Total Con-struc-tion
	Total	Money Invest-ment	Collective-Farm Investment in Kind	Road-Building in Kind				
	(1)	(2)	(3)	(4)	(5)	(6)	(7)	(8)
1928	2.64	2.64	0.0	0.00	0.26	2.38	1.71	4.09
1929	3.69	3.61	0.0	0.08	0.36	3.33	1.60	4.93
1930	5.99	5.87	0.0	0.12	0.59	5.40	0.87	6.27
1931	10.14	9.96	0.0	0.18	1.00	9.14	0.76	9.90
1932	13.4	13.1	0.1	0.2	1.3	12.1	0.2	12.3
1933	11.6	10.7	0.6	0.3	1.5	10.1	0.2	10.3
1934	15.8	14.6	0.8	0.4	1.6	14.2	0.3	14.5
1935	19.5	17.4	1.2	0.9	1.4	18.1	0.5	18.6
1936	25.1	22.7	1.3	1.1	1.4	23.7	0.7	24.4
1937	23.5	20.7	1.7	1.1	1.4	22.1	0.7	22.8
1938	25.0	23.0	0.7	1.3	1.6	23.4	0.6	24.0
1939	28.1	25.9	0.8	1.4	1.9	26.2	0.6	26.8
1940	31.9	28.9	1.5	1.5	2.2	29.7	0.5	30.2
1941 1st Half	18.4	--	--	--	1.3	17.1	--	17.1
1941 2nd Half	6.5	--	--	--	0.8	5.7	--	5.7
1942	14.4	13.2	0.3	0.9	1.8	12.6	0.3	12.9
1943	17.7	16.1	0.6	1.0	2.3	15.4	0.3	15.7
1944	26.7	24.0	1.6	1.1	3.6	23.1	0.5	23.6
1945	30.3	27.7	1.5	1.1	3.7	26.6	0.8	27.4
1946	38.9	35.0	1.5	2.4	4.3	34.6	1.3	35.9
1947	44.2	39.8	1.7	2.7	4.4	39.8	1.8	41.4
1948	55.8	50.9	2.0	2.9	5.1	50.7	2.7	53.4
1949	83.4	78.0	2.5	2.9	6.9	76.5	3.2	79.7
1950	91.8	86.4	2.4	3.0	6.7	85.1	3.2	88.3
1951	103.5	97.9	2.6	3.0	7.5	96.0	2.9	98.9
1952	116	110	3	3	9	107	4	111
1953	120	114	3	3	9	111	6	117
1954	136	129	4	3	10	126	6	132
1955	138	130	5	3	10	128	6	134
1956	153	145	5	3	11	142	6	148
1957	170	--	--	--	12	158	7	165
1958	193	--	--	--	14	179	8	187
1959	222	--	--	--	16	206	9	215
1960	246	--	--	--	18	228	10	238
1961	257	--	--	--	19	238	10	248

outlays. In the Soviet source from which they were originally drawn, TsSU-32, p. 296, private rural construction was apparently estimated from the peasant budget studies (see the discussion of these studies pp. 56–57 above). The source shows most private construction to have occurred in the agricultural sector and indicates in connection with another table (pp. 652–53), which gives similar agricultural investment series, that the latter are drawn from the peasant budget studies. The figures should, therefore, encompass, at least in principle, all such private investment, including investment in kind. The Table A–7 series beyond 1932 is too roughly approximate to justify any precise statement as to its coverage, although from 1932 it relates essentially to private residential construction only. No attempt is made to reconcile these data with those for investment in private housing in physical units, shown in Table 3–2. At least for the years beyond 1932, the private investment figures serve only to round out the totals.

In detail, sources for Table A–7 are the following.

Column 1

1928–34: TsUNKhU–36, pp. 407–9.

1935–36: Computed as in Powell–59, p. 65, but without deducting investment in kind.

1937–40: Computed sums of columns 2, 3, and 4.

1941, 1st half: Extrapolated from 1940 on column 8.

1941, 2nd half: Extrapolated from 1942 on column 8.

1942–56: Computed sums of columns 2, 3, and 4.

1957–60: Figures are extrapolated from 1956. In Powell–59, p. 68, 1956 socialized construction and installation other than in capital repairs and in collective farms is estimated as 109 billion rubles. This component is extrapolated on the official series in July 1, 1955, prices (TsSU–61, p. 591), inflated to current prices by the official index of construction and installation costs (*ibid.*, p. 628). Collective-farm 1956 money investment in construction and installation is estimated in Powell–59, *loc. cit.*, as 10 billion rubles; investment in kind is estimated in Table A–7 as 5 billion. The two collective-farm components are extrapolated in combination on the official series in July 1, 1955, prices for collective-farm financed investment in construction and installation (TsSU–61a, p. 164); the series is inflated to current prices by the official cost index referred to above. Totals for column 1 are then extrapolated on the sums of the two indicated components.

1961: Extrapolated as in 1957–60, except that the collective-farm component is extrapolated on the official series for total investment in this sector. The necessary data are given in TsSU–62, pp. 290–91, 293, and 303.

Column 2

1928–36: Computed as column 1 minus columns 3 and 4.

1937: Computed as the sum of 19.86 billion for sectors other than collective farms and .87 billion for collective farms. The derivation of these components is explained in Powell–59, p. 65, except that the investment totals shown there should read 32.3 and 3.1 billion.

1938–40: Computed as the sum of separate estimates for sectors other than collective farms and for collective farms. The first is extrapolated from 1937 on the official series for construction and installation other than in collective farms, in prices of July 1, 1955 (TsSU–61, p. 590). The grounds for treating this series in the prewar years as in current prices are explained in Powell–59, pp. 66–67. The collective-farm component is extrapolated from 1937 on total money investment in collective farms, given in Kaplan–56, p. 29.

1942–56: Reproduced from Powell–59, pp. 64 and 72.

Column 3

1928–37: See Table D–9.

1938–40: Computed as the difference between total and money investment in collective farms, both given in Kaplan–56, p. 29.

1942–55: Investment in kind equaled 28 percent of collective-farm money investment during the period 1946–50 and 23 percent during 1951–53 (see *loc. cit.*). We assume this ratio was 28 percent from 1942 to 1949, 25 percent in 1950, and 23 percent from 1951 to 1955. Annual money investment is given *loc. cit.* or in unpublished calculations made by Kaplan.

1956: Extrapolated from 1955 on the official series for collective farms' investment from their own resources in construction and installation, nominally in constant prices (see TsSU–61a, p. 164).

Column 4

1928–34: TsUNKhU–36, p. 384.

1935–36: See Moorsteen–62, Table G–2.

1937: Road-building in kind is assumed to have equaled 3 percent of total socialized money investment, which was its average relative magnitude in 1933–37. See *loc. cit.* for both investment and road-building figures.

1938–56: Road-building in kind in real terms is assumed to have been constant at the 1937 level throughout 1938–40 and 1946–56 and to have been half the 1937 level from 1942 through 1945. The current-price value of the category is estimated by inflating the value in 1937 prices by the index of money wages in construction given in Powell–59, p. 78.

Column 5

1928–32: Installation is assumed equal to 10 percent of money investment in construction and installation, which is the average of its share in 1933–36. Investment in kind is unlikely to include any significant amount of installation.

1933–34: Computed difference between columns 1 and 6.

1935–36: Total socialized construction and installation is assumed divided between its components in the ratios shown in Powell–57, Part II, p. 422. That the ratios referred to are inclusive of investment in kind is argued in Moorsteen–62, pp. 428 ff.

1937–39: Interpolated on money investment in socialized construction and installation on the assumption the division of the total changed linearly from 1936 to 1940.

1940: Estimated from money investment in socialized construction and installation and the percentage breakdown shown in Powell–57, Part II, p. 425. The breakdown is judged from its date of publication to refer to money investment only.

1941, 1st half: Extrapolated from 1940 on column 1.

1941, 2nd half: Extrapolated from 1942 on column 1.

1942–56: Computed difference between socialized construction and installation and construction alone as shown in Powell–59, pp. 64 and 72.

1957–61: Extrapolated from 1956 on column 1.

Column 6

1928–32: Column 1 minus column 5.

1933–34: TsUNKhU–36, pp. 404–5.

1935–61: Column 1 minus column 5.

Column 7

Private construction is assumed to include no installation.

1928–32: Powell–59, p. 64.

1933–36: Interpolated from 1932 and 1937 on socialized construction.

1937, 1940, 1944, 1948–55: The figures are Bergson's "allowance for private housing construction"; see Bergson–61, p. 381.

1938–39, 1942–43, 1945–47: All are interpolated or extrapolated on socialized construction: 1938–39 from 1937 and 1940, 1942–43 from 1944, and 1945–47 from 1944 and 1948.

1956–60: Extrapolated on data for retail sales of building materials given in TsSU–60, p. 648, and TsSU–61, p. 691.

1961: Extrapolated from 1960 on column 6.

Column 8

1928–40: Figures are sums of columns 6 and 7.

1941: Construction indexes for the first and second halves of 1941 in 1937 prices are given in Table A–6. From similar values for 1940 and 1942 and from the current-price totals shown in the present table, it may be inferred that construction prices rose by 40 percent from 1940 to 1942. Price indexes for the two halves of 1941 are interpolated on a straight line and the constant-price valuation inflated correspondingly.

1942–61: Figures are sums of columns 6 and 7.

Construction Exclusive of Capital Repairs

The construction indexes of Table A–6 are inclusive, at least in principle, of materials allocated to capital repairs of structures and are for that reason interpreted as measures inclusive of such repairs. We obtain estimates of the volume of construction exclusive of capital repairs from the inclusive series and the data in Table A–8, which shows the relative share of capital repairs in construction and installation together, for money investment in the socialized sectors only, in current prices. Doubtless with some inaccuracy, these same ratios are assumed to hold for construction alone, in the entire economy, and in the constant prices of the three weight years.

The Table A–8 data are obtained as follows.

Column 1: Figures are from Table A–7, column 2.

Column 2

1928–30: Column 1 multiplied by column 3.

1931–33: Computed as 61/39 of repairs to equipment. See Table A–9 and the accompanying description of sources.

1934–36: Computed from total repairs and repairs on equipment as estimated in Moorsteen–62, p. 448.

1937–56: Computed as 61 percent of total repairs as given in Kaplan's unpublished estimates. The 61 percent figure is the fraction of repairs not attributed to equipment by Moorsteen (see *loc. cit.*).

Column 3

1928–30: The repairs shares for these years are computed from data for socialized investment in three sectors only: industry, rail transportation, and housing. The resulting percentages are assumed to apply to the whole of socialized money investment in construction and installation. Component data are the following (billion rubles):

	Construction and Installation			Capital Repairs		
	1928	1929	1930	1928	1929	1930
VSNKh industry	.778	1.113	2.212	.080	.092	.086
Other industry	.206	.272	.374	.021	.022	.015
Rail transportation ...	.419	.472	.639	.107	.117	.163
Housing	.300	.326	.413	.030	.033	.041
Total	1.703	2.183	3.638	.238	.264	.305

All figures for construction and installation are derived from TsSU–32, pp. 294–96. In 1928 and 1929 the source does not distribute total construc-

TABLE A-8

SHARE OF CAPITAL REPAIRS IN MONEY INVESTMENT IN SOCIALIZED
CONSTRUCTION AND INSTALLATION, IN CURRENT PRICES,
1928-61

	Construction and Installation (Billion Rubles) (1)	Capital Repairs (Billion Rubles) (2)	Repairs as Per-cent of Total (3)
1928	2.64	0.37	14.0
1929	3.61	0.44	12.1
1930	5.87	0.49	8.4
1931	9.96	0.66	6.6
1932	13.1	0.80	6.1
1933	10.7	0.94	8.8
1934	14.6	1.3	8.9
1935	17.4	1.6	9.2
1936	22.7	2.0	8.8
1937	20.7	2.3	11.1
1938	23.0	3.1	13.5
1939	25.9	3.2	12.4
1940	28.9	4.0	13.8
1941, 1st Half.	--	--	13.8
1941, 2nd Half.	--	--	4.5
1942	13.2	0.6	4.5
1943	16.1	1.2	7.5
1944	24.0	2.4	10.0
1945	27.7	4.3	15.5
1946	35.0	6.1	17.4
1947	39.8	7.9	19.8
1948	50.9	9.8	19.3
1949	78.0	13.4	17.2
1950	86.4	15.9	18.4
1951	97.9	17.6	18.0
1952	110.0	19.3	17.5
1953	114.0	21.3	18.7
1954	129.0	23.2	18.0
1955	130.0	24.4	18.8
1956	145.0	25.6	17.7
1957	--	--	17.7
1958	--	--	17.7
1959	--	--	17.7
1960	--	--	17.7
1961	--	--	17.7

tion and installation in industry among component categories of industry; the distribution is here assumed proportionate to total investment.

Repairs in VSNKh industry are computed from data given in Moorsteen–62, p. 447, by procedures parallel to those used there for estimating repairs to equipment. Repairs in other industry are assumed the same share of construction and installation as in VSNKh industry. Repairs in rail transportation are derived from Moorsteen, *loc. cit.* Repairs to housing in each year are assumed to have equaled 10 percent of the investment figures on the basis of a statement that socialized investment in housing during the First Five-Year Plan amounted to about 4 billion rubles and capital "renovations" of housing to 400 million rubles (Anonymous–35, p. 211).

1931–40: Column 2 divided by column 1.
1941, 1st half: Assumed the same as 1940.
1941, 2nd half: Assumed the same as 1942.
1942–56: Column 2 divided by column 1.
1957–61: Assumed the same as in 1956.

Equipment in 1937 and Current Prices

The original study from which our equipment investment series are drawn contains no estimates in 1937 or current prices for the years 1931–33, 1941–43, 1947–48, and 1957–60. For present purposes, we have made interpolations and extrapolations to include those years.

(*i*) Table A–9 shows our interpolations for 1931–33. Equipment investment, including capital repairs, in current prices, for the socialized sector of the economy (row 7), is obtained by subtracting items of nonequipment investment (rows 2, 3, 4, and 6) from total money investment (row 1). Private investment in equipment (row 8) is added (row 9). The total is divided into capital repairs and equipment investment exclusive of capital repairs (rows 10 and 11). Thus far the methodology and data employed are comparable to those used for other years. The deflators (rows 12 and 14), however, are not derived directly from price data but are estimated by interpolation between 1930 and 1934. While the price movements indicated by the interpolated indexes are believed to be in the right direction, i.e., uniformly upward, the timing of the price changes is unknown, and the estimates of investment in 1937 prices (rows 13 and 15) may err accordingly.

Sources for Table A–9 are these.

Row 1: TsUNKhU–36, p. 384.

Row 2: Ibid., p. 407.

TABLE A-9

DERIVATION OF GROSS INVESTMENT IN EQUIPMENT,
IN CURRENT AND 1937 PRICES, 1931-33
(Billion Rubles)

	Prices	1931	1932	1933
1. Total Investment, Including Capital Repairs, Socialized Sector	Current	15.681	20.086	18.432
2. Construction and Installation, Socialized	Current	10.138	13.439	11.587
3. Land Betterment.	Current	0.118	0.107	0.095
4. Research and Surveying	Current	0.219	0.281	0.258
5. Equipment and Other Acquisitions, Socialized	Current	5.206	6.259	6.492
6. Nonequipment Acquisitions, Socialized	Current	0.971	0.813	1.054
7. Equipment Acquisitions, Socialized .	Current	4.235	5.446	5.438
8. Private Investment in Equipment. . .	Current	0.175	0.088	0.000
9. Total Investment in Equipment, Including Capital Repairs	Current	4.410	5.534	5.438
10. Capital Repairs to Equipment	Current	0.421	0.512	0.604
11. Total Investment in Equipment, Excluding Capital Repairs	Current	3.979	5.022	4.834
12. Price Index for New Equipment (1937 = 100).		71	79	83
13. Total Investment in Equipment, Excluding Capital Repairs	1937	5.60	6.36	5.85
14. Price Index for Equipment Capital Repairs (1937 = 100)		65	71	77
15. Capital Repairs to Equipment	1937	0.65	0.72	0.78

Row 3: The 1933 figure is from *ibid.,* p. 404. The 1931 and 1932 figures are estimated by interpolating between that for 1933 and a 1930 figure estimated at 129 million rubles; for the latter, see Moorsteen–62, p. 427.

Row 4: Estimated in each year at 1.4 percent of row 1, the relationship which prevailed in 1930; see *loc. cit.*

Row 5: Row 1 minus rows 2, 3, and 4.

Row 6: The sum of: (*i*) investment in livestock acquisitions, as given in Kaplan–51, p. 102; plus (*ii*) investment in small-valued and short-lived durables in agriculture, estimated as the difference between agricultural investment in all durables less investment in agricultural machines, tractors, and vehicles (see *loc. cit.*); plus (*iii*) nonagricultural investment in small-valued and short-lived durables, estimated by interpolation between figures for 1930 and 1934 given in Moorsteen–62, p. 433.

Row 7: Row 5 minus row 6.

Row 8: Assumed negligible in 1933. For 1931 and 1932, the figures are interpolations between 1930 and 1933. For 1930, see Moorsteen–62, p. 444.

Row 9: Row 7 plus row 8.

Row 10: Estimated from row 1 on the basis of the relationship between capital repairs and total investment for 1933–36 and the share of equipment in total capital repairs in 1941 (Plan); see Moorsteen–62, pp. 448–49.

Row 11: Row 9 minus row 10.

Row 12: Estimated by interpolation between the corresponding 1930 and 1934 index numbers; see Moorsteen–62, Table G–20. (The figure shown for 1933, 83, would better be 87, but the interpolation is crude in any case, and correction of the error, which was discovered at a late date, would be excessively costly).

Row 13: Row 11 divided by row 12.

Row 14: Estimated by interpolation between the corresponding 1930 and 1934 index numbers; see Moorsteen–62, Table G–21.

Row 15: Row 10 divided by row 14.

(*ii*) Investment in equipment in 1937 prices, inclusive and exclusive of capital repairs, during the first half of 1941 is assumed to amount to half of that for 1940. This figure is inflated by an appropriate price index number to obtain investment in current prices. In the second half of 1941, investment in 1937 and current prices is assumed to equal half of the corresponding 1942 amount.

(*iii*) Interpolations for 1942 and 1943 are shown in Table A–10, which is self-explanatory. The estimates for these years are intended to round out our calculations but can scarcely be very reliable viewed in isolation.

Sources to Table A–10 are as follows.

Row 1: Unpublished estimates of Norman Kaplan.

Row 2: The sum of (*i*) the share of total money investment going to equipment requiring installation; plus (*ii*) half of the share of total investment going to all "acquisitions" (i.e., acquisitions of equipment not requiring installation plus livestock); see Moorsteen–62, Table G–5.

Row 3: Row 1 times row 2.

Row 4: The corresponding price index number for 1944 is used; see Moorsteen–62, Table G–20.

Row 5: Row 3 divided by row 4.

Row 6: Total capital repairs in 1942 and 1943 are estimated by Kaplan as about 1.0 and 2.0 billion rubles respectively. It is assumed that equipment accounted for about 40 percent of the total, as in 1941 (Plan); see Moorsteen–62, pp. 448–49.

Row 7: The corresponding price index number for 1944 is used; see Moorsteen–62, Table G–21.

Row 8: Row 6 divided by row 7.

TABLE A-10

DERIVATION OF GROSS INVESTMENT IN EQUIPMENT,
IN CURRENT AND 1937 PRICES, 1942-43

		1942	1943
1.	Total Money Investment, Excluding Capital Repairs (Billion Current Rubles)	20	22
2.	Percentage Share of Equipment Acquisitions in Total Investment	21.1	17.4
3.	Investment in Equipment, Excluding Capital Repairs (Billion Current Rubles)	4.22	3.83
4.	Price Index for New Equipment (1937 = 100)	114	114
5.	Investment in Equipment, Excluding Capital Repairs (Billion 1937 Rubles)	3.70	3.36
6.	Capital Repairs to Equipment (Billion Current Rubles)	0.4	0.8
7.	Price Index for Equipment Capital Repairs (1937 = 100)	132	132
8.	Capital Repairs to Equipment (Billion 1937 Rubles) . . .	0.38	0.76

(*iv*) Investment in equipment in 1937 prices, both inclusive and exclusive of capital repairs, in 1947 and 1948 is estimated by straight-line interpolation between the corresponding figures for 1946 and 1949. Our current-price estimates are extrapolated from the 1946 figure by means of an official index of machinery investment in "constant" prices. As explained in Moorsteen–62, pp. 88–89, the official index seems to have been compiled on the assumption of a constant price level for machinery from 1945 through 1948 and hence would serve as an indicator of the change in current investment.

(*v*) For 1957–61, equipment investment in 1937 and current prices is extrapolated from our 1956 figures by means of official Soviet data on investment in July 1, 1955, prices. This use of the official data is based on the finding in Moorsteen–62, pp. 96 ff., that, for 1950–56, the Soviet equipment investment series moves with his deflation of current investment into 1937 prices and the fact that, so far as we know, no important changes in machinery prices occurred during 1956–61 (see Moorsteen–62, pp. 166–67 and TsSU–61a, p. 258). Various Soviet data on investment in 1956–60 are shown in Table A–11. The figures in the first column include all investment in equipment by state and co-operative organizations, exclusive of collective farms. Soviet sources do not presently show equipment investment by collective farms separately, but they do provide a basis for dividing total collective-farm investment in productive fixed assets at least roughly into two components: construction-installation work and a residual category including equipment and miscellaneous, or "other," investment. In columns 2–6 of Table A–11, we estimate the share of collective-farm investment in equipment in this more inclusive residual series. State, co-operative, and collective-farm investment in equipment are summed to produce the equipment investment series (columns 7 and 8) which we use to extend our calculations to 1960.

Total equipment investment in 1961 is computed by analogous, but slightly cruder, methods. According to TsSU–62, pp. 291–93, investment in equipment in 1961 by state and co-operative organizations, exclusive of collective farms, in prices of July 1, 1955, was 100.75 billion, while total investment by collective farms was 30 billion rubles, 6.75 percent less than in 1960. If collective-farm investment in equipment changed with total collective-farm investment, then state, co-operative, and collective-farm equipment investment would have amounted in all to 107.5 billion rubles, which is the figure shown in Table A–11, column 7, for 1961.

In Table A–11, the data in columns 1–3 and 5 are from TsSU–61a, pp. 8, 44, 155, 160, 164. For columns 4, 6–8, see the discussion above. The collective-farm investment data for 1958 and preceding years do not include outlays for used equipment purchased from Machine-Tractor Stations.

Investment in equipment and "other" is computed as total investment for productive purposes less construction-installation work for productive purposes. In the case of collective farms, the latter series is described in the source as work "charged to the resources of collective farms" (*za schet sredstv kolkhozov*). This may mean that the series is exclusive of expenditures financed out of bank loans. However, the meaning is not clear, nor is it clear, if such an exclusion is intended, that it would be sizable in amount. We use the figures as though inclusive of essentially all construction and installation work performed by collective farms. The alternative interpretation, that a substantial amount of outlays are excluded, would imply significantly smaller figures for collective-farm investment in equipment than we have calculated in column 6. This, however, seems unlikely. Thus an earlier estimate of collective-farm equipment investment in 1956 placed it at 6.0 billion rubles (Moorsteen–62, p. 437), as compared with the 5.7 billion rubles computed here.

Equipment in 1928 and 1950 Prices

The equipment investment study cited earlier, together with the interpolations just described, yield a continuous series for investment in equipment in 1937 prices. This series is deflated by the price index numbers shown in Table A–12 to produce two further series, one in 1928 prices (using the deflator of column 2) and one in 1950 prices (using the deflator of column 3). These deflators are price index numbers for the indicated years, based on 1937 and variably weighted by the value of output in 1937 prices in the given year, as indicated in column 1. Thus the index numbers are of the form

$$\frac{\Sigma \, (P_W/P_{37}) \, (P_{37}Q_0)}{\Sigma \, (P_{37}Q_0)},$$

where (P_W/P_{37}) is the 1937-based price index number for the new weight year (1928 or 1950) for a specific kind of equipment and $(P_{37}Q_0)$ is the value in 1937 prices of investment in that kind of equipment in the given year. The multiplication of annual investment in 1937 prices, $\Sigma \, (P_{37}Q_0)$, by such an index number yields a series, $\Sigma (P_W Q_0)$, for the same investment expressed in prices of the new weight year. The weights used for the 1st half of 1941 actually refer to data for the 1941 annual plan; the weights for the 2nd half of 1941 to 1945, to actual output in 1945 only.

The application of the procedure described to obtain 1950-price valuations for 1957–61—over which interval the 1937-price series are extrapolated on official data in prices of July 1, 1955—involves an excessive refinement which might better have been foregone. The resulting 1950-price series differs insignificantly, however, from that which would be obtained by extrapolating directly on the official data. Also, because of rounding

TABLE A-11

GROSS INVESTMENT IN EQUIPMENT, EXCLUDING CAPITAL REPAIRS, OFFICIAL DATA
IN PRICES OF JULY 1, 1955, 1956–61

| | State and Co-operative Investment in Equipment (Billion Rubles) (1) | State, Co-operative, and Collective-Farm Investment for Agricultural Purposes | | | Collective-Farm Investment for Agricultural Purposes | | State, Co-operative, and Collective-Farm Investment in Equipment, Col. 1 plus Col. 6 | |
		Equipment and "Other" (Billion Rubles) (2)	Equipment (Billion Rubles) (3)	Equipment as Share of Equipment plus "Other" (Percent) (4)	Equipment and "Other" (Billion Rubles) (5)	Equipment Estimated as Col. 4 times Col. 5 (Billion Rubles) (6)	(Billion Rubles) (7)	(1956 = 100) (8)
1956	62.75	20.90	17.91	85.7	6.65	5.70	68.45	100.0
1957	70.17	22.39	19.08	85.2	6.13	5.22	75.39	110.0
1958	77.14	25.64	22.03	85.9	11.37	9.77	86.91	126.9
1959	83.40	23.50	19.59	83.4	12.71	10.60	94.00	137.2
1960	93.06	22.85	17.28	75.6	9.51	7.19	100.25	146.4
1961	--	--	--	--	--	--	107.50	157.0

TABLE A-12

PRICE INDEX NUMBERS FOR EQUIPMENT,
1928 AND 1950 RELATIVE TO 1937 PRICES

Weights of the Year:	1928/1937	1950/1937
(1)	(2)	(3)
1928	70	291
1929	74	282
1930	80	271
1931	91	243
1932	110	222
1933	124	213
1934	131	210
1935	131	212
1936	138	208
1937	141	197
1938	150	193
1939	150	189
1940	139	185
1941, 1st Half	133	188
1941, 2nd Half-45	152	160
1946	142	173
1947	138	178
1948	140	183
1949	142	189
1950	141	191
1951	132	191
1952	134	188
1953	135	186
1954	137	184
1955	137	186
1956	135	187
1957	131	188
1958-61	129	186

errors, the procedure yields, in Table A–4, a slightly different figure for 1950 investment in 1950 prices from the current-price figure given in Table A–5.

The price index numbers in Table A–12 are aggregations of price index numbers for 19 categories of machinery, weighted by the value of output of the year shown in column 1. The weights are from Moorsteen–62, Table D–2. The category price index numbers are from *ibid.*, Table E–1. Within individual categories, the price relatives for specific items of machinery are variously weighted: for the weight years 1945–58, intracategory weights of 1955 are used; for the weight years 1938–41 (Plan), intracategory weights of 1941 (Plan) are used; for 1928 and 1937, intracategory weights of 1928 and 1937 respectively are used. For 1929–36, two sets of over-all price index numbers were computed, each using weights of the indicated year between categories, but using, alternatively, weights of 1928 and 1937 within categories. The resulting pairs of index numbers are averaged, using respective weights which shifted gradually from 88/12 (for the weight year 1929) to 50/50 (for 1932) to 10/90 (for 1936). Thus, for example, the 1929-weighted index number for 1950 in the table is an average of (*i*) an aggregate of 19 category index numbers for 1950, weighted by 1928 weights within categories and by 1929 weights between categories; and (*ii*) an aggregate of index numbers for 1950 for the same 19 categories, using 1937 weights within categories and 1929 weights between categories. The over-all index is computed giving component (*i*) a weight of 88 and component (*ii*) a weight of 12.

For purposes of this table, the distinction between the Soviet fiscal years, 1927/28, 1928/29, and 1929/30, and the corresponding calendar years, 1928, 1929, and 1930, have been ignored.

Installation in Constant Prices

The value of installation in current prices is estimated in Table A–7 above (the data are for installation in the socialized sectors only, but these would account for virtually the whole). The series is not, however, highly reliable, and, in any case, we lack suitable deflators. We therefore estimate the volume of installation investment in constant prices, instead, on the assumption that it changed at rates intermediate to those displayed by investment in construction, on the one hand, and in equipment on the other. The rationale of this assumption is discussed on p. 48 of the text.

CONSTRUCTION ESTIMATED BY INPUT-PRICE DEFLATION

We consider in Chapter 2, Section 3, the consequences of replacing the construction series (in 1937 prices) based on materials inputs with one derived by deflating the value of construction in current prices with an index of input prices. The price index employed and the resulting deflated series for construction are shown in Table A–13.

The price index is the weighted average of indexes of wage rates in construction and of materials prices at the construction site. For 1928–40, 1945–46, 1950–51, and 1954–56, the index is computed with given-year quantity weights; it is reproduced without alteration from Powell–59, p. 85. The large statistical deficiencies of the component price indexes and of the weights are described in Powell–59 and, more extensively, in Powell–57. It need be noted here only that both the wage index and the labor series used in obtaining weights are thought to omit labor engaged in collective-farm and road-building construction in kind. For years between 1940 and 1945, 1946 and 1950, and 1951 and 1954, values of the price index are obtained by interpolation on a similar index composed with 1937 quantity weights, which is also given in Powell–59, p. 85. The differences between the given-year and 1937-weighted indexes are not so great as to suggest that large errors should arise from this procedure.

The series for construction is obtained, for 1928–40 and 1942–56, by deflating construction inclusive of capital repairs in current prices (Table A–7, column 8) by the index of input prices, and subtracting capital repairs equal to the percentages shown in Table A–8. As in the estimates from materials inputs, the 1st half of 1941 is assumed equal to one half of 1940, the 2nd half of 1941 to one half of 1942.

We lack data on input prices for years after 1956 and, in their absence, extrapolate the deflated series from 1956 to 1961 on the series derived from materials inputs (Table A–2). The reason for adopting this procedure is that over these years materials inputs and labor inputs appear to move quite closely together (1956 = 100):

Year	Materials Inputs	Labor Inputs
1956	100	100
1957	109	113
1958	122	125
1959	136	135
1960	146	145
1961	154	150

For this comparison, the materials series unadjusted for capital repairs is used (Table A–6). The labor series is computed from reported data on employment "in construction-installation work" (Powell–59, p. 73; TsSU–61, p. 626; and TsSU–62, p. 311), which, however, are known to be of incomplete coverage. Since a combined index of labor and materials inputs is likely to behave like a deflated index (see Powell–57, Part I, pp. 35–37), we infer from the above correspondence that the materials index is a fair approximation to a deflated series over this period. The calculation, taken with the value of construction in current prices, implies a 9 percent rise in input prices from 1956 to 1961.

TABLE A-13

DERIVATION OF CONSTRUCTION, EXCLUDING CAPITAL REPAIRS,
BY INPUT-PRICE DEFLATION, IN 1937 PRICES, 1928-61

	Prices of Construction Inputs (1937 = 100)	Input-Price Deflated Value of Construction (Billion Rubles--1937 Prices)
1928	43.4	8.10
1929	43.7	9.92
1930	44.0	13.05
1931	48.3	19.15
1932	58.1	19.88
1933	63.2	14.87
1934	72.1	18.32
1935	82.2	20.55
1936	92.6	24.03
1937	100	20.27
1938	107	19.40
1939	120	19.56
1940	132	19.72
1941, 1st Half	--	9.86
1941, 2nd Half	--	3.77
1942	163	7.55
1943	176	8.25
1944	187	11.36
1945	193	12.00
1946	197	15.05
1947	211	15.74
1948	212	20.33
1949	335	19.70
1950	287	25.11
1951	284	28.55
1952	269	34.04
1953	269	35.36
1954	273	39.65
1955	266	40.91
1956	263	46.31
1957	--	50.33
1958	--	56.35
1959	--	63.03
1960	--	67.71
1961	--	71.40

Appendix B

The Fixed Capital Stock

on January 1, 1928

The parameters of the initial stock of fixed capital are derived in Table B–1. These data underlie the discussion in Section 4 of Chapter 2, including Table 2–5.

The organization of Table B–1 is as follows: The "net" (straight-line depreciated) value in 1928 prices of the stock on January 1, 1928, by economic sector and kind of asset, as distributed in the Soviet source, is shown in column 1. For several classes of assets, the source also indicates depreciation rates relative to the assets' net values and replacement costs, i.e., "gross" values (columns 2 and 3), from which we estimate the ratio of net to gross values (column 4) and absolute gross values (column 5). Within each group, a division is estimated between structures, equipment, and installation (columns 6 through 11). Finally, by means of deflators (those for equipment only being shown in columns 12 and 13), we revalue the initial stock in prices of 1937 (columns 14 through 19) and of 1950 (columns 20 through 25). The table also shows service lives for different groups of assets (columns 26 through 28), as estimated in Appendix C of this study; the years of service estimated to remain for each group of assets (columns 29 through 31); and the annual straight-line depreciation rates implied by the service lives (columns 32 through 34). The latter, which differ from the official Soviet rates shown in the table (column 3) for reasons explained in Chapter 2 (Section 4), are the rates applied to the initial stock in estimating straight-line depreciation.

The sources of the data in Table B–1 are as follows, in the order of the columns.

Column 1: Gosplan–30, pp. 446–53. The figures shown are obtained by straight-line interpolation between figures given in the source for October 1, 1927 and 1928. The figures in the source are in prices of 1926/27 but are used here as estimators of the same values in 1928 prices. All assets shown in the source are included in Table B–1 except livestock, land melioration, and "transport, other agricultural and small-valued durables." Livestock are considered separately in this study. Our investment data for subsequent years do not, in principle, extend to expenditures for melioration, and hence this class of capital is excluded from our estimates throughout.

TABLE B-1

PARAMETERS OF THE FIXED CAPITAL STOCK, JANUARY 1, 1928

	Net Value of Stock in 1928 Prices (Million Rubles) (1)	Depreciation Charged in Soviet Accounts as Percent of:		Ratio of Net to Gross Value (Percent) (4)
		Net Value (2)	Gross Value (3)	
1. Industry	7,734	5.6	3.84	69
2. Electric Power	720	5.4	--	69
3. Agriculture:				
3a. Machines and Tools	1,009	11.4	6.8	60
3b. Tractors	53	20.0	14.0	70
3c. Productive Structures	5,143	7.6	4.9	64
3d. Irrigation Works	495	4.3	3.0	70
4. Railroads:				
4a. Structures	6,630	2.6	--	73
4b. Rolling Stock	3,462	5.6	--	73
5. Water Transport:				
5a. Waterways	115	4.4	--	70
5b. Ports	201	3.5	--	70
5c. River Craft	255	6.0	--	70
5d. Sea Craft	106	6.2	--	70
6. Motor Transport:				
6a. Roads	630	2.4	--	70
6b. Vehicles	4	--	7.0	70
7. Communications	242	5.1	--	70
8. Trade	567	5.0	--	70
9. Municipal Facilities	2,173	4.1	--	70
10. Education	1,826	1.8	1.25	69
11. Health	954	1.8	1.22	68
12. Administration	556	2.9	2.19	76
13. Housing:				
13a. Socialized Urban	7,235	3.1	2.19	71
13b. Private Urban	5,034	3.6	2.53	70
13c. Rural	10,896	5.8	3.7	64
14. Total	56,040	--	--	--

TABLE B-1 (continued)

PARAMETERS OF THE FIXED CAPITAL STOCK, JANUARY 1, 1928

	Gross Value of Stock in 1928 Prices (Million Rubles)	Net Value of Stock in 1928 Prices (Million Rubles)		
		Structures	Equipment	Installation
	(5)	(6)	(7)	(8)
1. Industry	11,209	3,325	3,326	1,083
2. Electric Power	1,043	402	217	101
3. Agriculture:				
3a. Machines and Tools	1,682	--	1,009	--
3b. Tractors	76	--	53	--
3c. Productive Structures	8,036	5,143	--	--
3d. Irrigation Works	707	495	--	--
4. Railroads:				
4a. Structures	9,082	6,630	--	--
4b. Rolling Stock	4,742	--	3,462	--
5. Water Transport:				
5a. Waterways	164	115	--	--
5b. Ports	287	201	--	--
5c. River Craft	364	--	255	--
5d. Sea Craft	151	--	106	--
6. Motor Transport:				
6a. Roads	900	630	--	--
6b. Vehicles	6	--	4	--
7. Communications	346	166	42	34
8. Trade	810	454	113	--
9. Municipal Facilities	3,104	1,738	435	--
10. Education	2,646	1,826	--	--
11. Health	1,403	954	--	--
12. Administration	732	556	--	--
13. Housing:				
13a. Socialized Urban	10,190	7,235	--	--
13b. Private Urban	7,191	5,034	--	--
13c. Rural	17,025	10,896	--	--
14. Total	81,896	45,800	9,022	1,218

TABLE B-1 (continued)

PARAMETERS OF THE FIXED CAPITAL STOCK, JANUARY 1, 1928

	Gross Value of Stock in 1928 Prices (Million Rubles)			Price Index Numbers for Equipment (1928 = 100)	
	Structures (9)	Equipment (10)	Installation (11)	1937 (12)	1950 (13)
1. Industry	4,820	4,820	1,569	109	227
2. Electric Power	583	314	146	109	227
3. Agriculture:					
3a. Machines and Tools	--	1,682	--	193	729
3b. Tractors	--	76	--	48	122
3c. Productive Structures	8,036	--	--	--	--
3d. Irrigation Works	707	--	--	--	--
4. Railroads:					
4a. Structures	9,082	--	--	--	--
4b. Rolling Stock	--	4,742	--	139	380
5. Water Transport:					
5a. Waterways	164	--	--	--	--
5b. Ports	287	--	--	--	--
5c. River Craft	--	364	--	143	416
5d. Sea Craft	--	151	--	143	416
6. Motor Transport:					
6a. Roads	900	--	--	--	--
6b. Vehicles	--	6	--	41	71
7. Communications	238	60	48	143	416
8. Trade	648	162	--	143	416
9. Municipal Facilities	2,483	621	--	143	416
10. Education	2,646	--	--	--	--
11. Health	1,403	--	--	--	--
12. Administration	732	--	--	--	--
13. Housing:					
13a. Socialized Urban	10,190	--	--	--	--
13b. Private Urban	7,191	--	--	--	--
13c. Rural	17,025	--	--	--	--
14. Total	67,135	12,998	1,763	--	--

TABLE B-1 (continued)

PARAMETERS OF THE FIXED CAPITAL STOCK, JANUARY 1, 1928

	Net Value of Stock in 1937 Prices (Million Rubles)			Gross Value of Stock in 1937 Prices (Million Rubles)		
	Structures (14)	Equipment (15)	Installation (16)	Structures (17)	Equipment (18)	Installation (19)
1. Industry	6,800	3,625	1,673	9,857	5,254	2,424
2. Electric Power	822	237	156	1,192	342	226
3. Agriculture:						
3a. Machines and Tools	--	1,947	--	--	3,246	--
3b. Tractors	--	25	--	--	36	--
3c. Productive Structures	10,517	--	--	16,434	--	--
3d. Irrigation Works	1,012	--	--	1,446	--	--
4. Railroads:						
4a. Structures	13,558	--	--	18,573	--	--
4b. Rolling Stock	--	4,812	--	--	6,591	--
5. Water Transport:						
5a. Waterways	235	--	--	335	--	--
5b. Ports	411	--	--	587	--	--
5c. River Craft	--	365	--	--	521	--
5d. Sea Craft	--	152	--	--	216	--
6. Motor Transport:						
6a. Roads	1,288	--	--	1,841	--	--
6b. Vehicles	--	2	--	--	2	--
7. Communications	339	60	53	487	86	74
8. Trade	928	162	--	1,325	232	--
9. Municipal Facilities	3,554	622	--	5,078	888	--
10. Education	3,734	--	--	5,411	--	--
11. Health	1,951	--	--	2,869	--	--
12. Administration	1,137	--	--	1,497	--	--
13. Housing:						
13a. Socialized Urban	14,796	--	--	20,839	--	--
13b. Private Urban	10,295	--	--	14,706	--	--
13c. Rural	22,282	--	--	34,816	--	--
14. Total	93,659	12,009	1,882	137,293	17,414	2,724

TABLE B-1 (continued)

PARAMETERS OF THE FIXED CAPITAL STOCK, JANUARY 1, 1928

	Net Value of Stock in 1950 Prices (Million Rubles)			Gross Value of Stock in 1950 Prices (Million Rubles)		
	Structures (20)	Equipment (21)	Installation (22)	Structures (23)	Equipment (24)	Installation (25)
1. Industry	17,769	7,550	5,218	25,758	10,941	7,559
2. Electric Power	2,148	493	487	3,116	713	703
3. Agriculture:						
3a. Machines and Tools	--	7,356	--	--	12,262	--
3b. Tractors	--	65	--	--	93	--
3c. Productive Structures	27,484	--	--	42,944	--	--
3d. Irrigation Works	2,645	--	--	3,778	--	--
4. Railroads:						
4a. Structures	35,431	--	--	48,534	--	--
4b. Rolling Stock	--	13,156	--	--	18,020	--
5. Water Transport:						
5a. Waterways	615	--	--	876	--	--
5b. Ports	1,074	--	--	1,534	--	--
5c. River Craft	--	1,061	--	--	1,514	--
5d. Sea Craft	--	441	--	--	628	--
6. Motor Transport:						
6a. Roads	3,367	--	--	4,810	--	--
6b. Vehicles	--	3	--	--	4	--
7. Communications	887	175	164	1,272	250	231
8. Trade	2,426	470	--	3,463	674	--
9. Municipal Facilities	9,288	1,810	--	13,269	2,583	--
10. Education	9,758	--	--	14,140	--	--
11. Health	5,098	--	--	7,498	--	--
12. Administration	2,971	--	--	3,912	--	--
13. Housing:						
13a. Socialized Urban	38,664	--	--	54,455	--	--
13b. Private Urban	26,902	--	--	38,429	--	--
13c. Rural	58,228	--	--	90,982	--	--
14. Total	244,755	32,580	5,869	358,770	47,682	8,493

TABLE B-1 (continued)

PARAMETERS OF THE FIXED CAPITAL STOCK, JANUARY 1, 1928

	Service Lives for Assets When New (Years)			Service Lives Remaining for Assets in Initial Stock (Years)		
	Structures (26)	Equipment (27)	Installation (28)	Structures (29)	Equipment (30)	Installation (31)
1. Industry	55	25	40	38	17	28
2. Electric Power	55	25	40	38	17	28
3. Agriculture:						
3a. Machines and Tools	--	8	--	--	5	--
3b. Tractors	--	12	--	--	8	--
3c. Productive Structures	40	--	--	26	--	--
3d. Irrigation Works	40	--	--	28	--	--
4. Railroads:						
4a. Structures	50	--	--	37	--	--
4b. Rolling Stock	--	45	--	--	33	--
5. Water Transport:						
5a. Waterways	50	--	--	35	--	--
5b. Ports	50	--	--	35	--	--
5c. River Craft	--	45	--	--	32	--
5d. Sea Craft	--	45	--	--	32	--
6. Motor Transport:						
6a. Roads	40	--	--	28	--	--
6b. Vehicles	--	8	--	--	6	--
7. Communications	40	25	40	28	17	28
8. Trade	65	25	--	46	17	--
9. Municipal Facilities	50	25	--	35	17	--
10. Education	80	--	--	55	--	--
11. Health	80	--	--	54	--	--
12. Administration	80	--	--	61	--	--
13. Housing:						
13a. Socialized Urban	90	--	--	64	--	--
13b. Private Urban	70	--	--	49	--	--
13c. Rural	50	--	--	32	--	--
14. Total	--	--	--	--	--	--

TABLE B-1 (concluded)

PARAMETERS OF THE FIXED CAPITAL STOCK, JANUARY 1, 1928

	Applicable Depreciation Rates, Excluding Funding for Capital Repairs (Percent)		
	Structures (32)	Equipment (33)	Installation (34)
1. Industry	1.82	4.00	2.5
2. Electric Power	1.82	4.00	2.5
3. Agriculture:			
3a. Machines and Tools	--	12.50	--
3b. Tractors	--	8.33	--
3c. Productive Structures	2.50	--	--
3d. Irrigation Works	2.50	--	--
4. Railroads:			
4a. Structures	2.00	--	--
4b. Rolling Stock	--	2.22	--
5. Water Transport:			
5a. Waterways	2.00	--	--
5b. Ports	2.00	--	--
5c. River Craft	--	2.22	--
5d. Sea Craft	--	2.22	--
6. Motor Transport:			
6a. Roads	2.50	--	--
6b. Vehicles	--	12.5	2.5
7. Communications	2.50	4.00	--
8. Trade	1.54	4.00	--
9. Municipal Facilities	2.00	4.00	--
10. Education	1.25	--	--
11. Health	1.25	--	--
12. Administration	1.25	--	--
13. Housing:			
13a. Socialized Urban	1.11	--	--
13b. Private Urban	1.43	--	--
13c. Rural	2.00	--	--
14. Total	--	--	--

The item, "transport, other agricultural and small-valued durables," is believed to consist largely of small-valued, short-lived assets, which we include in inventories (see fn. 30, p. 39).

Column 2: Gosplan–30, pp. 446–53. The figures shown are depreciation charges during the Soviet fiscal year 1927/28 as a percent of the October 1, 1927, net value of the items against which the charge was made.

Column 3: Ibid., pp. 462–65. The figures shown are depreciation rates relative to the gross value of the items against which the charge was made. For row 1, industry, the figure shown in the table is an average of the rate for industrial structures, 2.09 percent, and the rate for industrial equipment, 5.59 percent, equal weights being accorded each rate; see the distribution of assets between structures and equipment in columns 6 and 7 of the table. For row 3d, irrigation works, see Gosplan–28, p. 526.

Column 4: For items 1, 3a, 3b, 3c, 10, 11, 12, 13a, 13b, and 13c, the figures in column 3 are divided by those in column 2. For item 2, the ratio for item 1 is used. For each of the items 4a and 4b, a Soviet estimate for 1927, compiled for all fixed capital in railroading taken together, is used; see Strumilin–58, p. 649. For the remaining items, which account collectively for about 9 percent of the net value of the initial stock, the ratio of net to gross value is taken as 70 percent, i.e., roughly the level prevailing for the items listed just above.

Column 5: Column 1 divided by column 4.

Columns 6, 7, and 8: In these three columns, the total net values shown in column 1 are distributed between structures, equipment, and installation. Items 3a, 3b, 4b, 5c, 5d, and 6b are taken, from their designation in the source, to consist of equipment only. Items 3c, 3d, 4a, 5a, 5b, 6a, 10, 11, 12, 13a, 13b, and 13c are taken to consist only of structures, again on the basis of their designation in the source and of data in Gosplan–28, pp. 522–23, which show equipment to have been a negligible part of current investment for these items.

The installation component of items 1 (industry), 2 (electric power), and 7 (communications) is estimated as follows: Installation work, which occurs mainly in these three sectors, is estimated, roughly, as 0.26 billion current rubles in 1928 (Table A–7), or about 14 percent of the 1.82 billion rubles of total investment in industry, electric power, and communications for the year (TsSU–32, pp. 294–95). For each sector, the stock of installation is taken as 14 percent of the total shown in column 1.

The remaining industrial capital is distributed between structures and equipment in the proportions 1/1. According to TsSU–32, p. 20, structures accounted for 50.3 percent of the industrial capital stock on October 1, 1927, with power and operating machinery, tools, other durables, and means of transport accounting for the remainder. The breakdown does not show installation separately, and, for present purposes, we proceed as if it were distributed equally between the structural and nonstructural components. For the definitions of the components shown in TsSU–32, see Arakelian–38, pp. 14 ff. Capital other than installation in electric power is distributed between structures and equipment in the proportions 65/35, again on the basis of the components shown in TsSU–32, p. 20.

Capital other than installation in communications (item 7) and all capital in trade (item 8) and municipal facilities (item 9) is distributed between structures and equipment in the proportions 8/2. These figures are more or less arbitrary. In choosing them, however, we are guided in part by the relative importance of construction and installation in total investment during 1928–34, as given in TsUNKhU–36, pp. 384, 407.

Columns 9, 10, and 11: The distribution of the total gross values shown in column 5 is made on the same assumptions used for net values in columns 6, 7, and 8.

Columns 12 and 13: These are index numbers for domestic prices of Soviet machinery, drawn from Moorsteen–62. For items 1 and 2, index numbers aggregated with Soviet 1927/28 output weights for 14 categories of machinery used in industry (as defined in the capital stock breakdown, i.e., inclusive of manufacturing, extraction, public utilities, and, apparently, construction) are employed. The 14 categories are: construction and road-building machines, diesels, locomobiles, oil engines, steam turbines, water turbines, electrical machines, horse-drawn vehicles, steam boilers, pumps and compressors, lifting and handling equipment, woodworking and handling equipment, metalworking machines, and pneumatic hand tools. The indexes in the table are computed from 1927/28-weighted price indexes for the listed categories (*ibid.*, Table E–1), and 1927/28 value of category output weights (*ibid.*, Table D–2). For items 3a, 3b, 4b, and 6b, 1927/28-weighted price index numbers for agricultural machines, tractors, railroad rolling stock, and motor vehicles respectively (*ibid.*, Table E–1) are used. For the remaining items, 1927/28-weighted price indexes for all Soviet machinery (*ibid.*, Table E–2) are used.

Columns 14 and 16: The 1937 price levels of construction and installation implied by our investment series are (1928 = 100, 1928 quantity weights) 204.5 and 154.5, respectively; see Tables A–2 and A–3. The figures in 1937 prices in columns 14 and 15 are obtained from those in 1928 prices in columns 6 and 8 by applying these price index numbers.

Column 15: Column 7 times column 12.

Columns 17, 18, and 19: Obtained from columns 9, 10, and 11 by means of the same price index numbers as for columns 14, 15, and 16.

Columns 20 and 22: The 1950 price levels of construction and installation (1928 = 100, 1928 quantity weights) implied by our investment series are 534.4 and 481.8, respectively; see Tables A–3 and A–4. The figures in 1950 prices in columns 20 and 22 are obtained from those in 1928 prices in columns 6 and 8 by applying these price index numbers.

Column 21: Column 7 times column 13.

Columns 23, 24, and 25: Obtained from columns 9, 10, and 11 by means of the same price index numbers as for columns 20, 21, and 22.

Column 26: Table 2–10.

Column 27: The figures shown are chosen from the estimated service lives of Table 2–10 as follows: for items 1, 2, 7, 8, and 9, a service life of 25 years (that for electrical equipment, lifting and handling equipment, woodworking equipment, metalworking machines, leather and shoemaking machines, printing machines, and metallurgical machines) is used; for item 3a, that for agricultural machines; for item 3b, that for tractors; for items 4b, 5c, and 5d, that for railroad rolling stock; for item 6b, that for motor vehicles.

Column 28: See p. 67.

Columns 29, 30, and 31: The corresponding figures in columns 26, 27, or 28 are multiplied by the figures in column 4. Under straight-line depreciation, the ratio of net to gross value is also the ratio of remaining to total service life. See, however, the discussion in Chapter 2, Section 4, of the Soviet valuation procedures underlying the net figures.

Columns 32, 33, and 34: The figures are the reciprocals of the corresponding figures from columns 26, 27, or 28.

Appendix C

Service Lives of Fixed Assets

The purpose of this appendix is to explain the sources and methods used in obtaining the service-life data for individual kinds of equipment and structures shown in Table 2–10, p. 63, and also the derivation of the average depreciation rate and service life applied to annual investment in structures. The discussion turns first to equipment, then to structures.

EQUIPMENT

Three sets of estimates of average service lives for various categories of equipment are shown in Table C–1, columns 1–3. The estimated lives used in this study (shown in column 4) are selected from these. For items not represented in columns 1–3, estimated service lives in column 4 have been extrapolated from figures for similar or related equipment categories.

The estimates in column 1 are obtained from data on deliveries of equipment to agriculture during 1951–60 and the stock of such equipment at the end of 1960, the lives shown representing the period over which gross acquisitions cumulate to the terminal stock. The underlying data are shown in Table C–2. From these it may be seen, for example, that during ten years, 1951–60, agriculture received a total of 1,175 thousand tractors, while at the end of that period the total stock remaining was 1,122 thousand, that is, approximately the amount of deliveries during the preceding ten years. If all tractors had the same service life, this would be sufficient to indicate its magnitude, about ten years. In fact, as within all categories of equipment, retirements are distributed and not uniform. In the absence of a secular trend, this kind of data will still indicate the average about which actual lives are distributed. As the sources to Table C–2 reveal, there was no marked trend during 1951–60 in deliveries of the machines considered here. Another difficulty exists, however, in that the data refer to the end of the period covered by this study and may not be representative of earlier years. If, as seems likely, Soviet policy respecting the retirement of aging machines has grown more liberal, the lives implied by this material may be shorter than the average for the whole of the period. The Table C–2 data for deliveries are from *Pravda*, January 21, 1955; TsSU–57, p. 164; TsSU–59, p. 493; and TsSU–61, p. 491. The stock figures are from TsSU–61, pp. 485, 489.

The data in column 2 of Table C–1 are from a recent Soviet study by Ia. Kvasha of actual terms of service for equipment retired during the

TABLE C-1

DERIVATION OF SERVICE LIVES OF EQUIPMENT
(Years)

	Average Life Computed by Comparing Postwar Acquisitions and Stocks in Agriculture (1)	Average Life Estimated from Age of Equipment Scrapped during 1954-57 (2)	Expected Lives Used in Establishing Official Amortization Rates (3)	Service-Life Estimates Used in This Study (4)
Construction and Road-Building Equipment..........	--	--	7-12	10
Railroad Rolling Stock	--	45	20-85	45
Diesel Engines	--	--	30	30
Locomobiles	--	--	--	30
Oil Engines	--	--	30	30
Steam Turbines	--	--	30	30
Water Turbines	--	--	40	40
Electrical Equipment......	--	--	25-30	25
Tractors.........	10	10-19	--	12
Motor Vehicles..........	8	7-11	5	8
Horse-Drawn Vehicles.....	--	--	10-12	11
Steam Boilers	--	--	30	30
Pumps and Compressors ...	--	6-11	--	11
Lifting and Handling Equipment..........	--	--	--	25
Woodworking and Handling Equipment..........	--	6-33	--	25

TABLE C-1 (continued)

DERIVATION OF SERVICE LIVES OF EQUIPMENT
(Years)

	Average Life Computed by Comparing Postwar Acquisitions and Stocks in Agriculture (1)	Average Life Estimated from Age of Equipment Scrapped during 1954-57 (2)	Expected Lives Used in Establishing Official Amortization Rates (3)	Service-Life Estimates Used in This Study (4)
Textile and Sewing Machines	--	40-60	--	50
Metalworking Machines	--	27-31	--	25
Pneumatic Hand Tools	--	2-4	--	3
Agricultural Machines	5-8	8-13	--	8
Leather and Shoe-making Machines	--	--	--	25
Printing Machinery	--	--	--	25
Metallurgical Equipment	--	--	--	25
Coal Mining Machines	--	4-5	--	5
Petroleum Extraction and Refining Equipment	--	--	--	20

TABLE C-2

DELIVERIES OF EQUIPMENT TO AGRICULTURE, 1951-60,
AND THE STOCK OF EQUIPMENT IN AGRICULTURE, JANUARY 1, 1961
(Thousands)

	Deliveries to Agriculture during:					Stock in
	1951-1960	1953-1960	1954-1960	1955-1960	1956-1960	Agriculture, January 1, 1961
Tractors	1,175	--	--	--	--	1,122
Trucks	--	780	--	--	--	778
Grain Combines	--	512	471	--	--	497
Plows, Tractor.	--	--	--	793	698	782
Cultivators, Tractor . . .	--	--	--	827	721	755
Seed Drills, Tractor . . .	--	--	1,135	1,041	--	1,049

mid-1950's; see Kvasha–59, chap. 3. Using sample data from several industries, the average age of various kinds of equipment retired during 1954–57 was determined (for individual kinds of assets, see *ibid.*, pp. 149, 157–58, 160–61, 167, 172, 178, 188, 191, 221). The interpretation of these data encounters two difficulties. In the first place, inasmuch as the terms of service of any type of equipment acquired in a single year will be distributed, rather than uniform, the average age of retirements during any set period reflects not only the average service life but also the time distribution of previous acquisitions. In the case of tractors and grain combines, the author is able to make at least a rough adjustment for the distribution of acquisitions, but not for the other items. Rates of acquisition varied unevenly in the years preceding 1954–57 because of the war, and it is difficult to judge, therefore, what their effect on the average age of retirements during that interval would be. Secondly, as a result of the low acquisition rates and capital losses caused by the war, service lives were stretched out during the immediate postwar period. Thus, the capital stock may have been atypically aged just prior to the interval considered. In choosing among the data presented in this source, we proceed on the assumption that they tend to be on the high side in the interval considered. For individual categories of assets, our final estimates (Table C–1, column 4) do not coincide precisely with those made by the author (p. 225), though the comparisons are sometimes obscured by differences in scope. The average life we compute for all equipment, 21 years, on the other hand, is only slightly shorter than his, 23 years. See p. 69, for our estimate, Kvasha–59, p. 225, for his.

The expected lives used in establishing Soviet amortization rates (column 3) have various origins, but, for the most part, they apparently rest on "expert appraisals" rather than empirical investigations of actual service lives under Soviet conditions as they prevailed in the period studied by us. The figures for construction and road-building equipment are from Pavlov–57, p. 199. Those for rolling stock are from Kvasha–59, p. 203. The remaining figures are from Ministerstvo finansov–56, pp. 84, 129, 138.

STRUCTURES

The service lives shown in Table 2–10 for particular kinds of structures represent a considerably more impressionistic reading of the Soviet sources than do the lives cited for equipment, and the Soviet sources, in turn, are rarely explicit about the ultimate origins of the data they present. They are in agreement, however, that little firm knowledge is available on actual service lives of structures, which is almost unavoidably true of structures built during the Soviet period. On the whole, the lives we cite are probably best characterized as "expert appraisals." For several categories of structures used in Table 2–10, the figures are rough averages of lives reported for various structures which presumably are included in them. Though no systematic weighting of the lives of such components is attempted, the single lives chosen are meant to reflect weights proportionate to shares in annual investment rather than in the total stock of structures. The lives shown by kind of structure are obtained as follows.

Lives of housing of various wall materials are based on data given in Ministerstvo finansov–56, pp. 120–23, and Filatov–58, pp. 197–98 and 206–7. The figure for masonry buildings is the lower limit of a range commonly given and is characterized in *ibid.*, p. 199, as a conventional life. "Other" materials include mud brick, pressed board, and similarly cheap and impermanent materials.

Reported lives for nonresidential buildings are less consistent than those for housing, and we lack weights for buildings of different materials. The figure in Table 2–10 is estimated from data in Ministerstvo finansov–56, pp. 69 and 121–23; Bunich–57, p. 112; and Kvasha–59, pp. 137, 143, and 195.

Lives for other structures (*sooruzhenie*) are generally reported in the range of 25 to 50 years, excepting wood structures, for which lives of 11–12 years are indicated, and very long-lived structures such as steel or masonry bridges (cf. Ministerstvo finansov–56, pp. 12 and 128, and Kvasha–59, pp. 145 and 193 ff.). We take the average of 25 and 50 years.

The figure for roads, roadbeds, and squares is based on fragmentary data for roadbeds and for various road surfacings and materials, including rails and ties. See Kvasha–59, p. 193, and Ministerstvo finansov–56, p. 127.

The life for canals, wells, and reservoirs, and that for mine works, are from *ibid.*, p. 128. That for power transmission lines is from Kvasha–59, p. 196, where it is given for lines in rail transportation only. Dredging is a trivially small component of annual construction (see Table C–3), and the life ascribed to it is a guess.

The lives shown in Table 2–10 by economic sector, excepting those for housing, are rough estimates based on the lives by kind of structure and on the assumed composition of structures within each of the indicated sectors. We are guided here also in part by the depreciation charges in Soviet accounts shown in Table B–1, columns 2 and 3.

For housing, we have in Table 2–7 (p. 55), column 5, the distribution by wall materials of urban socialized and urban private housing in 1926 at 1926 prices. We assume the distribution was the same in 1928 for both socialized and private housing taken separately. For the materials categories used in Table 2–7, we assume lives of 100 years for masonry, 80 years for mixed masonry and wood, 70 years for wood (log and frame combined), and 30 years for other materials. The weighted average lives implied by these assumptions are 92 years for socialized housing and 69 years for private. We round these to 90 and 70 years respectively.

For rural housing we have no direct information on service lives. We estimate an average life instead from the ratio of the depreciation rates

TABLE C-3

DISTRIBUTION OF CONSTRUCTION BY COMPONENTS, 1934
(Billion Rubles--Current Prices)

	Total (1)	Housing (2)	Non-residential Buildings (3)	Other Structures (Sooruzhenie) (4)	Roads, Roadbeds, Squares (5)	Canals, Wells, Reservoirs (6)	Dredging (7)	Power Transmission Lines (8)	Mine Works (9)
1. Principal Economic Commissariats	7.608	1.116	3.163	1.739	0.851	0.087	0.012	0.213	0.425
2. Commissariat of Local Industry	0.253	0.050	0.144	0.059	0.000	0.000	0.000	0.000	0.000
3. Commissariat of Agriculture	1.194	0.115	0.767	0.312	0.000	0.000	0.000	0.000	0.000
4. Commissariat of State Farms	0.302	0.116	0.132	0.054	0.000	0.000	0.000	0.000	0.000
5. Commissariat of Transportation	1.874	0.160	0.171	0.171	1.371	0.000	0.000	0.000	0.000
6. Chief Administration of the Northern Sea Route	0.026	0.006	0.014	0.006	0.000	0.000	0.000	0.000	0.000
7. Central Union of Consumers' Co-operatives	0.214	0.036	0.160	0.018	0.000	0.000	0.000	0.000	0.000
8. Industrial Co-operatives	0.078	0.016	0.044	0.018	0.000	0.000	0.000	0.000	0.000
9. Education	0.305	0.000	0.305	0.000	0.000	0.000	0.000	0.000	0.000
10. Public Health	0.284	0.000	0.284	0.000	0.000	0.000	0.000	0.000	0.000
11. Urban Housing (Executive Committees and Co-operatives)	0.442	0.442	0.000	0.000	0.000	0.000	0.000	0.000	0.000
12. Municipal Facilities	1.010	0.000	0.718	0.291	0.000	0.000	0.000	0.000	0.000
13. Other	0.622	0.076	0.388	0.158	0.000	0.000	0.000	0.000	0.000
14. Total Socialized Construction	14.212	2.133	6.290	2.826	2.222	0.087	0.012	0.213	0.425
15. Private Construction	0.300	0.300	0.000	0.000	0.000	0.000	0.000	0.000	0.000
16. Total Construction	14.512	2.433	6.290	2.826	2.222	0.087	0.012	0.213	0.425
Of Total Housing:									
17. Masonry		1.506							
18. Wood Log		0.429							
19. Other, Including Wood Frame		0.498							

on rural housing to that on private urban housing shown in Table B–1, column 3.

Average Service Life and Depreciation Rate

The service lives by sectors (and corresponding depreciation rates) are applied separately to the construction categories shown in Table B–1, for the initial stock, and no average life or depreciation rate is required for our calculations. For annual investment in construction, on the other hand, we do utilize a single life and depreciation rate.

For this purpose, the lives of individual kinds of structures are taken to be those shown in Table 2–10; the depreciation rate for each is assumed equal to the reciprocal of its life. Lives and rates are then weighted by the values of investment in structures of various kinds in the single year 1934. The choice of this year is occasioned by the availability of relatively detailed data for it on the composition of investment in structures. It is thought also that 1934 is likely to be reasonably representative of the composition of construction in the whole period covered here, but substantial variations undoubtedly occurred over time. The weights are faulty, moreover, in that they are inclusive of capital repairs and in that they are in 1934 prices instead of the prices of any one of our weight years. The prices are probably closer to those of 1937 than of either of the other weight years. The average life so computed is 57 years. The average depreciation rate is 2.00 percent.

The 1934 weights employed are those shown in Table C–3 (column 2, rows 17–19, and columns 3–9, row 16), and are derived as follows.

Column 1: Figures for socialized construction are from TsUNKhU–36, p. 405. Private construction is from Table A–7, column 7.

Column 2, rows 1 to 16: Socialized housing is from TsUNKhU, *op. cit.*, p. 402; figures for two minor sectors are inclusive of municipal facilities. Housing is assumed to account for the whole of estimated private construction.

Column 2, rows 17 to 19: For 1934 investment in socialized housing, we have the following data on the distribution of wall materials.

Wall Material	Percentage Share of Area	Cost Per Cu. M. (Rubles)	Percentage Share of Value
Brick	50.3	52.1	59.3
Stone	12.2	41.1	11.3
Wood log	17.0	34.1	13.1
Other	20.5	35.0	16.3

The distribution of the total area by materials is given in Neifel'd–35, p. 136. The unit of measure is not specified. The cost data are from an unsigned article in *Nashe stroitel'stvo*, 1936:22, p. 36, except that the figure for "other" materials is estimated from figures given in the source of 22.7 for clay and 39.1 for "other" materials. Both sources probably refer to housing completed or occupied during 1934 rather than to that put in place. Both evidently include wood construction other than log with "other" materials. The distribution by value is computed from the area and cost data.

We distribute the total for socialized housing in column 2, row 14, in proportion to the value shares computed above. Brick and stone are combined in the masonry category. We assume private housing was divided equally between wood log and "other" materials. The figures shown for total housing are the sum of socialized and private housing.

Columns 3 to 9, row 1: Computed on the assumption that the 7.608 billion total for current investment in construction was distributed among components in the same proportions as were structures "put into operation" in these same commissariats, which are given in TsUNKhU–36, pp. 398–99. The latter data are evidently valued at acquisition costs and, insofar as structures put into operation in 1934 were acquired in part or whole in earlier years, must differ somewhat from valuations at 1934 prices (see, however, fn. 66, p. 61); the data exclude capital repairs. The breakdown referred to evidently includes housing in a single category for buildings; nonresidential buildings are here computed as the difference between total buildings and housing as previously estimated.

Columns 3 to 9, rows 2, 3, 4, 6, 8, 12, 13: That part of construction in each sector which is not accounted for by housing is assumed to be divided between nonresidential buildings and other structures in the same proportions as in the principal economic commissariats, i.e., 71.1/28.9. This assumption is undoubtedly inaccurate for any single sector, and the composition of structures in any such sector should not be read from the table. It is hoped that the assumption is reasonably accurate for all seven sectors in combination.

Columns 3 to 9, row 5: Construction other than in housing is assumed distributed 10 percent nonresidential buildings, 10 percent other structures, and 80 percent roadways.

Columns 3 to 9, row 7: Construction other than in housing is assumed distributed 90 percent nonresidential buildings and 10 percent other structures.

Columns 3 to 9, rows 9 and 10: All construction is assumed to be nonresidential buildings.

Columns 3 to 9, row 14: Totals are computed sums of components.

Columns 3 to 9, row 15: Private construction is assumed to consist solely of housing.

Columns 3 to 9, row 16: Totals are computed sums of components.

Appendix D

Nonagricultural Fixed Capital

Estimates of the stock of nonagricultural fixed assets in 1937, 1928, and 1950 prices are shown in the Tabular Section, Tables T–12, T–13, and T–14. These figures are variously derived for the three categories of capital, that is, structures, equipment, and installation.

In the case of installation, the estimates obtained for all branches of the national economy are also used for the nonagricultural sector. Most of the equipment acquired for agricultural use—tractors, trucks, combines, plows—requires no installation. Given this, the relatively minor role of installation in total fixed assets, and the roughness of the estimates we are able to make for it, no further adjustment is made to exclude the small part of installation work occurring in the agricultural sector.

The stock of nonagricultural structures is estimated by the same methods employed for the total stock of structures. Of the structures in the initial stock, all are included except those used in agricultural production (see Table B–1; the excluded items are those in rows 3c, productive agricultural structures, and 3d, irrigation structures). As will be explained in detail, series for annual investment in nonagricultural structures (shown in Table D–8 below) are compiled for the years from 1928. Present values of these two groups of assets are then computed, using the methods and service life data described in Chapter 2, Section 5. Each group of nonagricultural structures in the initial stock is assigned the same service life as in our basic calculations. For annual investment, the average depreciation rate and service life are compiled as in the basic calculations (i.e., using the service lives for individual kinds of structures in Table 2–10 and the 1934 investment weights of Table C–3), except that only the nonagricultural elements are aggregated. The average depreciation rate for nonagricultural investment in structures is 2.0 percent; the average service life, 57 years. That these figures are the same as those computed for all investment in structures is coincidental.

In the case of equipment, we estimate first the stock of equipment for agricultural use and then, by subtracting from our basic estimates for all equipment, the stock of nonagricultural equipment. Of the equipment items in the initial stock, agricultural machines and tractors (Table B–1, rows 3a and 3b) are considered to be for agricultural purposes. Annual investment in equipment acquired for agricultural use (shown in Tables D–2 and D–6, below) is also estimated, by methods explained later in this appendix. Present values for the initial stock and annual investment are

427

TABLE D-1

DISTRIBUTION OF RETIREMENTS AND AVERAGE DEPRECIATION CHARGES
FOR AGRICULTURAL INVESTMENT IN EQUIPMENT
(Percent)

Years after Acquisition of Asset	Gross Value of Assets Remaining in Existence as a Share of Total Investment in:			
	1928	1937	1955	Composite
0–8	100.0	100.0	100.0	100.0
9–11	13.7	24.0	36.3	24.7
12	1.0	20.9	33.3	18.4
Over 12	0.0	0.0	0.0	0.0

Years after Acquisition of Asset	Annual Depreciation Chargeable against Assets Remaining in Existence as a Share of Total Investment in:			
	1928	1937	1955	Composite
0–8	12.0	11.5	11.0	11.5
9–11	1.2	2.0	3.0	2.1
12	0.1	1.7	2.8	1.5
Over 12	0.0	0.0	0.0	0.0

again computed by means of the service-life data in Table 2–10. The treatment of the initial stock items is the same as in our basic calculations. For annual investment, we compile distributions of retirements and depreciation charges analogous to those used in the basic calculations, but with coverage restricted to equipment for agricultural uses: tractors, agricultural machinery, horse-drawn vehicles, and trucks. The results are shown in Table D–1. The service lives for individual kinds of equipment are from Table 2–10. The weights again are, respectively, the 1927/28, 1937, and 1955 value of output in 1937 prices from Moorsteen–62, Table D–2. The composites are simple averages of the three weight-year calculations. In applying the weights, all output of tractors, agricultural machinery, and horse-drawn vehicles, and 30 percent of motor vehicle output are used (the relative importance of agriculture as a consumer of Soviet motor vehicle production is shown in Table D–4 below). In each of the three investment years considered—1928, 1937, and 1955—rates of retirement and depreciation are similar or identical for the first eight years after acquisition, though substantial variations appear during the four remaining years of service. Since the values estimated for the nonagricultural equipment stock are relatively insensitive to the treatment of agricultural equipment over eight years old, we apply the composite rates of Table D–1 to all annual investment in agricultural equipment. (Retirement and depreciation rates for nonagricultural equipment show an even greater diversity among investment years, a fact which has dictated the indirect approach to estimating the nonagricultural stock employed here.)

The remainder of this appendix is devoted to the derivation of the series for annual investment in agricultural equipment and nonagricultural structures.

AGRICULTURAL INVESTMENT IN EQUIPMENT IN 1937 PRICES

We present in Table D–2 our 1937-price estimates for total investment in equipment (repeated from Table A–2), the agricultural component, the

TABLE D-2

GROSS AGRICULTURAL AND NONAGRICULTURAL INVESTMENT IN EQUIPMENT,
EXCLUDING CAPITAL REPAIRS, IN 1937 PRICES, 1928-61

	Total Investment (Billion Rubles) (1)	Agricultural (Billion Rubles) (2)	Nonagricultural (Billion Rubles) (3)	Nonagricultural as a Share of Total (Percent) (4)
1928	2.02	0.49	1.53	75.7
1929	2.73	0.61	2.12	77.7
1930	4.73	1.06	3.67	77.6
1931	5.60	1.32	4.28	76.4
1932	6.36	1.16	5.20	81.8
1933	5.85	1.62	4.23	72.3
1934	5.90	1.63	4.27	72.4
1935	7.60	2.08	5.52	72.6
1936	10.80	2.73	8.07	74.7
1937	11.00	2.46	8.54	77.6
1938	12.20	2.10	10.10	82.8
1939	11.50	1.87	9.63	83.7
1940	11.10	1.40	9.70	87.4
1941, 1st Half	5.55	0.70	4.85	87.4
1941, 2nd Half	1.85	0.35	1.50	81.1
1942	3.70	0.00	3.70	100.0
1943	3.36	0.00	3.36	100.0
1944	8.60	0.37	8.23	95.7
1945	12.10	0.73	11.37	94.0
1946	13.50	1.21	12.29	91.0
1947	15.20	1.75	13.45	88.5
1948	16.90	2.60	14.30	84.6
1949	18.50	4.51	13.99	75.6
1950	24.20	6.14	18.06	74.6
1951	25.50	6.20	19.30	75.7
1952	25.10	5.87	19.23	76.6
1953	28.20	6.00	22.20	78.7
1954	33.80	6.62	27.18	80.4
1955	41.40	7.83	33.57	81.1
1956	52.10	8.84	43.26	83.0
1957	57.31	9.42	47.89	83.6
1958	66.11	10.88	55.23	83.5
1959	71.48	9.67	61.81	86.5
1960	76.27	8.53	67.74	88.8
1961	81.80	9.16	72.64	88.8

nonagricultural component (computed from columns 1 and 2), and also the ratio of nonagricultural investment to the total (computed from columns 1 and 3). The derivation of the estimates for agricultural investment in equipment is explained in the discussion following. The investment referred to is that made for agricultural purposes, although some of the data from which we proceed refer to investment made by agricultural enterprises. The discussion is arranged in terms of time intervals, taken in sequence, over which the origins of the column 2 estimates are substantially homogeneous.

1928–35

The estimates shown in Table D–2 are, with a slight modification, those derived in Table D–3, row 18. The latter, which are obtained by deflation of current-price data, include investment in four kinds of machinery used for agricultural purposes: agricultural machines, tractors, trucks, and other means of transport (for example, horse-drawn vehicles). Some equipment

TABLE D-3

DERIVATION OF GROSS AGRICULTURAL INVESTMENT IN EQUIPMENT, INCLUDING CAPITAL REPAIRS,
IN 1937 PRICES, 1928-35

	Unit	1928	1929	1930	1931	1932	1933	1934	1935
Agricultural Machines									
1. Investment, Socialized Sector	million current rubles	45.2	118.6	323.7	530.0	447.1	513.1	455.9	531.7
2. Investment, Private Sector	million current rubles	188.1	155.2	67.0	33.5	0.0	0.0	0.0	0.0
3. Investment, All Sectors	million current rubles	233.3	273.8	390.7	563.5	447.1	513.1	455.9	531.7
4. Agricultural Machinery Price Index	1937 = 100	51.8	52.9	53.6	58.3	63.1	67.8	72.6	81.2
5. Investment, All Sectors	million 1937 rubles	450.4	517.6	728.9	966.6	708.6	756.8	628.0	654.8
Tractors									
6. Investment, Socialized Sector	million current rubles	9.5	41.1	111.5	187.2	208.2	424.4	674.4	1,046.2
7. Tractor Price Index	1937 = 100	103.4	95.6	94.6	95.0	96.0	97.0	97.5	98.2
8. Investment, Socialized Sector	million 1937 rubles	9.2	43.0	117.9	197.1	216.9	437.5	691.7	1,065.4
Trucks									
9. Investment, Socialized Sector	million current rubles	0.0	0.0	0.0	0.0	91.3	176.2	181.1	272.5
10. Motor Vehicle Price Index	1937 = 100	--	--	--	--	131.0	131.0	122.3	84.7
11. Investment, Socialized Sector	million 1937 rubles	0.0	0.0	0.0	0.0	69.7	134.5	148.1	321.7
Other Means of Transport									
12. Investment, Socialized Sector	million current rubles	7.4	33.9	155.7	147.1	146.6	276.2	204.6	160.7
13. Investment, Private Sector	million current rubles	32.0	26.4	11.4	5.7	0.0	0.0	0.0	0.0
14. Investment, All Sectors	million current rubles	39.4	60.3	167.1	152.8	146.6	276.2	204.6	160.7
15. Horse-Drawn Vehicle Price Index	1937 = 100	50.0	50.0	50.0	50.0	50.0	59.0	59.0	59.0
16. Investment, All Sectors	million 1937 rubles	78.8	120.6	334.2	305.6	293.2	468.1	346.8	272.4
All Machinery, Tractors, and Vehicles									
17. Investment, All Sectors	million current rubles	282.2	375.2	669.3	903.5	893.2	1,389.9	1,516.0	2,011.1
18. Investment, All Sectors	million 1937 rubles	538.4	681.2	1,181.0	1,469.3	1,288.4	1,796.9	1,814.6	2,314.3

TABLE D-4

DELIVERIES OF EQUIPMENT TO AGRICULTURE COMPARED
WITH TOTAL PRODUCTION, 1936-60
(Deliveries as Percentage of Total Production)

	1936-1938	1940	1946	1946-1950	1950	1951-1955	1955	1956-1960	1960
Tractors	72	64	83	84	85	71	75	71	66
Plows, Tractor	--	100	100	108	71	97	92	97	96
Paring Plows, Tractor	--	100	--	--	75	84	82	--	--
Seed Drills, Tractor .	--	100	96	102	101	99	97	97	90
Cultivators, Tractor .	--	100	91	101	99	98	94	97	93
Grain Combines	--	100	87	99	99	96	96	99	97
Mowers, Tractor. . . .	--	100	--	--	100	99	99	98	100
Rakers, Tractor	--	100	--	--	91	99	98	101	100
Trucks	--	13	48	31	30	30	34	26	13

purchased for agricultural purposes is therefore excluded, such as pumps used for irrigation. For 1928–31, an effort is made to estimate private as well as socialized investment, but, for the years after 1931, the magnitudes involved become small, and we assume private investment to have been negligible. The price index numbers for the most part are drawn from Moorsteen–62 and, where appropriate, are intended to take account of differences between prices of domestic and imported machines and of subsidies accorded agricultural purchasers of tractors. However, many of the price index numbers for 1931–33 are interpolations. The Table D–3 (row 18) data include capital repairs; in Table D–2 they are more or less arbitrarily reduced by 10 percent to obtain investment exclusive of repairs.

Sources of the Table D–3 data are the following.

Rows 1, 6, 9, 12 (investment, socialized sector): For 1928–33, see TsUNKhU–35, p. 287. For 1934–35, see TsUNKhU–36a, p. 243. In addition to the figures shown in the table, these sources indicate significant amounts to have been invested in other producers' durables used for agricultural purposes. These are omitted here, as they probably consisted primarily of small-valued, short-lived durables which we exclude from fixed capital (see fn. 30, p. 39). The sources also show investment in structures and equipment used for nonagricultural purposes by agricultural enterprises. These amounts, too, are omitted from the series in the table.

Row 2 (investment in agricultural machines, private sector): For 1928–30, see TsSU–32, p. 142. Investment in 1931 is set arbitrarily at half the 1930 amount and, in subsequent years, at zero.

Rows 3, 5, 8, 11, 14, 16–18: Figures are computed.

Row 4 (agricultural machinery price index): The series is the given-year weighted price index for agricultural machines from Moorsteen–62, Table E–1, and refers to wholesale prices of domestically produced machines. In this connection, it is noted (*i*) that the investment series include acquisitions by both socialized and private enterprises and (*ii*) that these acquisitions consist of both imported and domestically produced machines, sold at different price levels. However, private peasants and collective farms purchased machinery on the same terms during the period in which private investment was significant; see Gosplan–30, p. 307. In 1928, prices of imported agricultural machinery exceeded those for Soviet produced counterparts by about 15 percent; see Moorsteen–62, Table F–4. Judging from the volume of imports shown in TsUNKhU–35, pp. 583, 585, relative to total investment as given in Table D–2, imported agricultural machinery satisfied about 10 percent or less of Soviet demand during the years considered here. Hence, no adjustment to allow for the price level of imports has been made.

Row 7 (tractor price index): The series is an index of prices paid for tractors by Soviet agriculture. For 1928–30 and 1934, the figures shown are obtained from given-year weighted index numbers of factory prices for domestically produced equipment from Moorsteen–62, Table E–1, discounted by the amount of the subsidy accorded agricultural purchasers, i.e., 50 percent in 1928–30 and 15 percent in 1934; see Moorsteen–62, p. 28, fn. 14. For 1932 and 1933, the figures shown are index numbers of prices paid by agricultural purchasers, from Moorsteen–53, p. 90a. The 1931 figure is interpolated. For 1935, the domestic price index number for 1935, reduced by the amount of the 1934 subsidy, 15 percent, is used. In the years for which data are available, prices paid by agricultural purchasers were the same for imported and domestically produced tractors; see Moorsteen–62, Table F–6.

Row 10 (motor vehicle price index): For 1933–35, the given-year weighted price index for motor vehicles from Moorsteen–62, Table E–1, is used. For 1932, the 1933 index number is used.

Row 13 (investment in other means of transport, private sector): The figure shown for 1928 is the amount of purchases of horse-drawn vehicles by individual peasants in 1927/28; see Moorsteen–62, Table G–12. For 1929 and subsequent years, investment in other means of transport is assumed to move with private investment in agricultural machines, as shown in row 2.

Row 15 (horse-drawn vehicle price index): The figures shown for 1928 and 1934 are given-year weighted price index numbers for domestically produced equipment; see Moorsteen–62, Table E–1. Imports of these vehicles were negligible; see *ibid.*, p. 445. For 1929–32, the 1928 index number is used; for 1933 and 1935, the 1934 index number is used.

1936–40 (and 1945–55)

Adequate data on agricultural investment in equipment are not available for any of the period from 1936 to 1955. Except for the war years, the real change in such investment is estimated instead from data on production and deliveries of equipment to agriculture. Clearly, data on deliveries bear the closer relationship to agricultural investment. On the other hand, the production data are available in greater detail and for a larger range of items. Our calculation includes four categories of equipment: agricultural machines, tractors, horse-drawn vehicles, and trucks. Of these, the first three are groups for which domestic production and acquisitions by agriculture have moved closely together, because of the dominance of agriculture in the demand for them. In the case of trucks, by contrast, only a small and varying fraction of output has normally gone to agriculture. The relation between production and agricultural acquisitions can be judged from Table D–4. The data shown there for 1936–38 are from Kvasha–59, p. 176, and TsSU–57a, p. 226. Those for 1940–55 are from TsSU–57, p. 164; TsSU–57a, pp. 223, 226, 230–31; and Moorsteen–62, Table D–1. Those for 1956–58 and 1959–60 are from TsSU–59, pp. 242–44, 493, and TsSU–61, pp. 291–93, 491, respectively.

In Table D–5, we construct an interpolating index spanning the interval 1935–56 as the sum of the value in 1937 factory prices of all production of agricultural machinery, tractors, and horse-drawn vehicles, plus the value in the same prices of deliveries of trucks to agriculture. In order to take some account of the change in the mix of trucks acquired, deliveries in physical units are valued in different years at the average value in 1937 prices of all Soviet production in the corresponding year (for an indication of the change in truck size, see TsSU–57, pp. 155, 163, which shows the agricultural stock of trucks both in physical units and in horsepower). The index so obtained is shown in row 3b of the table. Taking 1935 as 100, it stands at 389.4 in 1956. According to our estimates of the absolute volume of investment in 1935 and 1956, however, 1956 was 425.5 percent of the 1935 level; see Table D–2. The interpolating index is adjusted to agree with the volume estimates; see row 4 of Table D–5. The difference between the two indicators for 1956 is not great—about 9 percent—and the adjustment to the computed interpolating index is made freehand. The index is then multiplied by 2.08 billion rubles, the absolute value of investment in 1935, to obtain the Table D–2 estimates for 1936–40 and 1945–55.

The production and deliveries data of Table D–5 are obtained as follows.

Row 1: Moorsteen–62, Table D–2.

Row 2: The figures are the product of the number of trucks delivered times the corresponding 1937 representative price. The delivery data for 1935, 1940, 1946–56 are from TsUNKhU–36, p. 253; TsSU–57, p. 164; TsSU–59, p. 493, and *Pravda*, January 20, 1949, January 18, 1950, January 23, 1952, and January 21, 1955. For 1936–37 and 1938–40, we assume deliveries to be equal to the increase in the stock of trucks in agriculture as given in TsUNKhU–36a, p. 248, and TsSU–57, p. 155. Deliveries within these two-year intervals are distributed between years in the proportions of motor vehicle output as given in TsSU–57a, p. 223. For 1945, deliveries are extrapolated from the 1946 figure by means of the change in motor vehicle production; see *loc. cit.* Our series for deliveries of trucks to agriculture, in thousands, is 1935, 27.1; 1936, 31; 1937, 45; 1938, 33; 1939, 31.5; 1940, 17.5; 1945, 33.3; 1946, 45.6; 1947, 49.4; 1948, 35; 1949, 64; 1950, 87.1; 1951, 59; 1952, 54; 1953, 68.9; 1954, 116; 1955, 110.6; 1956, 114.2.

The 1937 prices used to value these deliveries are obtained by dividing total output of motor vehicles in each year (from TsSU–57a, pp. 223, 428) into the value of all motor vehicle output in 1937 prices (from Moorsteen–62, Table D–2). The value-of-output data in the latter source reflect changes in the composition of truck output. They also include the value of trailers, as well as motor vehicles proper; thus the procedure just described also involves a corresponding imputation.

1941–44

Data on agricultural investment during World War II are few and of doubtful reliability; see, for example, the discussion of official, pre-1950 investment series in Moorsteen–62, pp. 98 ff. Given the circumstances, however, it is no doubt safe to assume that the supply of equipment for agricultural purposes was minimal. In particular, the years 1942–43, after military activity had enveloped the principal tractor and agricultural ma-

TABLE D-5

DERIVATION OF INDEX OF GROSS AGRICULTURAL INVESTMENT IN EQUIPMENT, IN 1937 PRICES, 1935-40 AND 1945-56

	1935	1936	1937	1938	1939	1940	1945	1946	1947
1. Value of Production (Billion 1937 Rubles)									
1a. Agricultural Machinery.............	0.5076	0.8072	0.8609	0.6039	0.4668	0.3917	0.0260	0.1273	0.2395
1b. Tractors..........	0.6596	0.7582	0.3844	0.4888	0.4702	0.3298	0.0648	0.1177	0.2982
1c. Horse-Drawn Vehicles	0.0449	0.0505	0.0562	0.0618	0.0673	0.0730	0.0393	0.0629	0.0865
2. Value of Deliveries to Agriculture (Billion 1937 Rubles)									
2a. Trucks.............	0.2378	0.2803	0.4032	0.3124	0.2983	0.1779	0.3796	0.5213	0.5623
3. Sum of Rows 1a, 1b, 1c, and 2a									
3a. In Billion 1937 Rubles	1.4499	1.8962	1.7047	1.4669	1.3027	0.9724	0.5097	0.8292	1.1865
3b. As an Index, 1935 = 100	100	130.8	117.6	101.2	89.8	67.1	35.2	57.2	81.8
4. Interpolating Index, 1935 = 100	100	131	118	101	90	67	35	58	84

TABLE D-5 (continued)

DERIVATION OF INDEX OF GROSS AGRICULTURAL INVESTMENT IN EQUIPMENT, IN 1937 PRICES, 1935-40 AND 1945-56

	1948	1949	1950	1951	1952	1953	1954	1955	1956
1. Value of Production (Billion 1937 Rubles)									
1a. Agricultural Machinery............	0.5967	1.1219	1.7766	2.1965	1.9387	1.6829	1.6179	1.8925	2.2627
1b. Tractors...........	0.6511	1.0693	1.2250	1.1083	1.1398	1.2527	1.4743	1.7560	1.9668
1c. Horse-Drawn Vehicles...........	0.1101	0.1337	0.1573	0.1573	0.1573	0.1573	0.1573	0.1573	0.1573
2. Value of Deliveries to Agriculture (Billion 1937 Rubles)									
2a. Trucks...........	0.3956	0.7160	0.9741	0.6495	0.5959	0.7589	1.2694	1.2106	1.2592
3. Sum of Rows 1a, 1b, 1c, and 2a									
3a. In Billion 1937 Rubles..........	1.7535	3.0409	4.1330	4.1116	3.8317	3.8518	4.2344	5.0164	5.6460
3b. As an Index, 1935 = 100..........	120.9	209.7	285.1	283.6	264.3	265.7	292.0	346.0	389.4
4. Interpolating Index, 1935 = 100	125	217	295	298	282	288	318	376	424.5

chinery producing centers of Kharkov, Stalingrad, and Rostov-on-Don, have been described as a period in which deliveries of equipment to agriculture "virtually ceased"; see Shigalin–60, p. 209, and Kvasha–59, p. 176. We set real investment in equipment for agricultural purposes in the 1st half of 1941 at half that of 1940, investment in the 2nd half of 1941 at half that of the 1st half, and investment in 1944 at half that of 1945. Investment in 1942 and 1943 is assumed to be negligible.

1945–55

See the discussion of 1936–40, above.

1956–60

The figures are derived from official investment statistics, given in TsSU–61a, p. 159, which are described in the source as the value in July 1, 1955, prices of "acquisitions of tractors, means of transport, agricultural machines, equipment and durables not included in project cost estimates," in "investment by state and collective farms in agriculture." They exclude outlays for capital repairs and for collective-farm purchases of used machinery from Machine-Tractor Stations in 1958 (see *ibid.*, pp. 7, 9, 159). We accept this official series on the grounds, stated on p. 43 of the text, which lead us to accept the corresponding series for total investment in equipment.

The agricultural series cited is reduced by 10 percent to allow for acquisitions by agricultural enterprises of equipment for nonagricultural uses, which it evidently includes. According to TsSU–60a, p. 386, the "productive basic funds of socialist agricultural enterprises, at acquisition cost" at the end of 1956 included tractors (7.8 percent of the total), motor vehicles (4.3 percent), horse-drawn vehicles (3.2 percent), agricultural machines (17.6 percent), other equipment used for agricultural purposes (3.7 percent), and basic funds used for nonagricultural purposes (7.7 percent). If, say, half of the last item consisted of equipment, then equipment of all sorts accounted for 40.5 percent of all basic funds, of which equipment used for agricultural purposes accounted for 36.6 percent.

The adjusted official series, in July 1, 1955, prices, is deflated into prices of 1937 by the price index number (1937 = 100) of 182.3. This index number is computed as a weighted harmonic mean, as would be appropriate for a given-year, current-value weighted index, of 1937-based price index numbers for tractors, motor vehicles, horse-drawn vehicles, and agricultural machines. The weights are proportionate to the shares of the indicated categories in "basic funds" given in the preceding paragraph. The price index numbers, with 1937 = 100, are 176.6 for tractors, 132.3 for motor vehicles, 243.5 for horse-drawn vehicles, and 194.1 for agricultural machines. These are given-year weighted indexes for 1956, from Moorsteen–62, Table E–1. As is explained in the latter source, p. 166, the prices of July 1, 1955, are best reflected by the index numbers computed for the calendar year 1956.

1961

The share of agricultural in total investment in equipment is assumed the same as in 1960.

AGRICULTURAL INVESTMENT IN EQUIPMENT IN 1928 AND 1950 PRICES

The series for agricultural investment in equipment in 1937 prices derived in the preceding section is repeated in Table D–6, column 1. The next two columns of the table show price index numbers for 1928 and 1950 for the same kinds of equipment, based on 1937 and variably weighted by the value in 1937 prices of investment in the given year (see the discussion in Appendix A of similar indexes in Table A–12). The multiplication of annual investment in 1937 prices by these index numbers yields series for the same investment expressed in prices of the new weight year. The series thus obtained, in prices of 1928 and 1950, are shown in columns 4 and 5 of the table.

The price index numbers in columns 2 and 3 are aggregations of price index numbers for four categories of equipment used in agriculture—agricultural machines, tractors, trucks, and horse-drawn vehicles—from Moorsteen–62, Table E–1. Ideally, these price index numbers too should be computed with given-year weights, but such index numbers are not available. As an approximation, therefore, the following substitutions are made: For the given years 1928–34, category indexes using 1927/28 output weights are used; for·the given years 1935–37, 1937 output weights are used; for 1938–41, 1941 (Plan) output weights are used; for 1944–61, 1955 output weights are used. These category price index numbers are shown in Table D–7.

The weights used in aggregating the category price index numbers are the value of investment in 1937 prices as shown in Table D–3 (for 1928–35) and Table D–5 (for 1936–40 and 1945–56). For 1941, the 1940 weights are used; for 1944, the 1945 weights; for 1957–61, the 1956 weights.

NONAGRICULTURAL CONSTRUCTION

Gross nonagricultural investment in structures in 1937, 1928, and 1950 prices is estimated in Table D–8 as the product of our series for total investment in structures excluding capital repairs (Tables A–2, A–3, and A–4) and the estimated share of nonagricultural sectors in the total (column 1 of Table D–8).

As will be explained shortly, the latter series is computed from data which are in prices of various years and which in many cases include, rather than exclude, capital repairs. Its use for present purposes yields proper results only insofar as the ratio of nonagricultural to total construction is the same in the various prices employed and the same for capital repairs as for other outlays. Given the preponderance of the nonagricultural share, these conditions probably prevail in the main, though concrete evidence on the matter is lacking. In addition, however, the reliability of many of the data used is unknown, and on both counts the resulting nonagricultural construction series should be taken as of a lower order of reliability than those for total construction.

The relative importance of nonagricultural investment in structures during 1928–37 is computed in Table D–9, in which total construction

TABLE D-6

DERIVATION OF GROSS AGRICULTURAL INVESTMENT IN EQUIPMENT,
EXCLUDING CAPITAL REPAIRS, IN 1928 AND 1950 PRICES, 1928-61

	Investment in 1937 Prices (Billion Rubles) (1)	Price Index Numbers		Investment in 1928 Prices (Billion Rubles) (4)	Investment in 1950 Prices (Billion Rubles) (5)
		1928/1937 (2)	1950/1937 (3)		
1928	0.49	54.2	360.2	0.27	1.76
1929	0.61	61.3	.351.2	0.37	2.14
1930	1.06	66.8	335.5	0.71	3.56
1931	1.32	72.2	339.0	0.95	4.47
1932	1.16	87.8	321.6	1.02	3.73
1933	1.62	103.3	304.4	1.67	4.93
1934	1.63	126.0	293.0	2.05	4.78
1935	2.08	164.6	246.6	3.42	5.13
1936	2.73	159.8	246.8	4.36	6.74
1937	2.46	148.2	242.6	3.65	5.97
1938	2.10	166.6	237.5	3.50	4.99
1939	1.87	174.2	235.0	3.26	4.39
1940	1.40	162.1	240.5	2.27	3.37
1941, 1st Half	0.70	162.1	240.5	1.13	1.68
1941, 2nd Half	0.35	162.1	240.5	0.57	0.84
1942	0.00	--	--	0.00	0.00
1943	0.00	--	--	0.00	0.00
1944	0.37	213.1	201.4	0.79	0.75
1945	0.73	213.1	201.4	1.56	1.47
1946	1.21	196.7	209.6	2.38	2.54
1947	1.75	189.1	219.6	3.31	3.84
1948	2.60	168.3	236.0	4.38	6.14
1949	4.51	167.2	235.2	7.54	10.61
1950	6.14	158.7	235.7	9.74	14.47
1951	6.20	141.9	241.7	8.80	14.99
1952	5.87	145.8	241.6	8.56	14.18
1953	6.00	156.9	238.2	9.41	14.29
1954	6.62	182.2	247.6	12.06	16.39
1955	7.83	168.2	234.6	13.17	18.37
1956	8.84	165.1	235.9	14.59	20.85
1957	9.42	165.1	235.9	15.55	22.22
1958	10.88	165.1	235.9	17.96	25.67
1959	9.67	165.1	235.9	15.97	22.81
1960	8.53	165.1	235.9	14.08	20.12
1961	9.16	165.1	235.9	15.12	21.61

(row 1) is reduced by the amount of agricultural construction (rows 2a–2c). The data are in current prices and include outlays on capital repairs.

The series for total construction is that used elsewhere in this study; see Table A–7, column 8. Three categories of agricultural construction are distinguished: (*i*) Money investment in the socialized sector of agriculture includes money outlays for construction for agricultural purposes by state, co-operative, and collective-farm organizations. The data for 1928–35 are cited directly from Soviet sources (see TsUNKhU–35, p. 287, and TsUNKhU–36, p. 243; following Moorsteen–62, p. 427, we assume half of expenditures for land betterment and irrigation to be for construction). The figures for 1936–37 are extrapolated from 1935 on a series for total socialized money investment in agriculture (see Kaplan–51, p. 214). (*ii*) Data on the magnitude of collective-farm investment in kind are available only from 1932, and even then may be inferred only indirectly from Soviet data by subtracting money investment from total investment by collective

TABLE D-7

PRICE INDEX NUMBERS FOR CATEGORIES OF EQUIPMENT EMPLOYED
IN AGRICULTURE, 1928 AND 1950 RELATIVE TO 1937 PRICES

For Given Years:	Agricultural Machines	Tractors	Trucks	Other Means of Transport (Horse-Drawn Vehicles)
		1928/1937		
1928-34	51.8	206.8	241.6	50.0
1935-37	79.2	224.7	236.4	50.0
1938-41	71.2	254.4	236.9	50.0
1944-61	74.7	232.8	236.1	50.0
		1950/1937		
1928-34	377.7	252.1	172.4	272.8
1935-37	268.8	246.7	178.7	272.8
1938-41	269.4	237.7	168.6	272.8
1944-61	255.5	244.2	183.0	272.8

farms (see Kaplan–56, p. 29). Furthermore, for the period 1933–37 only a single such figure is available, 5.6 billion rubles. In Table D–9 this has been distributed among years in the proportions of collective-farm money investments (see Kaplan–56, p. 29; these estimates differ from those in Moorsteen–62, Table G–2, in which collective-farm investment in kind was erroneously taken as 33 percent, rather than 56 percent, of money investment during 1933–37). Investment in kind by collective farms before 1932 and by state and co-operative organizations in all years is taken to be negligible. (*iii*) The figures on private agricultural construction for 1928–30 are Soviet estimates, drawn apparently from peasant budget surveys and, in principle at least, inclusive therefore of all such investment, including investment in kind (see TsSU–32, pp. 295, 652–53). However, the figure for 1931 is an extrapolation (following Powell–57, Part II, p. 429), while for 1932–37 it is simply assumed that, relative to total construction, private agricultural construction was negligible.

For 1938–60, the nonagricultural share of total construction is computed from the following identity:

$$C_a/C_t = [C_a/(C_s + I_s)] [(C_s + I_s)/C_t],$$

where C_a is agricultural construction; C_t is total construction; C_s is all socialized construction, agricultural as well as nonagricultural; and I_s is all socialized installation. The calculation is shown in Table D–10. For purposes of comparison with the findings for 1928–37 explained just above, the calculations in Table D–10 have been extended to 1933–37 as well, although no other use of the findings for that period is made.

The ratios in the first column are obtained from Table A–7 of this study and are computed from data in current prices, inclusive of capital repairs. The ratios in the second column are derived from the following three series in a recently published Soviet statistical handbook (TsSU–61a, pp. 44, 164): (*a*) all construction-installation work by state and co-operative enterprises and organizations, exclusive of collective farms; (*b*) construction-installation work for agricultural purposes financed by the state; and (*c*) construction-installation work for agricultural purposes financed by collective farms. The figures shown in the table are the ratio: $[(b) + (c)]/[(a) + (c)]$. Inasmuch as collective farms do some construction for nonagricultural purposes, the denominators are slightly too small. As may be seen by comparing the coverage of these Soviet series with the identity cited

TABLE D-8

DERIVATION OF NONAGRICULTURAL CONSTRUCTION, EXCLUDING CAPITAL
REPAIRS, IN 1937, 1928, AND 1950 PRICES, 1928-61

	Nonagricultural as a Share of Total Construction (Percent)	Nonagricultural Construction (Billion Rubles)		
		1937 Prices	1928 Prices	1950 Prices
	(1)	(2)	(3)	(4)
1928	84.6	6.09	2.98	15.91
1929	86.2	7.78	3.88	20.79
1930	89.3	10.98	5.55	29.33
1931	88.4	11.99	6.07	31.66
1932	91.1	12.41	6.30	33.11
1933	85.5	10.17	4.95	26.80
1934	87.1	12.50	6.12	32.58
1935	88.7	15.66	7.75	40.52
1936	89.6	21.43	10.77	55.20
1937	86.6	17.55	8.82	45.62
1938		17.08	8.53	43.54
1939		17.69	8.81	45.53
1940	87.7	17.40	8.54	44.31
1941, 1st Half		8.71	4.27	22.17
1941, 2nd Half		2.91	1.45	7.45
1942		5.87	2.91	14.89
1943	87.7	5.92	2.96	15.05
1944		7.50	3.79	19.08
1945		7.25	3.69	18.40
1946		10.39	5.27	26.11
1947		12.46	6.35	31.22
1948	85.9	16.75	8.58	42.31
1949		21.89	11.09	54.80
1950		24.77	12.53	61.89
1951	85.4	28.10	14.29	70.55
1952	86.9	32.04	16.35	80.72
1953	87.7	35.27	17.99	88.31
1954	86.1	38.47	19.67	96.23
1955	83.4	40.76	20.97	101.93
1956	84.1	43.71	22.54	108.69
1957	83.6	47.23	24.38	117.83
1958	84.2	53.25	27.57	133.05
1959	85.0	60.13	31.04	149.65
1960	86.0	65.35	34.00	161.89
1961	86.0	68.91	35.92	169.03

above, the ratios are suitable for present purposes only on the assumption
that both private agricultural construction and socialized agricultural installation were negligible. Neither assumption should be greatly in error
for the period in question.

The Soviet data used in computing the second set of ratios are described
in the source as exclusive of capital repairs and expressed in prices of
July 1, 1955 (see TsSU–61a, p. 9). That they are what they purport to be,
however, is by no means clear (for comment on such official series in general, see Chapter 7, Section 2). The series for all socialized, noncollective-
farm, construction and installation—series (a) above—appears to have been
derived directly from undeflated current-price data, when referring to prewar years, and from current-price data deflated by input price indexes for
at least part of the postwar years (see Powell–57, Part II, pp. 511 ff., and
Powell–59, pp. 8 ff.). The data in series (b) and (c) have not been published
before, and the source does not reveal how they have been derived. If, for
all the series, analogous methods have been employed for each time pe-

TABLE D-9

DERIVATION OF THE SHARE OF NONAGRICULTURAL IN TOTAL CONSTRUCTION, 1928-37*

	1928	1929	1930	1931	1932	1933	1934	1935	1936	1937	1928-1932	1933-1937
						Billion Rubles						
1. Total Construction	4.09	4.93	6.27	9.90	12.3	10.3	14.5	18.6	24.4	22.8	37.49	90.6
2. Agricultural Construction												
2a. Socialized Money Investment	0.075	0.148	0.424	0.93	1.05	0.88	1.09	0.94	1.20	1.34	2.63	5.45
2b. Collective-Farm Investment in Kind .	0.00	0.00	0.00	0.00	0.05	0.61	0.78	1.16	1.33	1.72	0.05	5.60
2c. Private Investment, Money and in Kind	0.555	0.531	0.249	0.22	0.00	0.00	0.00	0.00	0.00	0.00	1.56	0.00
3. Nonagricultural Construction	3.46	4.25	5.60	8.75	11.20	8.81	12.63	16.50	21.87	19.74	33.25	79.55
						Percent						
4. Nonagricultural as a Share of Total Construction	84.6	86.2	89.3	88.4	91.1	85.5	87.1	88.7	89.6	86.6	88.7	87.8

*Data are in current prices and inclusive of capital repairs.

TABLE D-10

DERIVATION OF THE SHARE OF NONAGRICULTURAL IN TOTAL
CONSTRUCTION, 1938-60*
(Percent)

	Socialized Construction and Installation Relative to Total Construction $[(C_s + I_s)/C_t]$	Agricultural Construction Relative to Socialized Construction and Installation $[C_a/C_s + I_s)]$	Nonagricultural Construction Relative to Total Construction $\{1-[C_s + I_s)/C_t]$ $[C_a/C_s + I_s)]\}$
	(1)	(2)	(3)
1933-37	105.4	11.1	88.3
1938-41, 1st Half	105.4	11.7	87.7
1941, 2nd Half-45	112.1	11.0	87.7
1946-50	105.2	13.4	85.9
1951	104.7	13.9	85.4
1952	104.5	12.5	86.9
1953	102.6	12.0	87.7
1954	103.0	13.5	86.1
1955	103.0	16.1	83.4
1956	103.4	15.4	84.1
1957	103.0	15.9	83.6
1958	103.2	15.3	84.2
1959	103.3	14.5	85.0
1960	103.4	13.5	86.0

*Coverage and price weights of the data are explained in the text.

riod, the ratios computed from them may indeed reflect the distribution of construction between the agricultural and nonagricultural sectors, even though the underlying series do not give an accurate picture of year-to-year change in real terms. But whether this is the case cannot be known until more information about the origins of the agricultural components of the series is available. That the results produced by the present use of the data are at least plausible is suggested by comparison with the calculations made above for 1928–37; see Table D–9. According to the latter, nonagricultural construction accounted for about 85–90 percent of total construction during 1928–37, as compared with 83–88 percent for 1938–60, as computed in Table D–10. For the five years 1933–37, for which the two calculations overlap, they yield about the same results, 87.8 percent from Table D–9 as opposed to 88.3 percent from Table D–10.

In computing annual figures for nonagricultural construction in Table D–8, the share figures obtained in Table D–10 for periods of several years' duration are assumed to hold for each year within a period.

For 1961, no independent information on the share of nonagricultural construction is available, and the 1960 figure is used.

Appendix E

Fixed Capital Investment

Projects in Progress

Table E–1 presents estimates of the value of fixed capital investment projects in progress. The figures reflect expenditures for new fixed assets which, although included in our investment and capital stock series, are not yet completed. They are intended to measure the difference between capital in place and capital available for operation.

This appendix explains the sources and methods underlying these estimates. In anticipation of that discussion, however, it may be helpful first to describe briefly the principal relevant Soviet accounting concepts. In part this recapitulates the discussion of Chapter 2, Section 3.

In Soviet accounts, and therefore in our calculations, capital investments are considered to have occurred as stages of the investment project are completed. When the work of preparing the site (or laying the foundation, or placing the roof) is finished, but not before, all expenditures made for the purpose are counted as part of investment. In the case of equipment, the investment is considered to occur as machines are taken from the warehouse of the project for the purpose of beginning installation or, for equipment requiring no installation, when the machines are first received into the project warehouse. Expenditures for installation enter the investment accounts as the emplacement of individual units of equipment or equipment aggregates is completed. For each project, a good deal of capital is put into place before the project as a whole is ready to begin operations. Our calculations include only the three elements just discussed: construction, installation, and equipment. Soviet series, it will be recalled, also contain "other" investments, including "investments not increasing the stock of fixed capital," of which it will be necessary to say more shortly.

Soviet accounts also record the value of "completed" capital investments. As with the concept of "capital investment," the governing criteria are accounting conventions and are to some extent arbitrary. The two components of "completed" investment are completed "investments which do not increase the stock of fixed capital" and "assets put into operation." The criteria of completion for "investments which do not increase the stock of fixed capital" are not known to us—nor are they significant for present purposes. With respect to "assets put into operation," equipment not re-

TABLE E-1

FIXED CAPITAL INVESTMENT PROJECTS IN PROGRESS,
IN ACQUISITION, 1937, 1928, AND 1950 PRICES, 1928-62
(January 1--Billion Rubles)

	Acquisition Prices	1937 Prices	1928 Prices	1950 Prices
	(1)	(2)	(3)	(4)
1928	1.57	3.03	1.63	8.17
1929	2.22	4.29	2.31	11.5
1930	3.09	5.91	3.27	16.0
1931	5.22	9.96	5.80	26.9
1932	8.02	12.5	7.72	32.9
1933	10.1	12.6	8.56	32.3
1934	10.8	12.7	9.28	31.8
1935	12.4	13.5	10.0	33.3
1936	11.6	12.1	9.07	29.8
1937	12.0	12.6	9.81	30.8
1938	13.8	14.1	11.5	33.9
1939	--	14.1	11.5	33.9
1940	--	14.1	11.5	33.9
1941	--	14.1	11.5	33.9
1944	--	5.1	4.4	11.4
1945	--	7.5	7.3	15.8
1946	--	10.3	11.4	20.9
1947	--	13.2	14.0	27.4
1948	--	16.4	16.2	34.9
1949	--	20.4	19.5	44.6
1950	--	25.6	23.6	57.3
1951	77.4	32.3	30.0	72.6
1952	91.4	41.1	37.1	92.5
1953	105.0	48.0	41.7	109.0
1954	117.0	55.1	47.9	124.0
1955	128.0	60.9	54.2	136.0
1956	137.0	69.0	63.2	153.0
1957	147.0	78.3	73.9	172.0
1958	161.0	86.1	81.2	189.0
1959	160.0	84.9	79.3	186.0
1960	174.0	90.8	84.3	198.0
1961	196.0	100.0	92.6	218.0
1962	--	107.1	99.4	232.3

quiring installation is apparently considered in the main to be put into operation as soon as received, which is to say, as soon as it enters the capital investment account. For construction, installation, and equipment requiring installation, a formal document drawn by a commission of inspection is issued to indicate the date. The document denotes the completion of all the work on a productive unit. In some cases, therefore, productive use of the asset begins while completion of the final stages of construction and installation work are still in progress, that is, before the actual issuance of the document. On the general concept of assets put into operation, see TsSU–44, pp. 202–3, and, with respect to the treatment of equipment not requiring installation, Savvin–59, p. 31.

Between these two streams lies a pool, known in Soviet parlance as "unfinished construction," which is augmented by the inflow of capital investments and depleted by the outflow of "completed" investments. The magnitude of this stock is also kept in Soviet accounts, though the information has not been published with much regularity. By comparing the inflow and outflow, we see that "unfinished construction" includes the following: (*i*) construction and installation work which has progressed to the point of completing some technical stage indicated by the project specifications, but not to the point of permitting actual operation of the asset to begin; (ii) equipment in the process of being installed or installed in structures not yet completed; (iii) "other" investments in progress; and (iv) assets not formally completed but in fact already in productive operation. This is also the scope as specified in Soviet sources; see, e.g., Savvin–59, pp. 27–28.

Of these four items, only the last, item (iv), operates as fixed capital. Item (iii) is excluded entirely from our calculations. Items (i) and (ii) we would prefer to treat as inventories. In addition, "unfinished construction" excludes, while our fixed capital stock estimates include, (v) equipment which does not require installation but which is still in the project warehouse, that is, which is inoperative because the project for which it is intended has not begun to function. Finally, as may also be convenient to recall, both our fixed capital estimates and the Soviet category "unfinished construction" exclude, while our inventory estimates include, (vi) equipment requiring installation which is still in the project warehouse and (vii) construction and installation work which has commenced but not yet progressed to the point of satisfying one of the prescribed technical stages necessary for classification as "capital investment."

The purpose of this appendix, then, is to estimate values for items (i), (ii), and (v), which may be subtracted from our estimates of fixed capital in place to obtain that available for operation. In the remaining sections of the appendix, we first derive a series in acquisition prices for "unfinished construction," according to the Soviet concept for selected years; from this, we estimate the value in acquisition prices of items (i), (ii), and (v); finally, by deflation and extrapolation, we obtain figures for all years in prices of 1937, 1928, and 1950.

"UNFINISHED CONSTRUCTION," SOVIET CONCEPT

The value of "unfinished construction" in acquisition prices is shown in Table E–2. The data refer to the socialized sector of the economy only.

We begin with the figures in the first column of the table. For 1933–35 and 1951–61, these are taken directly from Soviet statistical handbooks; see TsUNKhU–36, p. 393, and TsSU–61a, p. 126.

For 1928–32, Soviet sources report only the value of "unfinished construction" in large-scale industry, which is used together with data on the value of "unfinished construction" of industrial commissariats for 1933–35 in extrapolating total values backward from 1935. The industry data for 1928–32 are in Putilov–32, p. 105; for 1933–35 in TsUNKhU–36, p. 393. Although the scope of these two series does not precisely coincide, it is no doubt safe to assume that both include virtually all "unfinished construction" in industry (both also include housing built by industrial commissariats). The method of extrapolation is as follows: On January 1 of the years 1933–35, industry accounted for 56–62 percent of all "unfinished construction," the average for the three years being 59 percent. During the three years 1932–34, industry accounted for 49–53 percent of all capital investment, the average being 52 percent; see Kaplan–51, p. 91. The relative importance of industry in "unfinished construction" was about 13 percent greater than in investment. The volume of "unfinished construction" is presumably a function of the amount of investment in the preceding period and the length of the building cycle. We take it from the comparison just cited that the cycle in industry was greater than in the economy generally. Taking the January 1 share of "unfinished construction" in industry to be about 13 percent greater than industry's share in investment in the preceding year, we estimate the former shares as: for 1928, 54 percent; for 1929, 52 percent; for 1930, 51 percent; for 1931, 50 percent; for 1932, 57 percent. (The investment data used are of uniform scope and are from Kaplan–51, p. 91. The figures for 1927 include the last three months of 1926.) *Total* "unfinished construction" is then computed from the figures for industry only in Putilov–32, p. 105.

TABLE E-2

"UNFINISHED CONSTRUCTION" IN THE SOCIALIZED SECTOR,
IN ACQUISITION PRICES, 1928-38, 1951-61
(January 1--Billion Rubles)

	Varying Coverage[a] (1)	Adjusted Coverage[b] (2)
1928	1.66	1.61
1929	2.43	2.36
1930	3.47	3.37
1931	6.08	5.90
1932	9.41	9.13
1933	11.97	11.61
1934	12.85	12.46
1935	14.63	14.20
1936	13.78	13.37
1937	14.22	12.79
1938	16.4	15.9
1951	87	89
1952	102	105
1953	117	121
1954	129	134
1955	141	147
1956	150	158
1957	160	169
1958	176	185
1959	175	184
1960	190	200
1961	214	225

[a] Figures for 1928–38 include, while those for 1951–61 exclude, capital repairs and "unfinished construction" of collective farms.

[b] All figures exclude capital repairs and include "unfinished construction" of collective farms.

For 1936–37, we follow the method of computation shown in TsUNKhU–36, p. 393, which derives the annual increment in "unfinished construction" as (total investment) minus (special purpose expenditures) minus (capital investments put into operation). To obtain the January 1 stock of "unfinished construction" for 1936–37, we compute increments during 1935–36 from the following data: For total investment and investments put into operation, see *Planovoe khoziaistvo*, 1937:3, pp. 222–25. Special purpose expenditures are estimated from Moorsteen–62, pp. 422, 428, multiplying their relative importance in total investment by the absolute value of investment. The investment and "capital put into operation" data are of the scope of annual plan investment statistics and hence exclude some items included in the TsUNKhU–36 data: (*i*) certain outlays for small equipment and small repairs; (*ii*) housing repairs; (*iii*) collective-farm investments; and (*iv*) investment in kind in road-building (see Kaplan–51, p. 100). That the investment figures do include all "special purpose" expenditures may be inferred by comparing the figures of annual plan scope for 1933 and 1934 plus the listed omissions, given in Kaplan–51, pp. 98, 100, with the totals inclusive of special purpose expenditures in TsUNKhU–36, p. 393. The omitted categories apparently are not subject to special purpose expenditures; see TsUNKhU–36a, pp. 348–49. Accordingly, the increments computed for "unfinished construction" also exclude these categories. Judging from the increments indicated for 1933–35, the excluded increments for this period should be quite small; see TsUNKhU–36, p. 393.

For 1938, we again add the increment to "unfinished construction" realized during 1937 to the 1937 stock. Total investment in 1937 is taken as 29.5 billion rubles, assets put into operation as 26.5 billion, and special purpose expenditures as 0.8 billion. The increment to "unfinished construction," thus, is 2.2 billion rubles (29.5 − 26.5 − 0.8 = 2.2). The figures for investment and assets put into operation are from the 1938 budget reports in *Pravda*, August 11, 1938, and August 12, 1938, which give planned figures for 1938 relative to preliminary realized figures for 1937. Special purpose expenditures are not reported, and we use the 1936 figure. For this reason, and because the scope of reported investment was subject to (partially unknown) variation at this time, the increment calculated for 1937 is especially tentative (on the changes in investment reporting, see Kaplan–51, pp. 124–30).

As noted in Table E–2, the figures in column 1 are of varying coverage, in that the prewar data include, while the postwar exclude, capital repairs and "unfinished construction" of collective farms. Neither item is very large, but for the sake of consistency with our fixed capital estimates, adjustments are made (in column 2) to obtain a series intended uniformly to exclude capital repairs but include "unfinished construction" of collective farms.

In Table A–1, capital repairs in 1937 prices are shown as about 9 percent of all investment (including capital repairs) over the period 1928–37 as a whole. However, the construction time, and therefore the carry-over of "unfinished construction," for capital repairs must be substantially less than for new investment projects. We reduce the unadjusted series for "unfinished construction" for 1928–37 by 3 percent, to exclude capital repairs.

According to Garbuzov–57, p. 168, "unfinished construction" of collective farms as of the first of the year (in billion rubles) was 2.2 in 1951, 6.1 in 1955, 7.6 in 1956, and 8.5 in 1957. We estimate values for 1952–54 from the figures in column 1 by interpolating on the ratio of collective-farm to total noncollective-farm in 1951 and 1955. For 1958–61, the value of the collective-farm share is assumed to be 5 percent of total noncollective-farm, the proportion of 1957.

INVESTMENT PROJECTS IN PROGRESS IN ACQUISITION PRICES, 1928–38, 1951–61

On the basis of data for 1958, the only year for which they are available, we estimate the value of investment projects in progress in acquisition prices, socialized sector, for all years at 87 percent of "unfinished construction" according to the Soviet concept (Table E–2, column 2).

According to Savvin–59, p. 28, "unfinished construction" on January 1, 1958, was distributed as follows: construction and installation work, 80.0 percent; equipment in the process of installation, 9.6 percent; "other," 10.4 percent. Of this total, however, 7.5 percent was in assets which actually had begun to operate, even though not yet formally certified as "put in óperation." Eliminating the category "other," as not pertaining to our concept of investment or capital, and reducing the remainder by 7.5 percent, to exclude assets actually operating, we arrive at 82.9 percent of "unfinished construction" as consisting of investment projects in progress. This is increased to 87 percent to allow for equipment not requiring installation but not yet in operation. According to Savvin–59, p. 28, uninstalled equipment still in project warehouses was of about the same value as equipment in the process of installation in 1958, that is, equal to about 9.6 percent of all "unfinished construction." Of the total in warehouses, we take half as equipment requiring installation but not yet taken from the warehouse for the purpose—thus not yet in the capital investment or "unfinished construction" figures—and half as equipment not requiring installation—thus counted as "put into operation" as soon as received in the warehouse and hence included in capital investment but excluded from "unfinished construction." It is the latter half which we here wish to include in total work in progress. (The 87 percent figure cited results from a rounding downward of 87.7 which was inadvertent but of trivial consequence.)

As noted, the figures derived in the preceding paragraph refer to the socialized sector only. In the case of equipment and installation, however, the relative importance of the private sector is certain to be trivial. In the case of construction, it is noted that private investment activity in the period studied is restricted almost entirely to small houses and, in the earliest years, productive structures on peasant holdings. The building time for such structures is short and, given the seasonality of construction activity under Soviet climatic conditions, starts must tend to bunch in the spring and the carry-over of structures not yet put to use, as of January 1, must be very small. We assume it to amount to 10 percent of all private construction during the preceding year (as shown in Table A–7, column 7). For January 1, 1928, however, the January 1, 1929, figure is used. After 1932, the amounts decline to less than 1 percent of the socialized total and no further allowance is made for the private sector.

INVESTMENT PROJECTS IN PROGRESS IN CONSTANT PRICES, 1928–38, 1951–61

The acquisition price values (Table E–1, column 1) are deflated by the implied price indexes of the total investment series in Tables A–2 through A–5. The deflators are constructed on the assumption that work in progress at the first of the year consists essentially of investments made during the two preceding years, though with the proportion of carry-over from the later year greater in the ratio of 2/3. Thus, for example, to deflate the acquisition price figure for January 1, 1933, into 1937 prices, the deflator is the quotient of [2 × (1931 investment in 1937 prices) + 3 × (1932 investment in 1937 prices)] divided by [2 × (1931 investment in 1931 prices) + 3 × (1932 investment in 1932 prices)]. The weights are impressionistic. In part, however, we are guided by the discussion in Savvin–59, p. 32. For January 1, 1928 and 1929, however, the deflator used is computed from investment data for the year 1928 only.

INVESTMENT PROJECTS IN PROGRESS IN CONSTANT PRICES, 1939–41, 1944–50, 1962

We have discovered no quantitative information that bears directly on the stock of investment projects in progress during these years. The estimates in Table E–1, therefore, are extrapolations, made rather freely on the basis of the constant-price investment series (Tables A–2 through A–4).

In those tables it may be observed that investment in constant prices varied rather little during the period 1937–40. We assume that the real volume of work in progress at the beginning of the years 1939–41 remained at the level of January 1, 1938.

The estimates for 1944–50 and 1962 are based on the series in Table E–3, which shows work in progress related to investment in the two preceding years. The figures in the table are ratios, reflecting the same as-

TABLE E-3

FIXED CAPITAL INVESTMENT PROJECTS IN PROGRESS AT THE BEGINNING
OF THE YEAR RELATIVE TO INVESTMENTS MADE IN PRECEDING
TWO YEARS, 1930-62
(Percent)

1930	53.2
1931	64.3
1932	65.1
1933	61.8
1934	65.5
1935	67.5
1936	50.0
1937	39.1
1938	41.6
1939	43
1940	43
1941	43
1944	48
1945	50
1946	52
1947	54
1948	56
1949	58
1950	60
1951	62.7
1952	70.1
1953	76.1
1954	80.3
1955	78.5
1956	77.4
1957	76.2
1958	75.1
1959	66.1
1960	63.5
1961	64.7
1962	65

sumptions as the deflators explained in the preceding section. For each ratio, the numerator is work in progress on January 1, the denominator the sum of 60 percent of investment in the year just preceding plus 40 percent of investment in the year before that. The ratios in the table for 1930–41 and 1951–61 are computed from values in 1937 prices, though, because of our method of deflation, the results would be the same for 1928 or 1950 prices. The figures for 1944–50 are freehand extrapolations, backward from 1951. As the table shows, the ratio of work carried forward to work begun increases markedly during 1951–54. In part the rapidity of this rise must reflect dislocations associated with the Korean War. It does seem likely, however, that there was a continuing tendency throughout the period following World War II toward undertaking projects with lengthening completion cycles. Given the scarcity of investment funds and the priority that must have been given to rehabilitation, projects with short cycles no doubt predominated in the immediate postwar years, gradually giving way to larger and more lengthy projects as the 1950's approached. The ratios in the table are chosen to show a continuing increase during 1944–51, though at a slower rate than that observed for 1951–54. From 1959, there is no marked trend in the observed ratios, and we arbitrarily set the estimated ratio for 1962 at about the 1961 level. The absolute value of work in progress for 1944–50 and 1962, as shown in Table E–1, is computed for each set of constant prices by applying the ratio in Table E–3 to the appropriate investment figures in Tables A–2 through A–4. The ratios for 1930–41 in Table E–3 are shown for purposes of comparison but do not directly enter the calculations.

Appendix F

Average Realized Prices

of Livestock

The average realized livestock prices shown in Chapter 4, Table 4–2, are obtained as follows.

1928 PRICES

TsSU–29, pp. 134 and 166–67, gives the value in "1927 prices" and the number of private holdings of various kinds of livestock in 1926. The prices shown in Table 4–2 are calculated by dividing value by number. The source does not give the value of pigs separately, and this figure is calculated as the difference between the value of all livestock holdings and the kinds separately itemized (inadvertently, the price of pigs was entered in Table 4–2 as 11.5 rubles instead of the correct figure of 11.1; because the error is small and was discovered at a late date, it has been left uncorrected). The source gives only the total value of cows and other cattle, taken together. It is assumed, as for 1937 (see below), that prices for cows are approximately double that for other cattle. Although the data used refer to 1926, we take the resulting prices as representative also of 1928 price levels; see Karcz–57, p. 340, which indicates a change in the price of meat between the two years of only 4 percent.

1937 PRICES

The 1937 prices are estimates, derived from prices and quantities of livestock marketed in that year. The calculations for sheep, hogs, and cattle other than cows are shown in Table F–1. The price obtained there for sheep is used to value both sheep and goats. Sheep typically account for 85 percent or more of the total head of both kinds of animal; see TsSU–57c, p. 6. In recent years, procurement prices for goats have been about 15 percent below those for sheep; see Anoynmous–55, pp. 342, 474. The prices used for horses and cows are derived from the price for cattle other than cows by means of Soviet coefficients for conversion of various animals into "mature cattle equivalents." These place the value of a cow or horse as equivalent to two head of cattle fattening for slaughter; see TsSU–44, p.

91. It will be noted that the 1937 prices in Table F–1 are computed first per ton liveweight (row 5) and are thereafter converted into prices per head on the basis of average herd weights in 1932, the only year for which herd weight data are available.

TABLE F-1

DERIVATION OF AVERAGE PRICES PER HEAD OF CATTLE
OTHER THAN COWS, OF SHEEP, AND OF HOGS, IN 1937*

		Cattle Other than Cows	Sheep	Hogs
1.	Compulsory Deliveries by Collective Farms and Individuals:			
	1a. Marketings (thousand tons)	403	105	186
	1b. Price per Ton (rubles)	220	220	700
2.	State Purchases from Collective Farms and Individuals:			
	2a. Marketings (thousand tons)	571	148	263
	2b. Price per Ton (rubles)	1,370	1,630	2,650
3.	State Farm Deliveries:			
	3a. Marketings (thousand tons)	165	43	76
	3b. Price per Ton (rubles)	242	242	770
4.	Collective-Farm Market Sales of Livestock on the Hoof:			
	4a. Marketings (thousand tons)	412	165	263
	4b. Price per Ton (rubles)	1,900	2,400	3,600
5.	Average Realized Price per Ton (rubles)	1,092	1,455	2,325
6.	Average Weight of Herds, on the Hoof, in 1932 (kg.)	179	33	60
7.	Average Price per Head (rubles)	195	48	140

*Prices and marketings refer to live weights.

In this, our practice differs from that followed by the source from which most of our price and marketing data are drawn, Karcz–57, in which an average liveweight price for all meat is computed from prices of five kinds of marketings, the four in Table F–1 plus collective-farm sales of meat in cuts. In addition, we take account of the revised price estimates in Karcz–61. As a result of these differences, our average livestock prices also differ both in level and structure from those in Bergson–61, p. 394, which are based on the data in Karcz–57. The average liveweight price for all meat marketings in 1937 in the latter source (p. 33) is 1900 rubles per ton, whereas the average implied by our estimates is just under 1500 rubles, or about 20 percent less.

Sources to Table F–1

Rows 1a, 2a, 3a, 4a (marketings): The data are from Karcz–57, which gives the total in million tons of meat sold under each type of marketing (p. 284), and the percentage distribution by kind of animal (pp. 288, 296). Collective-farm marketings of livestock on the hoof include animals sold live and also sales of meat in cuts. The price differential between these two kinds of sales is interpreted as a charge for slaughtering, butchering, and sale in small quantities.

Rows 1b, 2b, 3b, 4b (prices): The compulsory delivery prices are from the same source (p. 288), but reduced by 12 percent to take account of the revised estimate in Karcz–61, p. 22. State purchase prices are from Karcz–57, p. 289. We follow Karcz–57 in setting state farm delivery prices 10 percent above compulsory delivery prices (pp. 292–93); in deriving the liveweight prices of animals sold on the hoof on collective-farm markets from meat prices (p. 296) by using the liveweight to slaughter-weight factors of 2.22 for cattle and sheep, 1.5 for hogs (p. 288); and in assuming that prices for animals sold on the hoof were about 60 percent of prices for meat sold in cuts (pp. 296–97).

Row 5: The prices for each kind of animal in rows 1–4 are averaged, using the marketing data as weights.

Row 6: The average weights for cattle and hogs are from Gosplan–36, pp. 598–99; the figures shown are weighted averages for state-farm and collective-farm herds for 1932. For sheep, a figure for 1932 average slaughter weight is used; see TsUNKhU–36, p. 216.

Row 7: The average weight (row 6) is multiplied by the average price per ton (row 5).

1950 AND 1955 PRICES

Hoeffding–59, p. 60, gives average realized prices for cows, other cattle, hogs, sheep and goats, obtained by means of price index numbers from those for 1937 in Bergson–61, p. 394. As noted above, the 1937 prices in the latter source are not entirely consistent with ours, either in structure or level. We adjust for the difference in level by reducing the cited prices by 20 percent, but retain the structure to illustrate differences in the measurement of the value of livestock herds produced by varying relative price weights. The prices shown in Table 4–2 are rounded. For horses, we use the prices for cows.

1958 PRICES

The prices for cows, other cattle, hogs, and sheep and goats are from Nimitz–62, p. 28, but here are rounded. For horses, the price of cows is used.

Appendix G

Inventories in Current Prices

This appendix consists solely of explanations of the derivation of the estimates in current prices shown in Table G–1. The general logic of our interpretation of data drawn from Soviet sources and of various estimating procedures is discussed in Chapter 5 and not repeated here. The table, it should be noted, omits inventories in nonstate agriculture and inventories of uninstalled equipment, n.e.c., for which we do not make current-price estimates. The explanations are arranged by dates.

1928–30

The estimates for these three years commence from data, largely reported, for October 1, 1927, 1928, and 1929, which are assembled in Table G–2. The October 1 figures provide the basis for January 1 estimates, which are presented in Table G–3. Adjustments for coverage are made in the latter to arrive at the estimates shown in Table G–1.

Sources to Table G–2

Most of the figures shown in the table appear both in Gosplan–29, p. 432, and in Rozentul–29, p. 307, though there are some minor differences between the two. Both sources (p. 434 in the first and p. 303 in the second) give partial descriptions of the origins of the data, from which it is evident that they are of very unequal reliability. Some of the data are from enterprise balance sheets; some are extrapolations from past periods or related sectors or sample surveys; some are derived from norms or are simply "expert appraisals." On the whole, the data appear to have some objective basis, but they cannot be highly accurate. The figures are described as for "commodity-material" assets and are clearly exclusive of goods shipped.

One deficiency in the data is that those for 1929 are planned rather than realized and those for 1928 are probably preliminary rather than final. The probable error from this source can be tested by the following comparisons. Total nonagricultural inventories according to Gosplan–29 were 7.87, 8.53, and 9.41 billion rubles on the three successive dates under consideration. In Gosplan–30, pp. 420–21, which contains no sector breakdowns, total nonagricultural inventories are given as 7.35, 7.98 and 8.85 billion, and the figure for 1929 is described as "preliminary." Although the figures from the later source are smaller (for reasons not known), they are smaller by an almost constant percentage. Also, as is explained below,

TABLE G-1

INVENTORIES IN CURRENT PRICES, BY SECTORS*, 1928-62
(January 1--Billion Rubles)

	1928	1929	1930	1931	1932	1933	1934	1935	1936	1937	1938
Producer Goods Industries											
Inventories on Hand	2.50	2.87	3.43	4.31	6.44	8.4	9.8	12.4	16.0	22.3	25.0
Goods Shipped	0.42	0.48	0.57	0.72	1.07	1.4	1.7	2.0	2.9	4.1	4.5
Consumer Goods Industries											
Inventories on Hand	3.20	3.25	3.01	3.84	5.56	7.2	8.4	9.2	15.7	19.6	20.9
Goods Shipped	0.71	0.72	0.67	0.85	1.24	1.6	2.1	1.9	4.0	5.0	5.2
Transportation and Communications											
Inventories on Hand	0.74	0.76	0.79	--	1.8	1.9	2.2	2.7	3.4	3.1	3.0
State Agriculture											
Inventories on Hand	0.05	0.11	0.14	--	1.7	2.2	2.4	2.9	4.2	4.6	5.0
Goods Shipped	0.00	0.00	0.00	--	0.0	0.0	0.0	0.0	0.1	0.1	0.1
Procurement											
Inventories on Hand	0.36	0.51	0.67	--	1.3	1.4	1.6	2.0	3.2	2.5	2.9
Goods Shipped	0.03	0.04	0.05	--	0.1	0.1	0.3	0.3	0.6	0.5	0.6
Domestic Trade											
Inventories on Hand	2.36	2.61	2.80	--	4.3	5.9	6.9	9.3	13.3	16.8	19.3
Goods Shipped	0.24	0.27	0.28	--	0.4	0.6	0.7	0.8	1.3	1.7	1.9
Contract Construction											
Inventories on Hand	0.04	0.06	0.09	--	--	--	--	--	--	--	--
Other Nonagricultural Sectors											
Inventories on Hand	0.20	0.22	0.24	--	1.5	1.5	1.7	1.7	1.8	2.1	2.2
Goods Shipped	0.01	0.01	0.02	--	0.1	0.1	0.2	0.2	0.2	0.2	0.2
Total											
Inventories on Hand, Excluding Contract Construction	9.41	10.33	11.17	--	22.6	28.5	33.0	40.2	57.6	71.0	78.3
Inventories on Hand, Including Contract Construction	9.45	10.39	11.26	--	--	--	--	--	--	--	--
Goods Shipped	1.41	1.52	1.59	--	2.9	3.8	5.0	5.2	9.1	11.6	12.5

*Inventories in nonstate agriculture and inventories of uninstalled equipment, n.e.c., are omitted.

TABLE G-1 (continued)

INVENTORIES IN CURRENT PRICES, BY SECTORS*, 1928-62
(January 1--Billion Rubles)

	1939	1940	1941	1944	1945	1946	1947	1948	1949	1950	1951
Producer Goods Industries											
Inventories on Hand	28.7	33.7	39.9	--	--	51.3	56.6	63.8	112.0	104.9	113.5
Goods Shipped	4.8	6.3	9.7	--	--	11.0	11.4	12.6	21.7	19.7	20.9
Consumer Goods Industries											
Inventories on Hand	25.0	30.8	26.7	--	--	19.2	19.9	24.1	43.2	59.1	59.0
Goods Shipped	5.9	8.2	9.5	--	--	5.9	5.9	6.9	12.1	16.0	15.5
Transportation and Communications											
Inventories on Hand	2.8	4.0	3.8	--	--	4.1	4.7	5.2	7.3	6.1	6.7
State Agriculture											
Inventories on Hand	6.6	7.0	6.7	--	--	4.6	5.7	5.3	--	--	9.3
Goods Shipped	0.1	0.1	0.1	--	--	0.1	0.1	0.1	--	--	0.2
Procurement											
Inventories on Hand	3.5	2.9	3.4	--	--	4.6	4.4	5.9	7.9	9.0	8.3
Goods Shipped	0.7	0.6	1.0	--	--	1.1	1.0	1.3	1.7	1.9	1.7
Domestic Trade											
Inventories on Hand	18.9	20.4	24.9	10.3	14.1	19.6	29.0	40.8	63.2	76.1	67.4
Goods Shipped	1.8	2.1	3.4	1.4	1.9	2.6	3.7	5.2	7.5	8.4	6.8
Contract Construction											
Inventories on Hand	--	--	3.7	--	--	--	4.9	--	--	--	10.6
Other Nonagricultural Sectors											
Inventories on Hand	2.2	2.8	3.3	--	--	2.9	5.7	6.7	6.7	7.6	9.5
Goods Shipped	0.2	0.3	0.4	--	--	0.3	0.6	0.7	0.7	0.8	1.1
Total											
Inventories on Hand, Excluding Contract Construction	87.7	101.6	108.7	95.8	98.3	106.3	126.0	151.8	--	--	273.7
Inventories on Hand, Including Contract Construction	--	--	112.4	--	--	--	130.9	--	--	--	284.3
Goods Shipped	13.5	17.6	24.1	18.9	19.4	21.0	22.7	26.8	--	--	46.2

TABLE G-1 (concluded)

INVENTORIES IN CURRENT PRICES, BY SECTORS*, 1928-62
(January 1--Billion Rubles)

	1952	1953	1954	1955	1956	1957	1958	1959	1960	1961	1962
Producer Goods Industries											
Inventories on Hand	122.0	139.6	152.5	151.8	134.6	137.3	148.1	166.1	179.6	200.1	228
Goods Shipped	22.0	24.6	26.5	26.3	24.0	25.2	25.0	27.4	30.5	33.0	37
Consumer Goods Industries											
Inventories on Hand	62.6	65.0	71.0	71.6	81.5	99.6	110.0	130.1	138.0	147.6	152
Goods Shipped	15.9	15.8	16.9	16.9	20.9	24.9	25.7	31.2	32.1	34.0	36
Transportation and Communications											
Inventories on Hand	7.0	6.7	8.1	6.9	7.7	7.0	7.9	8.9	9.8	10.1	12
State Agriculture											
Inventories on Hand	--	9.2	11.5	10.9	13.9	14.1	19.0	21.6	26.6	31.7	36
Goods Shipped	--	0.1	0.1	0.1	0.1	0.1	0.2	0.2	0.3	0.4	0
Procurement											
Inventories on Hand	8.3	10.8	6.6	7.1	8.0	15.3	13.0	18.3	37.5	43.9	49
Goods Shipped	1.7	2.3	1.5	1.7	1.9	3.5	2.7	3.3	5.5	6.5	7
Domestic Trade											
Inventories on Hand	82.0	98.9	99.4	92.7	108.5	126.1	132.4	165.1	192.2	200.2	226
Goods Shipped	7.6	8.4	7.7	6.4	6.7	7.4	7.1	8.2	8.4	8.8	10
Contract Construction											
Inventories on Hand	13.5	14.9	17.9	17.2	17.6	19.5	21.7	22.1	25.7	28.0	30
Other Nonagricultural Sectors											
Inventories on Hand	11.8	9.7	6.0	7.8	8.8	13.5	17.2	19.4	27.2	28.8	32
Goods Shipped	1.3	1.1	0.7	0.9	1.0	1.5	1.9	2.1	3.0	3.2	3
Total											
Inventories on Hand, Excluding Contract Construction	--	339.9	355.1	348.8	363.0	412.9	447.6	529.5	610.9	662.4	735
Inventories on Hand, Including Contract Construction	--	354.8	373.0	366.0	380.6	432.4	469.3	551.6	636.6	690.4	765
Goods Shipped	--	52.3	53.4	52.3	54.6	62.6	62.6	72.4	79.9	85.9	93

TABLE G-2

REPORTED INVENTORIES ON HAND, BY SECTORS,
IN CURRENT PRICES, 1927-29
(October 1--Billion Rubles)

	1927	1928	1929
Industry, Excluding Syndicates	4.06	4.64	4.78
State (Census).	3.88	4.41	4.50
Planned VSNKh.	3.23	3.68	3.79
Private	0.04	0.04	0.04
Raional Power Stations.	0.05	0.05	0.05
Industrial Co-operatives.	0.09	0.14	0.19
Syndicates	0.50	0.55	0.67
Industry, Including Syndicates	4.56	5.19	5.45
Producer Goods	2.02	2.39	2.86
Consumer Goods.	2.54	2.80	2.59
Transportation and Communications.	0.50	0.50	0.52
State Agriculture	0.26	0.31	0.40
Procurement	0.39	0.55	0.71
Trade	2.06	2.26	2.49
State	0.64	0.68	0.75
Co-operative	0.92	1.24	1.43
Private	0.50	0.34	0.31
Contract Construction	0.03	0.05	0.07
Other Nonagricultural Sectors.	0.18	0.20	0.22
Total.	7.98	9.06	9.86

the figures used in the table for VSNKh industry are from a later source and are realized.

Industry, excluding Syndicates: Computed sum of components.

State (Census) Industry: Gosplan–29, p. 432, gives figures of 3.664, 3.834, and 4.132 billion rubles for the three years in sequence. These are assumed to be understated by the same proportion in each year as are the data for VSNKh industry (see below).

Planned VSNKh Industry: The data for this sector are from Putilov–32, p. 103 (see also, for the dating of the figures cited, p. 112). The author asserts, p. 102, that earlier figures were understated (the Gosplan–29 figures are 3.051, 3.200, and 3.478).

Private Industry, Industrial Co-operatives, Raional Power Stations: Gosplan–29, p. 432. Rozentul includes industrial co-operatives in trade, on the grounds (p. 303) that it is difficult to distinguish their industrial from their trade operations. We include them with industry for greater consistency with our treatment of them in later years. They are not large enough, in any case, to much affect the results.

Syndicates: Rozentul–29, pp. 305 and 307, gives figures for VSNKh industry inclusive and exclusive of syndicates and for state trade inclusive and exclusive of syndicates. The two sets of syndicate figures that can be computed as residuals diverge slightly from one another and their averages are used here.

It should be noted that recent Soviet publications provide data for these years that differ somewhat from those accepted here. Rubinshtein–58, p. 47, gives inventories in state industry, inclusive of syndicates, as 3.9 billion

on October 1, 1927. Atlas–52, p. 67, gives inventories in VSNKh industry
as 3.98 billion on October 1, 1928. There is no reason to suppose these
figures are superior to those used.

Industry, including Syndicates: Computed sum of industry excluding
syndicates and syndicates. The industry totals are repeated in the table in
order to show the division between producer and consumer goods.

Producer and Consumer Goods Industries: Putilov–32, *loc. cit.*, divides
his VSNKh totals between "A" and "B" sectors. We estimate producer
goods industry as the sum of his "A" industry inventories, raional power
stations, and a proportion of inventories held by syndicates equal to the
"A" share in VSNKh industry. All other industrial inventories are attributed to consumer goods. The distribution of syndicate inventories is
arbitrary, but we have no direct evidence on the point, and we hesitate
to be guided here by the division of inventories in sales-supply in later
years.

Transportation and Communications: Gosplan–29, p. 432. These figures are slightly in error, since the source indicates (p. 434) that data for
water transport are for January 1.

State Agriculture: Data are taken from Rozentul–29, p. 307, because
figures for this sector in Gosplan–29 are indicated (p. 434) to be for January 1. The data cover only state farms.

Procurement: We enter here data given in Gosplan–29, p. 432, for
"agricultural co-operatives." This procedure is highly questionable and, at
best, makes the figures for procurement in this period incomparable with
those for later years. The agricultural co-operatives were procurement organizations, for procurements from the private peasantry, but they also
performed trade and credit operations (cf. Kistanov–57, pp. 79–80). On the
other hand, state procurement organizations are presumably included in
the data for other sectors. The two errors may be roughly offsetting.

Domestic Trade: Total trade is the sum of components. State trade is
computed by deducting from the figures given in Gosplan–29, p. 432, the
estimates for syndicates made above (that syndicates are included here is
clear from Rozentul). Consumer co-operatives and private trade are also
from the Gosplan source.

We hereafter treat the trade figures as for domestic trade alone, though
this may be incorrect. Foreign trade is not explicitly accounted for in our
sources.

Contract Construction: Gosplan–29, p. 432.

Other Nonagricultural Sectors: Figures are the sums of those given in
Gosplan–29, p. 432, for housing co-operatives (which in fact are for January 1) and for municipal economy. These may not much resemble the
components of the "other" category in later years which, in particular, are
inclusive of foreign trade.

Of all the sectors shown in Gosplan–29, we omit banks (the assets of
which are shown inclusive of precious metals and foreign exchange), governmental organs (trivial amounts are shown, and such bodies are thought
to be excluded from data for later years), and private and collective-farm
agriculture.

Total: Sum of components.

Sources to Table G–3

As noted, we undertake in Table G–3 to estimate inventories for January 1 from those obtained in Table G–2 for the preceding October 1. Basically, our procedure is interpolation or extrapolation with crude adjustments for seasonal variations in the more important sectors.

Producer and Consumer Goods Industries: For 1928 and 1929, we proceed as follows. From graphs given in *Statisticheskoe obozrenie*, 1930:5, p. 172, it is possible to read approximate monthly values for the gross output of large-scale state industry, in 1926/27 prices (million rubles):

Date	Producer Goods	Consumer Goods
October, 1927 345		445
December, 1927 345		500
January, 1928 352		510
September, 1928 380		490
October, 1928 430		515
December, 1928 425		570
January, 1929 435		590
September, 1929 510		615
October, 1929 560		665

From these data, we interpolate 1st-of-month figures from contiguous monthly totals (percentage changes from September to October, 1927, are assumed the same as in 1928). We compare the January 1 figures so computed with those that would result from straight-line interpolations from October 1 data. We assume the percentage difference between actual and interpolated production—for industry of this limited coverage and in nominally constant prices—is also the percentage difference between actual inventories and those that can be interpolated from the Table G–2 figures for October 1.

For 1930, we assume that the percentage increase in inventories during 1929 was equal to that during 1928/29 (Table G–2). This is a questionable assumption, but it is thought that the major changes occurring shortly after

TABLE G-3

UNADJUSTED ESTIMATES OF INVENTORIES ON HAND, BY SECTORS,
IN CURRENT PRICES, 1928-30
(January 1--Billion Rubles)

	1928	1929	1930
Producer Goods Industries	2.14	2.46	2.94
Consumer Goods Industries................	2.92	2.97	2.75
Transportation and Communications	0.50	0.51	0.53
State Agriculture........................	0.05	0.10	0.13
Procurement	0.35	0.49	0.64
Domestic Trade	2.25	2.49	2.67
State	0.69	0.74	0.83
Co-operative.........................	1.06	1.38	1.59
Private	0.50	0.37	0.25
Contract Construction....................	0.03	0.05	0.07
Other Nonagricultural Sectors	0.19	0.21	0.23
Total...........................	8.43	9.28	9.96

October, 1929, would not, with the possible exception of collectivization, have had much impact before the beginning of 1930.

Transportation and Communications: 1928 and 1929 are straight-line interpolations from the Table G–2 data. 1930 is estimated as for industry.

State Agriculture: 1928 and 1929 are from Gosplan–29, p. 432 (see notes for Table G–2). 1930 is estimated as for industry.

Procurement: As a pure guess, figures on January 1 are assumed 10 percent below the preceding October 1 (see discussion of this sector in notes for Table G–2).

Domestic Trade: Monthly percentage changes in inventories in trade, wholesale and retail, for state, co-operative, and private trade separately, were reported monthly in *Statisticheskoe obozrenie* until early 1930 (data used here are taken from issues of 1927:11 to 1930:2). These were based on reports from a limited number of trading enterprises, covered stocks of finished goods for sale only, and not all of the latter (see Fomin–28, pp. 67 ff.). Though it is not entirely clear, the way the percentages are used in context suggests that they refer to monthly average inventories. If the monthly changes are linked in sequence and 1st-of-month figures interpolated, the following indexes can be computed (October 1, 1927 = 100):

Date	State		Co-operative		Private	
	Wholesale	*Retail*	*Wholesale*	*Retail*	*Wholesale*	*Retail*
Oct. 1, 1927......100.0		100.0	100.0	100.0	100.0	100.0
Jan. 1, 1928......119.9		101.1	121.6	108.8	102.0	99.0
Oct. 1, 1928......107.4		106.8	136.9	123.2	62.8	73.8
Jan. 1, 1929......132.2		118.0	150.1	142.8	79.8	76.0
Oct. 1, 1929......135.1		149.1	151.0	162.3	52.6	70.8
Jan. 1, 1930......185.0		155.9	178.3	175.6	36.4	59.6

Except for state trade from October 1, 1928 to 1929, the changes indicated by these series correspond closely to those shown by the data in Table G–2.

No data are available on the division of total inventories in each sector between wholesale and retail trade. As a rough guess, based largely on data for later years (see Table K–1), we assume that wholesale trade accounted for one third of total inventories in each sector on October 1, 1927. Given this, an index for total inventories can be computed for each sector.

For January 1, 1928 and 1929, we assume that figures interpolated from the October 1 data of Table G–2 understate true inventories by the same percentages as do similar interpolations from the series composed above (approximately 5–10 percent).

For January 1, 1930, we accept the changes indicated by the above series from October 1, 1929, to January 1, 1930, for co-operative and private trade. For state trade, we assume that the increase between these two dates was the same as that in co-operative trade (11.3 percent), since that indicated for state trade (14.7 percent) appears dubious in the light of the 1928/29 figures.

Total trade inventories are sums of components.

Contract Construction: Though the trend in construction inventories was sharply upward, there is probably a substantial seasonal decline between October 1 and January 1. We therefore assume inventories unchanged from the preceding October 1.

Other: For 1928 and 1929, interpolated from Table G–2 data; 1930 is estimated as for industry.

Total: Computed sum of components.

Derivation of Table G–1 Estimates

In Table G–1, the figures for January 1, 1928–30, are derived from those in Table G–3 as follows:

(*i*) Small tools are assumed to have accounted for the same share of the value of total inventories on hand as in 1937 or, for contract construction, 1951 (see Table H–1 and the accompanying discussion). For other nonagricultural sectors, for which no estimate is included in Table H–1, we make an arbitrary upward adjustment of 5 percent.

(*ii*) No adjustment is made for expenses of future periods. Descriptions given in the sources of the October 1 data do not explicitly include such assets and quite strongly suggest their exclusion (cf. Rozentul–29, p. 301; Putilov–32, pp. 101 and 112). Other sources from this period which give more detailed breakdowns of short-term assets do not include an item for expenses of future periods (cf. VSNKh–27, pp. 398 ff.; *Economic Survey,* February 15, 1930, p. 2), though these may be included in another category. According to Shenger–40, p. 58, expenses of future periods were among those assets for which the STO decree of July 23, 1931, provided financing solely from owned working capital, and the earliest reference we have observed to the account is in a 1931 source, Khavin–31, p. 8. We do not know, however, but what the account was in use earlier.

(*iii*) No attempt is made to correct for the possible inclusion of some livestock in the inventory figures for state agriculture.

(*iv*) Goods shipped are estimated on the assumption that their ratio to inventories on hand in each sector was the same as in 1933.

1931–32

We estimate industrial inventories for both of these years but inventories in other sectors for 1932 only. We commence with the estimates for industry, for inventories on hand only.

According to Putilov–32, p. 103, VSNKh inventories on January 1, 1931, were 4,892 million (see the discussion of this source in notes for 1928–30). According to Atlas–58, p. 124, "material values" in VSNKh industries increased during 1931 by 2,313 million, which implies a January 1, 1932, total of 7,205. We expand these figures to derive inventories in all industry, both state and co-operative.

(*i*) On October 1, 1929 (see Table G–2), syndicate inventories amounted to 17.7 percent of those in VSNKh. We assume the same ratio held on January 1, 1931 and 1932.

(*ii*) On October 1, 1929, VSNKh and syndicates combined accounted for 81.8 percent of inventories in all industry (Table G–2). On January 1, 1933, state industry other than local accounted for 79.9 percent of inventories in all industry (Table G–4, except that industrial co-operatives are extrapolated on bank loans from 1937; on the latter, see notes for 1933–39). We assume that the appropriate ratio for 1931 and 1932 is 80.0 percent.

(*iii*) We divide the totals so derived between producer and consumer goods industries. For 1931, this is done on the basis of data for "A" and "B" Groups in VSNKh, given in Putilov, *loc. cit.*, by the same procedures as for Table G–2. The further assumption is required here that inventories in raional power stations changed from October 1, 1929, in proportion to those in VSNKh industries. For 1932, we interpolate a distribution on a straight line from those for 1931 (as described) and 1933 (Table G–4 and the estimate referred to for co-operatives).

(*iv*) We adjust for the omission of small tools by assuming their share in the value of total inventories in both industrial sectors was the same as in 1937 (see Table H–1 and the explanatory notes thereto). Since these estimates, which are those entered in Table G–1 for inventories on hand, derive basically from Putilov, no adjustment for expenses of future periods appears in order (see notes for 1928–30).

For sectors other than industry, in 1932, we extrapolate inventories on hand and goods shipped in combination from 1933 on bank loans (Table I–1). Because of the nearness of this date to the end of the Credit Reform, the procedure is unlikely to be accurate. Loans to foreign trade are included with other nonagricultural sectors.

Though total loans on goods shipped are available for both 1932 and 1933 (Table J–1), we hesitate to extrapolate goods shipped on the corresponding loans because of the likelihood that loans for this purpose were not yet at their normal level by the beginning of 1932. Instead, we extrapolate goods shipped by sectors from 1933 on inventories on hand, for the industrial sectors, or on inventories on hand plus goods shipped, for other sectors. The resulting total for goods shipped, 2.9, compares with a figure of 2.1 that would result from extrapolation on loans on goods shipped. There is an obvious inconsistency here in utilizing bank loans to estimate total inventories and not the goods-shipped component, but the discrepancy is small for the total and may be offset by other peculiarities in the loan figures for 1932.

In 1931, loan data are clearly unusable as extrapolators because of the effects of the Credit Reform then in progress, and we have no other data for nonindustrial sectors. For industry, we assume the ratio of goods shipped to inventories on hand was the same as in 1933.

Other data for these two years which are available but are not employed in the foregoing estimates include the following:

(*i*) Campbell–58a, p. 4, cites S. Rubinshtein, *Oborotnye sredstva*, 2nd edition, Moscow, 1934, p. 33, to the effect that, in 1932, short-term liabilities consisted 44.2 percent of owned working capital, 36.8 percent of bank loans, and 19 percent of other sources, and, p. 31, that industry accounted for 57.3 percent of the total working capital assets of the socialized economy. Any reliable estimate of total inventories from these data is forestalled by the existence of two different loan totals for 1932 (see notes to Table I–1), by the strong possibility that the sector coverage is restricted (see notes for 1933–39), and by the lack of any information on the ratio of inventories to total assets or liabilities. Rough computations made on various assumptions suggest that Rubinshtein's data are reasonably consistent with the estimates made here.

(*ii*) A similar conclusion can be drawn for a figure for the increase of "working capital" during 1932 of 4.1 billion rubles, which appears in Gosplan–34, Vol. 1, p. 541. This is probably for owned capital and is likely to be restricted in sector coverage. Its order of magnitude appears consistent with the 1932 increase implied by the Table G–1 estimates.

(*iii*) Omel'chenko–39, p. 12, cites a figure from a 1931 source of 4,475 million rubles for "mobile working capital" of "combines of Union industry," evidently within VSNKh, on January 1, 1931. This appears consistent with Putilov's somewhat larger figure for the whole of VSNKh industry.

(*iv*) Campbell–58a, *loc. cit.*, cites from D. Shvartsman, "Finansovyi plan promyshlennosti v 1931 godu," *Finansy i sotsialisticheskoe khoziaistvo*, 1931:36, pp. 13–16, a figure for the increase of industrial inventories during 1931 of 2.8 billion. Assuming that the coverage of this figure is somewhat broader, it appears consistent with the increase of 2.3 billion in VSNKh alone cited from Atlas.

In addition to the foregoing, there are several inventory series, running from the late 1920's into the years considered here, which we cannot reconcile at all with other published data:

(*i*) Ragol'skii–32, p. 142, gives figures, in context as though of quite comprehensive coverage, for annual increases of "so-called supplies," of 1,446 million in 1928, 1,346 in 1929, 2,143 in 1930, and 2,300 in 1931. The figures for 1930 and 1931 appear totally implausible.

(*ii*) Atlas–52, p. 150, indicates that "material stocks" in VSNKh industry on October 1, 1930, were 89 percent, and on October 1, 1931, 195 percent, above the level of October 1, 1929. The VSNKh data we have used (from Putilov–32 and Atlas–58) indicate totals on January 1, 1931, 29 percent and on January 1, 1932, 90 percent, above those of October 1, 1929.

(*iii*) Somewhat similar data are given in Golev–47, p. 117, for "material stocks" in heavy VSNKh industry. Relative to October 1, 1928, these are indicated to have increased by 31 percent by October 1, 1929, by 96 percent by January 1, 1931, and by 193 percent by January 1, 1932. The figures used here imply increases to the same dates of 17, 51, and roughly 125 percent.

It is perhaps worth noting that the annual increases implied by Atlas' data for 1930/31 and by Golev's for 1931 are quite consistent with our data for 1931 above. The discrepancies arise in the earlier years.

1933–39

Our estimates for these years rest on a considerable body of reported data, the meaning and coverage of which, however, are exceedingly ambiguous. We have attempted in Table G–4 to identify and fit together the various reported figures, by detailed sectors, without undertaking there to adjust for minor deficiencies in coverage or to fill in all gaps with estimates. The table does include some estimates, made to assist in the identification of reported data. To move from the Table G–4 figures to those entered in Table G–1, we estimate missing figures, make adjustments for uniformity of coverage, and consolidate the detailed data for major sectors, all by procedures which are described at the end of the notes for this period.

The reason for treating at one time so long a span of years as 1933–39 is that the several sources to be reconciled cover overlapping portions of that period. Because of the character of the data, the process of inferring their meaning and coverage can more easily be described in terms of their sources than by dates or categories. Hence, the notes to Table G–4, which follow, are arranged by sources. In general, however, we commence with sources relating to 1936 and work outward from that date. Also, we have indicated in Table G–4 the location of the notes which explain the derivation of each figure.

For interpretations of much of these same data which differ considerably from those made here, see Campbell–58a, pp. 5 ff.

Sources to Table G–4

Sobol'–37: This source provides the following information:

(*i*) (p. 137) The total working capital of producing *khozraschet* enterprises (excluding construction) subordinate to economic commissariats and institutions was 51.9 billion rubles on January 1, 1935, 69.8 on January 1, 1936.

In context, it is clear that these figures refer to total assets, physical and financial. Besides the indicated exclusion of construction, there is a reference subsequently in the source (p. 150) to the exclusion of collective farms. The exclusion of private agriculture is implied by the stated coverage of the data (we assume hereafter, throughout the remainder of this appendix, that private agriculture is omitted from all data). Though the source gives no evidence of further exclusions, we conclude below (see notes on Usoskin–39) that the 1936 total of 69.8 billion excludes also industrial co-operatives, transportation and communications, and minor "other" sectors.

Sobol' notes, p. 137, that his 1935 and 1936 figures for total assets imply an increase in the course of 1935 of 17.9 billion rubles and adds that the increase exclusive of monetary assets and *debitory* was 16 billion.

(*ii*) (p. 143) In 1936, goods in process and semifabricates for the entire economy were 8,391.5 million rubles.

(*iii*) (p. 145) In 1936, total finished products were 21,313 million, of which industry held 5,682.9, sales-supply 3,531.2, and trade 11,077.4. Of the total, 1,022 million is unaccounted for. Given the conclusion referred to above on the sector coverage of Sobol's data, this latter residual must represent procurement and state agriculture.

(*iv*) (p. 150) In 1936, total *debitory* were 7,952.7 million, of which *state* industry, presumably excluding sales-supply, held 2,090.3. The latter figure is given also as 7.0 percent of the total assets of state industry, implying a figure for the latter of about 29.9 billion.

(*v*) (p. 151) In 1936, "goods unpaid for" in *state* industry amounted to 765 million rubles. This category, which does not appear in our other sources, is described by Sobol' as similar to *debitory*, representing goods shipped which have not been paid for in the time legally allowed because of a lack of money on the part of the buyer. This presumably is elsewhere included with *debitory*.

TABLE G-4

REPORTED NORMED ASSETS AND GOODS SHIPPED, BY SECTORS,
IN CURRENT PRICES, 1933-39
(January 1--Billion Rubles)

	1933		1934		1935		1936		1937		1938		1939	
	Normed	Normed and Shipped	Normed	Normed and Shipped	Normed	Normed and Shipped	Normed	Normed and Shipped	Normed	Normed and Shipped	Normed	Normed and Shipped	Normed	Normed and Shipped
State Industry, Excluding														
Sales-Supply	--	--	--	--	--	--	23.4[a]	25.7[a]	32.4[a]	36.8[a]	38.8[a]	43.8[a]	--	--
Sales-Supply	--	--	--	--	--	--	3.7[a]	5.7[a]	6.1[a]	10.5[a]	6.2[a]	10.6[a]	--	--
State Industry, Including														
Sales-Supply	13.0[e]	--	15.4[d]	17.7[d]	18.0[a]	20.4[a]	27.1[a]	31.4[a]	38.5[a]	47.3[a]	45.0[a]	54.4[a]	52.9[e]	63.3[e]
Heavy	5.5[b]	--	6.4[b]	--	9.0[b]	--	12.1[b]	--	--	--	--	--	--	--
Timber	2.1[c]	--	2.5[c]	--	2.0[c]	--	2.2[c]	--	--	--	--	--	--	--
Food	2.3[c]	--	3.2[c]	--	3.1[c]	--	5.8[c]	--	--	--	--	--	--	--
Light	1.6[c]	--	2.2[c]	--	2.1[c]	--	4.4[c]	--	--	--	--	--	--	--
Local	1.5[c]	--	1.1[c]	--	1.8[c]	--	2.6[c]	--	--	--	--	--	--	--
Industrial Co-operatives	--	--	--	--	--	--	--	--	1.9[f]	2.2[f]	--	--	--	--
Transportation and Communications	--	--	--	--	--	--	--	--	2.6[f]	2.6[f]	--	--	--	--
State Agriculture	3.4[c]	--	3.6[c]	3.6[c]	4.4[a]	4.4[a]	6.4[a]	6.5[a]	7.2[a]	7.3[a]	8.0[a]	8.1[a]	10.6[e]	10.7[e]
Procurement	1.3[c]	--	1.5[c]	1.7[d]	1.9[a]	2.1[a]	3.1[a]	3.5[a]	2.5[a]	3.0[a]	2.9[a]	3.5[a]	3.5[e]	4.2[e]
Domestic Trade	5.7[c]	--	6.7[c]	7.2[d]	9.0[a]	9.6[a]	12.8[c]	13.8[a]	16.5[a]	18.2[a]	19.4[a]	21.3[a]	19.0[e]	20.8[e]
Other Nonagricultural Sectors	--	--	--	--	--	--	--	--	2.0[f]	2.2[f]	--	--	--	--

[a] See notes for Usoskin--39.
[b] See notes for Omel'chenko--39.
[c] See notes for Shenger--36.
[d] See notes for Konovalov--34.
[e] See notes for Rubinshtein--58.
[f] See notes for Bogolepov--37.

(vi) (p. 148) In 1936, the bank deposits of *union* industry were 1,186.7 million rubles or 4.7 percent of total assets; till cash was 52.7 million or 0.2 percent of the total. The implied total asset figure for union industry, of about 25 billion, is implied also by data given in the source for goods in process and semifabricates held in union industry.

Atlas–37: Atlas, writing at about the same time as Sobol', states (p. 119) that on January 1, 1936, three fourths of all working capital assets of "socialist economic organizations" were normed. Of total normed assets, production supplies constituted 34.6 percent, goods in process and semifabricates 16.7 percent, finished products 42 percent, monetary assets 4.3 percent, and other assets 2.4 percent. Monetary assets which were not normed amounted to 3.4 billion rubles or 18.2 percent of the total of nonnormed assets.

If we take the last two figures to compute nonnormed assets and take Sobol's figure for total assets (Atlas' figure of three fourths is clearly rounded) we can convert Atlas' percentages to absolute figures (billion rubles):

Production supplies	17.7
Goods in process and semifabricates	8.5
Finished products	21.5
Normed monetary assets	2.2
Other normed assets	1.2
Total normed	51.1
Nonnormed monetary assets	3.4
Other nonnormed	15.3
Total nonnormed	18.7
Total assets	69.8

The resulting figures for goods in process and for finished products correspond closely to those given in Sobol', and the two sources can be inferred to be drawing from the same basic data.

Usoskin–39: Data from this source are taken from notes provided by Robert W. Campbell, who very generously made them available to us. We consider first various groups of data given by Usoskin which can be demonstrated to be, or which appear to be, interrelated. All figures are for January 1.

(i) (p. 86) "The total of working capital invested in material assets" amounted to (billion rubles):

1935	36.5
1936	55.3
1937	75.8
1938	87.3
1939	98–100

Usoskin refers to these figures as for "the socialist economy." Elsewhere (Usoskin–46, p. 37), the same author gives totals, similarly described, of 36.7 in 1935, 75.8 in 1937, and "about 100" in 1939. We disregard the slight discrepancy in the figures for 1935.

(ii) (p. 84) Sources of finance of working capital of "basic branches" of the economy, as percents of total:

	1935	1936	1937	1938
Owned working capital and equivalents	41.3	40.0	41.4	40.4
Bank loans	33.2	34.2	33.7	34.5
Kreditory and other	25.5	25.8	24.9	25.1
	100.0	100.0	100.0	100.0

(*iii*) (p. 87) Percentage shares of sectors in total "planned" ("normed") assets of "basic branches":

	1935	1936	1937	1938
Industry	56.0	46.4	48.6	50.2
Agriculture	12.0	11.8	9.6	9.3
Trade and sales-supply	25.1	30.6	31.4	31.2
Procurement	6.9	11.2	10.4	9.3
	100.0	100.0	100.0	100.0

(*iv*) (p. 86) Percentage shares of normed and nonnormed assets in total assets of "basic branches":

	1935		1936		1937		1938	
	(1)	(2)	(1)	(2)	(1)	(2)	(1)	(2)
Industry	80.8	19.2	82.0	18.0	81.1	18.9	82.2	17.8
Agriculture	83.3	16.7	87.6	12.4	85.0	15.0	84.1	15.9
Trade and sales-supply	80.8	19.2	74.4	25.6	76.3	23.7	76.7	23.3
Procurement	70.0	30.0	73.4	26.6	71.1	28.9	70.0	30.0
Total	80.0	20.0	79.0	21.0	79.0	21.0	79.0	21.0

(1) *Normed*
(2) *Nonnormed*

(*v*) (p. 80) Equivalents to owned working capital as a percentage of owned working capital (no indication of sector coverage given):

1935.................9.4
1936.................8.3
1937.................6.1
1938.................6.4

(*vi*) (p. 87) Sources of finance of normed assets of basic branches as per-cent—evidently—of normed assets:

	1935			1936			1937			1938		
	(1)	(2)	(3)	(1)	(2)	(3)	(1)	(2)	(3)	(1)	(2)	(3)
Industry	56.0	36.2	7.8	58.6	31.7	9.7	64.5	28.7	6.8	63.0	29.1	7.9
Agriculture	80.0	14.3	5.7	76.8	15.0	8.2	82.3	12.7	5.0	82.8	15.6	1.6
Trade and sales-supply	36.8	50.4	12.8	39.2	55.9	4.9	35.5	57.5	7.0	30.4	60.5	9.1
Procurement	6.5	93.5	—	14.0	86.0	—	5.8	94.2	—	7.3	92.7	—
Total	51.6	41.1	7.3	50.3	43.2	6.5	52.5	43.0	4.5	51.0	43.5	5.5

(1) *Owned working capital and equivalents*
(2) *Bank Loans*
(3) *Other*

The source states that "other" represents the net balance of *kreditory* and sundry assets.

TABLE G-5

REPORTED WORKING CAPITAL ACCOUNTS (from Usoskin-39), BY SECTORS, IN CURRENT PRICES, 1935-39

(January 1--Billion Rubles)

| | Liabilities | | | | | Assets | | | | | | | | | |
	Owned Working Capital (1)	Equivalents (2)	Bank Loans (3)	Kreditory and Other (4)	Total (5)	Production Supplies (6)	Goods in Process and Semi-fabricates (7)	Expenses of Future Periods (8)	Finished Products (9)	Other (10)	Total Normed (11)	Goods Shipped (12)	Total Normed and Shipped (13)	Monetary Assets and Debitory (14)	Total (15)
Industry, Excluding Sales-Supply															
1935	11.4		7.4	6.4	25.2	--	--	--	--	--	--	--	20.4	4.8	25.2
1936	15.1		8.1	8.1	31.3	--	--	--	--	--	--	--	25.7	5.6	31.3
1937	23.7		10.6	11.1	45.4	--	--	--	--	--	--	--	36.8	8.6	45.4
1938	27.6		12.7	13.0	53.3	--	--	--	--	--	--	--	43.8	9.5	53.3
Agriculture															
1935	3.5		0.6	1.2	5.3	--	--	--	--	--	--	--	4.4	0.9	5.3
1936	5.0		1.0	1.4	7.4	--	--	--	--	--	--	--	6.5	0.9	7.4
1937	6.0		0.9	1.7	8.6	--	--	--	--	--	--	--	7.3	1.3	8.6
1938	6.7		1.3	1.6	9.6	--	--	--	--	--	--	--	8.1	1.5	9.6
Procurement															
1935	0.6		2.3	0.7	3.6	--	--	--	--	--	--	--	2.5	1.1	3.6
1936	1.1		5.3	2.0	8.4	--	--	--	--	--	--	--	6.2	2.2	8.4
1937	1.6		7.4	2.1	11.1	--	--	--	--	--	--	--	7.9	3.2	11.1
1938	1.9		7.5	2.2	11.6	--	--	--	--	--	--	--	8.1	3.5	11.6
Trade and Sales-Supply															
1935	3.4		4.6	3.4	11.4	--	--	--	--	--	--	--	9.2	2.2	11.4
1936	6.6		9.4	6.7	22.7	--	--	--	--	--	--	--	16.9	5.8	22.7
1937	8.4		13.7	9.1	31.2	--	--	--	--	--	--	--	23.8	7.4	31.2
1938	8.3		16.5	10.7	35.5	--	--	--	--	--	--	--	27.2	8.3	35.5
Total															
1935	17.2	1.6	15.1	11.6	45.5	11.8	5.8	0.7	14.9	0.1	33.3	3.2	36.5	9.0	45.5
1936	25.8	2.1	23.9	18.0	69.8	17.7	8.5	1.1	22.0	0.3	49.5	5.8	55.3	14.5	69.8
1937	37.6	2.3	32.5	24.0	96.3	24.0	11.3	1.0	28.2	0.2	64.7	11.1	75.8	20.5	96.3
1938	41.7	2.7	37.9	27.6	110.0	29.2	14.0	0.9	31.0	0.3	75.3	12.0	87.3	22.7	110.0
1939	--	--	--	--	--	--	--	--	--	--	--	--	99.0	--	--

(*vii*) (p. 71) Percentage share of owned working capital in total working capital:

	1935	1936	1937	1938
"Basic branches"	51.6	50.3	52.5	51.0
Food industry	34.6	30.2	34.1	31.3
Procurement	22.3	18.5	19.8	23.4

(*viii*) (p. 40) Percentage shares of kinds of assets in total "material assets" in "basic branches":

	1934	1935	1936	1937	1938
Production supplies	32.3	32.2	32.0	31.6	33.4
Goods in process and semifabricates	16.5	16.0	15.3	14.9	16.0
Expenses of future periods	2.8	2.0	1.9	1.3	1.0
Finished products	37.8	40.7	39.8	37.2	35.5
Goods shipped	9.9	8.7	10.5	14.7	13.8
Other	0.7	0.4	0.5	0.3	0.3
	100.0	100.0	100.0	100.0	100.0

Usoskin's data pose several interdependent questions. Are the absolute figures shown in Paragraph (*i*) for assets or liabilities? (The expression "working capital invested in material assets" is wholly ambiguous.) If the figures are for assets, what kinds of assets do they include? Are the several percentage breakdowns related to the absolute figures and to one another, or are they of varying and inconsistent coverage? If the data are mutually consistent, what sectors do they include? The conclusions we come to are that the absolute figures are for normed assets in the usual sense and goods shipped, that the percentage breakdowns are consistent with the absolute totals and with one another, and that the sectors covered are in all cases "basic branches" only (i.e., industry, including sales-supply, state agriculture, domestic trade, and procurement). These conclusions rest in part on the calculations shown in Table G–5.

In Table G–5, the Paragraph (*iii*) distribution of "normed assets"—in Usoskin's terminology—by sectors is applied to the absolute figures of Paragraph (*i*) and the resulting sector figures entered in column 13, for "normed assets and goods shipped." That the latter expression is the correct interpretation of Usoskin's "normed assets" (identified hereafter by quotation marks) is argued below.

Total assets by sectors (column 15) are computed from normed assets and goods shipped (column 13) and the sector ratios of "normed" to total assets given in Paragraph (*iv*). Total assets for all sectors are computed as the sum of the component sectors. The totals thus obtained can be compared with those which can be computed directly from normed assets and goods shipped in all sectors and the Paragraph (*iv*) ratio of "normed" to total assets for all sectors (billion rubles):

	Sum of components	Computed totals
1935	45.5	45.6
1936	69.8	70.0
1937	96.3	95.9
1938	110.0	110.9

Though there are slight discrepancies between the two sets of figures, the Paragraph (*iv*) percentages for all sectors in combination are obviously rounded to the nearest full percentage point whereas the percentages for component sectors are carried to one decimal point. The sums of the components are presumably more accurate. In any case, the near correspondence of the figures is a first verification of the internal consistency of the data.

Taking total liabilities (column 5) as necessarily equal to total assets (column 15) and applying the Paragraph (*ii*) distribution of liabilities, we obtain owned working capital and equivalents, bank loans, and *kreditory* and other liabilities, for all sectors in combination. Equivalents are separated from owned capital on the basis of the Paragraph (*v*) percentages. The results are shown as totals in columns 1–4.

The Paragraph (*vi*) distribution of liabilities for component sectors is stated to relate to "normed assets" only, but Usoskin is not explicit that the base of the percentages is the total of "normed assets"; this, however, is quite clearly the case. What the author has evidently done is to show the whole of owned capital and bank loans as percentages of "normed assets" and then attribute to other liabilities only that part of "normed assets" which is not covered by the first two sources. This would account for the low share of other liabilities in the total. In the case of procurement, however, the sum of owned capital and bank loans evidently exceeds the total of "normed assets"; other liabilities are shown as a blank and owned capital is here treated as the residual. On the last point, note that in Paragraph (*vii*) the share of owned capital in procurement is shown as much higher than in (*vi*), yet the percentages for all sectors combined is the same in both sets of data. There remains a slight discrepancy, which we cannot explain and which we disregard, between the ratios of total owned capital to bank loans in Paragraphs (*vi*) and (*ii*).

On the foregoing interpretations, we compute owned capital *cum* equivalents and bank loans for industry, agriculture, and trade and sales-supply (columns 1–3) from their normed assets and goods shipped (column 13) and from the Paragraph (*vi*) percentages. For procurement, we compute owned capital and equivalents from the Paragraph (*vii*) percentage, bank loans from Paragraph (*vi*). For all sectors, *kreditory* and other liabilities (column 4) are computed as total liabilities minus owned capital and loans.

The liabilities by sectors computed in this fashion sum to totals which diverge by no more than 0.2 billion rubles from the totals previously computed. Internal consistency is again demonstrated. No adjustment is made for the slight discrepancies.

We compute assets by kind (columns 6–10 and 12) from the totals of normed assets and goods shipped (column 13) and the percentage breakdowns of "material assets" given in Paragraph (*viii*). The combined sum of monetary assets and *debitory* (column 14) is computed as the difference between total assets (column 15) and normed assets and goods shipped (column 13). Normed assets (column 11) are computed by deducting goods shipped from the combined total.

The foregoing computations appear to establish that Usoskin's Paragraph (*i*) totals are for "normed assets" in his sense of the term and that his various data can be combined with some positive evidence of internal consistency and no evidence of significant inconsistency. The computations do not establish what assets are included by Usoskin in "normed assets" and whether his breakdown of assets by kind is consistent with the other data. Both points can be settled fairly conclusively by reference to external evidence.

There is, first, suggestive evidence in the terminology used. Though the meaning of "normed assets" varies in Soviet usage, it does not ordinarily include, as we have assumed it does in this source, goods shipped. However, the same author in a later work, Usoskin–46, more or less completely assimilates goods shipped into the category of normed assets. On p. 75 of the work referred to, he divides total assets between normed and non-normed assets; he refers to the latter as inclusive of "monetary assets, *debitory*, etc."; and, in a numerical breakdown, he shows "normed assets and goods shipped" as accounting for 80 percent of the total, "nonnormed assets" for 20 percent. On p. 76, he refers to the composition of "normed assets (including goods shipped)" and presents a table which includes goods shipped as a component but which is entitled simply "structure of normed assets." The latter table is stated to refer to basic branches in a prewar year. It is identical with the breakdown of "material assets" shown for 1938 in Paragraph (*viii*) above. That Usoskin might in the 1939 work refer to a total inclusive of goods shipped as for normed assets therefore seems entirely possible. Since the term which appears in the description of Paragraph (*viii*), "material assets" (*material'nye fondy*), appears also in the description of Paragraph (*i*), it is possible also that the absolute totals of Paragraph (*i*) embrace the same assets as the percentages of Paragraph (*viii*), i.e., normed assets in the usual sense and goods shipped.

Secondly, the breakdown of total assets by kind for 1936 which we derive from Usoskin can be compared with those derived previously from Sobol'–37 and Atlas–37 (where the total asset figure for Atlas is taken from Sobol'). Figures are billion rubles.

	Usoskin	Sobol'	Atlas
Production supplies	17.7	—	17.7
Goods in process and semifabricates	8.5	8.4	8.5
Expenses of future periods	1.1	—	—
Finished products	22.0	21.3	21.5
Other on hand	0.3	—	1.2
Goods shipped, monetary assets, and *debitory*	20.3	—	20.9
Total	69.8	69.8	69.8

Though there are some discrepancies, the correspondences are much too close to leave serious doubt that, in 1936 at least, Usoskin's "normed asset" totals are inclusive of goods shipped and that his distribution of assets by kind belongs to an internally coherent set of accounts which, in addition, is the same as that used by Sobol' and by Atlas. (This comparison appears to establish also that Usoskin's normed assets exclude normed monetary assets; cf. the discussion of Atlas–37.)

The Usoskin figure for total assets on January 1, 1935, 45.5 billion, is not consistent with Sobol's figure of 51.9 billion, and this inconsistency is one of the least explicable puzzles of the data for this period. The difference between the two, however, evidently arises in larger part from their figures for monetary assets and *debitory*. According to Sobol', total assets increased in the course of 1935 by 17.9 billion, assets other than monetary (i.e., normed assets and goods shipped) by 16 billion, and, by implication, monetary assets and *debitory* by about 1.9 billion. The corresponding figures from Usoskin are 24.3 for the total, 18.8 for normed assets and goods shipped, and 5.5 for monetary assets and *debitory*. The discrepancy between 18.8 and 16 billion is not trivial, but it is less extraordinary than is the discrepancy in the totals for all assets. Given that Usoskin's data are more complete and are consistent internally, and given further checks of them provided by material cited hereafter, we accept the increase obtained from them in preference to that given by Sobol'.

Two further questions with respect to the Usoskin data remain: how comprehensive is their coverage of sectors and how have assets and liabilities been distributed among the sectors included?

As has been noted, Sobol' indicates no exclusions from his figures except for contract construction and collective farms. Usoskin also refers to his absolute totals as for "the socialist economy," which would suggest relatively comprehensive coverage. But Usoskin's percentage breakdowns, which we have now determined are congruent with his absolute totals, are nearly all described as for "basic branches" only. Evidence indicates that "basic branches" is the accurate description.

We compare below Usoskin's bank loan figures, by sectors (Table G–5, column 3), with reported loans as compiled in Table I–1 (billion rubles; the Table I–1 figures for 1938 are themselves derived largely from loan data given directly in Usoskin–39, p. 71):

	1935	1936	1937	1938
1. Table I–1: State industry, including sales-supply	6.6	12.5	18.7	20.9
2. Usoskin: Industry, excluding sales-supply ...	7.4	8.1	10.6	12.7
Row 1 minus Row 2	—0.8	4.4	8.1	8.2
3. Table I–1: State agriculture	0.9	1.2	1.2	1.5
4. Usoskin: Agriculture	0.6	1.0	0.9	1.3
Row 3 minus Row 4	0.3	0.2	0.3	0.2
5. Table I–1: Procurement	2.0	3.0	2.8	3.3
6. Usoskin: Procurement	2.3	5.3	7.4	7.5
Row 5 minus Row 6	—0.3	—2.3	—4.6	—4.2
7. Table I–1: Domestic trade	5.9	7.5	9.4	11.5
8. Usoskin: Trade and sales-supply	4.6	9.4	13.7	16.5
Row 7 minus Row 8	1.3	—1.9	—4.3	—5.0
9. Table I–1: Total of indicated sectors	15.4	24.2	32.1	37.2
10. Usoskin: Total of indicated sectors	15.1	23.9	32.5	37.9
Row 9 minus Row 10	0.3	0.3	—0.4	—0.7

From the close correspondence of the loan totals, we infer that Usoskin's data are of limited sector coverage; in particular, they exclude industrial co-operatives, transportation and communications, foreign trade and "other" sectors, in addition to construction and collective farms. From the extreme differences between loans for particular sectors, we infer that Usoskin's distribution of assets and liabilities by sectors is novel and, moreover, is not precisely as he describes it. Both of these conclusions are borne out by data for individual sectors which are cited in the discussion following.

It should be noted, first, that Usoskin's sector breakdowns for 1935 are almost certainly not comparable with those for the three subsequent years. Though his bank loan breakdown for 1935 does not fit at all precisely that from Table I–1, the differences are generally smaller than in 1936–38 and in two cases are of different signs. His figures for normed assets and goods shipped in industry and trade loosely resemble those cited below from Shenger–36 for industry inclusive of sales-supply and trade exclusive of sales-supply (both for normed assets only). His 1935 figure for inventories in procurement looks at least plausible relative to bank loans (Table I–1) and to data for postwar years, which is not true of his procurement figures for 1936–38. We assume from this evidence that Usoskin's 1935 figures are in fact for industry inclusive of sales-supply, trade exclusive of sales-supply, and for procurement in something close to the usual meaning of that term.

Usoskin's figures for loans and inventories in agriculture, unlike those for the other three sectors, do not appear to change their coverage from 1935 to the later years. We are unable to account for the discrepancies between his loans figures for this sector and those taken from Table I–1, and these may indicate a consistent understatement in his figures for agricultural inventories. However, we assume they are comprehensive (on this point, see the discussion of Shenger–36).

For 1936–38, Usoskin's figures for industry appear to be accurately described in the source, i.e., as exclusive of sales-supply. (*i*) The 4.4 billion difference in loans to industry in 1936, computed above, looks consistent with Sobol's figure of 3.5 billion for finished products in sales-supply, allowance being made for other inventories on hand and for goods shipped. (*ii*) The 1938 difference in loan figures, 8.2 billion, compares with a reported figure for loans to sales-supply on January 1, 1941, of 10.5 billion (Table I–3). These two figures amount to 39 percent and 34 percent respectively of total loans to state industry in the same years (totals are from Table I–1). (*iii*) We have from Sobol' that in 1936 state industry excluding sales-supply held total assets of 29.9 billion, of which 2.1 were *debitory* and 0.8 goods unpaid for. Usoskin's figure for normed assets and goods shipped is 25.7 or 4.2 less than Sobol's total assets. Deducting *debitory* and goods unpaid for from the latter leaves a residual for monetary assets in state industry of 1.3, which compares with Sobol's total for deposits and cash in *union* industry of 1.2. (This particular check argues rather strongly against the hypothesis, offered in Campbell–58a, p. 7, that Usoskin has excluded from industry and attributed to procurement a portion of assets usually included in industry. On this, see also the discussion above of Sobol's data on finished products.)

The most peculiar feature of Usoskin's sector distributions for 1936–38 is his treatment of trade and procurement. What he appears to have done is to attribute to procurement a substantial part of assets and liabilities that by usual sector classification would be attributed to trade. (*i*) If, in the bank loan calculation above, we subtract the apparent loans to sales-supply from Usoskin's total for trade and sales-supply combined, Usoskin's loans to trade alone fall short of those taken from Table I–1 by 2.1 billion in 1936, 3.5 in 1937, 4.0 in 1938. These compare with a difference in the opposite direction for loans to procurement of 1.9, 4.3, and 5.0. (*ii*) Usoskin's 1936 figure for normed assets and goods shipped in trade and sales-supply, 16.9, compares with Sobol's total of finished products in the same two sectors of 14.6. The difference between the two is much too small to allow for other normed assets and, especially, for goods shipped. (*iii*) Usoskin (p. 29), gives a percentage distribution by sectors of finished products, which we have not previously cited:

	1935	1936	1937	1938
Producing enterprises of basic branches ...28.7	24.3	24.2	22.4
Trade, sales-supply, and procurement 71.3	75.7	75.8	77.6
Of which, sales-supply			
and procurement 33.0	42.3	43.1	42.3

Since the sector categories used here are different from those used else-where by Usoskin, it is possible that this breakdown is not congruent with his other data. Moreover, it is unclear whether the percentages for sales-supply and procurement refer to total finished products or to the total exclusive of producing enterprises. However, applying these breakdowns to Usoskin's absolute totals for finished products yields this distribution in billion rubles (variants are shown to allow for the alternative possible meanings of the procurement and sales-supply percentages):

	1935	1936	1937	1938
Producing enterprises 4.3	5.3	6.8	6.9
Sales-supply and procurement .. 4.9 (3.5)	9.3 (7.1)	12.2 (9.2)	13.1 (10.2)
Trade 5.7 (7.1)	7.4 (9.6)	9.2 (12.2)	11.0 (13.9)
Total 14.9	22.0	28.2	31.0

For 1936, these data can be compared with Sobol's similar breakdown of 5.7 in industry, 3.5 in sales-supply, 1.0 evidently in procurement and agri-culture (judging from postwar data, agricultural holdings would be very small), and 11.1 in trade. By either possible reading of his breakdown, Usoskin appears to have attributed too little of inventories to trade, too much to procurement, in comparison with Sobol' and with other related breakdowns. (See also the discussion of the distribution of assets by kind in 1937 in Appendix H.)

Given the above readings of Usoskin's data, we make use of them in deriving the figures in Table G–4 as follows.

(*i*) We accept for all years his total figures for normed assets and goods shipped, 36.5 in 1935, 55.3 in 1936, etc. For 1939, we take the midpoint of the range given, 98–100. We assume that these totals cover consistently and comprehensively state industry, sales-supply, state agriculture, pro-curement, and domestic trade.

(*ii*) We accept his industry figures for normed assets and goods shipped in all years for which they are given, but interpret the 1935 figure as in-cluding, the 1936–38 figures as excluding, sales-supply.

(*iii*) In 1951 (see Table G–6 and notes for Table H–1, for 1951), finished products in sales-supply accounted for 95.5 percent of normed assets, ex-cluding small tools, in that sector. We assume that the same ratio held in 1936 and estimate total normed assets in sales-supply as 3.7 billion from Sobol's figure for finished products of 3,531 million.

(*iv*) We accept Usoskin's figures for normed assets and goods shipped in agriculture in all years, 1935–38.

(*v*) We estimate normed assets and goods shipped in procurement, 1935–38, from our Table I–1 figures for bank loans to this sector and Usoskin's ratio of loans to "normed assets" (in his sense), Paragraph (*vi*) of the data reproduced from the source. For consistency, we use this procedure for 1935, although Usoskin's figure for this date evidently does refer to procurement in the usual sense (the difference is between 2.1 and 2.5).

(*vi*) From Shenger–36, q.v., we take a figure for domestic trade normed assets in 1936 of 12.8 billion. Given this, we have normed assets, either with or without goods shipped, for all sectors covered by Usoskin for 1936. From Tables G–6 and H–1, we have ratios of goods shipped to normed assets (including expenses of future periods but excluding small tools) in 1951. We apply these ratios to the 1936 sector figures and adjust the results to the total of goods shipped, 5.8 billion, derived from Usoskin. By appropriate additions and subtractions, this gives us for each of Usoskin's sectors, and for industry and sales-supply separately, normed assets with and without goods shipped in 1936.

(*vii*) Given 1936 normed assets with goods shipped in sales-supply, we extrapolate similar totals in 1937 and 1938 from bank loans to this sector computed above of 4.4 billion in 1936, 8.1 in 1937, and 8.2 in 1938. This is a palpably crude procedure but the best available to us.

(*viii*) Step (*vii*) permits us to compute domestic trade normed assets with goods shipped in 1937 and 1938 as that part of Usoskin's totals which is not accounted for by other sectors. Since for 1935 sales-supply is included with industry, we similarly compute trade as a residual in that year. For a measure of the reliability of these trade estimates, see Paragraph (*ix*) following.

(*ix*) For 1935, 1937, and 1938, we distribute Usoskin's totals for goods shipped by the same procedure as in 1936, with this difference: in deriving the 1951 ratios of goods shipped to the combined total, we include one half of the value of small tools for the 1937 estimate and all of small tools for the 1938 estimate. For 1935, the division of their combined total between industry and sales-supply is assumed the same as in 1936.

Since our estimates of trade assets in these three years are derived as residuals, it is worth noting that their rough accuracy is substantiated by other evidence. The 1935 figure for normed assets, 9.0 billion, is precisely the same as that given by Shenger–36. The figures for 1936–38, 12.8, 16.5, and 19.4, compare with figures (Table K–1) for inventories in trade of finished products valued at retail prices of 14.6, 19.3, and 22.5, respectively.

(*x*) For 1934, we use Usoskin's ratio of goods shipped to normed assets and goods shipped, Paragraph (*ix*), to derive an absolute figure for goods shipped (see notes for Konovalov–34).

It should be stressed that our conclusion on the sector coverage of Usoskin's data largely predetermines our interpretation of much of the other data—of purportedly comprehensive coverage—for the years considered here: Usoskin's data clearly cover basic branches only; other data are consistent with Usoskin's; hence other data are also limited to basic branches.

Omel'chenko–39: This source (p. 11) reports working capital in the Commissariat of Heavy Industry (January 1—million rubles):

$$
\begin{array}{ll}
1933\dots & 5,483 \\
1934\dots & 6,418 \\
1935\dots & 9,008 \\
1936\dots & 12,120 \\
\end{array}
$$

In the text the author refers to these figures as for "supplies of commodity-material values," from which we infer that they are for normed assets. The source gives figures (p. 10) for the share of finished products in the total which are large enough to indicate that the totals are inclusive of sales-supply. We use Omel'chenko's figures on these interpretations. See also notes on Shenger–36 and Khromov–37.

Shenger–36: With an exception to be explained, this source provides, pp. 21–24, the information tabulated below for settlement accounts (deposits at Gosbank) held by the indicated sectors, in million rubles and as percentage ratios to "total material values."

	1933		1934		1935		1936	
	Rubles	Percent	Rubles	Percent	Rubles	Percent	Rubles	Percent
Industry	1,312	9.8	1,186	9.7	1,128	6.9	2,163	7.4
Heavy	426	7.3	620	9.1	578	6.6	989	7.2
Timber	115	5.2	97	5.8	80	4.7	—	—
Food	413	17.1	269	12.9	213	7.9	—	—
Light	165	9.9	123	8.4	149	8.4	—	—
Local	193	12.7	77	8.8	108	7.3	—	—
Agriculture	295	6.3	253	5.0	203	3.3	272	2.9
Domestic trade	528	9.3	494	7.4	502	5.6	677	5.3
Total	2,135	9.7	1,933	8.5	1,833	5.9	3,112	6.0

The exception referred to is that, for component industries in 1934, the settlement account figures are not given in Shenger but are taken from Gosbank–35, pp. 58–59. The latter source gives deposit figures for 1933 and 1935 which are virtually identical with Shenger's, and the components for 1934 sum to Shenger's industry total for that date. Total deposits are computed sums.

Shenger indicates his figures for component industries are for the corresponding commissariats; Gosbank–35, however, identifies the deposit figures for timber as covering all timber and not the commissariat alone. This source also identifies the deposit figures for trade as for domestic trade only.

From the above data it is possible to compute "material values" by sectors, with the results shown below. The sums of the industry components differ slightly from the totals calculated directly and are adjusted to the latter. For agriculture, the deposit figures are shown in Shenger as for the Commissariats of Agriculture and of State Farms, but the ratios are stated to include in addition agriculture subordinate to the Commissariat for Food. This difference presumably accounts for the quite substantial difference in 1933 and 1934, and a small difference in 1935 and 1936, between the sums of component sectors and the totals computable from total deposits. We show without parentheses agriculture computed from the data given for that sector and the total as the sum of components. Figures within parentheses are totals computed from the deposit figures and agriculture computed as a residual. Figures are in billion rubles.

	1933	1934	1935	1936
Industry 13.4		12.2	16.3	29.2
Heavy 5.7		6.5	8.7	13.7
Timber 2.2		1.6	1.7	—
Food 2.4		2.0	2.7	—
Light 1.6		1.4	1.8	—
Local 1.5		0.7	1.5	—
Agriculture 4.7 (2.9)		5.1 (3.8)	6.2 (5.8)	9.4 (9.9)
Domestic trade 5.7		6.7	9.0	12.8
Total 23.8 (22.0)		24.0 (22.7)	31.5 (31.1)	51.4 (51.9)

It is clear from the terms used in the source that industry here is state industry only, presumably inclusive of sales-supply. Agriculture excludes collective farms; the comparison made below suggests it includes procurement which is not otherwise accounted for. From the expression, "material values," and from the general orders of magnitude of the figures, we assume that the data are for normed assets.

For such sectors as we can, we compare below Shenger's figures with those available from other sources. We treat his agriculture figures as inclusive of procurement. Since they provide a better fit with other data, we use Shenger's agriculture figures derived from data for that sector and we use the corresponding totals. Figures attributed to sources other than Shenger are those used in Table G–4, except where the latter are themselves derived from Shenger. The 1934 figure for total state industry used in the comparison is from the source discussed below as *Den'gi i kredit*, 1939:4. The 1936 figure for trade is estimated by increasing Sobol's figure for finished products, 11,077 million, by 13 percent. Lifits–50, p. 521, states that raw and other materials held by the Commissariat of Trade equaled 13 percent of finished products in *1937*; the commissariat accounted for only part of trade and the 1937 ratio need not have been close to that for 1936. Figures are billion rubles.

This comparison suggests that the sector coverage of Shenger's data is essentially the same as that of Usoskin–39, i.e., basic branches only are included. As is explained in the discussion of the latter source, it may understate assets in agriculture; the apparent substantiation of our assumption that Shenger includes procurement with agriculture may, on this account, be spurious. That uncertainty aside, however, Shenger's figures appear to fit closely with those from other sources except for material discrepancies for industry, which in turn clearly account for almost all of the discrepancies in the totals. We accept the industry totals (and heavy industry figures) from other sources in preference to Shenger's.

Shenger's data (taken as for normed assets) are incorporated in Table G–4 as follows.

	1933	1934	1935	1936
State industry				
1. Shenger 13.4		14.2	16.3	29.2
2. Other 13.0		15.2	18.0	27.1
Row 1 minus Row 2 .... 0.4		—3.0	—1.7	2.1
Heavy				
3. Shenger 5.7		6.5	8.7	13.7
4. Other 5.5		6.4	9.0	12.1
Row 3 minus Row 4 .... 0.2		0.1	—0.3	1.6
State agriculture and procurement				
5. Shenger .... —		—	6.3	9.5
6. Other .... —		—	6.1	9.3
Row 5 minus Row 6 .... —		—	0.2	0.2
Domestic trade				
7. Shenger .... —		—	9.0	12.8
8. Other .... —		—	9.0	12.5
Row 7 minus Row 8 .... —		—	0.0	0.3
Total of indicated sectors				
9. Shenger .... —		24.0	31.5	51.4
10. Other .... —		27.2	33.3	49.5
Row 9 minus Row 10 .... —		—3.2	—1.8	1.9

(*i*) His figures for domestic trade in 1933, 1934, and 1936 are entered without adjustment.

(*ii*) His—larger—figures for agriculture in 1933 and 1934 are assumed to cover both agriculture and procurement. Procurement is extrapolated from 1935 on the basis of bank loans (Table I–1). Agriculture is computed as a residual. We have not much confidence in these estimates for agriculture, but they are of little consequence for present purposes.

(*iii*) For state industry in 1933–35, the difference between normed assets in total state industry and in heavy industry is distributed among the remaining four industrial sectors in the proportions indicated by Shenger. This is not likely to be a highly accurate procedure for individual industries, though consumer goods industries in combination undoubtedly account for most of the whole.

(*iv*) For state industry in 1936, we extrapolate normed assets in sectors other than heavy industry from 1935 on bank loans (Table I–1) and adjust the resulting estimates proportionately to the difference between total and heavy industry. These estimates may be compared with figures for October 1, 1935, which are cited below from Khromov–37.

Konovalov–34: Konovalov, p. 179, states that working capital assets (*oborotnye fondy*) of the national economy were planned to rise to 37.1 billion on January 1, 1935, or an increase of 6.9 billion over January 1, 1934; the implied actual figure for 1934 is 30.2 billion. The publication date of the source makes the meaning of its terminology uncertain, but a further statement that the 6.9 billion increase was to be financed by 4.5 billion of owned capital and 2.4 billion of bank loans suggests that the totals are for normed assets plus goods shipped. The sector coverage of the data is not specified. However, the planned total for 1935, 37.1 billion, compares with Usoskin's realized total for normed assets and goods shipped in basic branches of 36.5 billion. That Konovalov's coverage is the same as that of Usoskin and of Shenger is borne out also by component sector data which are cited below.

We accept Konovalov's asset total for 1934, as for the coverage indicated. From Usoskin (see Paragraph [*viii*] of the data cited from this source), we have the share of goods shipped in normed assets and goods shipped on this date as 9.9 percent. This percentage, coupled with the 30.2 billion total, implies 3.0 billion of goods shipped and 27.2 billion of normed assets. From the latter figure, we subtract the Table G–4 figures (derived from Shenger) for normed assets in agriculture, procurement, and trade, which leaves a residual for state industry, including sales-supply, of 15.4 billion. We would place little reliance on this figure were it not that it differs only slightly from an estimate of 15.2 billion which can be derived from an independent source (see notes on *Den'gi i kredit*, 1939:4). We retain the figure of 15.4 billion.

The 3.0 billion of goods shipped is distributed among major sectors by extrapolating from 1935 on normed assets and adjusting the results proportionately to the known total.

Rubinshtein–58: This source, p. 47, provides balance sheets, derived from TsSU sources, for state industry inclusive of sales-supply, on January 1, 1933 and 1939 (billion rubles):

	1933	1939
Owned working capital	10.5	36.9
Bank loans	3.0	25.5
Kreditory	8.4	16.4
Total	21.9	78.8
Working capital assets	13.0	52.9
Resources in settlements and *debitory*	8.9	25.9
Total	21.9	78.8

Rubinshtein's loan figure for 1933 is markedly smaller than that derivable from Table I–1 (3.0 to 3.7 billion); that for 1939 is relatively close to that from Table I–1 (25.5 to 24.7 billion). His 1933 figure for working capital assets, which is clearly normed assets in the usual sense, is close to that from Shenger–36 (13.0 to 13.4 billion); his 1939 figure is at least plausible relative to that for 1938 derived from Usoskin–39. Monetary assets are evidently included here with resources in settlements and *debitory*.

We accept Rubinshtein's normed asset figures for both 1933 and 1939.

To complete the 1939 distribution, we:

(*i*) Take total normed assets and goods shipped in basic branches to have been 99.0 billion (Table G–5).

(*ii*) Extrapolate total goods shipped in the same sectors from 1938 (Table G–5) on loans on goods shipped (Table J–1). This distributes 13.0 billion of the total to goods shipped and 86.0 billion to normed assets.

(*iii*) Extrapolate normed assets with goods shipped in trade from 1938 on inventories of finished products at retail prices (Table K–1).

(*iv*) Extrapolate goods shipped from 1938 on normed assets in industry, on normed assets with goods shipped in trade, and on bank loans in agriculture and procurement, and adjust the component estimates proportionately to the known total. Bank loans are those shown in Table I–1, except that we deduct from loans to agriculture on January 1, 1938, 87 million of loans to the MTS's. Gosbank ceased in the course of 1938 to make such loans (cf. Atlas–58, p. 192).

(*v*) From the results of the preceding steps, we calculate normed assets with goods shipped in agriculture and procurement together as a residual. This total is divided by extrapolating normed assets with goods shipped in each sector from 1938 on bank loans (Table I–1, corrected as above) and adjusting to the known total. Goods shipped are subtracted to obtain normed assets. While the estimates for these two sectors cannot be accurate, the plausibility of their order of magnitude appears to substantiate our general procedures for 1939.

Khromov–37: The entries we have made in Table G–4 thus far derive principally from reported data on working capital assets. Before turning to liability data, which are required for the completion of the table, we briefly consider asset data which are not actually employed in our calculations. The source here considered and the two following contain data of this sort.

Khromov–37, pp. 70–71, reports "material working capital" on October 1, 1935 (billion rubles):

Commissariat of Heavy Industry 12.222
Commissariat of Food Industry 5.084
Commissariat of Light Industry 1.576
Commissariat of Timber Industry 1.746
Chief Administration for the Film Industry .... .097

      Total 20.725

These figures appear reasonably consistent with those for normed assets on January 1, 1936, used in Table G–4, except that light industry is much smaller. Conceivably, Khromov's figure is for light industry exclusive of textiles. Whatever the explanation, the figure is almost certainly an understatement of inventories in this sector in its usual meaning.

Batyrev–40: Campbell–58a, p. 11, cites a source which is not available to us, V. M. Batyrev and V. I. Sitnin, *Organizatsiia i planirovanie finansov sotsialisticheskoi promyshlennosti*, Moscow-Leningrad, 1940, pp. 66–67, as reporting working capital assets in socialist industry on January 1, 1938, of 54 billion rubles. Campbell infers from other evidence in the source that the total includes monetary assets and goods shipped but excludes *debitory*, and that it is for state industry, including sales-supply but excluding local industry. The figure is in fact, although perhaps coincidentally, identical with that we derive (in Table G–4) from Usoskin–39 for state industry, including sales-supply and local industry, for normed assets and goods shipped. See also the further discussion of this source in notes to Table H–1 for 1937.

Mitel'man–40: Herein, p. 50, are given data purportedly for union, republican, and local industry, and including sales-supply (January 1—billion rubles):

	1933	1938	1939
Raw materials and goods in process 5.6	25.7	29.0
Finished products 2.7	9.1	10.2
Sum 8.3	34.8	39.2

The total figures amount to 64, 77, and 74 percent respectively of those for total normed assets in state industry used in Table G–4. Some large but unidentifiable omission unquestionably occurs in the Mitel'man data.

Bogolepov–37: We turn at this point to consideration of liability data and, in particular, data for owned working capital. The principal use we make of such data for the years under consideration, 1933–39, is to estimate inventories for the single year 1937 in sectors other than basic branches, i.e., in transportation and communications, industrial co-operatives, and other nonagricultural sectors (including foreign trade). For 1940–41, however, we have no reported asset data and must proceed from bank loans and owned capital. It will be useful, therefore, to comment here on the general character of the owned capital statistics which were released in prewar Soviet sources for the late 1930's and 1940–41. The bulk of these statistics appeared in the annual budget messages and related reports of the Commissar of Finance. Comments on individual sources appear hereafter.

We find no way of interpreting the whole of the prewar reported owned capital totals, other than on wholly arbitrary assumptions, which firmly establishes their meaning and coverage or makes them fully consistent with one another. It appears clear that almost all of them are restricted in sector coverage beyond the usual omissions of contract construction and nonstate agriculture, but there are variations in the sectors excluded. Evidence on sector coverage relates in part to annual increments, and it is by no means certain that increments are homogeneous with totals appearing in the same source. Evidence is largely or wholly lacking on the treatment of equivalents to owned capital, of capital gains on inventories, and of inventories acquired with the new territories. Consequently, such of our estimates as rest on these data are subject to considerable errors.

Bogolepov–37, p. 115, provides the one substantial clue available to us on the size of inventories in other than basic branches in the 1930's. He states, p. 115, that owned working capital of economic organizations was 42 billion on January 1, 1937, and was planned to reach 58.8 billion on January 1, 1938 (he states also that the increment in the course of the year was to be 15 billion and 35.7 percent of the initial total, which implies a planned total of only 57 billion). He gives in addition an allocation of the 1938 planned aggregate by sectors: 33.2 billion in industry, 7.7 in agriculture, 3.4 in transportation and communications, 8.6 in trade and procurement, and 5.9 in "other" branches. Judging from their date of publication, the data are almost certainly exclusive of equivalents to owned capital.

From Usoskin–39 (see Table G–5), we have a figure for owned capital in basic branches on January 1, 1937, of 37.6 billion. This would appear to be effectively identical with a figure for the same date, of unspecified coverage, of 37.3 billion given in Grin'ko–37, which source gives a planned total for January 1, 1938 of 48 billion (see notes on this source). In Zverev–46 (see notes thereon), the 1938 planned total is given as 49 billion, which may be a later but conceptually unchanged version of Grin'ko's 48 billion (Grin'ko and Zverev were successive Commissars of Finance). The strategic point of comparison is that Bogolepov's 1938 planned figures for industry, agriculture, trade, and procurement sum to 49.5 billion, or close to the Grin'ko and Zverev figures. The remaining 9.3 billion of Bogolepov's 1938 planned total explicitly covers transportation and communications and "other" branches. Presumably, this is the coverage also of the roughly 5 billion difference between Bogolepov's 1937 total and that given by Grin'ko.

Lacking contrary evidence, we assume that this 5 billion represents the whole of sectors not included in basic branches: industrial co-operatives, transportation and communications, and "other" branches. We proceed as follows.

(*i*) From Smigla–37 (see notes thereon) we have owned capital in transportation and communications on January 1, 1937, as 2.7 billion. This figure is for union enterprises only, but is likely to be comprehensive. Assuming that the ratio of owned capital to equivalents was the same in this sector as in basic branches (see Table G–5), equivalents amounted to an additional 0.2 billion. Bank loans were 0.8 billion (Table I–1), and the sum of these three sources 3.7 billion. The ratio of these same sources to normed assets (excluding one half of small tools) in 1951 was 69 percent (see Tables G–6 and H–1), which ratio we assume, doubtless inaccurately, held also in 1937. We assume that goods shipped were negligible in transportation and communications.

(*ii*) We have a remainder of owned capital of some 2.3 billion and bank loans to industrial cooperatives, foreign trade, and "other" sectors of 1.7 billion. The first figure, however, is rough, and our loan figures for both industrial co-operatives and "other" sectors are interpolations. As an impressionistic guess—based on postwar data, current data for basic branches, the ratio of loans to inventories in local industry, and the probability that loans were large relative to inventories in foreign trade—we take total normed assets and goods shipped as 2.2 in industrial co-operatives and an equal amount in "other" sectors including foreign trade. On similar grounds, we assume that 0.3 of the total in co-operatives and 0.2 in other sectors represented goods shipped.

In company with his data for 1938 Plan, Bogolepov provides figures also for actual owned working capital on January 1, 1933: 8.7 billion in industry, 0.9 in agriculture, 0.5 in transportation and communications, 1.7 in trade and procurement, and 0.5 in "other" sectors. A rough calculation which is not reproduced here (employing the Table I–1 loan data and Usoskin's 1935 data for short-term liabilities and assets) suggests that Bogolepov's owned capital figures are rather low relative to the inventory figures we accept for this date. His owned capital figure for industry, 8.7 billion, compares with that given by Rubinshtein for the same date of 10.5 billion, and his figures for other sectors appear quite implausibly low relative to Usoskin's figures for 1935. On this evidence, we assume some systematic undercoverage in Bogolepov's 1933 data and do not attempt to make use of them.

Grin'ko–37: Grin'ko, p. 30, reports total owned working capital on January 1, 1937, as 37.3 billion, which was approximately 10 billion over January 1, 1936, and that planned for January 1, 1938, as 48 billion and an increase in the year of about 11 billion.

In our discussion of Bogolepov–37, we have concluded that the 1937 and planned 1938 totals from Grin'ko are for basic branches only. For 1936, the implied total of 27.3 compares with the figure derived from Usoskin (Table G–5) for owned capital in basic branches of 25.8 billion. This discrepancy may reflect some difference in coverage, though it is too small to be clearly significant.

In this source, as in others considered here, the owned capital totals appear in context to be meant to be comprehensive. It is our inference from the data in Usoskin–39 that they are not.

Smigla–37: Smigla, p. 118, gives some data which are clearly identical with those cited from Grin'ko: owned capital on January 1, 1937, was 37.3 billion; during 1936 it increased 9.9 billion; during 1937 it was planned to increase 11 billion.

In addition, Smigla, p. 119, provides a detailed breakdown of owned capital of *union* enterprises (billion rubles):

	January 1, 1937	Increase Planned during 1937
Industry	21.835	5.849
Commissariats of Heavy and Defense	13.867	3.609
Commissariat of Light	2.865	.723
Commissariat of Timber	.990	.480
Commissariat of Food	3.367	.925
Transportation and communications	2.662	1.191
Agriculture	5.471	1.356
Commissariat of Agriculture	3.618	.851
Commissariat of State Farms	1.853	.505
Trade and procurement	2.274	.627
Total	32.284	9.201

Given the exclusion of nonunion enterprises from these figures, they appear, taken with total bank loans by sectors, at least broadly consistent with our inventory estimates for 1937. However, the fact that Smigla includes transportation and communications in her data for union enterprises raises a question about our interpretation of the 37.3 billion figure for total owned capital.

If the latter is, as we suppose, comprehensive of basic branches only, then it excludes transportation and communications. Smigla's total for union enterprises exclusive of this category is 29.6 billion, which leaves 7.7 billion of owned capital to be attributed to nonunion enterprises in basic branches. We have from Sobol'–37, q.v., that union industry in 1936 accounted for about 84 percent of gross assets in state industry (the difference presumably representing republican and local industry). If we make the crude assumption that this ratio held in 1937 and for owned capital, the size of the latter in republican and local industry would have been about 4 billion. Secondly, we have from Usoskin–39 (see Table G–5 and the discussion of the 1935 data shown therein) a figure for owned capital in all trade on January 1, 1935, of 3.4 billion. From 1935 to 1937, normed assets and goods shipped in trade increased 90 percent (Table G–4), bank loans increased 60 percent (Table I–1). If owned capital increased in a roughly similar proportion, its total on January 1, 1937, would have been on the order of 5–6 billion, or 3–4 billion more than Smigla attributes to union trade organs, including procurement. Generous allowance being made for error in these calculations, they seem to leave little room for any sector but nonunion basic branches in the 7.7 billion residual. Evidently, the sector coverage of Smigla's data for union enterprises is greater than that of the 37.3 billion total. Compare on this point also Smigla's implied planned totals for January 1, 1938, with those cited above from Bogolepov–37. As is explained in the discussion of the latter source, we use Smigla's 1937 figures for transportation and communications in estimating inventories for that sector.

Zverev–46: This volume consists of Zverev's annual budget messages, 1938 to 1945. The original dates of release of material contained in it, therefore, vary, and no homogeneity of coverage can be inferred from the common source. The apparent inconsistencies in the source, indeed, are among the largest which we encounter.

Zverev reports, p. 19, total owned working capital on January 1, 1938, as 45.7 billion, as against a planned total for that date of 49 billion and a planned increment during 1938 of 8.9 billion. The apparently implied total planned for January 1, 1939, is 54.6 billion.

The 49 billion planned figure for 1938 looks to be a later version of Grin'ko's figure of 48 billion, which we have concluded refers to basic branches only (see notes on Bogolepov–37). Zverev's realized figure of 45.7 billion for 1938, however, is substantially larger than Usoskin's figure for basic branches, excluding equivalents to owned capital, of 41.7 billion (see Table G–5). His implied planned figure of 54.6 billion for 1939, moreover, is substantially larger than a figure which he himself gives later, p. 51, of 49.2 billion.

Elsewhere (Zverev–38, p. 41), Zverev gives a sector breakdown of the 8.9 billion increment planned for 1938 (billion rubles):

Industry	5.735
Agriculture	.884
Transportation and communications	.552
State trade and procurement	.708
Other organizations	.147
Co-operatives	.826
Total	8.853

That Zverev's totals of 45.7 billion for 1938 and 54.6 for 1939 Plan comprehend more than owned capital in basic branches is reasonably clear. Though it could be that his coverage is still for basic branches and that he has merely included equivalents to owned capital, the date is too early to make this plausible, and the correspondence to Usoskin's total inclusive of equivalents (Table G–5) is not convincingly close. His breakdown of the 1938 increment, on the other hand, suggests that his figures may be fully comprehensive (with the usual exclusions of contract construction and nonstate agriculture). However, the 4 billion difference between Zverev's 45.7 billion for 1938 and Usoskin's 41.7 appears too small to represent all sectors other than basic branches. In particular, it is rather close to the

3.9 billion figure for owned capital in transportation and communications planned for 1938 according to Smigla–37. But we conclude only that Zverev here includes more than basic branches and less than all sectors.

As noted, Zverev, p. 51, gives owned capital planned for January 1, 1939, as 49.2 billion. With this, he gives owned capital *requirements* (presumably normed amounts) for January 1, 1940, as 56.7 billion and the planned increment in owned capital of *state* enterprises during 1939 as 10.1. The difference between the 49.2 billion planned figure for 1939 and that cited above of 54.6 billion suggests that Zverev may here have reverted to a coverage of basic branches only. If we subtract the planned increment for state enterprises from the 1940 planned requirements, the resulting total of 46.6 billion for January 1, 1939, resembles a figure of 48 billion which we cite below from Shenger–40 and identify as for basic branches and exclusive of equivalents. It falls short of a figure of 52.1 billion which we derive below from D'iachenko–40 and which evidently includes more than basic branches.

Data from Zverev for 1940, 1941, and 1945 are discussed in notes to Table G–1 for those dates.

Shenger–40: Shenger, p. 25, gives a figure, which he attributes to the Commissariat of Finance, of "about" 48 billion rubles for owned working capital on January 1, 1939. He does not state whether or not equivalents to owned capital are included in the figure, but since he discusses these at length elsewhere and is generally a careful writer, it is reasonable to infer that they are excluded. In the same paragraph, he gives the total of working capital as "approximately 98–100 billion." The latter figures are the same as those given by Usoskin–39 which we have identified as for normed assets and goods shipped in basic branches. It appears likely that Shenger's 48 billion of owned capital refers also to basic branches, which reading fits our interpretation of data for 1939 from Zverev–46 and D'iachenko–40.

D'iachenko–40: D'iachenko, p. 405, gives a planned total of owned working capital for January 1, 1941, of 71.1 billion, a planned increment during 1940 of 10.4, and a preliminary realized increment during 1939 of 8.6. The apparently implied 1939 total is 52.1 billion. The difference between this figure and Shenger's 48 billion resembles the difference between Zverev's 1938 figure of 45.7 billion and Usoskin's of 41.7. D'iachenko probably includes more than basic branches but less than all sectors; he may exclude equivalents to owned capital. See also the discussion of this source in notes to Table G–1 for 1940–41.

Den'gi i kredit, 1939:4: In an unsigned article, this source provides, p. 12, a percentage distribution of short-term liabilities for the commissariats of heavy, timber, food, light, and local industries, as of January 1:

	1934	1938
Owned working capital	47.7	44.5
Bank loans	26.7	37.2
Kreditory	25.6	18.3
Total	100.0	100.0

For 1934, the source (pp. 10–11) reports bank loans as 1.102 billion for heavy industry, 1.377 for light, 2.022 for food. Loans to timber and local industries are not given in the source but are elsewhere given as .630 and .243 respectively (Gosbank–35, p. 10; we here take loans to the timber industry as for the commissariat only). The sum of bank loans to these five sectors is 5.374 billion, which, with the above percentages, implies owned capital of 9.6 billion, *kreditory* of 5.2, and total liabilities of 20.2. These figures are at least plausible relative to those for 1935 derived from Usoskin (see Table G–5; note that we interpret Usoskin's 1935 data for industry as inclusive of sales-supply).

As a means of checking our estimate of normed assets in state industry in 1934, which is derived from Konovalov, we make a rough estimate of the same item implied by the above data. From Usoskin's data for industry in 1935 and assuming that equivalents were the same ratio to owned capital in industry as in all basic branches, we can compute that the ratio of owned capital plus bank loans to normed assets was 98.9 percent. If the same ratio held in 1934, the 15.0 billion of owned capital and loans computed above implies normed assets of 15.2 billion. This compares with the 15.4 billion figure which we derive from Konovalov.

We cannot repeat the same kind of calculation with the 1938 breakdown because we lack usable data on the ratio of owned capital and loans to assets in industry inclusive of sales-supply. However, the same percentage breakdown is given in Granovskii–40, p. 553, together with a loan total of 21.3 billion. The implied total of owned capital plus bank loans, 46.7 billion, appears roughly consistent with Usoskin's total (Table G–5) of owned capital, equivalents, and bank loans, for state industry excluding sales-supply, of 40.3 billion (*kreditory* in the 1938 breakdown appear to be net of *debitory*).

Atlas–58: Atlas, p. 148, reports for January 1, 1938, owned working capital and equivalents as 7.7 billion in the Commissariat for Light Industry, 9.2 in the Commissariat for Food Industry, and bank loans to the two as 6.6 and 8.5 respectively. The bank loan figures do not diverge greatly from those used in Table I–1, though they are somewhat higher. The owned capital figures look implausibly large, in comparison especially with the planned figures for this date (for union industry) given in Smigla–37. We cannot account for this seeming discrepancy.

Derivation of the Table G–1 Estimates

The figures shown in Table G–1 are derived from those compiled in Table G–4 by a series of extensions and adjustments, the intermediate results of which are not shown here.

In effect, we first complete Table G–4.

(*i*) We extrapolate total goods shipped in state industry (including sales-supply), agriculture, procurement, and domestic trade from 1934 to 1933 on total loans on goods shipped (Table I–1). The total is divided by extrapolating goods shipped for the same sectors from 1934 on normed assets and adjusting to the total.

(*ii*) For 1933 to 1936, we distribute total goods shipped in state industry (including sales-supply) between producer goods (heavy and timber) and consumer goods (food, light, and local) by extrapolating from 1951 on normed assets and adjusting to the known totals. For simplicity, this extrapolation is done from the Table G–1 data for inventories on hand and goods shipped in 1951. The resulting estimates for producer and consumer goods are distributed among their component industries in proportion to normed assets.

(*iii*) For 1937 to 1939, we extrapolate total normed assets and goods shipped in component state industries (including sales-supply) on bank loans (Table I–1) and adjust the results proportionately to the known totals. The division between normed assets and goods shipped is similarly extrapolated by component sectors from 1936, and the results are adjusted to the known totals.

(*iv*) For all years except 1937, we extrapolate both normed assets and goods shipped in industrial co-operatives, transportation and communications (where goods shipped are negligible), and other nonagricultural sectors from 1937 on bank loans (Table I–1). Loans to foreign trade are included with those to "other" sectors. These extrapolations disregard some possible changes in the ratio of bank loans to assets which are allowed for in the estimates for other sectors. The magnitudes involved, however, are too small to call for precision at this point.

Secondly, we undertake to adjust the figures resulting from the above procedures to obtain inventories on hand and goods shipped of coverage appropriate to our purposes.

(*i*) For 1935 through 1938, we have from Usoskin–39 (Tables G–5) absolute totals of expenses of future periods in basic branches (state industry, state agriculture, procurement, and domestic trade). For 1934, we compute a similar figure, of 0.8 billion, from the percentage breakdown given by Usoskin–39 (see Paragraph [*viii*] of the data transcribed from this source in notes for Table G–4) and the total figure given by Konovalov–34 (see notes thereon for Table G–4).

In deriving Table H–1, we distribute 0.6 billion of the 1.0 total in 1937 to state producer goods industries, 0.3 to state consumer goods, and 0.1 to domestic trade. We apply the 1937 ratios of expenses of future periods to normed assets in these three sectors to the sector totals for other years, 1934–38, and adjust the results proportionately to the known totals. For 1933 and 1939, we assume these ratios were the same as in 1934 and 1938 respectively.

For the remaining, minor, sectors, we assume on the basis of 1951 data (see Table G–6) that expenses of future periods were of trivial magnitude in the years covered here.

(*ii*) We consolidate the data for component industries into producer goods (heavy and timber) and consumer goods (food, light, local, and industrial co-operative) industries.

(*iii*) In Table H–1 we estimate the 1937 values of small tools in all sectors except other nonagricultural sectors. We assume that the ratio of small tools to other inventories on hand (as computed to this point) was the same in all years, 1933 through 1936, and increase the estimates correspondingly. Inventories in "other" sectors are raised arbitrarily by 5 percent in 1933–36, 2.5 percent in 1937. In 1938 and 1939 the whole of small tools are assumed to have been included in reported inventories.

(*iv*) We deduct immature livestock from inventories in state agriculture in all years on the assumption their share in the total was the same as in 1937 (see notes for Table H–1).

(*v*) In Table G–4 and from procedures described above, we have estimates of goods shipped in each sector for all years 1933–39, as they were carried on enterprise books. However, the extension during 1936 of the allowed period of payment for goods (see Chapter 5, p. 126) presumably accounts in substantial part for the large increase in recorded goods shipped between January 1, 1936 and 1937. To reduce the distortion resulting from this change, we adjust upward the 1936 estimates of goods shipped, by sectors, to equate their ratios to inventories on hand with those of 1937. We make an equal percentage adjustment in the estimates for 1933–35. In effect, we chain the 1933–36 series for goods shipped to those for 1937–39. The procedure implies that of the total increase during 1936 in the book value of goods shipped, 5.3 billion, 2.8 was due to the lengthening of the payment period.

1940–41

The estimates for 1940 and 1941 are extrapolated from 1939, chiefly on bank loans and owned working capital. The uncertainties involved in the interpretation of owned capital data in this period are discussed in the notes to Table G–4 for Bogolepov–37. Adjustments for the effects of the territorial acquisitions are made after estimates have been composed on the basis of data as they were reported.

(*i*) According to Zverev–46, p. 80, total owned capital planned for January 1, 1941, was 71.1 billion or 10.3 billion over January 1, 1946, which implies a realized figure for 1940 of 60.8 billion (reference should be made to the discussion of this source in notes for Table G–4). Subsequently, p. 108, Zverev gives the planned 1941 total for state organs only as 68.4 billion and indicates that this plan was underfulfilled by 2.7 billion. Assuming the percentage underfulfilled of the 71.1 billion goal was the same, the realized figure of the latter coverage for 1941 was 68.3 billion. D'iachenko–40, p. 405, gives a planned 1941 total and a planned 1940 increment effectively identical with Zverev's and a 1939 increment which implies a total on January 1, 1939, of 52.1 billion. We have previously (see notes to Table G–4) surmised that D'iachenko's data include more than owned capital of basic branches but less than owned capital and equivalents for all sectors. We now make the assumption that the coverage of Zverev's data is the same as D'iachenko's. This yields a seemingly homogeneous series of 52.1 billion for 1939, 60.8 for 1940, and 68.3 for 1941.

In a postwar source, Atlas–58, p. 242, the following information is given: sources of finance consisted in 1941 of 52.9 percent owned capital, 34.2 percent bank loans, and 12.9 percent *kreditory* net of *debitory*; in 1951 the same shares were 46.0 percent, 45.0 percent, and 9.0 percent, respectively; in 1951 owned capital was 211.2 percent of its 1941 level, bank loans 296.0 percent, and *kreditory* net of *debitory* 167.6 percent. As can be seen, the 1951/1941 ratios are not consistent with the changes in the percentage shares. In the discussion below of 1951 and related years, we conclude that Atlas' percentage breakdown for 1951 and a similar one for 1956 are congruent with the TsSU–61 data which we use for those years, excluding contract construction. Applying Atlas' 1951/1941 ratios to totals given in Table G–6, net of contract construction, yields 1941 figures of

56.3 billion for bank loans and 75.1 billion for owned working capital, presumably inclusive of equivalents. The loan figure corresponds fairly closely to the reported loan total for that date of 55.0 billion (Table I–1). The owned capital figure differs from the 68.3 billion derived from Zverev by an amount which could plausibly represent owned capital equivalents and minor sectors omitted by Zverev. If, however, owned capital is computed from Atlas' percentage breakdown and 55.0 billion of loans, the implied figure is 85.1 billion. We are unable to account for the discrepancy between this figure and that of 75.1 billion, although Atlas may here have omitted some part of bank loans (his 1941 percentage breakdown appears also on p. 187, where it is coupled with Usoskin's 1938 breakdown for basic branches). Because it is more plausible, we accept 75.1 billion as the proper 1941 total for owned capital inclusive of equivalents and comprehensive of all sectors (except contract construction and nonstate agriculture). We raise the totals previously derived for 1939 and 1940 in the ratio 75.1/68.3.

(*ii*) To provide a base for the extrapolation, we compose a distribution of owned capital plus equivalents in 1939 from data for 1951 (Table G–8; figures shown there for sales-supply are distributed proportionately among component state industries). Owned capital and bank loans in combination are extrapolated from 1951 to 1939 by sectors on inventories on hand plus goods shipped (the derivation of the 1939 asset estimates for detailed industrial sectors is described in the notes for 1933–39; figures for other sectors are from Table G–1). The resulting estimates are adjusted proportionately to the sum of owned capital (estimated above) and total bank loans (Table I–1). Loans to collective farms are excluded and loans to foreign trade are combined with those to "other" sectors. From the combined sum of owned capital and bank loans for each sector, loans are deducted to obtain owned capital alone.

From the data for 1939, owned capital in all sectors except domestic trade is extrapolated to 1940 and 1941 on bank loans. For trade, owned capital plus bank loans are extrapolated on inventories of finished products in retail prices (Table K–1) and owned capital computed as a residual. Owned capital in all sectors except trade is adjusted to the known totals net of capital in trade.

Combined sums of inventories on hand and goods shipped are extrapolated by sectors from 1939 on owned capital plus bank loans and, for domestic trade, on inventories of finished products in retail prices.

Estimates for component industrial sectors are at this point consolidated into totals for producer goods industries and consumer goods industries.

(*iii*) Total goods shipped are extrapolated from 1939 on loans on goods shipped (Table J–1). Distributions between inventories on hand and goods shipped are extrapolated from 1939 by sectors and adjusted to the known totals.

(*iv*) For 1941 only, we estimate a figure for inventories on hand in contract construction by extrapolating from 1951 on loans to contract construction for procurement of materials (Table J–1). The reliability of this procedure, which is not great, is considered in Appendix J.

The estimates made thus far contain no deliberate adjustments for the territorial acquisitions of 1939 and 1940. From the character of the data employed, it is clear that the estimates cannot include more assets in the new territories than those held in enterprises which had been "socialized" by January 1, 1940 or 1941, and they may not include that much. The acquisitions of 1939 came late in the year, and we find no suggestion that our data for January 1, 1940, include any assets in the acquired territories. We assume, therefore, that no such assets are included and, following our procedure with fixed capital, raise our estimates for the beginning of 1940 by 5 percent. Doubtless improperly, we apply the same percentage to all sectors and to both inventories on hand and goods shipped.

By 1941, our data clearly do reflect some part of the assets in the new territories, including those acquired in the course of 1940. We are told (Edinovich–57, p. 14) that the Bank of Lithuania was converted into the Lithuanian Branch of Gosbank in October, 1940. Reported totals of Gosbank loans for January 1, 1941, are explicitly inclusive of loans in the Baltic Republics (see Popov–57, p. 246), though the total, 533 million rubles, looks relatively small. Since reported data for state and co-operative trade in 1940 include trade in the new territories (cf. TsSU–56, p. 31), it is reasonable to suppose that the data for trade inventories on January 1, 1941, do also. We assume, lacking firmer evidence, that by the beginning of 1941 all inventories in the territories acquired in 1939 are covered in our data and that half of those in the 1940 acquisitions are covered. As a rough correction for the understatement, we raise our estimates for all sectors by 2.5 percent.

The estimates for 1941 do not incorporate some data appearing in Soviet sources. In *Den'gi i kredit*, 1954:1, p. 6, the "prewar" share of bank loans in total working capital is given as 31.5 percent as against a "present" share of 41.2 percent. These same figures are reproduced in later sources. In the absence of additional data, their coverage is not identifiable. In Mitel'man–58, p. 43, total owned working capital on January 1, 1941, is given as "about 100" billion rubles. This appears to be an erroneous figure.

1944–45

The only usable data available for these years are the series for finished products in trade at retail prices (Table K–1) and total bank loans (Table I–2; we do not attempt to employ the 1944 figure for loans to industry shown in that table). We extrapolate inventories in trade, both on hand and shipped, from 1946 on the finished products series. Total inventories, excluding construction, are extrapolated similarly on total bank loans. The latter estimates are understood to give only a very rough guide to the probable behavior of total inventories in these years.

A reported figure for total owned capital on January 1, 1945, is available (see notes for 1946), but it is not usable because of the lack of a 1945 breakdown of bank loans by sectors.

1946

Zverev–46, p. 154, reports total owned working capital planned for January 1, 1946, as 66.0 billion and an increase of 6.8 billion over 1945 (implying a realized total for 1945 of 59.2). How nearly the 1946 planned total was realized is not known. If the ratio of owned capital to bank loans (see Table I–2) remained at the 1945 level, realized owned capital on January 1, 1946, would have been 64.0 billion. We have noted in the discussion of data for the late 1930's and for 1940–41 the uncertain and evidently varying coverage of Zverev's owned capital totals. For 1941, Zverev's total of 68.3 billion compares with a total which we take to be comprehensive except for the exclusion of contract construction of 75.1 billion.

We can estimate 1946 owned capital by sectors, excluding contract construction, from 1951 (Table G–8). For domestic trade, owned capital and bank loans in combination are extrapolated on finished products in retail prices (Table K–1), and owned capital is computed as a residual. For all other sectors, owned capital is extrapolated on bank loans (Table I–3). The sum of the sector estimates derived in this manner is 70.5 billion, which differs from 64.0–66.0 billion by about the same percentage as does 75.1 billion from 68.3. On this evidence, we extrapolate inventories on hand plus goods shipped by component sectors directly from 1951: domestic trade on inventories of finished products, all other sectors on bank loans. Foreign trade is included with "other" sectors in the extrapolation.

Total goods shipped are extrapolated from 1951 on loans on goods shipped (Table J–1). Goods shipped by component sectors are extrapolated from 1951 on the combined sums of inventories on hand and goods shipped and adjusted to the known totals. Inventories on hand are computed as residuals. Estimates for detailed industrial component sectors (see Table G–7) are consolidated into producer and consumer goods industries.

1947–48

Combined inventories on hand and goods shipped are extrapolated by sectors from 1951 by the same procedures as for 1946. The division of loans between heavy and timber industries, which is not shown in Table I–3, is interpolated on a straight line between 1946 and 1951. The ratio of goods shipped to inventories on hand in each sector is assumed to have changed linearly from 1946 to 1951. Component industrial sectors are consolidated as in 1946.

For 1947, a figure for inventories on hand in contract construction is extrapolated from 1951 on bank loans to contract construction for procurement of materials (Table J–1). On the reliability of this procedure, see Appendix J.

1949, 1950, and 1952

We consider these three years together, because they pose a common problem. On January 1 of each, a general revision of industrial prices was made effective. The only basis we have for estimating inventories in these years is bank loans. The question which arises is how far the January 1 price changes are reflected in the loan data.

From the order of magnitude of the loan figures (see Table I–3), especially for January 1, 1949, when the price change was very large, we assume that the loan data do reflect in some degree the January 1 price revisions, although it is not clear from the loan figures that this assumption is correct for all sectors. If the usual principles of inventory valuation (see the discussion in Chapter 5) were applied in these instances, inventories on hand were revalued with the price changes, but goods shipped were not. If the usual principles of bank lending held, bank loans on inventories on hand were revalued, but loans on goods shipped were not. We assume that the usual principles in fact were operative and estimate inventories for most sectors by first converting the reported loan figures to their equivalents at valuations in prices made effective on January 1. If our assumptions are correct, the resulting estimates for inventories on hand should correspond to their book values, but the estimates for goods shipped will differ from their book values in proportion to the difference between prices preceding and following the January 1 changes. For domestic trade, we follow a different procedure, and our estimates for that sector may not adequately reflect the January 1 price changes. We do not attempt to estimate figures for state agriculture.

Producer Goods Industries

The estimating method for this sector will serve as a prototype for others and hence is described in detail.

(*i*) We commence from the Table I–3 loans for producer goods industries proper and for producer goods sales-supply organs. No attempt is made here to treat heavy and timber industries separately.

(*ii*) We have for 1956 (see notes for 1951 and related years) that loans on normed assets accounted for 17.7 out of 37.6 billion or 47.1 percent of total loans to producer goods industries. The bulk of the remaining loans represent those on goods shipped, although some small portion may have been on assets that were revalued. Minor adjustments might also be made in the ratio for known changes in the composition of inventories and of bank loans, but they are too small, relative to the crudity of the procedure, to be justified. We therefore assume that the 47.1 percent ratio would have held in each of the three years considered if uniform prices had applied to all kinds of inventories.

Using the deflators calculated in Table L–2 for prices before and after the January 1 changes, we calculate the share of loans on normed assets in total loans as actually valued. From this and from the reported loan totals cited above, we calculate absolute values for total loans at the price levels which became effective on January 1.

(*iii*) For sales-supply, we estimate a loan composition at uniform prices from data for 1951. In that year, goods shipped were 8.9 billion (Table G–7), and we assume that loans on goods shipped were the same. Total bank loans on the same date were 12.5 billion (Table I–3). We assume all loans not on goods shipped, or 28.8 percent of the total, were on normed assets. This probably overstates the share of loans on normed assets in sales-supply, but our estimate for industry proper may understate the portion of loans affected by the price change. We proceed from this share as from the similar share for industry proper.

(*iv*) The foregoing operations yield total loans to industry, inclusive of sales-supply, at prices effective on January 1, of 42.3 billion in 1949, 40.2 in 1950, and 46.9 in 1952. Because of the roughness of the calculation, we simply interpolate inventories on hand and goods shipped in combination on these loan totals, between 1948 and 1951 and between 1951 and 1953. Loan totals for the latter three years are from Table I–3; asset figures are from Table G–1. The divisions between inventories on hand and goods shipped are interpolated linearly between the same years.

Consumer Goods Industries

The procedure is the same as that used for producer goods industry. Total bank loans for consumer goods industry (component industries are not treated separately) and for the related sales-supply organs are from Table I–3. The normal ratio of loans on normed assets to total loans in industry proper is taken to be that of 1956 (see notes for 1951 and related years) and in sales-supply that of 1951 (goods shipped are from Table G–7). The necessary price indexes are given in Table L–3.

Transportation and Communications

We have no basis for determining how far bank loans to this sector might have reflected price changes occurring on January 1, and the magnitudes of the loan figures do not suggest a single assumption which would yield plausible results for all three years. Quite arbitrarily, we assume that reported loans (Table I–3) reflect valuations that are midway between those preceding and following the January 1 changes (see Table L–4). Reported loans are then adjusted by the ratio of the post-change prices to the average so calculated. The derivation of the inventory figures from the adjusted loan totals follows the procedures used for the industrial sectors.

Procurement

The procedure is the same as that used for industry. Total reported loans are taken from Table I–3. Loans on goods shipped in 1951, which is taken as the normal year, are assumed equal to goods shipped (Table G–1). All other loans are assumed, probably with some inaccuracy, to be on normed assets. The necessary price indexes are given in Table L–5.

Domestic Trade

Inventories on hand and goods shipped in combination are interpolated between 1948 and 1951 and 1951 and 1953 on inventories of finished products at retail prices (Table K–1). The share of goods shipped is interpolated linearly between the same dates. The resulting estimates doubtless do not reflect accurately the effects of the January 1 price changes, which presumably altered both the ratio of book values to retail prices of inventories of finished products and the ratio, in current prices, of finished products to other kinds of inventories in trade. This deficiency in the trade estimates is not peculiar to the three years under consideration, but it may be especially large for them. As in other years for which the finished product series are the basis of the Table G–1 estimates, the latter are not utilized in deriving indexes of trade inventories in constant prices. The Table G–1 estimate for January 1, 1950, does affect our estimate of the absolute level of trade inventories in 1950 prices (see Appendix M), but errors in it are likely to be of minor consequence in that calculation.

Contract Construction

Data are lacking for 1949 and 1950. For 1952, the procedure is the same as that used for transportation and communications. The reported loan

TABLE G-6

REPORTED WORKING CAPITAL ACCOUNTS, BY MAJOR SECTORS, IN CURRENT PRICES, 1951, 1956, 1959, AND 1960

(January 1--Billion Rubles)

	Industry, Total				State Industry				Industrial Co-operatives			
	1951	1956	1959	1960	1951	1956	1959	1960	1951	1956	1959	1960
Assets												
1. Normed Assets	155.7	196.7	260.8	274.7	149.0	186.4	--	--	6.7	10.3	--	--
2. Inventories on Hand	151.5	190.8	253.8	266.5	145.0	180.8	--	--	6.5	10.0	--	--
3. Immature Livestock	0.0	0.0	0.0	0.0	0.0	0.0	--	--	0.0	0.0	--	--
4. Expenses of Future Periods	4.2	5.9	7.0	8.2	4.0	5.6	--	--	0.2	0.3	--	--
5. Goods Shipped and Services Rendered	20.9	28.1	37.4	39.2	19.4	26.5	--	--	1.5	1.6	--	--
6. Monetary Assets	12.6	14.8	18.4	18.6	10.7	13.2	--	--	1.9	1.6	--	--
7. Debitory	18.6	13.5	10.8	11.0	17.2	12.8	--	--	1.4	0.7	--	--
8. Other Assets	1.5	2.0	0.7	0.7	1.4	1.9	--	--	0.1	0.1	--	--
Liabilities												
1. Owned Working Capital and Equivalents	106.5	137.2	155.5	164.5	98.8	127.9	--	--	7.7	9.3	--	--
2. Bank Loans	69.3	87.5	126.6	132.2	68.0	84.3	--	--	1.3	3.2	--	--
3. Kreditory	30.1	27.3	37.7	38.5	28.1	25.5	--	--	2.0	1.8	--	--
4. Other Liabilities	3.3	3.1	8.2	8.9	2.8	3.1	--	--	0.5	0.0	--	--
Total	209.3	255.1	328.0	344.2	197.7	240.8	--	--	11.6	14.3	--	--

REPORTED WORKING CAPITAL ACCOUNTS, BY MAJOR SECTORS, IN CURRENT PRICES, 1951, 1956, 1959, AND 1960

(January 1--Billion Rubles)

	Sales-Supply				Transportation and Communications				State Agriculture			
	1951	1956	1959	1960	1951	1956	1959	1960	1951	1956	1959	1960
Assets												
1. Normed Assets	21.0	25.3	42.4	51.2	7.0	7.9	9.0	9.9	14.9	19.8	33.7	42.8
2. Inventories on Hand	21.0	25.3	42.4	51.1	6.7	7.7	8.9	9.8	9.3	13.9	21.6	26.6
3. Immature Livestock	0.0	0.0	0.0	0.0	0.0	0.0	0.0	0.0	5.6	5.7	11.9	15.9
4. Expenses of Future Periods	0.0	0.0	0.0	0.1	0.3	0.2	0.1	0.1	0.0	0.2	0.2	0.3
5. Goods Shipped and Services Rendered	15.5	16.8	21.2	23.4	1.0	1.3	1.4	1.4	0.2	0.1	0.2	0.3
6. Monetary Assets	3.2	3.3	3.4	3.1	5.0	6.1	6.8	7.6	1.0	2.8	2.9	2.4
7. Debitory	7.8	4.9	3.2	3.5	1.4	2.0	1.8	1.9	0.6	2.1	1.3	1.5
8. Other Assets	0.0	0.1	0.1	0.1	0.0	0.0	0.2	0.2	0.5	0.4	1.1	1.7
Liabilities												
1. Owned Working Capital and Equivalents	10.7	12.3	16.9	19.6	6.2	7.2	8.3	9.2	10.2	14.4	22.6	28.9
2. Bank Loans	25.0	27.0	39.9	47.2	2.3	2.3	2.7	2.5	5.1	5.8	10.6	13.8
3. Kreditory	11.6	10.9	12.6	13.4	5.5	7.0	6.9	7.4	1.2	4.0	3.0	3.3
4. Other Liabilities	0.3	0.2	0.8	1.1	0.5	0.7	1.3	2.0	0.7	1.0	3.1	2.7
Total	47.6	50.4	70.2	81.3	14.4	17.3	19.2	21.0	17.2	25.2	39.3	48.6

TABLE G-6 (continued)

REPORTED WORKING CAPITAL ACCOUNTS, BY MAJOR SECTORS, IN CURRENT PRICES, 1951, 1956, 1959, AND 1960

(January 1--Billion Rubles)

	Procurement				Domestic Trade				Contract Construction			
	1951	1956	1959	1960	1951	1956	1959	1960	1951	1956	1959	1960
Assets												
1. Normed Assets	8.3	8.0	18.4	37.5	67.7	108.9	165.4	192.6	10.9	18.1	22.6	26.3
2. Inventories on Hand	8.3	8.0	18.3	37.5	67.4	108.5	165.1	192.2	10.6	17.6	22.1	25.7
3. Immature Livestock	0.0	0.0	0.0	0.0	0.0	0.0	0.0	0.0	0.0	0.0	0.0	0.0
4. Expenses of Future Periods	0.0	0.0	0.1	0.0	0.3	0.4	0.3	0.4	0.3	0.5	0.5	0.6
5. Goods Shipped and Services Rendered .	1.7	1.9	3.3	5.5	6.8	6.7	8.2	8.4	0.6	0.9	1.6	1.9
6. Monetary Assets	0.8	1.1	0.9	1.5	3.6	5.2	6.7	6.5	1.3	2.6	7.0	8.6
7. Debitory	1.4	1.5	0.6	2.3	6.5	5.7	6.1	7.5	5.0	11.4	13.1	14.5
8. Other Assets.	0.0	0.1	0.4	0.4	0.2	0.3	0.2	0.2	0.0	0.0	0.0	0.1
Liabilities												
1. Owned Working Capital and Equivalents	2.6	3.0	3.4	6.8	17.5	48.5	58.2	64.5	1.5	7.8	15.0	17.0
2. Bank Loans	7.9	8.3	16.8	34.1	50.3	59.6	104.7	125.4	4.1	4.4	5.2	7.4
3. Kreditory.	1.3	1.3	3.0	5.7	16.5	17.6	22.6	23.9	12.0	20.7	22.8	25.5
4. Other Liabilities	0.5	0.1	0.3	0.7	0.5	1.0	1.1	1.3	0.1	0.2	1.3	1.4
Total.	12.2	12.7	23.5	47.2	84.8	126.7	186.6	215.1	17.7	33.0	44.3	51.3

TABLE G-6 (concluded)

REPORTED WORKING CAPITAL ACCOUNTS, BY MAJOR SECTORS, IN CURRENT PRICES, 1951, 1956, 1959, AND 1960
(January 1--Billion Rubles)

	Other Sectors				Total			
	1951	1956	1959	1960	1951	1956	1959	1960
Assets								
1. Normed Assets	10.0	8.5	20.7	28.1	295.5	393.2	572.8	663.1
2. Inventories on Hand	9.5	8.8	19.4	27.2	284.3	380.6	551.6	636.6
3. Immature Livestock	0.3	-0.1	0.7	0.7	5.9	5.5	12.6	16.6
4. Expenses of Future Periods	0.2	-0.2	0.3	0.3	5.3	7.1	8.6	9.9
5. Goods Shipped and Services Rendered	1.1	1.0	2.1	3.0	47.8	56.8	75.4	83.2
6. Monetary Assets	2.9	1.6	4.7	5.9	30.4	37.5	50.8	54.0
7. Debitory	5.6	5.0	9.3	13.7	46.9	46.1	46.3	55.7
8. Other Assets	-0.1	-0.1	-0.4	-0.8	2.1	2.7	2.2	2.6
Liabilities								
1. Owned Working Capital and Equivalents	5.0	4.5	14.0	15.8	160.2	234.9	293.8	326.3
2. Bank Loans	6.9	4.1	9.1	14.3	170.8	199.0	315.5	376.9
3. Kreditory	6.8	6.2	11.7	18.1	85.0	94.9	120.4	135.7
4. Other Liabilities	0.8	1.2	1.7	1.7	6.8	7.5	17.9	19.7
Total	19.5	15.9	36.4	49.8	422.8	536.3	747.7	858.6

totals used are those shown in Table J–1 for loans for procurement of materials. Deflators are shown in Table L–7.

Other Nonagricultural Sectors

Taking into account the calculations made for other specified sectors of the difference between loans as reported and loans adjusted to reflect fully the January 1 price changes, we raise the reported bank loans to other nonagricultural sectors (Table I–3; loans to foreign trade are included) by 20 percent in 1949 and lower them by 4 percent in 1950 and 1 percent in 1952. Our procedures thereafter are the same as for industry.

1951, 1956, 1959, 1960

Sources to Table G–6

The inventory estimates for these four years derive for the most part from exceptionally comprehensive and detailed balance sheets published in TsSU–61, pp. 92–101. Data provided by this source are presented in Table G–6, though not all the detail available in the source is retained here.

Except for the division of total industry (which is given exclusive of sales-supply) between state industry and industrial co-operatives, total assets and normed assets for each sector and for the combined total are given directly in TsSU–61. All the remaining figures are computed from these absolute data and from percentage breakdowns given in the source, except for "other sectors," for which no percentage breakdown is given. Figures for the latter, except those for total and normed assets, are computed as residuals: as that part of total assets in each category which is not accounted for in the specified sectors. The asset categories shown in Table G–6 are the same as those used in the source, except that all normed assets other than immature livestock and expenses of future periods are here classed as inventories on hand. The sector categories are the same as those in the source, except that "domestic trade" in the table is given in the source merely as "trade." That foreign trade is excluded from the trade figures and included with "other sectors" is argued below.

The division of total industry between state and co-operative industry is based on data published in *Vestnik statistiki*, 1957:2, pp. 94–96. These are identified as the antecedents of the breakdowns for 1951 and 1956 given in TsSU–61 (see *Vestnik statistiki*, 1961:6, p. 88, fn.). They differ from the latter principally in that (*i*) they consist of percentage breakdowns only, (*ii*) contract construction is omitted, (*iii*) the "other" asset category is lacking, (*iv*) goods shipped and *debitory* are combined in a single category, (*v*) some immature livestock are shown for nonagricultural sectors, and (*vi*) percentage breakdowns are given both for total industry and for state industry. It is from the last that we estimate the share of state in total industry in 1951 and 1956. In all categories excepting "other assets" and the subcomponents of normed assets, shares in state industry are assumed to differ from those in all industry by the percentages implied in the *Vestnik statistiki* breakdowns. The share of "other assets" is assumed the same in state as in all industry. The shares of immature livestock and of expenses of future periods in total normed assets are assumed the same in state as in all industry (they are the same in the *Vestnik statistiki* data), and inventories on hand are computed as a residual. The resulting percentage breakdowns for state industry are converted to absolute figures on the basis of total bank loans to state industry, which are taken to equal total loans (Table G–6) minus loans to industrial co-operatives (Table I–3). Figures for industrial co-operatives, other than loans, are computed as residuals. Since the division of bank loans between state and co-operative industry is not entirely reliable (see both the notes to Table I–3 and the discussion below of the Table G–6 loan figures), the estimates may err on this account, though they appear plausible.

Returning to the TsSU–61 data, we note first that there is evidence of some internal inconsistency. Asset categories computed as residuals for "other sectors" are in some instances negative and in others behave erratically over time (this is true of detailed categories additional to those shown in Table G–6). The cause of these discrepancies is unclear. Since they are small and affect only minor asset categories of no immediate concern, we make no effort to correct for them.

The character of the sector classifications in the TsSU–61 data can be inferred by comparison of the bank loan figures derived in Table G–6 with reported bank loans shown in Table I–3 (billion rubles):

	Table I–3	Table G–6	Table I–3 minus Table G–6
Industry			
1951	69.8	69.3	0.5
1956	88.7	87.5	1.2
1959	131.8	126.6	5.2
1960	137.3	132.2	5.1
Sales-supply			
1951	25.8	25.0	0.8
1956	27.1	27.0	0.1
1959	40.3	39.9	0.4
1960	47.2	47.2	0.0
Transportation and communications			
1951	2.3	2.3	0.0
1956	2.3	2.3	0.0
1959	2.8	2.7	0.1
1960	2.5	2.5	0.0
Agriculture and procurement			
1951	13.3	13.0	0.3
1956	16.5	14.1	2.4
1959	32.2	27.4	4.8
1960	59.1	47.9	11.2
Trade			
1951	54.9	50.3	4.6
1956	63.5	59.6	3.9
1959	112.3	104.7	7.6
1960	135.4	125.4	10.0

	Table I–3	Table G–6	Table I–3 minus Table G–6
Contract construction			
1951	6.1	4.1	2.0
1956	10.9	4.4	6.5
1959	10.7	5.2	5.5
1960	12.3	7.4	4.9
Other sectors			
1951	1.1	6.9	—5.8
1956	1.7	4.1	—2.4
1959	1.4	9.1	—7.7
1960	1.5	14.3	—12.8
Total			
1951	173.3	170.8	2.5
1956	210.7	199.0	11.7
1959	331.5	315.5	16.0
1960	395.4	376.9	18.5

Both sets of loan data originate in the same agency, i.e., TsSU. Both are arranged and captioned in their sources in much the same way.

The loan figures in the two for sales-supply and for transportation and communications correspond closely. Loans shown for other sectors differ, but for reasons which can be identified.

(*i*) Loans to industry not accounted for in Table G–6 are approximately equal to loans issued by Gosbank for "the introduction of new techniques and mechanization," and for "the increased production of consumer goods" (see Table J–1 for reported figures for 1951, 1956, and 1959). While loans for these purposes are included with short-term loans in published statistics, they are issued essentially for fixed capital purposes. TsSU presumably has excluded them and the assets they finance from the present accounts.

(*ii*) The data for agriculture in Table G–6 are explicitly for state agriculture; the difference between the two loan series for agriculture and procurement presumably represents loans to collective farms. We have no reported data for the latter as of January 1 (those shown in Table I–3 are derived from Table G–6). As of July 1, loans "for the productive needs of collective farms" are given in Popov–57, p. 76, as 1.5 billion in 1951 and 4.8 billion in 1956, which appear consistent with the residuals computed above. The large increase in the residual from 1959 to 1960 is probably explained in part by changes which occurred in the course of 1959 in the Bank's procedures for lending to collective farms (see Korovushkin–60, p. 9).

(*iii*) The differences in the loan figures for trade in 1951 and 1956 correspond closely to reported loans to foreign trade of 4.7 and 3.7 billion rubles respectively (see Table I–2). We infer that the trade data in Table G–6 are for domestic trade only. Reported figures for loans to foreign trade are not available for 1959 and 1960, but the calculated residuals look like plausible values for such loans.

TABLE G-7

WORKING CAPITAL ACCOUNTS FOR INDUSTRY AND SALES-SUPPLY, SELECTED ITEMS, IN CURRENT PRICES, 1951, 1956, 1959, AND 1960

(January 1--Billion Rubles)

	1951				1956			
	Owned Working Capital	Bank Loans	Normed Assets	Goods Shipped	Owned Working Capital	Bank Loans	Normed Assets	Goods Shipped
Industry								
Heavy.	81.0	24.3	95.3	11.0	101.8	26.3	114.1	14.4
Timber.	2.6	7.2	8.9	1.0	4.0	9.5	12.1	1.5
Food.	1.5	20.5	19.1	3.1	2.5	29.9	27.6	4.9
Light.	11.4	14.9	22.8	3.8	14.7	16.6	26.7	4.7
Local	2.3	1.1	2.9	0.5	4.9	2.0	5.9	1.0
Industrial Co-operatives.	7.7	1.3	6.7	1.5	9.3	3.2	10.3	1.6
Sales-Supply								
Producer Goods	8.3	12.2	12.1	8.9	8.6	10.4	12.2	8.1
Consumer Goods	2.4	12.8	8.9	6.6	3.7	16.6	13.1	8.7

	1959				1960			
	Owned Working Capital	Bank Loans	Normed Assets	Goods Shipped	Owned Working Capital	Bank Loans	Normed Assets	Goods Shipped
Industry								
Heavy.	103.2	37.3	132.1	16.3	116.1	55.3	161.3	20.0
Timber.	7.1	14.9	20.8	2.5				
Food.	4.1	42.8	42.3	7.3				
Light.	27.0	27.0	48.6	8.5	48.4	76.9	113.4	19.2
Local	5.0	1.8	6.1	1.1				
Industrial Co-operatives.	9.1	2.8	10.9	1.7				
Sales-Supply								
Producer Goods	10.6	12.5	17.3	8.6	13.2	16.9	23.1	10.5
Consumer Goods	6.3	27.4	25.1	12.6	6.4	30.3	28.1	12.9

(*iv*) Loans to contract construction not accounted for in Table G–6 are approximately equal to loans (by the long-term banks) to construction organizations "on stocks of equipment" (see Table J–1). As in industry, TsSU has presumably here excluded from short-term liabilities a source of finance which it views as related to fixed capital investment and excluded as well the corresponding assets.

(*v*) The differences in the loan figures for "other sectors" correspond roughly to the differences, of opposite sign, for trade. This sector can therefore be inferred to include foreign trade. The residuals for "other sectors" probably reflect also the discrepancies in the accounts commented upon above.

We conclude from the foregoing that the sector classifications of Table G–6 are essentially identical with those of Table I–3, allowance being made for the identified omissions and reclassifications. With respect to the latter table, we cite evidence from Zverev–58, p. 144 (see the introductory discussion in Appendix I), that its sector classifications are based in some part on the operations of individual enterprises, and we conclude that the classifications are relatively invariant to administrative reorganizations. The same conclusions can appropriately be drawn for the Table G–6 data. It is to the point also that an owned capital total for January 1, 1956, of 236.3 billion, given by Zverev, *loc. cit.*, differs insignificantly from the Table G–6 total of 234.9 billion.

On the other hand, it is clear that the sector classifications of Table G–6 have not been made on a purely commodity basis. In the detailed data of the source, the normed assets of nonagricultural sectors are shown to include inventories held by subsidiary agricultural organs (these amount to about 5 billion rubles in all four years). Since the construction sector is explicitly contract only, force-account construction is undoubtedly included in other sectors. There are probably other points at which administrative arrangements affect the classifications.

Sources to Table G–7

The principal deficiency of the Table G–6 data is that they lack distributions of the totals for industry and for sales-supply organs among component industries, other than the separation of state and co-operative industries for 1951 and 1956. Errors in estimating these distributions will affect all of the postwar inventory calculations, since the latter rest on the estimates made for the four years considered here. The available data relating to these distributions are fragmentary and ambiguous, and error undoubtedly occurs in the estimates derived from them. The impact of such errors is likely to be greatest on the division of total inventories in industry between producer and consumer goods. Their impact elsewhere is limited by the existence of known totals.

Our procedure is to utilize reported data for the single year 1956 and to distribute the totals for the other three years by extrapolation from 1956. We retain in these calculations more detail for component sectors than is shown in the inventory estimates in order to have a firmer basis for estimating other postwar years than would be provided by data for major sectors alone. We retain only so much detail for component assets and liabilities as is useful for the estimates for other years. The distributions arrived at are shown in Table G–7.

The estimates for 1956, for industry proper, are derived in the following steps.

(*i*) A distribution of bank loans by purpose and between producer and consumer goods is composed from reported data (billion rubles):

	Producer Goods	Consumer Goods	Total
On normed assets 17.7		37.1	54.8
On goods shipped 16.3		12.6	28.9
For new techniques, etc. 0.6		1.1	1.7
Other loans 3.0		3.7	6.7
Total 37.6		54.5	92.1

The data are obtained as follows.

On normed assets: The components are from Kazantsev–61, pp. 13–14. The total is the computed sum. The latter is not entirely consistent with a statement by the author, p. 12, that loans on normed assets equaled 56.5 percent of total loans. Kazantsev–61, it should be noted, is the principal source for the whole of our 1956 breakdown. Reference should be made to the discussion of this source in the notes to Table I–3, industry components.

On goods shipped: The figure for producer goods is computed as the residual of total loans to the sector and loans in the other categories. That for consumer goods is from Kazantsev–61, p. 14. The total is the sum of components. The loans in this category are both those on settlement documents and "payment credits" (see Appendix J).

For new techniques, etc.: The figure for producer goods is the residual of total loans and consumer goods for this category. That for consumer goods is from Kazantsev–61, *loc. cit.* The total figure is from Table J–1.

Other loans: For producer goods, Popov–57, p. 66, gives loans for purposes other than the three specified here, in 1957, for producer goods as classified in Gosbank loan data (see Appendix I), as 3.7 out of a total of 45.8 billion rubles. We assume the relative share was the same in 1956 for loans as classified here, i.e., by TsSU classifications. For consumer goods, "other loans" are the unaccounted for residual for this sector in Kazantsev–61, *loc. cit.* The total is the sum of components.

Total loans: All figures are derived from Kazantsev–61. See notes to Table I–3, industry components.

(*ii*) The foregoing loan breakdown is adjusted to the Table G–6 figure for total loans to industry by excluding loans for new techniques, etc., and reducing all other components equiproportionately (billion rubles):

	Producer Goods	Consumer Goods	Total
On normed assets 17.1		35.9	53.0
On goods shipped 15.8		12.2	28.0
Other loans 2.9		3.6	6.5
Total 35.8		51.7	87.5

(*iii*) From loans so distributed, the distribution of assets is computed (billion rubles):

	Producer Goods	Consumer Goods	Total
Normed assets	126.2	70.5	196.7
Goods shipped	15.9	12.2	28.1
Total	142.1	82.7	224.8

The asset totals by kind are from Table G–6. Normed assets in consumer goods industries are computed from loans on normed assets and a statement in Kazantsev–61, p. 12, that loans financed 50.9 percent of such assets—in 1957 and in industry under the *sovnarkhozy*. Normed assets in producer goods industries are computed as a residual. Goods shipped in each sector are assumed proportionate to loans on goods shipped, the proportion being virtually 100 percent.

To distribute the estimated assets among more detailed component sectors, we derive the loan distribution shown in Table G–7. Figures for heavy and timber industries from Table I–3 are adjusted proportionately to the total for producer goods computed in Paragraph (*ii*). Figures from Table I–3 for food, light, and local industries are similarly adjusted to the total for consumer goods net of loans to industrial co-operatives. The figure for co-operatives is taken from Table G–6 without adjustment.

(*v*) We find no data on the ratio of bank loans to assets for these detailed sectors in which loans and assets are classified in accordance with TsSU sector classifications. Lacking these, we resort to data provided in Popov–57, pp. 65, 66, and 71, which are almost certainly based on Gosbank classifications. This source gives (or suggests) ratios of bank loans to *total assets* of 17.6 percent in heavy industry, 60 percent in timber, 62 percent in food, and 40 percent in light. The ratio for heavy industry is given as for non-seasonal heavy industries, including machine-building, chemicals, ferrous metallurgy, and coal. The figure for timber is for 1957 rather than 1956. The food and light figures are our guesses, based on figures in Popov of 75.8 percent for the fish industry, 60.2 percent in industry of "provisionary commodities," and 42 percent in textiles. We are guided also by data in other sources, including Lovtsov–56, p. 12, but we make no attempt to reconcile other data with Popov's. For local industry, we assume a comparable ratio of 22 percent, which is the ratio for industrial co-operatives in Table G–6. We are guided also by prewar data for inventories on hand and bank loans in local industry (see Tables G–4 and I–1). The asset totals arrived at in Paragraph (*iii*) for producer goods and consumer goods (exclusive of industrial co-operatives) are then distributed among the component industries of each in proportion to the totals implied by the loan and loan/asset figures. Assets in industrial co-operatives are taken from Table G–6.

(*vi*) Owned working capital is distributed on the assumption that the ratio of owned capital plus bank loans to normed assets plus goods shipped is the same in all state industries. The resulting figure for the food industry is almost certainly too low, but we have no basis for correcting it, and its effects upon our inventory estimates are necessarily slight. Owned capital in industrial co-operatives is from Table G–6.

The estimates for 1956 for sales-supply organs are composed as follows.

(*i*) Totals for loans, normed assets, and goods shipped, are taken from Table G–6.

(*ii*) The division of total loans between producer and consumer goods is assumed that shown in Table I–3.

(*iii*) The distribution of the asset categories between the two sectors requires assumptions that cannot be accurate but appear not highly implausible: that loans on goods shipped equal goods shipped (which is virtually the case for industry proper); that loans other than on goods shipped in the two component sectors bear the same ratio to normed assets as in producer and consumer goods industries (loans are those computed in Paragraph [*ii*] of the industry discussion, excluding loans on goods shipped; normed assets are those computed in Paragraph [*iii*] of that discussion); and that the ratio of goods shipped to normed assets is the same in both sales-supply components. These assumptions imply total normed assets of 26.3 billion and goods shipped of 17.4 billion, which differ little from the known totals. The estimated assets for each component are adjusted proportionately to the known totals.

(*iv*) Owned working capital is distributed on the same assumptions as for industry.

Given the Table G–7 breakdown for 1956, we proceed to those for the other three years, for both industry and sales-supply, as follows.

(*i*) All items for industrial co-operatives in 1951 are taken from Table G–6. References hereafter to "known totals" (which are those in Table G–6) are exclusive in 1951 and inclusive in 1959 and 1960 of industrial co-operatives.

(*ii*) Bank loans are extrapolated from 1956 to 1951 and 1959 on the Table I–3 loan series and adjusted to the known totals. Since loans to industry in 1959 are distributed in Table I–3 only between producer and consumer goods, we divide these totals in the 1958 proportions (estimates for detailed industrial components in 1959 are required for interpolations that are made elsewhere). Loans in 1960 are extrapolated from 1959 on the Table I–3 series and adjusted to the known totals.

(*iii*) Owned working capital items are estimated in 1951 and 1959 from their ratios to bank loans in 1956, and in 1960 from the same ratios in 1959, and adjusted to the known totals. In the calculations for 1959 and 1960, however, loans to heavy industry are taken net of loans on nonseasonal inventories (see Table J–1); the combined sum of owned capital and net bank loans is estimated; and owned capital is computed as the difference between the combined sum and bank loans gross of those on nonseasonal inventories. The value of the latter loans in 1956 is assumed the same as in 1957 (Table J–1).

(*iv*) Combined sums of normed assets and goods shipped are estimated on the assumption that their ratio to owned capital and bank loans is uniform for all sectors composing each known total. Divisions of the combined totals between normed assets and goods shipped are estimated from 1956 in 1951 and 1959, and from 1959 in 1960, and adjusted to the known totals.

Sources to Table G–8

The calculations in Tables G–6 and G–7 require a few further adjustments, the results of which are shown in Table G–8. Normed assets in industry and sales-supply are there reduced to inventories on hand by deducting expenses of future periods; the latter are assumed distributed in proportion to normed assets. Goods shipped in transportation and communications and in contract construction are assumed zero. It is clear from the source of the data that the "services rendered" portion of the category, "goods shipped and services rendered," applies solely to these two sectors. It seems probable from the character of their operations that services rendered account for the whole of the category in these sectors.

For ease of cross reference, we assemble in Table G–8 data by detailed sectors both for inventories and for the liability categories that are of principal use for estimates of other years. Except for the adjustments described above, all data are transcribed from Tables G–6 and G–7.

Derivation of Table G–1 Estimates

The asset figures in Table G–1 are taken from Table G–8. The figures for producer goods industries are the sum of those for heavy and timber industries and producer goods sales-supply. The figures for consumer goods industries are the sum of those for food, light, and local industries, and industrial co-operatives and consumer goods sales-supply. The "other sectors" of Table G–8 are the "other nonagricultural sectors" of Table G–1.

Reported Data Not Utilized

We disregard in the computations for these four years some other data which are available in Soviet sources.

(*i*) Atlas–58, pp. 242 and 283, reports distributions of total working capital of 46.0 percent owned capital, 45.0 bank loans, and 9.0 *kreditory* net of *debitory*, in 1951; 49.2, 41.4, and 9.4, for the same categories in 1956. The figures are stated to exclude contract construction, collective farms, and municipal economy. Assuming that "other" liabilities and assets are included in net *kreditory*, Atlas' distribution for 1956 is close to that of TsSU–61, excluding contract construction, for 1956, less close to that for 1951. For both years, Atlas' divisions between owned capital and bank loans are close to those of the *Vestnik statistiki* antecedents of the TsSU–61 breakdowns. Atlas' figures appear effectively congruent with those we have used. Whether the exclusion of municipal economy is peculiar to Atlas or common to all our data is uncertain.

(*ii*) Usatov–60, p. 43, gives data for owned capital, total and by sectors, in 1959, which are entirely different from those we have used (parts of the same data for 1959 and similar data for 1960 have appeared in other sources). His figures are identified by Usatov as for normed rather than actual amounts of owned capital, and the total is elsewhere (*Pravda*, December 23, 1958) stated to cover state enterprises only.

(*iii*) In Korovushkin–59, p. 9, bank loans are indicated to have accounted for "over 40 percent" of total working capital in 1959; in Koro-

WORKING CAPITAL ACCOUNTS BY DETAILED SECTORS, SELECTED ITEMS, IN CURRENT PRICES, 1951, 1956, 1959 AND 1960

(January 1--Billion Rubles)

	1951				1956			
	Owned Working Capital	Bank Loans	Inventories on Hand	Goods Shipped	Owned Working Capital	Bank Loans	Inventories on Hand	Goods Shipped
Industry								
Heavy	81.0	24.3	92.7	11.0	101.8	26.3	110.7	14.4
Timber	2.6	7.2	8.7	1.0	4.0	9.5	11.7	1.5
Food	1.5	20.5	18.6	3.1	2.5	29.9	26.8	4.9
Light	11.4	14.9	22.2	3.8	14.7	16.6	25.9	4.7
Local	2.3	1.1	2.8	0.5	4.9	2.0	5.7	1.0
Industrial Co-operatives	7.7	1.3	6.5	1.5	9.3	3.2	10.0	1.6
Sales-Supply								
Producer Goods	8.3	12.2	12.1	8.9	8.6	10.4	12.2	8.1
Consumer Goods	2.4	12.8	8.9	6.6	3.7	16.6	13.1	8.7
Transportation and Communications	6.2	2.3	6.7	0.0	7.2	2.3	7.7	0.0
State Agriculture	10.2	5.1	9.3	0.2	14.4	5.8	13.9	0.1
Procurement	2.6	7.9	8.3	1.7	3.0	8.3	8.0	1.9
Domestic Trade	17.5	50.3	67.4	6.8	48.5	59.6	108.5	6.7
Contract Construction	1.5	4.1	10.6	0.0	7.8	4.4	17.6	0.0
Other Sectors	5.0	6.9	9.5	1.1	4.5	4.1	8.8	1.0
Total	160.2	170.8	284.3	46.2	234.9	199.0	380.6	54.6

WORKING CAPITAL ACCOUNTS BY DETAILED SECTORS, SELECTED ITEMS, IN CURRENT PRICES, 1951, 1956, 1959, AND 1960

(January 1--Billion Rubles)

	1959				1960			
	Owned Working Capital	Bank Loans	Inventories on Hand	Goods Shipped	Owned Working Capital	Bank Loans	Inventories on Hand	Goods Shipped
Industry								
Heavy	103.2	37.3	128.6	16.3	116.1	55.3	156.5	20.0
Timber	7.1	14.9	20.2	2.5				
Food	4.1	42.8	41.2	7.3				
Light	27.0	27.0	47.3	8.5	48.4	76.9	110.0	19.2
Local	5.0	1.8	5.9	1.1				
Industrial Co-operatives	9.1	2.8	10.6	1.7				
Sales-Supply								
Producer Goods	10.6	12.5	17.3	8.6	13.2	16.9	23.1	10.5
Consumer Goods	6.3	27.4	25.1	12.6	6.4	30.3	28.0	12.9
Transportation and Communications	8.3	2.7	8.9	0.0	9.2	2.5	9.8	0.0
State Agriculture	22.6	10.6	21.6	0.2	28.9	13.8	26.6	0.3
Procurement	3.4	16.8	18.3	3.3	6.8	34.1	37.5	5.5
Domestic Trade	58.2	104.7	165.1	8.2	64.5	125.4	192.2	8.4
Contract Construction	15.0	5.2	22.1	0.0	17.0	7.4	25.7	0.0
Other Sectors	14.0	9.1	19.4	2.1	15.8	14.3	27.2	3.0
Total	293.8	315.5	551.6	72.4	326.3	376.9	636.6	79.9

vushkin–60, p. 7, a similar figure is given of "about half" for 1960. It is impossible to identify the coverage of these percentages.

1952

See the discussion for 1949 and related years.

1953–54

All figures for these years are interpolated, except for sales-supply in 1954. Estimates for industry and sales-supply are made by detailed components and consolidated into the Table G–1 categories. The results of intermediate calculations are not shown.

(*i*) According to Chernyshova–59, pp. 29–30, working capital in sales-supply in 1954 consisted 24.8 percent of owned capital and 52.3 percent of bank loans and, on the asset side, 50.2 percent normed assets ("commodity-material values") and 31.7 percent goods shipped. The source gives similar percentages for 1951 which are identical with those in TsSU–61, and the coverage of Chernyshova's data for other years can reasonably be inferred to be consistent with those from the former source (see notes for 1951 and related years). For 1954, we compute absolute totals of both kinds of assets from bank loans (see below) and distribute them between producer and consumer goods by interpolation on bank loans between 1951 and 1955. For 1953, asset totals in both component sectors are interpolated on bank loans between 1951 and 1954 and their division between inventories on hand and goods shipped interpolated on a straight line between the same years.

(*ii*) In domestic trade, combined inventories on hand and goods shipped are interpolated on inventories of finished products (Table K–1) between 1951 and 1956; the division between the two components is assumed to have changed linearly between the same dates.

(*iii*) In contract construction, inventories on hand are interpolated on loans for procurement of materials (Table J–1) between 1951 and 1956.

(*iv*) In all other sectors, the two asset categories together are interpolated on bank loans between 1951 and 1955 and their relative shares in the total assumed to have changed linearly between the same dates. The requisite loan series, including those for the sales-supply estimates, are interpolated on the Table I–3 loan series between 1951 and 1956 (Table G–8).

We make no use in the estimates for 1954 of a statement in Atlas–55, p. 25, that in 1954 bank loans accounted for 41 percent of total working capital (this is presumably the same as a figure of 41.2 percent "at the present time" given in *Den'gi i kredit*, 1954:1, p. 6). The coverage of the single percentage is not identifiable.

1955

According to Pessel'–58, p. 31, bank loans accounted for 38.2 percent and *kreditory* for 15.4 percent of total working capital; the remainder presumably represents owned capital and other liabilities. Similar percentages given by Pessel' for 1957 (see notes for that year) can be inferred to be consistent with the TsSU–61 data for 1951 and related years except that contract construction is excluded. We assume the coverage of the percentages is the same for 1955 as for 1957. We estimate the owned capital share in 1955 as 44.8 percent by interpolating a ratio between owned capital and other liabilities from those for 1951 and 1956 (Table G–8). The implied share of owned capital in the sum of owned capital and bank loans, 54.0 percent, compares with a share of 54.3 percent implied by data given in other sources but of uncertain coverage (*Den'gi i kredit*, 1956:9, pp. 8–9, and Rubinshtein–58, p. 49, distribute total working capital 49.2 percent to owned capital, 41.4 to bank loans, and 9.4 to *kreditory; kreditory* here are clearly net of *debitory* and perhaps inclusive of "other" liabilities). We compute total owned capital exclusive of construction as 219.1 billion, from the Pessel' percentage and from the absolute volume of bank loans (see below).

Given the owned capital total, the inventory estimates are derived as follows.

(*i*) Bank loans for detailed component sectors other than contract construction are interpolated between 1951 and 1956 (Table G–8) on the TsSU loan series (Table I–3).

(*ii*) For sales-supply, total owned capital is interpolated on bank loans between 1954 and 1956 (for 1954, see the discussion of Chernyshova–59 in notes for that year; for 1956 see Table G–6). Owned capital in the sales-supply components is interpolated between 1951 and 1956 (Table G–8) on bank loans and adjusted proportionately to the known total. For domestic trade, the combined sum of owned capital and bank loans is interpolated between 1951 and 1956 on finished products in trade (Table K–1) and owned capital computed as a residual. Owned capital in all other sectors is interpolated between 1951 and 1956 on bank loans and the resulting estimates adjusted proportionately to the total net of the amounts attributed to sales-supply and trade.

(*iii*) Combined sums of inventories on hand and goods shipped are interpolated: on sums of owned capital and bank loans in sales-supply, between 1954 and 1956 (see the references in Paragraph [*ii*]), and in all other sectors except trade and construction, between 1951 and 1956; on inventories of finished products (Table K–1) in trade between 1951 and 1956; and on loans for procurement of materials (Table J–1) in contract construction between 1951 and 1956.

(*iv*) The division of their combined sums between inventories on hand and goods shipped in each sector is interpolated between 1951 and 1956 in all sectors except sales-supply. For the latter, the division of the entire sector is interpolated between 1954 and 1956 (see the references in Paragraph [*ii*]), and the asset totals divided between the component sectors in proportion to the sum of their owned capital and bank loans.

(*v*) The component estimates for industry and sales-supply are consolidated into estimates for producer goods and consumer goods sectors.

1956

See the discussion for 1951 and related years.

1957

A relatively detailed breakdown of owned working capital can be composed for this date from reported data (billion rubles):

Industry	143.5
Sales-supply	14.5
Transportation and communications	6.9
State agriculture	15.1
Procurement	2.7
Domestic trade	49.8
Unaccounted for	20.1
Total	252.6

Except for sales-supply and the unaccounted for residual, all figures are given directly in Zverev–58, p. 144. The total is presumably inclusive of contract construction since a total for 1956 given *loc. cit.* is demonstrably so (see notes for 1951 and related years). Industry is indicated explicitly to include industrial co-operatives. Agriculture is inferred to be state only. Owned capital in sales-supply is computed from bank loans (see below), on the basis of figures for shares in total working capital of 25.4 percent for owned capital and 52.8 percent for bank loans, which are given in Chernyshova–59, p. 30. We cite evidence elsewhere (see the introductory discussion to Appendix I and the discussion in the present appendix for 1951 and related years and for 1954) of the homogeneity of both Zverev's and Chernyshova's data with those from TsSU–61, which are the foundation of our postwar inventory estimates.

Given the owned capital data, the inventory estimates are derived as follows.

(*i*) Bank loans for detailed component sectors, other than contract construction, are interpolated between 1956 and 1959 (Table G–8) on the TsSU loan series (Table I–3). Loans to contract construction are interpolated on loans other than on stocks of equipment (Table J–1). No deliberate adjustment is made in the loan interpolations for changes in the relative size of loans for new techniques, etc., to industry, though a rough adjustment results from the interpolations.

(*ii*) The owned capital figures shown above are accepted and the totals for industry, sales-supply, and the unaccounted for residual distributed by interpolation between 1956 and 1959. For heavy industry, the sum of owned capital and bank loans is interpolated on bank loans net of loans on nonseasonal inventories (Table J–1), and owned capital is computed as the difference between the combined sum and total bank loans. Owned capital in all other industrial components is interpolated on bank loans. The estimated industry components are adjusted proportionately to the known total. Sales-supply components are interpolated on bank loans and adjusted to the known total. For contract construction, owned capital and bank loans are interpolated on inventories (see below), and owned capital computed as a residual. The remainder of the unaccounted for owned capital is attributed to "other" sectors.

(*iii*) Except for sales-supply, domestic trade, and contract construction, the sum of inventories on hand and goods shipped in each sector is interpolated between 1956 and 1959 on the sum of owned capital and bank loans. For sales-supply, total inventories and total goods shipped are calculated from shares in working capital of 54.4 percent and 33.1 percent respectively, given in Chernyshova–59, p. 29, and the absolute value of liabilities derived from the same source. Each of the asset categories is distributed between the two component sectors of sales-supply in proportion to the sums of their owned capital and bank loans. Inventories on hand and goods shipped in domestic trade are interpolated on inventories of finished products (Table K–1); those in contract construction are interpolated on loans for the procurement of materials (Table J–1).

(*iv*) Total goods shipped are estimated from loans on goods shipped (Table J–1), on the assumption the ratios between the two changed linearly from 1956 to 1959. Shares of goods shipped in combined asset totals are, except for sales-supply, assumed to have changed linearly between the same dates, and the resulting estimates for goods shipped are adjusted proportionately to the known total minus goods shipped in sales-supply. Inventories on hand are then computed as residuals.

(*v*) Component estimates for producer and consumer goods industries, including sales-supply, are aggregated.

Our estimates for 1957 do not incorporate data given in Pessel'–58, p. 31. According to Pessel', bank loans accounted for 41.2 and *kreditory* for 14.9 percent of total working capital, the remaining 43.9 percent presumably representing owned capital and other liabilities. The relatively small size of *kreditory* suggests that these figures omit contract construction. Assuming that to be the case, the 43.9 percent can be distributed 42.2 percent owned capital and 1.7 percent other liabilities by interpolating the ratio between the two from those for 1956 and 1959, for sectors other than construction (see Table G–6). The implied share of owned capital in the sum of owned capital and bank loans, 50.6 percent, compares with a similar share implied by our estimates of 50.5 percent. Pessel's data appear to be consistent with those we have used.

1958

Kazantsev–61, p. 11, reports shares in total working capital in industry of 50.2 percent for owned capital and 36.1 percent for bank loans. These figures appear together with breakdowns for 1956 and 1960 which are identical with those given—for state and co-operative industry but exclusive of sales-supply—in TsSU–61 (see notes for 1951 and related years). We infer that the 1958 breakdown is homogeneous with data from the latter source. We assume the percentage for loans to refer to total loans to industry, 110.1 billion (Table I–3), minus loans for new techniques, etc., 4.3 billion (Table J–1), or 105.8 billion. Owned working capital in industry can then be computed as 147.1 billion. Given total owned capital, we estimate inventories on hand and goods shipped in combination, for component industrial sectors, by procedures parallel to those used for 1957.

Data on owned capital for sectors other than industry are not available. For these, we interpolate combined sums of inventories on hand and goods shipped between 1957 and 1959. Domestic trade is interpolated on the series for inventories of finished products (Table K–1), contract construction on loans for the procurement of materials (Table J–1), all other sectors on total loans (interpolated between the 1956 and 1959 values shown in Table G–8 on the Table I–3 series).

Total goods shipped are estimated as in 1957. Shares of goods shipped in the sector totals for inventories on hand and goods shipped are assumed to have changed linearly from 1957 to 1959 and the resulting estimates of goods shipped adjusted proportionately to the known total. Inventories on hand are computed as residuals.

Component estimates for producer and consumer goods industries, including sales-supply, are consolidated.

1959–60

See the discussion of 1951 and related years.

1961–62

Figures for these years are extrapolations from 1960, adjusted to owned working capital totals of 360 billion in 1961 and 401 billion in 1962 and an owned capital figure for industry and construction in 1962 of 246 billion. The 1961 total is given in Usatov–61, p. 26, as "over 36 billion" new rubles "at the present time"; we infer that it is for January 1, 1961, and is comprehensive of all sectors, including contract construction, from comparison with a total derived from unadjusted extrapolations. The 1962 figures are from the Minister of Finance's budget message (*Pravda*, December 7, 1961); we infer that "industry and construction" are inclusive of sales-supply from comparison with unadjusted extrapolations.

(*i*) Bank loans by sectors are extrapolated from 1960 (Table G–8) on the Table I–3 loan series. The sector detail of the extrapolations, here and in the subsequent steps, is the same as that of 1960 (Table G–8). Loans to contract construction in 1961–62 are not known and are not estimated.

(*ii*) Owned working capital in producer goods industry in 1961 is estimated by extrapolating from 1960 the combined sum of owned capital and bank loans net of those on nonseasonal inventories (Table J–1) and deducting total loans from the combined sum. Owned capital in this sector is extrapolated from 1961 to 1962 on total loans, since loans on nonseasonal inventories in 1962 are not known. Owned capital in consumer goods industry and in both sales-supply components is extrapolated from 1960 to 1961 and 1962 on bank loans.

The foregoing extrapolations yield an owned capital total for industry and sales-supply in 1962 of 226.0 billion, which compares with the reported figure for "industry and contract construction" of 246 billion. The difference of 20 billion appears a plausible estimate for owned capital in construction, which was 17.0 billion in 1960 (Table G–8). On this evidence, we use without adjustment the owned capital extrapolations for industry and sales-supply in both 1961 and 1962 and the contract construction figure for 1962. We interpolate a 1961 figure for construction of 18.5 billion from the 1960 and 1962 figures.

(*iii*) Owned capital in domestic trade in 1961 is estimated by extrapolating the combined sum of owned capital and bank loans from 1960 on inventories of finished products (Table K–1) and deducting bank loans from the total. Owned capital in trade is extrapolated from 1961 to 1962 on bank loans, since the inventory series is unavailable for 1962. Owned capital in all other sectors is extrapolated on bank loans from 1960 to 1961 and 1962.

Of the owned capital totals of 360 and 401 billion, the estimates of industry, sales-supply, and construction leave 137 unaccounted for in 1961 and 155 in 1962. The sums of the unadjusted extrapolations for transportation and communications, state agriculture, procurement, domestic trade, and other sectors are 134.2 billion in 1961 and 150 billion in 1962. We distribute the differences equiproportionately among the components (excluding trade in 1961 and including it in 1962).

(*iv*) The ratio of inventories on hand and goods shipped to owned capital plus bank loans in each sector is assumed the same as in 1960, except that owned capital alone is used for construction. The ratio of inventories on hand to goods shipped in each sector is also assumed the same as 1960, since loans on goods shipped are not known for 1961–62.

(*v*) Industry components are consolidated into producer and consumer goods categories as in other years.

We disregard in these calculations a statement in Korovushkin–62, p. 3, that bank loans on January 1, 1962, accounted for "about half" of total working capital. See comments on similar statements from the same author for earlier years in the notes for 1951 and related years.

After the completion of the inventory estimates for 1961 and 1962 and their incorporation in other calculations in this study, data were released which indicate that our current-price totals for these years are overstated by some 2–3 percent. From data, similar to that cited above from TsSU–61, given in TsSU–62a, pp. 70 ff., it can be computed that in 1961 inventories on hand amounted to 677.3 billion rubles, goods shipped to 81.4, and the two together to 758.7. These figures compare with our Table G–1 estimates of 690.4, 85.9, and 776.3 billion rubles, respectively. As among sectors, the errors appear to be (the TsSU–62a data by sectors are not complete) about the same in industry as in the total, negligible in domestic trade, and relatively large in the estimates for procurement and for other nonagricultural sectors.

According to Birman–63, pp. 40–41, total working capital at the beginning of 1962 was 1,004 billion rubles, of which "over 78 percent" was "commodity-material values" and "about 9 percent" goods shipped and services rendered. A rough allowance being made for the immature livestock, expenses of future periods, and services rendered included in these figures, they suggest a percentage overstatement in our 1962 estimates of inventories on hand and goods shipped of about the same magnitude as in 1961. Birman does not give a sectoral breakdown. Data for trade inventories of finished goods at retail prices, released in TsSU–62a, p. 643, indicate an overstatement in our 1962 estimates for that sector of 3–4 percent.

These errors are not significant for our estimates of the total capital stock or for the discussion of the role of capital in growth, and for this reason we have not undertaken the very extensive recomputations which their correction would require. They are more consequential for the analysis of inventories alone, especially in their exaggeration of the increment occurring in the course of 1960.

Appendix H

Distribution of Inventories on

Hand by Kind

Data are assembled here, in Table H–1 (p. 520), on the distribution of inventories on hand by kind, within component sectors and in current prices, as of three selected dates. The principal purpose of these estimates is to provide weights for the deflation of inventories by sectors. However, they serve additional subsidiary functions, and we include several estimates which are not employed in the deflators.

The deflated inventory series are meant to be in average annual prices of 1928, 1937, and 1950. The distributions calculated here are for the beginning of the first two years and for the end of the last, and are therefore not entirely appropriate. Data limitations, the probable relative stability of the distributions through the years involved, and the unavoidable approximateness of the distributions as they stand, rule out any attempt at greater precision.

Data released in Soviet sources on the composition of inventories by kind are sparse and difficult to interpret. For 1951, we have quite complete information, except that separate breakdowns for producer and consumer goods industries are lacking (the estimates are deficient at this point in all three years). For 1937, we have a fairly complete breakdown of total inventories by kind, but data for sector distributions are largely lacking. For 1928, we have—partial—data for industry only, and we make estimates for the industrial sectors only.

Given the inadequacies of the information available, we are forced to rely heavily on various extrapolations. Although these could possibly be improved by systematically incorporating in them the data on relative price movements which are assembled in Appendix L, the complexities of this procedure would scarcely be justified by the gains in accuracy. We have, instead, permitted ourselves considerable discretion in determining the ways in which the Table H–1 estimates are used.

In the explanatory notes following, we cite only those sources that have been drawn on directly in the derivation of the estimates. Our impressions of plausible magnitudes have been affected as well by other data, of which we merely cite the sources: Atlas–52, p. 67; Barngol'ts–57, p. 30; Birman–

56, pp. 46–48; *Economic Survey*, October 1, 1929; Kasimovskii–40, p. 20; Katsenelenbaum–58, p. 42; Khavin–31, p. 8; Omel'chenko–39, p. 10; Rovinskii–51, p. 129; VSNKh–27, pp. 398 ff.

For brevity, we frequently use the term, "goods in process," to include semifabricates.

Since goods shipped are shown separately in Table G–1, they are not included in the present breakdowns.

1928

For 1928, we estimate a breakdown of inventories by kind for industry only, and this largely on the basis of data given in Putilov–32. The same source underlies our Table G–2 estimates of total industrial inventories.

Putilov, pp. 103 and 112–13, gives absolute and percentage data for VSNKh industry, excluding syndicates, from which the following partial breakdowns can be compiled. Absolute figures implied by percentages given in the source are not fully consistent, and averages are therefore employed.

Figures are in billion rubles for October 1 of the year indicated.

	Goods in Process	Finished Products	Other	Total
VSNKh industry				
1927	.51	.84	1.88	3.23
1928	.74	.85	2.09	3.68
Group "A"				
1927	—	—	—	1.71
1928	—	—	—	2.04
Group "B"				
1927	—	—	—	1.52
1928	—	—	—	1.64

The "other" category here is a computed residual. In context, it appears fairly clear that Putilov's goods in process are that category in its strict meaning and are exclusive of semifabricates (and expenses of future periods, which we have assumed were omitted entirely in these years). The residual thus includes both raw materials and semifabricates.

We have no reliable way of estimating semifabricates in this period. For lack of better, we estimate them from goods in process, on the basis of data for October 1, 1935, given in Khromov–37, p. 72 (see the discussion of this source in the notes following for 1937). Khromov's data imply a ratio of semifabricates to goods in process for heavy and timber industries combined of 17.8 percent, for food of 27.5 percent, and for light of 45.6 percent. We combine the latter two ratios with equal weights to obtain a ratio for all consumer goods of 36.5 percent. Using Putilov's figures for Groups "A" and "B" as weights, we obtain percentages for all industry of 26.6 percent in 1927, 26.2 in 1928. These ratios applied to the above figures for goods in process imply semifabricates of .14 in 1927, .19 in 1928. Deducting these from the "other" category leaves raw materials of 1.74 and 1.90.

From Table G–2, we have inventories in syndicates of .50 in 1927, .55

in 1928. As in Table G–3, we assume these are divided between Groups "A" and "B" in the same proportions as the VSNKh inventories. We assume the distribution by kind of syndicate inventories, for both industrial groups, was the same as in sales-supply organs in 1937 (see the notes following for that date).

To distribute total inventories by kind between producer and consumer goods (which are assumed synonymous with Group "A" and Group "B"), we apply to the totals for each of the two the 1937 percentage compositions by kind, excluding small tools, for state industry (see notes for that date) and adjust the results sequentially to the known totals by kind and by sector to consistency with both.

Given the breakdowns for October 1, 1927, and October 1, 1928, we interpolate on a straight line a breakdown for January 1, 1928, with these results (percent of total):

	Producer Goods	Consumer Goods
Raw materials	38.4	56.5
Goods in process, etc.	22.6	13.9
Finished products	39.0	29.6
Total	100.0	100.0

Though the above percentages apply to VSNKh industry only, it is doubtful, in view of the manner of their derivation and of the lack of information on other industry, that better estimates than these could be derived for total industry. We therefore assume that the composition of inventories in producer and consumer goods industries of all administrative subordinations were the same as those of VSNKh industries alone.

The preceding estimates make no adjustment for small tools. To allow for these, we assume that the value of tools in each of the two industrial sectors was the same share of total inventories as in 1937. This is scarcely a defensible assumption. It implies a stock of tools in industry in 1928 equal to about 13 percent of the stock in 1937, both valued in current prices. In Moorsteen–62, pp. 433 ff., it is estimated that annual investment in small tools in 1928 in industry, transportation, communications, and trade was about 11 percent of its level in *1936*. However, as is explained in the notes following for 1937, the absolute level of the investment estimates is grossly inconsistent with that of the stock estimates made here.

The percentage breakdowns entered in Table H–1 are those shown above, after adjustment to include small tools. The absolute figures are computed from the percentages and the totals given in Table G–3 plus small tools.

1937

The estimates for 1937 begin with a distribution of inventories in "basic branches" (see the notes to Table G–4 on Usoskin–39, which source is the principal basis of the present calculations) by asset categories as they were reported at the time. Figures are billion rubles.

	Production Supplies	Goods in Process and Expenses of Future Periods	Finished Products	Total
State industry, excluding sales-supply	17.6	8.5	6.3	32.4
Sales-supply	0.3	0.0	5.8	6.1
State agriculture	3.0	3.7	0.5	7.2
Procurement	0.9	0.0	1.6	2.5
Domestic trade	2.3	0.1	14.1	16.5
Total	24.1	12.3	28.3	64.7

(*i*) Total inventories by sector are from Table G–4. That is, they are essentially reported figures, unadjusted for expenses of future periods, immature livestock, and small tools.

(*ii*) Total inventories by kind are from Table G–5, except that 0.2 billion of "other" inventories are distributed among the three specified categories in their proportions exclusive of other inventories.

(*iii*) Totals by sector are divided between finished products and the

TABLE H-1

DISTRIBUTION OF INVENTORIES ON HAND BY KIND, IN CURRENT PRICES, 1928, 1937, AND 1951

(January 1)

	1928		1937		1951	
	Billion Rubles	Percent of Total	Billion Rubles	Percent of Total	Billion Rubles	Percent of Total
Producer Goods Industries						
Raw Materials	0.82	32.9	6.8	30.5	38.5	33.9
Small Tools	0.36	14.4	3.2	14.4	12.7	11.2
Goods in Process	0.48	19.3	5.0	22.4	24.3	21.4
Finished Products	0.84	33.4	7.3	32.7	38.0	33.5
Total	2.50	100.0	22.3	100.0	113.5	100.0
Consumer Goods Industries						
Raw Materials	1.65	51.6	9.7	49.5	30.9	52.4
Small Tools	0.28	8.7	1.7	8.7	4.2	7.1
Goods in Process	0.41	12.7	2.7	13.8	7.6	12.9
Finished Products	0.86	27.0	5.5	28.0	16.3	27.6
Total	3.20	100.0	19.6	100.0	59.0	100.0
Transportation and Communications						
Raw Materials	--	--	2.0	63.0	4.2	63.0
Small Tools	--	--	1.0	32.7	2.2	32.7
Goods in Process	--	--	0.0	1.4	0.1	1.4
Finished Products	--	--	0.1	2.9	0.2	2.9
Total	--	--	3.1	100.0	6.7	100.0
State Agriculture						
Raw Materials	--	--	2.8	60.8	5.3	57.3
Small Tools	--	--	0.4	8.7	0.8	8.3
Goods in Process	--	--	0.9	19.6	2.2	23.5
Finished Products	--	--	0.5	10.9	1.0	10.9
Total	--	--	4.6	100.0	9.3	100.0
Procurement						
Raw Materials	--	--	0.8	32.0	2.5	30.2
Small Tools	--	--	0.1	4.0	0.4	4.3
Goods in Process	--	--	0.0	0.0	0.1	1.5
Finished Products	--	--	1.6	64.0	5.3	64.0
Total	--	--	2.5	100.0	8.3	100.0
Domestic Trade						
Raw Materials	--	--	1.9	11.8	5.8	8.6
Small Tools	--	--	0.8	4.8	3.0	4.5
Goods in Process	--	--	0.0	0.0	0.3	0.4
Finished Products	--	--	14.1	83.9	58.3	86.5
Total	--	--	16.8	100.0	67.4	100.0
Contract Construction						
Raw Materials	--	--	--	--	7.8	73.7
Small Tools	--	--	--	--	2.2	20.6
Goods in Process	--	--	--	--	0.6	5.7
Finished Products	--	--	--	--	0.0	0.0
Total	--	--	--	--	10.6	100.0

other two categories by applying the 1951 shares of finished products in comparable combined totals and adjusting the results sequentially to the known totals by kind and by sector. The 1951 ratios used in this calculation are computed from totals inclusive of expenses of future periods, immature livestock, and 50 percent of small tools (for the necessary data, see Tables G–6 and H–1 and the notes for 1951 below). The 50 percent figure reflects the assumption which we make throughout that half of the actual value of small tools was included in reported inventories by January 1, 1937. The finished products estimates look plausible, at least as rough orders of magnitude, in comparison with figures for 1936 reported in Sobol'–37 (see notes to Table G–4). The implied share of finished products in total trade inventories, 85 percent, appears roughly consistent with a 13 percent ratio of raw and other materials to finished products in 1937 in the Commissariat of Trade, reported in Lifits–50, p. 521.

(*iv*) The combined totals of production supplies and goods in process and expenses of future periods in each sector are divided in ratios given for 1937 in Usoskin–39, p. 31 (percent):

	Production Supplies	*Goods in Process and Expenses of Future Periods*
Industry, excluding sales-supply	67.5	32.5
Agriculture	44.8	55.2
Procurement	99.0	1.0
Trade and sales-supply	96.9	3.1

The resulting sector estimates sum precisely to the known asset totals, an outcome which supports somewhat the credibility of our procedures. (As is explained in the notes for Table G–4, we do not accept Usoskin's division of total inventories between procurement and trade. Since the percentages involved in the present calculation are much the same for these two sectors, this inconsistency in our treatment of Usoskin's data has no significant consequence.) The figures for trade and sales-supply in combination are 2.6 billion of production supplies and 0.1 billion of goods in process and expenses of future periods. From the data for 1951, we assume the 0.1 billion is attributable to trade and distribute the 2.6 billion between the two sectors so as to exhaust their totals.

We proceed next to distribute inventories in state industry, inclusive of sales-supply, between producer and consumer goods industries, and to adjust the estimates for small tools and for expenses of future periods.

(*i*) Khromov–37, pp. 70–72, provides absolute data for October 1, 1935, from which it is possible to compute the percentage composition of inventories in the four commissariats indicated:

	Heavy	*Timber*	*Food*	*Light*
Production supplies	32.4	40.0	45.5	46.9
Goods in process and expenses of future periods	28.0	14.2	8.0	32.4
Finished products	39.6	46.5	46.5	20.7
Total	100.0	100.0	100.0	100.0

In this source, goods in process and semifabricates, which are here combined, are given separately. Expenses of future periods, which are not expressly accounted for, are presumably included in goods in process. Khromov does in one breakdown include in, and in another (which we follow) exclude from, total inventories other than finished products an item, "materials and *inventar'* intended for sale." This category could possibly correspond to Usoskin's "other" inventories, though Khromov's absolute figures are very small, even in comparison with Usoskin's "other."

The absolute totals to which Khromov's breakdowns refer are reproduced in the notes to Table G–4, where it is also pointed out that, with one exception, they appear reasonably consistent with inventories on January 1, 1936, for state industry inclusive of sales-supply. The exception is light industry, for which Khromov's coverage appears very limited, possibly by the exclusion of textiles. Though we hereafter use Khromov's breakdown for light industry as though it were representative of the whole of that sector, this may be inaccurate.

It should be noted that Khromov's data underlie our division of particular kinds of inventories between producer and consumer goods not only in 1937 but in 1928 and 1951 as well. Errors from this source are considerably constrained by the known data on distributions of inventories in industry as a whole, but the use of 1935 breakdowns for years remote from 1935 or separated from it by large price changes may produce substantial inaccuracies.

Since Khromov gives no breakdown for local industry, we assume for simplicity that it equaled the average of those given for light and food industries.

(*ii*) Our distribution by sectors of the 1937 total of state industrial inventories, including sales-supply, prior to adjustment for expenses of future periods and small tools, is the following (billion rubles; these figures are not shown elsewhere, but their derivation is explained in Appendix G, notes for 1933–39):

Heavy	19.3
Timber	2.0
Food	6.5
Light	7.4
Local	3.3
Total	38.5

We apply to these totals the Khromov ratios of finished products in total inventories and adjust the results to the known total. We make no allowance here for the differential effects of the partial inclusion of small tools in the 1937 sector totals.

(*iii*) Usoskin–39, p. 50, gives the percentage division in 1937 of inventories other than finished products in the Commissariats of Heavy and Food Industries:

	Heavy	*Food*
Production supplies	57.8	83.3
Goods in process, semifabricates, and expenses of future periods	42.2	16.7
Total	100.0	100.0

These figures do not explicitly include sales-supply organs, but inventories other than finished products held by the latter are trivial in any case. Moreover, a similar breakdown given by Usoskin for January 1, 1936, corresponds closely to that for October 1, 1935, cited above from Khromov. We apply the percentages to the totals net of finished products for the two sectors indicated.

For the remaining three sectors, we divide inventories other than finished products in the proportions indicated by Khromov and adjust the results sequentially to the known totals by kind and by sector to consistency with both.

From the several preceding steps, we obtain estimates for state producer (heavy and timber) and consumer (food, light, local) goods industries as follows (billion rubles):

	Producer Goods	Consumer Goods	Total
Production supplies	8.4	9.5	17.9
Goods in process and expenses of future periods	5.6	2.9	8.5
Finished products	7.3	4.8	12.1
Total	21.3	17.2	38.5

(*iv*) Adjustments must now be made in this breakdown for small tools, one half of which we assume included in production supplies by the beginning of 1937 and all of which thereafter. Our one piece of evidence on the volume of small tools for any date earlier than 1951 is given by Birman–56, p. 41, who indicates that on January 1, 1940, small tools accounted for 31.9 percent of production supplies in Group "A" industry and 14.4 in Group "B." Applying these percentages to the 1937 data above, on the assumptions specified, yields figures for small tools of 3.2 billion in producer goods industries and 1.5 billion in consumer goods. (See the comments below on the whole of our estimates for small tools.)

The plausibility of our estimates to this point for state industry as a whole can be checked by comparison with similar reported data for January 1, 1938. Campbell–58a, p. 11, cites from Batyrev–40 data for industry in 1938 which imply a distribution of inventories of 41.3 percent production supplies, 19.6 goods in process, and 39.1 finished products on hand and shipped. We have elsewhere (Appendix G, 1933–39) concluded that a 54 billion figure given in this source is probably for inventories in state industry, inclusive of sales-supply and of goods shipped, and we have estimated (Table G–4) 1938 goods shipped in state industry as 9 billion. From these data we compose a breakdown from Batyrev exclusive of goods shipped, which we can compare with our own estimates, one half of small tools being added to production supplies as shown above (percent):

	Present Estimates (*1937*)	Batyrev (*1938*)
Production supplies	49.6	49.5
Goods in process and expenses of future periods	20.8	23.6
Finished products	29.6	26.9
Total	100.0	100.0

The comparison appears to corroborate reasonably well our 1937 estimate for state industry as a whole.

(*v*) We undertake, finally, to remove expenses of future periods from their combined totals with goods in process. From Table G–5, we have expenses of future periods in all basic branches on January 1, 1937, as 1.0 billion. On the basis of data for 1951 (see Table G–6), we assume these were distributed 0.9 billion to state industry and 0.1 to domestic trade. We assume that the industry figure is divided between producer and consumer goods in proportion to their totals of goods in process and expenses of future periods, i.e., 0.6 and 0.3 billion respectively.

(*vi*) Our final breakdowns for state industry are derived by subtracting one half of small tools from production supplies as shown above, including the whole of small tools in the total of inventories, and deducting expenses of future periods both from their combined total with goods in process and from total inventories. The results are these (billion rubles):

	Producer Goods	Consumer Goods	Total
Raw materials	6.8	8.7	15.5
Small tools	3.2	1.5	4.7
Goods in process	5.0	2.6	7.6
Finished products	7.3	4.8	12.1
Total	22.3	17.6	39.9

The figures for producer goods industries are those used in the table. State consumer goods industries are combined with industrial co-operatives (see below).

For basic branches other than state industry, it remains to estimate small tools, expenses of future periods, and, in the case of agriculture, immature livestock. From the calculation made in Paragraph (*v*) above, we take expenses of future periods to have been 0.1 billion in domestic trade and zero in both agriculture and procurement. On the basis of the fact that the share of small tools in total inventories in state industry was of the same order of magnitude in 1937 as in 1951 (see notes for 1951 following), we assume the share in other sectors was equal in 1937 to that of 1951 (see Table H–1). The adjustments for expenses of future periods and small tools are handled in the same way as for state industry.

In state agriculture, immature livestock accounted in 1951 for 38.6 percent of inventories on hand inclusive of immature livestock and of one half of small tools (see Tables G–6 and H–1). We assume, doubtless inaccurately, that the share was the same in 1937 and the absolute amount was 2.8 billion. In the 1951 data (see Table G–6), immature livestock are included with production supplies. From comparison of the reported 1937 breakdown (see above) and that for 1951 (Table H–1), it appears unlikely that in the former livestock could be included in production supplies but quite possible that they are included in goods in process. Rather arbitrarily, we assume that the latter is the case. We make very limited use of the data for state agriculture.

For sectors other than basic branches, we have from Table G–4 unadjusted inventory totals of 1.9 billion in industrial co-operatives and 2.6

billion in transportation and communications. On the basis of postwar data (Table G–6), we assume expenses of future periods were negligible in these sectors and distribute the totals plus one half of small tools in the same proportions as in 1951 (data for industrial co-operatives are given in the notes for 1951).

The resulting estimates for industrial co-operatives (1.0 billion raw materials, 0.2 small tools, 0.1 goods in process, and 0.7 finished products) are added to those derived above for state consumer goods industries to obtain total consumer goods industries.

Except for transportation and communications, all percentage breakdowns in Table H–1 are computed from the absolute figures. Because of rounding errors, the computed percentages differ in some instances from the percentages used in obtaining the absolute figures.

A further comment is in order on our 1937 estimates of small tools. For the sectors covered, these sum to 7.2 billion rubles. In Moorsteen–62, pp. 433 ff., estimates are made of annual investments in small tools which appear extremely small relative to the 1937 figure for the stock. For example, investment in these assets in 1936 in industry, transportation and communications, and trade is estimated at 600 million rubles, in socialized agriculture 190 million rubles. Even if our supposition is right that small tools, like other inventories, are revalued with price changes, the stock and flow figures could be reconciled only on the assumption of implausibly long service lives.

We cannot satisfactorily account for this discrepancy. We retain the present estimates because they rest on a fragment of evidence on the *stock* of tools and because, taking account of price movements from 1937 to 1951, they look more plausible in comparison with the known 1951 stocks than would any figure for 1937 which could be derived by cumulating the annual investment figures.

1951

Except for the distribution of inventories in industry and sales-supply between producer and consumer goods, all figures for 1951 derive from detailed breakdowns given in TsSU–61, pp. 92–101. Reference should be made to the discussion of this source in Appendix G, notes for 1951. Our treatment of data in the source requires these explanations.

(*i*) All inventories described as "production supplies" are included here in raw materials, except small tools and immature livestock. Spare parts, which are classed as production supplies, might in principle be better treated separately, but their amount is small.

(*ii*) "Goods in process and internally produced semifabricates" are classed as goods in process. It may be peculiar to TsSU–61 that it includes purchased semifabricates (of unspecified amount) with production supplies, though we have no evidence on the point.

(*iii*) "Supplies and goods in process of subsidiary agricultural organs" are divided between raw materials and goods in process in the proportions attributed to these categories exclusive of agricultural subsidiaries. The amounts involved are small.

(*iv*) "Other normed assets," which are very small, are distributed proportionately among the four categories in Table H–1.

(v) The 0.6 billion of goods in process (literally, "unfinished production") shown for contract construction is indicated in the source to consist of 0.1 billion of industrial and 0.5 billion of nonindustrial goods in process. The former may refer to goods held in the industrial subsidiaries of contract construction organizations. The latter evidently refers to construction and installation work which has not yet been classified as "capital investment" (see Appendix E, p. 445). On this point, Birman–56, p. 53, cites data for four construction trusts in 1954 in which unfinished production accounts for 2 percent of total normed assets. Birman states further, p. 52, that unfinished production includes as a rule only unfinished "constructional elements" which have not been paid for, and that the category is therefore small. His 2 percent figure is smaller than that which we cite, for all contract construction, but the orders of magnitude are similar. Since "constructional elements" are probably paid for as they are completed, his explanation of this category appears consistent with that cited in Appendix E.

(vi) Sector totals are from Table G–1.

Data available in TsSU sources permit the breakdown of inventories in industry and sales-supply only to the following extent (billion rubles):

	State Industry	Sales-Supply	Industrial Co-operatives
Raw materials	65.4	0.8	3.2
Small tools	15.9	0.2	0.8
Goods in process	31.4	0.1	0.4
Finished products	32.3	19.9	2.1
Total	145.0	21.0	6.5

Data for state and co-operative industry combined and for sales-supply are derived from TsSU–61 as for other sectors. The division of the industry totals between state and co-operative is made on the basis of data in *Vestnik statistiki*, 1957:2, pp. 94–96, by procedures analogous to those described in Appendix G, notes for 1951 and related years.

We have elsewhere (see Table G–8) attributed 113.5 billion of total inventories in state industry and sales-supply to producer goods, 52.5 billion to consumer goods. We apply to these totals the 1937 percentage shares of inventories by kind for each of the two sectors (see notes for 1937) and adjust the results sequentially to the known totals by kind and by sector to consistency with both sets of totals. To the resulting figures for state consumer goods we add industrial co-operatives to obtain the totals shown in Table H–1. Percentages in the table for industrial sectors are computed from the absolute figures.

Distribution of Short-Term

Bank Loans by Sector

The inventory estimates are dependent at numerous points upon data for short-term bank loans, which are assembled here. Data for the prewar years are shown in Table I–1. Those for postwar years are shown in two variants, in Tables I–2 and I–3. Figures for 1941 are also included in the latter tables.

Typically, Soviet sources do not explain the basis on which distributions of loans by sector are made. It is reasonably clear, nevertheless, that the distributions are based almost entirely upon administrative rather than product classifications. That this is the case is more or less explicit in a few sources (for example, where the breakdown is by ministries). That it is can also be inferred from the obvious conceptual difficulties in allocating total loans to a borrowing organization among its several products. Loan series, even if given in a single source, may therefore reflect organizational changes occurring over the span of years covered. Loan series pieced together from various sources are still more likely to be affected by such changes.

On the other hand, it is clear that loan breakdowns reported for any given date do not necessarily reflect the organizational structure of that date. This is indicated by the existence of different breakdowns for the same date (which may be due also to differences in the administrative level at which the classifications are made) and by occasional references in the literature to the classification of borrowers on a given date in accord with administrative subordinations of an earlier date. In some degree, Soviet sources attempt to stabilize sector classifications, presumably in order to improve the comparability of the data over time. In sum, available loan distributions employ sector classifications which are partly stabilized and partly varying, and it is rarely possible to establish the classification principle of any given series.

For the prewar years in particular, the number of alternative distributions is so large and their inconsistencies so numerous that a complete reconciliation has not been attempted. The series put together in Table I–1 have been chosen largely on the basis of the authority of their sources, their consistency with inventory data used elsewhere, and their apparent "fit" with one another. Some obvious discontinuties produced by organiza-

TABLE I-1

DISTRIBUTION OF SHORT-TERM BANK LOANS BY SECTOR, 1932-41

(January 1--Billion Rubles)

	1932	1933	1934	1935	1936	1937	1938	1939	1940	1941
Heavy Industry	0.51	0.85	1.27	1.95	2.84	5.0	5.48	6.19	6.76	9.7
Timber Industry	0.58	0.52	0.73	0.71	0.91	0.9	1.00	1.28	1.91	1.9
Food Industry	1.01	1.10	1.89	2.45	5.38	6.8	8.00	9.15	9.14	10.3
Light Industry	0.80	1.00	1.25	1.05	2.59	4.9	6.18	7.78	10.35	8.6
Local Industry	0.30	0.24	0.24	0.45	0.78	1.1	0.28	0.29	0.38	0.5
Industrial Co-operatives	0.40	0.44	0.42	0.49	0.58	0.6	0.53	0.56	0.73	1.1
Transportation and Communications	0.37	0.40	0.46	0.55	0.72	0.8	0.92	0.85	1.15	1.2
Agriculture	0.79	1.04	0.91	1.00	1.33	1.4	1.79	2.01	2.01	2.2
State	0.75	0.97	0.87	0.92	1.18	1.2	1.47	1.78	1.78	1.9
Collective-Farm	0.04	0.07	0.04	0.08	0.15	0.2	0.32	0.24	0.24	0.3
Procurement	1.35	1.47	1.68	2.00	2.99	2.8	3.29	3.85	3.07	4.0
Domestic Trade	1.85	2.58	4.39	5.86	7.46	9.4	11.52	11.80	10.94	13.5
Foreign Trade	0.30	0.31	0.46	0.38	0.36	0.3	0.32	0.17	0.44	0.7
Other Sectors	0.45	0.44	0.40	0.48	0.60	0.8	0.91	1.02	1.08	1.2
Total	8.71	10.39	14.11	17.39	26.56	34.8	40.22	44.95	47.95	55.0

TABLE I-2

DISTRIBUTION OF SHORT-TERM BANK LOANS BY SECTOR, GOSBANK CLASSIFICATIONS, 1941, 1944-62

(January 1--Billion Rubles)

	1941	1944	1945	1946	1947	1948	1949	1950	1951	1952
Heavy Industry	11.2	36.3	--	18.2	22.1	24.5	30.1	43.0	35.0	39.7
Timber Industry	2.1		--	1.2					7.3	8.3
Food Industry	10.7		--	8.3	9.2	11.8	20.8	30.1	27.5	30.1
Light Industry	9.1		--	7.9	7.2	6.7	10.1	17.5	19.7	20.4
Local Industry	1.4	--	--	0.4	0.5	0.7	0.9	1.3	1.1	1.2
Industrial Co-operatives		--	--	0.7	0.8	1.1	1.6	1.6	1.3	1.8
Transportation and Communications	1.2	--	--	2.4	2.7	2.9	2.9	3.7	3.6	4.0
Agriculture	2.2	--	--	1.8	2.2	2.2	3.4	5.6	5.5	5.7
Procurement	3.3	--	--	2.4	2.3	3.3	4.6	6.1	6.2	6.6
Domestic Trade	12.3	--	--	14.3	20.1	28.6	53.2	62.2	49.8	59.2
Foreign Trade	0.9	--	--	1.3	1.3	3.3	2.6	4.0	4.7	6.3
Other Sectors	0.5	--	--	0.6	0.8	1.0	0.9	0.8	1.2	1.0
Total	55.0	53.6	55.0	59.5	70.8	86.1	131.1	175.9	162.9	184.3

	1953	1954	1955	1956	1957	1958	1959	1960	1961	1962
Heavy Industry	44.3	45.7	45.7	35.8	35.4	40.0	147.0	159.0	171.0	183.0
Timber Industry	9.3	10.3	9.8	9.8	10.4	12.1				
Food Industry	30.1	27.7	26.8	33.8	37.3	42.0				
Light Industry	20.7	18.8	19.7	18.2	22.9	25.8				
Local Industry	1.5	1.7	3.1	2.1	2.1	1.6				
Industrial Co-operatives	3.3	3.3	3.1	3.3	3.3	2.5				
Transportation and Communications	2.3	1.7	3.8	3.5	3.4	3.5	4.0	4.3	4.0	5.0
Agriculture	3.8	4.4	9.0	10.7	10.4	27.5	34.0	59.8	70.0	77.0
Procurement	5.8	5.4	6.0	6.1	17.1					
Domestic Trade	72.1	77.6	58.1	70.1	93.9	99.0	124.0	146.5	153.0	171.0
Foreign Trade	3.6	2.9	3.9	3.7	4.9	6.2	7.6	10.0	10.0	11.0
Other Sectors	1.4	1.6	2.2	2.3	2.4	3.0	3.5	3.9	4.0	4.0
Total	203.4	207.5	190.0	199.4	243.5	263.2	320.1	383.5	412.0	451.0

tional changes have been crudely corrected for. The loans shown in Table I–1 are those issued by Gosbank only.

For the postwar years, most reported data can be attributed to one of two distributions, which, on the basis of the sources from which they emanate, are here referred to as Gosbank and TsSU distributions.

The Gosbank distributions, shown in Table I–2, are probably the more similar to the prewar data, which also come largely from bank sources. The sector classifications in the postwar Gosbank distributions appear to have been stabilized to some extent, since prewar data given in the same sources differ from those published in prewar sources, and the 1957 reorganization has no obvious impact on the series. Examination of the data leaves little doubt, however, that some major reclassification of sectors occurs between January 1, 1953, and January 1, 1954. This is evidently due chiefly, though perhaps not solely, to the reorganization of sales-supply agencies which occurred in the course of 1953 (see *Sovetskoe gosudarstvo i pravo*, 1953:5, p. 21). Popov–57, p. 82, which is a chief source of the Gosbank distributions, refers explicitly to an increase in loans to trade resulting from the transfer to trade of the sales organs of light industry. But more changes than this appear to be reflected in the data.

We do not adjust the Gosbank distributions for the apparent change in classifications because, with minor exceptions, they are not used directly in the derivation of the inventory estimates. They are included here, instead, to provide a means of distributing the categories of the TsSU distributions among more detailed sectors than are given in the sources and to extend the TsSU series to years not covered in the published data. The Gosbank distributions cover loans from Gosbank only.

The TsSU distributions, shown in Table I–3, include loans both from Gosbank and from the long-term banks (in 1959, the functions of these banks were transferred to a single long-term bank and to Gosbank). Short-term loans from these banks are thought to be restricted largely to contract construction organizations, and subtraction of loans to construction from the TsSU totals leaves residuals which are virtually identical with total Gosbank loans, with the single exception of 1951. The cause of the discrepancy in that year is unknown, but the TsSU totals for loans from all banks are here accepted as accurate.

Some evidence on the character of the TsSU breakdowns has been released. A partial loan distribution for January 1, 1957, given in Zverev–58, p. 144, compares as follows with the TsSU data (billion rubles):

	Zverev	TsSU
Industry	97.2	97.2
Transportation and communications	1.2	1.8
Agriculture	8.3 ⎫	
Procurement	17.2 ⎬	25.6
Trade	88.4 ⎭	88.4

Zverev explains that his distribution is a revision, presumably from the Gosbank classifications, and that the classification of loans is based not only on the operations of ministries and administrative bodies but on those of individual enterprises. The apparent implication is that the TsSU data are still based on administrative rather than commodity categories. But

TABLE I-3

DISTRIBUTION OF SHORT-TERM BANK LOANS BY SECTOR, TsSU CLASSIFICATIONS, 1941, 1946-62

(January 1--Billion Rubles)

	1941	1946	1947	1948	1949	1950	1951	1952	1953
Industry	21.3*	25.2	27.3*	31.7	46.0	69.4	69.8*	75.6*	82.8*
Heavy	--	11.9	14.9	17.0	21.4	31.3	24.4	27.1	31.0
Timber	--	1.2					7.2	8.0	9.2
Food	--	5.6	6.2	8.2	14.8	22.1	20.7	22.2	22.8
Light	--	5.5	5.0	4.8	7.4	13.1	15.1	15.4	16.0
Local	--	0.4	0.5	0.7	0.9	1.3	1.1	1.2	1.5
Industrial Co-operatives	--	0.6	0.7	1.0	1.5	1.6	1.3	1.7	2.3
Sales-Supply	10.5*	10.1	10.1*	11.7	17.2	26.0	25.8*	25.9*	24.1*
Producer Goods	--	6.0	5.9	6.8	8.6	12.6	12.5	12.9	12.7
Consumer Goods	--	4.1	4.2	4.9	8.6	13.4	13.3	13.0	11.4
Transportation and Communications	0.7*	1.4	1.6*	1.8	1.8	2.3	2.3*	2.5*	2.3*
Agriculture and Procurement	8.9*	7.0	7.4*	8.6	11.3	14.8	13.3*	13.3*	15.7*
Agriculture	--	2.5	3.1	2.9	4.1	6.1	5.4	5.2	5.0
State	--	2.5	3.1	2.9	4.0	5.8	5.1	4.9	4.7
Collective-Farm	--	0.0	0.0	0.0	0.1	0.3	0.3	0.3	0.3
Procurement	--	4.5	4.3	5.7	7.2	8.7	7.9	8.1	10.7
Trade	13.4*	16.5	24.3*	33.4	57.8	67.7	54.9*	66.2*	76.3*
Domestic	--	15.2	21.4	30.1	55.2	63.7	50.3	59.9	72.7
Foreign	--	1.3	2.9	3.3	2.6	4.0	4.6	6.3	3.6
Contract Construction	0.4*	--	3.0*	--	--	--	6.1*	8.8*	10.6*
Other Sectors	0.5*	0.4	0.5*	0.7	0.7	0.7	1.1*	1.1*	2.6*
Total	55.7*	--	74.2*	--	--	--	173.3*	193.4*	214.4*

*Figures reported in TsSU sources.

TABLE I-3 (continued)

DISTRIBUTION OF SHORT-TERM BANK LOANS BY SECTOR, TsSU CLASSIFICATIONS, 1941, 1946-62
(January 1--Billion Rubles)

	1954	1955	1956	1957	1958	1959	1960	1961	1962
Industry.................	92.3*	93.2*	88.7*	97.2*	110.1*	131.8*	137.3*	150.5	161.0
Heavy....................	34.4	34.9	26.6	26.4	30.3 ⎫	54.2	57.3	63.8	73.0
Timber..................	10.2	9.9	9.6	10.2	12.1 ⎭				
Food....................	25.2	24.7	30.4	33.9	39.0 ⎫				
Light...................	17.7	18.8	16.9	21.4	24.6 ⎭	77.6	80.0	86.7	88.0
Local...................	3.2	1.8	2.0	2.1	1.6				
Industrial Co-operatives..	1.6	3.1	3.2	3.2	2.5				
Sales-Supply............	25.4*	24.0*	27.1*	30.4*	31.7*	40.3*	47.2*	47.7	52.0
Producer Goods..........	13.0	12.3	10.4	11.4	11.7	12.6	16.9	16.7	18.0
Consumer Goods..........	12.4	11.7	16.7	19.0	20.0	27.7	30.3	31.0	34.0
Transportation and Communications..	2.8*	2.4*	2.3*	1.8*	2.3*	2.8*	2.5*	2.5	3.0
Agriculture and Procurement..	13.4*	14.4*	16.5*	25.6*	25.5*	32.2*	59.1*	69.0	76.0
Agriculture.............	6.6	6.8	8.2	8.3	12.3	15.4	25.0	29.2	32.0
State...................	5.7	5.3	5.8	5.8	8.5	10.6	13.8	16.1	18.0
Collective-Farm........	0.9	1.5	2.4	2.5	3.8	4.8	11.2	13.1	14.0
Procurement............	6.8	7.6	8.3	17.3	13.2	16.8	34.1	39.8	44.0
Trade...................	73.2*	54.9*	63.5*	88.4*	92.8*	112.3*	135.4*	141.0	157.0
Domestic................	70.3	51.0	59.6	83.5	86.6	104.7	125.4	131.0	146.0
Foreign.................	2.9	3.9	3.9	4.9	6.2	7.6	10.0	10.0	11.0
Contract Construction...	11.2*	11.3*	10.9*	10.7*	12.3*	10.7*	12.3*	--	--
Other Sectors...........	1.1*	1.6*	1.7*	0.8*	1.3*	1.4*	1.5*	2.0	2.0
Total.............	219.4*	201.8*	210.7*	254.9*	276.0*	331.5*	395.4*	--	--

*Figures reported in TsSU sources.

the classification at the enterprise level, to whatever extent that has been used, should more nearly approximate a commodity classification than do the Gosbank breakdowns. It should also make the loan distributions invariant to organizational changes which affect merely the administrative subordination of individual enterprises. (Zverev indicates that his trade figure is for domestic trade only, but this appears to be an error.)

Through 1953 (i.e., in 1941, 1947, and 1951–53), the TsSU distributions correspond quite closely to the Gosbank distributions, if the Gosbank category for industry is assumed to include sales-supply and the TsSU trade category is assumed to include foreign trade. From 1954 on, the TsSU industry (plus sales-supply) figures are much larger than the Gosbank figures, the TsSU figures for trade much smaller. The apparent explanation for these differences is that the TsSU categories were unaffected by the organizational changes of 1953. The TsSU series also show no discontinuities with the 1957 reorganization, and, indeed, it is probable that these distributions were prepared by TsSU to provide series of comparable coverage before and after the 1957 reorganization. So far as one can judge by inspection, the TsSU series are of relatively stable coverage throughout the postwar years.

In years since 1957, Gosbank sources have on occasion reported breakdowns which can be inferred to be a mixture of Gosbank and TsSU categories. We have judged the coverage of particular figures from internal evidence and general orders of magnitude.

SOURCES TO TABLE I–1

1932–35

Data are taken largely from Gosbank–35, p. 58, though similar data appear in TsUNKhU–36, p. 674. Unlike the latter, Gosbank–35 excludes from total short-term loans a portion of loans subject to funding but not yet funded as of the beginning of 1932 (this difference explains the larger TsUNKhU total, of 10.31 billion); includes timber enterprises of several sectors, rather than of the commissariat alone, in the timber category; and includes agricultural co-operatives in the "other" category. Timber excepted, loans are classified by administrative categories, generally at the commissariat level.

Data from the source cited have been adjusted and supplemented in two respects. Loans given separately for the food industry and for procurement in 1932 are redivided in the 1933 proportions; data published in this and other sources for these sectors in 1932 appear incomparable with those of succeeding years. Loans to collective farms for 1932–34 are taken from Efimov–34, p. 16; those to state agriculture are computed as residuals. For 1935, the share of collective farms in total loans to agriculture is assumed to have changed linearly from 1934 to 1938.

1936

The share of collective farms in total agriculture is interpolated between 1934 and 1938. All other data are derived from a detailed breakdown given in Gumilevskii–36, p. 21. Data in this source appear at least roughly consistent in coverage with those for 1935. For five major sectors,

Gumilevskii's figures can be approximated by adding to the 1935 figures increments for the year reported in Grin'ko–36, p. 7. Gumilevskii gives separate figures for timber enterprises not under the commissariat, which are included in the timber category in Table I–1.

1937

Figures for this date are drawn from a number of sources and are of questionable consistency with one another and with data for contiguous years.

Heavy industry is computed as a residual of total loans and loans to all other sectors. A figure for this date is available (in *Kredit i khozraschet*, 1937:1, p. 2) of 4.4 as against the estimated 5.0 billion, but there is reason to believe that this, like nearly all other figures for heavy industry reported for the years 1937–40 in prewar (and some postwar) sources is exclusive of loans to the defense industry. Defense industry was separated administratively from heavy industry in 1936. At least one commonly cited figure for heavy industry, 4.8 billion in 1939, is explicitly stated to exclude defense industry (cf. *Den'gi i kredit*, 1939:4, p. 11). Very detailed breakdowns of loans by sectors for years in the late 1930's give no figure for defense industry and show loans to "other sectors" which are disproportionately high relative both to those for the early 1930's and to those shown for the late 1930's in postwar sources (which presumably include defense with industry).

Our general procedure for years from 1937 to 1940 is to disregard reported "other" figures and compute these instead from the 1936 ratio of other to total loans and, given the other category, to compute total heavy industry as a residual. The implied estimates of loans to defense industry—differences between reported and estimated loans to heavy industry—are 0.6 billion in 1937, .87 in 1938, 1.37 in 1939, and 1.55 in 1940.

Timber is estimated from a figure of 820 million for the commissariat alone given in Grin'ko–37, p. 7, and from the share of the commissariat in the total in 1936 and 1938 (see sources cited for those dates).

Food and procurement are from *Kredit i khozraschet*, 1937:1, p. 2.

Light and local are from Grin'ko–37, p. 7.

Industrial co-operatives and transportation and communications are both straight-line interpolations between 1936 and 1938.

Total agriculture and total loans are from Rovinskii–37, p. 15. The division of agriculture between its components is interpolated between 1934 and 1938.

Domestic trade is computed from the 1936 total and an increase during 1936 of 1.9 billion given in Shvarts–37, p. 4.

Foreign trade is computed from a total of foreign and domestic trade of 9.7 billion, given in Rovinskii–37, p. 15, and the computed figure for domestic trade.

"Other sectors" are assumed the same share of total loans as in 1936.

1938–39

Data are derived for the most part from detailed breakdowns given in Usoskin–39, p. 71. Usoskin's categories resemble closely those used by Gumilevskii for 1936. The sharp decline from 1937 to 1938 in loans to local industry, however, probably reflects a change in classification.

As in 1937, loans to "other sectors" are estimated from their 1936 share in the total; loans to heavy industry are computed as residuals. Usoskin's figures for the latter category are 4.61 billion in 1938 and 4.82 in 1939.

The estimated 1938 figure for heavy industry, 5.48 billion, compares with a figure of 5.45 billion reported in *Den'gi i kredit*, 1938:7–8, p. 53; the latter presumably is inclusive of defense industry. The sum of loans to state industry in 1939, 24.69 billion, compares with a reported figure, evidently inclusive of defense industry, of 25.5 billion, given in Rubinshtein–58, p. 47.

1940

Data are based largely on a detailed but incomplete breakdown given in D'iachenko–40, pp. 523–24. D'iachenko's categories are clearly not identical with those used by Usoskin and Gumilevskii, and several adjustments have been made in them to increase their comparability with data for earlier years.

(*i*) For timber, D'iachenko gives loans to the commissariat only (1.66). A more inclusive figure has been taken from Gerashchenko–39, p. 12; this source gives figures for several other sectors which are identical with D'iachenko's.

(*ii*) The combined total for local industry and industrial co-operatives is divided between the two components in the 1939 proportions.

(*iii*) D'iachenko's figures for agriculture are not comprehensive. The figure used is computed from total loans and a percentage breakdown given in Atlas–47, p. 338. The total for agriculture is assumed distributed as in 1939.

(*iv*) Comparison of D'iachenko's component data for domestic trade with similar breakdowns for 1939 (in *Den'gi i kredit*, 1939:4, p. 10, and Sokolov–39, p. 38) indicates that his figure for "other trade" is of smaller coverage than that of figures used for preceding years. We assume the ratio of "other" to state and co-operative trade was the same in 1940 as in 1939 (see the *Den'gi i kredit* citation).

(*v*) Foreign trade is a straight-line interpolation between 1939 and 1941.

(*vi*) As in 1937, we assume that loans to "other sectors" were the same share of total loans as in 1936 and compute heavy industry as a residual. The sum of D'iachenko's figures for this sector is 5.21 billion.

(*vii*) Total loans are from Proselkov–40, p. 9.

1941

Data are not available in prewar sources for this date and those published in postwar sources are clearly affected by changes from prewar classifications. Our procedure is essentially to extrapolate the Table I–1 1938 breakdown to 1941, using a postwar breakdown for both dates (Popov–57, p. 243); the resulting estimates are adjusted to the known total. Some variations on this procedure are required.

(*i*) The figure for transportation and communications is taken from Popov without adjustment, since the extrapolating procedure yields an implausible result (cf. on this, data in Golev–47, p. 127).

(*ii*) Heavy and timber industry are estimated together. The increase in timber is then assumed that shown by a breakdown given in Golev, *loc. cit.*

(*iii*) The increase in foreign trade is also taken from Golev, *loc. cit.*

(*iv*) Loans to "other sectors" are computed without adjustment as in 1937, from total loans.

(*v*) The combined sum of local industry and industrial co-operatives is divided between its components in the 1939 proportions; total agriculture is similarly distributed among its components.

SOURCES TO TABLE I–2

1941

Popov–57, p. 243, except that loans to timber and foreign trade are from *ibid.*, pp. 65 and 200.

1944

The total figure is computed from a statement in Atlas–58, p. 212, that loans on nonseasonal inventories on this date were 5.9 billion rubles and 11 percent of total loans.

The figure for industry is estimated from a statement in Atlas–52, p. 204, that the share of industry in total loans rose from 59 percent in 1941 to 66 percent in 1944. The 1941 percentage appears from data given in *ibid.*, p. 199, to exclude local industry and industrial co-operatives; the 1944 percentage is assumed to have the same coverage. The latter implies loans to industry in 1944 of 35.4 billion. This is increased in the ratio of 33.1/32.3, which is the 1941 ratio of loans of this coverage given in Atlas–52 to those used in Table I–2.

1945

Total loans are assumed equal to those of 1941 on the basis of statements that during 1944 they approached (Atlas–45, p. 14), and after the end of the war exceeded (Popov–57, p. 34), the prewar level.

1946–56

All data are from Atlas–58, pp. 246 and 289, except that timber in 1946 is from Popov–57, p. 65. The latter source, p. 243, gives complete distributions for several of these same dates which are fully consistent with those given in Atlas.

1957

Figures are from Popov–57, p. 243, with these exceptions: timber is from *ibid.*, p. 65; foreign trade is extended from 1956 on an index given in *ibid.*, p. 208; "other sectors" are computed as a residual; the combined total of local industry and industrial co-operatives is divided in the 1956 proportions.

1958

Figures are from Atlas–58, p. 351, with these exceptions. (*i*) Atlas gives only a total for producer goods industries, of 52.1 billion. From its size, we assume that the TsSU figure for timber (see Table I–3) is also the Gosbank figure, and we compute heavy industry as a residual. (*ii*) Atlas' figure for consumer goods industries is 71.9 billion. On the assumption that the Gosbank and TsSU values for local industry and industrial co-operatives are unlikely to differ substantially, we use the TsSU figures for these two sectors in combination and divide the total in the 1956 proportions. The remaining loans to consumer goods industries are divided between food and light in the 1957 proportions. (*iii*) Atlas gives a combined total for foreign trade and "other sectors" of 9.2 billion. We divide the total in the 1957 proportions.

1959

Total loans are from *Den'gi i kredit*, 1959:8, p. 92. Industry, agriculture and procurement, and domestic trade are from Korovushkin–59, p. 9. Foreign trade is the TsSU figure (see notes to Table I–3 on loans to foreign trade). The remainder is divided between transportation and communications and "other sectors" in their 1958 proportions.

1960

The figures for total loans and for domestic trade are from Korovushkin– 60, pp. 7–8. Loans to industry are given *loc. cit.* as "almost" 140 billion, but this is probably the TsSU figure of 137.3. Loans to agriculture and procurement are given in *ibid.*, p. 9, as 55 billion on January 1, 1960, and are stated to have increased during 1959 by 24 billion rubles or 76 percent. The implied figure for January 1, 1959, is 31 billion. The figures for 1959 and 1960 differ from their TsSU counterparts, but that for 1959 differs also from the 34 billion figure given by the same author a year earlier. We assume that a change in classification is responsible for the difference and estimate 1960 loans to agriculture and procurement as 76 percent greater than those of 1959.

Foreign trade, as in 1959, is the TsSU figure. Remaining loans are distributed among industry, transportation and communications, and "other sectors" in the 1959 proportions.

1961

Total loans, industry, agriculture and procurement, and domestic trade are from *Den'gi i kredit*, 1961:10, pp. 14–15. The figure for agriculture and procurement is given in the source merely as "over 7 billion new rubles," and it is uncertain whether it corresponds to the 1959 or 1960 figures given by Korovushkin (see above). A figure of 70 billion (old) rubles, however, leaves a residual which is plausible in comparison with earlier years. The residual is distributed among transportation and communications, international trade, and "other sectors" in the 1960 proportions.

1962

Total loans, industry, and domestic trade are from Korovushkin–62, pp. 3 and 8. The remainder is distributed in the 1961 proportions.

The various estimates made here in extending the Gosbank series beyond 1957 are required to complete the TsSU breakdowns for the same years. They are, doubtless, not highly accurate.

SOURCES TO TABLE I–3

Table I–3 is constructed upon a framework of data reported, for broad categories and for only part of the years covered, in standard publications of TsSU. These data are identified in the table by asterisks. Fragmentary data available from other sources are inserted which distribute the industry total among its components in a few years, the agriculture and procurement total similarly among its components, and the trade total between domestic and foreign trade. All remaining figures are interpolated or extrapolated on the basis of the Gosbank loan breakdowns (Table I–2). Much of Table I–3 is in the nature of a worksheet and has little merit apart from its present use.

Industry, Total

1941, 1947, 1951–60: Vestnik statistiki 1960:2, p. 86, and TsSU–61, p. 849.

1946, 1948–50, 1961: Computed sum of components.

1962: Extrapolated from 1961 on the Gosbank series.

Industry, Components

Reported information permits distribution of the industry total among its components to the following extent (billion rubles):

	1956	1958	1959	1961	1962
Industry, total	88.7	110.1	131.8	150.5	—
Producer goods	36.2	42.4	54.2	63.8	73.0
Heavy	—	30.3	—	—	—
Timber	—	12.1	—	—	—
Consumer goods	52.5	67.7	77.6	86.7	—
Food	—	39.0	—	—	—
Light	—	24.6	—	—	—
Local	—	1.6	—	—	—
Industrial co-operatives	—	2.5	—	—	—

The industry totals for 1956, 1958, and 1959 are reproduced from Table I–3.

The division between producer and consumer goods in 1958 and 1959 is based on a statement in Korovushkin–59, p. 9, that during 1958 loans to "Group A" industry increased by 11.6 billion or 27.4 percent, loans to "Group B" by 9.6 billion or 14.2 percent. These figures imply loans outstanding (billion rubles):

	1958	1959
Group A	42.3	53.9
Group B	67.6	77.2
Total	109.9	131.1

Korovushkin's totals are almost identical with the reported TsSU totals, and it is reasonable to infer that his components are classified in a way consistent with the totals. The components are adjusted equiproportionately to accord precisely with the TsSU figures.

The division between producer and consumer goods in 1956 and 1961 is based on data given in Kazantsev–61, pp. 10, 14, and 15 (billion rubles):

	1956	1961
Heavy	37.6	63.8
Light and food	54.5	86.7
Sales-supply	9.5	20.3
Total	101.6	170.8

All figures shown are given directly in the source, except that heavy industry is computed as a residual. The latter, however, is precisely consistent with a statement in the source that loans to heavy industry increased 70 percent between the two dates.

Kazantsev's total figure for 1956 is close to the Gosbank total (101.6 as against 103.0) for all industry, including local and industrial co-operatives; his 1961 total is identical with the Gosbank total. The sum of his heavy and light and food figures for 1956 is close to the TsSU industry total (92.1 as against 88.7). While the fit is not perfect, it appears that Kazantsev here reconciles the Gosbank and TsSU industry figures, removing from the Gosbank totals so much of loans to sales-supply as are included with industry in that distribution.

Kazantsev's heavy category and light and food category quite clearly comprehend the whole of producer and consumer goods respectively. We distribute the TsSU total for 1956 between these two components in the proportions shown by Kazantsev. For 1961 we use his absolute figures for the components and compute total loans to industry as their sum.

For producer goods in 1962, Korovushkin–62, p. 4, states that loans to "heavy" industry increased 14.4 percent during 1961 and accounted for 41.7 percent of total loans to industry on January 1, 1962. The 14.4 percent increase applied to the 1961 loan figure derived from Kazantsev implies a 1962 figure for producer goods of 73.0 billion. The 41.7 percent applied to the Gosbank industry total (Table I–2) implies a figure of 76.3 billion. There is a rough fit among all the data, but we use the 73.0 billion figure as probably more consistent with Kazantsev's figure for 1961.

The more detailed allocation for 1958 is based on a distribution given by Zlobin–58, p. 37 (billion rubles):

Heavy and machine-building	29.7
Timber and paper	11.8
Food	39.0
Light	24.6
Agriculture	12.2
Procurement	13.1
Trade	105.6
Other	27.5
Total	263.5

Zlobin's total figure resembles the Gosbank total in that it evidently excludes construction, and his figure for trade is almost identical with the sum of the Gosbank figures for domestic and foreign trade. The sum of his heavy and timber figures, however, is almost identical with the producer goods total derived above from Korovushkin–59, and the sum of his agriculture and procurement figures nearly coincides with the reported TsSU total for this category. The sum of his food and light is smaller than total consumer goods both as derived from Korovushkin and as reported in the Gosbank distribution.

On the basis of Zlobin's data, we divide total producer goods in the proportions shown by him for heavy and timber. With less confidence, we assume that his light and food figures are literally for the two sectors named and are in accord with TsSU classifications, and we assume that the remainder of consumer goods represents local industry and industrial co-operatives. We divide the combined total of the latter two categories in the proportions for 1956 given in the Gosbank breakdown.

From the partial reported data, the component industry figures in all years are derived as follows.

1946: All components are extrapolated from 1947 on the Gosbank series. Heavy and timber are extrapolated together, but timber alone is assumed equal to the Gosbank figure and heavy industry computed as a residual.

1947: Extrapolated from 1951 on the Gosbank series and adjusted proportionately to the known total.

1948–50: Interpolated between 1947 and 1951 on the Gosbank series.

1951–52: Extrapolated from 1953 on the Gosbank series and adjusted to the known totals.

1953: Because of the evident reclassification of sectors in the Gosbank data between 1953 and 1954, special assumptions are required to link the TsSU series at this point. The assumptions made are (*i*) that the TsSU figures for local industry and industrial co-operatives in 1953 are the same as those given by Gosbank (loans to these sectors are small and, in any case, inexplicably erratic) and (*ii*) that all other components increased equiproportionately from 1953 to 1954.

1954–55: Extrapolated from 1956 on the Gosbank series and adjusted to the known totals.

1956: Extrapolated from 1958 on the Gosbank series and adjusted to the totals computed above for producer and consumer goods separately.

1957: Interpolated between 1956 and 1958 on the Gosbank series and adjusted to the known total.

1958–59: Figures are those computed above from reported data.

1960: Shares of components in the total are interpolated between 1959 and 1961.

1961: Figures are those computed above from reported data.

1962: Producer goods industry is the figure computed above from reported data. Consumer goods are computed as a residual.

Sales-Supply, Total

1941, 1947, 1951–60: Vestnik statistiki, 1960:2, p. 86, and TsSU–61, p. 849.

1946, 1948–50, 1961–62: Sums of components.

Sales-Supply, Components

The division of the sales-supply total between its two components where the total is known, and the estimation of the absolute values of the components where the total is not known, are based entirely on the differences between the TsSU and Gosbank loan distributions. From 1946 to 1953, the difference between the two distributions for loans to heavy and timber industries is used as an estimator for the producer goods components of sales-supply, the difference between loans to food and light industries for the consumer goods component. From 1954 on, the difference between loans to domestic trade is included in the estimator for the consumer goods component. For years prior to 1953, the sum of the loan differences approximates fairly closely the sales-supply total in the years when it is known. For years after 1953, the sum of the differences falls significantly short of the known total.

1946: Components are extrapolated from 1947 on the loan differences described above.

1947: The known total is distributed in the proportion of the loan differences.

1948–50: Interpolated between 1947 and 1951 on the loan differences.

1951–58: Known totals are distributed in the proportions of the loan differences.

1959–60: The difference between industry loan figures is known only for industry as a whole. The division of this total is extrapolated from 1958 on the TsSU figures for loans to industry proper. The estimates are otherwise composed as in 1951–58.

1961–62: The total industry difference is divided as in 1959–60. Components are then extrapolated from 1960 on the loan differences.

Transportation and Communications

1941, 1947, 1951–60: Vestnik statistiki, 1960:2, p. 86, and TsSU–61, p. 849.

1946, 1948–50, 1961–62: Interpolated or extrapolated from 1947, 1947 to 1951, and 1960, respectively, on the Gosbank series.

Agriculture and Procurement, Total

1941, 1947, 1951–60: Vestnik statistiki, 1960:2, p. 86, and TsSU–61, p. 849.

1946, 1948–50: Sum of components.

1961–62: Extrapolated from 1960 on the Gosbank series.

Agriculture and Procurement, Division between Agriculture and Procurement

1946: The two components are extrapolated separately from 1947 on their corresponding Gosbank loan series.

1947: Extrapolated separately from 1951 on the Gosbank loan series and adjusted to the known total.

1948–50: Interpolated separately between 1947 and 1951 on the Gosbank loan series.

1951: Procurement is from Table G–6 (see the notes to that table for discussion of the correspondence of loan data therein to the TsSU loan breakdowns). Agriculture is computed as a residual.

1952–55: Division of the known totals is interpolated between 1951 and 1956 on the Gosbank loan series.

1956: Derived as in 1951.

1957–58: Zverev–58, p. 144, gives figures of 8.3 billion for agriculture and 17.2 billion for procurement in 1957; Zlobin–58, p. 37, gives figures of 12.2 and 13.1 billion for 1958. These are adjusted for their slight discrepancies from the known totals.

1959–60: Derived as in 1951.

1961–62: Division of the total is assumed to have remained the same as in 1960.

Agriculture, Division between State and Collective-Farm

1946: Division of the total is extrapolated from 1947.

1947: According to Popov–57, p. 76, loans for "the productive needs of collective farms" were 133 million rubles on July 1, 1946, as against 1,529 million on July 1, 1951. From this and from the Table I–3 figure for January 1, 1951, we assume that loans to collective farms on January 1, 1947, were less than 50 million rubles. All loans to agriculture are attributed to the state sector.

1948–50: Division of the total is interpolated between 1947 and 1951.

1951: Loans to state agriculture are from Table G–6; those to collective farms are the residual.

1952–55: The share of state agriculture in the total is assumed to have remained constant from 1951 to 1953 and then to have fallen linearly to 1956. Loans to collective farms are the residual.

1956: Derived as in 1951.

1957–58: Division of the total is assumed to have changed linearly from 1956 to 1959.

1959–60: Derived as in 1951.

1961–62: Division of the total is extrapolated from 1960.

Trade, Total

1941, 1947, 1951–60: Vestnik statistiki, 1960:2, p. 86, and TsSU–61, p. 849.

1946, 1948–50, 1961–62: Sum of components.

Trade, Domestic

1946: Extrapolated from 1947 on the Gosbank series.

1947: Computed difference between total and foreign trade.

1948–50: Interpolated between 1947 and 1951 on the Gosbank series.

1951: Table G–6.

1952–55: Computed difference between total and foreign trade.

1956: Table G–6.

1957–58: Computed difference between total and foreign trade.

1959–60: Table G–6.

1961–62: Extrapolated from 1960 on the Gosbank series.

Trade, Foreign

1951, 1956, 1959–60: Computed differences between total and domestic trade.

All other years: The figures derived as residuals for 1951 and 1956 are close to the reported Gosbank figures for the same dates (the Table I–2 figures for 1959 and 1960 are not reported but are assumed the same as the TsSU figures). For all years other than the four derived as residuals, we assume the TsSU values for foreign trade are the same as the Gosbank values.

Contract Construction

Figures for all years shown are from *Vestnik statistiki*, 1960:2, p. 86, and TsSU–61, p. 849.

Other Sectors

1941, 1947, 1951–60: Vestnik statistiki, 1960:2, p. 86, and TsSU–61, p. 849.

1946, 1948–50, 1961–62: Interpolated or extrapolated from 1947, 1947 to 1951, and 1960, respectively, on the Gosbank series.

Total Loans

Figures for all years shown are from *Vestnik statistiki*, 1960:2, p. 86, and TsSU–61, p. 849. For other years, totals are not computed for lack of estimates of contract construction. However, the sums of the estimates for sectors other than contract construction are reasonably close to the Gosbank totals (Table I–2), allowance being made for the effect upon estimates for other years of the discrepancy, previously commented upon, between the TsSU and Gosbank figures for 1951.

Data released at a late date indicate considerable error in our Table I–3 figures for 1961. In TsSU–62a, p. 765, loans are given as 147.2 billion to industry, 56.1 to sales-supply, 3.2 to transportation and communications, 62.6 to agriculture and procurement, 140.0 to trade, 15.7 to contract construction, and 2.6 to other sectors.

Distribution of Short-Term

Bank Loans by Purpose

We have occasion in the current-price inventory estimates to make use of data on the distribution of bank loans classified according to the purposes for which the loans are granted. Complete distributions of this sort are not required but only a few selected categories, and it is the latter for which data are assembled here, in Table J–1 (p. 546).

The category shown in the table as "loans on goods shipped," which is for Gosbank loans only, includes both loans described in Soviet sources as on "settlement documents, accreditives, and special accounts" and those described as "payments credits" (*raschetnye kredity*). Loans on settlement documents are essentially loans against bills for goods shipped which are to be paid under the so-called "acceptance method"; these account for the bulk of the category in which they are included. Accreditives and special accounts are forms of letters of credit. "Payments credits" include a variety of loans made to permit or insure the rendering of certain payments but, in the years in which they have been quantitatively significant, they appear to have consisted principally of loans to enterprises rendering payments to one another through clearing arrangements (in Atlas–58, p. 319, the whole of payments credits are identified as "serving clearing systems"). For years up to 1941, no separate category is shown in Soviet sources for payments credits and we assume they were included with loans on settlement documents, etc. By 1941, payments credits accounted for only 5 percent of the combined total (see Popov–57, p. 245); their share became significant in the postwar years with the expansion of clearings.

Our main use for the series on loans on goods shipped is as an extrapolator for goods shipped. That there should be a functional relation between goods shipped and loans on settlement documents, etc., is obvious. The same is less obvious for payments credits, but it is our understanding that the latter serve in substantial part as substitutes for the former. For this reason, we include payments credits in the Table J–1 series.

Goods shipped (as reported and without adjustments) and loans on them can be compared for a few years in which reported data are available for both (figures are for January 1):

Year	Goods Shipped (Billion Rubles)		Total Loans on Goods Shipped as Percent of Goods Shipped	
	In "Basic Branches"	In "Basic Branches" and Other Sectors	In "Basic Branches"	In "Basic Branches" and Other Sectors
1934 .... 3.0		—	79.3	—
1935 .... 3.2		—	95.0	—
1936 .... 5.8		—	76.9	—
1937 ....11.1		—	84.1	—
1938 ....12.0		—	82.8	—
1951 ....43.6		46.2	102.1	96.3
1956 ....52.0		54.6	97.9	93.2
1959 .... —		72.4	—	92.4
1960 .... —		79.9	—	89.7

The figures for goods shipped in basic branches cover state industry, including sales-supply, state agriculture, procurement, and domestic trade. Those for basic branches and other sectors include, in addition, industrial co-operatives and sundry "other" sectors but exclude nonstate agriculture, for which we do not have data, and contract construction and transportation and communications, for which goods shipped are assumed to be negligible. Figures for 1934–38 are derived from Usoskin–39 (see Table G–5 and, for 1934, the discussion of Konovalov–34 in the notes to Table G–4); figures for 1951–60 are from Table G–6. For both calculations, bank loans are the whole of those shown in Table J–1.

Loans on goods shipped are evidently not a highly accurate basis for estimating goods shipped. Our procedures are such, however, that the estimates are not affected by the difference in the general levels of the calculated ratios between prewar and postwar years.

The second category shown in Table J–1, loans for the introduction of new techniques and mechanization and loans for increased production of consumer goods, are of interest here chiefly because balance sheets appearing in postwar publications exclude them from sources of finance for short-terms assets (see Appendix G, for 1951 and related years). The apparent reasoning behind this exclusion is that the loans relate essentially to fixed capital assets. Because the total of these loans is small, we make little effort to adjust our sector distributions of bank loans for them. We do adjust our total loan data for them. The series shown refers to Gosbank loans only.

Loans shown in Table J–1 to heavy industry on nonseasonal inventories are those identified in Soviet sources as loans "on the turnover of material values." The lending arrangement to which they refer dates from 1939 but was of no quantitative significance until 1957. From 1957 to 1960 their volume expanded rapidly, and they accounted for more than half of the increase of loans to producer goods industries over that interval. In Soviet financial practice, such loans are regarded as replacing owned working capital, and a change in their relative size alters the relation between owned capital and bank loans. In order to be able to take account of this change in deriving our inventory estimates, the necessary loan data are recorded here. Loans of this sort are issued by Gosbank only.

The data shown in the table for loans to contract construction are given in their source as loans "by the Construction Bank," but the totals are virtually identical with those in Table I–3 for loans to contract construc-

TABLE J-1

DISTRIBUTION OF SHORT-TERM BANK LOANS BY PURPOSE, SELECTED CATEGORIES, 1932-61
(January 1--Billion Rubles)

	1932	1933	1934	1935	1936	1937	1938	1939	1940	1941	1946	1947
Loans:												
On Goods Shipped	1.04	1.84	2.38	3.04	4.46	9.33	9.94	10.79	13.39	18.88	20.2	--
For the Introduction of New Techniques and Mechanization and for Increased Production of Consumer Goods	--	--	--	--	--	--	--	--	--	0.11	0.1	--
To Heavy Industry on Non-seasonal Inventories	--	--	--	--	--	--	--	--	--	--	--	--
To Contract Construction, Total	--	--	--	--	--	--	--	--	--	0.52	--	2.95
On Stocks of Equipment	--	--	--	--	--	--	--	--	--	0.10	--	2.15
For Procurement of Materials	--	--	--	--	--	--	--	--	--	0.39	--	0.53
Other	--	--	--	--	--	--	--	--	--	0.03	--	0.28

	1951	1952	1953	1954	1955	1956	1957	1958	1959	1960	1961
Loans:											
On Goods Shipped	44.5	--	--	--	--	50.9	58.2	58.0	66.9	71.7	--
For the Introduction of New Techniques and Mechanization and for Increased Production of Consumer Goods	0.2	--	--	0.2	0.5	1.7	3.1	4.3	5.0	--	--
To Heavy Industry on Non-seasonal Inventories	--	--	--	--	--	--	1.0	4.6	11.9	13.8	14.6
To Contract Construction, Total	5.79	8.24	10.34	11.10	11.21	10.81	10.51	12.24	10.41	12.39	--
On Stocks of Equipment	1.54	2.39	2.87	3.61	5.66	6.52	5.29	5.83	5.27	4.39	--
For Procurement of Materials	1.14	1.58	1.74	2.18	2.19	2.35	2.68	3.08	3.24	3.11	--
Other	3.11	4.28	5.72	5.31	3.35	1.93	2.54	3.33	1.90	4.88	--

tion. We employ the series for loans for procurement of materials as an estimator in some years of inventories in contract construction. That this is not a highly accurate procedure may be judged from the relation of such loans to inventories in years in which both are known. Inventory data are from Table G–1. Figures are for January 1.

	Loans for Procurement of Materials (Billion Rubles)	Inventories (Billion Rubles)	Loans as Percent of Inventories
1951	1.14	10.6	10.8
1956	2.35	17.6	13.4
1959	3.24	22.1	14.7
1960	3.11	25.7	12.1

Loans for materials, however, appear a better guide to the behavior of inventories than do total loans to contract construction or any other component loan series.

Sources of the Table J–1 data are these.

Loans on Goods Shipped

1932–34: Efimov–34, p. 17.

1935: Computed from the 1934 total and an increase during 1934 of 656 million rubles given in Shvarts–35, p. 5.

1936–37: Computed from percentage shares in total loans of 16.8 percent in 1936 and 26.8 percent in 1937 given in Gorfinkel'–37, pp. 4–5, and total loans shown in Table I–1.

1938–39: Usoskin–46, p. 142.

1940: Computed from the 1939 total and an increase during 1939 of 2.594 billion given in Gerashchenko–39, p. 12.

1941–57: Popov–57, p. 245.

1958: Atlas–58, p. 319.

1959–60: Computed from percentage shares of 20.9 percent in 1959 and 18.7 percent in 1960 given in Barkovskii–60, p. 23, and total loans shown in Table I–2.

Loans for Introduction of New Techniques and Mechanization and Loans for Increased Production of Consumer Goods

1941–57: Popov–57, pp. 85, 86, and 245.

1958: Atlas–58, p. 319.

1959: Korovushkin–59, p. 9.

Loans to Heavy Industry on Nonseasonal Inventories

1957: Den'gi i kredit, 1958:9, p. 2.

1958–59: Figures for these years are rough interpolations between 1957 and 1960, made on the assumption that the total increase was distributed among the three years in proportion to the annual increases in total loans to the heavy and timber industries (Table I–3). However, the figure estimated for the beginning of 1959 of 11.9 billion appears reasonable in the light of a statement in Den'gi i kredit, 1959:8, p. 3, that such loans had reached 9 billion by mid-1958 and were planned to reach 11 billion by the end of the 3rd quarter of that year.

1960: Petrov–60, p. 35, gives a figure of 14.746 billion for loans on non-seasonal inventories to all industry but attributes .923 billion to light industry. We take the difference between the two figures as presumably more comparable with our data for other years.

1961: Kazantsev–61, p. 13.

Loans to Contract Construction

Data for all years are from *Vestnik statistiki,* 1960:2, p. 88. The other category in the table is the sum of loans "on settlements" and "for other purposes" in the source.

Appendix K

Inventories of Finished

Products in Domestic Trade

in Current Retail Prices

Beginning in 1956, TsSU released an extensive body of statistics on inventory holdings in retail and wholesale trade in current prices, which are reproduced in Table K–1. The figures, other than estimates, shown in the table for total and co-operative trade are taken from TsSU–61, pp. 698 and 701, and, for 1944–45, from TsSU–56, pp. 84 and 87. Figures for state trade are computed residuals. The estimated figures are explained below. These data underlie part of the estimates of trade inventories in current prices and much of the estimates in constant prices. Their meaning and coverage are considered in this appendix. The conclusions drawn here are consistent with and largely derived from those drawn in Campbell–58, pp. 561–62, and Bergson–61, pp. 396 ff.

What kinds of enterprises are covered by the data is quite clear for retail inventories, less clear for wholesale inventories. Data given in TsSU–56, pp. 108–10, indicate that retail inventories include (in 1956) those held by enterprises of the Ministry of Trade, the *glavursy*, specialized retail establishments of a few ministries, and—in co-operative trade—the consumers' co-operatives and a trivially small quantity held by industrial co-operatives. The wholesale trade inventories evidently include, in addition to those held in wholesale organs proper, some part of finished consumer goods held by producing enterprises or their sales organs: tables in TsSU–56, pp. 80 ff., are described as for commodities "in organs of wholesale trade and in industry"; Campbell–58, p. 562, fn., cites evidence of a general statistical practice of including some industrial inventories in trade.

Whether the coverage of the data is consistent over time and consistent with that of other inventory data is impossible to establish firmly. It is noteworthy that the TsSU series for total trade inventories moves closely with the TsSU series for bank loans to trade (see Table I–3) from 1953 to 1954 and therefore appears, like the latter, to be unaffected by the reorganization of sales-supply organs in the course of 1953 (see the intro-

TABLE K-1

INVENTORIES OF FINISHED PRODUCTS IN DOMESTIC TRADE, IN CURRENT RETAIL PRICES, 1933-61
(January 1--Billion Rubles)

	1933	1936	1937	1938	1939	1940	1941	1944	1945	1946	1947	1948
State Trade												
Retail	--	7.4	9.4	10.7	9.4	9.7	12.7	7.9	11.0	15.5	22.9	31.9
Wholesale	--	4.8*	6.1*	7.0	6.8*	7.8*	10.6	3.7*	5.2*	7.4*	10.9*	15.1*
Total	--	12.2*	15.5*	17.7	16.2*	17.5*	23.3	11.6*	16.0*	22.9*	33.8*	47.0*
Co-operative Trade												
Retail	--	1.5	2.3	2.9	3.5	3.2	3.7	2.1	2.7	3.6	4.9	6.8
Wholesale	--	1.0	1.5	1.9	2.3	2.1	2.3	1.5	1.8	2.3	3.8	5.9
Total	--	2.4	3.8	4.8	5.8	5.3	6.0	3.6	4.5	5.9	8.7	12.7
Total Trade												
Retail	2.4	8.8	11.7	13.6	12.9	12.9	16.4	10.0	13.7	19.1	27.8	38.7
Wholesale	--	5.8*	7.6*	8.9	9.1*	9.9*	12.9	5.2*	7.0*	9.7*	14.7*	21.0*
Total	--	14.6*	19.3*	22.5	22.0*	22.8*	29.3	15.2*	20.7*	28.8*	42.5*	59.7*

	1949	1950	1951	1952	1953	1954	1955	1956	1957	1958	1959	1960	1961
State Trade													
Retail	46.5	54.4	47.4	56.8	69.0	68.5	63.8	70.7	84.5	84.6	101.8	118.3	124.0
Wholesale	22.1*	25.8*	22.5	23.4	20.5	15.6	7.7	11.0	11.0	16.7	30.0	32.1	31.2
Total	68.6*	80.2*	69.9	80.2	89.5	84.1	71.5	81.7	95.4	101.3	131.8	150.4	155.1
Co-operative Trade													
Retail	13.1	18.0	16.7	20.0	24.2	25.8	26.2	28.2	34.9	38.6	46.2	56.0	57.8
Wholesale	10.1	11.5	9.7	11.4	15.1	14.0	13.2	14.7	16.7	16.5	19.8	23.1	26.3
Total	23.1	29.4	26.4	31.5	39.3	39.8	39.4	42.9	51.6	55.1	66.0	79.1	84.1
Total Trade													
Retail	59.5	72.3	64.1	76.9	93.2	94.3	90.0	98.9	119.4	123.2	148.0	174.3	181.8
Wholesale	32.2*	37.3*	32.2	34.8	35.6	29.6	20.9	25.7	27.7	33.2	49.8	55.2	57.5
Total	91.7*	109.6*	96.3	111.7	128.8	123.9	110.9	124.6	147.0	156.4	197.8	229.5	239.2

*Estimated.

ductory discussion in Appendix I). Some kinship between these two series and also with other postwar inventory data released by TsSU (see notes to Table G–1 for 1951 and related years), appears likely. From context, it is reasonably clear that the inventory data cover domestic trade only.

It is clear from their sources that the data include inventories only of finished products and not of packaging materials, fuels, small tools, etc. It appears unlikely that they include goods in transit as recorded in the books of sellers, but they may include those recorded in the books of buyers.

The TsSU sources are explicit that inventories are valued in current prices, and they contain evidence that prices are those of the particular date to which the data refer (cf. TsSU–56, p. 85, fn.) rather than average annual prices. Both Campbell and Bergson have inferred (see citations above) that the prices are not acquisition costs but current retail prices for both wholesale and retail inventories. This inference is supported by the inclusion in the sources of series for the number of days of trade turnover which are covered by stocks on hand (according to TsSU–61, p. 894, these are calculated from the ratio of January 1 stocks to sales of the preceding quarter). Data for wholesale inventories valued in retail prices have also appeared elsewhere (see *Vestnik statistiki*, 1962:4, p. 91).

Assuming that the TsSU data are for finished products at retail prices, they can be compared for a few dates with reported figures (or figures derived principally from reported data) for inventories valued at acquisition cost (billion rubles):

	1936	1937	1938	1951	1956	1959	1960
Finished products at retail prices	14.6	19.3	22.5	96.3	124.6	197.8	229.5
Finished products at acquisition cost	11.1	—	—	58.3	95.7	149.7	175.7
Total inventories at acquisition cost	14.6	18.5	21.2	74.2	115.2	173.3	200.6

The figure for finished products at acquisition cost in 1936 is from Sobol'–37, p. 144. Those for other years are computed from absolute totals for normed assets and percentage shares of finished products given in TsSU–61, pp. 92 and 101 (see notes to Table G–1 for the same years). Total inventories at acquisition cost are from Table G–1; both inventories on hand and goods shipped are included. The total figures for the prewar years involve considerable amounts of estimation, as do the TsSU figures for 1936 and 1937.

The TsSU figures exceed the acquisition cost figures for finished products by approximately one third in all years except 1951 but in 1951 by almost two thirds. Variations in this margin presumably reflect, in addition to changes in the ratio of retail prices to acquisition costs in each sector, changes in the shares of wholesale and retail trade in total inventories and, possibly, differences in coverage. Changes in the ratio of the TsSU data to total inventories at acquisition cost reflect in addition changes in the share of finished products in total inventories. As is evident, the ratio between the TsSU series and total inventories is by no means stable, though 1951 is again the markedly exceptional year. The interpolations and extrapolations of total inventories which we make on the TsSU series are therefore subject to substantial error.

The question remains of what retail prices were used for the TsSU data in rationing periods, when more than one retail price level existed. Comparison of the inventory figures for 1944–47 with available data on retail sales and bank loans to trade suggests, although not strongly, that in these years the inventory figures are in actual retail prices rather than in ration prices alone. The single figure from the earlier rationing period, for retail inventories in 1933, looks implausibly small in comparison with total inventories at cost for the same date (see Table G–1). Conceivably, the 1933 figure is valued at ration prices, but its small size may be otherwise accounted for, and we make no effort to employ it in our estimates.

As can be seen from Table K–1, the TsSU series lack figures for inventories in state wholesale trade for a number of years in which data are given for other component sectors. As is also evident from the table, state wholesale inventories behave exceedingly erratically. We have, nevertheless, attempted to estimate these inventories for a number of years.

The prewar estimates are made on the assumption that the ratio of wholesale to retail inventories in state trade was the same in 1936–37 as in 1938 and from 1938 to 1941 changed linearly.

For the years 1944 through 1950, two alternative estimates are considered. In one, inventories in state wholesale trade are again extrapolated on those in retail trade, on the assumption that the 1951 ratio between the two was maintained throughout. In the second, total trade inventories are extrapolated on bank loans to domestic trade (Table I–3), from the 1951 ratio of TsSU inventories to loans, and the known amounts of inventories other than in state wholesale are deducted from the totals. The two procedures yield these results (January 1—billion rubles):

	Estimated Inventories in State Wholesale Trade	
	On Bank Loans	On Inventories in State Retail Trade
1944	—	3.7
1945	—	5.2
1946	7.7	7.4
1947	9.4	10.9
1948	13.0	15.1
1949	36.1	22.1
1950	38.2	25.8

The two estimates show some similarity in 1946–48, but none at all in 1949–50. There is reported evidence (see Atlas–58, pp. 240 ff.), however, that in the late 1940's there was a large build-up of trade inventories in anticipation of annual retail price cuts and that Gosbank financed a disproportionately large share of this increase. From this, we judge that the extrapolation on retail inventories is the more reliable for 1949–50 and we employ it for all the postwar estimates.

It should be added that in Bergson–61, pp. 396 ff., these same data are used to estimate inventories in state wholesale trade, but on the assumption that the ratio of total wholesale to retail inventories was in 1948 at approximately the 1941 level and thereafter fell to the 1951 level. This assumption is not demonstrably inferior to the one made here, although the ratio of wholesale to retail inventories was substantially higher in 1941 than in any other year for which data are reported.

Appendix L

Inventories in 1937

Prevailing Prices

We present here explanations of the estimates of inventories in prevailing prices (i.e., prices unadjusted for turnover taxes and subsidies) of 1937, which are shown in Table L–1. The estimates are discussed by sectors in the notes following. Preliminary comment may be made on two common elements in their derivation.

For the most part, the estimates are derived by deflating current-price values by price indexes. In principle, it would be desirable to obtain separate deflators for inventories on hand and goods shipped. However, the imprecision both of the deflators available and of the current-price estimates makes separate treatment of the two components unjustified and they are, in effect, deflated together. Since goods shipped are necessarily finished products, we regard them as such in determining weights for categories of inventories in the sector deflators.

Secondly, all sector deflators are intended to be weighted, as is appropriate, with given-year quantity weights. This intention is not realized in all cases, either for the components of the sector deflators or in the combining of the component indexes. The weights actually used are described in the notes for each sector.

PRODUCER GOODS INDUSTRIES

The series for this sector are derived entirely by deflation of the Table G–1 data in current prices. As with other sectors, the deflators used rest basically on indexes of selling prices—of commodities either produced by or purchased by enterprises within the sector. In the case of producer goods industries, however, this procedure cannot be relied upon entirely because of wide variations over time in the ratio of prices to money costs. Divergences of prices from costs are thought to have become particularly large between 1928 and the general price reform of 1936 and in the postwar years preceding the price reforms of 1949–50, i.e., in the periods in which producer goods industries were heavily subsidized. In order to correct for this deficiency of the product price indexes, we undertake to compose an index of wage costs per unit of output. This is used principally to adjust

TABLE L-1

INVENTORIES IN 1937 PREVAILING PRICES, BY SECTORS, 1928-62

(January 1--Billion Rubles)

	1928	1929	1930	1931	1932	1933	1934	1935	1936	1937	1938
Producer Goods Industries											
Inventories on Hand	4.2	4.9	5.9	7.2	10.0	12.5	14.5	17.8	22.3	22.3	24.5
Goods Shipped	0.7	0.8	1.0	1.2	1.7	2.1	2.5	2.9	4.0	4.1	4.4
Consumer Goods Industries											
Inventories on Hand	15.6	15.0	12.7	14.8	17.3	15.8	15.9	15.0	18.8	19.6	21.0
Goods Shipped	3.5	3.3	2.8	3.3	3.9	3.5	4.0	3.1	4.8	5.0	5.2
Transportation and Communications											
Inventories on Hand	1.4	1.5	1.6	2.6	3.6	3.6	3.3	3.6	4.6	3.1	3.0
Procurement											
Inventories on Hand	1.0	1.4	1.7	2.2	2.7	2.7	2.8	3.3	3.8	2.5	2.9
Goods Shipped	0.1	0.1	0.1	0.2	0.2	0.2	0.5	0.5	0.7	0.5	0.6
Domestic Trade											
Inventories on Hand	20.4	21.0	20.6	18.5	16.4	11.3	11.2	12.8	13.1	16.4	19.8
Goods Shipped	2.1	2.2	2.1	1.8	1.5	1.1	1.1	1.1	1.3	1.7	1.9
Contract Construction											
Inventories on Hand	0.1	0.1	0.2	0.8	1.1	1.0	0.6	0.7	1.0	1.7	2.1
Other Nonagricultural Sectors											
Inventories on Hand	0.9	1.0	1.0	2.4	3.9	2.8	2.8	2.5	2.2	2.1	2.2
Goods Shipped	0.0	0.0	0.1	0.2	0.3	0.2	0.3	0.3	0.2	0.2	0.2
Uninstalled Equipment, n.e.c.											
Inventories on Hand	0.1	0.2	0.3	0.5	0.6	0.6	0.6	0.6	0.6	0.6	0.6
Total Nonagricultural Sectors											
Inventories on Hand	43.7	45.1	44.0	49.0	55.6	50.3	51.7	56.3	66.4	68.3	76.1
Goods Shipped	6.4	6.4	6.1	6.7	7.6	7.1	8.4	7.9	11.0	11.5	12.3
Total	50.1	51.5	50.1	55.7	63.2	57.4	60.1	64.2	77.4	79.8	88.4
Agriculture											
Inventories on Hand	13.5	13.8	12.9	12.2	11.1	10.0	10.9	11.6	13.7	12.3	15.0
Total											
Inventories on Hand	57.2	58.9	56.9	61.2	66.7	60.3	62.6	67.9	80.1	80.6	91.1
Goods Shipped	6.4	6.4	6.1	6.7	7.6	7.1	8.4	7.9	11.0	11.5	12.3
Total	63.6	65.3	63.0	67.9	74.3	67.4	71.0	75.8	91.1	92.1	103.4

TABLE L-1 (continued)

INVENTORIES IN 1937 PREVAILING PRICES, BY SECTORS, 1928-62
(January 1--Billion Rubles)

	1939	1940	1941	1944	1945	1946	1947	1948	1949	1950	1951
Producer Goods Industries											
Inventories on Hand	26.9	28.3	31.1	--	--	32.7	34.9	39.6	36.1	39.6	43.8
Goods Shipped	4.5	5.3	7.6	--	--	7.0	7.0	7.8	7.0	7.4	8.1
Consumer Goods Industries											
Inventories on Hand	24.8	29.1	22.3	--	--	12.5	11.3	11.8	16.9	24.4	27.2
Goods Shipped	5.9	7.7	7.9	--	--	3.8	3.4	3.4	4.7	6.6	7.1
Transportation and Communications											
Inventories on Hand	2.7	3.6	3.1	--	--	3.2	3.7	4.1	2.5	2.5	2.8
Procurement											
Inventories on Hand	3.5	2.8	3.2	--	--	4.3	4.0	5.4	5.2	4.8	4.4
Goods Shipped	0.7	0.6	0.9	--	--	1.0	0.9	1.2	1.1	1.0	0.9
Domestic Trade											
Inventories on Hand	19.1	20.2	20.3	9.4	11.6	14.5	11.8	17.1	26.9	36.1	38.6
Goods Shipped	1.8	2.1	2.8	1.3	1.6	1.9	1.5	2.2	3.2	4.0	3.9
Contract Construction											
Inventories on Hand	2.2	2.8	2.9	1.2	1.7	1.9	3.3	3.4	3.9	4.3	3.8
Other Nonagricultural Sectors											
Inventories on Hand	2.1	2.6	2.7	--	--	2.0	3.3	3.7	2.5	3.2	4.4
Goods Shipped	0.2	0.3	0.3	--	--	0.2	0.3	0.4	0.3	0.3	0.5
Uninstalled Equipment, n.e.c.											
Inventories on Hand	0.6	0.6	0.6	--	0.3	0.5	0.6	0.8	0.9	1.2	1.5
Total Nonagricultural Sectors											
Inventories on Hand	81.9	90.0	86.2	65.6	68.3	71.6	72.9	85.9	94.9	116.1	126.5
Goods Shipped	13.1	16.0	19.5	13.3	13.6	13.9	13.1	15.0	16.3	19.3	20.5
Total	95.0	106.0	105.7	78.9	81.9	85.5	86.0	100.9	111.2	135.4	147.0
Agriculture											
Inventories on Hand	13.8	14.6	16.6	--	9.8	11.2	12.3	15.7	17.3	17.7	17.5
Total											
Inventories on Hand	95.7	104.6	102.8	75.4	78.1	82.8	85.2	101.6	112.2	133.8	144.0
Goods Shipped	13.1	16.0	19.5	13.3	13.6	13.9	13.1	15.0	16.3	19.3	20.5
Total	108.8	120.6	122.3	88.7	91.7	96.7	98.3	116.6	128.5	153.1	164.5

TABLE L-1 (concluded)

INVENTORIES IN 1937 PREVAILING PRICES, BY SECTORS, 1928-62

(January 1--Billion Rubles)

	1952	1953	1954	1955	1956	1957	1958	1959	1960	1961	1962
Producer Goods Industries											
Inventories on Hand	49.0	56.1	61.5	61.7	57.5	59.2	64.4	72.2	78.1	87.0	99.1
Goods Shipped	8.8	9.9	10.7	10.7	10.2	10.9	10.9	11.9	13.3	14.4	16.1
Consumer Goods Industries											
Inventories on Hand	30.4	31.7	35.7	35.1	37.6	44.1	48.2	56.8	60.3	64.4	66.4
Goods Shipped	7.7	7.7	8.5	8.3	9.6	11.0	11.3	13.6	14.0	14.8	15.7
Transportation and Communications											
Inventories on Hand	3.2	3.0	3.7	3.1	3.8	3.5	3.9	4.4	4.9	5.0	6.0
Procurement											
Inventories on Hand	4.5	5.3	2.6	2.4	2.5	4.3	3.5	4.6	9.4	10.9	12.2
Goods Shipped	0.9	1.1	0.6	0.6	0.6	1.0	0.7	0.8	1.4	1.6	1.7
Domestic Trade											
Inventories on Hand	47.4	57.5	61.3	57.8	63.4	74.8	78.7	98.9	115.5	121.0	138.3
Goods Shipped	4.4	4.9	4.7	4.0	3.9	4.4	4.2	4.9	5.1	5.3	6.1
Contract Construction											
Inventories on Hand	5.3	5.9	7.1	6.8	7.8	8.6	9.6	9.7	11.3	12.3	13.2
Other Nonagricultural Sectors											
Inventories on Hand	5.6	4.6	2.9	3.8	4.3	6.5	8.3	9.4	13.1	13.8	15.5
Goods Shipped	0.6	0.5	0.3	0.4	0.5	0.7	0.9	1.0	1.4	1.5	1.5
Uninstalled Equipment, n.e.c.											
Inventories on Hand	1.9	2.2	2.5	2.8	3.2	3.6	4.0	3.9	4.2	4.6	4.9
Total Nonagricultural Sectors											
Inventories on Hand	147.3	166.3	177.3	173.5	180.1	204.6	220.6	259.9	296.8	319.0	355.6
Goods Shipped	22.4	24.1	24.8	24.0	24.8	28.0	28.0	32.2	35.2	37.6	41.1
Total	169.7	190.4	192.1	197.5	204.9	232.6	248.6	292.1	332.0	356.6	396.7
Agriculture											
Inventories on Hand	16.5	17.7	18.3	18.8	21.0	24.2	24.2	26.8	27.1	27.4	28.2
Total											
Inventories on Hand	163.8	184.0	195.6	192.3	201.1	228.8	244.8	286.7	323.9	346.4	383.8
Goods Shipped	22.4	24.1	24.8	24.0	24.8	28.0	28.0	32.2	35.2	37.6	41.1
Total	186.2	208.1	220.4	216.3	225.9	256.8	272.8	318.9	359.1	384.0	424.9

the price indexes within the intervals 1928–37 and 1937–50 and does not alter the long-term trend determined from the price indexes over those periods. From 1950, wage costs and prices change similarly.

Both inventories on hand and goods shipped are deflated, in years through 1958, by the inventory deflator shown in Table L–2. For 1939, 1940, and 1941, the deflator used is the average of the figures shown in the table for prices before and after changes effective on January 1. The differences are small in 1939 and 1941; in 1940, the difference is moderate and the dating of the price change is not certain (see notes on the index of basic industrial prices). In any case, no allowance has been made in the current-price estimates for these three years for the effects of price changes occurring on January 1. For 1949, 1950, and 1952, the current-price estimates are for valuations at prices made effective on January 1 (see Appendix G); the corresponding deflator is used. For 1959 through 1962, the deflator is assumed to have remained at the 1958 level. Although no general change in selling prices occurred in this period, particular changes were made (cf. Kaplan–63, p. 97, text and fn. 3), and wage costs may have departed somewhat from the 1958 level.

TABLE L-2

DERIVATION OF DEFLATOR, TO 1937 PRICES, OF INVENTORIES
IN PRODUCER GOODS INDUSTRIES, 1928-58*
(1937 Average = 100)

	Basic Industrial Prices, Excluding Petroleum (January 1)		Machinery Prices (January 1)		Wage Rates (Annual Average)	Wage Costs (January 1)	Inventory Deflator (January 1)	
1928	57.7		70		27.4	58.8	59.4	
1929	56.5		70		30.1	59.2	58.6	
1930	55.5		70		32.5	60.1	58.1	
1931	54.9		70		37.2	67.3	59.5	
1932	55.1		75		46.3	84.5	64.4	
1933	56.3		81		52.3	91.0	67.2	
1934	57.4		89		60.6	87.8	67.6	
1935	58.3		93		74.7	92.1	69.5	
1936	59.5		91		94.0	98.2	71.7	
1937	100		100		100	100	100	
1938	100		100		114	107	102	
1939	104	(103)	100		129	119	107	(106)
1940	126	(116)	103	(100)	140	128	122	(116)
1941	133	(133)	114	(110)	--	136	129	(128)
1944	142		110		199	--	--	
1945	142		115		199	225	151	
1946	142		123		206	251	157	
1947	142		127		237	275	162	
1948	142		129		245	277	161	
1949	382	(142)	273	(130)	259	262	310	(156)
1950	321	(382)	196	(273)	273	259	265	(306)
1951	315		186		287	257	259	
1952	299	(315)	165	(186)	300	257	249	(259)
1953	299		165		306	259	249	
1954	299		165		314	253	248	
1955	299		165		320	247	246	
1956	284		135		330	237	234	
1957	284		136		343	231	232	
1958	284		134		357	222	230	

*Figures in parentheses are for prices prior to changes effective on January 1.

The derivation of the deflator is explained in the notes following.

Basic Industrial Prices, excluding Petroleum

The series, through 1956, derives entirely from that of the same title composed by Abram Bergson and his associates. It differs from the Bergson series only in that January 1 values have here been estimated from annual averages. The bulk of the data employed are those shown in Bergson–56, p. 322 (1937 is here set equal to 100), and in Turgeon–57, p. 13. For the dating of price changes and for detailed component indexes, we have made reference to the various RAND memoranda cited in Bergson–55, pp. iii and iv.

The Bergson index employs constant, 1937, quantity weights. However, partial recomputation of the index (inclusive of petroleum products) with 1928 weights (Bergson–55, p. 69b) shows no difference in the indicated price change from 1928 to 1937. A similar recomputation with 1955 weights (Turgeon–57, p. 16) shows a considerable difference from the 1937-weighted index for the interval from 1948 to 1951 but no difference from 1951 to 1952 and 1956. On this evidence, which the compilers do not present as conclusive, we treat the 1937-weighted index as though it had given-year weights.

Our reason for using the Bergson index exclusive of petroleum products is that purchases of such products by other industries appear to be small (cf. Kaplan–52, p. 7, and TsSU–61, pp. 104 ff.).

1928: Extrapolated from the 1928 average and the figure for January 1, 1929.

1929–35: Because the change in annual average prices over these years is small, January 1 figures are computed simply as the average of those of contiguous years.

1936: Extrapolated from the 1935 average and the figure for January 1, 1935.

1937–38: The index is assumed equal to the 1937 average. No significant price changes occurred during 1937 or on January 1, 1938.

1939–41: All indexes are recomputed from detailed data given in Bergson and in the underlying memoranda. It should be noted that the difference in the two indexes for January 1, 1940, is due largely to changes in the prices of ferrous metals, which were decreed on December 9, 1939, and which are merely assumed to have become effective on January 1, 1940.

1944–48: January 1 values are assumed to equal annual averages, since the averages are unchanging.

1949: The price change in 1949 occurred on January 1. The index after the change is taken to equal the 1949 average, before the change to equal the 1948 average.

1950: Prices changed in this year on January 1 and July 1. The index for January 1, inclusive of the change of that date, is computed from the 1950 average and the index for January 1, 1951, on the assumption the latter has a 50 percent weight in the 1950 average. Prices before the January 1 change are taken to equal the 1949 average.

1951–56: All indexes are read directly from the annual averages and dates of changes given in the sources. Each price level was in effect through at least one calendar year.

1957–58: No general price change occurred after July, 1955, and prices are assumed to have remained at the level of January 1, 1956. Some changes in individual producer goods prices did occur after that date (cf. Kaplan–63, p. 97, and Nimitz–62, p. 10), but we are unable to take these into account.

Machinery Prices

The index is a somewhat freehand adaptation of the index of average annual prices compiled in Moorsteen–62, p. 72, and, for 1931–33, in Table A–9 of the present study. The Moorsteen index is consistently weighted with given-year weights on a base of 1937. Because the shifting of weights produces quite continuous variations in the index, January 1 values are in large part simply interpolated from contiguous annual averages.

1928–31: The Moorsteen index is virtually unchanged near a value of 70 from 1927/28 to 1931. We assume a value of 70 for January 1.

1932–35: Computed as averages of the annual averages of contiguous years.

1936: Assumed to equal the 1935 average: the 1936 average is dominated by price changes occurring within that year.

1937–39: Indexes for January 1 are assumed unchanging at 100, since annual averages, 1936 through 1939, are virtually unchanging.

1940–41: The Moorsteen annual averages are 100 for 1939, 106 for 1940, and 114 for 1941. The price changes producing these increases occurred partly on January 1, 1940, partly in the course of 1940, and partly on January 1, 1941 (see Moorsteen–54, p. 109). We assume the prechange level of January 1, 1940, was 100; the postchange level of the same date was the average of 100 and 106; the prechange level of January 1, 1941, was the average of 106 and 114; and the postchange level of that date was 114.

1944–48: Computed as averages of the annual averages of contiguous years. The 1943 average is assumed the same as that of 1944.

1949: The change in prices was effective January 1; the index for that date is equal to the annual average. Prices before the change are assumed equal to the 1948 average.

1950: Prices following the January 1 change are estimated from the 1950 average and from those in effect from July 1, 1950 (which are the same as the 1951 average). Prices prior to the January 1 change are the same as the 1949 average.

1951: Assumed equal to the annual average.

1952: Prices following the January 1 change are equal to the 1952 average; those preceding the change to the 1951 average.

1953–55: Average prices remained unchanged from 1952 through mid-1955.

1956: Assumed equal to the annual average.

1957: Interpolated between the 1956 and 1957 averages.

1958: The Moorsteen figure is for January 1.

Wage Rates

The wage series presented here is meant to approximate average annual wages and salaries in producer goods industries. It can do so only roughly.

1928–35: Annual relatives are derived from data for average annual wages and salaries in large-scale industry, TsUNKhU–36, pp. 512–13. No adjustment is made for the inclusion of large-scale producers of consumer goods or the omission of small-scale producers of producer goods. Data given in the same source for average *monthly* wage rates in individual (large-scale) industries suggests the series is reasonably reliable for our purposes.

1935–38: The foregoing series is extended from 1935 on the basis of figures for average annual wages and salaries in the economy as a whole. Data are from TsUNKhU–36, *loc. cit.*, for 1935; Bergson–47, p. 236, for 1936; Gosplan–39, p. 228, for 1937; and TsUNKhU–39, p. 20, for 1938.

1939: Interpolated on a straight percentage line between 1938 and 1940.

1940 and 1944: Bergson–61, p. 422. The series cited here and below from Bergson is for annual wages of all industrial workers.

1945: Assumed the same as 1944.

1946: Linked to 1947 by a percentage increase in wages in the economy as a whole estimated in Kaser–55, p. 40, fn. 57.

1947: Linked to 1948 by a percentage increase in the economy as a whole estimated in Yanowich–55, p. 218, fn.

1948–55: Bergson–61, *loc. cit.*

1956: Linked to 1955 by a percentage increase in the economy as a whole, *Pravda,* January 31, 1957.

1957–58: Linked to 1956 by percentage increases for the economy as a whole, which are cited from a Soviet source in Turgeon–59, p. 321.

Wage Costs

The index labeled, somewhat inaccurately, as for wage costs is meant to provide a basis for deflating value added to inventories within individual enterprises as against the value of externally purchased inventories. The need for such an index is explained above. Because the cost index we can contrive is highly unreliable, we restrict its long-run effects by fixing values for it in 1928, 1937, and 1950 on the basis of selling prices alone. The crudity of our procedures will be evident from the description which follows. The results of intermediate calculations are not shown.

(*i*) We compose weighted averages of the indexes of basic industrial prices and machinery prices of 59.0 in 1928, 100 in 1937, and 261 in 1950. The reference in each case is to average annual prices. The annual averages for the components are from the sources from which we derive January 1 values. The assumptions made here are that, in these three years, selling prices reflected production costs and, what is considerably more questionable, that the costs of inventories moved with the production costs of the sector in which the inventories were held.

Basic industrial prices and machinery prices are combined with given-year weights. According to Omel'chenko–39, p. 11, machine-building accounted for 4,844 million rubles or 40 percent of a total of 12,120 million of inventories on hand in the Commissariat for Heavy Industry on January 1, 1936 (see the discussion of this source in Appendix G, notes for 1933–39; the figures are for inventories as accounted at the time; similar ratios indicated for earlier years are 49 percent in 1933, 49 percent in 1934, and 40 percent in 1935). On January 1, 1936, the timber industry held an additional 2.2 billion rubles of inventories (see Table G–4), so the machine-building share in the whole of producer goods inventories was approximately 34 percent. In the course of 1936, basic industrial prices increased much more than machinery prices, but production costs in the two sectors doubtless showed no similar divergence, and we wish to give some weight to machinery prices in the deflation of inventories in defense industries. We therefore take the appropriate weight in 1937 for machinery prices to be one third, or approximately the same as at the beginning of 1936. From their 1937 shares and on the basis of production indexes for machinery, munitions, and other producer goods (the series are those underlying the industrial production estimates in Table P–1), we estimate 1928 quantity weights of 15 percent for machinery prices and 85 percent for basic industrial prices, and 1950 weights of 45 percent and 55 percent respectively.

(*ii*) We convert the index of wage rates, computed previously, to an unadjusted index of wage costs by dividing it by an index of labor productivity. Productivity in 1928, 1937, 1940, 1950, 1955, and 1956 is computed from an index of output in producer goods industries (series are those underlying the industrial production estimates of Table P–1); a 1937 weight for civilian producer goods is estimated from the 1950 weights and from quantity indexes given in Kaplan–60, Vol. II, p. 235, and average annual employment in the same industries (*ibid.*, p. 266). Productivity estimates for other years are interpolated or, for 1957–58, extrapolated, on an index composed from total industrial production (from the Table P–1 series; the civilian industry and munitions components are combined with 1937 weights) and total industrial employment (Powell–62; the series cited derives largely from estimates presented in Kaplan–60, Vol. II, p. 264, and Hodgman–54, p. 112).

The resulting index of average annual wage costs is set equal to the 1928, 1937, and 1950 values previously calculated. Values are then interpolated on the unadjusted index between the three benchmark years and extrapolated from 1950 to 1958. January 1 values are interpolated on the annual averages, except that January 1, 1928, 1941, and 1945, are extrapolated on the annual averages.

Inventory Deflator

We again take the appropriate values for 1928, 1937, and 1950 annual averages to be those computed above from the basic industrial and machinery price indexes, which are combined with what are essentially sector weights. Values of the inventory deflator for all other years are obtained from an index in which the weights are determined by the composition of inventories by kind.

We have in Table H–1 the distribution by kind of inventories on hand on January 1, 1937. To this we add goods shipped (Table G–1), which are treated as finished products. Raw materials are largely purchased assets, and it is unlikely that they include significant purchases of machinery. We therefore attribute the whole share of raw materials to the basic industrial price index. Small tools are also purchased; here and elsewhere we distribute their share equally between basic industrial and machinery prices. Both goods in process and finished products include the value of purchased materials but also value added within the production process. We make a rough division between these two components, as follows.

Granovskii–40, pp. 505–6, provides data on the percentage share of wage costs (including supplements) in the combined total of wage and materials costs in eight producer goods industries in 1937:

```
Coal ........................73.1
Petroleum  extraction .........69.9
Iron mining ..................64.9
Brick ......................61.7
Machine-building ............44.0
Basic chemicals ..............33.4
Sawmilling ..................30.5
Ferrous metallurgy ...........30.1
```

The approximate median of these figures is 50 percent, which we take as the appropriate figure for producer goods industries as a whole.

Assuming that the costs of inventories of finished products (including goods shipped) are distributed in about the same proportion as production costs, we allocate 50 percent of the weight of finished products to the wage cost index, 50 percent to the index of basic industrial prices. On the assumption that the progression from raw material to finished product is steady, the weight of goods in process is allocated 25 percent to wage costs and 75 percent to basic industrial prices.

The resulting weights for the whole of inventories on January 1, 1937, are 67.6 percent for basic industrial prices, 6.1 percent for machinery prices, and 26.3 percent for wage costs. The three component indexes are combined with these weights in all years. The resulting index is used to interpolate between the three benchmark years and to extrapolate from 1928 average to January 1, 1928, and from 1950 average to 1951–58.

No use is made here of the Table H–1 distribution of assets by kind for January 1, 1928 and 1951, since the 1928 and 1950 values of the index are determined from sector distributions.

CONSUMER GOODS INDUSTRIES

Inventories on hand and goods shipped are derived essentially by deflating the Table G–1 series in current prices by the Tables L–3 inventory deflator. For 1940, the deflator used is the average of the alternative figures shown (see the discussion of producer goods industries). For 1949, 1950, and 1952, the deflator is that for prices effective on January 1, since the current-price estimates are in these prices. The appropriate deflator for 1960–62 is assumed to have remained at the 1959 level.

The derivation of the inventory deflator is explained in the notes following.

Agricultural Procurement Prices, Adjusted for Subsidies

For 1928 to 1952, the index is identical with that shown in Table L–5. In the post-Stalin period, however, increases in procurement prices have been countered for a time after their occurrence by budget subsidies to procurement organizations, with the consequence that the increases have not been fully and immediately reflected in the prices paid for agricultural raw materials by processing industries (see Nimitz–62, pp. 91–92). The Table L–5 index is adjusted here for the effects of these subsidies.

Data on the value at current prices of state and decentralized procurements, which is the coverage of the Table L–5 index, for 1951–58, are given in Hoeffding–59, p. 57, and Nimitz–62, p. 148. Subsidies to procurement organizations in the same years are given in Hoeffding–59, pp. 143 and 213, and Nimitz–62, p. 90. From these, we compute the ratios of procurements net of subsidies to their gross values and apply those ratios to average annual prices gross of subsidies (Table L–5). January 1 values are interpolated from the annual averages by the same procedure as in Table L–5. The resulting series is linked at 1952 to the index unadjusted for subsidies. The figure for January 1, 1959, which cannot be interpolated, is estimated from the behavior of the averages.

The price index for 1959 adjusted for subsidies is 17 percent below its unadjusted counterpart. Since we make no allowance in our deflation of inventories for a further rise in the adjusted index beyond 1959, our calculations may, on this account, be inaccurate. Nimitz–62, p. 92, however, notes that subsidies occasioned by the 1958 price increases continued through 1959 and, at least in the case of meat, through 1960.

Agricultural Procurement Prices, excluding Grain (Annual Average)

The index is derived by procedures identical with those by which the Table L–5 index of all procurement prices, for the dates shown, is obtained. The original sources are Karcz–57a and Hoeffding–59. The series is unadjusted for subsidies.

Agricultural Procurement Prices, excluding Grain, Adjusted for Subsidies (January 1)

The adjustment for subsidies refers to the years 1953–56 only.

1928–29: Prices other than for grain are assumed to have increased during 1928 by 15 percent, or the same amount as for all agricultural products (see notes for Table L–5). The annual average is assumed to have equaled the average of the year-end values.

1937–52: January 1 values are derived from annual averages as in the estimates for the same years for all agricultural products (see notes for Table L–5).

1953–56: To adjust for subsidies in these years, we make the crude assumption that 85 percent of subsidies from 1951 to 1954 and 50 percent of the (small) subsidies in 1955 were for products other than grain (cf. Nimitz–62, p. 91). We relate these to the procurement total for all products (see above) minus grain procurements (Hoeffding–59, p. 186). Our procedures thereafter are the same as for all agricultural prices. For January 1, 1956, we assume a figure equal to the unsubsidized 1955 average.

Retail Prices of Grain Products

The index is essentially one presented in Chapman–59, with some extensions made here.

1928–29: The Chapman index, with given-year weights and on a 1937 base, is 8.5 for the 1928 annual average. According to *Statisticheskoe oboz-*

TABLE L-3

DERIVATION OF DEFLATOR, TO 1937 PRICES, OF INVENTORIES IN CONSUMER GOODS INDUSTRIES, 1928-59*

(1937 Average = 100)

	Agricultural Procurement Prices, Adjusted for Subsidies (January 1)	Agricultural Procurement Prices, Excluding Grain (Annual Average)	Agricultural Procurement Prices, Excluding Grain, Adjusted for Subsidies (January 1)	Retail Prices of Grain Products (January 1)	Average of Retail Prices Adjusted and Unadjusted for Turnover Tax (January 1)	Inventory Deflator (January 1)
1928	29.5	20.6	19.2	8.1	13.5	20.5
1929	33.7	--	22.0	8.9	14.5	21.7
1930	37.3	--	--	--	--	23.9
1931	41.4	--	--	--	--	28.6
1932	45.8	--	--	--	--	35.3
1933	50.7	--	--	--	--	45.5
1934	56.2	--	--	--	--	51.3
1935	62.2	--	--	--	--	62.2
1936	90.3	--	--	--	--	83.6
1937	100	100	100	100	102	100
1938	100	--	100	100	99	99.5
1939	100	--	--	--	--	101
1940	101	101	101	100	103	107 (105)
1941	101	--	101	108	125	120
1944	--	104	--	--	--	--
1945	100	--	104	108	150	134
1946	101	--	--	--	--	153
1947	102	--	--	--	--	176
1948	103	105	105	270	270	205
1949	104	--	105	270	266	257 (204)
1950	161	171	171	242	244	242 (257)
1951	161	171	171	174	205	217
1952	161	182	171	148	194	206 (210)
1953	172	225	182	127	190	205
1954	189	274	188	115	178	199
1955	236	302	221	109	173	204
1956	307	--	302	109	173	217
1957	341	--	--	--	--	226
1958	346	--	--	--	--	228
1959	350	--	--	--	--	229

*Figures in parentheses are for prices prior to changes effective on January 1. For basic industrial prices (excluding petroleum), machinery prices, and (unadjusted) retail prices, which are also incorporated in the deflator, see Tables L-2 and L-6.

renie, 1929:1, p. 157, prices of grain products in socialized trade increased by 9.2 percent during 1928. We assume the annual average equaled the average of the year-end values.

1937–38: Both are assumed equal to the 1937 average. According to Chapman–59, prices did not change during 1937.

1940–41: According to Chapman–59, prices were still at the 1937 level at the beginning of 1940. Prices of some products rose about 15 percent during 1940 but those of others remained constant. We take 8 percent as the average increase.

1945: Assumed equal to the 1941 level. Mrs. Chapman indicates in private correspondence that ration prices of food products remained constant until September 16, 1946.

1948–49: Both are assumed equal to the Chapman index for the 1948 average.

1950–55: Chapman estimates indexes of 127 for prices effective from April 1, 1952, to March 31, 1953, and 109 for prices made effective on April 1, 1954. We take these as the appropriate indexes for January 1, 1953 and 1955, respectively. Values for 1950, 1951, 1952, and 1954 are interpolated on an official index for retail prices of bread and grain products (TsSU–56, p. 132). The latter shows prices in effect for the period after each major price change.

1956: Assumed the same as 1955, since the official index for average annual prices is unchanged from 1955 to 1956.

Average of Retail Prices Adjusted and Unadjusted for Turnover Tax

The index derives from an index of "prices of industrial inventories of finished consumers' goods" shown in Bergson–61, p. 416, which is computed by Bergson as the arithmetic average of indexes of retail prices adjusted and unadjusted for turnover tax. We use the ratio of Bergson's finished consumer goods index to his unadjusted retail price index to adjust our Table L–6 index of retail prices as of January 1.

1928–29, 1937–38: We assume the ratio between the Bergson indexes holds for the termini of both 1928 and 1937.

1940: Since retail prices were changed little from 1937 to the beginning of 1940, we assume the Bergson ratio for 1937 holds for January 1, 1940.

1941: The Bergson ratio for 1940 applied to the January 1, 1941, retail price index (Table L–6) implies an index of 127. To allow for a greater impact of turnover taxes by the year's end than on the average for 1940, we reduce the index to 125.

1945: Bergson does not provide an estimate for the immediate postwar years. According to Voznesenskii–47, p. 127, state wholesale prices for the output of the light and food industries in 1942 were 20 percent over the prewar level. The behavior of such prices is what the index computed here is meant to approximate (see the discussion below of the inventory deflator). Having in mind the near stability through the war of both retail prices and prices of materials purchased by consumer goods industries, we assume that the 20 percent increase was the whole of that occurring through 1944. We take January 1, 1945, to be 120 percent of the January 1, 1941, figure.

1948: The Bergson ratio for the 1948 average is applied to the retail price index for the beginning of the year.

1949–55: January 1 values for the Bergson ratio are interpolated between annual averages and applied to the corresponding retail price indexes.

1956: Assumed the same as 1955. Bergson's average annual index for finished consumer goods is unchanged.

Inventory Deflator

On the rationale of this deflator in particular, reference should be made to Bergson's discussion (Bergson–61, pp. 417–19).

(*i*) We first combine five indexes, which are or approximate given-year weighted indexes, with 1937 weights to obtain an index for the years 1928–29, 1937–38, 1940–41, 1945, and 1948–56. The component indexes and their 1937 weights are these (percent):

Basic industrial prices (excluding petroleum) 20.0
Machinery prices 3.5
Agricultural procurement prices, excluding
   grain and adjusted for subsidies 21.3
Retail prices of grain products 7.1
Average of retail prices adjusted and
   unadjusted for turnover tax 48.1
      Total 100.0

The first two indexes are shown in Table L–2, the remainder in Table L–3.

The weights are based on the Table H–1 distribution of inventories on hand by kind and the Table G–1 figure for goods shipped as of January 1, 1937.

Of the total share of raw materials, 30 percent is attributed to the basic industrial price index as representing "supplementary materials" and fuel. In Khromov–37, p. 72, this ratio is indicated to have been 25.9 percent in the food industry and 42.2 percent in light industry on October 1, 1935 (see the discussion of this source in Appendix G, notes for 1933–39). In Birman–56, p. 41, the ratio is indicated to have been 28.5 percent in "Group B" industry on January 1, 1940.

Of the remaining raw materials, we assume the bulk, 90 percent, represented materials of agricultural origin and attribute 10 percent to basic industrial prices. Following Bergson, we attribute 75 percent of total agricultural raw materials to products other than grain and 25 percent to grain. For the former, we use the procurement price index exclusive of grain (adjusted for subsidies); for the latter, we use the index of the retail price of grain products. The index for prices other than grain products makes no allowance for turnover taxes incorporated in the costs of processing industries. The grain price index reflects the whole of the turnover tax on grain, a large part of which is incorporated in processors' costs (see Bergson–61, p. 418). The errors in these two indexes are presumably offsetting to some degree.

Small tools, as elsewhere, are divided equally between basic industrial prices and machinery prices.

The entire weight of finished products, including goods shipped, is attributed to the index which is the average of retail prices inclusive and exclusive of turnover taxes. This index is intended to provide a further allowance for the effects of turnover taxes upon industrial costs.

The value of goods in process is distributed equally between the deflator for finished products and the deflator for raw materials. The components of the latter are given shares equal to their shares in the raw materials total.

No attempt is made here, as is for producer goods industries, to include a wage cost index in the composite deflator. The share of wages in the total of wage and materials costs in consumer goods industries is relatively small (the range is from 10 to 19 percent for five component industries in 1937 in data given in Granovskii–40, pp. 505–6). Subsidization of these industries is thought to have been slight.

(*ii*) To fill in the missing years in the foregoing index (i.e., 1930–36, 1939, 1946–47, and 1957–59), we compose a similar but cruder index by combining the indexes of basic industrial prices, machinery prices, agricultural procurement prices for all products (Table L–3), and retail prices unadjusted for turnover tax (Table L–6). The first two are given the same 1937 weights as previously. Procurement prices are given the combined weight of grain and other agricultural materials. Unadjusted retail prices are given the weight of finished products and goods shipped. Again, the exclusion of all turnover taxes from the procurement price index is offset in some degree by the inclusion of all turnover taxes in the retail price index. Though the procedure is crude in this respect, larger errors are likely to result from inaccuracies in the component indexes for procurement and retail prices (see discussions of both).

We make an exception to the general procedure for 1946 and 1947. We are hesitant to assume that in these years retail prices, for which our estimates are questionable in any case, provide an acceptable measure of the behavior of the cost of inventories of finished products in consumer goods industries. We assume, instead, that costs rose at a constant (percentage) rate from 1945 to 1948. The assumption is obviously arbitrary, and the resulting deflator is particularly unreliable.

The index described here is used to interpolate values for the index described in Paragraph (*i*) between 1929 and 1937, 1938 and 1940, and 1945 and 1948, and to extrapolate values from 1956 to 1959. Basic industrial and machinery prices are assumed to have remained unchanged from 1958 to 1959.

(*iii*) We adjust the index in which the components are aggregated with 1937 weights to one which approximates a given-year weighted index. Weights are computed for January 1, 1928, and January 1, 1951, for raw materials, small tools, and finished products (including goods shipped) from Table H–1 and Table G–1 data. The deflators for each of these categories implied by our previous calculations are recombined with the 1928 and 1951 weights to relate these two years to 1937. The resulting index with 1951 weights differs by a fraction of 1 percent from that calculated with 1937 weights, and the latter index is therefore retained without alteration for all dates from January 1, 1938, on. The 1928-weighted index differs significantly from its 1937-weighted counterpart. The former is used, and values for all years from 1928 to 1937 are interpolated on the 1937-weighted index.

To summarize, the inventory deflator employs a somewhat mixed system of weights. The price indexes with which we begin—industrial prices, machinery prices, etc.—are either literally given-year weighted indexes or are thought to approximate such indexes. The deflator for each individual category of inventories, excepting finished products which have a single deflator, are combined with 1937 weights. (Data are not available for given-year weights within each category.) The deflators for the several categories of inventories are combined in the final deflator with weights that approximate those of the given year.

TRANSPORTATION AND COMMUNICATIONS

Figures are obtained by deflation of the Table G–1 current-price series by the Table L–4 inventory deflator except that 1931 is interpolated between 1930 and 1932, and 1959–62 are extrapolated from 1958 on the current-price series. For 1934, the smaller value of the deflator is used on the assumption that price changes made on January 1 would not at that date have been reflected immediately in inventory valuations. In 1939–41, the average of the alternative deflators is used (see the discussion of these years for producer goods industries). In 1949, 1950, and 1952, the post-change index is used for correspondence with the current-price valuation in Table G–1.

The plausibility of the resulting series appears highly questionable. We regard it as usable only as a component of the inventory totals, in which its weight is small. It may be noted that, from an analytical point of view, the bulk of inventories in this sector are goods in transit, which are otherwise accounted for.

The derivation of the deflators is explained below.

Basic Industrial Prices, including Petroleum

Purchases of petroleum products by transportation and communications are large (cf. Kaplan–52, p. 7, and TsSU–61, pp. 136–37), and it therefore appears appropriate to use for this sector the basic industrial price index inclusive of such products. Average annual indexes are taken from Bergson–55, p. 69a, and Turgeon–57, p. 13. The conversion of the average indexes to January 1 values follows precisely that used with the index exclusive of petroleum products (see notes for Table L–2) with two exceptions. For January 1, 1934, we extrapolate a figure for prices effective after changes made on that date from the 1934 average and from January 1, 1935 (the annual averages are virtually identical in 1934 and 1935). For January 1, 1934, prior to changes effective on that date, we make a rough interpolation between the 1933 average and the postchange figure for the beginning of 1934. We are guided here by the discussion of the timing of changes in petroleum prices in Nimitz–55, pp. 27–28. Secondly, we recompute the index from its components from January 1, 1937, to January 1, 1941, since significant changes in the prices of petroleum products occurred during 1937.

Inventory Deflator

The deflator is the weighted average of basic industrial prices, including petroleum, and machinery prices (Table L–2). The weights, which are constant, are derived from the Table H–1 breakdown of inventories by

TABLE L-4

DERIVATION OF DEFLATOR, TO 1937 PRICES, OF INVENTORIES
IN TRANSPORTATION AND COMMUNICATIONS, 1928-58*
(1937 Average = 100)

	Basic Industrial Prices, Including Petroleum (January 1)		Inventory Deflator (January 1)	
1928	46.0		51.3	
1929	44.0		49.7	
1930	44.0		49.7	
1931	44.0		49.7	
1932	44.0		50.7	
1933	44.0		52.1	
1934	67.5	(60.0)	72.2	(66.3)
1935	68.5		73.9	
1936	69.5		74.1	
1937	99.4		99.5	
1938	101		101	
1939	104	(103)	103	(102)
1940	119	(112)	116	(109)
1941	124	(124)	122	(121)
1944	128		124	
1945	128		125	
1946	128		127	
1947	128		128	
1948	128		128	
1949	303	(128)	296	(128)
1950	261	(303)	247	(296)
1951	251		237	
1952	236	(251)	221	(237)
1953	236		221	
1954	236		221	
1955	236		221	
1956	220		201	
1957	220		202	
1958	220		201	

*Figures in parentheses are for prices prior to changes effec-
tive on January 1. For machinery prices, which are also incorporated in the deflator, see Table L-2.

kind for January 1, 1951, for which date the data are clearly more reliable than are our estimates for 1937. Goods in process and finished
products are disregarded as trivially small; total inventories are divided
in the proportions shown between raw materials and small tools. The
weight of the former is attributed to basic industrial prices; the weight
of the latter is divided equally between basic industrial prices and machinery prices. The resulting weights for January 1, 1951, are 82.9 percent
and 17.1 percent for basic industrial and machinery prices respectively.

PROCUREMENT

With exceptions to be noted, the estimates are composed by deflating
the Table G–1 current-price values of both inventories on hand and goods
shipped by the inventory deflator shown in Table L–5. For the years for
which alternative values are shown for the deflator, the average of the
two is used for 1940 (see the discussion of this year for producer goods
industries); the figures outside brackets are used for 1949, 1950, and 1952
(the current-price estimates are for values in prices made effective on Janu-

ary 1). For 1931, inventories in 1937 prices are interpolated between the contiguous years. For 1961 and 1962, the deflator is assumed to have remained at the 1960 level.

The behavior over time of the deflated series is not obviously plausible, though plausibilities are difficult to judge for this sector. Since both the underlying current-price data and the deflators are subject to large errors, we take the deflated series to be usable only as a component of inventory totals, its weight in which is small.

The derivation of the deflator is explained below.

Agricultural Procurement Prices, Annual Average

1928, 1937, 1940, 1944, 1948, 1952: Figures are reproduced from Karcz–57a. The index is computed from data for eight agricultural products. It refers to prices realized in centralized and decentralized procurements (excluding collective-farm market sales and institutional deliveries), and is weighted with given-year weights. Some of the data underlying the index cited have been revised by their author (see Karcz–61), but the revisions do not permit correction of the particular index used here. A value of the index for 1954 which is also given by Karcz coincides with that derived below.

1950–51, 1953–55: These years are linked to 1952 by an index computed from price and quantity data for 1950–55 provided in Hoeffding–59, pp. 186 ff., and from Karcz's 1937-price data. The products and markets covered are the same as Karcz's; weights are those of the given year.

1956–59: Figures are crude extrapolations from 1955 on an index composed from an official index (TsSU–60a, p. 117) of average procurement-purchase prices paid to collective farms and individuals and an index of state-farm prices. The official index, with 1952 equal to 100, is 209 in 1955, 251 in 1956, 266 in 1957, 296 in 1958, and 302 in 1959. State-farm prices are assumed to have remained at the 1955 level except for a small increase in grain prices in 1958 (see Nimitz–62, pp. 40 and 46). The components are combined with 1955 weights computed from data for 11 products given in Hoeffding–59, pp. 186 ff.

Agricultural Procurement Prices, January 1

1928–29: From data given in Karcz–57, pp. 340 and 345 ff., we make a rough guess that procurement prices rose 15 percent during 1928. We assume that the annual average was at the mid-point between the year-end values.

1930–36: The evidence available for these years is scant. It is clear, however, that a disproportionate part of the increase over the entire period occurred in 1935. Grin'ko–36, p. 9, states that there was a large increase in procurement prices of cotton, flax, hemp, and other agricultural raw materials; grain prices were raised somewhat. The increase in cotton prices is elsewhere given as "threefold" (Mar'iasin–36, p. 14). The increase in compulsory procurement prices for grain was 10 percent (Karcz–57, p. 376). Centralized procurement prices for eggs were raised (*ibid.*, p. 300). Premia for above-quota deliveries of technical crops were introduced (*ibid.*, p. 39). Prices of potatoes, milk, and meat were not raised (*ibid.*, p. 39, fn.). The money incomes of collective farms reportedly increased by 68 percent (Plot-

TABLE L-5

DERIVATION OF DEFLATOR, TO 1937 PRICES, OF INVENTORIES
IN PROCUREMENT, 1928-60*
(1937 Average = 100)

	Agricultural Procurement Prices (Annual Average)	Agricultural Procurement Prices (January 1)	Inventory Deflator (January 1)
1928	31.5	29.5	34.3
1929	--	33.7	37.7
1930	--	37.3	40.3
1931	--	41.4	43.9
1932	--	45.8	47.5
1933	--	50.7	51.8
1934	--	56.2	56.5
1935	--	62.2	61.5
1936	--	90.3	85.0
1937	100	100	100
1938	--	100	100
1939	--	100	101
1940	101	101	105 (104)
1941	--	101	106
1944	99.5	--	--
1945	--	100	107
1946	--	101	108
1947	--	102	109
1948	103	103	110
1949	--	104	152 (111)
1950	161	161	189 (199)
1951	161	161	188
1952	171	161	185 (188)
1953	217	186	205
1954	285	240	250
1955	309	293	294
1956	361	326	319
1957	380	367	353
1958	418	392	374
1959	425	420	397
1960	--	425	401

*Figures in parentheses are for prices prior to changes effective on January 1.
For basic industrial prices (excluding petroleum), which are also incorporated in
the deflator, see Table L-2.

nikov–48, p. 116) whereas agricultural output, from all producers, increased by only 18 percent (see Table P–1). On this evidence and taking into account 1937 weights shown in Karcz–57a, we assume that prices in the course of 1935 increased by 45 percent.

In all other years, we assume the percentage rate of increase of prices was uniform and of an amount, 10.8 percent per annum, sufficient to account for the total increase from 1929 to 1937 not accounted for in 1935. For evidence that procurement prices were rising substantially in the late 1920's and early 1930's, see TsSU–32, pp. 341 ff.

1937–49: Figures are freehand interpolations on the virtually unchanging annual averages.

1950–52: January 1 values are assumed equal to the annual averages because of the stability of the latter.

1953–59: Figures are interpolated from the annual averages with the preceding year weighted two thirds and the following year one third. Presumably January 1 prices typically are closer to those of the preceding harvest than of the harvest following.

1960: Assumed equal to the 1959 average.

Inventory Deflator

The index is the weighted average of the procurement price index computed here and the index of basic industrial prices exclusive of petroleum shown in Table L–2. The latter is assumed to have remained at the 1958 level to 1959 and 1960. Because of data limitations and because of the insignificance of the sector, the two components are combined with constant weights. The weights are based on the distribution of inventories by kind on January 1, 1951 (Table H–1 for inventories on hand and Table G–1 for goods shipped), because the data for that year are more reliable than those for 1937; the choice makes little difference to the results. Procurement prices are attributed the share in inventories of finished products on hand, goods shipped, and goods in process, the weight of the last being trivial. These account in 1951 for 71 percent of the total. Basic industrial prices are attributed the share of raw materials and small tools, the weight of the latter being trivial. These account in 1951 for 29 percent of the total.

In composing this deflator, we assume that in the 1950's, when procurement agencies were subsidized (see the discussion of consumer goods industries), their inventories of agricultural products were valued gross of subsidies. This would appear consistent with the general principle that inventories are valued at acquisition cost, but we find no direct evidence on the point.

DOMESTIC TRADE

Our procedure for deflating trade inventories differs from that used for other sectors in that, for the years 1936 through 1961, we do not deflate the Table G–1 series but the Table K–1 series for inventories of finished products valued at retail prices. The reasons for this are the availability of retail price indexes and the fact that the Table G–1 series is itself largely derived from the finished products series and, hence, is an inaccurate measure of total inventories at acquisition cost. The resulting deflated index may err both because of differences in the behavior of finished product inventories at retail prices and at acquisition cost and because of variations in the share of inventories other than finished products in the total. The latter share appears typically to have been small (see Table H–1) but, at least in current prices, subject to considerable variation (according to Lifits–50, p. 521, stocks of raw and other materials held by the Ministry of Trade increased from 13 percent of "commodity supplies" in 1937 to 26 percent at the beginning of 1941; see also the detailed breakdown of inventories by kind in TsSU–61, pp. 92 ff.).

The deflator used, which is shown in Table L–6, is basically the retail price index given in Chapman–59, with given-year weights on a 1937 base, extended to some additional years in Bergson–61, pp. 307–8, and extended to the remaining years by exceedingly crude devices improvised here. The figures for 1928–30 are inclusive of private trade but are thereafter for state and co-operative trade only. Our detailed explanations commence with that for the deflator.

1928–29: Chapman's index for average retail prices in 1928, with 1928 quantity weights and with the 1937 average equal to 100, is 11.5. According to the TsSU's "All-Union index of retail prices," which appears to be the most authoritative of the several indexes published at the time, retail prices in all trade increased by 7.4 percent during 1928 (*Statisticheskoe obozrenie*, 1929:1, p. 157). We do not know how closely this index may approximate one appropriate for our purposes (on its general characteristics, see Chapman–59), but we have no superior alternative. We link the official index to Chapman's on the assumption that the annual average equaled the average of the year-end values.

1930: According to the TsSU's "All-Union decentralized index of retail prices," which replaced that cited for 1928, retail prices in all trade during 1929 increased by 9.5 percent (see *Ekonomicheskoe obozrenie*, 1930:3, p. 189). We assume an equivalent increase in our index.

TABLE L-6

DEFLATOR, TO 1937 PRICES, OF INVENTORIES
IN DOMESTIC TRADE, 1928-62
(January 1--1937 Average = 100)

1928	11.1
1929	11.9
1930	13.0
1931	14.3
1932	25.0
1933	50.0
1934	59.0
1935	69.6
1936	96.9
1937	102
1938	99.0
1939	100
1940	103
1941	129
1944	141
1945	156
1946	172
1947	312
1948	303
1949	297
1950	264
1951	217
1952	205
1953	195
1954	176
1955	167
1956	171
1957	171
1958	173
1959	174
1960	173
1961	172
1962	170

1931: According to the same index as that cited for 1930 but now restricted to socialized trade only, retail prices inclusive of alcoholic beverages were, on a 1913 base, 208 on January 1, 1930, and 206 on December 1, 1930; exclusive of alcoholic beverages, prices were 196 on January 1, 1930, and 192 on January 1, 1931 (see *Ekonomicheskoe obozrenie, loc. cit.,* and *Economic Survey,* December, 1930, p. 9, and February, 1931, p. 12). Private trade was reportedly abolished in the course of 1930 (cf. TsSU–56, pp. 14–15), and it might appear from this fact and from the claimed behavior of prices in socialized trade, that prices in all trade in fact declined during 1930. On the other hand, Polliak–31, p. 68, presents a cost of living index which indicates a large rise (45–63 percent depending upon weights) in prices by October, 1930, relative to a year earlier. While this may be attributable in part to private trade, which we take to have been negligible by the end of the year, or to services rather than commodities, some rise in all retail prices appears to be implied. Having in view also the total increase in prices to be accounted for by January 1, 1932, we assume a 10 percent increase in the course of 1930.

The 1931 index is not used in our estimates of trade inventories for that date, but it is employed elsewhere in the study.

1932–33: Sovetskaia torgovlia, 1957:11, p. 59, contains an index of the "physical volume" of state and co-operative retail trade: 1928 = 100, 1932 = 134, and 1937 = 199. The volume of trade in current prices in the same years was 11.8, 40.4, and 125.9 billion rubles respectively (TsSU–56, p. 7). The implied price index, shifted to a 1937 base, is 1928 = 18.7, 1932 = 47.7, 1937 = 100. As Chapman notes (Chapman–59), the 1928/1937 ratio implied by this index does not differ greatly from that implied by her index with *1937* weights, which suggests that it may have some foundation in fact. If we use the official index to interpolate a 1932 average value for our Table L–6 index (interpolating on a straight percentage line), we obtain a figure of 36.4. This appears to be the best evidence available to us on the level of retail prices reached in the early 1930's.

It is clear that, in the course of 1932, prices were increased greatly (cf. Jasny–51, p. 31; see also the various data assembled in Hubbard–38, pp. 269 ff.), but the amount of the increase is highly uncertain. Having in mind the total increase to be accounted for from January 1, 1931, to the 1932 average, we assume that prices doubled during 1932, or rose from 25 to 50 in the Table L–6 series.

The figure for January 1, 1932, implies that retail prices rose by 75 percent in the course of 1931, which result is not easily substantiated. However, some considerable increases between 1930 and 1931 in average annual prices in co-operative trade are shown for a few products among several for which data are given in TsSU–32, pp. 348–49. Schwarz–51, p. 138, states that prices "actually skyrocketed from the spring of 1931 on." Significantly, the large increase in retail trade in current prices from 1930 to 1931 (cf. TsSU–56, p. 14) was accompanied by a large increase in budget receipts from indirect taxes (cf. Holzman–55, p. 142). Significantly also, perhaps, the publication of official price indexes ceased from early 1931. We may, nevertheless, be seriously in error at this point.

We should note also that the 1932 value derived from the official index is implicitly inclusive of prices in so-called commercial trade, as well as of ration prices. It is questionable whether the difference between ration and commercial prices was reflected fully in the valuation of inventories, but our estimates are too crude to justify any deliberate allowance for this possibility. For the whole of the ration period, our estimates of retail prices are best read as inclusive of commercial trade, and we employ them elsewhere on the assumption that this is their coverage. The share of commercial in total trade reportedly rose from 3 percent in 1931 to 24 percent in 1934 (Lifits–50, p. 88).

1934–35: The evidence for these years is fragmentary. From 1933 to the beginning of 1935, ration prices quite clearly rose (see Jasny–51, pp. 21 and 31 ff.), the share of commercial trade rose (see above), but commercial store prices may have fallen. The rise of prices with the abolition of bread rationing on January 1, 1935, was evidently large (see Jasny–51, p. 21); bread prices were reduced in October, 1935, but prices of a number of other products, then derationed, were raised (see Pinus–35, pp. 7 ff.). On balance, it appears likely that the effective price increase during 1935 was greater than in either of the two preceding years. We assume it was twice as great and divide the remainder of the total increase from January 1, 1933, to January 1, 1936, equally between 1933 and 1934. Our estimate for January 1, 1935, is intended to exclude price increases occurring on that date, since it is unlikely that our figure for trade inventories (Table G–1) reflects the price change.

1936: Prices are assumed to have been 5 percent below those of January 1, 1937. Average prices in 1936 appear to have been about the same as in 1937 (Mrs. Chapman in private correspondence), but some upward movement appears to have occurred in the course of 1936 (cf. *Quarterly Bulletin of Soviet-Russian Economics,* November, 1939, p. 55, and the individual price quotations shown in Trivanovitch–38, pp. 27–28).

1937–38: The relation of January 1, 1937 and 1938, to the 1937 average is that estimated in Bergson–61, p. 399.

1939: We assume that of the 4 percentage point rise from January 1, 1938 to January 1, 1940, one point occurred during 1938, the remainder during 1939.

1940–41: The Chapman index for the 1940 average is 126. The relation of January 1, 1940 and 1941, to the average is estimated in Bergson–61, p. 399.

1944–47: While we undertake to compute directly price indexes for these years, the results are, for reasons to be explained, somewhat implausible. The indexes entered in the table, therefore, are averages of the directly computed index and an implicit deflator derived on a simple assumption about the behavior of inventories in constant prices (see below).

Annual volumes of trade of various categories in current prices can be estimated as follows (billion rubles):

	1943	1944	1945	1946	1947
Ration trade and restaurants	75.3	101.0	128.1	180.9	221.5
Commercial trade	0.0	6.0	15.4	44.0	86.0
Special rural trade	8.7	12.3	16.6	22.3	23.3
Total	84.0	119.3	160.1	247.2	330.8

Total trade figures are from TsSU–56, p. 20. They are for all state and co-operative trade, inclusive of restaurants.

Ration trade and restaurants is computed as the difference between the total and the other two components.

Commercial trade was introduced in the course of 1944 and therefore was zero in 1943. The 1944 figure is from Chapman–59. Figures for 1945 and 1947 are computed from the totals and from ratios of commercial trade in the total of 9.6 percent and 26 percent given in Anonymous–57, p. 10. The similar ratio for 1946 is interpolated.

Special rural trade refers to the sale of manufactured goods to the rural population at prices above the ration level, which was introduced in 1942 (Chapman–59). The figure shown for 1944 is Chapman's estimate. The share of such sales in the total of rural sales is assumed the same in all other years as in 1944. Total rural sales for 1945–47 are given in TsSU–56, p. 21; for 1943–44, they are assumed the same share of the total as in 1945.

From these annual trade data, we first derive distributions as of January 1; for 1944, on the assumption it was the same as in 1943; for 1945 to 1947, on the assumption the distribution equaled the average of those in the two contiguous years. Using the price indexes shown below, we recompute the shares of each kind of trade to valuations in ration prices.

Prices in each kind of trade are assumed to have behaved as follows, with 1937 weights and with 1937 = 100 (January 1):

	1944	1945	1946	1947
Ration	143	143	143	320
Commercial	—	1,520	1,180	915
Special rural	330	330	330	330

The indexes of ration and special rural prices were very kindly provided by Mrs. Chapman; we assume that prices on January 1, 1944, were the same as the average of that year.

Chapman has estimated also that the average index for commercial prices in 1944 was 2,200, and that the index for January, 1947, was 900–930 (we take the average of the latter figures). Chapman's 1944 estimate is based on the assumption that commercial prices equaled collective-farm market prices in that year, or an index of 2,200. By January 1, 1945, however, collective-farm market prices had declined to 68.9 percent of their 1944 average (see the indexes given in Zverev–57, p. 39, which are the same as those used by Chapman). We assume that commercial prices fell proportionately. Commercial prices in 1946 are estimated on the assumption that the percentage rates of change in 1946 and 1947 were equal.

Applying to these indexes the weights computed above yields combined indexes of 152 for 1944, 164 for 1945, 174 for 1946, and 375 for 1947. These, however, approximate 1937-weighted indexes. Chapman's given-year weighted index is 94.9 percent of her 1937-weighted index for January 1, 1941, 90.1 percent for 1948 average. We assume the 1948 difference held on January 1 of that year and interpolate adjustments for 1944–47 along a straight line. The resulting indexes with, so to speak, given-year weights, are 141 in 1944, 151 in 1945, 159 in 1946, and 341 in 1947.

If, then, we deflate the reported series for inventories of finished products (Table K–1) with these indexes, we arrive at the following estimates of inventories in 1937 prices. The years, 1941, adjusted for territorial coverage, and 1948, are included for comparison. Figures are billion rubles on January 1.

1941	23.3
1944	10.8
1945	13.7
1946	18.1
1947	12.5
1948	19.5

That some considerable reduction in trade inventories occurred during 1946 is by no means improbable, in view of the reportedly poor harvest and of the postponement of the abolition of rationing announced for that year (cf. Prokopovicz–52, p. 433). A substantial build-up of inventories during 1947, in anticipation of the abolition of rationing in mid-December of that year, is also probable (cf. Atlas–58, p. 248). Moreover, if the increase in ration prices in September, 1946, was anything close to the 124 percent rise estimated by Chapman (the weight of other prices is relatively small), it is unlikely that the indicated decline in inventories during 1946 is entirely spurious.

Nevertheless, we are reluctant to assume so violent a fluctuation in trade inventories during 1946–47 as the above estimates imply. As a device for smoothing these in some degree, we estimate as well the change in prices that would be implied if the physical volume of inventories had risen at a constant percentage rate from January 1, 1944, to January 1, 1948 (the Table K–1 data are again taken for inventories in current prices). With 1944 set equal to 141, this yields indexes of 166 in 1945, 199 in 1946, and 253 in 1947. Since the presumptive reliability of these indexes is considerably less than that of the indexes computed directly, we combine the two with weights of one third and two thirds respectively. The resulting indexes are those entered in the table.

1948–49: Figures are computed from the Chapman index for the 1948 average and a 2 percent decline in the course of 1948 estimated in Bergson–61, p. 397. Bergson, p. 399, indicates the price change occurred in mid-1948; we assume the average of the year-end figures equaled the annual average.

1950–55: Derived from Chapman's annual averages and Bergson's interpolations on the basis of the official retail price index (see Bergson–61, pp. 307–8). The relation of the year-end values to the annual averages is interpolated from the official index on the assumption that the divergence of the official index from Chapman's on January 1 equals the average of the divergence in the two contiguous years. We do not use the ratios shown in Bergson–61, p. 397, of year-end to average values since, for the years considered here, they are computed from the official index.

1956–62: Figures for these years are based on the official retail price index, which, for the immediately preceding years, does not diverge greatly from Chapman's.

Average annual values of the official index, with January 1, 1941, equal to 100, are these:

1955	134
1956	135
1957	135
1958	138
1959	137
1960	136
1961	135

Data through 1960 are from TsSU–59, p. 771, and TsSU–61, p. 716. The 1961–62 link is computed from data for retail trade in current and constant prices given in *Vestnik statistiki*, 1962:2, p. 12.

The average 1955 value of the Chapman-Bergson index is 170. We link the official index to this value and estimate January 1 values as the average of those of the contiguous years, except that January 1, 1962, is estimated from January 1, 1961, and the 1961 average.

Given the Table L–6 price indexes, we estimate trade inventories on hand in these steps:

(*i*) We compose an index for 1928–30 and 1932–36 by deflating the Table G–1 data in current prices with the Table L–6 price index.

(*ii*) We interpolate a value for inventories in 1931 on a straight line between 1930 and 1932.

(*iii*) We link to the foregoing series, at 1936, one derived by deflating the Table K–1 series for inventories of finished products by the Table L–6 price index. We raise the series for finished products by 5 percent in 1940 and 2.5 percent in 1941 to correct for a supposed territorial undercoverage (see notes to Table G–1 for these years), and we extend the series from 1961 to 1962 on the Table G–1 series for inventories on hand.

(*iv*) To establish an absolute value for this series in 1937, we compute average trade inventories at acquisition cost from the beginning- and end-of-year values shown in Table G–1. We equate to this the 1937 average, similarly computed, of the inventory index described above.

Goods shipped are estimated in all years on the assumption that their ratio to inventories on hand was the same in constant prices as in current (Table G–1). The ratio for 1931 is interpolated from that in 1930 and 1932.

We note that TsSU–56, p. 16, contains a series for inventories in *retail* trade valued in prices of January 1, 1941, for January 1, 1941, 1951, 1955, and 1956. Comparison of this series with the current-price series given in the same source (see Table K–1) suggests that the current-price series has been deflated simply by the official index of retail prices.

CONTRACT CONSTRUCTION

For years in which Table G–1 includes figures for inventories in current prices (1928–30, 1941, 1947, and 1951–62), the 1937-price series are deflated. The deflator for years through 1958 is shown in Table L–7. The figure outside parentheses is used for 1952, for correspondence with the current-price estimate. For 1959–62, prices are assumed to have remained at the 1958 level.

All remaining years are interpolated (from 1930 to 1941, 1941 to 1947, and 1947 to 1951) on a series for contract construction and installation in 1937 prices, which is composed as follows.

(*i*) Total construction and installation in 1937 prices is computed as the sum of these two categories shown in Table A–1.

(*ii*) For 1929–32, the share of contract in total construction and installation is computed from absolute figures for contract construction and installation (reproduced from Pokrovskii–36, pp. 53–54, in Powell–57, Part II, p. 430) and for total construction and installation (computed from Table A–7 as the sum of construction and socialized installation). Both series are in current prices.

(*iii*) For 1933–50, the share of contract in the total is computed as the product of the share of money investment in socialized construction and installation in the total and the share of contract in socialized money investment. The first share is computed from the data in Table A–7, which are in current prices. The second is assumed to equal the share of contract in total money investment in socialized construction and installation other than that of collective farms, nominally in July 1, 1955, prices, which is given in official sources (see TsSU–61, p. 606). The two ratios used here are incomparable in that the first includes and the second excludes money investment by collective farms, but the difference is inconsequential for present purposes.

TABLE L–7

DERIVATION OF DEFLATOR, TO 1937 PRICES,
OF INVENTORIES IN CONTRACT CONSTRUCTION, 1928–58*
(1937 Average = 100)

	Construction Materials Prices (January 1)		Inventory Deflator (January 1)	
1928	61.7		62.2	
1929	59.1		60.3	
1930	56.9		58.7	
1941	132		129	
1947	159		150	
1951	294		281	
1952	264	(294)	256	(281)
1953	259		253	
1954	259		253	
1955	259		253	
1956	230		227	
1957	230		227	
1958	230		227	

*Figures in parentheses are for prices prior to changes effective on January 1. For basic industrial prices (excluding petroleum) and machinery prices, which are also incorporated in the deflator, see Table L–2.

(*iv*) The preceding steps yield a series for annual contract construction and installation in 1937 prices. Inventories as of January 1 are interpolated on the construction and installation of the preceding year.

The derivation of the inventory deflator is described below.

Construction Materials Prices

The January 1 figures are derived from an index of average annual prices of construction materials at site, with given-year quantity weights, which is presented in Powell–59, p. 80.

1928: Extrapolated from the 1928 average and January 1, 1929.

1929–30: Computed as averages of contiguous annual averages.

1941, 1947, and 1951: Assumed the same as the annual averages.

1952: Prices effective after the change on January 1, 1952, are assumed the same as the 1952 average; those before the change the same as the 1951 average.

1953–55: Assumed equal to the 1953 and 1954 averages, which are the same.

1956: Assumed the same as the 1956 average.

1957–58: In the absence of a general price change, prices are assumed to have remained at the 1956 level. This is in error in that individual prices did change, most notably those of lumber being increased by 30 percent in April, 1957 (see Nimitz–62, p. 10).

Inventory Deflator

The deflator is the weighted average of basic industrial prices (excluding petroleum; Table L–2), machinery prices (Table L–2), and construction materials prices (Table L–7). The weights employed are for January 1, 1951, for which we have usable data. From the Table H–1 breakdown, we distribute total inventories 78.2 percent to raw materials and 21.8 percent to small tools, disregarding the trivial amount of goods in process. From data in TsSU–61, p. 97, we estimate that 81.1 percent of raw materials represent construction materials (those given in the source as "raw materials, basic materials, and purchased semifabricates") and attribute this weight to the construction materials index. The weight of the remaining raw materials (given in the source as "supplementary materials") and 50 percent of small tools we attribute to basic industrial prices. The weight of the remaining small tools is attributed to machinery prices. The 1951 weights which result from these assumptions are 25.7 percent for basic industrial prices, 63.4 percent for construction materials, and 10.9 percent for machinery prices.

OTHER NONAGRICULTURAL SECTORS

Except for 1931, all years are estimated on the assumption that the ratio of inventories on hand in other nonagricultural sectors to the sum of those in industry, transportation and communications, procurement, and domestic trade was the same in 1937 prices as in current prices (data for the latter are from Table G–1). The ratio of goods shipped to inventories on hand is also assumed the same in 1937 as in current prices; 1931 is interpolated between 1930 and 1932.

Uninstalled Equipment, n.e.c.

This category represents equipment held in the warehouses of construction projects, of a sort which ultimately requires installation but which has not yet been installed. That such equipment is not included in official data or in our estimates for fixed capital investment is explained in Appendix E. That it is not included in the reported data underlying our current-price estimates for inventories in contract construction can be inferred from the fact that the TsSU working capital accounts, on which we principally rely, exclude loans to contract construction on stocks of equipment and hence, presumably, the assets which such loans are considered to finance (see Appendix G, p. 503). Nor is there any category on the asset side of these accounts which appears likely to contain such equipment (on the coverage of "unfinished production" in contract construction, see Appendix H, p. 526.

In Appendix E, p. 448, we attribute to this category of uninstalled equipment, in 1958, a value equal to 4.8 percent of "unfinished construction," and we take fixed capital investment projects in progress to equal 87 percent of "unfinished construction." Uninstalled equipment, n.e.c., therefore amounts to 5.5 percent of investment projects in progress. Lacking other evidence, we assume this ratio held in all years and in 1937 prices, and estimate uninstalled equipment, n.e.c., from investment projects in progress, in 1937 prices, as given in Table E–1.

Clearly, these estimates serve only to round out the inventory—and total capital stock—estimates.

Erratum: Mistakenly, the Table L–1 calculations for this category were made with a percentage of 4.6 instead of the indicated 5.5, which error was not discovered until late in the course of the study. Since the calculation is very rough in any case and the error trivially small, amounting, for example, to 1.0 billion rubles in 1962, it has been left uncorrected.

TOTAL NONAGRICULTURAL SECTORS

Figures for all years except 1944 and 1945 are sums of the components shown in Table L–1. In the latter two years, we assume that inventories in all sectors other than domestic trade and contract construction were the same as in 1946 (and, in 1944, uninstalled equipment was the same as in 1945). The justification for assuming unchanging inventories in sectors other than those specified is that changes in total inventories in current prices over these years appear to be largely accounted for by changes in trade inventories (see Table G–1) and, secondly, that prices other than in retail trade appear to have been virtually constant (see the indexes assembled in the present appendix). No precision, however, can be attributed to the resulting estimates.

AGRICULTURE

We do not attempt to estimate agricultural inventories by deflation. Although a current-price series for state agriculture is included in Table G–1, its reliability is low, and little is to be gained by estimating a constant-price series for that component alone. Data for nonstate agriculture—collective farms and private agriculture—are extremely fragmentary. Our procedure, therefore, is to estimate the value of total agricultural inventories as of a single date and extrapolate figures for all other years on agricultural output. The resulting estimates can serve no purpose other than to permit a rough adjustment in the inventory aggregates and in their trends, it being reasonably certain that the rate of increase in agricultural inventories has been lower than that in the whole of nonagricultural sectors.

Our single estimate of the absolute value of inventories is for January 1, 1938, on which date we assume that prices were the same as the 1937 average. We have from Table G–1 that inventories on hand in state agriculture were 5.0 billion rubles. According to Sautin–39, p. 13, "products and materials" held by collective farms amounted to 6.9 billion rubles. The coverage of this figure, which is attributed to "annual accounts," is unexplained, but we assume from its caption and its date that it includes inventories of both agricultural and nonagricultural origin, that it excludes immature livestock, and that it excludes small tools. Sautin states also, p. 7, that at the end of 1936 "means of production" in the private property of collective farmers equaled approximately 15 percent of those held by the collective. This ratio presumably overstates the size of inventory holdings of collective farmers, since it reflects their relatively large holdings of livestock. On the other hand, an allowance needs to be made for inventories in other private agriculture, including the garden plots of urban workers. We take 15 percent of 6.9 or 1.0 billion to represent all private holdings of the same kinds of assets as are covered in Sautin's figure for collective farms.

With respect to small tools in agriculture, our firmest evidence is figures for "transport, other agricultural, and small-valued durables [*inventar'*]" in agriculture in the late 1920's (Gosplan–30, p. 448; this category is included in the source in fixed capital, from which we have excluded it; see p. 408). The category amounts to 1.5 billion rubles on October 1, 1927, and 1.6 billion on October 1, 1928. The prices of these inventories presumably rose between 1928 and 1937; their physical volume may well have declined (there is a suggestion in Gosplan–30, p. 463, that at least part of them was related to the number of horses); and on the order of 0.4 billion rubles of small tools is accounted for in our estimate of inventories in state agriculture on January 1, 1938 (cf. data for 1937 in Table H–1). An allowance of 2.0 billion rubles for small tools in nonstate agriculture appears to be ample.

The preceding estimates sum to a total of inventories on hand on January 1, 1938, in all agriculture of approximately 15 billion rubles, which is the figure we use.

Goods shipped are trivially small in the accounts of state agriculture (see Table G–1), and we suppose that goods shipped by nonstate agriculture are carried largely on the books of other sectors. We therefore assume them to be zero for all agriculture.

Given the value of inventories on hand on January 1, 1938, we extrapolate values in all other years on total agricultural production. Inventories as of January 1 are assumed a constant fraction of the output of the preceding calendar year. The resulting figure for January 1, 1940, is raised by 5 percent to allow for the effects of the 1939 territorial acquisitions, which we judge are not reflected in 1939 output. The output series used, for all years other than 1927 and 1944, is that shown in Table P–1. 1927 is extrapolated from 1928 on the official index of agricultural production, TsSU–61, p. 362. 1944 is extrapolated from 1945 on the basis of an estimate made in Bergson–61, p. 333, that agricultural production (in 1937 prices) in 1944 relative to 1945 was 55/69 or 79.7 percent. In context, this estimate appears to make no allowance for changes in livestock herds. Proceeding as for the Table P–1 series, we allow for herd changes and obtain a ratio of 87.1 percent.

The extrapolation of inventories on output may be questionable, among other reasons, in that we relate inventories to total agricultural production whereas we have made separate estimates of livestock. The procedure is not firmly defensible on this score, but our reasoning is the following. To the extent that livestock can properly be regarded as goods in process, it represents a form of inventory which is largely omitted in the present estimates: some goods in process are evidently included for state agriculture (see Table H–1), but none appear to be for private and collective-farm agriculture. To the extent that livestock consist of draft animals, breeding herds, and the like, it is probably more nearly a substitute for fixed capital than for inventories. On balance it appears preferable to estimate agricultural inventories on total agricultural production rather than on crops alone.

Evidence can be adduced that bears on the plausibility of our estimates for 1928. The figure for January 1, 1928, in 1937 prices, if converted to 1928 average prices by the deflator shown in Table M–3, comes to 5.0 billion rubles. According to Rozentul–29, p. 307, inventories in agriculture on October 1, 1927, of seed and feedstuffs and horticultural products intended for sale (see the explanation in *ibid.*, p. 303) amounted to 6.4 billion rubles. Such inventories, however, undoubtedly decline greatly from October 1 to January 1. In state farms alone (which accounted for a small share of the whole), they declined by four fifths in the last quarter of 1927 and two thirds in the last quarter of 1928 (see Tables G–2 and G–3). So large a decline in the whole of agriculture seems unlikely, but data on the timing of harvests in the late 1920's (Iurtsovskii–28, *passim*) and on the distribution by months of agricultural procurements in 1927 and 1928 (published serially in *Economic Survey*), suggest a decline on the order of one third to one half or a figure for January 1, 1928, of roughly 3.5 billion rubles. To this must be added 1.5 billion or so of small tools (see above) and presumably some small amount of other inventories of non-agricultural origin. The indicated total comes close to the 5.0 figure derived from our estimates. As a reading of the sources will make clear, however, all of the reported data cited are of highly questionable reliability and comparability. (We note that a figure for inventories in the "peasant economy" on October 1, 1927, of 9.7 billion rubles, which is given in Gosplan–29, p. 42, is indicated in Gosplan–30a, Vol. I, p. 9, to be inclusive of about 4 billion rubles of consumption stocks of peasant households.)

A similar conversion of our estimate in 1937 prices for January 1, 1951, to 1950 average prices yields a total of 31 billion rubles or slightly over twice the current-price figure for January 1, 1938. The Table G–1 estimates for state agriculture show a similar, though smaller, increase over the same period. We have no evidence on the behavior of nonstate agriculture.

TOTAL

Except for 1944, figures are sums of components. In 1944, agricultural inventories are arbitrarily assumed the same as in 1945.

Inventories in 1928 and

1950 Prevailing Prices

The estimates in 1928 and 1950 prevailing prices, which are shown in Tables M–1 and M–2, are derived from those in 1937 prices by quite limited and rule-of-thumb adjustments, and the results are far less reliable than the 1937-price estimates. The basic procedure is described first, and exceptions noted thereafter.

(*i*) The value of inventories on hand in 1937 prices in each sector in the middle of each of the three weight years, 1928, 1937, and 1950, is assumed equal to the average of the values at the beginning and end of each year (see Table L–1).

(*ii*) The mid-1928 and mid-1950 values in 1937 prices are converted to 1928 and 1950 prices by means of the sector price indexes with given-year weights shown in Table M–3.

(*iii*) The mid-1937 values in 1937 prices are converted to 1928 and to 1950 prices by means of the 1937-weighted sector price indexes shown in Table M–3.

(*iv*) Sector estimates in 1928 prices are interpolated between and extrapolated from the mid-1928 and mid-1937 figures in 1928 prices on the series in 1937 prices. Estimates in 1950 prices are similarly interpolated between and extrapolated from the mid-1937 and mid-1950 figures in 1950 prices.

(*v*) Goods shipped in each sector are assumed to bear the same ratio to inventories on hand as they do in current prices (Table G–1).

(*vi*) Totals are sums of components.

Exceptions to the foregoing procedures are made in the following instances.

(*i*) For domestic trade, our series for inventories on hand in 1937 prices is essentially an index of inventories of finished products with its 1937 values set equal to total inventories in current prices (see Appendix L). The conversions to 1928 and 1950 prices yield appropriate indexes in those prices but absolute values in 1928 and 1950 in prices of those years which are not necessarily consistent with the current-price totals shown in Table G–1. We therefore estimate mid-1928 and mid-1950 values for total trade inventories in 1928 and 1950 prices respectively from the Table G–1 data,

TABLE M-1

INVENTORIES IN 1928 PREVAILING PRICES, BY SECTORS, 1928-62

(January 1--Billion Rubles)

	1928	1929	1930	1931	1932	1933	1934	1935	1936	1937	1938
Producer Goods Industries											
Inventories on Hand	2.5	3.0	3.7	4.8	6.9	9.0	10.9	13.8	18.0	18.6	20.8
Goods Shipped	0.4	0.5	0.6	0.8	1.1	1.5	1.9	2.2	3.3	3.4	3.7
Consumer Goods Industries											
Inventories on Hand	3.3	3.3	2.9	3.6	4.4	4.2	4.4	4.3	5.6	6.1	6.7
Goods Shipped	0.7	0.7	0.6	0.7	0.9	0.9	1.1	0.9	1.4	1.6	1.7
Transportation and Communications											
Inventories on Hand	0.7	0.8	0.8	1.4	2.0	2.1	2.0	2.2	2.9	2.0	2.0
Procurement											
Inventories on Hand	0.4	0.5	0.6	0.8	1.0	1.0	1.0	1.2	1.4	0.9	1.1
Goods Shipped	0.0	0.0	0.0	0.1	0.1	0.1	0.2	0.2	0.3	0.2	0.2
Domestic Trade											
Inventories on Hand	2.4	2.6	2.7	2.5	2.3	1.7	1.7	2.0	2.2	2.8	3.4
Goods Shipped	0.2	0.3	0.3	0.2	0.2	0.2	0.2	0.2	0.2	0.3	0.3
Contract Construction											
Inventories on Hand	0.1	0.1	0.1	0.5	0.7	0.7	0.4	0.5	0.7	1.2	1.5
Other Nonagricultural Sectors											
Inventories on Hand	0.2	0.2	0.2	0.7	1.3	1.1	1.2	1.1	1.1	1.0	1.1
Goods Shipped	0.0	0.0	0.0	0.1	0.1	0.1	0.1	0.1	0.1	0.1	0.1
Uninstalled Equipment, n.e.c.											
Inventories on Hand	0.1	0.1	0.2	0.3	0.4	0.4	0.4	0.5	0.4	0.5	0.5
Total Nonagricultural Sectors											
Inventories on Hand	9.7	10.6	11.2	14.6	19.0	20.2	22.0	25.6	32.3	33.1	37.1
Goods Shipped	1.3	1.5	1.5	1.9	2.4	2.8	3.5	3.6	5.3	5.6	6.0
Total	11.0	12.1	12.7	16.5	21.4	23.0	25.5	29.2	37.6	38.7	43.1
Agriculture											
Inventories on Hand	5.0	5.1	4.8	4.6	4.1	3.7	4.1	4.3	5.1	4.6	5.6
Total											
Inventories on Hand	14.7	15.7	16.0	19.2	23.1	23.9	26.1	29.9	37.4	37.7	42.7
Goods Shipped	1.3	1.5	1.5	1.9	2.4	2.8	3.5	3.6	5.3	5.6	6.0
Total	16.0	17.2	17.5	21.1	25.5	26.7	29.6	33.5	42.7	43.3	48.7

TABLE M-1 (continued)

INVENTORIES IN 1928 PREVAILING PRICES, BY SECTORS, 1928-62
(January 1--Billion Rubles)

	1939	1940	1941	1944	1945	1946	1947	1948	1949	1950	1951
Producer Goods Industries											
Inventories on Hand	22.9	24.1	26.4	--	--	27.8	29.7	33.7	30.7	33.7	37.2
Goods Shipped	3.8	4.5	6.4	--	--	6.0	6.0	6.7	5.9	6.3	6.8
Consumer Goods Industries											
Inventories on Hand	7.9	9.2	7.5	--	--	4.0	3.6	3.7	5.4	7.7	8.6
Goods Shipped	1.9	2.5	2.7	--	--	1.2	1.1	1.1	1.5	2.1	2.3
Transportation and Communications											
Inventories on Hand	1.8	2.4	2.0	--	--	2.1	2.4	2.7	1.6	1.6	1.8
Procurement											
Inventories on Hand	1.3	1.0	1.2	--	--	1.6	1.5	2.0	1.9	1.8	1.6
Goods Shipped	0.3	0.2	0.4	--	--	0.4	0.3	0.4	0.4	0.4	0.3
Domestic Trade											
Inventories on Hand	3.3	3.5	3.5	1.7	2.0	2.5	2.1	3.0	4.7	6.4	6.8
Goods Shipped	0.3	0.4	0.5	0.2	0.3	0.3	0.3	0.4	0.6	0.7	0.7
Contract Construction											
Inventories on Hand	1.6	2.1	2.1	0.9	1.3	1.4	2.4	2.5	2.9	3.2	2.8
Other Nonagricultural Sectors											
Inventories on Hand	1.0	1.2	1.4	--	--	1.1	2.0	2.2	1.3	1.5	2.1
Goods Shipped	0.1	0.1	0.2	--	--	0.1	0.2	0.2	0.1	0.2	0.2
Uninstalled Equipment, n.e.c.											
Inventories on Hand	0.5	0.5	0.5	--	0.3	0.5	0.6	0.7	0.9	1.1	1.4
Total Nonagricultural Sectors											
Inventories on Hand	40.3	44.0	44.6	39.5	40.2	41.0	44.3	50.5	49.4	57.0	62.3
Goods Shipped	6.4	7.7	10.2	7.9	8.0	8.0	7.9	8.8	8.5	9.7	10.3
Total	46.7	51.7	54.8	47.4	48.2	49.0	52.2	59.3	57.9	66.7	72.6
Agriculture											
Inventories on Hand	5.1	5.4	6.2	--	3.7	4.2	4.6	5.9	6.5	6.6	6.5
Total											
Inventories on Hand	45.4	49.4	50.8	43.2	43.9	45.2	48.9	56.4	55.9	63.6	68.8
Goods Shipped	6.4	7.7	10.2	7.9	8.0	8.0	7.9	8.8	8.5	9.7	10.3
Total	51.8	57.1	61.0	51.1	51.9	53.2	56.8	65.2	64.4	73.3	79.1

TABLE M-1 (concluded)

INVENTORIES IN 1928 PREVAILING PRICES, BY SECTORS, 1928-62
(January 1--Billion Rubles)

	1952	1953	1954	1955	1956	1957	1958	1959	1960	1961	1962
Producer Goods Industries											
Inventories on Hand	41.7	47.7	52.3	52.4	48.9	50.3	54.7	61.4	66.4	73.9	84.2
Goods Shipped	7.5	8.4	9.1	9.1	8.7	9.2	9.2	10.1	11.3	12.2	13.7
Consumer Goods Industries											
Inventories on Hand	9.6	10.0	11.3	11.1	11.9	14.0	15.3	18.0	19.1	20.4	21.0
Goods Shipped	2.4	2.4	2.7	2.6	3.1	3.5	3.6	4.3	4.4	4.7	5.0
Transportation and Communications											
Inventories on Hand	2.1	2.0	2.4	2.0	2.5	2.3	2.6	2.9	3.2	3.3	3.9
Procurement											
Inventories on Hand	1.7	2.0	1.0	0.9	0.9	1.6	1.3	1.7	3.5	4.1	4.5
Goods Shipped	0.3	0.4	0.2	0.2	0.2	0.4	0.3	0.3	0.5	0.6	0.6
Domestic Trade											
Inventories on Hand	8.3	10.1	10.7	10.1	11.1	13.1	13.8	17.3	20.2	21.2	24.2
Goods Shipped	0.8	0.9	0.8	0.7	0.7	0.8	0.7	0.9	0.9	0.9	1.1
Contract Construction											
Inventories on Hand	3.9	4.3	5.2	5.0	5.7	6.3	7.1	7.1	8.3	9.1	9.7
Other Nonagricultural Sectors											
Inventories on Hand	2.7	2.2	1.4	1.8	1.9	2.9	3.7	4.0	5.5	5.9	6.6
Goods Shipped	0.3	0.2	0.2	0.2	0.2	0.3	0.4	0.4	0.6	0.7	0.6
Uninstalled Equipment, n.e.c.											
Inventories on Hand	1.7	1.9	2.2	2.5	2.9	3.4	3.7	3.6	3.9	4.3	4.6
Total Nonagricultural Sectors											
Inventories on Hand	71.7	80.2	86.5	85.8	85.8	93.9	102.2	116.0	130.1	142.2	158.7
Goods Shipped	11.3	12.3	13.0	12.8	12.9	14.2	14.2	16.0	17.7	19.1	21.0
Total	83.0	92.5	99.5	98.6	98.7	108.1	116.4	132.0	147.8	161.3	179.7
Agriculture											
Inventories on Hand	6.2	6.6	6.8	7.0	7.8	9.0	9.0	10.0	10.1	10.2	10.5
Total											
Inventories on Hand	77.9	86.8	93.3	92.8	93.6	102.9	111.2	126.0	140.2	152.4	169.2
Goods Shipped	11.3	12.3	13.0	12.8	12.9	14.2	14.2	16.0	17.7	19.1	21.0
Total	89.2	99.1	106.3	105.6	106.5	117.1	125.4	142.0	157.9	171.5	190.2

TABLE M-2

INVENTORIES IN 1950 PREVAILING PRICES, BY SECTORS, 1928-62

(January 1--Billion Rubles)

	1928	1929	1930	1931	1932	1933	1934	1935	1936	1937	1938
Producer Goods Industries											
Inventories on Hand	11.7	13.6	16.4	20.1	27.8	34.7	40.3	49.5	62.0	62.0	67.9
Goods Shipped	2.0	2.3	2.7	3.4	4.6	5.8	7.0	8.0	11.2	11.4	12.2
Consumer Goods Industries											
Inventories on Hand	35.9	34.5	29.2	34.0	39.8	36.3	36.6	34.5	43.2	45.1	48.0
Goods Shipped	8.0	7.6	6.5	7.5	8.9	8.1	9.2	7.1	11.0	11.5	12.0
Transportation and Communications											
Inventories on Hand	3.4	3.7	3.9	6.3	8.8	8.8	8.1	8.8	11.2	7.6	7.3
Procurement											
Inventories on Hand	1.9	2.6	3.1	4.1	5.0	5.0	5.2	6.1	7.0	4.6	5.4
Goods Shipped	0.2	0.2	0.2	0.3	0.4	0.4	1.0	0.9	1.3	0.9	1.1
Domestic Trade											
Inventories on Hand	39.6	40.7	39.9	35.9	31.8	21.9	21.7	24.8	25.4	31.8	38.2
Goods Shipped	4.0	4.2	4.0	3.5	3.0	2.2	2.2	2.1	2.5	3.2	3.7
Contract Construction											
Inventories on Hand	0.3	0.3	0.6	2.4	3.3	3.0	1.8	2.1	3.0	5.0	6.2
Other Nonagricultural Sectors											
Inventories on Hand	2.0	2.1	2.1	5.4	8.8	6.5	6.6	5.9	5.2	4.9	5.2
Goods Shipped	0.1	0.1	0.2	0.4	0.6	0.4	0.8	0.7	0.6	0.5	0.5
Uninstalled Equipment, n.e.c.											
Inventories on Hand	0.4	0.5	0.7	1.2	1.5	1.5	1.5	1.5	1.4	1.4	1.6
Total Nonagricultural Sectors											
Inventories on Hand	95.2	98.0	95.9	109.4	126.8	117.7	121.8	133.2	158.4	162.4	180.0
Goods Shipped	14.3	14.4	13.6	15.1	17.5	16.9	20.2	18.8	26.6	27.5	29.5
Total	109.5	112.4	109.5	124.5	144.3	134.6	142.0	152.0	185.0	189.9	209.5
Agriculture											
Inventories on Hand	24.0	24.6	23.0	21.7	19.8	17.8	19.4	20.6	24.4	21.9	26.7
Total											
Inventories on Hand	119.2	122.6	118.9	131.1	146.6	135.5	141.2	153.8	182.8	184.3	206.7
Goods Shipped	14.3	14.4	13.6	15.1	17.5	16.9	20.2	18.8	26.6	27.5	29.5
Total	133.5	137.0	132.5	146.2	164.1	152.4	161.4	172.6	209.4	211.8	236.2

TABLE M-2 (continued)

INVENTORIES IN 1950 PREVAILING PRICES, BY SECTORS, 1928-62

(January 1--Billion Rubles)

	1939	1940	1941	1944	1945	1946	1947	1948	1949	1950	1951
Producer Goods Industries											
Inventories on Hand	74.2	77.7	85.0	--	--	87.3	92.7	104.7	94.9	103.6	114.3
Goods Shipped	12.4	14.5	20.7	--	--	18.7	18.7	20.7	18.4	19.5	21.0
Consumer Goods Industries											
Inventories on Hand	56.8	66.4	50.8	--	--	28.0	25.2	26.3	37.5	54.0	60.1
Goods Shipped	13.4	17.7	18.1	--	--	8.6	7.5	7.5	10.5	14.6	15.8
Transportation and Communications											
Inventories on Hand	6.6	8.8	7.5	--	--	7.8	9.0	9.9	6.1	6.1	6.8
Procurement											
Inventories on Hand	6.5	5.2	5.9	--	--	8.0	7.5	10.1	9.8	9.0	8.3
Goods Shipped	1.3	1.1	1.7	--	--	1.9	1.7	2.2	2.1	1.9	1.7
Domestic Trade											
Inventories on Hand	36.7	38.6	38.6	17.5	21.5	26.7	21.5	31.0	48.4	64.6	68.7
Goods Shipped	3.5	4.0	5.3	2.4	2.9	3.6	2.8	4.0	5.7	7.1	6.9
Contract Construction											
Inventories on Hand	6.5	8.3	8.6	3.5	5.0	5.5	9.6	9.9	11.3	12.4	11.0
Other Nonagricultural Sectors											
Inventories on Hand	5.0	6.0	6.3	--	--	4.6	7.7	8.7	5.6	7.1	9.6
Goods Shipped	0.5	0.6	0.8	--	--	0.5	0.8	0.9	0.6	0.7	1.1
Uninstalled Equipment, n.e.c.											
Inventories on Hand	1.6	1.6	1.6	--	0.7	1.0	1.3	1.6	2.1	2.6	3.3
Total Nonagricultural Sectors											
Inventories on Hand	193.9	212.6	204.3	157.4	162.9	168.9	174.5	202.2	215.7	259.4	282.1
Goods Shipped	31.1	37.9	46.6	32.1	32.6	33.3	31.5	35.3	37.3	43.8	46.5
Total	225.0	250.5	250.9	189.5	195.5	202.1	206.0	237.5	253.0	303.2	328.6
Agriculture											
Inventories on Hand	24.6	26.0	29.5	--	17.4	19.9	21.9	27.9	30.8	31.5	31.2
Total											
Inventories on Hand	218.5	238.6	233.8	174.8	180.3	188.8	196.4	230.1	246.5	290.9	313.3
Goods Shipped	31.1	37.9	46.6	32.1	32.6	33.3	31.5	35.3	37.3	43.8	46.5
Total	249.6	276.5	280.4	206.9	212.9	222.1	227.9	265.4	283.8	334.7	359.8

TABLE M-2 (concluded)

INVENTORIES IN 1950 PREVAILING PRICES, BY SECTORS, 1928-62

(January 1--Billion Rubles)

	1952	1953	1954	1955	1956	1957	1958	1959	1960	1961	1962
Producer Goods Industries											
Inventories on Hand	127.9	146.4	160.5	161.0	150.1	154.5	168.1	188.4	203.8	227.1	258.7
Goods Shipped	23.1	25.8	27.9	27.9	26.8	28.3	28.4	31.1	34.6	37.4	42.0
Consumer Goods Industries											
Inventories on Hand	67.2	70.1	78.9	77.6	83.1	97.5	106.5	125.5	133.3	142.3	146.7
Goods Shipped	17.1	17.0	18.8	18.3	21.3	24.4	24.9	30.1	31.0	32.8	34.7
Transportation and Communications											
Inventories on Hand	7.7	7.3	9.0	7.5	9.2	8.5	9.4	10.6	11.9	12.1	14.5
Procurement											
Inventories on Hand	8.5	10.0	4.9	4.5	4.7	8.1	6.6	8.6	17.7	20.5	22.9
Goods Shipped	1.7	2.1	1.1	1.1	1.1	1.9	1.4	1.6	2.6	3.0	3.3
Domestic Trade											
Inventories on Hand	84.4	102.4	109.1	102.9	112.9	133.1	140.1	176.0	205.6	215.4	246.2
Goods Shipped	7.8	8.7	8.4	7.1	7.0	7.9	7.6	8.8	9.0	9.5	10.8
Contract Construction											
Inventories on Hand	15.3	17.1	20.5	19.7	22.5	24.9	27.7	28.0	32.7	35.5	38.1
Other Nonagricultural Sectors											
Inventories on Hand	12.4	10.1	6.5	8.3	9.3	14.1	18.0	20.2	27.9	29.5	33.1
Goods Shipped	1.4	1.1	0.8	1.0	1.1	1.6	2.0	2.2	3.1	3.3	3.1
Uninstalled Equipment, n.e.c.											
Inventories on Hand	4.3	5.0	5.7	6.3	7.0	7.9	8.7	8.6	9.1	10.0	10.7
Total Nonagricultural Sectors											
Inventories on Hand	327.7	368.4	395.1	387.8	398.8	448.6	485.1	565.9	642.0	692.4	770.9
Goods Shipped	51.1	54.7	57.0	55.4	57.3	64.1	64.3	73.8	80.3	86.0	93.9
Total	378.8	423.1	452.1	443.2	456.1	512.7	549.4	639.7	722.3	778.4	864.8
Agriculture											
Inventories on Hand	29.4	31.5	32.6	33.5	37.4	43.1	43.1	47.7	48.2	48.8	50.2
Total											
Inventories on Hand	357.1	399.9	427.7	421.3	436.2	491.7	528.2	613.6	690.2	741.2	821.1
Goods Shipped	51.1	54.7	57.0	55.4	57.3	64.1	64.3	73.8	80.3	86.0	93.9
Total	408.2	454.6	484.7	476.7	493.5	555.8	592.5	687.4	770.5	827.2	915.0

and set each series equal to its weight-year value so determined. For 1928, the mid-year value is computed as the average of the year-end values. For mid-1950, because of the timing of the change in retail prices of that year, we first deflate the January 1, 1950 and 1951, values to 1950 average prices with the index of retail prices (the index used is that with given-year weights shown for January 1 in Table L–6 and for 1950 average in Table M–3). There are some slight imprecisions in this latter operation, but they are of minor consequence.

(*ii*) Inventories in "other nonagricultural sectors" are computed as in 1937 prices from their ratio to inventories in other specified sectors in current prices (see the discussion in Appendix L).

(*iii*) Uninstalled equipment, n.e.c., is estimated as in 1937 prices (and with the same error) from the Table E–1 series for fixed capital investment projects in progress.

(*iv*) Inventories in agriculture in 1928 and 1950 prices are assumed to move with the 1937-price series. The latter, as is explained in Appendix L, is estimated from agricultural output in 1937 prices. Since measures of agricultural output appear relatively insensitive to price weights (cf. the Table P–1 series in 1937 prices with series in prices from the late 1920's and 1958 prices shown in Johnson–59, p. 204; note, however, that the former is and the latter are not adjusted for changes in livestock herds) and since, in any case, our estimates for agricultural inventories are rough, allowance for the effects of different price weights appears uncalled for.

(*v*) Totals for 1944 and 1945 are obtained as in the 1937 prevailing price estimates, by extension from 1946.

The derivation of the Table M–3 indexes is described below. Those labeled as component indexes are indexes which are combined to obtain the sector deflators. The weight-year attributions in some cases represent our assumptions rather than a literal description of the weights employed.

Basic Industrial Prices, including Petroleum

The index with 1937 weights is from Bergson–55, p. 69a. The index with given-year weights is assumed the same as with 1937 weights: see the notes for Table L–2.

Basic Industrial Prices, excluding Petroleum

The index with 1937 weights is from Bergson–56, p. 322; 1937 is set equal to 100. The index with given-year weights is assumed the same.

Machinery Prices

Both indexes are from Moorsteen–62, p. 72. 1928 is assumed the same as 1927/28.

This index is used in part as a deflator for small tools. It is undoubtedly true that a price index for small tools, if it were available, would show less sensitivity to the weights used than does the index of machinery prices. We do, however, combine the machinery price index with the basic industrial price index in deflating small tools, and our procedures elsewhere very probably understate the effects of weight changes on the deflators.

Agricultural Procurement Prices

The index with given-year weights is from Table L–5. The index with 1937 weights for 1928 is from Karcz–57a; that for 1950 is interpolated between Karcz's 1948 and 1952 figures on the Table L–5 index with given-year weights.

Agricultural Procurement Prices, excluding Grain

The index with given-year weights is from Table L–3. The adjustment for subsidies, referred to in the latter table, does not affect the dates under consideration here. The index with 1937 weights is derived from Karcz–57a in the same manner as for all procurement prices.

Retail Prices

Both figures for 1928 are from Chapman–59; that for 1950 with given-year weights is from Bergson–61, p. 416. Neither Chapman nor Bergson provides a 1950 figure with 1937 weights. However, the Chapman index for 1948 with 1937 weights is 109.8 percent of that with 1948 weights, and the similar ratio for 1952 is 108.0 percent. We assume the 1950 ratio was the average of those for 1948 and 1952.

Average of Retail Prices Adjusted and Unadjusted for Turnover Tax

The given-year weighted index is from Bergson–61, p. 416, where it is entitled "prices of industrial inventories of finished consumers' goods." The 1937-weighted index is computed from the unadjusted retail price index on the assumption that with 1937 weights it differs from its unadjusted counterpart by the same percentage as with given-year weights.

Retail Prices of Grain Products

Both figures for 1928 are from Chapman–59. The 1950 figure with given-year weights is computed from the Table L–3 figures for January 1, 1950 and 1951, with weights of 2/12 and 10/12 respectively (prices were changed on March 1, 1950; see TsSU–56, p. 132). Data are unavailable for calculation of a 1950 figure with 1937 weights, and it is therefore assumed the same as that with given-year weights.

Construction Materials Prices

All figures are from Powell–59, p. 80.

SECTOR DEFLATORS

Producer Goods Industries

The derivation of the given-year weighted index, which is the average of basic industrial prices (excluding petroleum) and machinery prices, is explained in the discussion of this sector in Appendix L. We there also estimate 1937 weights of 2/3 and 1/3 respectively for the two component indexes. The sector deflator with 1937 weights is obtained by weighting the two components, each with 1937 weights, in this ratio.

Consumer Goods Industries

The figure for 1928 with given-year weights is the average of the Table L–3 figures for January 1, 1928 and 1929. The figure for 1950 with given-year weights (the timing of changes in retail prices in this year forestalls averaging of the year's termini) and both figures with 1937 weights are

DERIVATION OF DEFLATORS, TO 1928 AND 1950 PRICES, OF INVENTORIES IN COMPONENT SECTORS,
1928 AND 1950 RELATIVE TO 1937
(1937 Average = 100)

	Given-Year Weights		1937 Weights	
	1928 Average	1950 Average	1928 Average	1950 Average
Component Price Indexes				
Basic Industrial Prices, Including Petroleum	45.0	256	45.0	256
Basic Industrial Prices, Excluding Petroleum	57.1	318	57.1	318
Machinery Prices	70	191	141	197
Agricultural Procurement Prices	31.5	161	33.1	158
Agricultural Procurement Prices, Excluding Grain	20.6	171	21.9	169
Retail Prices	11.5	222	16.8	242
Average of Retail Prices Adjusted and Unadjusted for Turnover Tax	14	210	20.4	229
Retail Prices of Grain Products	8.5	185	11.7	185
Construction Materials Prices	60.4	304	62.1	316
Sector Deflators				
Producer Goods Industries	59.0	261	85.0	278
Consumer Goods Industries	21.1	221	31.7	230
Transportation and Communications	50.5	242	65.6	244
Procurement	35.9	188	37.2	185
Domestic Trade	11.5	222	16.8	242
Contract Construction	61.2	289	73.6	242
Agriculture	37.3	178	--	--

computed averages of the indexes of basic industrial prices, machinery prices, agricultural procurement prices excluding grain, average of retail prices adjusted and unadjusted for turnover tax, and retail prices of grain products. Component indexes with given-year weights are used for the 1950 given-year weighted calculations; components with 1937 weights for the 1937-weighted calculations. The components are combined in all three cases with the 1937 weights computed in the notes for Table L–3. It is pointed out there that 1937 weights yield a figure for January 1, 1951, which differs insignificantly from one computed with weights from the latter date. We assume the same would be true for the 1950 annual average. The 1937 weights are conceptually appropriate for the 1937-weighted index.

Transportation and Communications

The indexes are weighted averages of basic industrial prices, including petroleum, and machinery prices. The weights are those for January 1, 1951, given in the Appendix L discussion of this sector. Component indexes for January 1, 1951, are from Table L–4 (for basic industrial prices), Table L–2 (for machinery prices with given-year weights), and Moorsteen–62, p. 72 (for machinery prices with 1937 weights; the index for 1951 average, 192, is taken as that for the beginning of the year also).

Procurement

For the index with given-year weights, annual averages are computed as for January 1 dates by combining the indexes of basic industrial (excluding petroleum) and procurement prices with quantity weights of January 1, 1951 (see the discussion of this sector in Appendix L). For the index with 1937 weights, we again combine the two component indexes with weights of January 1, 1951, but use the 1937-weighted variants of the components. The index of basic industrial prices on January 1, 1951, is given in Table L–2; that of procurement prices is assumed the same as the 1950 average on the basis of the behavior of procurement prices with given-year weights (see Table L–5).

Domestic Trade

The sector deflators are the same as the retail price indexes.

Contract Construction

The indexes are weighted averages of basic industrial prices (excluding petroleum), machinery prices, and prices of construction materials. The weights are those for January 1, 1951, derived in the discussion of this sector in Appendix L. The sources for January 1, 1951, values of the basic materials and machinery indexes are identified in the discussion above of the deflator for transportation and communications. Values for the construction materials price index are given in Powell–59, p. 80.

Agriculture

The index nominally composed with given-year weights is the average of the given-year weighted indexes of basic industrial prices (including petroleum), machinery prices, and procurement prices, combined with

1937 weights of 15 percent, 10 percent, and 75 percent respectively. The basic industrial price index inclusive of petroleum is chosen because agriculture is a large purchaser of petroleum products (cf. Kaplan–52, p. 7, and TsSU–61, p. 137). The procurement price index is deficient for present purposes in that it is likely to be a poor measure of production costs in agriculture, but we have no superior alternative. The weights are essentially guesses, based on the material relating to January 1, 1938, which is discussed in Appendix L, and on our supposition that inventories of non-agricultural origin other than small tools are unlikely to be large. Evidence that bears on the reliability of the sector deflator is discussed in Appendix L.

Since we estimate agricultural inventories in 1928 and 1950 prices on the assumption that they move with those in 1937 prices (see above), we do not compose a deflator using the 1937-weighted component indexes.

Inventories in 1937, 1928,

and 1950 Factor Costs

The estimates at factor cost valuations in the prices of all three weight years (Tables N–1, N–2, and N–3) are derived from the corresponding estimates in prevailing prices (Tables L–1, M–1, and M–2). Inventories in all sectors except consumer goods industries and domestic trade are assumed the same at factor cost as at prevailing prices, and entries are repeated in the tables. This assumption is not precisely accurate. However, the incidence of turnover taxes, which largely account for the difference between prevailing prices and factor costs, is principally upon consumer goods, as can be seen from Bergson's calculations of the distribution of GNP by use (see Bergson–61, pp. 130, 150, and 154). The single category of producer goods on which a large turnover tax is levied, petroleum products, appears to be a large input for the sectors considered here only in transportation and in agriculture (see the Appendix L discussion of these sectors). Total inventories in transportation are small. The amount of inventories in agriculture which would include petroleum products is thought to be small.

For domestic trade, we take the ratio of inventories on hand and goods shipped at factor cost to their values in prevailing prices to be that estimated by Bergson for annual investment in inventories in domestic trade: 54 percent in 1937, 78 percent in 1928, and 43 percent in 1950 (see Bergson–61, *loc. cit.*). For consumer goods industries, we assume that the comparable ratios lay midway between those for domestic trade and 100 percent: 77 percent in 1937, 89 percent in 1928, and 71 percent in 1950. The latter ratios are undoubtedly subject to considerable error, but the assumption made in their derivation is essentially the same as that made in obtaining deflators for the same sector (see Appendix L).

Total figures are sums of components, except that those for 1944 and 1945 are derived from 1946 by the same procedures as in the estimates in prevailing prices.

Scattered bits of evidence appear in Soviet sources which bear on—and in the main support—the plausibility of our constant-price estimates and which have not been employed in their derivation. We have not searched the sources systematically for evidence which could not be incorporated

TABLE N-1

INVENTORIES IN 1937 FACTOR COSTS, BY SECTORS, 1928-62

(January 1--Billion Rubles)

	1928	1929	1930	1931	1932	1933	1934	1935	1936	1937	1938
Producer Goods Industries											
Inventories on Hand	4.2	4.9	5.9	7.2	10.0	12.5	14.5	17.8	22.3	22.3	24.5
Goods Shipped	0.7	0.8	1.0	1.2	1.7	2.1	2.5	2.9	4.0	4.1	4.4
Consumer Goods Industries											
Inventories on Hand	12.0	11.5	9.8	11.4	13.3	12.2	12.2	11.5	14.5	15.1	16.2
Goods Shipped	2.7	2.5	2.2	2.5	3.0	2.7	3.1	2.4	3.7	3.9	4.0
Transportation and Communications											
Inventories on Hand	1.4	1.5	1.6	2.6	3.6	3.6	3.3	3.6	4.6	3.1	3.0
Procurement											
Inventories on Hand	1.0	1.4	1.7	2.2	2.7	2.7	2.8	3.3	3.8	2.5	2.9
Goods Shipped	0.1	0.1	0.1	0.2	0.2	0.2	0.5	0.5	0.7	0.5	0.6
Domestic Trade											
Inventories on Hand	11.0	11.3	11.1	10.0	8.9	6.1	6.0	6.9	7.1	8.9	10.7
Goods Shipped	1.1	1.2	1.0	1.0	0.8	0.6	0.6	0.6	0.7	0.9	1.0
Contract Construction											
Inventories on Hand	0.1	0.1	0.2	0.8	1.1	1.0	0.6	0.7	1.0	1.7	2.1
Other Nonagricultural Sectors											
Inventories on Hand	0.9	1.0	1.0	2.4	3.9	2.8	2.8	2.5	2.2	2.1	2.2
Goods Shipped	0.0	0.0	0.1	0.2	0.3	0.2	0.3	0.3	0.2	0.2	0.2
Uninstalled Equipment, n.e.c.											
Inventories on Hand	0.1	0.2	0.3	0.5	0.6	0.6	0.6	0.6	0.6	0.6	0.6
Total Nonagricultural Sectors											
Inventories on Hand	30.7	31.9	31.6	37.1	44.1	41.5	42.8	46.9	56.1	56.3	62.2
Goods Shipped	4.6	4.6	4.6	5.1	6.0	5.8	7.0	6.7	9.3	9.6	10.2
Total	35.3	36.5	36.2	42.2	50.1	47.3	49.8	53.6	65.4	65.9	72.4
Agriculture											
Inventories on Hand	13.5	13.8	12.9	12.2	11.1	10.0	10.9	11.6	13.7	12.3	15.0
Total											
Inventories on Hand	44.2	45.7	44.5	49.3	55.2	51.5	53.8	58.5	69.8	68.6	77.2
Goods Shipped	4.6	4.6	4.6	5.1	6.0	5.8	7.0	6.7	9.3	9.6	10.2
Total	48.8	50.3	49.1	54.4	61.2	57.3	60.8	65.2	79.1	78.2	87.4

TABLE N-1 (continued)

INVENTORIES IN 1937 FACTOR COSTS, BY SECTORS, 1928-62

(January 1--Billion Rubles)

	1939	1940	1941	1944	1945	1946	1947	1948	1949	1950	1951
Producer Goods Industries											
Inventories on Hand	26.9	28.3	31.1	--	--	32.7	34.9	39.6	36.1	39.6	43.8
Goods Shipped	4.5	5.3	7.6	--	--	7.0	7.0	7.8	7.0	7.4	8.1
Consumer Goods Industries											
Inventories on Hand	19.1	22.4	17.2	--	--	9.6	8.7	9.1	13.0	18.8	20.9
Goods Shipped	4.5	5.9	6.1	--	--	2.9	2.6	2.6	3.6	5.1	5.5
Transportation and Communications											
Inventories on Hand	2.7	3.6	3.1	--	--	3.2	3.7	4.1	2.5	2.5	2.8
Procurement											
Inventories on Hand	3.5	2.8	3.2	--	--	4.3	4.0	5.4	5.2	4.8	4.4
Goods Shipped	0.7	0.6	0.9	--	--	1.0	0.9	1.2	1.1	1.0	0.9
Domestic Trade											
Inventories on Hand	10.3	10.9	11.0	5.1	6.3	7.8	6.4	9.2	14.5	19.5	20.8
Goods Shipped	1.0	1.1	1.5	0.7	0.9	1.0	0.8	1.2	1.7	2.2	2.1
Contract Construction											
Inventories on Hand	2.2	2.8	2.9	1.2	1.7	1.9	3.3	3.4	3.9	4.3	3.8
Other Nonagricultural Sectors											
Inventories on Hand	2.1	2.6	2.7	--	--	2.0	3.3	3.7	2.5	3.2	4.4
Goods Shipped	0.2	0.3	0.3	--	--	0.2	0.3	0.4	0.3	0.3	0.5
Uninstalled Equipment, n.e.c.											
Inventories on Hand	0.6	0.6	0.6	--	0.3	0.5	0.6	0.8	0.9	1.2	1.5
Total Nonagricultural Sectors											
Inventories on Hand	67.4	74.0	71.8	58.4	60.1	62.0	64.9	75.3	78.6	93.9	102.4
Goods Shipped	10.9	13.2	16.4	14.3	14.5	14.6	14.4	13.2	13.7	16.6	17.8
Total	78.3	87.2	88.2	72.7	74.6	76.6	79.3	88.5	92.3	110.5	120.2
Agriculture											
Inventories on Hand	13.8	14.6	16.6	--	9.8	11.2	12.3	15.7	17.3	17.7	17.5
Total											
Inventories on Hand	81.2	88.6	88.4	68.2	69.9	73.2	77.2	91.0	95.9	111.6	119.9
Goods Shipped	10.9	13.2	16.4	14.3	14.5	14.6	14.4	13.2	13.7	16.6	17.8
Total	92.1	101.8	104.8	82.5	84.4	87.8	91.6	104.2	109.6	128.2	137.7

TABLE N-1 (concluded)

INVENTORIES IN 1937 FACTOR COSTS, BY SECTORS, 1928-62

(January 1--Billion Rubles)

	1952	1953	1954	1955	1956	1957	1958	1959	1960	1961	1962
Producer Goods Industries											
Inventories on Hand	49.0	56.1	61.5	61.7	57.5	59.2	64.4	72.2	78.1	87.0	99.1
Goods Shipped	8.8	9.9	10.7	10.7	10.2	10.9	10.9	11.9	13.3	14.4	16.1
Consumer Goods Industries											
Inventories on Hand	23.4	24.4	27.5	27.0	29.0	34.0	37.1	43.7	46.4	49.6	51.1
Goods Shipped	5.9	5.9	6.5	6.4	7.4	8.5	8.7	10.5	10.8	11.4	12.1
Transportation and Communications											
Inventories on Hand	3.2	3.0	3.7	3.1	3.8	3.5	3.9	4.4	4.9	5.0	6.0
Procurement											
Inventories on Hand	4.5	5.3	2.6	2.4	2.5	4.3	3.5	4.6	9.4	10.9	12.2
Goods Shipped	0.9	1.1	0.6	0.6	0.6	1.0	0.7	0.8	1.4	1.6	1.7
Domestic Trade											
Inventories on Hand	25.6	31.1	33.1	31.2	34.2	40.4	42.5	53.4	62.4	65.3	74.7
Goods Shipped	2.4	2.6	2.5	2.2	2.1	2.4	2.3	2.6	2.8	2.9	3.3
Contract Construction											
Inventories on Hand	5.3	5.9	7.1	6.8	7.8	8.6	9.6	9.7	11.3	12.3	13.2
Other Nonagricultural Sectors											
Inventories on Hand	5.6	4.6	2.9	3.8	4.3	6.5	8.3	9.4	13.1	13.8	15.5
Goods Shipped	0.6	0.5	0.3	0.4	0.5	0.7	0.9	1.0	1.4	1.5	1.5
Uninstalled Equipment, n.e.c.											
Inventories on Hand	1.9	2.2	2.5	2.8	3.2	3.6	4.0	3.9	4.2	4.6	4.9
Total Nonagricultural Sectors											
Inventories on Hand	118.5	132.6	140.9	138.8	142.3	160.1	173.3	201.3	229.8	248.5	276.7
Goods Shipped	19.5	20.0	20.6	20.3	20.8	23.5	23.5	26.8	29.7	31.8	34.7
Total	138.0	152.6	161.5	159.1	163.1	183.6	196.8	228.1	259.5	280.3	311.4
Agriculture											
Inventories on Hand	16.5	17.7	18.3	18.8	21.0	24.2	24.2	26.8	27.1	27.4	28.2
Total											
Inventories on Hand	135.0	150.3	159.2	157.6	163.3	184.3	197.5	228.1	256.9	275.9	304.9
Goods Shipped	19.5	20.0	20.6	20.3	20.8	23.5	23.5	26.8	29.7	31.8	34.7
Total	154.5	170.3	179.8	177.9	184.1	207.8	221.0	254.9	286.6	307.7	339.6

TABLE N-2

INVENTORIES IN 1928 FACTOR COSTS, BY SECTORS, 1928-62

(January 1--Billion Rubles)

	1928	1929	1930	1931	1932	1933	1934	1935	1936	1937	1938
Producer Goods Industries											
Inventories on Hand	2.5	3.0	3.7	4.8	6.9	9.0	10.9	13.8	18.0	18.6	20.8
Goods Shipped	0.4	0.5	0.6	0.8	1.1	1.5	1.9	2.2	3.3	3.4	3.7
Consumer Goods Industries											
Inventories on Hand	2.9	2.9	2.6	3.2	3.9	3.7	3.9	3.8	5.0	5.4	6.0
Goods Shipped	0.6	0.6	0.6	0.7	0.9	0.9	1.0	0.8	1.2	1.4	1.5
Transportation and Communications											
Inventories on Hand	0.7	0.8	0.8	1.4	2.0	2.1	2.0	2.2	2.9	2.0	2.0
Procurement											
Inventories on Hand	0.4	0.5	0.6	0.8	1.0	1.0	1.0	1.2	1.4	0.9	1.1
Goods Shipped	0.0	0.0	0.0	0.1	0.1	0.1	0.2	0.2	0.3	0.2	0.2
Domestic Trade											
Inventories on Hand	1.9	2.0	2.1	1.9	1.8	1.3	1.3	1.6	1.7	2.2	2.7
Goods Shipped	0.2	0.2	0.2	0.2	0.2	0.1	0.1	0.1	0.2	0.2	0.2
Contract Construction											
Inventories on Hand	0.1	0.1	0.1	0.5	0.7	0.7	0.4	0.5	0.7	1.2	1.5
Other Nonagricultural Sectors											
Inventories on Hand	0.2	0.2	0.2	0.7	1.3	1.1	1.2	1.1	1.1	1.0	1.1
Goods Shipped	0.0	0.0	0.0	0.1	0.1	0.1	0.1	0.1	0.1	0.1	0.1
Uninstalled Equipment, n.e.c.											
Inventories on Hand	0.1	0.1	0.2	0.3	0.4	0.4	0.4	0.5	0.4	0.5	0.5
Total Nonagricultural Sectors											
Inventories on Hand	8.8	9.6	10.3	13.6	18.0	19.3	21.1	24.7	31.2	31.8	35.7
Goods Shipped	1.2	1.3	1.4	1.9	2.4	2.7	3.3	3.3	5.1	5.3	5.7
Total	10.0	10.9	11.7	15.5	20.4	22.0	24.4	28.0	36.3	37.1	41.4
Agriculture											
Inventories on Hand	5.0	5.1	4.8	4.6	4.1	3.7	4.1	4.3	5.1	4.6	5.6
Total											
Inventories on Hand	13.8	14.7	15.1	18.2	22.1	23.0	25.2	29.0	36.3	36.4	41.3
Goods Shipped	1.2	1.3	1.4	1.9	2.4	2.7	3.3	3.3	5.1	5.3	5.7
Total	15.0	16.0	16.5	20.1	24.5	25.7	28.5	32.3	41.4	41.7	47.0

TABLE N-2 (continued)

INVENTORIES IN 1928 FACTOR COSTS, BY SECTORS, 1928-62

(January 1--Billion Rubles)

	1939	1940	1941	1944	1945	1946	1947	1948	1949	1950	1951
Producer Goods Industries											
Inventories on Hand	22.9	24.1	26.4	--	--	27.8	29.7	33.7	30.7	33.7	37.2
Goods Shipped	3.8	4.5	6.4	--	--	6.0	6.0	6.7	5.9	6.3	6.8
Consumer Goods Industries											
Inventories on Hand	7.0	8.2	6.7	--	--	3.6	3.2	3.3	4.8	6.9	7.7
Goods Shipped	1.7	2.2	2.4	--	--	1.1	1.0	0.9	1.3	1.9	2.0
Transportation and Communications											
Inventories on Hand	1.8	2.4	2.0	--	--	2.1	2.4	2.7	1.6	1.6	1.8
Procurement											
Inventories on Hand	1.3	1.0	1.2	--	--	1.6	1.5	2.0	1.9	1.8	1.6
Goods Shipped	0.3	0.2	0.4	--	--	0.4	0.3	0.4	0.4	0.4	0.3
Domestic Trade											
Inventories on Hand	2.6	2.7	2.7	1.3	1.6	1.9	1.6	2.3	3.7	5.0	5.3
Goods Shipped	0.2	0.3	0.4	0.2	0.2	0.2	0.2	0.3	0.4	0.5	0.5
Contract Construction											
Inventories on Hand	1.6	2.1	2.1	0.9	1.3	1.4	2.4	2.5	2.9	3.2	2.8
Other Nonagricultural Sectors											
Inventories on Hand	1.0	1.2	1.4	--	--	1.1	2.0	2.2	1.3	1.5	2.1
Goods Shipped	0.1	0.1	0.2	--	--	0.1	0.2	0.2	0.1	0.2	0.2
Uninstalled Equipment, n.e.c.											
Inventories on Hand	0.5	0.5	0.5	--	0.3	0.5	0.6	0.7	0.9	1.1	1.4
Total Nonagricultural Sectors											
Inventories on Hand	38.7	42.2	43.0	38.7	39.4	40.0	43.4	49.4	47.8	54.8	59.9
Goods Shipped	6.1	7.3	9.8	7.8	7.8	7.8	7.7	8.5	8.1	9.3	9.8
Total	44.8	49.5	52.8	46.5	47.2	47.8	51.1	57.9	55.9	64.1	69.7
Agriculture											
Inventories on Hand	5.1	5.4	6.2	--	3.7	4.2	4.6	5.9	6.5	6.6	6.5
Total											
Inventories on Hand	43.8	47.6	49.3	42.4	43.1	44.2	48.0	55.3	54.3	61.4	66.4
Goods Shipped	6.1	7.3	9.8	7.8	7.8	7.8	7.7	8.5	8.1	9.3	9.8
Total	49.9	54.9	59.1	50.2	50.9	52.0	55.7	63.8	62.4	70.7	76.2

TABLE N-2 (concluded)

INVENTORIES IN 1928 FACTOR COSTS, BY SECTORS, 1928-62
(January 1--Billion Rubles)

	1952	1953	1954	1955	1956	1957	1958	1959	1960	1961	1962
Producer Goods Industries											
Inventories on Hand	41.7	47.7	52.3	52.4	48.9	50.3	54.7	61.4	66.4	73.9	84.2
Goods Shipped	7.5	8.4	9.1	9.1	8.7	9.2	9.2	10.1	11.3	12.2	13.7
Consumer Goods Industries											
Inventories on Hand	8.5	8.9	10.1	9.9	10.6	12.5	13.6	16.0	17.0	18.2	18.7
Goods Shipped	2.1	2.1	2.4	2.3	2.8	3.1	3.2	3.8	3.9	4.2	4.5
Transportation and Communications											
Inventories on Hand	2.1	2.0	2.4	2.0	2.5	2.3	2.6	2.9	3.2	3.3	3.9
Procurement											
Inventories on Hand	1.7	2.0	1.0	0.9	0.9	1.6	1.3	1.7	3.5	4.1	4.5
Goods Shipped	0.3	0.4	0.2	0.2	0.2	0.4	0.3	0.3	0.5	0.6	0.6
Domestic Trade											
Inventories on Hand	6.5	7.9	8.3	7.9	8.7	10.2	10.8	13.5	15.8	16.5	18.9
Goods Shipped	0.6	0.7	0.6	0.5	0.5	0.6	0.5	0.7	0.7	0.7	0.9
Contract Construction											
Inventories on Hand	3.9	4.3	5.2	5.0	5.7	6.3	7.1	7.1	8.3	9.1	9.7
Other Nonagricultural Sectors											
Inventories on Hand	2.7	2.2	1.4	1.8	1.9	2.9	3.7	4.0	5.5	5.9	6.6
Goods Shipped	0.3	0.2	0.2	0.2	0.2	0.3	0.4	0.4	0.6	0.7	0.6
Uninstalled Equipment, n.e.c.											
Inventories on Hand	1.7	1.9	2.2	2.5	2.9	3.4	3.7	3.6	3.9	4.3	4.6
Total Nonagricultural Sectors											
Inventories on Hand	68.8	76.9	82.9	82.4	82.1	89.5	97.5	110.2	123.6	135.3	151.1
Goods Shipped	10.8	11.8	12.5	12.3	12.4	13.6	13.6	15.3	17.0	18.4	20.3
Total	79.6	88.7	95.4	94.7	94.5	103.1	111.1	125.5	140.6	153.7	171.4
Agriculture											
Inventories on Hand	6.2	6.6	6.8	7.0	7.8	9.0	9.0	10.0	10.1	10.2	10.5
Total											
Inventories on Hand	75.0	83.5	89.7	89.4	89.9	98.5	106.5	120.2	133.7	145.5	161.6
Goods Shipped	10.8	11.8	12.5	12.3	12.4	13.6	13.6	15.3	17.0	18.4	20.3
Total	85.8	95.3	102.2	101.7	102.3	112.1	120.1	135.5	150.7	163.9	181.9

TABLE N-3

INVENTORIES IN 1950 FACTOR COSTS, BY SECTORS, 1928-62

(January 1--Billion Rubles)

	1928	1929	1930	1931	1932	1933	1934	1935	1936	1937	1938
Producer Goods Industries											
Inventories on Hand	11.7	13.6	16.4	20.1	27.8	34.7	40.3	49.5	62.0	62.0	67.9
Goods Shipped	2.0	2.3	2.7	3.4	4.6	5.8	7.0	8.0	11.2	11.4	12.2
Consumer Goods Industries											
Inventories on Hand	25.5	24.5	20.7	24.1	28.3	25.8	26.0	24.5	30.7	32.0	34.2
Goods Shipped	5.7	5.4	4.6	5.3	6.3	5.7	6.5	5.1	7.8	8.2	8.5
Transportation and Communications											
Inventories on Hand	3.4	3.7	3.9	6.3	8.8	8.8	8.1	8.8	11.2	7.6	7.3
Procurement											
Inventories on Hand	1.9	2.6	3.1	4.1	5.0	5.0	5.2	6.1	7.0	4.6	5.4
Goods Shipped	0.2	0.2	0.2	0.3	0.4	0.4	1.0	0.9	1.3	0.9	1.1
Domestic Trade											
Inventories on Hand	17.0	17.5	17.2	15.4	13.7	9.4	9.3	10.7	10.9	13.7	16.4
Goods Shipped	1.7	1.8	1.7	1.5	1.3	1.0	0.9	0.9	1.1	1.4	1.6
Contract Construction											
Inventories on Hand	0.3	0.3	0.6	2.4	3.3	3.0	1.8	2.1	3.0	5.0	6.2
Other Nonagricultural Sectors											
Inventories on Hand	2.0	2.1	2.1	5.4	8.8	6.5	6.6	5.9	5.2	4.9	5.2
Goods Shipped	0.1	0.1	0.2	0.4	0.6	0.4	0.8	0.7	0.6	0.5	0.5
Uninstalled Equipment, n.e.c.											
Inventories on Hand	0.4	0.5	0.7	1.2	1.5	1.5	1.5	1.5	1.4	1.4	1.6
Total Nonagricultural Sectors											
Inventories on Hand	62.2	64.8	64.7	79.0	97.2	94.7	98.8	109.1	131.4	131.2	144.2
Goods Shipped	9.7	9.8	9.4	10.9	13.2	13.3	16.2	15.6	22.0	22.4	23.9
Total	71.9	74.6	74.1	89.9	110.4	108.0	115.0	124.7	153.4	153.6	168.1
Agriculture											
Inventories on Hand	24.0	24.6	23.0	21.7	19.8	17.8	19.4	20.6	24.4	21.9	26.7
Total											
Inventories on Hand	86.2	89.4	87.7	100.7	117.0	110.5	118.2	129.7	155.8	152.2	170.9
Goods Shipped	9.7	9.8	9.4	10.9	13.2	13.3	16.2	15.6	22.0	22.4	23.9
Total	95.9	99.2	97.1	111.6	130.2	123.8	134.4	145.3	177.8	174.6	194.8

TABLE N-3 (continued)

INVENTORIES IN 1950 FACTOR COSTS, BY SECTORS, 1928-62
(January 1--Billion Rubles)

	1939	1940	1941	1944	1945	1946	1947	1948	1949	1950	1951
Producer Goods Industries											
Inventories on Hand	74.2	77.7	85.0	--	--	87.3	92.7	104.7	94.9	103.6	114.3
Goods Shipped	12.4	14.5	20.7	--	--	18.7	18.7	20.7	18.4	19.5	21.0
Consumer Goods Industries											
Inventories on Hand	40.3	47.1	36.1	--	--	19.9	17.9	18.7	26.6	38.3	42.7
Goods Shipped	9.5	12.6	12.9	--	--	6.1	5.3	5.4	7.5	10.4	11.2
Transportation and Communications											
Inventories on Hand	6.6	8.8	7.5	--	--	7.8	9.0	9.9	6.1	6.1	6.8
Procurement											
Inventories on Hand	6.5	5.2	5.9	--	--	8.0	7.5	10.1	9.8	9.0	8.3
Goods Shipped	1.3	1.1	1.7	--	--	1.9	1.7	2.2	2.1	1.9	1.7
Domestic Trade											
Inventories on Hand	15.8	16.6	16.6	7.5	9.2	11.5	9.2	13.3	20.8	27.8	29.5
Goods Shipped	1.5	1.7	2.3	1.0	1.2	1.5	1.2	1.7	2.5	3.1	3.0
Contract Construction											
Inventories on Hand	6.5	8.3	8.6	3.5	5.0	5.5	9.6	9.9	11.3	12.4	11.0
Other Nonagricultural Sectors											
Inventories on Hand	5.0	6.0	6.3	--	--	4.6	7.7	8.7	5.6	7.1	9.6
Goods Shipped	0.5	0.6	0.8	--	--	0.5	0.8	0.9	0.6	0.7	1.1
Uninstalled Equipment, n.e.c.											
Inventories on Hand	1.6	1.6	1.6	--	0.7	1.0	1.3	1.6	2.1	2.6	3.3
Total Nonagricultural Sectors											
Inventories on Hand	156.5	171.3	167.6	139.3	142.5	145.6	154.9	176.9	177.2	206.9	225.2
Goods Shipped	25.2	30.5	38.4	28.2	28.4	28.7	27.7	30.9	31.1	35.6	38.0
Total	181.7	201.8	206.0	167.5	170.9	174.3	182.6	207.8	208.3	242.5	263.5
Agriculture											
Inventories on Hand	24.6	26.0	29.5	--	17.4	19.9	21.9	27.9	30.8	31.5	31.2
Total											
Inventories on Hand	181.1	197.3	197.1	156.7	159.9	165.5	176.8	204.8	208.0	238.4	256.7
Goods Shipped	25.2	30.5	38.4	28.2	28.4	28.7	27.7	30.9	31.1	35.6	38.0
Total	206.3	227.8	235.5	184.9	188.3	194.2	204.5	235.7	239.1	274.0	294.7

TABLE N-3 (concluded)

INVENTORIES IN 1950 FACTOR COSTS, BY SECTORS, 1928-62
(January 1--Billion Rubles)

	1952	1953	1954	1955	1956	1957	1958	1959	1960	1961	1962
Producer Goods Industries											
Inventories on Hand	127.9	146.4	160.5	161.0	150.1	154.5	168.1	188.4	203.8	227.1	258.7
Goods Shipped	23.1	25.8	27.9	27.9	26.8	28.3	28.4	31.1	34.6	37.4	42.0
Consumer Goods Industries											
Inventories on Hand	47.7	49.8	56.0	55.1	59.0	69.2	75.6	89.1	94.6	101.0	104.2
Goods Shipped	12.1	12.1	13.3	13.0	15.1	17.3	17.7	21.4	22.0	23.3	24.6
Transportation and Communications											
Inventories on Hand	7.7	7.3	9.0	7.5	9.2	8.5	9.4	10.6	11.9	12.1	14.5
Procurement											
Inventories on Hand	8.5	10.0	4.9	4.5	4.7	8.1	6.6	8.6	17.7	20.5	22.9
Goods Shipped	1.7	2.1	1.1	1.1	1.1	1.9	1.4	1.6	2.6	3.0	3.3
Domestic Trade											
Inventories on Hand	36.3	44.0	46.9	44.2	48.5	57.2	60.2	75.7	88.4	92.6	105.9
Goods Shipped	3.4	3.7	3.6	3.0	3.0	3.4	3.3	3.8	3.9	4.1	4.6
Contract Construction											
Inventories on Hand	15.3	17.1	20.5	19.7	22.5	24.9	27.7	28.0	32.7	35.5	38.1
Other Nonagricultural Sectors											
Inventories on Hand	12.4	10.1	6.5	8.3	9.3	14.1	18.0	20.2	27.9	29.5	33.1
Goods Shipped	1.4	1.1	0.8	1.0	1.1	1.6	2.0	2.2	3.1	3.3	3.1
Uninstalled Equipment, n.e.c.											
Inventories on Hand	4.3	5.0	5.7	6.3	7.0	7.9	8.7	8.6	9.1	10.0	10.7
Total Nonagricultural Sectors											
Inventories on Hand	260.1	289.7	310.0	306.6	310.3	344.4	374.3	429.2	486.1	529.3	588.1
Goods Shipped	41.7	44.8	46.7	46.0	47.1	52.5	52.8	60.1	66.2	71.1	77.6
Total	301.8	334.5	356.7	352.6	357.4	396.9	427.1	489.3	552.3	600.4	665.7
Agriculture											
Inventories on Hand	29.4	31.5	32.6	33.5	37.4	43.1	43.1	47.7	48.2	48.8	50.2
Total											
Inventories on Hand	289.5	321.2	342.6	340.1	347.7	387.5	417.4	476.9	534.3	578.1	638.3
Goods Shipped	41.7	44.8	46.7	46.0	47.1	52.5	52.8	60.1	66.2	71.1	77.6
Total	331.2	366.0	389.3	386.1	394.8	440.0	470.2	537.0	600.5	649.2	715.9

in the estimates, and that which we shall cite here refers solely to industrial inventories. For simplicity, the references hereafter to our estimates will be to those in 1937 prices (factor costs).

(*i*) Our estimates imply that industrial inventories (on hand) increased only slightly in the course of 1928 and declined absolutely, because of a considerable decline in consumer goods industries, in the course of 1929. Putilov–32, on whom, however, our current-price estimates for this period are based, attributes (p. 104) the decline in inventories of consumer goods industries to difficulties in the supply of raw materials and fuel and indicates also (p. 112) that the same difficulties were experienced in industry in general. Relevant to this also is the evidence of a rapid build-up of inventories in the years immediately preceding 1928, cited p. 12 above.

(*ii*) Our estimates imply that industrial inventories (on hand) increased by 25 percent during 1931 and by 6 percent during 1932. Atlas–58, p. 124, states that the reported rise in "material values" in VSNKh industry during 1931 of 2.3 billion rubles (in current prices) was 1.2 billion in excess of the planned increase and led to "above-plan" stocks at the beginning of 1932 of 1.2 billion also. The latter figure equals about 17 percent of total inventories held in VSNKh industry on that date (see Appendix G, notes for 1931–32). According to Atlas, from the second half of 1932, Gosbank began to apply "credit sanctions" to enterprises which did not fulfill their "tasks for the mobilization of internal resources," in consequence of which above-plan stocks had by the beginning of 1933 been reduced to 279 million rubles.

(*iii*) Our estimates for producer goods industries imply that inventories (on hand) were high—as high as immediately before the war—at the beginning of 1946, increased somewhat during 1946 and 1947, but declined absolutely during 1948 to a level not far above that of January 1, 1946. The statement appears in Usoskin–46, p. 71, fn., that during the war industrial enterprises formed large above-norm stocks of materials which, at the time of the return to civilian production, could not be used by the enterprises holding them. The government authorized managers, with the permission of their ministers, to sell to other enterprises and institutions materials which were in surplus on January 1, 1946. The "surplus" presumably was in the producer goods sector.

With respect to the same period, Zverev–49, p. 46, in a passage concerned with the excessive level of stocks relative to norms and to prewar ratios to sales, states that nevertheless stocks of "material values" in *union* industry on October 1, 1948, were below their levels both of January 1, 1948, and of January 1, 1947. Our estimate for *producer goods* inventories on hand on January 1, 1949, is below that for January 1, 1948, and slightly above that for January 1, 1947.

(*iv*) Relative to the absolute decline during 1955 in inventories (on hand) in producer goods industry and in all industry, Atlas–58, p. 290, attributes the decline in bank loans to *heavy* industry during that year to the reduction in prices which occurred but also to a "significant reduction in above-plan stocks." Reference is made also in Kisman–56, p. 94, to "a reduction of above-plan stocks of raw and other materials in industry" during 1955, and actual holdings are stated to have been approximately in accord with norms by January 1, 1956. However, Usatov–61, p. 28, states that nonseasonal inventories on hand in industry in excess of norms were only 2–3 percent of norms in 1953–54, which suggests the reduction on this account during 1955 would not have been large.

Unfortunately, we do not find statements of the foregoing sort to substantiate the extraordinarily large increase during 1935—of 21 percent for total inventories in all sectors—implied by our estimates. As a reading of Appendix G will make clear, the current-price data from Soviet sources for this period show various inconsistencies and have been subjected to rather elaborate, and hence questionable, interpretations by us. As is equally clear from Appendix L, the deflators we employ for this period are likely to be highly inaccurate. The increase in inventories estimated for 1935 may well, therefore, be quite wide of the mark.

We would note, however, that of the total estimated increase during 1935, of 13.9 billion rubles in 1937 factor costs, 4.5 billion or 32 percent is accounted for by inventories on hand in producer goods industries. The increase within this sector is not extraordinarily large in comparison with those of preceding years. The current-price figures for *heavy* industry come directly and with little manipulation from a seemingly reliable Soviet source (see the discussion of Omel'chenko–39 in Appendix G, notes for 1933–39) and are accepted in preference to those derived from an alternative source which imply an even larger increase (see the discussion of Shenger–36 in Appendix G, *loc. cit.*). Our inventory deflator (Table L–2) shows little increase during 1935, but no significant change is known to have occurred in selling prices relevant for this sector, and, while wage rates were rising rapidly, productivity was almost certainly increasing also.

Inventories on hand in consumer goods industries and domestic trade account for another 3.2 billion or 23 percent of the total increase. For these sectors, the current-price estimates are considerably shakier than those for producer goods industries, but a large error is more likely to result from our deflators. Relevant to the latter, one fragment of evidence can be cited which suggests that we have not grossly underestimated the extent of price rises affecting these two sectors.

In 1935, inventory gains resulting from price increases—of consumer goods in this instance—and on inventories which are regarded as financed by Gosbank were for the first time transferred to the Bank (cf. Pinus–35, *passim;* part of the transfer appears to have been credited first to the Budget and from there to the Bank). The procedure applied both to industry and to domestic trade. It undoubtedly did not apply to goods shipped or the loans against them. The amount of the transfer was approximately 1.7 billion rubles (the figure is given in Anonymous–38, p. 10; see also Lande–36, p. 131). Assuming that the share of consumer goods industries and trade in loans on goods shipped was the same as their share in goods shipped, loans to these two sectors other than on goods shipped amounted to 8.7 billion on January 1, 1935 (see Tables G–1, I–1, and J–1). The transfer, then, equals less than 20 percent of the loans to which it related, as of the beginning of 1935, whereas our inventory deflators indicate price rises during 1935 of 34 percent in consumer goods industries and 39 percent in trade (see Tables L–3 and L–6). This comparison is not conclusive, because too many uncertainties surround the method and comprehensiveness of the transfer referred to, but, so far as it goes, it suggests an understatement rather than an overstatement in our estimate of the increase in inventories during 1935. If we are wrong in assuming that the current-price data for January 1, 1935, do not reflect the price increases of that date (see Appendix L, p. 576), the implied understatement is even greater.

There is nothing we can add to what is said in the explanations of their derivation on the reliability of the 1935–36 estimates for other sectors or for goods shipped. Taken as a whole, the evidence seems convincing that the increase in total inventories during 1935 was exceptionally large, but we cannot verify that it was within a narrow range of the magnitude we estimate.

Appendix O

Official Soviet Data

on Fixed Capital

The purpose of this appendix is to explain and reconstruct the official Soviet data on investment in, and the stock of, fixed capital which are considered further in Chapter 7. The necessity for "reconstruction" arises because the official aggregative data, as presently published, do not coincide entirely, either in scope or concept, with the capital series developed in this study. The first section of the appendix is devoted to capital investment statistics, the second to data on the stock of fixed capital.

GROSS FIXED CAPITAL INVESTMENT

The required official data on investment in fixed capital are assembled in Table O–1. In many cases, Soviet sources report only separate series for investment by the state and co-operative sector of the economy, by collective farms, and by private individuals. The objective of Table O–1, therefore, is that of aggregating these series to provide global totals of approximately the same scope as our gross investment estimates.

The sources of the data in the table are as follows, in the order of the rows. For row 1a, see TsSU–62a, pp. 537–38. For row 1b, see TsSU–61a, p. 164. For row 1c, the annual data for 1956–60 and for the intervals 1946–50, 1951–55 are from TsSU–61a, p. 170; the annual figures for 1940, 1950, 1955, and 1961 are estimated at 70 percent of row 1a, approximately the relationship which prevailed in the interval 1951–55 and in the years 1956 and 1960; the figures for the intervals 1928 (4th quarter)–32, 1933–37, 1938–41 (1st half) and 1941 (2nd half)–45 are estimated at 111 percent of the corresponding figures in row 1b, approximately the relationship that prevailed during 1946–50. The figures in rows 2a and 2b are from TsSU–62a, pp. 537–38. For row 3, see TsSU–61a, pp. 188–89 and, for 1961 only, TsSU–62a, p. 535. Row 4a is the sum of rows 1a, 2a, and 3, except that the 1928 figure is obtained from TsSU–62a, p. 65. Row 4b is the sum of rows 1c, 2b, and 3. The figures in rows 4c are from Table A–11 of this study for 1956–61 and are derived by means of the same sources and methods as used in Table A–11 for all other years. Row 5 is from TsSU–61a, pp. 188–89 and, for 1961, from TsSU–62a, p. 541. Row 6 is computed as the difference between

TABLE O-1

GROSS INVESTMENT IN FIXED CAPITAL, OFFICIAL SERIES IN "1956 ESTIMATING PRICES," 1928-61
(Billion Rubles)

	1928	1940	1950	1955	1956	1957	1958	1959	1960	1961
1. Collective-Farm Investment										
1a. Total	--	4.36	7.51	21.20	22.64	22.04	28.43	35.26	31.66	31.55
1b. Productive Construction-Installation	--	--	--	--	--	--	--	--	--	--
1c. All Construction-Installation	--	3.05	5.26	14.84	15.75	15.66	16.75	21.78	21.70	22.08
2. State--Co-operative Investment (Excluding Collective Farms)										
2a. Total	--	47.29	96.30	164.55	191.23	215.76	245.15	274.07	307.95	327.47
2b. Construction-Installation	--	36.43	58.08	100.15	113.20	128.60	149.94	170.44	192.99	199.79
3. Private Investment in Housing	--	3.72	7.03	13.56	15.19	20.50	26.54	30.53	27.44	23.99
4. Socialized and Private Investment										
4a. Total	8.54	55.37	110.84	199.31	229.06	258.30	300.12	339.86	367.05	383.01
4b. Construction-Installation	--	43.20	70.37	128.55	144.14	164.76	193.23	222.75	242.13	245.86
4c. Equipment	--	--	--	--	68.45	75.39	86.91	94.00	100.25	107.50
5. Investment in Housing	--	9.59	20.23	37.98	44.69	62.15	75.36	83.19	82.75	78.79
6. Nonagricultural Investment	--	49.11	94.52	161.27	188.82	216.27	252.71	289.15	315.13	325.34

TABLE O-1 (continued)

GROSS INVESTMENT IN FIXED CAPITAL, OFFICIAL SERIES IN "1956 ESTIMATING PRICES," 1928-61
(Billion Rubles)

	1928 (4th Quarter)-32	1933-37	1938-41 (1st Half)	1941 (2nd Half)-45	1946-50	1951-55
1. Collective-Farm Investment						
1a. Total.....................	3.05	9.93	13.17	14.89	31.50	67.27
1b. Productive Construction-Installation.	2.41	7.33	9.69	11.39	21.57	39.78
1c. All Construction-Installation	2.68	8.14	10.76	12.64	23.94	47.72
2. State--Co-operative Investment (Excluding Collective Farms)						
2a. Total.....................	67.16	151.70	151.01	145.48	348.75	671.87
2b. Construction-Installation	55.45	119.38	115.66	110.96	220.43	420.31
3. Private Investment in Housing	4.02	6.48	11.75	17.17	39.15	52.51
4. Socialized and Private Investment						
4a. Total.....................	74.23	168.11	175.93	177.54	419.40	791.65
4b. Construction-Installation	62.15	134.00	138.17	140.77	283.52	520.54
4c. Equipment.................	7.94	23.39	26.50	25.02	106.76	205.36
5. Investment in Housing	11.90	21.99	30.82	28.45	83.24	156.99
6. Nonagricultural Investment.........	62.27	146.91	155.85	160.30	365.55	668.95

total investment, shown in row 4a, and agricultural investment as given in TsSU–61a, pp. 154–55 and, for 1961, TsSU–62a, p. 541.

THE GROSS FIXED CAPITAL STOCK

The most recently published Soviet data on the size and growth of the stock of fixed assets are compiled in accordance with the Soviet statistical concept "basic funds" (*osnovnye fondy*), the scope of which includes not only fixed assets as defined in this study—structures, installation, and equipment—but also draft and productive livestock and a residual category, "other." The livestock category is less comprehensive than the series computed in Chapter 4 of this study in that it excludes all immature animals and adult animals being fed for slaughter. The excluded kinds are considered in Soviet usage to belong to working capital rather than fixed, although it is not clear where or how consistently the dividing line is drawn in actual Soviet statistical practices (cf. Gozulov–59, p. 53, and Bunich–59, p. 44). The only items in the residual category we have succeeded in identifying are capitalized outlays for perennial plantings and for land betterment measures other than structures, although others may also exist.

TABLE O-2

GROSS "BASIC FUNDS" BY KIND OF ASSET, IN "1956 ESTIMATING PRICES,"
ON JANUARY 1, 1960
(Billion Rubles)

	Total	Livestock	"Other"	Fixed Capital
Total	2965	95	30	2840
Nonagricultural	2545	0	20	2525
Residential	942	0	0	942
Nonresidential	2023	95	30	1898

The purpose of this section is to isolate, so far as possible, the fixed asset components of the "basic funds" totals. For January 1, 1960, we estimate the distribution of basic funds between fixed assets, livestock, and "other." The results are shown in Table O–2. For other dates, we are able only to estimate basic funds exclusive of livestock, but including "other." As may be seen in Table O–2, however, the relative importance of "other" is small, and for most purposes the difference between "basic funds exclusive of livestock" and "fixed capital" will be of little significance. The derivation of the figures in Table O–2 is explained in the remainder of this section, the first part of which presents the available time series on basic funds exclusive of livestock, the second the estimation of "other" basic funds on January 1, 1960.

Basic Funds, excluding Livestock

Part A of Table O–3 reproduces the Soviet indexes—those referred to in Chapter 7 as the "revised" indexes—of the change in the stock of "basic funds." The figures are taken from two Soviet statistical handbooks, TsSU–61, p. 85, and TsSU–62a, p. 68. Neither source contains the complete set of indexes, but for overlapping dates the two give figures which are the same or, in the case of 1960, differ by very small relative amounts. We assume that such differences reflect minor corrections within a single set of indexes common to both sources. Where such differences occur, therefore, we use the figures appearing in the later source. The second of the two sources cited states that the data refer to the end of the years with which it identifies them. Although the first source does not so state, we assume that index numbers for years appearing only in that source—"1950" and "1955"—also refer to the end of the year. This is confirmed for the index numbers for agriculture in *Vestnik statistiki*, 1960:11, p. 18. For consistency with the dating used elsewhere in this study, we attribute the figures given for the end of a year to the January 1 of the year following.

The sources indicate that the indexes are computed in "comparable prices, gross of depreciation," but do not specify which prices are used. However, data are also given (see TsSU–60, p. 67) for the absolute value of all basic funds, distributed by economic sector, as of January 1, 1960—the results of the inventory discussed in Chapter 7. These figures are reproduced in Part B of Table O–3, in the 1960 column. If the two indexes for the productive and nonproductive sectors of the economy in Part A of the table (rows 2 and 7) are combined, using as weights the absolute figures for 1960 in Part B, the total index of Part A (row 1) is reproduced within the rounding error. If, similarly, the component indexes for both the productive and nonproductive totals are weighted with the 1960 absolute values, they leave "other" residuals (rows 14 and 17) which are plausible in that they are small, positive, and increase over time. In at least this limited sense, therefore, the "comparable prices" underlying the indexes are the same as those of the absolute data for 1960, which, as is explained in Chapter 7, are essentially 1956 estimating prices.

On the basis of the foregoing, absolute values for the stock of basic funds for years other than 1960 are computed in Part B from the Part A indexes and the 1960 absolute figures, the "other" categories, for which no indexes are given, being computed as residuals. Because of rounding, the productive and nonproductive subtotals do not sum exactly to totals.

Part C of Table O–3 shows "basic funds" exclusive of livestock. For all individual sectors except agriculture and for the aggregate series for all nonproductive sectors, "basic funds" inclusive and exclusive of livestock must be approximately the same. Hence the figures in Part C (rows 20 and 22–26) are simply repeated from Part B. It will be noted that Part A of the table contains two *indexes* of basic funds in agriculture, one inclusive, one exclusive of livestock. The absolute data in Part B are inclusive only, but, if it were possible to obtain an exclusive absolute figure for agriculture for any year, we could use the exclusive index of Part A to obtain exclusive absolute values for all other years and, hence, could complete Part C of the table.

Agricultural "basic funds" exclusive of livestock can be estimated for *1928* as follows. (*i*) TsSU–62a, p. 67, states that in 1928 the socialized sector of the economy accounted for 35.1 percent of all productive basic funds including livestock, but for 65.7 percent of all productive basic funds excluding livestock. (*ii*) According to Anonymous–36, p. 5, socialized holdings of livestock in June of 1928 amounted to 0.7 percent of the national total for horses, 0.5 percent for cows and other cattle, 0.5 percent for hogs, and

TABLE O-3

DERIVATION OF GROSS "BASIC FUNDS" EXCLUSIVE OF LIVESTOCK,
IN "1956 ESTIMATING PRICES," OFFICIAL SERIES, SELECTED YEARS
(January 1)

	1929	1941	1951	1956	1960	1961	1962
A. "Basic Funds" in "Comparable Prices," Including Livestock Except as Noted (1929 = 100)							
1. Total	100	230	273	395	558	612	668
2. Productive Sectors.	100	256	325	511	731	805	881
3. Industry and Construction	100	852	1343	2305	3284	3708	4121
4. Agriculture Including Livestock.	100	123	125	193	256	273	292
5. Agriculture Excluding Livestock.	100	227	236	447	623	677	739
6. Transportation and Communications	100	371	435	584	837	904	972
7. Nonproductive Sectors	100	211	230	300	418	456	495
8. Housing	100	188	200	245	348	374	398
B. "Basic Funds" in "1956 Estimating Prices," Including Livestock (Billion Rubles)							
9. Total	531	1222	1450	2099	2964.7	3252	3549
10. Productive Sectors.	238	609	773	1216	1739.3	1915	2096
11. Industry and Construction	26	222	349	600	854.5	965	1072
12. Agriculture	164	201	205	316	419.2	447	478
13. Transportation and Communications	46	172	201	270	387.4	419	450
14. Other Productive.	2	14	18	30	78.2	84	96
15. Nonproductive Sectors.	293	619	674	879	1225.4	1337	1453
16. Housing.	271	509	541	663	941.5	1012	1077
17. Other Nonproductive . . .	22	110	133	216	283.9	325	376
C. "Basic Funds" in "1956 Estimating Prices," Excluding Livestock (Billion Rubles)							
18. Total	419	1145	1365	2011	2869.5	3157	3455
19. Productive Sectors.	126	526	691	1132	1644.1	1820	2002
20. Industry and Construction	26	222	349	600	854.5	965	1072
21. Agriculture	52	118	123	232	324.0	352	384
22. Transportation and Communications	46	172	201	270	387.4	419	450
23. Other Productive.	2	14	18	30	78.2	84	96
24. Nonproductive Sectors	293	619	674	879	1225.4	1337	1453
25. Housing.	271	509	541	663	941.5	1012	1077
26. Other Nonproductive . . .	22	110	133	216	283.9	325	376

0.7 percent for sheep and goats. Similar figures are reported for 1927 and 1929 in TsUNKhU–32, pp. 4–5, which suggests that the cited proportions may be taken to characterize the whole of 1928. (*iii*) If we assume that overall socialized holdings of livestock accounted for 0.6 percent of the Soviet total in 1928, we may use the information from TsSU–62a, p. 67, in simultaneous equations to establish that livestock accounted for 47.0 percent of all productive basic funds, including livestock, in 1928. The equations are $.006L + S = .351(S + P + L)$ and $S = .657(S + P)$, where S stands for socialized productive basic funds, excluding livestock; P for private productive basic funds excluding livestock; and L for livestock. (*iv*) The absolute value of livestock at the end of 1928, i.e., on January 1, 1929, can be computed as 47.0 percent of 238 billion rubles (row 10), or 112 billion rubles. Subtracting this amount from agricultural basic funds including livestock, 164 billion rubles (row 12), we obtain the corresponding figure exclusive of livestock, 52 billion rubles, which is entered in row 21.

Applying the index of row 5 to the absolute value for 1928 in row 21, absolute values for agricultural basic funds exclusive of livestock are obtained for all other years. Total and productive basic funds, exclusive of livestock (rows 18 and 19), are then computed by summing appropriate components.

This calculation is subject to some important ambiguities. The data on the socialized share of productive basic funds in 1928 are given in the source without specification as to the prices in which they are expressed or indication of whether they refer to the beginning of the year, the end, or the annual average. We have used them as though they were consistent in these respects with the index numbers in Part A of Table O–3. The two sets of data occur on adjacent pages of a single source, but this need have no special significance. In the next paragraphs, therefore, we present some collateral information bearing on the plausibility of the results so far obtained.

Our calculations imply an absolute value for the livestock component of basic funds at the beginning of 1960 of 95 billion rubles (compare rows 9 and 18 of Table O–3). How does this figure compare with other data on livestock numbers and prices?

According to the authority cited earlier (p. 195, fn. 25), all values for basic funds in the January 1, 1960, data are in "contemporary prices." For fixed assets, as noted in Chapter 7, this probably means 1956 estimating prices. However, unlike structures and equipment, for which prices varied little between 1956 and 1960, livestock experienced a major increase in price in 1958, at which time uniform procurement prices for state and collective farms were introduced (see Nimitz–59, pp. 267 ff.). Furthermore, Soviet statistical sources published since 1959 revalue livestock for inclusion in collective-farm "indivisible funds" into the new 1958 prices (see, e.g., TsSU–61b, pp. 202–3). The global values for basic funds at the beginning of 1960, therefore, are also likely to include livestock at the 1958 procurement prices (these prices are believed to have prevailed through 1960 as well). TsSU–60a, pp. 306–9, shows the distribution of Soviet livestock herds at the end of 1959 by age and sex. From these figures, we have tried to distinguish the part of total herds corresponding to the livestock component of basic funds. The following categories are assumed to enter basic funds: breeding bulls, draft bullocks and oxen, cows; breeding boars, sows; breeding rams, ewes, other rams over one year old; male and female goats over one year old; breeding stallions, mares, other stallions and geldings over three years old. The following are assumed to be excluded: all bulls and bullocks other than draft and breeding heifers; shoats over six months and boars being reared for breeding, sucklings and shoats under six months, hogs fed for slaughter; lambs under one year; kids under one year; colts under three years. Valuing the included animals at 1958 prices, as shown in Table 4–2, yields a total of 122 billion rubles. If 1955 prices, also shown in Table 4–2, are used, the value is 71 billion rubles. Neither of these figures is very close to the 95 billion implied in Table O–3 and, while their calculation contains many possibilities for error, they seem to imply as well that the reliability of the 95 billion ruble figure is also low.

Relative to the total value of basic funds at the end of 1959, on the other hand, the total value of livestock is not large, and sizable errors in it, accordingly, are of limited consequences for the estimation of indexes for basic funds exclusive of livestock. To illustrate this, we recompute Part C of Table O–3 on the alternative assumptions that the livestock component at the end of 1959 was not 95 billion rubles but 122 or 71 billion. The only affected indexes are, of course, the total and the series for all productive funds. The absolute value of the agricultural series is altered, but not its change over time. For the former two series, the results of the alternative computations may be tabulated as follows (January 1):

	Assumed Value of Livestock, 1960 (billion rubles)	*Basic Funds, Excluding Livestock (1929 = 100)*						
		1929	*1941*	*1951*	*1956*	*1960*	*1961*	*1962*
Total 122		100	274	327	480	685	754	825
95		100	273	326	480	685	754	825
71		100	273	325	480	684	753	824
Productive 122		100	424	559	913	1326	1470	1616
95		100	417	548	898	1304	1445	1589
71		100	412	539	885	1284	1421	1564

The second series of each group is that implied by the absolute figures in our original calculation in Part C of Table O–3. Within each group, the alternative index numbers differ from those from Table O–3 by less than 2 percent. The corresponding absolute values, not reproduced here, would differ by 1 percent or less for the total series and by some 3 percent or less for the productive sector. For the agricultural sector alone, on the other hand, the absolute differences would amount to 13 percent or less. Thus the figures derived here for livestock alone or for agricultural funds exclusive of livestock are subject to substantial errors, but the error in the remaining series should be relatively limited.

"Other" Basic Funds. As remarked earlier, the only elements of this category we have identified are capitalized outlays for perennial plantings and land betterment (see Bunich–59, p. 44, and Petrov–61, p. 77). Presumably a large part of the assets of this kind are held in the agricultural sector, therefore, though some perennial plantings and more, perhaps, of the unidentified components must be found in other sectors as well (see Bunich–59, pp. 51–52).

Information on the magnitude of the category is largely unavailable. It is not treated separately in the data published on the value of all basic funds at the beginning of 1960. Some fragments of information exist, however. (*i*) TsSU–60, p. 69, shows a residual category of basic funds for non-budgetary state and co-operative organizations as of January 1, 1960, of 38.9 billion rubles. However, this item includes livestock as well as the narrower residual considered here. Of the larger figure, industrial funds are stated to account for 0.7 percent of all basic funds, or 5.8 billion rubles, a figure which is surely exclusive of livestock. As explained earlier, these values are gross values in 1956 estimating prices. (*ii*) A revaluation of basic funds conducted for collective farms at the end of 1961 showed "other" basic funds, mainly perennial plantings, to amount to 4.9 billion rubles, or 2.1 percent of all collective-farm basic funds (see TsSU–62a, p. 420). The underlying values are apparently also gross values in 1956 estimating prices (see Kaplan–63, pp. 102–3). (*iii*) TsSU–60a, p. 385, shows a percentage distribution by kind of all productive basic funds in the socialist sector of agriculture at acquisition cost. None of the items explicitly shown in the distribution belong to "other" assets, but there is an implicit residual of

2.9 percent for January 1, 1959, the last year covered by the data, which must be accounted for mainly or entirely by "other" funds. In revaluing basic funds into 1956 estimating prices, the Soviet statistical organs apparently retained perennial plantings and land betterment at acquisition cost (see Kaplan–63, p. 98). For all agricultural basic funds taken together, however, the effect of revaluation from acquisition to replacement cost was an increase in value of 7.4 percent for the state sector in the revaluation at the end of 1959, of 28 percent for collective farms in the revaluation at the end of 1961 (see TsSU–60, p. 73, and TsSU–62a, p. 424). Thus, at replacement cost, the value of "other" funds would be less than the 2.9 percent shown at acquisition cost. As the private sector must dispose of few assets of this type, the corresponding figure for *all* agriculture would be smaller still, perhaps on the order of 2–2.5 percent, or about 10 billion rubles on January 1, 1960 (see Table O–1 for all agricultural basic funds on that date). (*iv*) The residential component of basic funds is apparently restricted almost entirely to structures and, hence, contains little or no "other" component (see Bunich–59, p. 51).

From the foregoing, we estimate very roughly that "other" basic funds probably accounted for about 1 percent of the national total on January 1, 1960, or about 30 billion rubles in 1956 estimating prices, of which about 10 billion were in the agricultural sector, the remaining 20 billion in the nonagricultural nonresidential sector.

Appendix P

Gross and Net National Product

This appendix explains the Soviet national product data used in Part II of the study and included in the Tabular Section in Tables T–47 to T–49. As our standard of measurement, we take the calculations presented by Abram Bergson in Bergson–61. This work contains estimates for selected years of national product by use in 1937, 1928, and 1950 prices. Here, as elsewhere, we refer to Bergson's estimates at ruble factor cost. For the meaning of these costs and their difference from established ruble prices, see the summary discussion in Chapter 1 (Section 4) of this study and the more detailed examination in Bergson, *op. cit.*, chaps. 8 and 9. Where possible, we use Bergson's results without modification. For certain purposes, however, it has seemed desirable to consider, at least tentatively, estimates by originating sector or for years not included in Bergson's calculations. What we compile, therefore, are (*i*) annual series for the domestic product of the total economy and by sector of origin for the periods 1928–40 and 1945–61 in 1937 prices (factor costs) and (*ii*) series in 1928 and 1950 prices for income originating by sector in the two years covered by Bergson's estimates in 1928 prices and in selected years of those covered by Bergson in 1950 prices. Methods of estimation are set forth in the two main sections of the appendix.

It is to be emphasized here as in the text (see Chapter 8, Section 2) that these calculations are intended only to provide a context in which to explore, quite provisionally, some implications of the capital stock estimates. They are not among the primary findings of this study, and, as the subsequent exposition should make clear, many important questions concerning their reliability must go unanswered. The justification for the use made of them derives essentially from their relation to the Bergson calculations. Where we deal with years already covered by Bergson, this relation is close, and some of the authority of Bergson's results should also adhere to these elaborations. On the other hand, the annual estimates for years not considered by Bergson are significantly more speculative.

The annual series are computed by aggregating indexes of the physical volume of output by sectors of origin, using 1937 value-added weights. As originally undertaken, the calculation was intended only to provide a means for interpolating and extrapolating from Bergson's calculations for benchmark years. In the upshot, however, our Gross National Product index, as calculated before adjustment to fit Bergson's results, proved similar to his. To avoid the uncertainties that would be evoked by attempting to fit our index more precisely to Bergson's, therefore, we use the former as is, without further manipulation. In a purely formal sense, this means the introduction of a new GNP series, but it is to be understood that we attach no significance to the minor divergences between our index and Bergson's and that the validity of our index depends not on the confidence that would be inspired by the methods used in its derivation but on the *ad hoc* empirical finding that, for common years, it agrees closely with Bergson's. This should serve as well to emphasize the tentative character of our index numbers for years not covered by Bergson.

Our index for total GNP in 1937 prices is compared with Bergson's for years common to both series (and for 1944 *versus* 1945) in the following tabulation (1928 = 100):

Year	Present Estimates	Bergson's Estimates
1928	100	100
1937	172	162
1940	203	197
1944	—	175
1945	161	—
1948	203	202
1949	224	218
1950	246	243
1951	264	265
1952	284	287
1953	303	302
1954	327	319
1955	357	350

Our index is from Table P–1 of this appendix, Bergson's from Bergson–61, pp. 128, 210, 303. The figure for 1944 refers to domestic product, exclusive of Lend-Lease receipts. As may be seen, for common years, the two indexes differ by more than 3 percent only once, in 1937, for which our index exceeds Bergson's by 6 percent. Taken together, the two indexes imply a decline in domestic product of 8 percent between 1944 and 1945. It is possible that some decline did occur in this interval in connection with the reorientation of the economy as the war ended. The official Soviet index of industrial output shows a decline of about 12 percent (see TsSU–62a, p. 169). But most other sectors must have shown gains, which suggests that the decline in GNP, if any, would not have been so great as indicated here. Although the available data do not permit us to extend our series to 1944, it seems that the degree of consistency between our index number and Bergson's for 1944–45 is less than for other years. We would not, therefore, interpret the two indexes in combination as providing a measure of change during 1944–45, and instead we issue an additional *caveat* about the quality of our estimates for the immediate postwar years.

NATIONAL PRODUCT IN 1937 PRICES

Total Product

The derivation of the annual estimates of total national product, net and gross, is shown in Table P–1. Rows 1–7e of the table contain 1937-based indexes of productive activity by economic sector. Value added in the same sectors in 1937 at 1937 factor cost is shown in the first column of the table. Multiplying value added in 1937 by the corresponding indexes of productive activity and summing by years, we compute Net National Product in 1937 prices, row 8. However, for "services, including government," the five component indexes, rows 7a–7e, do not account for the whole. These are aggregated, using 1937 wage-bill weights (or pay and subsistence for military services), and the resulting index, row 7, is used thereafter to stand for all such services. Finally, straight-line depreciation, row 9, as computed in this study (Table T–11), is added to yield Gross National Product, row 10.

The data for value added by economic sector are from Bergson–60, p. 33, with the following exceptions. The distribution of "industry and construction" among civilian industry, munitions, and construction is from Bergson–61, p. 177. For value added in housing, we use the revised figure for gross rental outlays from Bergson–61, p. 316, arbitrarily reduced by 25 percent for depreciation. Thus the figure we show for "services, including government" excludes housing, and the inclusive figure given in Bergson–60, p. 33, 37.1 billion rubles, is reduced by 4.3 billion rubles, the unrevised amounts of net imputed rentals for owner-occupied houses (Bergson–60, p. 7) plus profits from socialized housing (Bergson–53, p. 127). The wage-bill data in rows 7a–7e are from Bergson–61, pp. 130, 318, 347, 355, 359–60.

The sources of the series in rows 1–7e of the table are given below.

Row 1 (Agriculture): The series from which we begin, but which is adjusted for changes in livestock herds, is an extension and recomputation into 1937 prices of the gross agricultural output series compiled by D. Gale Johnson and Arcadius Kahan (in Johnson–59). The physical output data used are, for 1928–38, 1940, 1950–57, those employed in the original series (see Johnson–59, pp. 231–32). For 1945 and 1958–61, we use the corresponding output data from TsSU–61, pp. 374, 378, and TsSU–62, pp. 176–79, 186 (for meat output in 1961, the slaughtered weight figure in TsSU–62 is converted to liveweight on the basis of the 1960 relationship between the two items; the sugar beet production data refer to beets raised for sugar production). In all cases, the data refer to gross output, and, for meat, output exclusive of changes in herds. Johnson and Kahan also develop "net" output series, i.e., net of certain losses and uses in production within agriculture, such as for seed and fodder. As these series are affected by the Soviet shift from animal to mechanical draft power, they seem less appropriate as an indicator of the change in agricultural value added than the gross output series.

The physical output series are summed arithmetically, using average realized 1937 prices as weights. The prices are those compiled by Karcz for Bergson–61 and presented in the latter, p. 324. For grain, potatoes, cotton, meat, and milk, however, we use the prices as revised by Karcz after the publication of Bergson–61 in his unpublished manuscript, Karcz–61, Table IV. The prices used, in rubles per ton or per 1,000 eggs, are: grain, 225; potatoes, 210; vegetables, 340; sunflower seed, 550; sugar beets, 44; seed cotton, 1,650; flax fiber, 1,050; wool, greasy weight, 7,500; milk, 570; meat, liveweight, 2,080; eggs, 320.

TABLE P-1

DERIVATION OF GROSS AND NET NATIONAL PRODUCT IN 1937 PRICES, 1928-61

	Income Originating in 1937 at 1937 Factor Cost (Billion Rubles)	1928	1929	1930	1931	1932	1933	1934	1935	1936	1937
					Index Numbers (1937 = 100)						
1. Agriculture	63.0	92.2	86.0	81.4	74.3	66.5	72.9	77.4	91.0	81.8	100.0
2. Industry and Construction	75.9										
2a. Civilian Industries	60.4	40.2	46.4	55.3	59.4	61.7	65.0	73.5	84.8	98.1	100.0
2b. Munitions Industries	5.0	4	5	6	6	6	16	35	60	80	100.0
2c. Construction	10.5	36.7	45.0	58.9	63.7	63.6	57.2	69.1	85.3	115.0	100.0
3. Transportation and Communications	16.8	27.9	34.0	43.6	50.3	58.1	56.5	63.8	75.1	90.2	100.0
4. Trade and Restaurants	10.4	91.8	97.1	99.2	98.4	78.0	66.6	71.7	74.2	86.4	100.0
5. Housing	2.1	81.1	83.3	85.4	87.6	89.8	91.9	93.9	96.0	98.0	100.0
6. Finance	1.9	49.2	56.0	52.3	60.1	66.3	68.4	69.4	78.8	89.1	100.0
7. Services, Including Government	32.8	51.7	53.3	57.2	64.4	71.0	72.6	76.4	82.2	91.0	100.0
7a. Health	3.2	35.4	39.0	42.8	50.9	59.4	62.4	67.4	73.6	86.9	100.0
7b. Education	9.8	34.0	35.3	40.0	50.9	60.9	65.5	70.3	77.3	88.6	100.0
7c. Government and Other Administration	3.1	67.9	72.6	85.0	99.0	110.9	101.9	97.1	100.9	100.4	100.0
7d. Military Services	3.4	32.1	32.1	32.1	32.1	32.1	36.5	48.7	61.0	80.0	100.0
7e. Repairs, Domestic Service, etc.	5.0	100.0	100.0	100.0	100.0	100.0	100.0	100.0	100.0	100.0	100.0
					Billion Rubles						
8. Net National Product		120.3	123.3	130.4	132.5	130.4	135.5	148.7	171.3	184.6	202.9
9. Depreciation		3.4	3.7	4.1	4.7	5.3	5.8	6.5	7.3	8.2	9.4
10. Gross National Product		123.7	127.0	134.5	137.2	135.7	141.3	155.2	178.6	192.8	212.3
					Index Numbers (1937 = 100)						
11. Gross National Product		58.3	59.8	63.4	64.6	63.9	66.6	73.1	84.1	90.8	100.0

TABLE P-1 (continued)

DERIVATION OF GROSS AND NET NATIONAL PRODUCT IN 1937 PRICES, 1928-61

	1938	1939	1940	1945	1946	1947	1948	1949	1950	1951
				Index Numbers (1937 = 100)						
1. Agriculture	92.0	92.8	110.9	74.8	82.0	104.4	115.4	117.9	116.9	110.3
2. Industry and Construction										
2a. Civilian Industries	101.6	105.0	105.6	54.3	67.4	82.6	106.4	129.4	148.4	167.4
2b. Munitions Industries	145	205	280	420	275	245	230	230	240	285
2c. Construction	98.8	101.0	101.0	42.9	64.2	79.4	106.0	135.0	155.0	176.0
3. Transportation and Communications	102.0	108.9	115.1	83.2	95.0	99.3	118.2	136.0	155.6	175.6
4. Trade and Restaurants	109.1	123.5	106.6	68.0	76.1	72.0	79.6	100.2	130.5	146.1
5. Housing	102.5	105.5	116.6	97.7	99.5	102.7	107.3	112.3	117.7	123.5
6. Finance	111.9	129.0	135.8	102.1	109.0	116.0	122.9	129.8	136.8	136.6
7. Services, Including Government	109.1	119.9	131.6	171.9	137.2	129.4	134.6	140.9	156.1	167.2
7a. Health	115.4	125.7	133.7	125.9	136.6	149.3	154.6	170.5	182.0	193.5
7b. Education	105.5	113.8	126.1	109.8	122.6	132.8	140.6	150.0	161.5	168.4
7c. Government and Other Administration	107.5	115.1	122.6	110.6	113.1	115.6	118.1	120.6	123.1	120.7
7d. Military Services	128.6	165.7	200.0	600.0	285.7	191.4	164.2	165.7	228.6	280.0
7e. Repairs, Domestic Service, etc.	100.0	100.0	100.0	70.0	80.0	90.0	100.0	100.0	100.0	100.0
				Billion Rubles						
8. Net National Product	205.5	217.9	236.9	186.9	185.9	207.2	236.5	262.4	287.5	308.1
9. Depreciation	10.6	11.6	13.6	12.1	12.5	13.3	14.2	15.3	16.8	19.0
10. Gross National Product	216.1	229.5	250.5	199.0	198.4	220.5	250.7	277.7	304.3	327.1
				Index Numbers (1937 = 100)						
11. Gross National Product	101.8	108.1	118.0	93.7	93.5	103.9	118.1	130.8	143.3	154.1

TABLE P-1 (concluded)

DERIVATION OF GROSS AND NET NATIONAL PRODUCT IN 1937 PRICES, 1928-61

	1952	1953	1954	1955	1956	1957	1958	1959	1960	1961
				Index Numbers (1937 = 100)						
1. Agriculture	118.0	122.2	125.2	139.9	161.2	161.4	178.7	180.5	182.9	188.2
2. Industry and Construction										
2a. Civilian Industries	177.5	195.1	218.7	243.4	272.1	296.2	325.1	350.7	369.7	391.9
2b. Munitions Industries	315	300	320	360	370	380	395	400	430	545
2c. Construction	196.0	217.0	239.0	264.0	277.0	301.0	337.0	377.0	405.0	427.0
3. Transportation and Communications	192.9	208.2	225.1	254.4	279.6	314.6	340.6	373.4	395.5	414.2
4. Trade and Restaurants	157.6	184.9	214.8	223.0	239.4	271.0	285.7	303.6	330.0	342.2
5. Housing	129.6	136.1	143.0	150.2	155.9	161.4	169.8	180.8	192.7	204.6
6. Finance	136.5	136.3	136.8	137.3	137.8	135.2	134.7	133.7	137.3	143.0
7. Services, Including Government	178.1	179.3	185.0	184.9	184.6	183.3	187.8	193.0	204.4	216.5
7a. Health	202.7	204.8	222.0	233.1	242.8	256.6	271.4	288.2	307.1	327.1
7b. Education	175.7	178.6	191.3	197.2	205.6	216.6	227.0	238.6	261.4	284.6
7c. Government and Other Administration	118.4	116.0	103.7	91.5	90.2	87.0	87.0	85.2	83.7	85.7
7d. Military Services	331.4	331.4	331.4	314.3	280.0	228.6	217.1	207.0	207.0	207.0
7e. Repairs, Domestic Service, etc.	100.0	100.0	100.0	100.0	100.0	100.0	100.0	100.0	100.0	100.0
				Billion Rubles						
8. Net National Product	330.4	351.1	378.5	413.2	451.8	478.3	518.7	549.1	577.0	610.6
9. Depreciation	21.4	23.5	25.6	28.4	31.6	35.7	40.2	45.2	50.0	55.8
10. Gross National Product	351.8	374.6	404.1	441.6	483.4	514.0	558.9	594.3	627.0	666.4
				Index Numbers (1937 = 100)						
11. Gross National Product	165.7	176.4	190.3	208.0	227.7	242.1	263.3	279.9	295.3	313.9

Given this initial output series (in billion rubles) for the years covered by it (1928–38, 1940, 1945, 1950–61), we adjust it for changes in livestock herds, as also seems appropriate for a measure of value added. The adjustment is made by adding net increases in herds and deducting net decreases, with values equal to our estimates of annual investment in livestock in 1937 prices (Table T–44). The resulting series is then set equal to 100 in 1937.

For the years not covered by the foregoing index, values are obtained from an official index of agricultural production (TsSU–61, p. 36), which is thought to be adjusted for changes in livestock herds (see Johnson–63, p. 207). For 1939, we extrapolate from 1938 on the official index, taking 1939 to be just less than 1 percent above 1938. For 1946–49, we interpolate between our 1945 and 1950 index numbers. Over the total interval 1945–50, the official index shows an increase of 62.8 percent, our index one of 56.3 percent.

The physical output series underlying our index, including those taken from Johnson and Kahan, are essentially officially published data also. As has been disclosed recently, the official figures for at least the years since 1957 are probably affected by falsification in reporting at the local level. An attempt to derive a measure of agricultural output which is corrected for such falsification has been made in Willett–62. In the case of grain, output is estimated on the basis of "reports on crop conditions, weather information and grain acreage. . . ." (p. 99). The estimating procedure for other products is not indicated, and, for the most part, the figures presented agree with those published officially. If, for the years since 1950, Willett's estimates are substituted for the physical output series used by us, the resulting index of agricultural production is materially altered, but the GNP series (row 10 of Table P–1) is not changed in any of the years by as much as 1 percent. We would not infer from this that our GNP estimates are not seriously affected by errors in the official agricultural output series, because of the possibility that Willett has been unable to make an adequate correction. However, it does not seem possible to much improve our GNP series on the basis of the data now available, and we therefore leave the estimates unadjusted. We do, however, make use of the agricultural estimates beyond their inclusion in the GNP totals, and the possibility of significant error in them should be kept in mind.

Row 2a (Civilian Industries): For the years for which it is available, the Kaplan-Moorsteen index of industrial output, which is weighted by *1950* prices and payrolls, is used (see Kaplan–60). For present purposes, this index has been extended by us to include years not considered in the original computations, i.e., 1929–31, 1933–36, 1938–39, and 1959–61. We explain below the methods used in extending the original calculations, and also some changes we have made in the original index for the years 1955–58.

The use of an index for this component which employs 1950 instead of 1937 weights is one of the more questionable approximations to which we resort, and, like others, must be defended principally on the grounds that it yields results for the GNP total which are reasonably consistent with Bergson's estimates. It is worth noting in addition, however, that Bergson's estimates in 1937 and 1950 prices appear to imply that civilian industrial production in the two sets of prices would behave much the same over time, with the possible exception of the immediate postwar years. In Powell–63, Table IV–9, series of (final) industrial product are computed which, for 1928, 1937, 1940, 1944, and 1948–55, are derived either from Bergson's GNP estimates or from component series similar to those underlying his estimates. With munitions production excluded, the value of industrial production in 1937 prices lies between 41 and 44 percent of the value in 1950 prices, except for 1944, in which it is 48 percent. The exception points again to the relative unreliability of our estimates for the immediate postwar years.

The Kaplan-Moorsteen calculations classify civilian industrial products into three groups: machinery, producer goods other than machinery, and consumer goods. For the last two groups, we extend the index by compiling physical output series for the years indicated above for the commodities included in the original calculations for benchmark years; see *op. cit.*, pp. 220, 224. In addition, where differences arise, we have replaced "preliminary" output data for 1958 with "final" figures from later sources. The series are aggregated by the same procedures and weights employed in the Kaplan-Moorsteen benchmark calculations. For machinery, for years prior to 1950, we obtain a 1950 price weighted production index from the 1937 price weighted production index in Moorsteen–62, p. 106, and the machinery price index numbers presented elsewhere in this study, Table A–12. For the years 1950–61, we employ investment in equipment in 1950 prices, exclusive of capital repairs, from Table A–4 above, to represent industrial output of civilian machinery. The substitution of the index of investment for that of machinery production permits us to extend the calculations to the years 1959–61 without compiling a separate index of machinery output and, additionally, is suggested by the discussion in Kaplan–60, p. 54, and Moorsteen–62, pp. 111–12, where it is argued that the original machinery production index probably understates the post-1950 growth of output, and in Moorsteen–62, p. 112, fn. 19, which argues the probable superiority of deflation, as opposed to the aggregation of physical output series, in measuring post-1950 machinery output. (Belatedly, it occurred to us that, both in principle and for symmetry with our procedures in estimating munitions production, q.v., it would have been appropriate to assume a time lag between the production of machinery and its incorporation into investment. This omission, however, is not of much consequence for the estimates.)

The sources of the physical output series employed are cited briefly below. In general, the effort was to obtain series similar to those used in the original calculation. Thus, for the period 1928–32, the possibility (discussed in Kaplan–60, pp. 8–13) that some of the series do not include output by small-scale industry applies to the present calculation as well. The implication is a possible overstatement of the rate of increase for these years.

As explained in Kaplan–60, pp. 3–4, some of the output data for the fiscal year 1927/28 in the Kaplan-Moorsteen index actually refer to the calendar year 1928. Furthermore, for most products, data are available either for 1927/28 or 1928, but not for both. For present purposes, we use the original index for 1927/28 to stand for 1928, even though it is probably closer to the former than to the latter year. For 1929–30, we sought, where possible, to obtain data for calendar years, but where such figures were not forthcoming, we have used data for the corresponding fiscal years.

For the years 1929–31, 1933–36, and 1938–39, the physical output series with which we extend the Kaplan-Moorsteen indexes are from TsSU–57 (pages as cited in Kaplan–60, pp. 195, 205, 211) and Nutter–62, Table B–2, with the following exceptions. For natural and manufactured gas, we interpolate between benchmark years, on the basis of the series given by Nutter for natural gas only. For all building materials, we use the output series compiled by Powell in Powell–57, Part II, and revised in Powell–59. For motorcycles, we use the series from TsUNKhU–35, p. 65, for 1929–31; from TsUNKhU–36a, p. 83, for 1933–34; and from *Planovoe khoziaistvo*, 1937:3, p. 233, for 1935–36. For cameras, we use the figure from TsUNKhU– 35, p. 65, for 1929. For *makhorka*, we use the series in TsUNKhU–36a, p. 221, for 1929–34, and in *Planovoe khoziaistvo*, 1937:3, p. 236, for 1935–36. For two series, syrup and dry starch, we interpolate between benchmark years, having reference for the purpose to the series shown in Nutter–62, *loc. cit.*, for syrup and dry starch combined. For television sets, vacuum cleaners, and washing machines during the intervals 1929–31, 1933–36, and 1938–39, and for refrigerators during 1929–31 and 1933–36, we estimate output at zero because output in the years preceding and succeeding the indicated intervals is known to have been nil or negligible. For cotton thread in 1930–35, we extrapolate forward and backward from the 1932 figure on the basis of the series in TsUNKhU–36a, p. 206; this series, like the one used in the Kaplan-Moorsteen calculations, expresses output in millions of spools, but for unknown reasons gives a different figure for 1932 from that used in the Kaplan-Moorsteen index.

For flour, having reference to the Johnson-Kahan estimates of grain available for human use in Johnson–59, p. 234, and data on Soviet grain exports in TsUNKhU–36a, pp. 428–29, we take output in 1929–30 to have been at the 1928 level, output in 1931 to have been at the 1932 level, and output in 1933–36 and 1938–39 to have been midway between the levels of 1932 and 1937. For the following series and intervals, we have located no suitable physical output data but have estimated output by simple interpolation: gypsum, construction lime, and technical lime in 1929–30; asbestos-cement pipe in 1929–31; fire clay brick, quartzite brick, and magnesite brick in 1938–39; shale in 1939; vodka in 1933–36, 1938–39; meat in 1939; *makhorka* in 1938–39; cotton thread in 1929, 1936, 1938–39; soap in 1929–31; hosiery and knitwear in 1929–31; motorcycles in 1938–39; timepieces in 1929–30 and 1939; cameras, radio receivers, and phonographs in 1939; refrigerators in 1938–39. Clearly, the estimated output figures listed in this paragraph are subject to substantial errors. In trial calculations not reproduced here, we also computed industrial production index numbers in which these figures, instead of being estimated, are omitted entirely from the calculation. For the years in question, the index numbers are computed from a smaller number of output series, the results being linked to the benchmark years of wider coverage by the method described in Kaplan–60, pp. 61–68. However, the final index obtained in this manner does not differ significantly from the one shown in Table P–1.

Output series for 1959–60, and also final figures for 1958 used to supplement the preliminary data used in the Kaplan-Moorsteen index, are from TsSU–61, pp. 235–37, 241, 246, 267, 269, 282, 297, 300, 302, 309, 314, 315, 319, 320, 340, 343, and TsSU–61b, p. 128. Our calculations for 1959–60 include the same products as the Kaplan-Moorsteen index for 1958, with two exceptions: (*i*) Four products included in the Kaplan-Moorsteen index for earlier years but omitted for 1958 because of the lack of data (construction lime, technical lime, gypsum, and phonographs) are included in our calculations. The four products are also included in our calculation for 1958. (*ii*) Two products (milk products and *makhorka*) included in the Kaplan-Moorsteen index for 1958 must be omitted from our calculation for lack of data. To allow for the diminution in coverage, we compute 1959–60 index numbers by branch of industry for the smaller group of products on a 1958 base, linking the resulting index to the corresponding 1950-based index numbers for 1958 and aggregating by the branch weights.

For 1961, the physical output data are from TsSU–62, pp. 122–30. The number of series for which information is available is substantially reduced. In addition to those omitted for 1959–60, the following are now excluded: manganese ore, peat, fire wood, sawnwood, plywood, cardboard, construction lime, technical lime, gypsum, fire clay brick, quartzite brick, magnesite brick, phonographs, cotton thread, refined sugar, margarine and compounds, macaroni products, alcoholic beverages, salt, flour, starch, cigarettes, and syrup. The total number of series for products other than machinery is reduced from 73 in the original Kaplan-Moorsteen calculations to 45.

Rows 2b (Munitions Industries) and 7d (Military Services): The two series we use for these components are essentially interpolations and extrapolations on Bergson's estimates of munitions procurements (with procurements assumed to lag production by six months) and real outlays on military pay and subsistence. In composing our estimates, we proceed from the data presented in Table P–2, of which the sources are the following.

Column 1 (Reported Defense Outlays): The figures for 1928–30 are interpolated from data for the Soviet fiscal years 1927/28–1929/30 and the last quarter of 1930, respectively: 789; 880; 1,046; and 434 million rubles. The 1928/29, 1929/30, and last quarter 1930 figures are from Plotnikov–48, p. 70. The 1927/28 figure is extrapolated from the 1928/29 figure and the change in outlays for administration and defense combined, in TsSU–32, p. 577. The figures for 1931–45 are from Plotnikov–48, pp. 70, 142, 303; that for 1946 from Anonymous–57, p. 216; that for 1947 from Bergson–49, p. 67; that for 1948, from Bergson–54, p. 23; those for 1949–54 from Hoeffding–59, p. 177; for 1955–56 from TsSU–59, p. 900; for 1957, from Nimitz–62, p. 127; for 1958–60, from TsSU–61, p. 844. For 1961 and 1962, see *Pravda*, December 7, 1961, which states that planned expenditures for 1962 "have been increased by 31.44 billion (old) rubles" and are to amount to 134.0 billion old rubles. The language is somewhat ambiguous, in that the base from which the "increase" is reckoned is not specified. Presumably, realized outlays in 1961 are compared with the 1962 Plan.

Although it may be true, as is often argued, that outlays of a military nature are also entered in the budget under other headings, the evidence presently available is by no means unambiguous. It is clearly impracticable

TABLE P-2

DERIVATION OF MUNITIONS PROCUREMENTS, IN 1937 PRICES, AND SIZE OF ARMED FORCES, 1928-62

	Defense Outlays Reported in State Budget (Including Pensions) (Billion Current Rubles) (1)	Reported Size of Armed Forces (Thousands) (2)	Gross Output of Defense Industry, Official Index (1937 = 100) (3)	Munitions Procurements, Bergson's Estimates in 1937 Prices (1937 = 100) (4)	Present Estimates	
					Munitions Procurements in 1937 Prices (1937 = 100) (5)	Size of Armed Forces (Thousands) (6)
1928	0.812	562	--	4.5[a]	4.5	562
1929	0.922	--	--	--	5	562
1930	1.212	--	--	--	7	562
1931	1.288	--	--	--	7	562
1932	1.296	--	--	--	7	562
1933	1.421	638	36	--	7	638
1934	5.019	--	--	--	30	852
1935	8.186	1,067	--	--	50	1,067
1936	14.883	--	83	--	90	1,400
1937	17.481	1,433	100	100	100	1,750
1938	23.2	--	137	--	135	2,250
1939	39.2	--	201	--	200	2,900
1940	56.7	3,500	--	282	282	3,500
1941	--	4,207	380[b]	--	380[b]	--
1944	137.7	12,000	--	675[c]	675[c]	12,000
1945	128.2	11,365	--	--	640[c]	10,500
1946	73.6	--	--	--	350	5,000
1947	66.4	--	--	--	300	3,000
1948	66.3	2,874	--	273	273	2,874
1949	79.2	2,900	--	273[a]	273	2,900
1950	82.8	4,000	--	266	266	4,000

DERIVATION OF MUNITIONS PROCUREMENTS, IN 1937 PRICES, AND SIZE OF ARMED FORCES, 1928-62

	Defense Outlays Reported in State Budget (Including Pensions) (Billion Current Rubles) (1)	Reported Size of Armed Forces (Thousands) (2)	Gross Output of Defense Industry, Official Index (1937 = 100) (3)	Munitions Procurements, Bergson's Estimates in 1937 Prices (1937 = 100) (4)	Present Estimates	
					Munitions Procurements in 1937 Prices (1937 = 100) (5)	Size of Armed Forces (Thousands) (6)
1951	93.9	4,900	- -	299	299	4,900
1952	108.6	5,800	- -	371	371	5,800
1953	105.0	5,800	- -	371	371	5,800
1954	101.8	5,800	- -	333	333	5,800
1955	107.4	5,763	- -	415	415	5,500
1956	97.3	5,123	- -	- -	430	4,900
1957	91.2	4,363	- -	- -	435	4,000
1958	93.6	3,923	- -	- -	460	3,800
1959	93.7	3,623	- -	- -	470	3,623
1960	93.3	3,623	- -	- -	470	3,623
1961	102.6	- -	- -	- -	535	3,623
1962	134.0[b]	- -	- -	- -	750[b]	3,623

[a]Relative obtained from data for all procurements for defense, i.e., munitions and "other."
[b]Planned.
[c]Excluding Lend-Lease.

for us to explore this complex question here, and, following Bergson, we employ the series shown as our indicator of the outlays in question.

Column 2 (Reported Size of Armed Forces): The data include the army, navy, and air force, but not internal security forces. Those for 1937, 1941, 1945, 1948, and 1955–60 are from a speech of Khrushchev's (*Pravda*, January 15, 1960) or computed from figures given by him and official Soviet announcements of force reductions (as cited in Nimitz–62, p. 50). Khrushchev's figures appear generally to refer to the beginning of the year, except that for 1945, which is for May. The 1928 figure is from a Soviet encyclopedia (as cited in Hoeffding–54, p. 111). The 1933 and 1935 figures are based on contemporary Soviet statements of army strength, adjusted to allow for other services, and are intended to be average annual figures; see Eason–59, pp. 394–95. The figures for 1940, 1944, and 1949–54 are Bergson's estimates of the average annual size of the forces; see Bergson–61, pp. 364–65.

Column 3 (Gross Output of Defense Industry): An official index of the gross output of "defense industry" can be pieced together for a few years from various Soviet sources. Figures for 1937, 1938, 1939, and 1941 Plan are cited by Bergson–61, p. 371. For 1933, see Sorokin–46, p. 41, who gives an index on a 1938 base. For 1936, see *Russian Economic Notes*, No. 367, 1938, p. 3.

The difficulty in using this information lies not only in the deficiencies of the "unchanging 1926/27 prices" in which the index is computed, but also in the ambiguity of the scope of the "defense industry." The data apparently refer to the gross output of a certain group of enterprises. The latter no doubt had defense output as their primary concern, but it is doubtful both that they were occupied entirely with this sort of production or that they alone were engaged in it. The precise significance of the index, thus, is by no means clear. We note, however, that, for 1937–41 Plan, the official index and Bergson's deflation of munitions procurements (column 4) appear mutually consistent.

Column 4 (Munitions Procurements, Bergson's Estimates): Bergson–61, pp. 366, 377. Bergson distinguishes four kinds of defense outlays, i.e., for military pay, military subsistence, munitions procurements, and "other." The latter category includes operating costs, such as procurement of petroleum, and certain kinds of military construction. For all of the years covered in the table, except 1928 and 1949, he provides separate figures for munitions and "other," and, with the exception of 1928 and 1949, therefore, the index shown in the table refers to munitions procurements only. For 1928, the relative shown refers to Bergson's estimate of all procurements, munitions and "other." For 1949, munitions procurements are assumed to be at the same level as in 1948, because the 1949 total of munitions and "other" procurements is the same as for 1948. The estimates of munitions procurements are obtained from Soviet budgetary data similar to those shown in column 1. Total current outlays are reduced by payments for pay and subsistence and expenditures for military procurements other than munitions. The residual is deflated into 1937 prices by estimated price index numbers for munitions. For a complete description of the calculations, see Bergson–61, Appendix E.

Columns 5 and 6 (Present Estimates): In describing our estimates, we begin with the series for force strength (column 6). Our figures are intended to be read as annual averages. For 1928, 1933, 1935, 1940, 1944, 1948–54, and 1959–60, we use the corresponding figures from column 2. For 1937 and 1955, we take Bergson's estimates of annual averages (Bergson–61, p. 364). For 1929–32, we use the 1928 figure, while for 1934, 1936, and 1938–39, we estimate by interpolation; for these years, see also Eason–59, pp. 394–95, and Nutter–62, p. 327. In estimating the rate of demobilization during 1945–48, we are guided mainly by data on the number of "workers and employees" in the Soviet economy. According to TsSU–57, p. 203, the latter were more numerous by about one million at the end of 1945 than on average during 1945. Between 1945 and 1946, their average annual number increased by 4 million, between 1946 and 1947 by 2.1 million, and between 1947 and 1948 by 1.6 million; see Weitzman–61, p. 60. Given that large numbers of demobilized soldiers must have returned to the collective farms (as opposed to joining the ranks of workers and employees) and that accretions to the noncollective-farm labor force from sources other than the armed forces must have been small, if not negative, in the immediate postwar years, we take these data to indicate a significant demobilization in operation as early as 1945, reaching a maximum rate during 1946, but continuing to some extent in 1947 as well. For 1956–58, we use annual averages computed from the official statements on force numbers and the timing of reductions as given in Nimitz–62, p. 33. For 1961 and 1962, the 1960 figure is used.

Our estimates of munitions procurements (column 5) are obtained as more or less freehand interpolations and extrapolations on Bergson's deflation of munitions procurements. We use Bergson's figure for procurements for 1928. For 1929–36, we also consider: (*i*) Probable changes in current outlays for pay and subsistence, as indicated by the size of the armed forces and money wages in the civilian economy; see column 6 of Table P–2; TsUNKhU–36a, pp. 368–69; and *Planovoe khoziaistvo*, 1937:3, p. 242, and 1939:5, p. 170. Given the contemporary decline in real civilian wages, money wages seem a more appropriate guide to money costs of pay and subsistence than at least one obvious alternative, retail prices. (*ii*) The balance of current defense outlays, after deducting pay and subsistence, together with the price index for civilian machinery, as an indicator of possible changes in real outlays on munitions. See Moorsteen–62, p. 72, and Table A–9 of this study for machinery prices; the index in reference is that using given-year weights. On the basis of the foregoing, it would seem that real outlays on munitions were low, less than a tenth of 1937, from 1928 through 1933, followed by sizable, successive, annual increases during 1934–37. This, however, is difficult to reconcile with the official index of "defense industry" production (column 3), which indicates a 1933 level of output over a third that of 1937. Perhaps budget accounting changed or the munitions produced in 1933 were not transferred to the Commissariat of Defense until 1934, resulting in a lag between output and expenditure. On the other hand, many other explanations are also possible, and, given the ambiguity surrounding most of the key magnitudes, there is obviously ample opportunity to go astray in trying to reconstruct the actual events. Without attempting precision, we proceed provisionally on the assumption that the various data cited in columns 1–3 of Table P–2 have at least some basis in reality, that is, that the period from 1928 to 1937 is divided into two fairly distinct subperiods, an early one of relative stability in real defense outlays and production and a later one of rapid increase. The apparently contradictory evidence for 1933 is taken as a difference in the timing of the transition as between production and expenditures. On this basis, and using the calculations described earlier in this paragraph as guidelines within subperiods, we obtain the index of munitions procurements shown in column 5.

For 1937, 1940, 1944, and 1948–55, we use Bergson's deflation of munitions procurements. We interpolate for 1938–39 and extrapolate to 1941 by means of the official index of defense industry production. The index of munitions procurements in 1945 is extrapolated from that for 1944. Money outlays for pay and subsistence probably changed little between the two years, declining numbers of men under arms being offset by rising costs. According to Bergson's estimates, munitions prices were relatively stable—i.e., rose about 10 percent—between 1944 and 1948; see Bergson–61, p. 367. Thus, the modest reduction in total budget outlays which occurred in 1945 suggests a larger proportional reduction in munitions procurements. Because we use the munitions index as an indicator of income originated by Soviet defense industries, we have adjusted both Bergson's 1944 munitions procurements figure and our extrapolated 1945 figure to exclude procurements of finished goods through Lend-Lease. For the same reason, we make no similar allowance for Lend-Lease shipments in the form of raw materials for industrial processing or consumers goods used for military subsistence. Bergson estimates that Lend-Lease shipments of military end products amounted to about 6.5 billion 1937 rubles in 1944, out of total procurements of 70.6 billion; see Bergson–61, pp. 99, 366. The volume of such shipments declined by about 70 percent between 1944 and 1945; cf. *Foreign Commerce Weekly*, June 29, 1946, p. 31. We estimate total munitions procurements for 1945 at about 63 billion 1937 rubles. Net of Lend-Lease shipments, therefore, they would come to about 61 billion, or 640 percent of Bergson's estimated 1937 level; see Bergson–61, p. 377.

The figures for 1946 and 1947 are extrapolated in much the same way from 1948. Although armed forces are assumed to decline significantly between 1946 and 1947, remaining roughly stable between 1947 and 1948, money outlays for pay and subsistence must have followed a different course. Pay rates may have risen, as they did in the civilian economy, and subsistence costs per man, insofar as they are reflected in prices for consumer goods, must have increased sharply between 1946 and 1947, only to decline modestly between 1947 and 1948; see Table P–3 below. Thus, total outlays for pay and subsistence probably changed rather little during 1946–48, and most of the change in the total defense budget would have been realized through changes in procurements. On this basis, and taking account of the relative stability of Bergson's munitions price index, we set munitions procurements in 1947 at about 10 percent above 1948 and in 1946 at about 15 percent above 1947. We make no allowance for Lend-Lease in these years, as shipments of military products had largely stopped by September of 1945; see *Foreign Commerce Weekly*, February 9, 1946, p. 40, and June 29, 1946, p. 31.

Our figures for 1956–62 are extrapolated from 1955 by adjusting total expenditures for changes in pay and subsistence and in munitions prices. For pay and subsistence in 1955, we use Bergson's figure of 40.6 billion rubles; see Bergson–61, p. 364. For subsequent years, we adjust this figure to allow for changes in armed force size (but not for changes in pay or subsistence costs per man); see column 6. Wholesale prices of civilian machinery declined about 12 percent between 1955 and 1956, remaining stable, so far as we know, thereafter; see Moorsteen–62, Table E–2, and TsSU–61a, p. 258. As our extrapolating index for munitions procurements after 1955, therefore, we use total current defense outlays, reduced by the amount of pay and subsistence and adjusted to allow for a 12 percent reduction in munitions costs between 1955 and 1956.

As noted earlier, the index of munitions industries production in Table P–1 (row 2b) is obtained from the index of munitions procurements by the introduction of a six-month lag. In deriving production index numbers for 1940 and 1961, the planned procurements index numbers for 1941 and 1962 are used. After 1933, the production index numbers are rounded to the nearest 5. The index of military services in Table P–1 (row 7d) is assumed to move with the size of armed forces (Table P–2, column 6).

Row 2c (Construction): The series is that for investment in construction in 1937 prices, including capital repairs, from Table A–1.

Row 3 (Transportation and Communications): The series used is the simple sum of ton-kilometers plus passenger-kilometers generated by the principal Soviet carriers. For the years 1928–50, the index refers to freight and passengers carried by railroads and river craft plus freight (but not passengers) carried by motor vehicles. For 1955–60, passengers carried by motor vehicles are also included. Three carriers (sea craft, airplanes, and pipelines) are omitted because of their relative unimportance and because data for them are available only for certain years. The following tabulation shows freight ton-kilometers plus passenger-kilometers moved by the carriers included in the index as a percentage of those moved by all Soviet carriers for selected years:

1928	93	1945	91
1932	92	1950	93
1937	92	1955	93
1940	95	1960	91

The data for freight and passenger transportation are from TsSU–57d, pp. 7, 12, 32, 116, 155, and TsSU–62, pp. 271, 273.

Row 4 (Trade): The series used is for the total volume of retail trade in 1937 prices, as computed in Table P–3. The data cover retail sales to households (including retail sales of producer goods), restaurant sales, and retail marketings to institutions, but exclude intravillage transactions and all trade by wholesale marketing enterprises. They fall short, therefore, of reflecting all value added in trade.

The method of computation is more or less apparent from the organization of Table P–3. The data on retail trade turnover in current prices (columns 1 and 4) are deflated by retail price indexes (columns 2 and 5) to obtain indexes of the volume of trade in 1937 prices (columns 3 and 6). The latter two series, which refer to state and co-operative trade, on the one hand, and to collective-farm market trade, on the other, are combined

TABLE P-3

DERIVATION OF RETAIL TRADE IN 1937 PRICES, 1928-61
(1937 = 100)

	State and Co-operative			Collective-Farm Market			Total
	Trade Turnover in Current Prices	Retail Price Index	Trade Turnover in 1937 Prices	Trade Turnover in Current Prices	Retail Price Index	Trade Turnover in 1937 Prices	Trade Turnover in 1937 Prices
	(1)	(2)	(3)	(4)	(5)	(6)	(7)
1928	12.1*	11.5*	105.2*	0.0	--	0.0	91.8
1929	13.9*	12.5*	111.2*	0.0	--	0.0	97.1
1930	15.9*	14.0*	113.6*	0.0	--	0.0	99.2
1931	22.2	19.7	112.7	0.0	--	0.0	98.4
1932	32.0	36.4	87.9	42.1	430	9.8	78.0
1933	39.5	54.5	72.5	64.6	250	25.8	66.6
1934	49.1	64.3	76.4	78.7	200	39.3	71.7
1935	64.9	83.2	78.0	81.5	170	47.9	74.2
1936	84.8	98.4	86.2	87.7	100	87.7	86.4
1937	100.0	100	100.0	100.0	100	100.0	100.0
1938	111.2	100	111.2	--	--	95.0	109.1
1939	123.7	102	129.1	--	--	85.0	123.5
1940	139.0	126	110.3	--	--	81.2	106.6
1944	94.7	149	63.6	--	--	10.0	56.8
1945	127.2	168	75.7	--	--	15.0	68.0
1946	196.3	237	82.8	--	--	30.0	76.1
1947	262.7	346	75.9	--	--	45.0	72.0
1948	246.3	300	82.1	--	--	62.5	79.6
1949	266.1	268	99.3	--	--	106.2	100.2
1950	285.5	222	128.6	--	--	143.7	130.5

TABLE P-3 (continued)

DERIVATION OF RETAIL TRADE IN 1937 PRICES, 1928-61

(1937 = 100)

	State and Co-operative			Collective-Farm Market			Total
	Trade Turnover in Current Prices	Retail Price Index	Trade Turnover in 1937 Prices	Trade Turnover in Current Prices	Retail Price Index	Trade Turnover in 1937 Prices	Trade Turnover in 1937 Prices
	(1)	(2)	(3)	(4)	(5)	(6)	(7)
1951	301.6	206	146.4	--	--	143.7	146.1
1952	312.5	198	157.8	--	--	156.2	157.6
1953	342.0	180	190.0	--	--	150.0	184.9
1954	382.6	170	225.1	--	--	143.7	214.8
1955	398.6	170	234.5	--	--	143.7	223.0
1956	434.7	171	254.2	--	--	138.0	239.4
1957	496.3	171	290.2	--	--	138.9	271.0
1958	537.7	175	307.3	--	--	137.2	285.7
1959	571.1	174	328.2	--	--	134.8	303.6
1960	623.7	173	360.5	--	--	120.2	330.0
1961	--	--	--	--	--	--	342.2

*Includes private trade.

into an index for total trade (column 7) as a weighted average. The weights
are the value of sales for consumption to households of each kind of trade
at 1937 factor cost, i.e., 57.7 and 8.4 billion rubles, respectively, as given
in Bergson–61, p. 128. For 1961, however, the value of all trade in 1937
prices is assumed to have increased over 1960 at the rate of the official
index of the physical volume of state and co-operative trade, i.e., by 3.7
percent; see TsSU–62, p. 358.

The series for state and co-operative turnover in current prices (column
1) includes the value of private trade for the years 1928–30, before such
trade was eliminated. The data are from TsSU–61, p. 681 (for state and
co-operative), from TsSU–56, p. 14 (for private). The series for collective-
farm market trade in current prices (column 4) is from *Planovoe khoziaistvo*, 1939:5, p. 171, and Stalin–52, p. 624.

The price index numbers for state and co-operative trade (including
private for 1928) are from Bergson–61, p. 416, for 1928, 1937, 1940, 1948–55.
For 1929, the simple mean of January 1 index numbers for state, co-operative, and private trade for 1929 and 1930 is used; see Table L–6 of this
study. The January 1, 1930, index number for state, co-operative, and
private trade is 13.0, that for January 1, 1931, for state and co-operative
trade only, 14.3; see Table L–6. Prices in private trade were rising and
were above those in state and co-operative trade at this time, though the
relative importance of private trade was rapidly declining; see *Ekonomicheskoe obozrenie*, 1930:3, p. 189, and TsSU–56, p. 14. We take the annual
average price level for 1930 for all forms of trade to be 14 percent of 1937.
For 1932, the average annual index number estimated for state and co-
operative trade in Appendix L, p. 575, is used. For 1931 and 1933–36 we
use straight-line, for 1938–39 free-hand, interpolations on the January 1
figures of Table L–6. For 1944–47, annual averages are derived from the
same sources and methods as employed for the January 1 figures of Table
L–6. Finally, the indexes for 1956–60 are official indexes, chained to 1955
in the manner explained in the discussion of Table L–6.

The price index numbers for collective-farm market trade for 1932–37
are from Holzman–60, p. 168.

The volume of collective-farm market trade in 1937 prices (column 6) is
obtained as the quotient of columns 4 and 5 for 1932–37. For 1938–39 and
1945–47, the figures are obtained by interpolating between preceding and
succeeding terminal dates. For 1940, 1944, 1948–55, the figures are from
Bergson–61, p. 312. The figures for 1956–58 are obtained from that for
1940 and a Soviet, 1940-based, index of the volume of collective-farm
market sales in TsSU–59, p. 788; those for 1959–60 are obtained from a
similar index in TsSU–61, p. 737.

Row 5 (Housing): The series is that for the average annual gross value
of the housing stock, computed from Table T–15. The 1939–40 territorial
acquisitions are handled as in fn. 10, p. 82.

*Rows 6 (Finance), 7a (Health), 7b (Education), 7c (Government and
Other Administration):* The indexes shown are for average annual employment of workers and employees in the indicated sectors. The underlying data, with exceptions noted below, are from Weitzman–61, p. 60, for
1928–59; TsSU–61, p. 637, for 1960; and TsSU–62, p. 312, for 1961. Following Weitzman–61, p. 93, the figures given in the sources for education for

1960 and 1961 have been adjusted to exclude employment in geological prospecting, etc. For the years 1938–39 and 1946–48, 1951–52, 1954, the employment series used for finance and for government administration are interpolations.

Row 7e (Repairs, Domestic Service, etc.): We follow Bergson–61, p. 318, in assuming the real volume of these services to be constant over the period studied, except for 1944–47. For 1945–47, we interpolate between Bergson's figures for 1944 and 1948.

Product by Sector

The estimates shown in Table T–47 of Gross and Net National Product by sector of origin, for such sectors as are distinguished in the text of Part II, are obtained from Table P–1 and from the depreciation series implicit in our capital stock calculations. Net product in housing and agriculture is obtained from the indexes and 1937 values for these sectors shown in Table P–1. Net product for nonresidential, nonagricultural, and nonagricultural nonresidential sectors are the appropriate remainders. Gross product is obtained by adding depreciation to net, the distribution of depreciation among sectors being calculated as in the capital service estimates (see fn. 37, p. 168).

NATIONAL PRODUCT IN 1928 AND 1950 PRICES

We obtain the product estimates in 1928 and 1950 prices (factor costs) shown in the Tabular Section, Tables T–48 and T–49, by procedures which are essentially the reverse of those employed for the 1937-price calculations. That is to say, we start with Gross National Product, taken from Bergson, deduct depreciation as estimated in this study, and then estimate net product in agriculture and housing to distribute total net product among the sectors we consider. Sectoral gross products are obtained by adding depreciation to net products. The several steps in the procedure are shown in Table P–4, except for the distribution of depreciation among sectors which parallels that in the 1937-price calculations. Sources of the data in Table P–4 are presented below, in the order of the rows.

Row 1 (Gross National Product): The figures are from Bergson–61, pp. 149, 153.

Row 2 (Depreciation): The figures are from this study, Table T–11.

Row 3 (Net National Product): Row 1 minus row 2.

Row 4 (Net Product in Agriculture): The figure for 1928 in 1928 prices is from Bergson–60, p. 33. For 1937, gross output exclusive of changes in livestock herds is computed in 1926/27 prices from price and quantity data given in Johnson–59, pp. 204 and 231–32; 1926/27 prices are assumed equivalent to 1928 prices. Net investment in livestock in each year (Table T–45 of this study) is added to the foregoing totals. The 1937/1928 output relative so obtained is applied to the 1928 net product total of Table P–4 to obtain the 1937 figure. On these various procedures, see the discussion of agriculture in the 1937-price calculations.

The figure for 1950 net product in agriculture in 1950 prices is derived

TABLE P-4

DERIVATION OF NATIONAL PRODUCT BY SECTOR OF ORIGIN
IN 1928 AND 1950 PRICES, SELECTED YEARS
(Billion Rubles)

		1928 Prices		1950 Prices				
		1928	1937	1928	1937	1940	1950	1955
1.	Gross National Product	29.56	81.3	298.6	478.4	561.7	694.1	1000.3
2.	Depreciation	1.80	7.4	9.3	23.3	32.2	36.9	61.2
3.	Net National Product. .	27.76	73.9	289.3	455.1	529.5	657.2	939.1
4.	Net Product in Agriculture	11.16	13.1	123.5	139.8	151.4	155.7	194.5
5.	Net Product in Housing	0.64	0.8	3.3	3.9	4.8	5.4	6.3
6.	Nonagricultural Net Product	16.60	60.8	165.8	315.3	378.1	501.5	744.6
7.	Nonresidential Net Product	27.12	73.1	286.0	415.2	524.7	651.8	932.8
8.	Nonagricultural Non-residential Net Product	15.96	60.0	162.5	311.4	373.3	496.1	738.3

in Table P–5. This table reproduces calculations made by Nancy Nimitz, whose generous co-operation and assistance is gratefully acknowledged. The calculations are intended to recapitulate the contribution of agriculture to Soviet national income as incorporated in the basic Bergson estimates used in row 1 of Table P–4—those presented in Bergson–61. Because the latter source presents accounts only on the outlay side, the income data needed here cannot all be read directly from it. Most of the data in Table P–5 are drawn from Hoeffding–59, therefore, which is also the basic source of the 1950 outlay accounts used in Bergson–61. Some of the 1950 figures in Bergson–61 reflect revisions made after the publication of Hoeffding–59. As it happens, however, all of these revisions are for items which occur on both the income and outlay side of the accounts in Hoeffding–59, and it has been possible, accordingly, to incorporate them into the calculation shown in Table P–5. Hoeffding–59 contains data in prevailing prices only. For those items for which factor cost differs from prevailing prices, the

TABLE P-5

DERIVATION OF INCOME ORIGINATING IN AGRICULTURE IN 1950,
IN 1950 PRICES
(Billion Rubles)

1.	Net Income of Households from Agriculture		
	1a. Wages of State Employed Farm Labor	17.9	
	1b. Wages of Farm Labor Hired by Collective Farms.	0.9	
	1c. Money Payments by Collective Farms to Members	11.4	
	1d. Net Income from Sale of Farm Products	42.1	
	1e. Consumption in Kind	68.9	
	1f. Net Investment in Kind (Livestock).	1.4	
	1g. Subtotal		142.6
2.	Net Income of Government and Economic Organizations from Agriculture		
	2a. Retained Income of Collective Farms	7.5	
	2b. Income Tax Paid by Collective Farms	2.9	
	2c. Profits of State Agricultural Organizations	1.9	
	2d. Social Insurance Charges	0.8	
	2e. Subtotal		13.1
3.	Net Income Originating in Agriculture, All Sectors . . .		155.7

appropriate adjustments have been introduced, using the allowances indicated in Bergson–61. As the present effort is concerned only with subtracting the agricultural contribution to national product as compiled for Bergson–61, the calculation in Table P–5 takes no account of information which became available after the preparation of Bergson–61.

Parenthetically we note, however, that in compiling Table P–4, one data inconsistency affecting the nonagricultural sector was left uncorrected. The 1950 income accounts in prevailing prices in Hoeffding–59 are based on an estimate of money subsidies of 27 billion rubles (p. 6). From information which became available subsequently, this estimate was changed to 15 billion rubles; see *ibid.*, p. 213, and Bergson–61, p. 151, fn. For the purposes of Bergson–61, no adjustment was made for this revision in the prevailing-price outlay account for 1950, but the revised subsidy figure was used in deriving outlays at factor cost from outlays in prevailing prices; see *loc. cit.* There is, thus, a relatively minor inconsistency between 1950 outlays at factor cost as given in Bergson–61 and the income account at factor cost implied by the underlying data. As the outlay accounts are used as weights in aggregating serial data to produce the GNP time series at 1950 factor cost (see *loc. cit.*), all years in the series are affected. Because the magnitude is slight and an extensive recalculation of the GNP series would be necessary to adjust for the inconsistency, we leave it uncorrected. The net effect on Table P–4 is an overstatement of nonagricultural income in 1950 equal to the difference between the revised and unrevised subsidy figures, i.e., 12 billion rubles.

The sources in detail of Table P–5 are as follows: For money incomes of households (rows 1a–1d), see Hoeffding–59, pp. 4–5. For household consumption and investment in kind (rows 1e–1f), see Bergson–61, p. 150. For convenience, all investment in kind is shown here as made by households. For retained income and income taxes of collective farms (rows 2a–2b), see Hoeffding–59, p. 6. Profits in the state agricultural sector (row 2c) are from *Planovoe khoziaistvo*, 1951:2, p. 27, which provides a sectoral distribution of the total profit figure used in Hoeffding–59, p. 119. This figure is for *khozraschet* organizations, gross of deductions to the state budget and subsidies. The figure shown for social insurance charges (row 2d) is 4.4 percent of the total wage bill in state agriculture, 17.9 billion rubles (row 1a). This is the rate applicable to agriculture and procurements, as given in Krulikovskaia–59, p. 18.

For years other than 1950, gross agricultural output, adjusted for herd changes, relative to 1950 is computed as in the 1928- and 1937-price calculations, and the relatives multiplied by the 1950 net product total to obtain net product in other years. The quantity data are from Johnson–59, pp. 231–32. The prices are average realized ruble prices of 1950. These, in rubles per ton or per 1,000 eggs, are: grain, 400; potatoes, 430; vegetables, 1,535; sunflower seed, 1,360; sugar beets, 105; seed cotton, 3,230; flax fiber, 4,270; wool, greasy weight, 11,300; milk, 855; meat, liveweight, 4,160; eggs, 545. The prices are from Bergson–61, p. 324, except for sugar beets and seed cotton. For the latter items, the prices are from Karcz–61, Table IV; they refer to 1952, but are evidently unchanged from 1950 (cf. Hoeffding–59, pp. 189 and 190).

Row 5 (Net Product in Housing): The figures shown are gross rentals, as indicated in Bergson–61, p. 316, arbitrarily reduced by 25 percent to allow for depreciation.

Row 6 (Nonagricultural Net Product): Row 3 minus row 4.

Row 7 (Nonresidential Net Product): Row 3 minus row 5.

Row 8 (Nonagricultural Nonresidential Net Product): Row 6 minus row 5.

Appendix Q

Employment

The labor series of which we make use in the study (see Table T–51) are for employment, in total and distributed between agricultural and non-agricultural sectors, adjusted and unadjusted for changes in hours worked per year. Their origins are explained in the two sections following.

EMPLOYMENT UNADJUSTED FOR CHANGES IN HOURS

Derivation of the estimates without adjustment for hours changes is shown in Table Q–1. The first two columns of the table show civilian employment divided between agricultural and nonagricultural organizations. In columns 3 and 4, the same data are reclassified to count as "nonagricultural" those persons working for agricultural organizations but engaged in nonagricultural activities. These two series together with armed force numbers (column 5) constitute our estimates of total employment (column 6). Because of Soviet reporting practices, however, the series apparently exclude employees of the internal security organs, the Ministry of Defense, the Communist Party, and the Young Communist League (see TsUNKhU–36b, pp. 360–61). Penal labor is also excluded. The figures are to be read as referring to man-years of work performed, in which the days per year and hours per day of work are those prevailing in the Soviet economy during the year in question. In the second section of this appendix, the same data are adjusted to allow for variations over time in days and hours worked.

The estimates of employment in nonagricultural organizations (column 1) are taken from, or patterned after, those in Eason–59, p. 121. His series is a summation over four socioeconomic groups: wage and salary earners, members of producers' co-operatives, independent artisans, and urban "bourgeoisie" (private entrepreneurs, a group which existed only in the earliest of the years considered here). Of these, the first accounts in all years for the bulk of the total. It includes all persons working for hire, with the exception of those employed by agricultural organizations, such as state farms, state subsidiary agricultural enterprises, machine-tractor stations, state veterinary stations, and the like. Employees of fishing and forestry enterprises are not excluded, however. The data refer to annual average employment, a Soviet statistical construct which is the quotient of (*i*) the total number of man-days in each month shown on the employment rosters of all employers, divided by (*ii*) the number of days in the month,

TABLE Q-1

DERIVATION OF EMPLOYMENT, UNADJUSTED FOR CHANGES IN HOURS, 1928-61
(Million Prevailing Man-Years)

	Civilian Employment in Nonagricultural Organizations (Workers, and Employees, Co-operative Members, Independent Artisans, Urban "Bourgeoisie")	Civilian Employment in Agricultural Organizations (Workers and Employees, Collective- Farm Members, Independent Peasants)	Civilian Non- agricultural Employment	Civilian Agricultural Employment	Armed Forces	Total
	(1)	(2)	(3)	(4)	(5)	(6)
1928	13.77	37.19	17.5	33.5	0.6	51.6
1929	14.53	35.96	18.1	32.4	0.6	51.1
1930	16.64	34.21	20.1	30.8	0.6	51.5
1931	20.08	32.13	23.3	28.9	0.6	52.8
1932	22.89	29.87	25.9	26.9	0.6	53.4
1933	21.74	31.89	24.9	28.7	0.6	54.2
1934	22.61	34.31	26.0	30.9	0.8	57.7
1935	23.82	37.86	27.6	34.1	1.1	62.8
1936	25.27	35.67	28.8	32.1	1.4	62.3
1937	26.53	37.75	30.3	34.0	1.7	66.0
1938	28.22	38.72	32.1	34.8	2.2	69.1
1939	29.98	38.75	33.8	34.9	2.9	71.6
1940	32.24	43.30	36.6	39.0	3.5	79.1
1945	26.52	37.57	30.3	33.8	10.5	74.6
1946	30.60	36.23	34.2	32.6	5.0	71.8
1947	31.83	38.09	35.6	34.3	3.0	72.9
1948	33.73	39.68	37.7	35.7	2.9	76.3
1949	35.56	42.24	39.8	38.0	2.9	80.7
1950	37.76	44.22	42.2	39.8	4.0	86.0
1951	39.39	42.74	43.7	38.5	4.9	87.1
1952	40.99	39.69	45.0	35.7	5.8	86.5
1953	41.99	40.59	46.0	36.5	5.8	88.3
1954	43.82	41.89	48.0	37.7	5.8	91.5
1955	44.38	44.48	48.8	40.0	5.5	94.3
1956	45.98	44.68	50.4	40.2	4.9	95.5
1957	47.84	45.03	52.3	40.5	4.0	96.8
1958	50.04	46.56	54.7	41.9	3.8	100.4
1959	52.44	45.31	57.0	40.8	3.6	101.4
1960	55.24	43.84	59.6	39.5	3.6	102.7
1961	58.34	43.24	62.7	38.9	3.6	105.2

(*iii*) averaged for the 12 months of the year (see, e.g., Kats–60, pp. 20–21). Thus, employees are counted as long as they remain on the roster, whether working or absent because of leaves, holidays, sickness, or the like. These data are reported more or less regularly, in a more or less straightforward fashion in Soviet statistical sources and are presumably among the most reliable information available on Soviet employment. For the remaining three groups, which account for about a quarter of the total in 1928 but never more than about 10 percent after 1932, the available data are less satisfactory. The membership of producers' co-operatives reported in Soviet sources tends to vary in coverage. As Eason–59 (pp. 378 ff.) explains, he has tried to assemble a series of comparable coverage over time, with the result, no doubt, that it is not fully comprehensive. Moreover, the extensions we have made to his series may have introduced variations in scope. Soviet data on independent artisans and "bourgeoisie" are available for the earliest years but must be roughly estimated for later ones.

In detail, the sources of the column 1 figures are these. Data for workers and employees in nonagricultural organizations for 1928–38, 1940, 1945–52, are from Eason–59, p. 224. For 1939, 1953–61, total employment of workers and employees (from Weitzman–61, p. 60, for 1939; from TsSU–61, p. 633, for 1940 and 1953–60; from *Pravda*, January 23, 1962, for 1961) is reduced by workers and employees of agricultural organizations. The data for the latter are from a forthcoming study by Nancy Nimitz. Following Eason–59, p. 220, and Weitzman–61, p. 59, we increase the figures for all workers and employees for 1939, 1953–61, which are given in the sources exclusive of domestic workers and day laborers, by 200,000 to adjust for the omission.

For members of producers' co-operatives, we use data from Eason–59, p. 360, for 1928–38; from TsSU–61, p. 633 for 1940, 1945, and 1950–60. For 1939, the 1938 figure is used. The figures for 1946–49 are straight-line interpolations. In 1960, the producers' co-operatives were transformed into state enterprises, and the members from that time are included in workers and employees; see TsSU–61, p. 633.

For independent artisans, see Eason–59, p. 379, for 1928–38. For 1939, the 1938 figure is used. For 1940, 1950, 1955–59, see Weitzman–61, p. 59. For 1945–49 and 1951–54, we extrapolate from the 1950 figure by means of the series for members of producers' co-operatives. For 1960 and 1961, the 1959 figure is used. For urban "bourgeoisie," see Eason–59, p. 360, for 1928–33. After 1933, this category is assumed to be negligible. The figures exclude "kulaks"; see Markus–36a, p. 381.

The data on employment by agricultural organizations (column 2) are from the Nimitz study, in which employment measured in man-days of work performed is estimated for state and institutional farms, MTS and RTS, state agricultural services, collective farms, and the private sector (independent peasant households and private plots of collective farmers, and of wage and salary earners). For the first three of these groups, the basic data are of the same nature as those for nonagricultural wage and salary workers, i.e., average annual employment as reported directly in Soviet statistical sources. Work performed for collective farms by members has, until quite recently, been recorded only in terms of the conventional units, "labor-days," against which collective-farm earnings are distributed. In addition, Soviet statisticians use peasant budget studies to estimate conversion factors, employed for present purposes by Miss Nimitz, from which the labor-day figures can be translated into man-days. Survey data of various dates are also available on labor inputs in man-days for different kinds of field crops and animal husbandry. Using these and statistics of private planting and livestock numbers, Miss Nimitz also estimates work performed in the private sector of agriculture. As with the other groups of agricultural organizations, the estimates include all work performed, direct and indirect labor inputs to agriculture and also nonagricultural activities by the indicated group workers. The method of estimation for the private sector is automatically inclusive of hired as well as own labor. An allowance is made for work hired, i.e., not performed by members, by collective farms.

In order to restate the original agricultural estimates, expressed in man-days, in terms more nearly comparable to those used for employment by nonagricultural organizations, we refer to the average number of days worked per year in large-scale industry as indicative of the number of days worked in the nonagricultural sector generally. Thus in column 2, the Nimitz estimates in man-days are translated into man-years, each of the number of days worked in the corresponding year in large-scale industry.

Although few of the employees of nonagricultural organizations are engaged in agricultural activities, the reverse cannot be said of those employed by agricultural organizations. In particular, collective farm members perform a variety of nonagricultural functions, such as production in subsidiary industrial enterprises, construction, or educational and cultural work. In Table Q–2, we show estimates of the relative importance of non-agricultural activities within agricultural organizations in various years. The figures show surprisingly little variation over time. Although we cannot hope for precision, the division of the total labor force between agricultural and nonagricultural pursuits would no doubt be improved if about 10 percent of those employed by agricultural organizations were counted in the nonagricultural part. In columns 3 and 4 of Table Q–1, the figures of columns 1 and 2 are adjusted accordingly.

TABLE Q-2

SHARE OF NONAGRICULTURAL WORK IN TOTAL WORK PERFORMED BY
FARM LABOR FORCE, SELECTED YEARS
(Percent)

	Scope of Data	Nonagricultural Work
1928	Productive work performed by agricultural population, measured in male-equivalent	10-15
1937	Work performed for labor-days by collective-farm members, measured in man-days	9
1940		10
1950	Work performed by collective-farm	10
1953	members, workers, and employees of	10
1955	state farms, MTS, RTS, and state	9
1956	subsidiary agricultural enterprises,	10
1957	exclusive of work performed on private	11
1958	plots, measured in average annual	10
1959	employment equivalents.	10
1960		9

The Table Q–2 figures are obtained, for 1928, from Bergson–61, p. 444. The author cites the following distribution of productive work done by the agricultural population during 1927/28 (in million male-equivalent years):

Arable agriculture, animal husbandry, work in pastures,
    gardens, vineyards 25.94
Forestry, fishing, hunting 1.21
Processing of agricultural products 2.60
Carting and other activities 4.90
      Total 34.65

From this he deducts 2.65 million man-years to allow for activities included in Eason's nonagricultural employment series. The deduction is not intended to include nonagricultural work such as forestry, fishing, hunting, etc., which is not in the latter series. The activities in the lower three rows of the tabulation, which presumably include all nonagricultural work, account after Bergson's deduction for 19 percent of the remaining total.

Assuming that nonagricultural work accounts for half to three quarters of this, such work would amount to 10–15 percent of the adjusted total.

For 1937, see Sautin–39, p. 97. The data presented are from a 1937 survey of 430 collective farms, in which labor performed, measured both in man-days and labor-days, was classified by activity into 13 categories. As nonagricultural activities, we take work for "construction and capital repairs," "subsidiary enterprises," "cultural-service establishments," "fulfillment of state and social obligations," and "work performed outside the collective farm."

For 1940, 1953, 1955, 1958–60, see TsSU–61, p. 521. For 1950, 1956–57, see TsSU–60a, p. 450.

The Table Q–1 series for armed force numbers (column 5) is Bergson's (Bergson–61, pp. 364–65), together with our interpolations and extrapolations, as explained in Appendix P of this study.

In general, our employment series are patterned after, and correspond closely to, those in Bergson–61, pp. 443 ff. The figures in column 1 differ only slightly from his series for "nonfarm" employment. Our figures for employment by agricultural organizations for years after 1928 differ somewhat more from his series for "farm" employment, because some data not previously employed have been introduced by Miss Nimitz and because we convert man-days to man-years by means of the days worked in industry rather than by a uniform 280 days per year. For reasons set forth in Chapter 9, we do not include, as Bergson does, estimates of penal labor.

It will be noted that the employment series, as is necessarily true for annual averages, are synthetic aggregates rather than head counts. The Soviet wage and salary earner series is itself a synthetic one. Soviet institutions make it possible to measure work performed in agriculture only in terms of statistical constructs, since the same individual is typically employed part time in the work of more than one enterprise. We refer to the series in Table Q–1 as "unadjusted" for changes in hours. This means that hours worked per year vary over time, in consequence of changes both in days worked per year and hours per day. For each year, however, the series is intended to aggregate man-years in all sectors of approximately the same number of *days*. Data are lacking on hours worked per day in agriculture; hence, it is not possible to determine differences in hours between the sectors.

EMPLOYMENT ADJUSTED FOR CHANGES IN HOURS

The only systematic data we have on days and hours worked in the Soviet economy refer to wage earners in large-scale industry. These are shown, without brackets, in columns 1–3 of Table Q–3. In column 4 of the table, these data are aggregated to form an index of hours worked per year. Although industry has usually accounted for only 30–40 percent of all non-agricultural employment in the Soviet economy, for want of better we use these data as indicative of trends generally in the nonagricultural sector. There is, no doubt, a tendency for hours in other sectors to change with those in industry. By the end of 1960, at least, the average workweek for all wage and salary earners was about the same as for wage earners in industry, 39.4 hours for the former versus 40 hours for the latter; see TsSU–61, p.

TABLE Q-3

DERIVATION OF HOURS WORKED PER YEAR BY WAGE EARNERS IN
LARGE-SCALE INDUSTRY, 1928-61[a]

	Average Number of Days Worked per Year (1)	Normal Working Day (Hours) (2)	Actual Working Day (Hours) (3)	Estimated Index of Actual Hours Worked per Year (1937 = 100) (4)
1928	263.0	7.8	7.37	106
1929	264.2	--	7.37	107
1930	252.7	--	7.38	102
1931	253.2	--	7.26	101
1932	257.2	--	7.16	101
1933	265.8	6.99[b]	7.11	104
1934	267.0	6.98	7.09	104
1935	268.0	(7.0)	7.06	104
1936	(264.1)	(7.0)	--	101
1937	260.3	(7.0)	--	100
1938	(260.3)	(7.0)	--	100
1939	(260.3)	(7.0)	--	100
1940	269.8	(7.5)	--	111
1944	(300.0)	(8.0)	(9.5)	156
1945	(292.0)	(8.0)	(8.5)	136
1946	(284.0)	(8.0)	--	125
1947	(276.3)	(8.0)	--	121
1948	(276.3)	(8.0)	--	121
1949	(276.3)	(8.0)	--	121
1950	276.3	(8.0)	--	121
1951	(275.7)	(8.0)	--	121
1952	(275.1)	(8.0)	--	121
1953	(274.5)	(8.0)	--	121
1954	(273.9)	(8.0)	--	120
1955	273.3	(8.0)	--	120
1956	272.1	7.96	--	119
1957	267.4	(8.0)	--	117
1958	268.0	7.4[c]	--	113
1959	266.5	7.3[c]	--	108
1960	(265.0)	6.67[c]	--	102
1961	(265.0)	--	--	97

[a] Figures in columns 1–3 in brackets are estimated.
[b] March.
[c] End of Year. Figures are weekly averages which allow for the reduction
in hours worked on Saturdays and before holidays.

645. But the coincidence can seldom be exact, and the adjustments we make here must be read with this source of error in mind.

Before discussing the data in Table Q–3 at greater length, it may be convenient to explain briefly the use made of them. In Table Q–4, the man-year employment series of Table Q–1 are adjusted so far as possible for changes in hours worked per year. The unadjusted figures for employment by nonagricultural organizations (Table Q–1, column 1) are multiplied by the index of man-hours per year in industry (Table Q–3, column 4). The result is intended to show man-years of work performed, in years having the same number of hours as 1937. Miss Nimitz's original estimates of employment by agricultural organizations, expressed in man-days, are now converted to man-years by dividing through uniformly by 260.3, the number of days worked in large-scale industry in 1937. The result is intended to show man-years of work performed, in years having the same number of days as in the nonagricultural sector in 1937. No adjustment for hours worked per day is made because we lack data on hours in agriculture and because no presumptive relationship exists between hours in that sector and hours in industry. As with the unadjusted series, 10 percent of employment by agricultural organizations is classified as nonagricultural employment. The resulting series for nonagricultural and agricultural employment, adjusted as indicated for changes in hours, are shown in columns 1 and 2 of Table Q–4. A soldier's life being what it is, we assume that adjustments for days per year or hours per day are not appropriate to the armed forces series and utilize the series from Table Q–1.

TABLE Q-4

DERIVATION OF EMPLOYMENT, ADJUSTED FOR CHANGES IN HOURS, 1928-61
(Million 1937 Man-Years)

	Civilian Nonagricultural Employment (1)	Civilian Agricultural Employment (2)	Armed Forces (3)	Total (4)
1928	18.4	33.8	0.6	52.8
1929	19.2	32.9	0.6	52.7
1930	20.3	29.9	0.6	50.8
1931	23.4	28.2	0.6	52.2
1932	26.1	26.6	0.6	53.3
1933	25.9	29.3	0.6	55.8
1934	27.0	31.7	0.8	59.5
1935	28.7	35.1	1.1	64.9
1936	29.1	32.6	1.4	63.1
1937	30.3	34.0	1.7	66.0
1938	32.1	34.8	2.2	69.1
1939	33.9	34.9	2.9	71.7
1940	40.3	40.4	3.5	84.2
1945	40.3	37.9	10.5	88.7
1946	42.2	35.6	5.0	82.8
1947	42.5	36.4	3.0	81.9
1948	45.0	37.9	2.9	85.8
1949	47.5	40.4	2.9	90.8
1950	50.4	42.2	4.0	96.6
1951	52.2	40.7	4.9	97.8
1952	53.8	37.7	5.8	97.3
1953	55.1	38.5	5.8	99.4
1954	57.0	39.7	5.8	102.5
1955	57.9	42.0	5.5	105.4
1956	59.4	42.0	4.9	106.3
1957	60.6	41.6	4.0	106.2
1958	61.3	43.1	3.8	108.2
1959	61.3	41.7	3.6	106.6
1960	60.8	40.2	3.6	104.6
1961	61.0	39.6	3.6	104.2

In summary, then, the adjusted total employment series (column 4 of Table Q–4) is intended to indicate employment in man-years, each year having the same number of days of work as 1937, and, for at least the nonagricultural part, each day having the same number of hours as in 1937. For agriculture the number of days are those of 1937 (in large-scale industry), but hours per day are uncertain.

The first column of Table Q–3 shows the average number of days worked per year. The figures include all days upon which any work at all was performed but exclude whole days missed for holidays, leave, sickness, equipment breakdowns, and the like. The second column shows the average "normal" working day, that is, the number of hours established for adult wage earners by regulation. The figures are weighted averages for the different branches of industry. The average "actual" working day, which differs from the "normal" by including overtime and excluding work stoppages of less than a whole day in duration, is shown in column 3. For the above definitions, see Kats–60, pp. 59–61, as well as the sources of the data cited in **Table Q–3.**

Data reported in Soviet sources are shown in the table without brackets and are obtained as follows.

Column 1 (Days Worked per Year): The data for 1929–35 are from Markus–36, p. 7. For 1934 and 1935, slightly different figures of 265.4 and 266.2 are given in TsUNKhU–35a, p. 142, and TsUNKhU–36b, p. 78. For 1937, 1940, 1950, 1955, and 1956, see *Vestnik statistiki*, 1957:2, p. 91. For 1957–59, see Shishkin–61, p. 69.

Column 2 (Normal Working Day): For 1928 and 1934, see TsUNKhU–36a, p. 386. For 1933, see TsUNKhU–35, p. 502. For 1956 and 1960, see TsSU–61, p. 645; for 1958, TsSU–59, p. 665; for 1959, TsSU–60, p. 596.

Column 3 (Actual Working Day): See Markus–36, p. 7, for 1928–35.

The reported data are supplemented for present purposes by estimates, which are enclosed in brackets in Table Q–3. To explain the estimates, it is necessary first to describe the main changes in work schedules over the period.

During the late 1920's and early 1930's, work schedules which were diverse with respect both to days per year and hours per day prevailed in different branches of industry. In 1929, a program was initiated, intended gradually to introduce a more or less uniform working day of seven hours (shorter hours were provided, however, for hazardous jobs, underground work, etc.). Judging from the data in Table Q–3, this objective was reached, at least on average, by March of 1933. Presumably, the seven hour "normal" day continued to predominate through the rest of the 1930's. A decree of June 26, 1940, increased the average length of the "normal" day to eight hours. It also provided that the working week be changed from five days of work out of every six, the pattern prevailing in most branches of industry during the 1930's, to six days of work out of every seven. The coming of the war affected work schedules in that overtime was encouraged, vacations were curtailed, etc. The "normal" day and week, however, were unchanged until 1956. The Twentieth Congress of the CPSU in February of that year called for the commencement in 1956 of a program designed gradually to reduce the standard workweek from 48 to 41 hours. The first step, promulgated in March of 1956, was a reduction in hours worked on Saturdays from eight to six. Thereafter, it was intended to reduce hours on week days from eight to seven, introducing the change gradually by enterprise and branch of industry. Where conditions were favorable, five eight-hour days out of seven were to be worked. These more consequential phases of the program apparently began slowly, and by the end of 1959, only about a quarter of all Soviet wage and salary earners were working according to the new regulations. By the end of 1960, however, the new hours had been established for all wage and salary earners.

The above account is drawn from Schwarz–51, pp. 259 ff., 268, 299, 302; TsUNKhU–36b, p. 80; *Pravda*, February 26, 1956; Anonymous–60a, pp. 137–38, 314; *Izvestiia*, July 13, 1960; and *Pravda*, October 14, 1960.

In estimating the number of days worked per year (Table Q-3, column 1), we have assumed that the figures for 1936, 1938–39, 1951–54, and 1960–61, would be closely related to those for proximate years in which the same basic regulations prevailed. For 1936, then, we interpolate between 1935 and 1937; for 1938–39, the 1937 figure is used; for 1951–54, we interpolate; for 1960, we extrapolate from 1959 and the 1957–59 rate of decrease; for 1961, the 1960 figure is used. According to Voznesenskii–47, p. 114, hours worked per month increased 22 percent "during two years" of World War II. If the actual working day just prior to the war were 8.5 hours (allowing for an excess of overtime over work stoppages) and days worked were at the rate of 1950, 276.3 per year, Voznesenskii's statement would imply a rate of work by mid-1943 of the order of 300 days per year, 9.5 hours per day (276.3 × 8.5 × 1.22 = 2,865.231; whereas 300 × 9.5 = 2,850). With this in mind, we put the 1944 work year at 300 days. More or less arbitrarily, we assume that the 1950 work year was attained by 1947. The intervening years, 1945–46, are interpolated.

The estimates of the "normal" working day are those indicated by the amount of work regulations given earlier. As noted there, the "normal" day is not uniform for all employees, but the seven-hour day prior to 1940 and the eight-hour day from mid-1940 to 1950 must have been predominant. As the 1940 change was decreed at the end of June, we use 7.5 hours for that year. For 1944, the estimate of 9.5 hours per actual working day corresponds to the estimate of days worked in that year, as explained above. The German surrender occurred about one third of the way through 1945. In 1945 as a whole, the average working day must have been substantially shorter than in 1944. We set it arbitrarily at 8.5 hours. In 1957–60, we assume that the normal day at the end of 1957 was still eight hours and compute annual average normal working days for 1958–60 (which are not shown in the table) as simple averages of the beginning and end of year figures.

We come finally to the index of hours worked per year, column 4. For the years 1928–35 and 1944–45, we compute hours worked per year as days worked (column 1) multiplied by actual hours worked (column 3). For all the remaining years except 1961, total hours are computed as days worked multiplied by the "normal" working day (column 2). For these years, we assume that work stoppages and overtime balance out. This was apparently true in the mid-1930's, but in 1928, as recently, the "normal" has tended to exceed the actual day (see, for example, columns 2 and 3 and Kats–60, p. 61). In the case of 1940, it is unlikely that the increased "normal" day went into practice as soon as decreed. This is suggested by the fact that the number of holidays decreased from 1937 to 1940 by 2.8, whereas the change from a five-day-out-of-six to a six-day-out-of-seven work rhythm would, during six months, produce a reduction of 4.5 days (see *Vestnik statistiki;* 1957:2, p. 91). The true "normal" day may have been shorter than 7.5 hours, but the actual day may have been even longer because of overtime. For 1961, hours worked are computed from days worked and the length of the "normal" day at the end of 1960.

Publications Cited

Citations in the text may be identified here by author's name and year of publication. Where more than one publication in a year is cited for the same author, identifying letters are shown in parentheses after date of publication.

ABRAMOVITZ, MOSES. "Resource and Output Trends in the United States since 1870," *American Economic Review*, May, 1956.

AFRUTKIN, SH. "O normalizatsii tovarnykh zapasov," *Voprosy ekonomiki*, 1962:12.

ANONYMOUS. *Gosudarstvennyi biudzhet Soiuza SSR za vtoruiu piatiletku (1933–1937)*. Leningrad, 1938 (?).

———— *Kratkii ekonomicheskii slovar'*. Moscow, 1958.

———— *Oxford Regional Economic Atlas: The U.S.S.R. and Eastern Europe.* Oxford, 1956.

———— *Sbornik zakonodatel'nykh aktov o trude.* Moscow, 1960(a).

———— *40 let sovetskoi torgovli.* Moscow, 1957.

———— *SSSR strana sotsializma.* Moscow, 1936.

———— *Summary of the Fulfillment of the First Five Year Plan.* Moscow, 1935.

———— "Tipovaia metodika opredeleniia ekonomicheskoi effektivnosti kapital'-nykh vlozhenii i novoi tekhniki v narodnom khoziaistve SSSR," *Planovoe khoziaistvo*, 1960:3.

———— *V pomoshch' predsedatelia kolkhoza, vypusk II.* Moscow, 1955.

ARAKELIAN, A. A. *Osnovnye fondy promyshlennosti SSSR.* Moscow, 1938.

ARNOLD, ARTHUR Z. *Banks, Credit, and Money in Soviet Russia.* New York, 1937.

ATLAS, M. (S.). "25 let kreditnoi reformy," *Den'gi i kredit*, 1955:2.

———— *Kreditnaia reforma v SSSR.* Moscow, 1952.

———— "Kreditnaia sistema SSSR v gody Velikoi Otechestvennoi voiny," *Sovetskie finansy*, 1945:6–7.

———— *Razvitie Gosudarstvennogo banka SSSR.* Moscow, 1958.

ATLAS, Z. (V.). "O planirovanii resursov Gosbanka i denezhnykh sredstv khozorganov i predpriiatii," *Planovoe khoziaistvo*, 1937:9–10.

———— and BREG'L, E. IA. *Denezhnoe obrashchenie i kredit SSSR.* Moscow, 1947.

BARKOVSKII, N. "Rol' Gosbanka v khoziaistvennoi zhizni strany," *Den'gi i kredit*, 1960:4.

BARNGOL'TS, S. B., and KHAVIN, I. E. *Puti uskoreniia oborachivaemosti oborotnykh sredstv v mashinostroenii.* Moscow, 1950.

———— and SUKHAREV, A. *Oborotnye sredstva promyshlennykh predpriiatii.* Moscow, 1957.

651

BATYREV, V. M. *Kreditnoe i kassovoe planirovanie.* Moscow, 1947.

———— and SITNIN, V. I. *Organizatsiia i planirovanie finansov sotsialisticheskoi promyshlennosti.* Moscow–Leningrad, 1940.

BAYKOV, ALEXANDER. *The Development of the Soviet Economic System.* Cambridge, 1948.

BECKER, GARY S. "Underinvestment in College Education," *American Economic Review,* May, 1960.

BERGSON, ABRAM. "National Income," in ABRAM BERGSON and SIMON KUZNETS (eds.), *Economic Trends in the Soviet Union.* Cambridge, 1963.

————"A Problem in Soviet Statistics," *Review of Economics and Statistics,* November, 1947.

———— *The Real National Income of Soviet Russia Since 1928.* Cambridge, 1961.

———— *Soviet National Income and Product in 1937.* New York, 1953.

———— BERNAUT, ROMAN, and TURGEON, LYNN. *Basic Industrial Prices in the U.S.S.R., 1928–1950: Twenty-five Branch Series and Their Aggregation.* The RAND Corporation, Research Memorandum RM–1522, August 1, 1955.

———— BERNAUT, ROMAN, and TURGEON, LYNN. "Prices of Basic Industrial Products in the U.S.S.R., 1928–50," *Journal of Political Economy,* August, 1956.

———— BLACKMAN, J. H., and ERLICH, A . "Postwar Economic Reconstruction and Development in the U.S.S.R.," *Annals of the American Academy of Political and Social Sciences,* May, 1949.

———— and HEYMANN, HANS, JR. *Soviet National Income and Product, 1940–1948.* New York, 1954.

———— HEYMANN, HANS, JR., and HOEFFDING, OLEG. *Soviet National Income and Product, 1928–1948: Revised Data.* The RAND Corporation, Research Memorandum RM–2544, November 15, 1960.

BIRMAN, A. M. *Planirovanie oborotnykh sredstv.* Moscow, 1956.

———— "Voprosy uluchsheniia organizatsii oborotnykh sredstv," *Voprosy ekonomiki,* 1963:1.

BOGOLEPOV, M. "Finansy SSSR nakanune tret'ei piatiletki," *Planovoe khoziaistvo,* 1937:3.

BOGOLIUBSKII, D. "Razmery sem'i krest'ianskogo khoziaistva i prirost chisla khoziaistv za 1916–1927 gg.," *Statisticheskoe obozrenie,* 1929:9.

BRACKETT, JAMES W. "Demographic Trends and Population Policy in the Soviet Union," in Joint Economic Committee, U.S. Congress, *Dimensions of Soviet Economic Power.* Washington, 1962.

BUNICH, P. *Amortizatsiia osnovnykh fondov v promyshlennosti.* Moscow, 1957.

———— *Osnovnye fondy sotsialisticheskoi promyshlennosti.* Moscow, 1960.

———— *Pereotsenka osnovnykh fondov.* Moscow, 1959.

CAMPBELL, ROBERT W. *Accounting in Soviet Planning and Management.* Cambridge, 1963.

———— "A Comparison of Soviet and American Inventory-Output Ratios," *American Economic Review,* September, 1958.

———— Statistical Appendix to Campbell–58, processed, 1958 (a).

CHAPMAN, JANET G. "Consumption," in ABRAM BERGSON and SIMON KUZNETS (eds.), *Economic Trends in the Soviet Union.* Cambridge, 1963.

———— *Retail Prices and Real Wages in the Soviet Union Since 1928,* preface dated 1959 (processed).

CHERNYSHOVA, T. "Planovye platezhi po spetsial'nym ssudnym schetam," *Den'gi i kredit,* 1957:8.

———— "Usilit' kontrol' banka za rabotoi snabzhencheskikh i sbytovykh organizatsii," *Den'gi i kredit,* 1959:1.

CLARK, M. G. *The Economics of Soviet Steel.* Cambridge, 1956.

Den'gi i kredit (serial).

DEWITT, NICHOLAS. "Costs and Returns to Education in the U.S.S.R.," unpublished doctoral dissertation, Harvard University, March, 1962.

D'IACHENKO, V. P. (ed.). *Finansy i kredit SSSR.* Moscow-Leningrad, 1940.

DOMAR, E. D. "On the Measurement of Technological Change," *Economic Journal,* December, 1961.

DONDE, IA. A., FREIDMAN, Z. M., and CHIRKOV, G. I. *Khoziaistvennyi dogovor i ego rol' v snabzhenii narodnogo khoziaistva SSSR.* Moscow, 1953.

DORFMAN, ROBERT, SAMUELSON, PAUL A., and SOLOW, ROBERT M. *Linear Programming and Economic Analysis.* New York, 1958.

EASON, WARREN W. "Labor Force," in ABRAM BERGSON and SIMON KUZNETS (eds.), *Economic Trends in the Soviet Union.* Cambridge, 1963.

———— *Soviet Manpower.* Princeton, 1959.

ECKSTEIN, ALEXANDER, and GUTMANN, PETER. "Capital and Output in the Soviet Union, 1928–1937," *Review of Economics and Statistics,* November, 1956.

Economic Survey (serial publication of the State Bank of the U.S.S.R.).

EDINOVICH, I. "Kredit i razvitie ekonomiki Litovskoi SSR," *Den'gi i kredit,* 1957:9.

EFIMOV, O. "1933 god v tsifrakh," *Kredit i khozraschet,* 1934:2.

Ekonomicheskoe obozrenie (serial).

ERLICH, ALEXANDER. *The Soviet Industrialization Debate, 1924–1928.* Cambridge, 1960.

EZHOV, A. I. *Statistika promyshlennosti.* 3rd ed. Moscow, 1957.

FEI, JOHN C. H., and RANIS, GUSTAV. "Innovation, Capital Accumulation, and Economic Development," *American Economic Review,* June, 1963.

FILATOV, N. "O normakh amortizatsii i zatratakh na remont zhilishchnogo fonda," in *Planirovanie i finansirovaniia kapital'nogo remonta osnovnykh fondov.* Moscow, 1958.

Finansy SSSR (serial).

FOMIN, A. "Torgovlia SSSR v 1-oi polovine 1927/28 g.," *Statisticheskoe obozrenie,* 1928:5.

Foreign Commerce Weekly (serial).

FREIMUNDT, D. T. *Ocherki po statistike natsional'nogo bogatstva SSSR.* Moscow, 1955.

FRONTAS'EVA, M. "Novye broshiury o raschetakh v narodnom khoziaistve SSSR," *Den'gi i kredit,* 1956:2.

GARBUZOV, V. F. "Rol' finansov v razvitii sotsialisticheskogo sel'skogo khoziastva," in *Finansy i sotsialisticheskoe stroitel'stvo.* Moscow, 1957.

GERASHCHENKO, V. "Gosudarstvennyi bank v 1940 godu," *Den'gi i kredit,* 1939:11–12.

———— "Kreditnyi plan vtorogo kvartala i zadachi Gosudarstvennogo banka," *Den'gi i kredit,* 1941:3.

———— "Nekotorye voprosy ukrepleniia khoziaistvennogo rascheta," *Den'gi i kredit,* 1957:7.

GERSCHENKRON, ALEXANDER. *A Dollar Index of Soviet Machinery Output, 1927–28 to 1937.* The RAND Corporation, Report R-197, April 6, 1951.

GIBSHMAN, A. "Zhilishchnyi fond i zhilishchnye usloviia nashikh gorodov," *Statisticheskoe obozrenie,* 1928:7.

———— and SIFMAN, P. "Stoimost' gorodskogo zhilishchnogo fonda," *Statisticheskoe obozrenie,* 1929:1.

GOLDSMITH, RAYMOND W. "The Growth of Reproducible Wealth of the United States of America from 1805 to 1950," in International Association for Research in Income and Wealth, *Income and Wealth,* Series II. Cambridge, 1952.

———— *The National Wealth of the United States in the Postwar Period.* Princeton, 1962.

———— "A Perpetual Inventory of National Wealth," in Conference on Research in Income and Wealth, *Studies in Income and Wealth.* Vol. 14. New York, 1951.

———— *A Study of Saving in the United States* (three volumes). Princeton, 1956.

GOLEV, IA. "Razvitiia sovetskogo kredita," in *Finansy SSSR za XXX let*. Moscow, 1947.

GORFINKEL', E. "Sezonnye kolebaniia bankovskogo kredita," *Kredit i khozraschet*, 1937:3.

GOSBANK. *Gosudarstvennyi bank k VII vsesoiuznomu s"ezdu sovetov*. Moscow, 1935.

GOSPLAN. *Kontrol'nye tsifry narodnogo khoziaistva SSSR na 1928/1929 god*. Moscow, 1929.

———— *Kontrol'nye tsifry narodnogo khoziaistva SSSR na 1929/1930 god*. Moscow, 1930.

———— *Kontrol'nye tsifry narodnogo khoziaistva SSSR na 1927/28 god*. Moscow, 1928.

———— *Piatiletnii plan narodno-khoziaistvennogo stroitel'stva SSSR*. 3rd ed. Moscow, 1930 (a).

———— *The Second Five Year Plan*. New York, 1936 (?).

———— *Tretii piatiletnii plan razvitiia narodnogo khoziaistva Soiuza SSR (1938–1942)*. Moscow, 1939.

———— *Vtoroi piatiletnii plan razvitiia narodnogo khoziaistva SSSR (1933–1937 gg.)*. Moscow, 1934.

GOZULOV, A. I. *Ekonomicheskaia statistika*. Moscow, 1953.

———— *Statistika sel'skogo khoziaistva*. Moscow, 1959.

GRANOVSKII, E. L., and MARKUS, B. L. *Ekonomika sotsialisticheskaia promyshlennosti*. Moscow, 1940.

GRANT, EUGENE L., and NORTON, PAUL T., JR. *Depreciation*. New York, 1949.

GRIN'KO, G. F. *Financial Program of the U.S.S.R. for 1936*. Moscow, 1936.

———— *Finansovaia programma Soiuza SSR na 1937 god*. Moscow, 1937.

GUMILEVSKII, A. "Raspredelenie operatsii mezhdu filialami banka," *Kredit i khozraschet*, 1936:23.

HODGMAN, DONALD R. *Soviet Industrial Production, 1928–1951*. Cambridge, 1954.

HOEFFDING, OLEG. *Soviet National Income and Product in 1928*. New York, 1954.

———— and NIMITZ, N. *Soviet National Income and Product, 1949–1955*. The RAND Corporation, Research Memorandum RM-2101, April 6, 1959.

HOLZMAN, FRANKLYN D. "Foreign Trade," in ABRAM BERGSON and SIMON KUZNETS (eds.), *Economic Trends in the Soviet Union*. Cambridge, 1963.

———— "Soviet Inflationary Pressures, 1928–1957: Causes and Cures," *Quarterly Journal of Economics*, May, 1960.

———— *Soviet Taxation*. Cambridge, 1955.

HUBBARD, LEONARD E. *Soviet Trade and Distribution*. London, 1938.

HUNTER, HOLLAND. *Soviet Transportation Policy*. Cambridge, 1957.

IURTSOVSKII, M. "Khod uborki po mnogoletnim dannym," *Statisticheskoe obozrenie*, 1928:7.

Izvestiia.

JASNY, NAUM. "Labor and Output in Soviet Concentration Camps," *Journal of Political Economy*, October, 1951 (a).

———— *The Socialized Agriculture of the U.S.S.R.* Stanford, 1949.

———— *Soviet Industrialization, 1928–1952*. Chicago, 1961.

———— *Soviet Prices of Producers' Goods*. Stanford, 1952.

———— *The Soviet Price System*. Stanford, 1951.

JASZI, GEORGE, WASSON, ROBERT C., and GROSE, LAWRENCE. "Expansion of Fixed Business Capital in the United States," *Survey of Current Business*, November, 1962.

JOHNSON, D. GALE. "Agricultural Production," in ABRAM BERGSON and SIMON KUZNETS (eds.), *Economic Trends in the Soviet Union*. Cambridge, 1963.

———— and KAHAN, ARCADIUS. "Soviet Agriculture: Structure and Growth," in Joint Economic Committee, U.S. Congress, *Comparisons of the United States and Soviet Economies*. Part I. Washington, 1959.

KANTOROVICH, L. V. *Ekonomicheskii raschet nailuchshevo ispol'zovaniia resursov.* Moscow, 1959.

KAPLAN, NORMAN M. "Capital Formation and Allocation," in A. BERGSON (ed.), *Soviet Economic Growth.* Evanston, 1953.

———— *Capital Investments in the Soviet Union, 1924–1951.* The RAND Corportion, Research Memorandum RM-735, November 28, 1951.

———— "Capital Stock," in ABRAM BERGSON and SIMON KUZNETS (eds.), *Economic Trends in the Soviet Union.* Cambridge, 1963.

———— *Collective Farm Investment in the U.S.S.R.* The RAND Corporation, Research Memorandum RM-1733, June 12, 1956.

———— and others, *A Tentative Input-Output Table for the U.S.S.R., 1941 Plan.* The RAND Corporation, Research Memorandum RM-924, September 2, 1952.

———— and MOORSTEEN, RICHARD H. *Indexes of Soviet Industrial Output* (two volumes). The RAND Corporation, Research Memorandum RM-2495, May 13, 1960.

KARCZ, JERZY F. "Indices of Prices Realized in Centralized and Decentralized Procurements, 1928–1954," unpublished memorandum, dated July 6, 1957 (a).

———— *Soviet Agricultural Marketings and Prices, 1928–1954.* The RAND Corporation, Research Memorandum RM-1930, July 2, 1957.

———— "Soviet Farm Prices, 1928–1952," unpublished memorandum, circulated 1961.

KASER, M. C. "Soviet Statistics of Wages and Prices," *Soviet Studies,* July, 1955.

KASIMOVSKII, E. "O kreditovanii gotovykh izdelii," *Den'gi i kredit,* 1940:6–7.

KATS, IA. D. *Ocherki statistiki truda.* Moscow, 1960.

KATSENELENBAUM, Z. S. *Osnovnye i oborotnye sredstva v mashinostroenie.* Moscow, 1958.

KAZANTSEV, A. "Gosbank i razvitie promyshlennosti," *Den'gi i kredit,* 1961:11.

———— "O kreditovanii khozorganov pod raschetnye dokumenty v puti," *Den'gi i kredit,* 1957:7.

KENDRICK, J. W. *Productivity Trends in the United States.* Princeton, 1961.

KHAVIN, I. "Kreditnaia reforma i khozraschet," *Problemy ekonomiki,* 1931:4–5.

KHRÓMOV, P. "K voprosu ob oborotnykh fondakh promyshlennosti," *Problemy ekonomiki,* 1937:1.

KISMAN, N., and SLAVNYI, I. *Sovetskie finansy v piatoi piatiletke.* Moscow, 1956.

KISTANOV, IA. A. "Kooperativnaia torgovlia v SSSR," in *40 let sovetskoi torgovli.* Moscow, 1957.

KOBALEVSKII, V. L. *Organizatsiia i ekonomika zhilishchnogo khoziaistva SSSR.* Moscow, 1940.

KONOVALOV, I. "Finansovyi plan na 1934 g.," *Planovoe khoziaistvo,* 1934:5–6.

KOROVUSHKIN , A. "Ocherednye zadachi Gosudarstvennogo banka," *Den'gi i kredit,* 1960:5.

———— "Za aktivnuiu tvorcheskuiu rabotu po vypolneniiu reshenii XXI s''ezda KPSS," *Den'gi i kredit,* 1959:6.

———— "Za dal'neishee uluchshenie raboty uchreshdenii Gosbanka," *Den'gi i kredit,* 1962:3.

KRAVIS, IRVING B. "Relative Income Shares in Fact and Theory," *American Economic Review,* December, 1959.

Kredit i khozraschet (serial).

KRULIKOVSKAIA, V., and others. *Planirovanie biudzheta gosudarstvennogo sotsial'nogo strakhovaniia.* Moscow, 1959.

KUZNETS, SIMON. "A Comparative Appraisal," in ABRAM BERGSON and SIMON KUZNETS (eds.), *Economic Trends in the Soviet Union.* Cambridge, 1963.

———— *National Product Since 1869.* New York, 1946.

KVASHA, IA. B. *Amortizatsiia i sroki sluzhby osnovnykh fondov.* Moscow, 1959.

LANDE, E. "Kredit i denezhnoe obrashchenie v 1935 g.," *Planovoe khoziaistvo,* 1936:4.

LAVROV, V. V. *Finansirovanie otraslei narodnogo khoziaistva.* Moscow, 1956.
LIFITS, M. M. *Ekonomika sovetskoi torgovli.* Moscow, 1950.
LOVTSOV, V. "Kredit i kontrol' rublem v legkoi i pishchevoi promyshlennosti," *Den'gi i kredit,* 1956:6.
MAKAROV, A. D. *Finansirovanie i kreditovanie sovetskoi torgovli.* Moscow, 1950.
MAR'IASIN, L. E. "Denezhnoe khoziaistvo i kredit," *Kredit i khozraschet,* 1936:2.
MARKUS, B. L. "The Abolition of Unemployment in the U.S.S.R.," *International Labor Review,* March, 1936 (a).
———— "The Stakhanov Movement and the Increased Productivity of Labour in the U.S.S.R," *International Labor Review,* July, 1936.
Ministerstvo finansov SSSR, Nauchno-issledovatel'skii finansovyi institut. *Amortizatsiia v promyshlennosti SSSR.* Moscow, 1956.
Ministerstvo vneshnei torgovli. *Vneshniaia torgovlia Soiuza SSR za 1959 god.* Moscow, 1960.
———— *Vneshniaia torgovlia Soiuza SSR za 1960 god.* Moscow, 1961.
MITEL'MAN, E. Review of P. Parfan'iak, "Voprosy bankovskogo kontrolia rublem v promyshlennosti," *Den'gi i kredit,* 1954:1.
———— "Effektivno ispol'zovat' oborotnye sredstva," *Den'gi i kredit,* 1958:12.
———— and AVERBAKH, I. "Oborotnye fondy sotsialisticheskoi promyshlennosti," *Planovoe khoziaistvo,* 1940:5.
MOORSTEEN, RICHARD H. "On Measuring Productive Potential and Relative Efficiency," *Quarterly Journal of Economics,* August, 1961.
———— *Prices and Production of Machinery in the Soviet Union, 1928–1958.* Cambridge, 1962.
———— *Prices of Prime Movers, U.S.S.R., 1927/8–1949.* The RAND Corporation, Research Memorandum RM-1225, March 30, 1954.
———— *Prices of Tractors, Trucks, and Automobiles, U.S.S.R., 1928–1949.* The RAND Corporation, Research Memorandum RM-1121, July 23, 1953.
Narkomzem and Narkomsovkhozov SSSR. *Sel'skoe khoziaistvo SSSR: ezhegodnik 1935.* Moscow, 1936.
Nashe stroitel'stvo (serial).
NEIFEL'D, L. "Zhilishchnoe stroitel'stvo v strane sotsializma," *Planovoe khoziaistvo,* 1935:11–12.
NIMITZ, NANCY, under the supervision of ABRAM BERGSON. *Prices of Refined Petroleum Products in the U.S.S.R., 1928–1950.* The RAND Corporation, Research Memorandum RM-1497, May 26, 1955.
———— "Soviet Agricultural Prices and Costs," in Joint Economic Committee, U.S. Congress, *Comparisons of the United States and Soviet Economies.* Part I. Washington, 1959.
———— *Soviet National Income and Product, 1956–1958.* The RAND Corporation, Research Memorandum RM-3112-PR, June, 1962.
———— *Soviet Statistics of Meat and Milk Output.* The RAND Corporation, Research Memorandum RM-2326, February 6, 1959 (a).
NKPS. *Sovetskii transport, 1917–1927.* Moscow, 1927.
NOVE, ALEC. *The Soviet Economy: An Introduction.* New York, 1961.
NOVIKOV, R. "Ob istochnikakh formirovaniia oborotnykh sredstv promyshlennykh predpriiatii," *Den'gi i kredit,* 1960:11.
NUSINOV, I. M. *Metodika finansovogo planirovaniia.* Moscow, 1937.
NUTTER, G. WARREN. *Growth of Industrial Production in the Soviet Union.* Princeton, 1962.
Oktiabr' (serial).
OMEL'CHENKO, A. I. (ed.). *O normakh proizvodstvennykh zapasov na zavodakh chernoi metallurgii.* Moscow, 1939.
PAVLOV, P. *Snashivanie i amortizatsiia osnovnykh fondov.* Moscow, 1957.
PESSEL', M. "Effektivnost' bankovskogo kontrolia," *Den'gi i kredit,* 1958:11.

PETROV, A. "Nekotorye voprosy vliianiia kredita na ukreplenia khozrascheta," *Den'gi i kredit*, 1960:7.

PETROV, A. I. *Kurs ekonomicheskoi statistiki*. 3rd ed. Moscow, 1961.

PINUS, A. "Pereotsenka khleba i drugikh produktov," *Kredit i khozraschet*, 1935:19.

Planovoe khoziaistvo (serial).

PLOTNIKOV, K. N. *Biudzhet sotsialisticheskogo gosudarstva*. Leningrad, 1948.

POLLIAK, G. "K voprosu ob urovne zhizni rabochego klassa SSSR," *Planovoe khoziaistvo*, 1931:5–6.

POKROVSKII, A. A. "Stroiindustriiu—na vyshuiu stupen' organizatsii," *Nashe stroitel'stvo*, 1936:4.

POPOV, V. F., and others. *Gosudarstvennyi bank SSSR: kratkii ocherk k soro-kaletiiu Oktiabria*. Moscow, 1957.

POWELL, RAYMOND P. "An Index of Soviet Construction, 1927/28 to 1955," *Review of Economics and Statistics*, May 1959 (a) .

———"Industrial Production," in ABRAM BERGSON and SIMON KUZNETS (eds.), *Economic Trends in the Soviet Union*. Cambridge, 1963.

——— *A Materials-Input Index of Soviet Construction 1927/1928 to 1955*. The RAND Corporation, Research Memoranda RM-1872 and RM-1873, February 14, 1957 (two parts).

——— *A Materials-Input Index of Soviet Construction, Revised and Extended*. The RAND Corporation, Research Memorandum RM-2454, September 28, 1959.

Pravda.

Problemy ekonomiki (serial).

PROKOPOVICZ, SERGE N. *Histoire économique de l' U.R.S.S.* Paris, 1952.

PROSELKOV, A. "Svodnyi godovoi otchet Gosbanka SSSR," *Den'gi i kredit*, 1940:1.

PUTILOV, A. "K voprosu o nakoplenii v promyshlennosti," *Planovoe khoziaistvo*, 1932:5.

Quarterly Bulletin of Soviet-Russian Economics (edited by S. N. PROKOPOVICZ).

RAGOL'SKII, M. "Itogi nakopleniia pervoi piatiletki," *Planovoe khoziaistvo*, 1932:3.

ROSENSTEIN-RODAN, P. N. "Les besoins de capitaux dans les pays sous-développés," *Économie appliquée*, January–June, 1954.

ROVINSKII, E. "Gosbank k XX godovshchine Velikoi Oktiabr'skoi sotsialistiche-skoi revoliutsii," *Kredit i khozraschet*, 1937:21.

ROVINSKII, N. N. *Organizatsiia finansirovaniia i kreditovaniia kapital'nykh vlo-zhenii*. Moscow, 1951.

ROZENTUL, S. "Protsessy nakopleniia v SSSR," *Planovoe khoziaistvo*, 1929:1.

RUBINSHTEIN, IA. *Ocherki razvitiia sovetskogo kredita*. Moscow, 1958.

Russian Economic Notes (serial publication of U.S. Department of Commerce).

SAUTIN, I. V. (ed.). *Kolkhozy vo vtoroi stalinskoi piatiletke*. Moscow-Leningrad, 1939.

SAVVIN, B., and SHER, I. "Nezavershennoe stroitel'stvo i puti ego sokrashcheniia," *Finansy SSSR*, 1959:3.

SCHWARZ, SOLOMON, M. *Labor in the Soviet Union*. New York, 1951.

SHABANOVA, N. "Osnovnye etapy rasvitiia khoziaistvennogo rascheta," *Den'gi i kredit*, 1957:10.

SHCHENKOV, S. A. *Bukhgalterskii uchet v promyshlennosti*. Moscow, 1955.

——— *Otchetnost' promyshlennykh predpriiatii*. Moscow, 1952.

SHENGER, IU. (E.) "Dvizhenie raschetnykh schetov i voprosy ikh planirovaniia," *Kredit i khozraschet*, 1936:21.

——— *Planirovanie finansov*. Moscow, 1940.

——— *Razvitie i organizatsiia kreditnoi sistemy SSSR*. Moscow-Leningrad, 1934.

SHER, I. *Finansirovanie kapital'nykh vlozhenii v promyshlennost' SSSR.* Moscow, 1958.

SHEREMET, A. *Oborotnye sredstva promyshlennogo predpriiatiia.* Moscow, 1956.

SHIGALIN, T. I. *Narodnoe khoziaistvo SSSR v period Velikoi Otechestvennoi voiny.* Moscow, 1960.

SHISHKIN, N. I. (ed.). *Trudovye resursy SSSR.* Moscow, 1961.

SHVARTS, G. "Kreditnyi plan i zadachi Gosbanka v 1937 godu," *Kredit i khozraschet,* 1937:4.

————— and KAGANOV, G. "Rost khoziaistvo—rost kredita," *Kredit i khozraschet,* 1935:4.

SMIGLA, ANTONINA. "Finansy sotsialisticheskogo gosudarstva," *Problemy ekonomiki,* 1937:2.

SOBOL', V. "Ob oborotnykh sredstvakh," *Problemy ekonomiki,* 1937:3–4.

SOKOLOV, N. "Bor'ba Gosbanka SSSR za khozraschet v tret'ei piatiletke," *Planovoe khoziaistvo,* 1939:6.

————— "Kreditnyi plan II kvartala i zadachi Gosbanka," *Den'gi i kredit,* 1939 (a):5.

SOLOW, ROBERT M. "Investment and Technical Progress," in *Mathematical Methods in the Social Sciences, 1959.* Stanford, 1960.

————— "Technical Change and the Aggregate Production Function," *Review of Economics and Statistics,* August, 1957.

SOROCHINSKII, V. "Oborotnye sredstva kolkhozov," *Den'gi i kredit,* 1956:2.

SOROKIN, G. *Stalinskie piatiletnie plany.* Moscow, 1946.

Sovetskaia torgovlia (serial).

Sovetskie finansy (serial).

Sovetskoe gosudarstvo i pravo (serial).

STALIN, J. V. *Problemy leninizma.* Moscow, 1952.

Statisticheskoe obozrenie (serial).

STRUMILIN, S. G. "Chto est' kommunizm," *Oktiabr',* 1960:3.

————— *Statistiko-ekonomicheskie ocherki.* Moscow, 1958.

TARASOV, E. M. "Sel'skoe stroitel'stvo," *Planovoe khoziaistvo,* 1927:10.

TERBORGH, GEORGE W. *Dynamic Equipment Policy.* New York, 1949.

————— *Realistic Depreciation Policy.* Chicago, 1954.

TIKTIN, G. "Funktsii i oblast' primeneniia sotsialisticheskogo kratkosrochnogo kredita," *Den'gi i kredit,* 1940:8–9.

TRIVANOVITCH, VASO. "Purchasing Power of Wages in the Soviet Union," National Industrial Conference Board, *Conference Board Bulletin,* March 7, 1938.

TsSU. *Chislennost' skota v SSSR.* Moscow, 1957 (c).

————— *Dostizheniia sovetskoi vlasti za 40 let v tsifrakh.* Moscow, 1957 (e).

————— *Kapital'noe stroitel'stvo v SSSR.* Moscow, 1961 (a).

————— *Krest'ianskie biudzhety 1925/26.* Moscow, 1929.

————— *Narodnoe khoziaistvo SSSR.* Moscow-Leningrad, 1932.

————— *Narodnoe khoziaistvo SSSR.* Moscow, 1956 (a).

————— *Narodnoe khoziaistvo SSSR v 1958 godu.* Moscow, 1959.

————— *Narodnoe khoziaistvo SSSR v 1959 godu.* Moscow, 1960.

————— *Narodnoe khoziaistvo SSSR v 1956 godu.* Moscow, 1957.

————— *Narodnoe khoziaistvo SSSR v 1960 godu.* Moscow, 1961.

————— *Narodnoe khoziaistvo SSSR v 1961 godu.* Moscow, 1962 (a).

————— *Posevnye ploshchadi v SSSR.* Moscow, 1957 (b).

————— Otdel Perepisi i Otdel Gorodskoi Statistiki, *Programmy i posobiia k razrabotke vsesoiuznoi perepisi naseleniia 1926 g. Vypusk v, proekt i form razrabotki vladenoi vedomosti i semeinoi karty o zhilishchakh.* Moscow, 1927.

————— *Promyshlennost' SSSR.* Moscow, 1957 (a).

————— *Sel'skoe khoziaistvo SSSR.* Moscow, 1960 (a).

————— Slovar'-spravochnik po sotsial'no-ekonomicheskoi statistike. Moscow, 1944.

————— Sovetskaia torgovlia. Moscow, 1956.

————— SSSR v tsifrakh. Moscow, 1958.

————— SSSR v tsifrakh v 1960 godu. Moscow, 1961 (b).

————— SSSR v tsifrakh v 1961 godu. Moscow, 1962.

————— Statisticheskii spravochnik SSSR za 1928 g. Moscow, 1929 (a).

————— Transport i sviaz' SSSR. Moscow, 1957 (d).

TsUNKhU. Socialist Construction. Moscow, 1936 (a).

————— Sotsialisticheskoe stroitel'stvo SSSR. Moscow, 1935.

————— Sotsialisticheskoe stroitel'stvo SSSR. Moscow, 1936.

————— Sotsialisticheskoe stroitel'stvo Soiuza SSR (1933–1938gg.). Moscow-Leningrad, 1939.

————— Trud v SSSR. Moscow, 1935 (a).

————— Trud v SSSR. Moscow, 1936 (b).

————— Zhivotnovodstvo SSSR v tsifrakh. Moscow, 1932.

TURGEON, LYNN. "Levels of Living, Wages and Prices in the Soviet and United States Economies," in Joint Economic Committee, U.S. Congress, Comparison of the United States and Soviet Economies. Part I. Washington, 1959.

————— and BERGSON, ABRAM. Prices of Basic Industrial Goods in the U.S.S.R., 1950 to 1956. The RAND Corporation, Research Memorandum RM-1919, June 12, 1957.

U.S. DEPARTMENT OF COMMERCE. Business Statistics. Washington, 1961.

U.S. TREASURY DEPARTMENT, INTERNAL REVENUE SERVICE. Bulletin "F" Tables of Useful Lives of Depreciable Property. Publication No. 173. Washington, 1955.

————— Depreciation Guidelines and Rules. Publication No. 456. Washington, 1962.

USATOV, I. "Izpol'zovanie oborotnykh sredstv v sotsialisticheskoi promyshlennosti," Den'gi i kredit, 1961:4.

————— "Uluchshat' normirovanie i organizatsiiu oborotnykh sredstv," Finansy SSSR, 1960:2.

USOSKIN, M. M. Organizatsiia i planirovanie kratkosrochnogo kredita. 2nd rev. ed. Moscow, 1956.

————— Osnovy kreditnogo dela. Moscow, 1946.

————— Osnovy kreditovaniia i raschetov. Moscow, 1939. (All citations to this source are based on notes provided by ROBERT W. CAMPBELL.)

Vestnik statistiki (serial).

VOLIN, LAZAR. A Survey of Soviet Russian Agriculture. Washington, 1951.

Voprosy ekonomiki (serial).

VOZNESENSKII, N. Voennaia ekonomika SSSR v period Otechestvennoi voiny. Moscow, 1947.

VSNKh. Svodnyi proizvodstvenno-finansovyi plan gosudarstvennoi promyshlennosti na 1926–27g. Moscow-Leningrad, 1927.

WEITZMAN, MURRY S., and ELIAS, ANDREW. The Magnitude and Distribution of Civilian Employment in the U.S.S.R., 1928–1959. Bureau of the Census, International Population Reports, Series P-95, No. 58. Washington, 1961.

WILES, P. J. D. The Political Economy of Communism. Oxford, 1962.

WILLETT, JOSEPH W. "The Recent Record in Agricultural Production," in Joint Economic Committee, Congress of the United States, Dimensions of Soviet Economic Power. Washington, 1962.

YANOWITCH, MURRAY. "Changes in the Soviet Money Wage Level Since 1940," The American Slavic and East European Review, April, 1955.

ZALESKII, EUGÈNE. "Les fluctuations des prix de détail en Union Soviétique," Études et Conjoncture, April, 1955.

ZLOBIN, I. D. Kredit i kreditnaia sistema SSSR. Moscow, 1958.

ZVEREV, A. G. "Finansy SSSR za 40 let sovetskoi vlasti," in *Finansy i sotsialisticheskoe stroitel'stvo*. Moscow, 1957.

———— "Gosudarstvennyi biudzhet chetvertogo goda poslevoennoi stalinskoi piatiletki," *Planovoe khoziaistvo*, 1949:2.

———— *Gosudarstvennye biudzhety Soiuza SSR: 1938–1945gg*. Moscow, 1946.

———— "O edinom Gosudarstvennom biudzhete Soiuza Sovetskikh Sotsialisticheskikh Respublik na 1938 god," in *Vtoraia sessiia Verkhovnogo soveta SSSR, 1-go sozyva*. Leningrad, 1938.

———— *Voprosy natsional'nogo dokhoda i finansov SSSR*. Moscow, 1958.

Indexes

Index of Names

The letter "n" following a page number indicates that the reference is to a footnote.

Subject Index

The letter "n" following a page number indicates that the reference is to a footnote; the letter "t," that the reference is to a table; the letter "c," that the reference is to a chart.

A

"Acceleration principle," 234, 237
Accounting procedures, Soviet
  for fixed capital, 38–39, 51, 81, 443–45
  for inventories, 39n, 112–19, 122–24, 134, 462
Armed forces; *see* Labor, in armed forces

B

"Basic funds," scope of, 195n, 613

C

Capital, human, 11, 248; *see also* Labor, quality change in
Capital-output ratio, 244, 252–54c, 367t–68t; *see also* Inventory-output ratio
"Capital repairs"; *see also* Fixed capital stock, effects on of capitalizing major repairs; Fixed capital stock, repairs of; Investment in fixed capital, capital repairs in
  definition of, 33n
Capital services; *see also* Depreciation, annual charges for, as component of capital services; Interest rate, relation of to capital services
  adjustments in for territorial acquisitions, 168n
  in alternative prices, compared, 169c
  calculation of, 168–70
  concept of, 10–11
  estimated with alternative depreciation methods, 170–71
  findings on, component sectors, 352t–57t
  findings on, total, 171–72, 352t–57t
  relation of to capital stock, 10–11, 22–32, 169n, 241n–42n
  reliability of estimates of, 169–71

Capital stock; *see also* Capital-output ratio; Capital services, relation of to capital stock; Equipment, stock of; Fixed capital stock; Installation, stock of; Inventories, stock of; Livestock, stock of; Structures, stock of
  age of, 164, 167–68, 307–8, 351t
  agricultural, 161, 163
  in alternative prices, compared, 144c, 154–56, 159–61, 164–66t
  compared with U.S., 181–83
  concept of, 2, 7–10, 185n
  contribution of to Soviet growth, 305–8
  distribution of by kind of asset, 156–61, 339t–41t
  distribution of by sector, 13, 161–65t
  effects on of territorial acquisitions, 144
  findings on, 143–45, 156, 339t–41t
  before 1928, 12
  nonagricultural, 161c–63, 166t, 342t–44t
  nonagricultural nonresidential, 161c, 163–64, 166t, 348t–50t
  nonresidential, 161c–62, 166t, 345t–47t
  policy on, 237–38
  quality change in, 8–10, 306; *see also* Technological change, embodiment of in capital
  relation of to investment flow, 237–38, 311
  relative to labor employed, 253–55c, 290–91, 298–99, 310, 369t
  reliability of estimates of, 12–16, 145–55, 162–63
  residential, 161–62
  scope of, 1, 11–13
  seasonal fluctuations in, 169–70
  service-life distribution of, 11
  valuation of, 2
  war losses of, 144
Claims, financial, exclusion of from capital stock, 11

666

This book has been set in 10 point and 9 point Baskerville, leaded 1 point. Part and number are in 14 point Baskerville; part title is in 24 point Baskerville Italics. Chapter and number are in 18 point Baskerville Italic; chapter title is in 24 point Baskerville roman. The size of the type page is 27 by 47½ picas.